Vinyl Leaves

Walt Disney World and America

INSTITUTIONAL STRUCTURES OF FEELING

George Marcus, Sharon Traweek,
Richard Handler, and Vera Zolberg, Series Editors

VINYL LEAVES

Walt Disney World and America

STEPHEN M. FJELLMAN

WESTVIEW PRESS

BOULDER · SAN FRANCISCO · OXFORD

Institutional Structures of Feeling

Copyright © 1992 by Westview Press, Inc.

Published in 1992 in the United States of America by Westview Press, Inc., 5500 Central Avenue, Boulder, Colorado 80301-2847, and in the United Kingdom by Westview Press, 36 Lonsdale Road, Summertown, Oxford OX2 7EW

Library of Congress Cataloging-in-Publication Data
Fjellman, Stephen M.
  Vinyl leaves : Walt Disney World and America / Stephen M. Fjellman.
      p.   cm. — (Institutional structures of feeling)
  Includes bibliographical references and index.
  ISBN 0-8133-1473-9. ISBN 0-8133-1472-0 (pbk.)
  1. Walt Disney World (Fla.)—Finance.   2. Walt Disney World
(Fla.)—History.   3. Leisure industry—United States—Case studies.
4. Leisure—Economic aspects—United States—Case studies.
5. United States—Popular culture—Economic aspects—Case studies.
I. Title. II. Series.
GV1853.3.F62W344   1992
381'.45179106875924—dc20   91-43693
                                                                      CIP

Printed and bound in the United States of America

The paper used in this publication meets the requirements of the American National Standard for Permanence of Paper for Printed Library Materials Z39.48-1984.

10   9   8   7   6   5   4   3   2   1

To Melina

Contents

Tables

Preface and Acknowledgments

It was about as nice as late April gets in Colonial Williamsburg. The sky was spring blue, cumulus puffs scudding east with the breeze. I had just heard a music lesson at the Mary Stith Shop and was readjusting to the sun.

I was standing on Duke of Gloucester Street in front of Chowning's Tavern, looking west. To my right stretched the lawn of Market Square, with its Courthouse of 1771 and Bowling Green; to my left the Guardhouse and Magazine.

I had come here two days ago, planning to spend a morning before heading on up the coast to Boston. Well, now it was early afternoon of the third day. I was, once again, hooked.

I have always found theme parks, open-air historical museums, heritage parks, and other such places with claims beyond carnival entertainment to be fascinating. Although I like my history neat, laid out on the printed page, I also love to walk through its remains, even to see it on the screen.

As I stood there in the sun that late April afternoon, I threw my figurative arms out shoulder-high and bellowed in my mind, "I love it here!" How could I spend more time in places like this, places where I am endlessly entertained? Where would I hang out if I could? And two thoughts came to mind simultaneously, jostling and connected: I have tenure, and I'm going to Disney World!

I work in the education business. I have been trained to pay deep attention to sources of information, rules of evidence, problems of sampling, limits to inference, and all the other spirits of careful inquiry and judicious report. I have learned to be subtle, skeptical, slow to conclude, dependent on further data — a real philosophical "show me" Missourian.

Yet if I ask myself, "How do I know things?"— the kinds of normal things about my own national tradition that I barely know I know or the stuff I picture about the rest of the world — much of it, I confess, comes from mass-mediated popular culture. I am quite convinced that Jack Lord was at the Continental Convention or at least that the character he plays in the Williamsburg orientation movie was there. When I see the paintings of the assembly at the Hall of Presidents in the Magic Kingdom, for example, I will ask, "Where's Jack Lord?"

And I'm supposed to know better.

But if I'm supposed to know better, what about all the people who are not supposed to do so, those whose knowing better might upset the way things are? How are we all — my friends, fellow citizens, and I — sold a bill of goods that is not good for us? I don't mean just the historical stories of Williamsburg; those aren't so dangerous. But there are stories about truth, justice, self-worth, the other, the gods, the land, power, the market, technology, and other big ideas — stories whose task it is to mythologize and mystify. As the United States unravels around us, these stories bear scrutiny.

So out in front of Chowning's Tavern, arms metaphorically akimbo, I heard the "voice" of C. Wright Mills (James Earl Jones, perhaps?), saying, "You have a job; show some sociological imagination." He told us years ago to undistance ourselves, to repudiate the deadening training-toward-safety of the academic apprenticeship (and its attendant murder of language), to seek the parts of social life where real live humans meet the social facts that sculpt their world.

Well, one place where *my* life meets those social facts is at Walt Disney World. This book argues that I'm not alone.

For five years it has been the eight hundred-pound gorilla that could sit wherever it wanted. It was written in many places: offices, living rooms, kitchens, bars, cafés, restaurants, planes, trains, and automobiles. It has been written on the beach, in Adventureland, at the mall, and lots of it in front of the TV.

The first words showed up on Great Tisbury Pond, Martha's Vineyard; the last in Coconut Grove. Much of it I don't remember writing at all. It was just sort of there, like Florida rain.

Its influences came from many places and many times. As a member of Gregory Bateson's Ecology of Mind — the thought-worker's Adventurers Club — I find that my head is a temporary storage place for all kinds of ideas, phrases, and fragments — what my friends call "junk." It's a kind of Chinese menu of the mind. Take one from column A and two from column B and there's an analogy or a metaphor. Make a bricolage, then search for the dump button to empty out some of the trash.

The result is, as in most of my life, that I can't remember where a lot of my ideas come from. I'm a really lousy scholar. What I heard yesterday on "Entertainment Tonight" goes into today's piece. Tomorrow I'll forget where I heard it. I'll probably tell some class it's from Heidegger.

I managed to keep some account of stuff I read for this book, so there are footnotes, but all sorts of things undoubtedly slipped through. I'm afraid that sometimes I just tore off the packaging and ate the ideas. I tried to be careful about potential litigation, but that may be where all my organizational concentration went. That and watching "L.A. Law" — just in case.

I'll state right now for the record that I don't have a clue as to who is responsible for the arguments in this book and its mistakes and slurs. It just wrote itself. We're probably all at fault.

Who is this "we," then, who will accompany me into the dock? Some watched me feed the gorilla from the box seats; others brought bananas.

The following people gave me enough help or support or showed enough interest — a few even by reading parts of the manuscript — that I remembered them when I put together this list. A few (*) were even fellow fieldworkers. So — Day-o! — thank you: Sandy Winters, Susan Whiting, John Whiting, Beatrice Whiting, Merry (Corky) White, *Tom Weathers, Barbara Watts, John van Maanen, Maria-Lydia Spinelli, Bruce Silver, *Melina Shepherd, Hallie Shepherd, Courtenay Selby, John Schenck, Meri-Jane Rochelson, Naomi Quinn, Vanessa Peterson, Joyce Peterson, Brian Peterson, Mark Miller, Jennifer Myers, Jeff Myers, *Pat Mahaffey, Barry Levine, Diane Klein, Terry Kandal, Howard Kaminsky, Jean Jackson, James Ito-Adler, Jeanne Irvine, Phyllis Hudson, Bob Hogner, Philip Harrington, Jane Guyer, Bernie Guyer, Camilla Guido, Mary Jo Good, Byron Good, Molly Goheen, *Mitzi Goheen, Mark Goheen, Mark Gladwin, Hugh Gladwin, Flora Gladwin, Christina Gladwin, Amy Gladwin, Debra Gewertz, Martha Fuller, Herb Fuller, Mary Free, Fred Errington, John Ernest, Becky Ernest, Mary Jane Elkins, Chuck Elkins, Bruce Detwiler, Roy D'Andrade, Jane Clarkson, Ron Casson, Mike Budd, Karen Brickman, Mary Yoko Brannen, Sy Bellin and the members of the Tufts University National Endowment for the Humanities 1987 Summer Institute on the history of technology in the United States, the staff of the Disney Archives at the Orlando Public Library, Florida International University, the FIU Foundation, from which I received two Faculty Development Grants, my colleagues and students at the Florida State University Florence (Italy) Study Center, and especially my colleagues at the North Miami Campus of Florida International University. Byron and Mary Jo Good connected me with Westview Press. Hugh Gladwin and Mary Free have been my good friends and Hugh has saved my life by typesetting this book.

The people at Westview Press — especially Julie Seko, Gordon Massman, Alice Levine, Cheryl Carnahan, and Libby Barstow — are good and true professionals and nice people. They bathed me in competence.

The Disney folks never tire of telling us that their parks are in continuous motion. New parks are built with some regularity. New hotels go up like mushrooms. Stores and restaurants change. Every glitch in this book's journey to publication means that names have been changed, numbers have gone up. What I offer here are ballpark numbers and ballpark names. Please take all the numbers to mean "lots." Do what you want with the names, although a bit of vinegar might come in handy. Walt Disney World is a place about which it is true to say, *plus c'est le même chose, plus ça change.*

So long book, short preface. Here we go. Choose an aisle and move all the way down. Eating and drinking are fine, but please, no flash photography.

Stephen M. Fjellman
El Portal, Florida

Vinyl Leaves

*Walt Disney World
and America*

1

Stalking Woozles

"It's a very funny thing," said Bear, "but there seem to be two animals now. This — whatever-it-was — has been joined by another — whatever-it-is — and the two of them are now proceeding in company. Would you mind coming with me, Piglet, in case they turn out to be Hostile Animals?"

—Winnie-the-Pooh[1]

There is a tree in central Florida. It is maybe ninety feet high and huge around the base and has a crown that stretches across almost as many yards as the tree is tall. From the top of this tree, when the wind is still, you can see almost to the Caribbean. The trunk looks about as much like that of a live oak as one might wish. The bark is deeply grained and covered with that pea-soup-green-colored stuff you see on trees in hot, wet places. It's a big, nice tree, a good place for the treehouse that adorns it.

But it's not made of wood.

The trunk and branches are formed out of prestressed concrete wrapped around a steel-mesh frame. The bark and green stuff that cover much of it are painted on. The leaves, all 800,000 of them, are made of vinyl.

This tree — *Disneyodendron eximus* ("out-of-the-ordinary Disney tree") in corporate parlance — holds the Swiss Family Island Treehouse, an attraction in the Adventureland part of Walt Disney World's Magic Kingdom. The Magic Kingdom, in turn, is part of the 27,400-acre Vacation Kingdom that is Walt Disney World (WDW) — a massive development that also includes (as of the end of 1990) EPCOT Center; the Disney-MGM Studios;

River Country; Discovery Island; Fort Wilderness; Walt Disney Shopping Village; Pleasure Island; Typhoon Lagoon; the Contemporary, Polynesian, Grand Floridian, Caribbean Beach, Swan, Dolphin, Yacht Club, Beach Club, and Port Orleans Resort Hotels; and three man-made lakes, a wildlife preserve, and thousands of acres of undeveloped scrub and swamp.

The Swiss Family Island Treehouse, shaded by its vinyl leaves, is a representation of the treehouse built by the Swiss Family Robinson in the 1960 Disney movie of the same name. It has four separate rooms built in different parts of the "tree," an outdoor kitchen with simulated food, an ingenious pulley system by which water is carried up to the highest point of the tree from the stream below, and a footbridge and stair structure to make it accessible to Disney's "guests." [2]

The movie *Swiss Family Robinson* — based on Johann Wyss's take off[3] on Daniel Defoe's *Robinson Crusoe* — is one in which, as in all "Disney versions," [4] art and history are transformed by dilution. So we have a fake tree holding a fake treehouse, representing a fake story told in a different medium from, but alluding to, a classic piece of literature, in an amusement park visited by 30 million people a year, most of whom are, like myself, enchanted.

What is going on here?

An answer to this question is not simple. To understand the Swiss Family Island Treehouse, we need to think a good bit about Walt Disney World (WDW) as a whole. To do this, however — to make sense of the Vacation Kingdom — we must ask a number of questions about the contemporary United States. Not only does an analysis of WDW require some attention to its political, economic, social, and cultural context, but that context itself — a particular version of America — relies in many ways on the stories told to millions of people by the Walt Disney Company. To explain WDW, then, is to explain a good deal about twentieth-century America.

Orwell and Huxley

In 1984 a number of people wandered around the globe, convening here and there at symposia to argue about whether or not George Orwell was right. Media, mass and otherwise, offered special features, editorials, upbeats, and downbeats about the state of the nation and the state of the world, for the prophetic year had arrived.

Orwell's *1984* described an imaginary totalitarian society in which the ruling party retained almost complete control of its population through constant surveillance, continuous indoctrination, behavioral modification, manipulation of language, and the general exercise of naked power. Only the Proles, in their tenements with their cheap gin and slovenly ways, were left more or less alone. It was a world that, Orwell said, "might happen."

The question for 1984 intellectuals was whether Orwell's satiric prophecies had come to pass. It was clear from the discussions I heard and read that there was a continuum of Orwellianism in the world. The exercise of naked power was evident in South Africa, Iran, Ethiopia, Guatemala, and so on. People argued that power wasn't too well clothed in many U.S. inner cities. Smoke aside, it was also pretty obvious that the middle-class U.S. world — to which most conferees and writers belonged — was deeply threatened by *1984*-like developments. Newspeak is real. Mainstream political and governmental language, which has become meaningless at best, is normally mystifying propaganda — world domination is represented as "keeping the peace," contras as "freedom fighters," and so forth. The possibilities for complete electronic surveillance of U.S. residents are increasingly real. The Reagan regime made sporadic use of its own version of the "three-minute hate." All in all, however, Orwellian arguments about contemporary U.S. society were and are not convincing — at least not yet.

What happened as 1984 passed by was that, although they honored Orwell, some people again began to think deeply about Aldous Huxley and his *Brave New World*. Huxley envisioned a far more efficient system of control than that of Orwell's Airstrip One, one based on the reinforcement of desired behavior by reward rather than by punishment.

As any number of political and social theorists have told us — among them Karl Marx, Max Weber, Antonio Gramsci, Peter Berger, and Thomas Luckmann — structures of power reproduce themselves best when people control themselves, spontaneously acting "correctly" because it is the right, normal, sane thing to do. Repressive sanctions need only come into play when there is a problem. Most of the time people will do what they are supposed to do.

A good way to make sure that people police themselves is to get them to believe essentially the same stories about what the world is and why the way it is is good, true, and beautiful. The world needs to be described, and it needs to be justified by arguments about nature, philosophical principle, history, or the gods. People will find their place in such a world. They will learn what hopes they might reasonably hold for themselves.

Because this world — any known world — contains an asymmetrical distribution of power and access to resources, something is always something at stake in these descriptions. Critical thought, anger, heresy, and action toward change are always possible. These possibilities must be stopped or tamed by deflecting them in harmless directions. Orwell showed us the obvious lie and a boot "stomping on a human face — forever." Huxley predicted that we might be tamed instead by desire and pleasure.

Both solutions draw our attention to the here and now. It is hard to think complex thoughts when a tooth nerve is exposed. It is also hard to pay attention when we are distracted by a flow of disconnected wants, the fear and envy that turn those wants into needs, and the fleeting satisfactions that sometimes answer them.

What neither Orwell nor Huxley predicted was the degree to which the Western world — especially the United States — would be taken over by the voracious nature of commodification. To mangle a cliché, commodities are — both literally and figuratively — the water we swim in and the air we breathe (both of which are polluted). To gain a commodity we must purchase it in the marketplace, taking part in a transaction through which rights are transferred from one person to another. Except by gift or theft, there is no other way to get a commodity. We can grow vegetables, hunt, or fish for our own use — if we have access to the appropriate environment. We can pick agates and shells from the beach. Most of us, however, need to enter the marketplace for the bulk of our material needs.

To participate in the world of commodities we must find a way to meet purchase prices. If we cannot, by falling on the wrong side of the division of spoils we can only do without. In the United States, doing without carries a moral charge. Those who must do without are often considered deeply unworthy. Their world can be very Orwellian.

What has happened in the United States under late capitalism is that commodification has metastasized. It has forced itself into every cell of human life. In recombinant fashion commodification has generated new forms of commodity life to dwell in new niches that may only be approached through market exchange. These are not just Koosh Balls, take-home sushi, and electric can openers, or even cruise control and remote control. The commodity form has increasingly taken away our dignity and our ability to live as human beings.

Over a hundred years ago, Karl Marx described the results of historical processes by which the factors necessary to what he called "species-being" were taken away from human beings by other human beings. Backed by instruments of power and through physical and ideological conflict, those who built the world of capital successfully brought factors of production into the market. Land, seeds, animals, tools, and especially human labor power came to be bought, sold, and withheld in the form of private property.

Particularly central for Marx was labor power — peoples' physical and mental ability to work — for he considered labor power to be the central human essence. To give over control of that essence through the wage-labor contract was to alienate the most crucial part of oneself. People without capital came to do that in order, through their wages, to purchase the necessities of life. Without land, seed, animals, or tools of one's own, one would have to purchase food, clothing, and shelter in the market.

Written in the immediate aftermath of the Industrial Revolution, Marx's picture of Europe was not pretty; yet in many ways the picture was clear. There were owners, workers, coal mines, big machines, and big factories spewing filthy smoke over the English gardens. Later, in the United States, things were also pretty clear — industrialists and their goons, backed by the state, fought against workers; railroad barons grabbed land; native Americans were decimated. But something was happening, especially in the United States, that would complicate things greatly.

By the late nineteenth century, U.S. manufacturing capabilities could produce not only big stuff but also little stuff — and lots of it. The question of what to do with the little stuff, the demand problem, was solved by the introduction of personal consumption on an increasingly mass basis. Assembly-line production, the great expansion of personal credit, the explosion of advertising — all were marshaled in the interests of efficient mass marketing.

Most important, during the first quarter of the twentieth century a new model of human nature was invented, developing out of but eventually annihilating the Enlightenment model of the rational, autonomous individual in whose name the modern, liberal Euro-American world had come into being. This new type of human was the consumer — a being of large mouth, large stomach, and, like Winnie-the-Pooh, very little brain.

Part of the promise of bourgeois democracy, of course, was abundance. Citizens were promised various economic and political rights, but they were also offered putative access to the good material things in life. With the invention and successful inculcation of the new ontological category of the consumer, one's piece of this abundance came to be seen as a natural right, perhaps the most important human entitlement. One's energy was directed toward fulfillment as a consumer.

What a consumer consumes are commodities, and the central historical process of the twentieth century is the triumph of the commodity form — nowhere more so than in the home of the free and the land of the brave. However they have been justified to the public, wars, police actions, trade and fiscal policies, legislative policies, judicial decisions, education and social policies, and the other paraphernalia of public life have been used to defend and extend commodification.

Control over commodities and over the access to commodities translates into control over people and their activities, especially in a world in which every part and parcel of human life has been drawn into the market. Commodification is like a "chaotic" fractal process,[5] repeating its patterns in branches and tendrils on an increasingly smaller scale as it fills the Mandelbrot sets of life. Even a short list of items available, often only available, in commodity form to those with the means of purchase or lease makes Marx's understanding of alienation seem Pollyannish. The list ranges from air, water, food, shelter, public office, personal image, information, love, and privacy to life-saving drugs, replacement body parts, and rented wombs.

What is characteristic of the postindustrial U.S. world is that the real material things available for consumption have been joined and crowded out by the ideas of things — symbols and images that circulate in the market as disconnected surrogates for substance. As consumers we are convinced not only of the justifiable insatiability of our desires but of new, unexpected needs, symbolically set before us and symbolically solved. Frederic Jameson has suggested that the culture of late capitalism has seen the spread of commodification into perhaps the last two available domains — the unconscious (pornography, psychotherapy, fantasy) and nature (wilderness parks, zoos, and anthropology[6]). Everything is for sale — or not, because property rights allow us to withhold food from a starving person.

The postmodern United States is a massive rush of disconnected commodities, each seeking a moment of our attention, a small but secure place inside our minds. Each must have a hook, a scary or amusing story, to overcome competing messages and move us to action. Half a century of advertising and mass media has severely shortened our attention spans. We have technical means of leaving stories that do not entertain us — we can turn them off — and as Neil Postman has written, we *must* be entertained.[7] Entertainment is the current form of public discourse. All public communication — advertisements, television shows, news, commentary — is packaged as entertaining bits that follow each other in series as items of the same weight and size. The great earthquake is no more important than the local car chase, the whale rescue, the wedding of television characters, or the latest escapades of the Energizer pink rabbit.

In a world of images to be consumed, it is hard not to be carried away. It becomes difficult to tell what is real and what is fake. In a time of creeping surrealism, as Joel Achenbach describes it, when we *can* tell the two apart, we often don't care which is which.[8] Simulations are fine. Why be too critical? Let's just tend our own gardens.

For those of us with wherewithal, the world is not an oppressive place weighed down by the stream of commodities. The things we gain as commodities obviously *do* fulfill many of our needs, even if only in symbolic form and only if those needs have become "real" in the interest of particular commodities (ring around the collar, halitosis, and the like). Given our times and circumstances, many commodities *are* pleasurable and fulfilling. They make us feel good. They may even temporarily take us away from the rat race, from the fear and discomfort of the everyday world of the pursuit of commodities. In this case particular commodities act as soma.

The denizens of Huxley's *Brave New World* were officially encouraged to take the soma drug, to go to "feelies," and to enjoy promiscuous sex in order to give them a stake in an ongoing life of pleasure and to capture their attention, deflecting it away from sustained critical thought about the organization of society. This was management by carrot. The easy availability of pleasure, Huxley believed, would make people self-policing and complicit in the reproduction of the status quo. Resources otherwise needed to maintain order — as in Orwell's Oceania — would be freed for other things. The insidious point of *Brave New World* was that except for the Savage, the people in London *did* have their needs met. They were quite happy. The Savage really was an oddball.

The postmodern United States is a world of commodities that act as discipline and as soma. We toe the line in order to get the means of existence, historically and broadly constructed — for such means are available only as commodities. We also get rewarded, pleased, entertained, and amused. We perceive these as our natural rights as consumers. As long as things are all right with ourselves and maybe with those immediately around us, we can avoid any systematic analysis of the institutional order. If a problem arises, we can rage at a particular subset of people involved — focusing our attention on doctors or lawyers or the police or the tax collector. Anything larger is the bureaucracy or City Hall, and you can't fight them.

Two things were particularly interesting about the Orwell conferences in 1984. First, there was a lot of discussion about media access. How were people to get the word about their Orwellian fears for the future out to the public when access to the mass media is denied to critical discourse? But the real problem is not the Orwell problem; it's the Huxley problem. No one wants to listen to critical analysis. It's too threatening to the accommodations people have made to the world as it is. It's not pleasant; it's not fun; it's boring. It's not soma.

Second, we were all having a real good time at these conferences. A couple of hours about Orwell and the iron boot, and we were off to trout almondine and pouilly-fuissé. During that year a lot of airplane tickets were bought, a lot of rooms rented, a lot of copies of *1984* and books about Orwell sold. A lot of commodities. It is all very complicated.

A World of Commodities

The world we live in is a world of commodities. Our physical survival and our relations with other people and with ourselves are increasingly mediated by the commodity form. Whatever particular items or experiences we gather to build our daily lives, they all come to us more and more through the same process. They are available in, and only in, the market. We can't even do the simple rituals that bind us together without purchasing paraphernalia. The commodity form, assumed and unremarkable, is the taken-for-granted structural principle of our times. It is *the* hegemonic truth of our times.

Antonio Gramsci describes hegemony as,

> the permeation throughout civil society . . . of an entire system of values, attitudes, beliefs, morality, etc., that is in one way or another supportive of the established order and the class interests that dominate it. . . . To the extent that this prevailing consciousness is internalized by the broad masses, it becomes part of "common sense." . . . For hegemony to assert itself success- fully in any society, therefore, it must operate in a dualistic manner: as a "general conception of life" for the masses and as a "scholastic programme." [9]

This "general conception of life" is what anthropologists mean when they talk about culture. It is not just that soma need be provided to keep people in line, or that the iron boot be used once in a while, but that the shared understandings by which people naturally construe their lives be shaped in certain ways. Culture is political in a deep sense. It is a lived-in thing, a seemingly transparent environment of symbols in which we live our normal lives. The meaning of things is obvious and unremarkable. Most of the time we don't even know we know things. How could they be otherwise? From the inside we don't live in a "culture"; we live in a world in which things just *are*.

It should be obvious, then, that it would be possible to benefit greatly in the distribution of power and resources if one could construe cultural meanings in one's favor. Others would become complicit in the main- tenance of one's position. The history of racism and sexism offers examples of the "naturalization" of categories to justify hierarchy.

Cultural control requires the invention and dissemination of stories as well as vigilance against counterstories. Culture is "relatively autonomous," as Louis Althusser would say, for the people who live it have room to maneuver — even in Orwell's Oceania. People often invent new pieces of potential culture and counterstories. The question is whether these survive to make a difference, whether they are suppressed and limited, or whether they are absorbed and assimilated.

Censorship is clearly part of the American way. More important, how- ever, is self-censorship, the repression of counterstories or counteraction out of the belief that they won't "sell" or the fear that we will lose our access to soma. Self-censorship is the result of a critical moment and a decision as to what to do about it. We see a possible course of thought or action but decide against it in order to avoid possible repercussions. It's not worth it. We sit back down and keep our mouths shut.

Most important is Gramsci's "scholastic programme," through which people are enculturated — taught how the world is and why it ought to be that way. Formal schooling, moral teaching, and the dissemination of well-shaped information and propaganda through mass media are all part of this "scholastic programme."

The hegemonic metamessage of our time is that the commodity form is natural and inescapable. Our lives can only be well lived (or lived at all) through the purchase of particular commodities. Thus our major existential interest consists of maneuvering for eligibility to buy such commodities in the market. Further, we have been taught that it is right and just — ordained by history, human nature, and God — that the means of life in all its forms be available *only* as commodities.

As the commodity form becomes a central part of culture, so culture becomes available for use in the interest of commodification as particular cultural items, as a source of commercial arguments,[10] and as symbolic legitimation for the entire system. Culture and the commodity form become dialectically intertwined. Americans live in an overcommodified world, with needs that are generated in the interests of the market and that can be met only through the market.

Who benefits from the current state of things? Obviously the corporations that produce, trade, finance, and sell pieces of life benefit. Their owners, managers, and major stockholders clearly have a vested interest in the commodity form. Their direct and indirect governmental hirelings, elected or otherwise, benefit from and support the world of commodities. Professionals who have made health, shelter, safety, and knowledge into private property get rich through the sale of their services.

But again things are not so simple, for in a rich, First World country we *all* benefit in a way — on the backs of workers and people in much of the rest of the world and over many of their dead bodies — from the commodity form, at least for now. This is what makes cultural criticism and other attempts to bring about change so difficult. Because the situation is complex and ambiguous, *we* are often ambivalent and inconsistent. In theoretical moments our critique may be clear: Television is bad; the world is full of kitsch; machines and tools are shoddy; politicians kill, as does cholesterol.

In the lived-in parts of our lives, however, we are often complicit in reproducing part of a situation we otherwise deplore. We make a brilliant public critique of television for its systematic confusion of reality and artifice, then go home and turn the machine on. Maybe it's showing sports, a concert, or the news, but maybe we're watching "Jeopardy." And maybe we're not just passively couched but actively engaged, shouting out answers from our own storehouse of trivia.

The commodification of culture acts on many levels. We are offered commodities to fill needs, some — like the contrived "need" for meat suggested by the Beef Council — artificial and manipulated but others real — stemming from the difficulties of life under the commodity form and the chaos the maldistribution of dignity and prospects through the market brings. The struggle for commodities, their vast numbers, the speed with which they pass before us, and the actions of those who cannot possess them all consume our energies. There is little time for sustained critique. We are tired; we need rest. We need, really need, soma. Thank God for plastic.

Walt Disney World

What does all this have to do with Walt Disney World?

I think this 27,400 acres of central Florida swamp and scrub forest, with its various theme parks and hotel complexes, is the most ideologically important piece of land in the United States. What goes on here is the quintessence of the American way.

First, of course, WDW is a set of amusement parks — the flagship Magic Kingdom, EPCOT Center with its Future World and World Showcase, the Disney-MGM Studios, River Country, Discovery Island, Typhoon Lagoon, and Pleasure Island. These venues, along with Walt Disney World Shopping Village and the various Disney resort hotels, are visited by over 30 million people a year, making WDW by far the most important entertainment center in the world.

But this Vacation Kingdom is more than just a set of amusement parks: It is the major middle-class pilgrimage center in the United States. Walt Disney, Mickey Mouse, Donald Duck, and the others are central U.S. icons. With the corporate capture as well of Peter Pan, Cinderella, Snow White, Pinocchio, the Three Little Pigs, even Winnie-the-Pooh and Kermit the Frog, WDW (together with California's Disneyland) has become the home of childhood. Not to bring our children there at least once, resuscitating our own childhood along the way, is to commit a grave moral offense. We abdicate our right to call ourselves parents.

Walt Disney World has become a pilgrimage site partly because of the brilliance of its cross-referential marketing and partly because its utopian aspects appeal strongly to real peoples' real needs in late capitalist society. Disney's marketing is unique. Not only has it captured the symbolic essence of childhood, but the Company has gained access to all public communication media. Movies, television shows, comic books, dolls, tee-shirts, and educational film strips all point to the parks and to each other.

Each advertises all the others as part of its content without the need for special commercial interruptions. Special advertising can be used sparingly and elsewhere.

We must always remember that the business of the Walt Disney Company is business. The theme park division is only part of a much larger conglomerate whose raison d'être is to sell commodities. Disney competes with a lot of other corporations for the discretionary leisure dollar, so however predatory Disney may be, it must and does sell something special. The Company — especially at its theme parks — produces, packages, and sells experiences and memories as commodities.

These in many ways are utopian experiences. From horseback riding to sashimi; golf to English high tea; mock historical tableaux to educational technological displays, song and dance reviews, parades, singing robot bears, films of all sorts, and Minnie Mouse in a kimono, WDW contains hundreds of separate events, all occurring more or less simultaneously. Each one has a consistent theme — a blend of architecture, art, craft, sound, even smell — that surrounds us like an envelope. The venues are organized into larger themes — fantasy, U.S. history, science and technology, world travel — in the major divisions of the parks.

The form that structures our experiences at WDW is the cinema. As we move around we enter into a series of activities constructed as movie scenes. We are in the middle with the action taking place all around us. We stand in, walk, or ride through these scenes as we move through the possible movies of our visit.

Often our experiences are passive as we are strapped into moving seats that carry us through particular scenes in absolute, fully programmed order. Sometimes we are dragged into participation by attendants who ask us to do something. But surprisingly often we are actively engaged with the show. There are countless effects at WDW, little hooks and traces of craft and memory. Surprises, such as the vinyl leaves after which this study is named, crop up constantly — some to be marveled at, some critiqued, but all there for active thought if noticed.

Madeleines bring remembrance. Disney simulations remind visitors of something they know, somewhere they've been, something they've seen or heard. We point things out, tell stories, argue about Disney's take on things. We decide what to see next, argue about where to eat, complain about the lines, and we walk — endlessly.

All of this takes place in an environment very different from that of our normal lives, for Disney is not just offering entertainment: The Company is also selling, to those of us who can afford it, an antidote to everyday life. Under the rule of the commodity, our lives have become fragmented and confusing. Our environments are dangerous and threatening. Our sense of powerlessness is fed by the institutions of modern life and by the uncontrollable behavior of others. What we buy at WDW is not just fun and souvenirs but is also a welcome civility on a human scale.

Other than the novelties, for instance, there are no vehicles on theme park streets. It is a pedestrian's world. We walk in the road. Except for the monumental architecture at Future World, everything is built to human scale, with upper stories foreshortened to give the illusion of height without overwhelming us. The disabled are well cared for.

The parks are impeccably clean. There are lots of restrooms. We can walk the streets at night without fear for ourselves or our pocketbooks. In a country in which it is often not wise to be out after dark, this freedom is enormously empowering.

People are civil — not just the employees, rhetorically dubbed "cast members," who have been trained to be polite at all times to the "guests" (as customers are called), but the guests themselves. Thousands of people, collected in the same space in the Florida heat, act well toward each other. WDW is a prime example in favor of an argument about the power of an environment to affect behavior. People are friendly, helpful, often (except with cameras in their hands) considerate, and sympathetic to parents with small children on hot afternoons. Children are safe and obviously welcomed.

However mysterious, the technology works. Food appears. There is air-conditioning. The trains run on time. This is clearly Oz (as well as Kansas). WDW's many utopian aspects undeniably answer the needs of its visitors. They are a major part of the draw. We have here utopia as a marketing device.

If we look at the context in which these needs are satisfied, however, we begin to see the other side of utopia, for the pleasantries are possible because this context is totally controlled. The promise of Disney's potential economic contribution to the Greater Orlando area was such that in 1967, the Florida State Legislature designated Disney's acres as the Reedy Creek Improvement District. This designation made the property, which straddles the line between Orange and Osceola counties, into an independent governmental unit, giving its citizens as much fiscal and administrative control as the state constitution offers its towns and cities. The few full-time residents of Bay Lake and Lake Buena Vista are Disney people. Thus, for all intents and purposes, the Company *is* local government.

Zoning, planning, bonding, developing, and the provision of most municipal services are under Disney control. So, by reason of Disney's enormous economic clout, are many of its relations with the counties and cities of central Florida, the state, and even the federal government. The Reedy Creek Improvement District is the local elephant, stepping — not without local opposition — pretty much where it wants.

Inside its property boundaries, Disney also sets the rules. From ticket pricing and operating hours to strict supervision of the behavior of its employees and security and operating practices, Big Brother is there. The public Disney "magic" is the product of a great deal of apparatus, such as the utility corridors beneath Cinderella's Castle, hidden from view.

WDW presents what Disney calls "family entertainment" — fun for all ages that is safe, clean, efficient, and uncontroversial; fun that is nice in a secular Sunbelt way. [11] Disney's greatest calling card is its image. This is the symbolic capital from which the real revenues flow. Insofar as the magic works, people purchase the experiences and the accompanying souvenirs. In order to feel safe, happy, clean, and civil — to feel what seems the antithesis to their normal lives — people are willing and trusting enough to put themselves into Disney's hands for a time.

These hands bear watching, for in their shaping of things lies danger. It is not just that our movements are constrained with the promise, usually fulfilled, of rewards. What is important is that our thoughts are constrained. They are channeled in the interests of Disney itself but also in the interests of the large corporations with which Disney has allied itself, the system of power they maintain, and the world of commodities that is their life's blood. Here in this hegemony of corporate power and the commodity form lurks Huxley's brave new world. Disney stories draw us further into the web.

We are told constantly how to feel about each WDW venue. They are called attractions; we are guests; Disney workers are cast members. Many are hosts and hostesses. The language for describing our experience is preempted by the Company. Everything is magical. Guide books, advertisements, and commemorative literature drip with description. This is "exhilirating"; that is "wonderful" or "amazing." We are told what is whimsical: "You don't want to miss X"; "everybody loves Y"; "we all become children at Z."

WDW literature is the retirement home of the inflationary descriptive adjective. We are ordered about by language that is constantly performative and directive. We are drained of interpretive autonomy. The rhetoric is so overexuberant that we stop noticing its intent: It is just normal Disneytalk. But the manipulative character of this language slides over into something much more sinister when we come to the corporate-sponsored descriptions of the world, its history, and its future at EPCOT Center.

The attractions at EPCOT Center, especially at Future World, are meant to be both entertaining and educational. Here we learn about the sea, hydroponic agriculture, energy, automobile design, and the human body. Our lessons are taught by Disney in collaboration with the giant corporations that sponsor the various pavilions — among them AT&T, General Motors, General Electric, Kraft Foods, Kodak, and United Technologies.

Each corporation tells stories centered around its own domain of production, but together these presentations form a rhetorical metastory of corporate ideology.

The past was zany, although there were some serious people around (Da Vinci, Michaelangelo) in the Italian Renaissance. The present is terrific, mostly because of the commodities the corporations have developed and marketed. The future, however, is full of challenges. New frontiers are everywhere, especially in space and in the oceans. On both sides of these new frontiers, the natural world exists only for human use. It has "gifts" for us. Potential difficulties and problems will challenge us, but "we" can overcome them if we are wise and if we have the will — if we dare to dream: "If we can dream it, we can do it."

Who is this "we"? The first-person plural at Future World is pure ideological gambit. It marks as natural an attempted alliance between the middle-class people who visit WDW and the giant corporations that would control our destiny. The problems of the future will be solved if "we" (the people) place ourselves in "our" (the corporations') hands. All these problems have technical solutions on which the developmental scientists of Exxon and United Technologies are working. We need only have the will, the courage, and the imagination to let them do it.

This is Bonapartist ideology. These corporations go beyond factions of the state to attempt a direct alliance between their imperial designs and the desires of the citizenry. They envision a global technocracy with which we will be complicit because, after all, we are all in this together. This technocracy will be universal and secular. [12] If we ally ourselves with corporate enterprise, we will have "progress." Progress toward what? Toward more and more.

What social critics sometimes forget in their discussions about the power of corporations vis-à-vis individuals, communities, and states is that the former exist because they produce and sell commodities. However cast, their messages to the world are either commercial rhetoric in particular or metaphysical discourse aimed at continually convincing people that the commodity form is natural. The corporate project is to bring everything associated with human life into the market and thus under control. The corporate project, then, is Disney's project, and Disney speaks for other corporations as well as for itself.

The semantics of this hegemonic speech are different at the various theme parks at WDW — nostalgia and fantasy at the Magic Kingdom, travel and culture at World Showcase, science and technology at Future World — but the syntax is the same. At all the parks we are overwhelmed by the number and velocity of messages. Images speed past us, disconnected from each other save for their tone. Disparate elements of design jumble our minds as we pass from theme to theme. Normal relations between building and façade do not hold. All tales seem the same size; difference is obliterated, overwhelmed. WDW is the postmodern sublime, and before it, lest we swoon, we enter a strange, hyperactive mental zone.

This buzz is precisely the state the purveyors of commodification would have us enter. The world of commodities presents itself in an onslaught of discrete, disconnected packages, and the pursuit of these packages — each designed to fill some artificially constructed need — leaves minimal space in our lives for coherent critical thought about what we are doing. We are encouraged to pay attention only to those things that are amusing and fun and to get through our other activities as expeditiously as possible.

At WDW we enter this state of commodity satori. It is the land of more. The 1988 Walt Disney World Resort Vacation Guide headlines its descriptive sections thus:

SO MUCH MORE THAN EVER BEFORE

MORE VACATION FUN THAN EVER BEFORE

MORE FANTASY IN THE MAGIC KINGDOM

MORE FUTURE AT EPCOT CENTER AND THE THRESHOLD OF TOMORROW!

MORE INTERNATIONAL EXCITEMENT TO EXPERIENCE IN WORLD SHOWCASE!

MORE PLACES TO PLAY IN THE WATERS OF RIVER COUNTRY

MORE WONDERS OF NATURE ON DISCOVERY ISLAND

MORE ACTIVITIES AT THE WALT DISNEY WORLD SHOPPING VILLAGE!

MORE RECREATION: We'll Fill Your Vacation with As Much Fun As You Can Handle!

MORE PLACES TO STAY AT THE GRAND FLORIDIAN BEACH RESORT

MORE CHOICES AT THE DISNEY VILLAGE RESORT

MORE RELAXATION AT THE DISNEY INN

MORE UP-TO-DATE ACCOMMODATIONS AT THE
CONTEMPORARY RESORT

MORE ISLAND PLEASURES AT THE POLYNESIAN
VILLAGE RESORT

MORE CAMPING FUN AT THE FORT WILDERNESS
CAMPGROUND RESORT

MORE TO COME! DISNEY'S CARIBBEAN BEACH
RESORT

Wow!

WDW is beyond excess — four or five standard deviations away from
the mean. It's beyond the horizon. It's not that things of excess are tasteless;
English high tea and the rijstaffel are not tasteless, nor are Angkor Wat,
King's College, Cambridge, or the Grand Canyon. In a different way, Miami
is not tasteless. It is, like much postmodernism, a-tasteful. Taste is irrelevant.

Although much of WDW has taste, the category is meaningless here as
well. In its destruction of the idea of excess, WDW is a constituting symbol
of a United States beyond excess. It is like a mutant growth, distilling the
commodity form to its core and presenting the postmodern world of late
capitalism — the vast market of image and mixed metaphor — in its essence.

Disney World and Me

I love it! I could live there. I love its infinitude, its theater, its dadaism. I
love its food, its craft, its simulations. It gets me to think, to remember, and
to make up new fantasies. I appreciate its civility and its safety. I crave its
contradictions. I like walking in its streets. I am writing this book because
it has allowed me to spend lots of time there — and lots of money. If ever
there were self-funded research, this is it.

But I am also writing this because I think it is important to do so. I want
to understand how culture is used in the interest of commodification
because I believe the commodity form is hegemonic in our times. I also want
to understand how that hegemony is reproduced, how we all become
complicit in the world of commodities, and how this complicity becomes
what Ludwig Wittgenstein called a "form of life."

We are not just passive beings with similar templates stamped into our brains by all-powerful modern institutions. We make history, as Karl Marx wrote, but under constraints. The constraints of late capitalism are subtle but strong. They are like the tiny Lilliputian strings that, all together, held Gulliver down.

These ties are subtle because we have been taught that our needs and wants can be met only through the market. Because we have taken commercially generated needs as natural needs, they often really can be filled in commodity form — just as we can buy safety and civility at the Magic Kingdom. Our ontological acceptance of the model of the consumer as the new human nature leads us to new natural rights of entitlement and to new evidence of fulfillment. Whether we police ourselves in order to play the game, or whether we step outside the rules as outlaw entrepreneurs, we "win" by consuming. Huxley was right.

The contradictions are many. I live them every day. I argue against the deadening impact of television — and I watch it nearly every day, actively engaged. I rail against the commodity form and impulse buy all the time. I love literal and metaphorical plastic. It's terrible, I know, but I do.

WDW is the teaching shrine for the corporate world of commodities. This is a cruel and contentious world. The hegemony of the commodity form threatens evolution on this planet and all living things. I hope WDW becomes the most important museum representing the historical period when commodification ruled. People can bring their children to see what life was like in those dangerous days.

Consider this book my application as a docent.

About My Application

This book is divided into five parts, each of which contains both description and theoretical discussion. At some point I will say something about every attraction at WDW, organizing these descriptions in terms of larger themes. Theoretical arguments are interwoven throughout the book, usually one major discussion to each part. There is no best, coherent way to see WDW, so, like a "guest," I will wander about in my own fashion.

Chapters 2-5 contain three different kinds of context-setting remarks: a general descriptive introduction to WDW; preliminary comments about culture, symbolic universes, maps, and territories, decontextualization, and unnatural selection; and a brief historical overview of the United States and the invention of the consumer. I then analyze how history is construed at WDW. This includes a tour of Frontierland, Liberty Square, the American Adventure at World Showcase, and various parts of Future World.

In Chapters 6-9 I discuss some of the political and economic aspects of WDW. This includes a bit of corporate history as well as a discussion of the impact of WDW on central Florida. Here I also analyze the Disney style of marketing and merchandising. This section ends with strolls down Main Street USA and Hollywood Boulevard.

Chapters 10-12 are about space. WDW has been considered by many urban planners to be a utopian urban space. In this part I discuss the urban planning and architecture of WDW. Following Howard Segal, I suggest that what we have here is a model of a technological utopia, one that has become a major U.S. pilgrimage site. Pictures of utopia, however, seldom tell us how the infrastructure works. Thus, this part begins with an extended discussion of the physical geography and physical planning of WDW. Here I say some things about transportation, energy, waste disposal, water control, and the like. I end with Disney's presentation of cultural geography — the world as a set of theme parks — in a tour of Adventureland and World Showcase.

Chapters 13-15 are about art, fantasy, and the postmodern world of late capitalism. A presentation of the cinematic structure of WDW, its approach to fantasy and the use of music is be followed by a visit to Fantasyland. Here there is a further discussion of the commodity form, advertising, and the relations between reality and artifice in the world of commodities. Chapter 15 is a centerpiece of the book.

In Chapters 16-18 I discuss science, technology, and the corporate Disney vision of the future. In a walk through Tomorrowland and Future World we see what General Motors, Exxon, and other corporations have in store for us and for nature, especially under what Langdon Winner calls "regimes of instrumentality." [13] Particularly interesting here are corporate notions about the future of agriculture and of work.

Now, a few words about the research. This study is the result of participant observation at WDW over a period of many years and through many visits. I paid my own way, and I wandered around just like any other visitor. I engaged in the kinds of normal conversations one has with other visitors, but I never initiated a research inquiry with a customer while at the parks. I overheard a lot of interesting conversation but never intruded on peoples' purchased holidays.

I have, however, talked to lots of people who have been to WDW or worked there. Much of what I have to say about visitors' responses comes from these conversations.

Every piece of literature I refer to is in the public record. Much of it I found in the Orlando Public Library at the Disney Depository. Other sources turned up in a number of libraries I visited around the country, when I sneaked off from official business to see if I could fill a gap in my growing files. I don't even want to think about how much money I spent on photocopying, but I can't carry the piles of Xeroxes by myself. I would especially like to acknowledge Steve Birnbaum's guides to WDW.[14] They contain an enormous amount of information. Don't leave home without one.

This book is full of details about WDW, perhaps numbingly so; but the number of details is part of the message. The message is about cognitive overload, but it is also about the possibilities for active recognition and response. There are many wonderful and surprising details at the parks — lots of things to notice, each one of which somebody thought to put there. If God is in the details, we will find the gods of the commodity form herein.

2

Culture and Context

George Washington may be the father of this country, Dad, but Walt Disney is its guardian.

—Dick Schaap's son[1]

Walt Disney World is an amusement park — the largest and most frequently visited part of the entire amusement park industry. It contains a concentrated distillation of one version of the United States and its view of the world, a version both mythical and real. This distillation is presented with great imagination and technical skill. Unlike many holy places, which become so through the unanticipated quirks of history, WDW is an *intended* shrine. It was built by a corporation for corporate purposes, and it has, as intended, transcended that corporation by assimilating and even inventing key symbols of the version of the United States it presents.

The park's main purpose is to make money for the Walt Disney Company. This it does in both direct and indirect ways. Most obviously, WDW charges an admission fee. This charge, surprisingly low if converted to dollars-per-hour in the park areas, admits one to most attractions and all transportation media. Some areas — River Country, Discovery Island, Pleasure Island, Typhoon Lagoon — require separate admissions. The other obvious daily charge is a parking fee. These fees add up, but they are not the only money-makers.

The three other largest direct sources of revenue at WDW are rents — collected at hotels, villas at Lake Buena Vista, and campsites and trailers at

Fort Wilderness — food, and the merchandise sold at ubiquitous themed shops. These are the costs most obvious to the visitor, the ones a friend of mine means when he says he walks around all day "feeling Walt's hand in my pocket."

As is often the case, however, behind appearance lies essence. Although many times bigger than Disneyland in Anaheim, the built-up area of the Vacation Kingdom is but a small portion of the 27,400 acres owned by the Walt Disney Company in central Florida. The rest, purchased by corporate agents in the 1960s at very low prices, is available for further development. For the most part, this development will be undertaken by corporate subsidiaries in concert with other corporations that have agreed to special fiscal arrangements with Disney. Further, Disney engineering subsidiaries market products, such as the WEDway PeopleMover, developed as part of the production of WDW.

Major corporations are generally fairly evident at WDW. For their own marketing purposes, these corporations pay sponsorship fees to Disney. Such fees underwrite much of the expense of constructing and maintaining attractions, stores, and restaurants. In return these corporations receive exclusive rights to presence at WDW and the use of the Disney connection in their own corporate advertising.

The Florida and California theme parks form part of a corporation that also makes movies and television shows and that merchandizes a wide range of commodities. All of these activities center around a set of Disney characters, invented or purloined, and a carefully constructed Disney image. These characters and images are not only leased to corporations but are also available for cross-referencing in Disney's own commercial activities. Disney film characters become park attractions. Character effigies sell as souvenirs of visits to WDW. The parks become venues for television shows. Corporate divisions point to other corporate divisions so that merchandizing by itself advertises other merchandizing.

Disney characters, images, and technical expertise have become franchised. A Tokyo Disneyland — to which the Walt Disney Company sold plans, technologies, and name — opened in 1983,[2] and an additional park, Euro Disney, outside Paris in 1992.

Finally, Disney stock trades on the New York Stock Exchange. Its fortunes have fallen and risen over recent years. The Company as a whole has been subject to greenmail and to friendly bailout. But through all of its recent financial history, Disney has continued to plan for further growth in Florida. In many ways WDW has become the cornerstone of the Disney empire.

The Vacation Kingdom carries a lot of weight on its shoulders. It is the most important forum in which the public meets the corporation. WDW not only must amuse its visitors, but it must do so in a manner that is both distinctive and appealing. This distinction and appeal protect the capital investments of Disney itself and also those of many others in the central Florida area who, having built motels, hotels, restaurants, service stations, industrial establishments, and similar institutions, depend on WDW for their continued existence. These are the people whose support Disney needs in the local political context. Disney's job is to lure visitors to central Florida in general and to its own theme parks in particular. As we will see, some contradiction is implied in these tasks.

WDW consists of a growing number of separate venues, each containing attractions that are designed to appeal, although not exclusively, to a different demographic category of visitors. The Magic Kingdom — the original theme park at Walt Disney World — is aimed at a young audience. EPCOT Center is constructed for adults and Pleasure Island for young adults. Each of the other establishments is designed to fill out the demographics. Among them all these sites capture around 30 million pilgrims a year.

Although each of these venues is constructed according to a more-or-less consistent theme, many are internally divided into areas with their own distinctive subthemes. The Magic Kingdom contains Adventureland, Frontierland, Liberty Square, Fantasyland, Mickey's Starland, Tomorrowland, and Main Street USA. EPCOT Center is divided into Future World and World Showcase. These areas are again subdivided, most more than once.

Each part and subpart of this multitheme resort carries a set of messages. Those of the timeless, a-historical world of Fantasyland are very different from the evolutionary messages of EPCOT Center's Universe of Energy and The Living Seas. The Diamond Horseshoe Jamboree seems worlds apart from the scene at the Rose and Crown Pub in World Showcase's United Kingdom. Yet Mickey Mouse shows up at the Golf Resort and Walt Disney World Marketplace as well as on Main Street USA.

The hierarchy of themes within themes is important in a number of ways. First, it lures visitors by providing differences, each of which is independently appealing. Second, it structures the flow of traffic for those who organize the progression of their days theme by theme. Third, it allows the Disney people to encapsulate their guests in the corporate version of each theme.

This envelopment-by-theme is effected by extremely skilled staging, research, and craft. Disney interpretations are packaged for material, emotional, and cognitive consumption. These packages are brief, multisensory, and discrete — each one seamlessly themed. A visitor's attention is focused on countless coordinated details passing by at high velocity, to the point that one's powers of discrimination can be overwhelmed. WDW is organized according to the principle of cognitive overload; it is with the overriding of visitors' capacities for making discriminations that Disney metathemes may take effect.

The volume and velocity of information are just two of the reasons many visitors implicate themselves in the Disney Project. The stories and media are compelling because they speak to real issues in the lives of Disney's visitors. There is, in a way, something for everyone — especially safety and cleanliness. The infrastructure — transportation, communication, climate control, and waste disposal devices — is extraordinary, as is the management of pedestrian circulation, lines, and services. There are day-care centers, kennels, wheelchairs, even rentable audio cassettes that describe the sights *and* artificial smells of each attraction for the blind.

The Vacation Kingdom is a surprisingly subtle place. Although some messages — such as those of the General Electric Company at its Carousel of Progress — are intrusively blatant, there are others of some delicacy. It is easy to note those elements of what William Leiss has called "the domination of nature" [3] in The Land Pavilion at EPCOT Center. Meanwhile, one has spent a day among endless horticultural experiments completely taken for granted on the Walt Disney World grounds. One can argue about the friendly fascism by which customers are managed throughout the various theme areas; yet it is seductive. The lines move, the restaurant tables and restrooms get cleaned, and the trains run pretty much on time. [4] Walt Disney World is not without its utopian aspects.

Along with other divisions of the Walt Disney Company, WDW performs key ideological functions in U.S. society. It has presented its constructions of the world to millions of people. WDW has acted, first and foremost, in its own corporate interests, presenting its stories in a way that will sell both stories and other Disney commodities. Disney has protected its commercial merchandizing, just as it has protected its movie-making, with what Pierre Bourdieu calls "symbolic capital." [5] This is what Mickey Mouse, Figment, friendliness, cleanliness, family values, and the general Disney image are about.

In protecting its own interest, however, the Walt Disney Company has become the muse of corporate capitalism, the defense and space establishments, and a version of the American way that might be called secular sunbelt culture. This, I think, is obvious to many visitors to Walt Disney World. What is less obvious is that Disney, with its bricolage of themes within themes, is also the muse of decontextualization. History, geography, politics, language, the present, nature, even nutrition are annihilated in WDW stories and practices. Through this process a huge space is opened up for a context-free vision of technology that, if "we" use "our" imagination, will allow "us" to control our "fun" future. As the old joke goes, "What do you mean *we*, kimosabe?"

This technology digitalizes the analog world, just as the Walt Disney Company — in content and in form — digitalizes the actual world in its merchandized fantasies. Disney not only sells its own bounded but cross-referenced commodities but, further, acts as a shill for decontextualized, digitalizing "hard-path" technologies, the corporations that control them, and the social and political interests on whose behalf they work. One of Disney's metathemes is found in what Max Weber called the "elective affinity" [6] between the bounded commodity and decontextualized technology, all marketed by enchanting stories about fantasy, history, and modern times in which culture has become ideology.

Before continuing with WDW, I need to explain two of the concepts I have begun to use: culture and decontextualization. First, culture.

Culture

One of my main conceptual tools in this book is one version of the anthropological notion of culture. As I use it, culture is a public, more-or-less shared set of symbols, meanings, understandings, and beliefs people use to make sense of and to reproduce their normal daily lives. I do not mean Culture with a capital C — that is, a received and explicit canon of activities and their products of putatively "correct value." Nor do I mean popular culture, the anti-elitist response to Culture. Those who argue that Walt Disney World is a mecca of popular culture are right, but they miss a much deeper and more important point. It is consistent with U.S. culture, in the anthropological sense, that there should be an academic response to Culture (with a capital C) in the name of the little people. I am interested in the taken-for-granted assumptions about how the world works that underly both positions. [7]

In the sense that I use it, culture has a number of characteristics. [8] First, it is learned. It is taught to children and other outsiders by means of talk, writing, and other available media. Once internalized, culture becomes a way — often the only way — of construing the world around us.

Second, culture is both shared and distributive; that is, there are levels of culture. Some of these are shared by most, if not all, people within their purview. American ideas about individualism, pragmatism, mom, and Mickey Mouse (as character and as silliness) are such notions. Other pieces of culture are indirectly available. One knows who knows them and how to reach those people. We can figure out where to go if we need a contractor, an airline reservation, a rabbi, a car mechanic, good barbecue, or maybe even a poet.

The issue of cultural purview is important, for although various symbols and understandings are shared by most Americans, others — such as some meanings shared by Catholics — are transnational. Still others are shared on local, regional, racial, ethnic, and even family levels. Conflicts between kinds of people are often fought through competing cultural understandings. The stories and symbols presented by the Walt Disney Company form one such set of cultural weapons.

Third, much of culture, especially that which is ubiquitous, is tacit. Once we learn them, these pieces of culture are backgrounded out of our normal awareness unless rules about them are broken. Beliefs about the individual, the gods, nature, etiquette, kinship, personal space, happiness, time, causality, fun, rules of evidence, responsibility, categories of people, the meaning of birth and death, the status of truth and lies — all of these are understandings that we learn, forget that we learned, and consider good, true, and beautiful or unfortunate but inevitable, but in any case universal.

People everywhere live in a "cultured" universe, the human and historical construction of which it is often difficult to notice. We are us; others are different. That is all.

Culture is made up of rules of interpretation and symbols in which these rules may be carried and embodied. Once such rules are historically established, they become available for normal, everyday understanding, but they can also be used by those who can constrain and control. Agents of change butt up against the inertia of received belief and feeling.

Most people who write about culture in the anthropological sense describe it as if it were "just there," in a kind of distinctive and timeless fashion. This is Nuer culture; this is Trobriand Island culture; over there is Hopi culture. These cultures are different from ours, but they should be respected and understood before we can make comments about universals in human behavior.

I am going to push the notion of culture a bit. Culture explains the world and provides the assumed background for action, but it also maps the world. It tells people what is reasonably (or theologically) out there in life. If one were to control the cultural apparatus, one could construct an "out there" to one's benefit. I think the Walt Disney Company does just that and more at Walt Disney World.

My use of culture is akin to the idea of legitimations as developed by Peter Berger and Thomas Luckmann in their *The Social Construction of Reality*.[9] They argue that the structural skeleton of any social group is formed by a set of everyday behaviors that are institutionalized; that is, these behaviors (or actions) are patterned, consistent, regular, and rule-governed such that people know what they are supposed to do under normal circumstances. When actions are institutionalized, people know what to expect from others in the course of everyday life. In this broad sense, institutionalization has the further characteristic that once it is completed, people take it for granted. It becomes backgrounded and out of normal awareness unless some problem arises to bring it to the fore.

Institutionalization ranges from the kinds of high-frequency, widely shared activities — conversations, shopping rituals, car driving practices, and other quotidian skills — studied by microsociologists and sociolinguists to large-scale activities such as war and politics. Berger and Luckmann argue that all aspects of social life require institutionalization;

otherwise, life would be impossibly random. Through this process we develop habits and skills that allow us to get through our days without having to start from scratch each time we act.

The problem with institutionalization, however, is one of coherence. There is no reason to believe, and there is infinite evidence to the contrary, that all the institutionalizations in a person's (or a group's) life will fit together without conflict or contradiction. Berger and Luckmann claim that whatever coherence *is* brought to the compartmentalized institutionalizations of life is brought on the cognitive level of human existence. They call the vehicles for this coherence "legitimations."

Legitimations come in many shapes and sizes, for they have a lot of tasks to perform. They help people — both socialized old-timers and especially newcomers such as children and immigrants — to understand daily life in a locally correct fashion. At the same time, legitimations justify the world. They tell us not only *what* our world is like but also *why* it is, and perhaps should be, as it is. When legitimations work, the gap between cognitions and justifications disappears. Legitimations are often stored out of normal awareness while we go on understanding and acting in the world. Only when a problem arises — a disagreement with another or a glitch in our endeavors — do we need to bring out a legitimation.

Many of the shared public symbols that make up culture are legitimations. One metaphor that is useful in understanding the relations between culture and legitimations is that of the map. Pieces of culture are like different-sized maps that represent various elements of a group's social and natural territory. They depict destinations, waystations, obstacles and hazards, and roadside rests — all in a territory that has been more-or-less bounded for representation.

As we go about our normal journeys, we use portions of the map we have already learned. We may try alternate pathways, or we may shy away from them, depending on our transportational equipment and what the legend says about the shape of the terrain. More distant journeys may be suggested to us by portions of the map depicting places we haven't yet visited. We may want to find another map, larger and with more detail, to get more information about these strange places. More often than not until we go there ourselves, what we know about strange territories comes from these maps. We may have heard some traveler's tales told by someone who has ventured out into *terra incognito* — probably bringing back slides — but these remain unofficial, idiosyncratic stories. We will surely want to consult a map.

We hope the map is correct. When it says there is a bridge across the river at the end of a long road in a wild place, we expect that bridge to be there. If it is, we continue to trust the map on the rest of our journey. If the bridge is not there, we have a problem. Not only is our day not made, but the accuracy of the map is jarringly called into question. So is the competence of its makers and distributors.

It is usually only when there is a problem or when we are searching for a particular kind of map that we even remember that maps are drawn (and caused to be drawn) by someone. We seldom ask, because the answer seems so obvious, why distribute a map at all?

Until the last few hundred years maps, for the most part, were jealously guarded. They contained information over which control was paramount to the interests of trade and war. Punishment for disclosing the information depicted on many such maps was severe. Over time, however, cartographic information escaped control and spread into the public domain.

As maps got better and better and people came to rely on the information presented on them, control over the cartographic enterprise itself became of central importance. If one could get lots of people to rely on the same maps, and if one could get them to think of the territory only in terms of those maps, one could control the flow of traffic and the selection of destinations by doing little more than presenting targets and pathways. By bounding the territory and placing warnings about dragons outside the boundaries, those in control of the cartography could get all but the most intrepid of travelers to remain in the territory.

Culture is made up of maps and sets of maps that serve as legitimations in Berger and Luckmann's sense. Whatever else it may be, culture also serves important ideological functions. Groups and categories of people in any society benefit differentially from the stories told and the symbols used to construct an understanding of everyday life. If the stories are good and the symbols are powerful, they will justify differences in access to power and resources as good, right, and beautiful. Institutionalized activity, channeled by mapped pathways and legitimated by cultural beliefs and values, is geared to maintain the normal world as it is.

Cultural items, especially those deep-seated items entirely taken for granted, have histories. They do not come from the gods or from nature, although many of us may become persuaded that they do. Instead they are survivors of a process by which alternative ways of conceptualizing ideas, things, and activities have been eliminated or marginalized. What we have, then, is a division of tasks among those who would control the production of culture in this broad sense. We might think of these as positive tasks and negative tasks.

The first, and most disorganized of these tasks is the invention of culture. People invent potential pieces of culture all the time. Many of these, such as bits of slang to be used with friends or the kind of tinkering engineers write about, are done essentially in play. Others are concocted as potential solutions to certain problems.

For the moment I will suggest three large classes of such problems: those of management and control, those of access to the market in market societies, and those pertaining to activities counter to the first two. In each of these cases, potential cultural solutions to problems are consciously sought.

However, one doesn't necessarily have to invent pieces of culture *de novo*. The most powerful and frequent use of culture in the interests of management, access to the market, and even rebellion involves the second task of cultural control — the capture and manipulation of already-existing stories and symbols. This is the task at which the Walt Disney Company excels. Most of the stories told at Walt Disney World make use of Disney versions of elements of U.S. (and world) culture. Notions about the home, family, and sex roles as well as historical characters such as Abraham Lincoln and Mark Twain are cleaned up and repackaged in the interest of Disney themes.

The two positive processes of invention and capture of culture can be done by anybody. The crucial question is whether or not anybody succeeds in disseminating them widely enough to become accepted as normal by a substantial number of people. Here is where the third task of cultural management — boundary maintenance — comes into play.

Cultural ideas and counterideas crop up like weeds. Some get nurtured; some get sprayed with metaphorical herbicide. If cultural constructions are to continue to have force (and thus those institutionalizations they define and explain are to persist), then the borders around these constructions must be patrolled. I call this process of boundary maintenance "unnatural selection." As in the biological process from which my trope is taken, forms — in this case cultural rather than biological forms — are pared away from the main body of cultural continuity by activities that dismiss or suppress them. What is left if this "negative" process works correctly is a kind of mainstream of cultural elements in which maps and legitimations of things as they are remains more or less intact.

Some of this paring away is done with systemic intent. There are agencies that perform censorship activities and cultural spin control, but because for the most part the policing of cultural boundaries is not organized by a positive conspiracy, those who have presented purely conspiracy theories to explain the protection of *ideology* have been unconvincing. [10]

The process of "universe-maintaining," in Berger and Luckmann's terms, is deep and subtle. Once members of a group have learned and internalized a discourse of fundamental assumptions about what is good, true, and beautiful, they will willingly police themselves in the normal course of events. Countermessages will be defined as heretical only if they force an explicit awareness of the parameters of the cultural map. Usually, however, such countermessages will be ignored or suppressed as sick, crazy, wacky, childish, or silly — not worthy of any serious mature contemplation. In their initial stages, before they had strengthened enough to be treated as heretical, all movements on behalf of civil rights in the United States were treated in this dismissive fashion.

A still more effective organization of unnatural selection may be produced if the cartographic enterprise can be managed so people do not even hear countermessages. If a voice is not heard, then it is truly in the wilderness. As it becomes louder in an attempt to break across the silence, it may be dismissed as intrusively shrill.

Alternate voices require silences (or a negotiation on when to use the floor) in order to be heard. Thus, another way to protect against such voices is to deny silence. Fill up the available sensory spaces with noise and people will find it difficult to hear new sounds, much less to concentrate on any specific extended message. This is one of the techniques used by the Party in Orwell's *1984*. Contemplative quiet destroyed by noisy technological intrusion is also, as Leo Marx reminds us in *The Machine in the Garden*, one of the central negative metaphors in the U.S. pastoral tradition. [11]

To be effectively distracting, noise need not be piercing. In fact, stridency calls such attention to the attack on silence that people may be strongly tempted to leave the premises. Noise works best when it fills the space with sounds that are either unobtrusively pleasant — and thus relatively un-noticed — or actually compelling in some safe way.

This invention of safe, compelling, ubiquitous noise is something the Walt Disney Company does better than any U.S. institution not based in Washington, D.C. At WDW the Company presents stories developed to become backgrounded depictions of U.S. history and the country's future, stories about the rest of the world, and stories about technology and nature. The content of these stories, inventing and purloining cultural icons, legitimates a particular version of the United States and its place in the world. The form in which these stories are told and the velocity with which they zoom past are consonant with a society based on the uncritical consumption of decontextualized, amusing commodities.

Walt Disney World is an important venue for the production of culture as ideology. It presents to around 30 million visitors a year, as well as to countless others who visit the park through television tie-ins, legitimations and maps for a Disney version of the world in particular and a U.S. corporate view in general.

Decontextualization

One of the ways people try to make sense out of their lives is to locate their activities in some sort of context. When we explain what we are doing and why we are doing it, we often describe the situation in which our actions make sense. Our response to queries — "I always do it this way," "I needed a change," "what I did was more efficient," or "the Devil made me do it" — assumes some common understanding of contexts. When a typology of contexts is shared and unproblematic, we can go our way without having to worry too much about the parameters of our lives.

The parameters within which our contexts are constructed are basic to the continuity of our maps, legitimations, and culture. They give us our normal notions about time, space, causality, ontology, and epistemology as well as of less abstract social units such as the individual, the family, and the community. Although these parameters and the criteria by which they are measured have historical roots, they tend to be turned into metaphysical categories; thus, they leave history and become embedded in a timeless tradition. Once parameters enter tradition, they become difficult to change.

If the meaning of things is found in their relations to contexts, then one way to gain control over these meanings is to capture the contexts. By doing so one can sever meanings from their previous environments and leave them hanging or separate, or one can reinsert them into new contexts. To manage either of these pieces of sleight of hand is to change the conceptual resources available to people.

By pulling meanings out of their contexts and repackaging them in bounded informational packets, decontextualization makes it difficult for people to maintain a coherent understanding about how things work. Meanings become all jumbled together — separate in that all are abstracted from their different environments and equal in that their packaging destroys any sense of scale by which they could be measured against each other. Differences are glossed over, and "differences that make a difference," as Gregory Bateson has put it, are neutralized. Disconnected information passes in front of us at high speed. It seems, as the apocryphal phrase about bad history has it, "like one damn thing after another."

Walt Disney World is an epicenter of decontextualization. In many of its attractions, pieces of literary tales are retold as if they were the whole story. Cuteness is injected, conflict removed. The Swiss Family Island Treehouse marks an indirect retelling of a literary classic, just as Peter Pan's Flight and Snow White's Scary Adventures redo important children's tales. The Big Bad Wolf and Captain Hook pop through doors at various points in the Magic Kingdom to entertain Disney guests.

History — with some problems, perhaps, but essentially zany — is disaggregated. Abraham Lincoln's speeches are mixed together. Benjamin Franklin and Mark Twain robots talk to each other about an American adventure in which barely related iconic images are surrounded by the silences of untold historical stories. Frontierland's façades form an extended collage of two hundred years of frontier architecture. Leonardo da Vinci is everywhere. As a Disney spokesperson explains the corporate approach to history, they are not telling history like it really was but as it should have been.

Geography is mixed up. The Jungle Cruise in Adventureland connects the Congo River to the Zambezi, the Amazon, and the Irrawaddy without a break. Adventureland itself is a pastiche of what visitors may take to be a reasonable evocation of tropical lands. In EPCOT Center's World Showcase, the Norway Pavilion sits cheek to jowl with Mexico on one side and the Peoples' Republic of China on the other. Across World Showcase Lagoon, The American Adventure leads to Japan and then to the Kingdom of Morocco. World Showcase is organized (or disorganized) like a World's Fair in a series of odd juxtapositions. As is all of Walt Disney World, it is a bricolage writ large in which all sorts of decontextualized messages make some kind of sense. "I'll meet you for lunch in Germany," someone says. "I'm on my way to Canada right now." The pavilions are built up of brilliantly realized collections of easily recognized national icons and motifs, most of which — such as France's Eiffel Tower overlooking a small-town Bel Epoque cul-de-sac — could only be found at Walt Disney World.

Literature, history, and geography are not the only things decontextualized at Walt Disney World. As I discuss later, nature, agriculture, work, architecture and design, food and nutrition, and technology and science are all given the disconnected Disney treatment.

But why take pieces of culture — especially those pertaining to time, space, nature, and technology — out of context? This question has a number of answers, most of which I try to find in this book. At this point let me suggest two of these reasons — recontextualization and consumption.

I have argued that the control of contexts — or of cartographic parameters — is a very useful thing. It can make the arrangement and labeling of features inside these contexts seem reasonable and inevitable. One can pull features apart from their normal attachments and reconceptualize them in new patterns. With this new reconceptualization, or recontextualization as I am using it here, it is possible to tell new stories and invent new legitimations. These new stories use familiar cultural elements that, if we are not sufficiently critical, we understand as if they still carried their previous meanings. As we try to make sense of this new information, we can easily miss the shift in parameters brought about by recontextualization. Leonardo can now be invoked as AT&T's favorite Renaissance Man. Mark Twain can speak, with only the faintest tinge of cynicism, in the interest of national chauvinism. Mae West becomes Kraft's Miss Cheese.

Because many of these images, icons, and symbols are widely shared by Disney's customers, the latter can be counted on to infer appropriate meanings for the new stories. Part of the Disney genius, both in the choice of public symbols it appropriates and in those the corporation itself has invented — Mickey, Donald, Figment, and the Veggie Combo — is that these are such famous or presumably harmless and attractive symbols that most people feel unthreatened by their incorporation into corporate tales. [12] What that has silly puns or Ben Franklin in it could be either misleading or dangerous? This charming insidiousness, as we shall see, allows recontextualized stories about the past, the present, and the future to be consumed in significant quantities by visitors in the name of good, clean, safe fun.

3

America and Consumption

*When economic necessity is replaced by the necessity for boundless economic develop-
ment, the satisfaction of primary human needs is replaced by an uninterrupted fabrication
of pseudo-needs which are reduced to the single pseudo-need of maintaining the reign of
the autonomous economy.*

—Guy Debord [1]

Recontextualization is the first practice abetted by decontextualization;
consumption is the second. The Walt Disney Company is clearly in the
business of enticing people into consuming its merchandise. Much of its
success is attributable to the skill with which it presents its various commodities in the marketplace. These commodities are surrounded by an aura
of Americanism that Disney people draw from and also help produce.

The job of a corporation in the entertainment business is, of course, to
entertain. This is a very risky business. Reading public taste in the contemporary United States is extremely difficult, especially those tastes that affect
the discretionary entertainment dollar. The Walt Disney Company was
notorious for resisting change in its public offerings from the 1950s through
the 1970s. These were years in which its market share in a booming industry
declined substantially. The result of this resistance to change after the death
of Walt Disney in 1966 was a series of management crises in the mid-1980s.

Yet throughout this period of intracorporate conflict, during which the
film division especially was in jeopardy, the two Disney theme parks —
Disneyland in California and, after 1971, Walt Disney World in Florida —

more than held their own. They were successful because they continued to appeal to the entertainment needs of millions of Americans, needs the Company had done much to produce in the first place. With the opening of EPCOT Center in 1981, Disney showed that to some extent it could move with the times and with the demographic realities that had altered the world of potential consumers.

In order to understand the importance of consumption and entertainment and to pursue the recontextualization of cultural symbols by the Walt Disney Company, we must take a brief look at U.S. history and contemporary society. This will allow us to see the ambiguous place of Walt Disney World in the United States and the ambivalence of the messages presented to its visitors.

America Now

If you listen to any amount of normal peoples' conversation these days, especially the kind of talk through which they try to understand their daily lives, you hear a great deal of confusion. People often talk about their lives as fractionated and disconnected. They talk of fear — fear of their places in the economy; fear of politicians, of bureaucracies that ignore personal characteristics in the interest of uniform treatment, especially fear of others who might hurt them and take away their possessions. Many people, overwhelmed by forces seemingly beyond their control — nuclear holocaust, chemical death, crime and drugs, and the like — numb themselves. "I don't want to talk about it," they often say. If they can they joke about these fears and their responses to them. There's a tee-shirt adorning some of those in academic environments in which a distraught comic book figure complains, "Nuclear war! There goes my career."

Powerlessness: That's what you hear about if you listen to people talk. "What can I do about it? It's too much. Too big." The moral moorings have become unglued, just as Emile Durkheim suggested. The stories many were told about the American dream and its truth, justice, and possibilities for individual happiness turned out to be untrue. People are scared and often surly. Streets aren't safe to walk; food isn't safe to eat; water isn't safe to drink; air isn't safe to breathe.

Some have argued that little of this fear and confusion is new. Pundits delight in pointing out that attitudes that seem screamingly new are but recapitulations of responses to some earlier set of conditions. They are often right, for responses take cultural forms that are resistant to change — a *plus ça change, plus c'est le même chose* kind of thing. Like the poor, they argue, alienation will always be with us.

But I think they misread the current public mood. People respond to the world, both cognitively and emotionally, with the symbolic tools available.

Yet these symbolic tools, as Karl Marx suggested over 120 years ago, have a kind of drag to them. They can become inappropriate as conditions change. And conditions have changed — not just in quantity, although numbers and speed of change continue to accelerate, but in quality as well. The qualitative changes brought about by nuclear science, computers, television, recombinant DNA, and similar developments relegate simple notions of cyclical oscillation to the compactor.

In 1970 Andrew Hacker wrote:

> America's history as a nation has reached its end. The American people will of course survive; and the majority will continue to exist quite comfortably. . . . But the ties that make them a society will grow more tenuous with each passing year. There will be undercurrents of tension and turmoil, and the only remaining option will be to learn to live with these disorders. For they are not problems that can be solved with the resources that we are willing to make available. [2]

This dire prediction seems today less a Jeremiad than a Pollyannad. The force of the "of course" phrase is no longer clear to many people. A short list of what are euphemistically termed "problems" makes the point: pollution, acid rain, chemical dumping, petrochemical smog, lead poisoning, PCBs, eutrophication of lakes, fertilizer runoff, waste disposal, fallout from nuclear tests, unsafe nuclear power plants, nuclear war, nuclear waste, cancer, AIDS, medical malpractice, the Middle East, the Persian Gulf, South Africa, Central America, Japan, international trade, budgetary deficits, jobs, runaway factories, Wall Street shenanigans, civil rights, affirmative action, race, sex, sexual preference, abortion, death, relations between church and state, housing, free speech, pornography, rape, crime, welfare, special interests, computerized surveillance, the erosion of personal rights, the upward redistribution of income, divorce, the demise of the family farm, the demise of the family.

It's not just that politicians and businesspeople have lied to us, because we have incorporated this knowledge into a normal understanding of the ways things work. But sportspeople, presented to us for whatever reasons as heroes, not only lie but are exonerated by editorials and letters to the editor for reasons of their age and the "misplaced" expectations put on them by the public. Preachers, especially those with access to the media, are exposed almost monthly as charlatans of the worst sort. Truth and honesty have been so devalued that their abrogation calls forth only cynical recognition.

Over all of these elements of postmodern times lie the clouds of disease — infectious ones such as AIDS and environmentally accelerated ones such as cancer — and the ultimate destroyer, not only of human life but potentially of all organic evolution on this planet — nuclear war. As Robert Nisbet bewails, the idea of "progress" has given way in the face of what many people take to be its terrifying unintended consequences. [3]

What kinds of responses do people make to the present situation? Many people have come together in attempts to affect these issues. Each of these issues, as well as countless others, has a set of constituents engaged on at least two sides. Battles are fought in communities, in the media, and especially in the courts.

The United States has become the most litigious nation in the world. "One million lawyers," sings Tom Paxton. "In ten years there're gonna be one million lawyers. How much can the poor nation stand?" There's a lot of litigation because there are a lot of lawyers but also because the courts are one of the few arenas people can turn to when they don't have many shared social institutions for resolving conflict. As many commentators have suggested recently, the demise of such institutions has disrupted the ability of Americans to share a common moral discourse through which to depict and judge their world. What remains, even among those who actively join together in social action, is a potpourri of disconnected special interest groups — each with its own particular exclusivist focus.

Many Americans, however, make a different sort of response to their confusion, alienation, and feelings of powerlessness. These responses are characterized by moves toward individuation and self-interest, the markers of which — both public and private — are the characteristics of ever-changing commodities available in the marketplace. The construction of life through the consumption of commodities — the symbolic forms of which are far more important than their various contents [4] — is clearly the solution to anxiety late capitalism depends on and promotes. It is also a solution applauded by the Walt Disney Company. How else could they sell vinyl leaves?

Inventing the Consumer

"On or about December 1910, human nature changed," Virginia Woolf remarked, putting her personal imprimatur on the new "modernist" aesthetic. Human nature, at least in the United States, *was* being remodeled in the early years of the twentieth century, but Woolf's remark caught only the edge of this change. The new human being that was being constructed was the consumer.

The U.S. industrial system had grown since Samuel Slater opened his watermill in Pawtucket, Rhode Island, in 1793. By the third quarter of the nineteenth century, what was called the American manufacturing process — with its mass production of interchangeable parts, machine tooled to repeatable tolerances — was in full swing. [5] In 1907 Henry Adams officially saluted the new industrial world in his response to the Chicago Columbian Exposition, "The Dynamo and the Virgin." [6]

By the turn of the twentieth century, the industrial plant was running. Railroads and other communication systems crossed the country. Steel mills and shipyards were in steady production. Electricity and the automobile were about to introduce their transformation of U.S. society. With Thomas Edison as a model, engineering and inventing were becoming cottage industries. The United States was, in the words of Cecelia Tichi, "a gear and girder world."[7]

But there was a problem. Karl Marx had predicted that industrial capitalism would be beset with the problem of overproduction. As the recessions at the end of the nineteenth century showed, this was the case in the United States. The industrial machine was too powerful. There was a persistent crisis of demand.

The response to this structural problem was a process — sometimes coordinated, sometimes disorganized — that continued into the late 1920s by which priorities in the economy were shifted from production to consumption. The key figures in this shift — people such as Henry Ford, Bruce Barton and Edward Filene — took as their mandate not only the retooling of practices of production but also the invention of a new kind of marketing. Their logic, which came to prevail in the economy, was based on the distribution of goods over the widest possible market. Costs of new items — such as the Model T — were held down. Style differences were kept to a minimum. Most important, credit was extended as widely as possible on the most liberal terms.

Intimately connected with this change in structural emphasis from supply to demand was another change. Ford, Barton, Filene, and others like them did not just want to sell large quantities of particular items: They wanted to invent a new ontological category of human being. Their interest was partly economic, but it was also philanthropic.[8] As did many others, they believed this new kind of person — the consumer — would be capable of living a rich human life far beyond the capabilities of his or her forebears.

This, of course, was not the first time human nature had been changed. As C. B. McPherson showed in *The Political Theory of Possessive Individualism*, over a somewhat longer period John Locke, Adam Smith, and others invented the "possessive individual," proprietor of his or her own self and talents and able to enter into contracts based on rational self-interest.[9] Constructed as part of the ideological battle between the bourgeoisie of Europe and various groups of the *Ancien Régime*, this model of human nature was enshrined in the core documents and practices of the victorious republicans in England, France, and the United States. Now, little over a century later, this rational possessive individual was transformed, in the interest of the economy, into a consumer — a being metaphorically linked to a mouth and a stomach.

How was this new consumer supposed to know how to act? He and increasingly she had to be taught what new commodities were available in the market, why they should want them, and — most important — why they should want to have lots of things in general. This required advertising on a vast new scale. Newspapers, magazines, and other vehicles for advertising received a substantial boost in income and circulation. Promotions were developed by which corporate names became household names through contests, samples, and the publication of corporate mythology.

In its early boom days (as it is today), advertising was profoundly ambivalent. It is true that people came to want to know what was out there in the marketplace; thus, advertising performed a specific educational function. But advertising also had a metaeducational, philosophical function. Whether through fear, envy, emulation, images of success and status, or images of youth and fun, advertising taught people first to want things and then turned these wants into needs. The combination of invention, design, marketing, advertising, and these wants and needs did construct a partial solution to the crisis of demand. The form of commodities changed so that they were available to an increasingly wide range of people at increasing speed. However, as Stuart Ewen argues in his study of this period of the history of advertising, *Captains of Consciousness*, the change in peoples' notions of the good life was not an unencumbered benefit. [10]

The invention of the consumer entailed a number of fundamental changes in U.S. social structure and in what Braudelians call the "American mentalité." The contradictions brought about by these changes are basic to an understanding of the Walt Disney Company's America.

First, in order to purchase some of a burgeoning mass of commodities for consumption, one has to be persuaded to desire these things. Because many of these things are new, consumers must be told why their purchase will make their lives better and more fulfilled. Stories need to be told that will create a feeling of lack in the hearts and minds of potential buyers.

This sense of missing out can be conveyed in a number of ways. People can be told that they are not modern or, in later parlance, "with it," without some commodity. They can be told that someone of high status or professional authority recommends a product. They can be convinced that they will be admired if others discover they have a certain commodity.

Potential consumers can be frightened by advertisements that tell them of a dangerous but fixible situation that they didn't even know about. Germs will kill their family if they don't use certain cleaning materials. People will say not that they have bad breath but that they have something even more sinister — halitosis — unless they use some kind of mouthwash.

Although it is true that the shift in emphasis from production to consumption brought about a democratization of the access to commodities — many of them time- and labor-saving and clearly useful — it also brought about the invention of commodities for which markets had to be forcefully created. Further, as the same kinds of commodities came to be produced by different companies, competition over market shares led to the differentiation of products through verbal, pictorial, and physical packaging.

As Ewen points out, by the mid-1920s we had in the United States a kind of corporate paternalism telling people what to do and how to be. Many of these messages were explicitly aimed at women and children, obvious new sources of untapped pressure for consumption. These messages promoted the assumption of abundance. Everyone could partake of the new world of goods. Those who were at the same time presentable (no dandruff) and popular (no dandruff) would be especially successful. These people would mark their popularity and prestige by public symbols in the form of commodities people admired and wanted for themselves.

The political organization of consumption turned wants into both needs and desires. Something becomes a need when, through historical and cultural processes, people come to think it is impossible or at least unreasonable to do without something that had been merely wanted. The contemporary bathroom and kitchen are filled with such items.

A commodity becomes desired in a somewhat different way. Things that are desired are often those pointed out as elements that will enhance the self in gratifying ways. Such enhancement to make oneself more attractive, more confident, and more distinctive and noticeable requires a conscious methodology that reminds one of Benjamin Franklin's endeavors, but it is based on quite different principles. Whereas Franklin assiduously dissected and recomposed his actions in the interest of public character, the U.S. consumer has been led to perform only the decomposition.

As structured by the invention of the consumer, desire is promoted in general by visions of abundance and in particular by the skills in packaging. In order for similar if not identical products to be differentiated from one another in the marketplace, each has to have a hook. This hook is constructed by taking some possible aspects the product might be said to have and connecting those aspects with a problem or lack in peoples' lives that the product might solve or fulfill. The consumer is then seen not as a person but as a bundle of characteristics, each one fair game for competition among purveyors of aspects. For the producers, hitting a collective nerve or correctly picking the right product aspect to emphasize translates into bigger market shares. For a time many people wanted to be a Marlboro man or a member of the Pepsi generation.

The consumer, meanwhile, becomes fractionated. Existential coherence becomes increasingly more difficult. People stop living lives and adopt lifestyles as they attempt to put together particular packages of commodities that seem pleasant. As the commodity system expands, products proliferate and packaging must scream to be noticed. Market shares become more differentiated and, in many cases, smaller. As Durkheim predicted over ninety years ago, the division of labor — now compounded by the division of markets — has led to increasing segmentation of a society whose people are held together by an increasingly diluted set of collective values. This segmentation within U.S. society is exacerbated by the internal segmentation of people brought about by the powerful and accelerating demands of modern commodity consumption.

A second contradiction brought about by the new emphasis on private consumption concerns American character. Here a little broadbrush historical sociology is useful. In *Great Transformation*, Karl Polanyi traced what he considered to be the central structural change brought about by the transition to capitalism in Europe. He described this change as the "disembedding of the economy." [11] What he meant by this was that prior to this time, those activities that had come to be regarded as strictly economic — in a logical sphere of their own — were embedded in social institutions. The production and distribution of goods and services were organized by the total institutional framework of society and performed in the service of that framework. The logic of economic activity was merely the logic of the social structure applied to production and distribution. In the anthropological world, the kinship system *was* the economic system.

Polanyi argued that the European transition to capitalism was characterized above all by the freeing of the economic realm as an autonomous system. This realm came in time to dominate the European and U.S. social world to the extent that, as Marshall Sahlins points out in *Culture and Practical Reason*, most of our social decisions are based on economic judgments, and much of our present discourse about social and political aspects of life is carried on in metaphors derived from economic language. [12]

The transition to capitalism, however, did not just take place in the structural arena. Intimately connected with this historical process was the philosophical invention of a new model of human nature — the aforementioned possessive individual. This possessive individual was required by the disembedded economy and reciprocally was used as a model of human nature to justify the disembedding as a natural process based on natural rights.

In order to be compelling to those whose daily activity would construct and maintain the new economy, the model needed to be fleshed out with moral injunctions and precepts for behavior. These precepts were presented by the Enlightenment philosophers. Locke, for instance, argued that property rightfully accrued to a person who used her or his own labor to appropriate some piece of the common. Yet he also stated that it would be morally illegitimate to take more than one's proper share, an act he operationally marked in terms of wastage: Take only as much as will not spoil under reasonable use.

The philosophers' prescriptions for proper behavior were augmented by another source. In *The Protestant Ethic and the Spirit of Capitalism*, Max Weber traced what he called the "elective affinity" between the activities useful to the development of a capitalist enterprise — frugality, sobriety, methodicality, and delayed gratification — and the behavioral evidence of resolutions to the psychological difficulties entered into by those who accepted the Calvinist teaching of predestination.[13] Weber wrote that a belief in predestination — that God had already chosen whether one were to be saved or damned independent of what one had done or might do in life — placed one in a severe psychological difficulty. A believer couldn't affect God's decision but suffered the torment of not knowing whether he or she would be among the elect. The psychological solution to this dilemma was for the believer to consider it obligatory that he or she *was* one of the chosen. One could not affect the attainment of salvation but could try to eliminate doubts, both one's own and those of others. Self-doubt was taken to be evidence of lack of grace and imperfect faith.

One could show evidence of grace and faith through worldly activities. Good works would be taken by others as a sign of election and at the same time could help one develop the self-confidence that would get a believer through life. These good works might include commercial activities. So long as time was not wasted through idleness, sobriety and seriousness were evinced, and the accumulation of material goods did not lead to pleasure for its own sake, public activity was valued and proper. Thus, Weber argued, the solution to the Calvinist problem of predestination led to precisely the kind of behavior that was appropriate to early capitalism.

Although one may not agree with the specifics of Weber's argument or with his relegation of Catholics and others to the edges of the commercial ethic, it is nonetheless true that by the end of the eighteenth century, an attenuated version of the Protestant ethic had become a central cultural model of character in the United States. This model, with its biblical tinge, methodicality, and seriousness, joined the republican model of Locke and Jefferson as a charter for revolutionary America. Our classic paradigm of American character, the one Weber himself put forth in his book, is Benjamin Franklin. Walt Disney's Franklin, as we shall see, is something else entirely.

In his autobiography, Benjamin Franklin reports that on his invention in 1742 of what came to be called the Franklin stove, the governor of Pennsylvania offered him a patent "for the sole vending of them for a term of years."[14] Franklin refused the patent under the principle "that as we enjoy great Advantages from the Inventions of others, we should be glad of an Opportunity to serve others by an Invention of ours, and this we should do freely and generously." Such a response would be more difficult to make a century later.

Michael Kammen has argued that Americans are a "people of paradox."[15] In their search for cultural models by which to guide their lives, Americans tend to pick polar opposite images and values between which they swing depending on the exigencies of life. Their belief system is like a pendulum but with no arc, only end states. The infinitely possible states on the arc are rejected in the interest of clarity. Yet Americans are Manichaean in an odd way. There are times when the cultural model allows a jump from one endstate to the other. Something considered good becomes, with the receipt of discrediting information, just as bad as it was previously good. Much of the time, however, Kammen argues, Americans are paradoxically capable of believing they may be reasonably characterized by both terms of an opposition. They are pragmatic but idealistic, gentle but tough. A classic U.S. cultural type, played by Senator Sam Ervin during the Watergate hearings, is the shrewdly sophisticated country bumpkin.

A paramount opposition — between the individual and the community — emerged in the nineteenth-century United States. This opposition fractured the kind of moral model signaled by Franklin's refusal to patent his stove. The philosophical wherewithal for this opposition emerged in Great Britain, but the ground that nurtured it was across the Atlantic.

In *The Wealth of Nations*, Adam Smith argued that civil society would be best served if all political fetters to economic self-interest were eliminated. The market, built out of the individual activities of people acting in their own best interests, would be run as if by an "invisible hand," which would guide the growth and distribution of increasing wealth. [16] Yet Smith, who also wrote *The Theory of Moral Sentiments*, [17] had not, in his more famous book, eliminated cooperation and altruism from his description of human nature. [18] His general notions about human character were of a piece with Franklin's.

But what exactly was self-interest? This question was answered in a powerful way by Jeremy Bentham in *Introduction to The Principles of Morals and Legislation*. [19] Conduct was to be judged in terms of its net utility, which for Bentham consisted of the balance of good over bad. Good, in turn, was defined as happiness, bad as unhappiness.

Three things might be said about Bentham's scheme, which came to be known as utilitarianism. First, as Gary Wills points out in *Inventing America: Jefferson's Declaration of Independence*, intellectuals in Europe and the United States in the second half of the eighteenth century were obsessed with the idea that everything was amenable to measurement. [20] Thus, Bentham's notion that happiness could be measured was in keeping with the times. By the twentieth century, with happiness as utility and money as its scale of measurement, Bentham's idea had become far more pernicious than it seemed at the time.

Second, Bentham and following him, John Stuart Mill, considered that each person's happiness was equal to anyone else's. [21] This equality was crucial; it enabled utilitarians to sum potential happiness and unhappiness across people, thus supporting both ethical and political theories.

Third, utilitarianism is what philosophers of ethics call a consequentialist theory. Such a theory requires that actions not be judged according to a priori principles but in terms of their results. Behavior is valued or not depending on what it leads to or, at the moment of decision, on what one thinks it will lead to. However, consequentialism in effect begs the question of what principles to use in judging the merits of potential outcomes. John Stuart Mill tried to solve this dilemma in *Utilitarianism* by trying to rank sources of happiness, with reason at the top.[22] But by then the genie had escaped the bottle.

By the time of de Tocqueville and Beaumont's arrival in Newport, Rhode Island, May 9, 1831, utilitarianism in the United States was on its way to "vulgar" pragmatism. Republicanism, the space afforded by the Louisiana Purchase, and the continuing military victories over native Americans in the western territories had led to a democracy of foot and wagon. Differences of opinion between communities and individuals could be solved by western migration on the part of the latter. As towns grew on the western frontier, community returned — often, ironically, in a more oppressive form than that which travelers had left earlier. For some, that meant moving once again.

De Tocqueville reported both the restless stirring and the structured banality of proper town life. What he saw, among other things, was an early stage in the process by which, given the opportunities afforded by space, values were making a post-Bentham transformation. It was bad enough that measurable happiness could be the central utility around which to build policy, but at least one could consider happiness a value and attempt, as Mill was later to do, to define it in terms of some presumed central element of human nature such as reason. What de Tocqueville saw in the United States of 1831 was that the concept of value was becoming diluted. Values were becoming preferences. Although there was much talk of shared beliefs about good, true, and beautiful values, de Tocqueville saw that people did what they wanted to do and then justified it, if need be, by recourse to interpretations of cultural values.

The transformations of values into preferences and happiness into pleasure took the nineteenth plus some of the twentieth century for U.S. culture to accomplish. This period saw the peopling of a United States that vastly expanded in size through purchase, conquest, and genocide. The Civil War was fought to decide whether two nations would become two nation-states or whether they would remain uneasily incorporated in one. Slavery ended, to be replaced after Reconstruction by rural poverty and Jim Crow. Native Americans were forcefully subdued and removed from the path of progress. Americans were taught that destiny had become "manifest" and self-justifying. Immigrants from Ireland, Scandinavia, southern and eastern Europe, China, and other places added their cultural patterns to the mix; so did the Spanish settlers of the southwest after the Mexican-American War.

Railroads spanned the continent, and, after less than two years of the Pony Express, so did the telegraph. Spurred by the Civil War, especially by the Union's need for replaceable rifle parts, mass production — of textiles, foodstuffs (including beef), and eventually such discretionary items as sewing machines and bicycles — spread everywhere as the industrial plant expanded. Petroleum replaced whale oil and other sources of energy and light. Manufacturing could now take place at night by what Marx called the relay system.

It seemed to many, especially to those in the eastern United States, as if things were getting out of hand. Emerson and Thoreau set the tone for a number of mid-nineteenth-century concerns. Among other things, they worried about the effects of technology on nature and people, the relation between the individual and the state, and the dilution of moral reason. For my purposes Thoreau is the more interesting of the two, even though there's no Thoreau robot at Walt Disney World.

Thoreau is one of the cultural champions of civil disobedience against the state, the brave stance taken by an individual whose moral values are deeply offended by the larger community. He is also the quintessential American model of the person who leaves society for the purifying experience of living simply and self-reliantly in nature. His stance on machines and technology, however — especially represented by the train that regularly passes by Walden Pond — is ambiguous. Sometimes it shatters his silence in both real and figurative ways. Sometimes the sound of the train draws him in, creating positive images of the ease of movement from Concord to Boston and back. Yet although great and transcendent issues fill *Walden*, along with the homely reports of daily routine, it is clear that Thoreau left Concord for the woods because he was bored — especially with the repetitive pettiness of neighbors whose values were becoming merely safe preferences. [23]

After Thoreau American literature returns to the great American themes — the individual and the community, the individual and morality, the individual and technology. Herman Melville's Ahab and Billy Budd, Stephen Crane's Civil War soldiers, Mark Twain's Huckleberry Finn, Walt Whitman's *Ur*-embrace in *Leaves of Grass* — all are *big* stories about *big* issues. Among all these voices, only Mark Twain (especially in *A Connecticut Yankee in King Arthur's Court* and *The Mysterious Stranger)* and Edgar Allen Poe deal specifically with the relations among technology, magic, and individual wants from which large questions of moral values have been expunged.

By the turn of the twentieth century, people were worried about the relationship between the individual and Tichi's "gear and girder world." One important voice was that of Henry Adams, the ironically self-styled eighteenth-century man confronting the twentieth-century world. Yet even as the historian Adams disavows competence in dealing with the modern dynamic world, he presents his quasi-scientific theory of the acceleration of progress. The pretend retrograde is captured by modernity.

Another voice, albeit from England, spoke clearly to the justifications required by the late-nineteenth-century robber barons. Herbert Spencer had reworked Darwin's theory of biological evolution into a justification for rapacious individuality under the guise of "the survival of the fittest."

Nevertheless, at the beginning of the twentieth century, people could puzzle about the relation of the autonomous and integral person to technology, politics, the economy, and the future. Yet the process set in motion by Bentham's notion of utility, replanted fortuitously in a land of relative plenty and reasonable geographic mobility, was about to surface. This process — the full transformation of values into preferences — would soon meet the invention of the consumer. The result would be the beginning of the final stage by which happiness would be turned into pleasure and, eventually, into amusement.

The Democratization of Consumption

In *The Cultural Contradictions of Capitalism*, Daniel Bell posits a modern disjunction among the three realms of bourgeois society — the technical-economic, political, and cultural realms of life. [24] These realms are based on what he calls axial principles, the logics of which define and explain each of them.

> The technical-economic realm, which became central in the beginning of capitalism, is, like all industrial society today, based on the axial principle of economizing: the effort to achieve efficiency through the breakdown of all activities into the smallest components of unit cost, as defined by the systems of financial accounting. . . . Necessarily individuals are treated not as persons but as "things," as instruments to maximize profit. . . .
>
> The political realm, which regulates conflict, is governed by the axial principle of equality: equality before the law, equal civil rights, and, most recently, the claims of equal social and economic rights. . . .
>
> The cultural realm is one of self-expression and self-gratification. It is anti-institutional and antinomian in that the individual is taken to be the measure of satisfaction, and *his* feelings, sentiments, and judgements, not some objective standard of quality and value, determine the worth of cultural objects. [25]

Bell argues that there is a deep antagonism among these three realms in the modern world. He bases his argument on the growing incompatibility of the principles and the institutional structures through which they are enacted. Central to his argument is the replacement of the Protestant ethic by a new creed based on short-term satisfaction of individual desires, a shift he locates in the realm of culture. Bell's culture, however, looks very much like culture with a capital C. He worries about artists and writers, the stances they generate, and their Pied Piper effect on others.

Yet although he misunderstands the locus of power in these transformations, Bell has correctly pointed toward a seminal change in U.S. society,
for just as Polanyi's economy was disembedded from the institutional order
of European societies during the seventeenth and eighteenth centuries, so
in the nineteenth century, U.S. culture in the anthropological sense began
to change in significant ways, pulled by a growing industrial plant and
shaped under the transplanted aegis of Bentham and Spencer.

In the 1830s de Tocqueville could write about the contradiction between
the principles of liberty and equality as he saw them played out during his
American journeys. De Tocqueville argued that these principles — representing Bell's technical-economic and political spheres — were by nature
inversely correlated. He was among the first to see that the discourse no
longer contained only two major categories: the economy, newly disembedded, and the polity. By the time of his visit secularized culture, with a
small c — de Tocqueville's mores — was recognizedly emerging as a third
sphere of social life, ready to bring its own contradictions into play. By the
turn of the century in the United States, civil secularization along with the
ideological and political machinery designed to turn enormous numbers
of immigrants into Americans had become a powerful social force.
Americans were ready to be transformed from producers into consumers.

The democratization of consumption and the accelerating reification of
the consumer have continued throughout the twentieth-century United
States. The main early avatar of consumption was Henry Ford, who understood his basic task as creating a market for his product. His strategy was
based on the mass distribution of affordable automobiles. The major thrust
of this strategy was low unit costs.

Ford kept unit costs low by standardizing his product. For many years
he produced only black Model Ts. Standardization led Ford to introduce
the assembly line on a large scale, allowing parts to be brought to workers
in an efficient and continuous manner. Efficiency, [26] raised at this time to the
center of U.S. values, was pursued by breaking previously continuous tasks
into their component parts and organizing activity around the rapid accomplishment of these new subtasks. Waste was to be eliminated by
introducing the kind of managerial techniques suggested by efficiency
experts such as Frederick Taylor. Such practices required new management
skills, for that is the area in which work practices would now be organized. [27]

Ford hired workers at his Highland Park, Michigan, plant at wages
considerably higher than those that prevailed in industry at the time — his
five-dollar-a-day plan. In turn he got worker support for his assembly-line
process. These wages also made it possible for many Ford workers to
purchase Model Ts for themselves. [28] The only hitch was that Ford made his
employees acquiesce in a paternalistic system that regulated more than
their work habits. Ford wished to hire and retain only those of good

character. He thus required his employees to undergo character training, and he monitored their behavior outside of the working day.

Ford attempted to inculcate in his employees a version of the sober, responsible Protestant ethic. Yet ironically, his production and financing practices were important factors in creating the consumer, through teaching people to pursue new commodity desires. By the mid-1920s, the United States had passed beyond Ford's practices. After years of foot-dragging, he introduced a new model — the Model A — and color options for his automobile. The new consumer market demanded differentiation, and other manufacturers were ready to meet these demands.

In the 1930s the demand problem surfaced with a vengeance. The U.S. industrial plant remained more productive than people normally remember; so, for a while, did U.S. agriculture. But as commodity prices fell, production made less and less sense. Fruit was left to rot on trees in the West; cotton was turned under in the South. Market prices for such products were so low that they couldn't repay labor and transportation costs. As unemployment reached 25 to 30 percent, people didn't have the purchase price for those things that could be produced. In an economic system that distributed commodities primarily through the market, as the market closed so did production.

Attempts to end the Great Depression under Franklin Roosevelt's New Deal followed Lord Keynes's advice that massive outlays of federal moneys be used to stimulate demand. Although there is disagreement as to how effective Roosevelt's programs were, it is clear that the major force in ending the Depression in the United States was World War II.

With global war, the problem of demand ended. The industrial plant was rejuvenated as war equipment, clothing, foodstuffs, and other mass-produced materials were distributed around the world for rapid and voluminous consumption. Unemployment was ended as thousands of men and women went to war in Europe, Africa, Asia, and the Pacific. Symbolized by Rosie the Riveter, women were drawn into production in great numbers. Consumer commodities were rationed as their component materials were directed at the war effort.

The United States emerged from the war as the most powerful nation on the globe — both economically and militarily. The industrial plant was rolling. Europe, the Soviet Union, and Japan were devastated. The United States had nuclear weapons and apparently was ready to drop them at will.

Hundreds of thousands of highly trained soldiers were coming home, seeking jobs if nothing else as a reward for their military service. Women were pressured to return to the home so the men could claim jobs in the peacetime world. The dollar was now the world's principal currency; thus, the United States was rich and powerful. The question was what was to be done to sustain this position.

With the war over and, with its end, the ability to absorb the country's industrial and agricultural output, the problems of demand resurfaced. The postwar attack on these potential difficulties took three general directions.

Three markets were created, partly to absorb U.S. productive capacity and partly to solve the political problem of global dominance. The first of these markets (although not chronologically) was created in Europe through the billions of dollars sent there through the Marshall Plan.

The second market was the military market. Spurred by the Truman Doctrine, which made the United States "policeman to the world," spending on military armaments, atomic weapons research, and the other continuing effluvia of the U.S. quest for empire has proven able to absorb enormous amounts of federal money and productive energy. The growth of this market required furious activity on the part of the political cartographers to justify the allocations of tax dollars to what is euphemistically called "defense." Thus the cold war and the McCarthy era.

The third market created after World War II was the domestic, non-military market. Men and women, with memories of the hardships of the Great Depression, had returned victorious from a war against consummate evil. They had fought for an American way many of them were just about to get.

The domestic market expanded rapidly in the postwar years. Veteran Housing Administration loans allowed returning soldiers to purchase single-family dwellings on easy terms. Housing construction soared. People got married, settled into their own houses, and began the baby boom. The automobile industry expanded, allowing much of the new housing stock to be built at the peripheries of U.S. cities.

The new suburbs brought a burst of merchandizing, some drawn out of urban cores but much of it generated anew as these peripheral areas grew in population. Postwar unemployment was low, particularly in the Northeast, the West, and the Great Lakes region. Interest rates were low. New markets for commodities opened everywhere, especially for consumer items such as televisions and major household appliances.

Advertising expanded, reaching out through the democratization of communication brought about by radio, television, and national magazines such as *Life* and *The Saturday Evening Post*. Marketing drove design as a way of generating product appeal. It was the age of Populuxe[29] and, as John Kenneth Galbraith would call it, the beginning of the affluent society.[30] Just over a decade after the end of World War II, during the Eisenhower years, Walt Disney opened Disneyland in Anaheim, California, to tap into the growing discretionary amusement dollar.

Yet all was not well and wonderful. Social commentators such as Vance Packard decried the dehumanizing and manipulating effects of advertising. David J. Riesman wrote of the lonely crowd. Paul Goodman claimed that Americans were growing up absurd, and Herbert Marcuse described the cultural and personality controls of capitalism as leading to the one-dimensional man. In *The Other America*, Michael Harrington pointed out that affluence was by no means shared by everyone. [31]

The atomic bomb hung over people's heads, as children practiced week-ly bomb drills in school and families debated building bomb shelters. The House Un-American Activities Committee and Senator Joe McCarthy taught Americans to be circumspect about espousing not only political beliefs but any potentially controversial beliefs. The secretary of state of New Jersey tried to ban the first rock and roll concert to take place in the state on the grounds that it was Satanic and probably communistic. Subur-ban life generated a kind of conformity that typed people growing up in the 1950s as the quiet generation.

Through the 1950s and 1960s, as commodity markets expanded, the struggle for black civil rights tore at U.S. society. The fight for women's rights began anew. The Vietnam War, brought nightly into U.S. homes by television, viscerally polarized the country. Political assassinations became altogether too commonplace. People went to the moon. The Russians loomed over our heads, as did nuclear annihilation. Rivers and lakes nearly died, and urban air turned yellow. The counterculture was absorbed into the world of merchandizing.

By the mid-1970s, as Americans shopped for Pet Rocks while thousands died of hunger in the Sahel, the United States was in a full crisis of legitimacy. Political leaders had lied about Vietnam, Watergate, their own financial interests, and, as far as most of us were concerned, most every-thing else as well.

The models for appropriate behavior under the circumstances were clearly based, for those who could follow them, on individualized self-in-terest. The avenue was consumption. The me-generation, soon followed by the yuppies, embraced the ideal of the consumer as the centerpiece of human existence. People such as Christopher Lasch, Richard Sennett, Mar-vin Harris, and Daniel Bell analyzed the sources and implications of what Lasch called the age of narcissism. [32]

What seems to have happened is that the solution to an essentially political problem — the construction of a just and safe world — has be-come sought in the world of privatized commodity consumption. This consumption is produced and rationalized by cultural understandings that put utilitarianism at the center of the human essence. In turn, these self-in-terested cultural assumptions are taught to people as ideology through educational mechanisms — schools, communication media, and the electronic church — whose interests are congruent with, if not the same as, those of the corporate world. The circle closes. We are driven to personalism as a response to a mad world built by corporations and those aligned with them. We are then given solutions to our confusion and anxiety that require that we define ourselves primarily as consumers so we may purchase surcease from divisions of these same corporations. The only escape is to buy things from those merchandizers who are local and have not yet been bought out by major corporations.

Furthermore, as Jules Henry pointed out in *Culture Against Man*, the logic of the personal ethic required by a system based on the consumption of commodities produced for exchange is one of disloyalty.[33] Marketing strategies ask us a hundred times a day to leave the product we have been using (and perhaps been faithful to) in favor of another product whose characteristics will enhance an aspect of our lives we may not have known needed enhancing until now. We will be better off, more popular, in with the right crowd if we buy the new product. No wonder a central problem in the United States today today is a crisis of commitment that has spread into all aspects of our social lives.

Underlying the varying experiences of most Americans since World War II — the conflicts and partial resolutions, the recessions and booms — is a secular trend toward personal fractionation. This trend is overdetermined in the sense that a number of seemingly different historical processes have run in parallel directions. The harmonies among these processes have become intricate and dense. Yet during this time the cartographers of U.S. ideology have remained relatively successful in masking the connections among the various story lines.

Building on the model of the human being as consumer, those who benefit from the political structure of the market system have been able to feed expanding U.S. desires sufficiently that this consumer model and the presumed entitlements attached to it have been accepted as true, beautiful, and universal. The result is that for many people, the tools for constructing themselves have become commodities that stand as symbols by which purchasers enhance aspects of a divided self.

As it has become more normal, the commodity form makes reasonable the division of things into bounded elements, each packaged and circulated according to its own market. The packaging of things — severing them from historical, social, biological, and geological contexts — takes on an ontological correctness as it expands into the interstices. Earth, water, and air are brought into the market. The courts measure unlived human life in dollars. Experience, as at Walt Disney World, is commodified.

In the United States commodities are soma. To be an American is to purchase commodities — to purchase soma. It is correct moral behavior and, incidentally, the kind of activity that is supposed to be useful in making one feel better about the fears and confusions of personal fractionation. Yet ironically, this fractionation is caused in part by the exigencies of the commodity market itself, with its packaging and advertising by aspects.

The emphasis on utilitarian self-interest in the U.S. cultural realm has made the kind of political world Bell and Sennett write about — with its citizens and public morality — obsolete. This cultural system has also repudiated the model of the Protestant ethic associated with early industry, commerce, and capital accumulation. It has instead been restructured by the needs of market expansion. Demanding equal access to soma in order to overcome envy and other forms of alienation, our attention has been drawn to commodities presented as solutions to invented personal difficulties. [34]

One of the great ironies of all this is that U.S. imaginative literature in the first half of the twentieth century tried to deal with the relation of the individual to the modern world. Some — Willa Cather, Theodore Drieser, Edith Wharton — saw the problem facing personal integrity in terms of modern science and technology; others — such as John Dos Passos, Ezra Pound, and even Ernest Hemingway — were comfortable with the new scientific world. [35] But the battle was misplaced; the horse was already out of the barn. The logic of the consumer had already eviscerated the individual as a reasonable unit of analysis. Autonomy was not so much in danger of being taken away by the bigger gun as it was by the erosion by small knife cuts.

Americans today, as Neil Postman has argued, are amusing ourselves to death. Keyed by Aldous Huxley, who pointed out in *Brave New World Revisited* that social critics had "failed to take into account man's almost infinite appetite for distraction," [36] Postman traces the implications for civility in a society "in which all public discourse increasingly takes on the form of entertainment." [37] Since around 1950 the media for public discourse have been channeled toward the form of presentation required by commercial television. With a sidelong glance at Marshall McLuhan, Postman writes that "the medium [television] is the metaphor" [38] and that this metaphor has, in Northrup Frye's terms, a "resonance" that captures possible modes of public epistemology.

As a medium, television is characterized by disconnection and decontextualization. Its content, whether program or news, is packaged in short pieces designed to appeal to some portion of an increasingly differentiated viewing public. The job of programmers is to retain current viewers and to seduce new ones so their numbers and demographics will generate advertising revenue. This task requires hooks and pizzazz because each program segment and each commercial must fight for attention against alternate, simultaneous ones. Any buildup of a coherent story risks viewer disaffection. Accustomed to the commercial pandering to short attention spans, Americans have learned how to be bored.

Postman argues that the prerequisite for television's packaged disconnection was the invention of the telegraph.

> Telegraphy gave a form of legitimacy to the idea of context-free information; that is to the idea that the value of information need not be tied to any function it might serve in social and political decision-making and action, but may merely attach to its novelty, interest, and curiosity. The telegraph made

information into a commodity, a "thing" that could be sold irrespective of its uses or meaning. [39]

The telegraph made possible the annihilation of space because information from anywhere might be transferred immediately to anywhere else. However, such information must be impoverished, for its context could not be transmitted as well. A double problem arises: First, information is stripped of context; second, information can be presented at high speed and in high volume. The potential, realized in the United States today, is information glut.

Postman claims that by the middle of the twentieth century, "where people once sought information to manage the real contexts of their lives, now they had to invent contexts in which otherwise useless information might be put to some apparent use." [40] Crossword puzzles, word games, television quiz shows, lately "Trivial Pursuit" all were marketed as "pseudo-contexts . . . structures invented to give fragmented and irrelevant information a seeming use." [41]

In today's United States, television has become the medium for the staging of world history as show. Beccause such a show must be entertaining, "television . . . has made entertainment itself the natural format for the representation of all experience." [42] In the interests of this entertainment, television has drained coherence out of the world. Because television resonates as metaphor throughout other media, the other media also become little more than collections of brightly packaged tidbits suitable for consumption on the run. "In the age of television," Postman writes, "the paragraph is becoming the basic unit of news in the print media." [43] *USA Today, People Magazine, Newsweek, Time,* and similar publications prove the point. "The public," says Postman, "has adjusted to incoherence and been amused into indifference." [44]

Television packages the world for us in discrete, amusing pieces. As the central model of our time, television conditions other media so that presentations of local and world events must become increasingly disconnected if these media are to remain in the market. Such packaging presents experience as commodity through a media structure the raison d'être of which is the advertising and sale of other commodities, including television sets, radios, movies, magazines, and newspapers.

Both public discourse and the cultural symbols through which people may make sense out of their personal lives are presented in commodity form. The structure of bounded media events and the structure of disconnected commodities, both aimed at utilitarian principles of immediate gratification of desires, are the same. This overdetermined disconnection is reinforced by commodity advertising that reproduces a fractionated personality whose only hope is to become a consumer agonist, polishing up pieces of a shattered self with the symbols of commerce. Further, the world in which this shattered self lives is riven with technological systems —

television, computers, nuclear and biological devices — that separate people from each other and make their individual lives increasingly insignificant. No wonder people want to be amused, even at the risk of ostrichity and death.

But there's more, for as Joshua Meyrowitz tells us in *No Sense of Place: The Impact of Electronic Media on Social Behavior*, the annihilation of space and time brought about by modern electronic media not only leads us toward new ways of being but pulls us away from previous lives. [45] It does this by breaking down the pattern of access to information that previously defined our social environment. Meyrowitz contends that "electronic media have tended to diminish the differences between live and mediated interaction. . . . The speech and appearance of others are now accessible without being in the same location." [46]

Various changes in social experience result. First, information appropriate to a particular situation, when taken up by electronic media, may bypass boundaries and informational gatekeepers and enter new situations. With their own access to television, children can learn information formerly available only to adults. As the secrets of adulthood become shared (or peeked into), the status boundaries between adult and child disintegrate; children become more like adults, adults more like children. Lines of command blur.

Second, "separation of situations allows for separation of behaviors." [47] Drawing on Erving Goffman's sociology, especially *The Presentation of Self in Everyday Life*, [48] Meyrowitz notes that electronic media mold situations. The distinction disappears between "frontstage" behavior, in which a crafted activity is publicly enacted, and "backstage" behavior, through which the show is put together with its practices and mistakes and in which performers relax with their cynicism toward the audience and their lack of decorum. Meyrowitz notes, "Television thrusts the personal, private realm into the public arena." [49]

Control over situations, as well as the attendant status hierarchies that such control supports, relies on the denial of access to information, especially that which demystifies holders of high status by presenting them as just like the rest of us in certain ways. Such demystification makes it difficult for authority to be performed. [50] Added to this is the problem that electronic media contain not just communication but personal expressions as well. The skills of a professional actor are required to control the information given off to the public.

Third, with increasing access to the information transmitted through the electronic media, "there is now much greater sharing of information among different sections of the population." [51] Yet this commodity-like information is diluted and disconnected. We know something about what other people are doing, but the stories are so short and pass so quickly that we can't tell what things are more important than other things. We have lost our ability to weigh information. The child in Iowa in search of a kidney is presented as being at least as important as the landslide in Colombia that kills hundreds or the military slaughter of thousands in East Timor.[52]

As former California governor Jerry Brown said, "The person picketing my office is going to have the same chance, the same thirty seconds, to get his message across to all the people watching the news as I will have."[53] Although this is clearly an overstatement, note that Governor Brown gave each person only thirty seconds. At that speed, as Richard Reeves remarks, "everyone is the same size on television."[54] Meyrowitz remarks, "When looked at as a whole, then, it becomes clear that much of the controversy surrounding television programming is not rooted in television content *per se*, but in the problems inherent in a system that communicates everything to everybody at the same time."[55]

At the same time national information is diluted and packaged into disconnected, evanescent symbols, the proliferation of media channels (cable TV, specialty magazines, and the like) constructs a "selective flow of information [which] may *create* 'sections' of the population by dividing people into very different information-systems."[56] "By altering the informational characteristics of place," Meyrowitz writes, "electronic media reshape social situations and social identities."[57] Group identities, stages of life, status and rank — all previously dependent on differentiation of access to information — blur together. Traditional distinctions become less and less operative. What are available to people in the ensuing confusion, brought to us by the very media that shift our moorings, are what Donald Horton and R. Richard Wohl have called "para-social interaction" — mediated relationships that psychologically resemble face-to-face interaction. We look to "media friends" for guidance and analysis.[58] Newscasters, talk show hosts, electronic preachers, the voices on call-in radio — these become our beacons of reality.

No wonder that in *Habits of the Heart*, Robert Bellah and his associates found among the Americans they interviewed a longing for some way of making sense out of their lives.[59] These writers argue that the traditional U.S. discourses — the biblical and republican models for life — have given way to two new forms. These new forms — the utilitarian individualism that constructs the entrepreneur and the expressive individualism that leads to commodity consumption — are the results of the disembedding of the economy, the relative autonomy of the sphere of culture, and the invention of the consumer. These processes lead to an existence in which the integrity of the person is problematic. Some of the available solutions — the pursuit of commodities, the search for self-actualization, and therapy — reproduce the fetish of possessive individualism that is one root of the problem.

Bellah and his associates claim that a solution to the dilemma for the people they talked to is a "community of memory."[60] To be found, perhaps, in a return to republican and biblical discourses, this community would provide people with a social group and social purpose that would reconnect them with one another and with some sense of the past. This community of memory would provide a shared tradition out of which would arise an ethic for meaningful activity in the world.

A community of memory is something Walt Disney World attempts to provide. It is one of the reasons the Disney theme parks are so successful and so ambiguous in their effects. The consummate irony, of course, is that this community of memory is presented as a myriad of commodities in the interests of the corporate world that has constructed the problem of broken ontology and fractured epistemology in the first place.

4

Distory: Disney History at the Magic Kingdom

It is possible that Walt Disney has taught people more history, in a more memorable way, than they ever learned in school.

—Mike Wallace [1]

By all accounts Walt Disney's midwestern childhood was not particularly joyous. His father was not prosperous. The family moved regularly, from city to country to town to city. Walt worked early and often. His budding drawing skills were supported only minimally and under duress. Falsifying his age, Walt left home as soon as he could by enlisting in the American Ambulance Corps, then serving in Europe in World War I. By the time he got there, the war was over, but he stayed for a year drawing cartoons and designing posters for the camp canteen.

Years later, by the time Walt was working on his plans for Disneyland, he had developed an orientation toward the past (including his own youth) that would form a metatheme for all of his parks. This orientation was called Disney realism. The past was to be cleaned up — "vacuum cleaned," in Mike Wallace's words. [2] Unpleasantries would be dropped from history, and stories of the past would be told in the carefully (and commercially) re-mythologized form to which Americans were becoming accustomed through the movies and television.

As Disneyland took shape during the Eisenhower fifties, Disney's Norman Rockwell view of history — Distory, if you will — was designed to soothe park visitors by leaping back across two world wars and a depression to more distant and hazy times. Colonial America, the American West, and the turn-of-the-century Victorian echoes of Main Street USA were meant to tap nostalgia and sneak past whatever grim realities attended those times and places.

The phrase "Disney realism" was meant to be ironic, although it is not so in a simple way. Disney people clearly knew they were not telling the truth. The point at Disneyland was to entertain people of all ages, not, as it would be later at EPCOT Center, to teach them a particular vision of the world. The past could be intrinsically entertaining, especially if visitors shared enough knowledge so historical symbols could be used in telling stories. But the Disney designers ("imagineers") were also Pollyannas. Many of them actually believed, in a relatively uncynical and optimistic fashion, that the world would be a better place if history could be rewritten, leaving in only the parts that "should have happened." Who better to do this than Disney engineers and craftspeople, whose expertise in fabricating the real is without peer.

Furthermore, this Distory did (and does) tap into people's nostalgic need for a false history — for the reasonably benign makings of a community of memory. Disney has not only told stories to help fill out those memories but has become a central part of U.S. shared experience — America's guardian, as Dick Schaap's son put it. [3] Finally, as visitors spend money to experience history as pastiche and to purchase souvenirs as tokens of their encounter with Disney, Disney realism keeps the comptroller happy.

Years after its creation, the model of Disneyland was transferred to central Florida. Walt Disney died and Corporate Disney came into being, transforming Walt's plans for EPCOT along the way. During those years, as the U.S. empire continued to crumble; as crises of political leadership and legitimacy grew; as the world economy shifted and U.S. wealth was redistributed upward; as race, sex, crime, drugs, religious fundamentalism, acid rain, chemical dumping, nuclear leaks, and the like began to affect most of us most of the time, the need grew for something of enduring interest and value to take us away for a while, to entertain us — perhaps something from the simpler past.

Our present times have made peoples' lives quite surreal. The search for an anchor of meaning has led many to the past. Unfortunately, the past is presently available mostly as commodity, as pieces of history as pastiche designed and marketed to assuage our nostalgia.

At WDW and especially at EPCOT Center, customers are offered ideas about history in a much more pedagogical fashion than at Disneyland. The tone has shifted from Walt's world, harkening back to a simpler, less sophisticated time, to the postmodern world of transnational corporations telling "histories they can live with." [4] These histories are a bit more complicated and contentious than those of Disneyland and of the Magic

Kingdom. I will come to them soon, but first a few words about Disney's presentation of time.

First, there is little about the present at WDW (and surprisingly little about the future). The point of a vacation is to change the here and now for a while. Although much of WDW is named for the future and the infrastructural technology points in that direction, much of the activity at the parks is wrapped up in the trappings of the past. Even the attractions at Future World are substantially about the past. The typical EPCOT story model — of which AT&T's Spaceship Earth, GM's World of Motion, GE's Horizons, and Delta's Dreamflight in Tomorrowland are variations (and Exxon's Universe of Energy and Kraft's The Land have touches) — takes riders on a journey through a whimsical past, mentions the present, and suggests some vague hint of a future in which technology and graphics will be important.

History at Future World has a different tone than it does at Disneyland and the Magic Kingdom. In the 1950s and the first part of the 1960s, history could be presented as if there had never been any problems, just continual progress through architecturally interesting times. By the late 1970s, when Future World was being planned, such a view of history could no longer be taken seriously: Too much had happened in the intervening years. Revisionist history and revisionist present had been conveyed to too many people through the mass media. Too many people had been involved in political activity to ignore. In terms of history writ large, the scientific-technological world view had rehabilitated evolutionary theory so that long-term stories could not be told without it. All of this required a history more risqué than that told at the Magic Kingdom, one that needed to be preempted by Disney's allied corporations.

A second interesting thing about Disneytime is that at both Disneyland and WDW, time is defined spatially. Tomorrow is not so much a time at the Magic Kingdom as a place — Tomorrow*land*. Each part of the Magic Kingdom has a temporal theme. Liberty Square represents colonial America and the War of Independence. Frontierland glosses the nineteenth-century American West. Main Street USA gives us a turn-of-the-century small town. Adventureland alludes to the history of empire — from the Spanish Main to the African safari. Even Fantasyland is about time, suggesting simultaneously the timelessness of fairy tales and children's stories and the romanticized medieval castles of central Europe with a bit of King Arthur thrown in.

Most of these historical moments — tomorrow included — are organized in lands.[5] At WDW we have the representation of spacetime; but this is not the space-time continuum of modernism, which, however folded, remains connected. Rather, here we have the disconnected, discrete spacetime packages of postmodernism — bounded, localized themes placed next to each other serially and, for the most part, randomly.[6]

Serious critics on the whole have excoriated Walt Disney's version of history. Indeed, they have accused him of historiography — a venal sin (whereas he claimed to be telling stories for their value as entertainment). I will add my brief to their case, but with a caveat or two. I agree with Mike Wallace that Walt and Corporate Walt are two different things, the latter being considerably more complicated and subtle (as well as divided into pre-Eisner and Eisner periods).[7] Corporate Walt histories are told for the most part at EPCOT Center and reflect the ideological necessities of the 1970s and 1980s rather than the Disneyland years.

Wallace's accusation of "historicide" invites some scrutiny. One question concerns the telling of particular histories — of the United States, the development of private transportation systems, and the like. Here, as we'll see, highly selective tales are told. But the Disney people have already 'fessed up, telling us not to take their histories seriously. They are giving us Disney realism — cleaned up, happy versions.

Sometimes the playfulness is clear, but sometimes the stories are pedagogically wrapped in seriousness. The problem comes in remembering that however dramatic, the stories are part of a purposeful pastiche — history as a commercial for optimistic individual consumerism and corporate management. What Disney does, perhaps, is kill the *idea* of history by presenting it as entertainment. If the truth value of parts of the past is indistinguishable from the truth value of fantasy and futurology, then what is history but crafted amusement?

How real is history, anyway — Walt's or anyone elses? Although I later dig more deeply into questions of the real, the fake, the surreal, and the relations among them, a few words are in order here.

Histories are constructs of the past produced by partisans in contemporary personal and social situations. As I suggested in Chapter 2, to produce a history is to make a map of some temporal-geographical territory from a particular point of view. The landmarks and other features posited for the territory are noticed because the cartographer is looking for them, and they are noted on the map as a rhetorical claim of importance. Histories remain in force when they are supported by enough authority, whether the information on which their claims rest is real, false, or incomplete.

Histories of various sorts construct scripts of time just as geographies domesticate space. They contain dominant, canonical accounts and silences — often vast ones — that result from the suppression or disregard of alternative voices. Historians and other partisans recover these voices by scanning the dial for faint or covered signals and boosting the volume. This recovered information is woven into new stories and counterstories.

Hayden White has directed our attention to the implications of the relation between history and narrative. He writes that "there has been a are: verbal fictions, the contents of which are as much *invented* as *found* and the forms of which have more in common with their counterparts in literature than they have with those in the sciences." [8] These "fictions" are what make sense out of history.

> Historians gain part of their explanatory effect by their success in making stories out of *mere* chronicles; and stories in turn are made out of chronicles by an operation . . . called "emplotment." And by emplotment I mean simply the encoding of the facts contained in the chronicle as components of specific *kinds* of plot structures, in precisely the way that (Northrop) Frye has suggested is the case with "fictions" in general. [9]

This emplotment is necessary because

> no given set of casually recorded historical events can in itself constitute a story; the most it might offer to the historian are story *elements*. The events are *made* into a story by the supression or subordination of certain of them and the highlighting of others, by characterization, motific repetition, variation of tone and point of view, alternative descriptive strategies, and the like — in short, all of the techniques that we would normally expect to find in the emplotment of a novel or a play. [10]

Further, as narrative the historical story must take a metahistorical literary tone: "Considered as potential elements of a story, historical events are value-neutral. Whether they find their place finally in a story that is tragic, comic, romantic, or ironic . . . depends upon the historian's decision to *con*figure them according to the imperatives of one plot structure or mythos rather than another." [11]

How do we learn history? Unless we are historians, we have learned much of our history through popular forms of narratives packaged for commercial purposes — historical novels, television series and docudramas, movies — or through the ideological programs of schools and churches. As audiences we bring our previous acquaintance with narrative forms into play when we approach history so that we understand a historical story as romantic, tragic, or comic. The genres, as Clifford Geertz has said, are "blurred." [12]

When Walt Disney presents history as a cartoon, he is perhaps less guilty of bad faith than the historian who considers her or his narrative a transparent channel for the truth. As noted earlier, Walt's people even tell you about their editing. "Walt's approach to the past," writes Wallace, "was thus not to reproduce it, but to improve it." [13]

Corporate Disney, however, is another matter. As the voice of Exxon, General Motors, United Technologies, and other corporations at EPCOT Center, the Walt Disney Company *does* attempt to capture history, to defang it and make it harmless. However, let's begin to look at Disney's version of history — Distory — in the Magic Kingdom.

Liberty Square

Because this is my first set of comments about specific parts of WDW, a few words of explanation are in order. Rather than approach the parks as I might as a customer — one park at a time, toured in a relatively systematic way based on the layout in place — I will describe the many venues according to my own organization of analytical themes. Sometimes, as in the case of Frontierland in this chapter, an entire "land" may appropriately be discussed in one place. At other times, attractions Disney has put together will be treated in different parts of the book. Such is the case, for example, with the pavilions of Future World, which I insert into many different discussions.

This is not meant to imply that Disney's attractions are univocal — that each fits perfectly into only one place. There is no such simplicity, not even in the case of Dumbo, the Flying Elephant. The ideological messages at WDW are wide-ranging and intricately woven and cross-referenced. Although teasing them apart for analytical purposes does some damage to their gestalt, it allows me to code them systematically enough to tell my story.

At the Magic Kingdom, for example, both Adventureland and Main Street USA have strong historical themes. It can be argued that the history of the United States leads from Liberty Square through Frontierland to Main Street USA, with a stop at Adventureland's colonialism on the way. I have chosen, however, to place Adventureland in my discussion of Disney's presentation of cultural geography. Main Street USA is found in Chapter 9, at the end of my treatment of commerce and merchandizing. [14]

As we reach the plaza at the end of Main Street USA, facing Cinderella's Castle, the entrance to Liberty Square hives off at ten o'clock. Ahead, across a dark wooden bridge, is a stone embankment overgrown with ivy behind which rise the variegated roofs of urban colonial America. Liberty Square is meant to represent the "idea" of America on the eve of independence from England: "Here life in the Thirteen Colonies and the Spirit of '76 have been reborn." [15]

The buildings are small, connecting with each other at odd angles. The façades show red brick and clapboard, and the roofs are topped with colonial weather vanes. These façades are styled as Georgian and federal architecture, although the Haunted Mansion outlier points to the Dutch manor houses of the Hudson River Valley, and the Columbia Harbour House restaurant near the entrance to Fantasyland is reminiscent of a New England seacoast town.

In *The Magic Kingdom Guide Book*, Liberty Square is presented together with Frontierland in Disney's imaginative reconstruction of U.S. history. It faces the east side of the Rivers of America, the canal that surrounds Tom Sawyer's Island and Fort Sam Clemens. Although its core is quite distinct,

centered more or less around the Liberty Tree, its boundaries with Frontierland are fuzzy.

To the north, the boundary cuts between the Haunted Mansion and the
waterside building containing Ichabod's Landing and the staging area for
the Mike Fink Keelboats, more thematically appropriate to Frontierland.[16]
Ichabod's Landing is a hybrid: Its architectural style and façade point to
Frontierland, but its merchandise — magic tricks and monster masks —
and its name make it an adjunct to the Haunted Mansion directly to the
north.

From the keelboats, the boundary passes down the street between the
entrance to the Liberty Square Riverboat and the public-punishment stocks
conveniently placed in the middle of the street for participatory photography. It then curls back to the east between the Liberty Tree Tavern and the
building containing the Diamond Horseshoe Jamboree. Beyond the Jamboree and next to the exit to Adventureland is another hybrid store, the
Tricornered Hat Shoppe, which incongruously sells western hats and
leather accessories. Because the U.S. frontier once began at the Atlantic
seacoast — as far as Europeans were concerned, anyway — perhaps the
fuzziness of the boundary is warranted.

The core of Liberty Square celebrates the ascendancy of commerce, a
celebration recapitulated on Main Street USA. It is an urban scene filled
with shops, taverns (each with its advertising sign and symbol hanging
over the street), and the Boston-Philadelphia meeting houses in which
commerce dispensed with its colonial trappings. Except for the Georgian
architecture reminiscent of Williamsburg, Virginia, there is nothing of the
south here — and little of Jefferson's yeoman farmers.[17] There is no sign of
the urban conflicts documented by Gary B. Nash in *The Urban Crucible*.[18]
What we do find is an underscoring of the "legends, real and fictional"
devised by canonical New England-Northeast history.[19]

To the right, after we cross the bridge from the plaza, is the Sleepy Hollow
snack bar (brownies, soft drinks, and Toll House cookies). This red brick
corner building — with its secluded outside patio, sloping red tile roof, and
stepped roof façade — recalls the New York Dutch version of a colonial
gabled house. Beyond Sleepy Hollow, past the Silhouette Cart — where a
Disney employee creates personal silhouettes "while you wait" — is
Heritage House. Here historical mementos and other Americana are sold.[20]
Here also is Mlle. Lafayette's Parfumerie, where fragrances may be custom
blended for customers. Each personal scent is given an identification number so it can be ordered by mail.[21] Beyond Heritage House, the square opens
out in front of the Hall of Presidents.

On the left side of the street, past the Parasol Cart, are Olde World
Antiques and the Silversmith. The former sells both actual one-of-a-kind
antiques and reproductions, and the latter offers decorative gifts and
jewelry. Behind them and the adjacent buildings is one of the more peaceful

garden rest spots in the Magic Kingdom. Umbrella-covered tables sit under the trees along the canal, just twenty feet from the throng. It is shockingly peaceful. At the garden's end is the seasonal Fife and Drum snack bar and an entrance to the Courtyard (garden and floral merchandise).

Beyond these stores and directly across from the Hall of Presidents is an arm of Liberty Square that contains its totems — a replica of the Liberty Bell and the Liberty Tree. Some forty feet tall and sixty feet wide and weighing over thirty-eight tons,[22] this live oak recalls the original Liberty Tree in Boston under which the self-styled Sons of Liberty gathered in 1765 to protest the Stamp Act. Hanging from its branches are lanterns that represent the thirteen original colonies.

Disney's Liberty Tree forms an interesting counterpoint to the tree holding the Swiss Family Treehouse not far away in Adventureland. Both evince a triumph of Disney technology over nature. The Swiss Family Treehouse, with its hundreds of thousands of vinyl leaves, is a fake — a "fake real" thing, as I suggest later. The Liberty Tree is a real tree, transplanted here from elsewhere on the property in a massive undertaking. Steve Birnbaum tells the story.

> Since the tree was so large (. . . with a root ball that measured some 18 by 16 by 4 feet around), lifting it by cable was out of the question — the cable would have sliced through the bark and into the trunk's tender cambrium layer, injuring the tree. Instead, 2 holes were drilled horizontally through the sturdiest section of the trunk; the holes were filled with dowels, and a 100-ton crane lifted the tree by these rods, which were subsequently removed and replaced with the original wood plugs. Unfortunately, the wood plugs had become contaminated, and a serious infection set in and rotted out a portion of the inside of the trunk. To save the tree, the plugs again were removed, the holes were filled in with cement, the diseased areas were cleaned out, and a young *Quercus virginiana* was grafted to the tree at its base, where it grows even today.[23]

Turning left past the Liberty Tree, we come to the Liberty Tree Tavern, one of the three full-service restaurants at the Magic Kingdom that requires reservations.[24] This eighteenth-century-style white clapboard inn, with entrance pillars fronting a small brick portico, contains six dining areas, each with a unique fireplace. The floors are oak, the wavy windows made from seed glass, and the curtains hung from cloth loops. Pewter mugs and ladder-backed chairs extend the theme. In the waiting area are a spinning wheel, a hope chest, and a writing desk. Copper pots and kettles flank the fireplace. Waitpersons in colonial garb serve simple "American" meals.

At the north end of Liberty Square, south of the Haunted Mansion and across the arch from the Columbia Harbour House, is Yankee Trader, a small New England-style building where cooking and serving accessories and Smucker's jams and jellies are sold. The fast-food Columbia Harbour House offers fried shrimp, clam chowder, and sandwiches in rooms filled with antique nautical paraphernalia.

Having waited for the Fife and Drum Corps to pass, we move back down the street, past the Liberty Square Potato Wagon toward the center of the square and the Hall of Presidents. The entrance to this federal-style red brick building with white trim faces the Liberty Tree across the square. A portico with grooved square pillars leads us into the marble-floored waiting area. In the center of the floor is embedded a replica of the seal of the United States.

Over the entrance is the golden date 1787 — the date the Constitution was ratified — and higher still, the white steeple with bell and clock. An American flag with thirteen stars stands on a pole to the left. Near it is the sign marking the attraction, with another U.S. seal and a replicated golden eagle on top. The façade is meant to recall the Philadelphia meeting house in which the Declaration of Independence was signed.

On the walls of the waiting area are copies of some of the eighty-five paintings created for the show inside. [25] Others may be seen in the Columbia Harbour House and the Liberty Tree Tavern, as well as on Main Street USA (in the City Hall and Penny Arcade). These latter placements tie the political Americana of the Hall of Presidents to the commercial Americana of Main Street USA. They echo the much clearer thematic connection between the Hall of Presidents and the American Adventure at EPCOT's World Showcase.

The ostensible theme of the show in the Hall of Presidents theater is the U.S. Constitution. This presentation is divided into two parts — the film and the robots. The relatively humorless patriotic film is visually constructed out of the eighty-five paintings shown on a segmented 70-millimeter screen. As panels of the screen turn on and off, the focus switches back and forth between the entire painting and particular portions of it, as guided by the script. Our visual attention thus is pulled here and there, and our heads are kept moving — stirred to match the stirring story backed by stirring music.

The film opens with the front center panels showing the shadows of people reciting the opening lines of the Preamble to the Constitution. We then see a copy of the original hand-written document. The chorus reciting "We the people of the United States of America" ironically includes the voices of women, who were disenfranchised at the time. We thus are confronted immediately with a central irony of all of Disney's historical productions: In order to suggest the appropriate "idea" of history, Disney pedagogy must suppress, rearrange, and invent history in the interest of safe dramatic presentation. Mike Wallace goes so far as to call Disney's practice "historicidal." [26]

Now a sonorant male voice sets the theme.

> *These immortal words, when first they were written, proclaimed to the world an idea new among men. They expressed a shining wish for a better way of life. This was the American Dream. But that golden goal was not to be had without cost. It was*

born in adversity, tested by time, perfected and proven only after long experience and trial. This is the drama of a new concept of freedom . . . of the inspired code of law creating that freedom.

We begin with "immortal words," just as the Abraham Lincoln figure ends the show's final speech with the immortality of man. Thus, the brackets of the presentation deny time. There are beginnings — words first written, an idea new among men, an adverse birth, and a new concept of freedom — but no end other than the ongoing stasis of the American dream, "perfected and proven." This American Dream — a "shining wish" — is the "golden goal" of the natural rights version of freedom. It is not about justice or equality, just a liberty of shining gold that will not be had "without cost."

What is interesting about the costs is that at the Hall of Presidents, they are most often paid by those who act in the name of liberty because the subtext of this drama is rebellion — one victorious and three suppressed. The show is an argument in favor of the executive branch of the federal government, embodied especially in George Washington, Andrew Jackson, and Abraham Lincoln.

The victorious rebellion is first. We are taken by painting to Philadelphia's Independence Hall in late summer 1787. Washington and Benjamin Franklin argue for the new document, flawed though it may seem to many. As the names of the states are intoned, we are told that thirty-nine of the forty-two delegates signed the document. [27]

This newly created document was unique. In a world of kings and emperors, would it work? The first test was not long in coming.

The first revolt was Pennsylvania's Whiskey Rebellion. Farmers, distillers, and traders objected to the levy of federal taxes on the interstate transportation of corn whiskey. In order to suppress the ensuing riots — actions taken in the same name of freedom the patriots had used only recently — President Washington overrode states' rights and called in the federal militia. The federal government needed the money, and Washington wanted to set the precedent. In the narrator's words,

Washington had shown his people that the government was prepared to ensure domestic tranquility when necessary.

We have slid from freedom to domestic tranquility, assured by a prepared government ready to act "when necessary." It is a small stretch to see this argument as having a pointed meaning during the late Woodstock years and the Vietnam War.

The second revolt is the South Carolina nullification campaign of 1832-1833 — a move in opposition to the federal government's newly imposed tariff acts. Here's Andrew Jackson.

Tell them for me that they can talk and write resolutions and print threats to their heart's content. But if one drop of blood is shed, they are in defiance of the laws of the

United States. I will hang the first man of them I can get my hands on to the first tree I can find.

The crisis passed as a martial Jackson "stood by the Constitution."

We now come to the centerpiece of the nonrobot part of the show. The Hall of Presidents presentation is built around "Great Moments with Mr. Lincoln," Disney's Illinois Pavilion offering from the 1964-1965 New York World's Fair. To a midwesterner like Disney, this "plainspoken man of the prairie" (who gives a number of hardly plainspoken speeches in this show, mixed and matched for dramatic effect) is the quintessential Disney president. We are leading up to the third rebellion — the Civil War; first, however, the scene is set with a representation of one of the 1858 debates between "the glib and talented Stephen Douglas and a self-taught lawyer named Abraham Lincoln."

On an outdoor stage surrounded by trees and draped with the U.S. flag, Lincoln gives a speech collage, and he is sometimes heckled by the crowd. [28] Douglas has a word here and there about Lincoln's "monstrous revolutionary doctrines" but mostly remains nonglibly mute. The audience is mostly male, all dressed up in frock coat, tie, and top hat. A small coterie of women sits off to the right, dressed in hoop skirts and holding parasols. The town band in its red uniforms stands in the bandstand to the left. One impassive Indian sits on the steps in front of the bandstand. Next to him is a black family — two adults and two children, one a babe in arms. This is obviously an event.

With solemn music the camera focuses on Lincoln's body, then on just his head. He does his "house divided" line and tells the people in the crowd that if they do not agree with the "sacred principles" of equality and political rights, they should rip out the pages of the Constitution wherein these principles are found.

Two years later we are taken to the White House where in a room with a highly polished floor, a very lonely Lincoln mutters a humble prayer to himself. Apparently the Constitution is the truth; the truth is everything; and with God's help he will not fail. After a minute or so of loud martial music played as paintings of Fort Sumter and various battlefields are shown, the war is over.

The Constitution had survived the fiery ordeal. America was one nation, finally and forever more.

Now comes Disney's favorite century, 1865-1965:

a time of . . . inventions, a time of unbounded creativity . . . a time of transition . . . a time of progress.

What Walt Disney liked most about this century were the inventors and entrepreneurs, who, like the postmortem-christening Mormons, he retroactively welcomed into the pantheon of "imagineers." These were the people with whom Disney felt the deepest affiliation. To Disney America meant the Wright brothers, Thomas Edison, Alexander Graham Bell, Andrew

Carnegie, and Henry Ford. The last war of any significance depicted at the
Magic Kingdom — except for the Indian campaigns alluded to at Fort Sam
Clemens — was the Civil War. After that were progress and unbounded
creativity.

As the show quickly passes through the century, Distory fills the screen
— the Golden Spike, the Wright brothers, Edison, an early twentieth-century car race, a crowd outside the nickelodeon, the demolition and building
of a city — no more wars, no flappers, no depression. We see a picture of a
farm, a town meeting (televised by WED-TV), and cubist churches. During
all this time, as Indians were being decimated, labor wars were being
fought, Woodrow Wilson was throwing leftists out of the country, blacks
were being disenfranchised, and women were considered second-class
citizens,

> *the fundamental philosophy of freedom, the belief in the rights of the individual
> and the dignity of man, remained unaltered. The Constitution was still the rock.
> Under its guarantees, men were free to speak, free to worship as they please, free to
> enjoy the fruits of their labor, and free to explore the energies of the universe.*

Aha! So that's it. The teleology is revealed. The meaning of America and
the goal to which all this history has led is the space program. [29] A man's
voice counts down as we see a rocket ready to go.

> *10-9-8-ignition sequence starts-6-5-4-firing-2-1. Up she goes. Look to the stars,
> said the wise men. There lies the future. In remote and distant worlds lies the riddle
> of tomorrow.*

This is what the Constitution is about — a "free world" in space.

> *If a free world is to endure, the principles of self-government must be perpetuated.
> The Constitution is the rock. And the leaders of tomorrow must be as dedicated to its
> preservation as were the leaders of yesterday, as are the leaders of today.*

Thus is made the transition to the second part of the show — the part
everybody has come to see.

> *In this Hall of Presidents, let us pay homage to the immortal men whose illustrious
> names have been indelibly inscribed on history's roll of honor.*

The curtain rises, and we are faced by extraordinary robotic likenesses
of some of the most unsavory characters in U.S. history — the presidents
of the United States. As the roll is called, a spotlight shines on each body.
The presidents are dressed in period costume. They sway back and forth,
turn from side to side, nod and fidget. Tyler whispers with Jackson, Arthur
with Garfield; Bush blinks. [30] The effect is extraordinary. The technical
wizardry overwhelms the memory of the film just seen. This is the message:
We can make robots look like real people. [31]

The presidents are arranged in clusters: Washington to John Quincy
Adams, Jackson to Grant, Hayes to Benjamin Harrison, Roosevelt to
Roosevelt, Truman to (so far) Bush, the latter ironically standing between
Lyndon Johnson and Truman, as if presidentiality wiped out partisanship.
Standing at front once again is Abe Lincoln. In another long, mixed-up

speech, Lincoln addresses the audience about liberty and independence. Again the message is that these will be preserved only if we guard ourselves against internal revolt. We must police our own citizenry. This is a far cry from Jefferson's justification for rebellion.

At what point shall we expect the approach of danger? By what means shall we fortify against it? Shall we expect some transatlantic giant to step across the ocean and crush us with a blow?

No. All the armies of Europe, Asia, and Africa combined could not by force take a drink from the Ohio, or make a track on the Blue Ridge.

At what point, then, is the approach of danger to be expected? I answer: If it ever reach us, it must spring up among us. It cannot come from abroad. If destruction be our lot, we ourselves must be its author . . . and its finisher.

As a nation of free men, we must live through all time or die by suicide.

This speech offers an interesting political contradiction. It is small comfort to the military-industrial establishment that captured the federal budget with its invention of the cold war and the deification of external threat. Neither does it support to the corporate world's transpacific economic fears. Lincoln's speech *is* in fact populist. Although its overtones are ominous, it credits the American people with having the spunk to keep foreign soldiers off the Blue Ridge and the intelligence and independence to be dangerous to the federal-business regime. One suspects that many of the robots behind him, were they live presidents, would have tried to muzzle old Abe.

His final words resonate with the expression of our nuclear fears. He speaks of a material mortality, not the bizarre apocalyptic spiritual mortality of a Ronald Reagan.

Surely God would not have created a being such as Man, with the ability to grasp the infinite, to exist for only a day.

No! No! Man was meant for immortality.

However, we are to remember the robot Lincoln, not his words — the robot presidents, not their deeds. Thus, we get a stirring patriotic ending. As the words of "The Battle Hymn of the Republic" boom out of the speakers, the sunset behind the presidents turns into the U.S. flag. We march out of the hall and into the heat and sunlight, past the Liberty Tree and on to Frontierland and more Distory. [32]

Frontierland

Frontierland consists of three sections of shops and attractions. First, the Rivers of America surround Tom Sawyer's Island and Fort Sam Clemens. On its waters float the Mike Fink Keelboats, the Liberty Square Riverboat, Tom Sawyer's Rafts, and — from time to time — the Indian Canoes. Second, east of the water sits Big Thunder Mountain and its roller coaster ride. Third, to the south is "civilization" — shops, restaurants, the Frontierland Shootin' Arcade, and the Country Bear Vacation Hoedown (also known as the Country Bear Jamboree). These venues share buildings with those of Adventureland to the south. Before I begin to describe Frontierland proper, however, I will look at an oddly placed Disney classic — the Diamond Horseshoe Jamboree.

Together, Liberty Square and Frontierland represent the border of the American West as it moved from New England and the eastern seaboard to the Appalachia of Davey Crockett, the Mississippi River of Mark Twain, the bear-filled Rockies, the desert Southwest and forests of the Northwest, and back to the country towns of the Great Plains. The carved wooden sign that marks the entrance to Frontierland sits next to the passageway from Adventureland. On the other side of the passage is the transition zone that contains the Tricornered Hat Shoppe and the Diamond Horseshoe.

The Diamond Horseshoe Jamboree is an incredibly corny western dance hall revue set inside a gray clapboard building in keeping with the architectural façades of Liberty Square (albeit with large fake diamonds running through its sign). According to the commemorative *Walt Disney World*,[33] the *Guinness Book of World Records* lists this revue — along with its elder sibling at Disneyland, the Golden Horseshoe Revue — as one of the longest-running shows in theatrical history. The show requires reservations, which are secured at the Hospitality House on Main Street USA each morning.[34]

The showroom is shaped like a horseshoe, open at the entrance with the stage in front. Along the left wall is a simulated bar with mirrors behind it. The tables are wood-grained formica. A balcony with tables runs along the top of the hall, its back walls adorned with western paintings. Longhorns wrapped with red velvet to match the stage curtains are hung on the balcony fronting. Minimal food and drink are available.

The show itself is built around the periodic visit of Miss Lily Langtree and her three can-can girls to the Diamond Horseshoe Saloon. Sam the bartender, his four-piece band, and three cowboy assistants wait for the ladies with double entendre-bated breath. They arrive and the show goes on, complete with harmlessly silly risqué asides. The show's theme concerns Sam's repeated attempts to convince Lily to be his woman and to let him be part of her show. Songs are sung (such as "Lily's Back in Town," a play on the standard, "Lulu's Back in Town"), dances are energetically danced, and audience participation is invoked. Toward the end, two older members of the audience are brought on stage to participate in a spoof of "Old McDonald Had a Farm." However corny the show is — and it verges on the unbearable — the audience appears to enjoy itself. The Diamond Horseshoe Jamboree is similar to the Hoop-Dee-Doo Review — a dinner show at Pioneer Hall in Fort Wilderness — but a lot less expensive.

Just east of the archway to Adventureland, right before the rocky creek that flows down the hill and under the wooden bridge to the Rivers of America, is the sign that welcomes visitors to Frontierland proper. Strung between wooden posts and topped by a rack of elk horns, the sign leads us into a conglomerate western town. Here the century between 1790 and 1890 — between Liberty Square and Main Street USA — is evoked. *Walt Disney World* introduces it thus.

> Walt Disney had a special respect for the men and women who pushed America's western boundary to the Pacific Ocean. Frontierland is his tribute to those hardy pioneers. Its landscape blends towering conifer forests of the Pacific Northwest, red-and-ochre-hued deserts of the Southwest, and Mississippi river landings. Its frontier way of life is symbolized by the coonskin cap and the cowboy hat, the calico sunbonnet and the plantation straw. [35]

Hitching posts front the street, and kerosene lamps dangle from the overhanging roofs. This is where all the earth tones at the Magic Kingdom are found — the dark browns of the unpainted board façades and the raised wood sidewalks fronting the buildings, the dusty red of the pavement, and the ochre and tan of the desert around Pecos Bill's restaurant and Big Thunder Mountain.

This western bricolage begins with Frontierland Wood Carving. Here Rubio artists cut personalized wooden signs on the first floor of a small building dressed as a fort, an echo of Fort Sam Clemens. Although the latter is a Great Plains stockade, this little log fort, with the stream and fir trees beside it, feels like the Northwest. The foreshortened second story, complete with shooting windows, is rotated forty-five degrees so its corners stick out over the walls below it. This would have given such a fort an octagonal rather than a square defensive posture.

Beyond Frontier Wood Carving the street opens up to the left in front of the Frontierland Shootin' Arcade. For twenty-five cents, customers can heft genuine refitted Hawkins 54-caliber buffalo rifles from their blankets and shoot infrared beams at targets scattered through the desert surrounding a mocked-up southwestern town. [36] In front of the arcade is Boot Hill, full of tombstones. Cow skulls litter the ground. An owl sits in a scraggly lodgepole pine. A groundhog pops out of its hole. High on the rocks to the left is a tarantula. With each bull's-eye comes a silly effect complete with sound; for example, a hit on the cloud makes a ghost rider gallop across the sky. The Arcade's portico pillars are designed with stylized pine tree boles.

Next is the Frontierland Trading Post, a building with slate-stone facing and rocking chairs in front. Toy pistols, hats (including Plains Indian headdresses), turquoise jewelry, beadwork, and Texas-style chili sauce are available here. This is also the epicenter of Frontierland's olfactory theme. Like the Morocco Showcase in EPCOT Center, Frontierland smells like leather as the aroma of leather goods at the Frontier Trading Post wafts across the land.

Across the street, sitting along the Rivers of America, are Big Al's (coonskin caps and Big Al merchandise) and the Frontierland and Westward Ho snack wagons. This is a good vantage point from which to watch the work that goes on (usually in January) when the canal is drained for refurbishing. Then one can see the track for the Riverboat and the configuration of Tom Sawyer's Island.

Beyond the Trading Post is Grizzly Hall, home of the Country Bear Jamboree and its current show, the "Country Bear Vacation Hoedown." With stone facing on the first floor and log facing on the second, Grizzly Hall is reminiscent of the Rockies. Inside in the waiting area, the wood plank floors are "scarred" as if by bear claws.[37] The fifteen-minute theater show is a revue played by seventeen audioanimatronic bears, one raccoon, and the heads of a moose, stag, and buffalo mounted over the exit doors. The bear puns are almost unbearable. The show parodies bluegrass, country, and dance hall standards. The cast includes the Five Bear Rugs (the house band — Zeke, Zeb, Ted, Fred, and Tennessee), Liver Lips McGrowl, Gomer (the microcephalic pianist), Terrence (with his Elvis embearsonation and love song to Delores, the octopus), Wendell (the overbearing bearitone with vacation slides), and Big Al (the depressive bass who has become the most important commercial character from the show.)

Along the way Trixie the Tampa Temptation sings the blues in all her weighty splendor, the baby Sunbonnets (Bunny, Bubbles, and Beulah) do their version of "I Wish They All Could Be California Bears," and Teddi Barra descends from the ceiling as Mae West, "Singing in the Rain." All of this is "organized" by Henry, the master of ceremonies, whose coonskin cap turns into a real robot raccoon for a duet near the end of the show. From time to time Melvin (the moose), Buff (the buffalo), and Max (the stag, with his John Deere cap) make off-the-wall comments on the show. By the end the audience claps and stomps along with the bears as they sing "Thank God I'm a Country Bear."

The exit bears us out into the Mile Long Bar. The heads of Max, Buff, and Melvin — still moving — are replicated on the wall. This restaurant sells Mexican food and shares a kitchen with Pecos Bill's Cafe. In a strange reversal, the plains-mountains-looking Mile Long Bar serves burritos, and the Southwest and Mexican-looking Pecos Bill's sells hamburgers and hot dogs. The latter has a patio filled with cactus, mesquite, and Peruvian pepper trees to replicate the Southwest desert.[38] This patio is a good place to sit and watch the daily Magic Kingdom parade(s), which wind up nearby.

From Pecos Bill's a visitor may turn south into Adventureland's Caribbean Plaza, continue west past the Briar Patch cart (stuffed animals and woven blankets) to Big Thunder Mountain,[39] or turn back east into town. For the moment, I will do the latter: partly because we have missed a shop but mainly to look at the façades.

Tucked up front between Grizzly Hall and the Mile Long Bar is Bearly Country ("where Grandma would love to browse") — a store with stuffed bears, country crafts, and clothing. From the street, the stretch between

Grizzly Hall and Pecos Bill's is a Disney version of what belongs in a late-nineteenth-century western plains town. The names on the two-story painted clapboard façades tell the tale. Over Bearly Country is a sign for the Seed and Hardware store. Over the street exit from the Country Bear Jamboree is the Gold Road Stagecoach office. A saloon sign sits over the Mile Long Bar, which also has a Herrick's vegetable pill sign in its window. Next is the faded red brick Town Hall, with its belfry and bell, and finally — before we come to Pecos Bill's desert — a Chinese laundry. This is the "tamed" West of Marshall Dillon, to which upright citizens can return after they have survived the Big Thunder Mountain Railroad.

Towering over the western end of Frontierland are the buttes of Big Thunder Mountain. In Florida towering comes easy. Big Thunder Mountain is 197 feet high. The highest point in the state, near the Alabama border in the Florida panhandle, is 345 feet in elevation. On its WEDway People-Mover in Tomorrowland, Disney announces that the 180-foot-tall Space Mountain is the third-highest mountain in Florida; WDW thus has two of the top three. The facts that Disney's "mountains" are not natural and that high points in Florida are not mountains add to the creeping surrealism we will experience in Chapter 15.[40] Let me turn to Birnbaum for statistics.

> The summit of the mountain, whose name refers to an old Indian legend about a sacred mountain in Wyoming that would thunder whenever white men took out its gold, is entirely Disney-made. It was in the planning for some 15 years and under construction for 2, and required some 650 tons of steel, 4,675 tons of cement and 16,000 gallons of paint;[41] hundreds of rock-makers contributed, applying multiple coats of cement and paint, throwing stones at the mountain, kicking dirt on it, and banging it with sticks and picks to make the whole thing resemble the rocks of Monument Valley, Utah — that is as if Mother Nature herself had created it. . . . The total cost was about $17 million, which, give or take a few million, was as much as it cost to build all of California's Disneyland in 1955.[42]

We approach the redstone mountain by way of a climb up a hill, past cacti and desert scrub, to the weathered wood building that stages the Big Thunder Mountain Railroad. Along the way we pass antique gold-mining equipment gathered from throughout the Southwest. Snaking through the building and down its central ramp, we come to the ride itself.

The "wildest ride in the wilderness" is a three-minute, 2,780-foot-long roller-coaster whirl in a cute, simulated mining train through a western desert potpourri.[43] The ride begins inside a cavern, climbs up past phosphorescent cave pools, and crests (for the first of three times) as we break through a waterfall for our first descent. On wooden trestles we zoom past audioanimatronic goats, burros, possums, and wildcats, turn out over the Rivers of America, and head back past volcanic pools that recall those at Mammoth Hot Springs in Yellowstone National Park.

The train hurtles through Tumbleweed, a gold-mining town that flooded out due to the overzealous ministrations of Professor Cumulus Isobar, the visiting rainmaker. Partying drunks on the second floor of the Gold Dust Saloon don't seem too worried. A citizen in long johns spins comfortably through the flood in a bathtub, stared at by a couple of chickens.

Spinning out of a 720-degree double loop, we pass under the bleached bones of a partially buried dinosaur as the ride nears its end. The exit takes us past the observation point where those who have been warned off by the entrance signs — no bad backs or heart conditions — or those too young to be allowed on the train have been waiting. [44]

The third section of Frontierland consists of the Rivers of America and the islands therein. The Rivers of America is actually one more-or-less figure-eight canal almost entirely contained in Frontierland. Four sets of craft ply the canal; three circumnavigate Tom Sawyer Island and Fort Sam Clemens, and one — the Tom Sawyer Rafts — provides the sole access to the islands.

The Mike Fink Keelboats — the "Gullywhumper" and the "Bertha Mae" — leave from the landing near the Haunted Mansion. Having slid "cheek-to-cheek, bumper-to-bumper, whichever comes first," as we have been ordered by the fast-talking guide, we sit on an open top or an enclosed main deck for our journey. The backwoods folksiness of this ride, named for a river boat captain who rode the waters in the first quarter of the nineteenth century, allows the Davy Crockett-clad hosts more license than usual. There is a lot of banter back and forth between audience and guide. Complaining children are asked, "Do you want to go home? To Erie?" Rain is explained away as just another Disney special effect.

As with the Riverboat, this ride is a tour in which ads for the attractions we see along the way are interspersed with the spiel. Backing and filling to avoid other river traffic, the free-floating keelboat takes us around the islands. We pass the Riverboat landing and Aunt Polly's restaurant on Tom Sawyer's Island and, avoiding the rafts and Indian canoes, glide by Big Thunder Mountain. On the far side of the Rivers, we pass a jumble of western effects — audioanimatronic deer and moose, a burning house (perhaps set ablaze by river pirates), Alligator Swamp (where Beacon Joe strums on his shack porch to his dog Rufus), a peaceful Indian village complete with children, dogs, canoes, and tepee, and an Indian burial platform. From a cave come the sounds of river pirates celebrating one thing or another. Shots from Fort Sam Clemens ring out as kids take aim at us. Turning a bend, we leave the wilderness, enter the Hudson, and float by the Haunted Mansion to the landing.

The Richard F. Irvine Liberty Square Riverboat travels the same route but with different style. Named for an important Disney designer, the riverboat is an actual steamboat — a white triple-decker with a pilot house on top and filigreed railings on its top two passenger decks — built to recall those that traveled the Ohio and Mississippi rivers in the nineteenth century.[45] The boat rides slowly, majestically, and breezily on a submerged rail as Dixieland music is broadcast over the sound system.

The Riverboat Landing — built of wood and framed by extraordinary stonework — sits on the water at the end of the main street through Liberty Square. It is, metaphorically, a transition ride. We leave the East (and its shops and stocks) for a taste of the barely tamed West, by way of southern swamps. But with a sigh of relief, we turn back toward town. Some, though, bitten by the bug (and sick or scared of the stocks), head off to join Tom and Huck.

Tom Sawyer's Island is reached by river raft from Tom's Landing, on the way to Big Thunder Mountain. In a strange juxtaposition, the entrance is marked by totem poles. Packed in and standing, perhaps on the Becky Thatcher raft, we cut across the river toward Harper's Mill. This mill — with its interlocking wheel mechanism, cobwebs, and owl in the rafters — has a working water wheel that creaks along, marking our way back to the landing.

Tom Sawyer's Island is distinctive as one of the few places we can escape the constant sensory assault at the Magic Kingdom. It is boring to some, but offers peace and relief to others. Parents can let children run around freely, knowing it will be difficult for them to get off the island. At the southeast end, the patio of Aunt Polly's Landing (sandwiches, snacks, and lemonade — presented by Smuckers) looks out over the Riverboat Landing and Liberty Square. The hum of the crowds is noticeable but seems blissfully distant. There is quiet piano-roll and banjo music, and off to the side is Tom's half-whitewashed fence.

There are no sidewalks here. Grass-edged footpaths meander around the island, up to the top of peaceful, usually empty Cardiff Hill and on the caves and bridges. Cardiff Hill has its own sound curtain. Woodsy sounds come from speakers sitting in fake tree stumps. There are two caves — the tilted, dark Magnetic Mystery Mine and Injun Joe's, a larger passage with wind sounds, owls, colored lights, and fake passages. Behind Cardiff Hill is a small wood building that hums, presumably from the machinery locked inside. An old-fashioned swinging suspension bridge takes us to Aunt Polly's, and a barrel bridge at the north end leads to Fort Sam Clemens.

These islands (along with the Jungle Cruise in Adventureland) are the horticultural center of the Magic Kingdom. They are backwoods green. Birnbaum lists oaks, pines, sycamores, red maples, and elms, as well as dwarf azaleas, firethorn, and American holly as growing here.[46] As with the Jungle Cruise, many of the trees do not belong here either ecologically or thematically, but they are included for their flowering activity. There are Brazilian pepper trees and, near the fort entrance, a pineapple guava from South America.[47]

Fort Sam Clemens is a wooden back-country stockade with two main buildings four corner "rifle roosts" complete with air rifles and misspelled

Huck Finn-type signs with backward esses. Guard rails and rocks are painted green to simulate wood mold. At the entrance is a robot drunk, perhaps a guard, snoring away next to his snoring dog. In the fort's courtyard near a modern water fountain is a well.

The building to the right holds the canteen and powder rooms. To the left is the blacksmith's shop. Here we find an audioanimatronic blacksmith, his assistant, a dog, two horses, and some hens surrounded by saddles, harnesses, tools, a broom, and various casks and burlap sacks. Over the shop is Cannon Nest. Under the right-rear rifle roost is the dark escape tunnel that leads out of the fort to the river.

River Country and Fort Wilderness

The rustic tone of Tom Sawyer's world is echoed elsewhere in WDW in the countrified atmosphere of River Country and Fort Wilderness. The former, set around an arm of Bay Lake called Bay Cove, is designed as a modern version of an old swimmin' hole. It is similar in structure to the later-built Typhoon Lagoon.

The core of River Country is Bay Cove, a section of the lake walled off by a flexible boom that keeps the level of Bay Cove six inches higher than that of the rest of the lake. [48] Around the cove are two beaches, one for adults and one for children. The larger part of the cove contains rope swings, automobile tire swings, and a swinging ship's boom to hang and fall from.

Tucked in behind the beaches is a heated swimming pool with a pair of water slides dropping from Disney-made rock hills. On the other side of Bay Cove are two flumes and an inner-tube ride. The flumes — one 260 feet long, the other 100 feet shorter — drop from the top of Whoop-'n-Holler Hollow. The fake rocks that make up this ridge were designed by the same crew that created Big Thunder Mountain, Schweitzer Falls (in the Jungle Cruise), and the caves on Tom Sawyer's Island. [49] The inner-tube ride, White Water Rapids, starts from the adjacent Raft Rider Ridge. Both dump riders into Bay Cove. "Lake water is pumped to the top of two giant flumes and a raft ride at the rate of 8,500 gallons a minute. Since gravity causes water to seek its own level, the River Country water spills over the top of the tube back into Bay Lake, providing needed circulation." [50]

River Country has a snack stand (Pop's Place), lockers, a concession stand (where towels can be rented), picnic tables, and a nature trail. Admission is separate — although it can be combined with a Discovery Island ticket — and River Country place closes at dusk.

River Country is tucked into a corner of the 650-acre Fort Wilderness Resort and Campground. Sprinkled here among cypress and slash pines are 1,190 upscale campsites laid out in a number of loops. Visitors can bring their own RVs and tents or rent one of Disney's fully furnished Fleetwood trailers, complete with maid service. The Meadow Trading Post, near the center of the campgrounds, and the Settlement Trading Post, near Fort Wilderness, supply campers with staples and souvenirs. Disney buses travel the main roads from the parking lot to Pioneer Hall, passing the two swimming pools and the tennis and volleyball courts.

The social center of Fort Wilderness is Pioneer Hall, where the campground meets the lake. Pioneer Hall was "designed to resemble a lodge in the Northwest Territory at the turn of the nineteenth century. It was constructed with 1,283 hand-fitted logs shipped by rail from Montana." [51]

On the right side of this sprawling building is Crockett's Tavern, a table-service restaurant with a bar. A wide porch with chairs and benches borders the restaurant on two sides. Just beyond it is a playground with a western theme. To the left of the tavern is the Trails End Buffet.

The focus of Pioneer Hall is the two-storied building where the Hoop-Dee-Doo Revue dinner show (sponsored by Fleetwood Recreation Vehicles) takes place twice each night. As waitpersons slap plates of fried chicken and barbecued ribs down on the tables with crashing gusto, the Pioneer Hall Players present a show similar in tone to the Diamond Horseshoe Jamboree — although because a lot of children visit from the campground, this show's wit is perhaps even broader. Again, audience participation is required.

Behind Pioneer Hall are the Tri-Circle-D Ranch [52] and the Petting Farm, the latter sponsored by Gaines Foods and filled with goats, sheep, chickens, rabbits, and a baby Brahma bull. At the ranch visitors can watch a blacksmith at work fitting the draught horses that pull the trolleys down Main Street USA with polyurethane-covered, steel-cored horseshoes. [53]

Fort Wilderness is replete with outdoor activities. Birnbaum lists the following: pool and lake swimming, bicycling (bikes can be rented at the Bike Barn), boat and canoe rentals, fishing on Bay Lake and in the canals, jogging on the jogging and exercise trail, horseback trail rides, waterskiing, and walking the Wilderness Swamp Trail. [54] There are also campfire program near the Meadow Trading Post, a part canoe-part hiking trip that ends in a campfire marshmallow roast (the Marshmallow Marsh Excursion), [55] and a nightly hayride from Pioneer Hall. The Headless Horseman has been known to ride by Pioneer Hall at hayride time.

Carousel of Progress

What can we say of the history presented at Liberty Square and Frontierland? This is public history, but it is an edited version that suggests U.S. history "as it should have been." Here, history is fun. The only transparent pedagogy is found in the Hall of Presidents. Here, history is nostalgia.

Regional and emblematic designs invoke the places of U.S. myth — places that are uncontaminated by people. Lincoln and company aside, most of the creatures represented here are bears. The serious ideological messages — the "dreamers-and-doers" theme, the saga of progress, the dissatisfactions turned into opportunities in disguise, the "challenges of new frontiers" — await us at EPCOT Center.

This is a "safe" century — from independence to the taming of the West. It is much safer than the previous 150 years, and its puritan-Protestant ethic overtones are out of sync with the commodificatory pageant of the twentieth century. Mike Wallace has suggested that in the Disney version of history, "the silences get louder the closer the show gets to the present," [56] and once we get past the time of Main Street USA, they do. But the silences from the opening of the Bering Strait until Santa Fe, Saint Augustine, and Jamestown and from 1621 to the Stamp Act are barely noticed. We have not returned to the childhood of America here but to that of the nation-state.

Frontierland and Liberty Square (along with Adventureland) serve, as Wallace has suggested, "as ritual reassurance of Main Street's triumph over its opponents," including, ironically, the nation-state itself. [57] This victory is the story of EPCOT Center, but our way leads first through the "paean to progress" sung for us at the General Electric (GE) Carousel of Progress in a Tomorrowland that is really about yesterday. [58]

Another product of the 1964-1965 New York World's Fair, the carousel is the pivotal hinge between the mythological history at the Magic Kingdom and the corporate view of technological empire at Future World. GE would have us believe that the way to progress — Disney's central descriptive theme for the twentieth century — leads through the "availability of emancipatory consumer goods." [59] What makes people free are electric ovens, televisions, and weight-reduction machines — all available as commodities for household purchase. The research "fellows" at General Electric are the liberators of our time — making this, as the carousel's insipid ditty goes, "the best time of your life."

In the Carousel of Progress, we sit in a theater that revolves around four sets that depict the kitchen and ancillary rooms of a middle-class robot family. [60] The sets show four time slices — the turn of the century (pre-electricity), the 1920s, the 1940s, and the present. It's a sort of Disney *Our Town*. In the first three scenes, the father-robot sits in the kitchen with his pipe and robot dog, telling us how liberty is spelled e-l-e-c-t-r-i-c d-e-v-i-c-e. In the fourth scene, he is behind the free-standing modern stove cooking omelettes *superbes avec jambon*. In each scene, electricity has changed the family's life. The family members have been freed from inconvenience and are electrically empowered. It is the best time of their lives, but things will be even better if the rumors are true about the things going on at GE.

The opening voice-over sets the tone, as we wait for the theater to turn to the first act.

> *On this and every turn we'll be making progress. And progress is not just moving ahead. Progress is dreaming, working, building a better way of life. Progress is commitment to people. A commitment to making today and tomorrow the best time of your life. It wasn't always easy. At every turn in our history there was always someone saying, "Turn back! Turn back!" But there was no turning back. Not for us; not for our carousel. A challenge always lies ahead. And as long as man dreams and works and builds together, these years, too, can be the best time of your life.*

With complete inexorability — for there is no turning back in this moving theater — and with our own voices silenced, we dreamily face the challenge of Scene 1.

It is spring, just before the turn of the century, and "things couldn't be any better than they are today." Father (John) points around the kitchen to the new telephone, gas lanterns, cast-iron coal stove, and ice box with a large block of ice in it. There are rumors in the air about Tom Edison's new snap-on lights.

A left side panel lights up. Through the gauzy curtain we can see Mother (Sarah) ironing.

Mother:	*With my new wash table marvels, it takes only five hours to do the wash. Imagine.*
Father:	*That's right, folks. Now mother has time for recreation, like . . .* [61]
Mother:	*Like canning and polishing the stove.*
Father:	*Okay, Mother. You just iron the wrinkles out of my shirt.*
Mother:	*Yes, dear.*

What we see here, as we move around the stage sets, is GE's saga of women's liberation by way of electronic device. [62]

In side panels we see cute scenes of the family's young son looking through a stereoscope at scenes from the St. Louis World's Fair (including a hoochy-koochy dancer) and the teenage daughter (Jane) getting ready for an electric streetcar ride (in lieu of a hayride).

Father:	*It's hard to imagine how life could be any easier. But there's a new company working on bringing the same power that runs the trolley into folks' homes. Hmmm. And because those fellas are working that out, one thing is certain.*

Then comes the song "Now Is the Best Time of Your Life," and the theater turns to the second set.

It's summer, twenty years later. Fluorescent wires lace the kitchen, connected to "Mother's new electrical servants" — sewing machine, coffee percolator, toaster, waffle iron, refrigerator — all of which go on at once at one point in a mechanical revolt. Father is still in the kitchen. Rover has become Queenie.

Father:	*Well, we've progressed a long way since the turn of the century twenty years ago. But no one realized then that this would*

be the Age of Electricity. Everyone uses it: farmers, fac-
tories, whole towns.

Mother is now embroidering in her free time. Grandma and Grandpa are listening to the new crystal set as in a sudden leap of time, Lindbergh's flight across the Atlantic is announced. Daughter Jane argues with her father about looking for a job.

Daughter:	*I don't see any harm in looking for a job, daddy.*
Father:	*It's a man's world out there, Jane.*
Daughter:	*Well, it won't always be, father.*
Queenie:	*Arf! Arf!*
Father:	*Now cut that out, Queenie. You're supposed to be man's best friend.*

Cousin Orville is in the bathroom, sitting in the bathtub wiggling his toes, with an electric fan blowing air toward him over a block of ice.

Father:	*You know, considering all the conveniences we have, it looks as though we've made real progress in making our lives easier. And when we read about the things those research people are working on, well, you can be sure of one thing.*

Again the song.

Now it's autumn in the Frantic Forties. Queenie is now Sport. What happened to the war?

Father:	*It's amazing how our new kitchen wonders are helping to take over the hard work. Everything's improved. The electric range and refrigerator are bigger, and [the refrigerator] makes a lot of ice cubes. But my favorite is the electric dish-washer. Now Mother spends less time in the kitchen, and I don't have to dry the dishes anymore.*

Grandma and Grandpa are watching television — which "has changed our lives and brought a whole new world of culture to our home." When he snoozes, she flips to wrestling. Son is working on a model airplane. Jane is now in her first year of college. She is on the telephone, talking to a friend about boys and being jiggled by an electric strap-type exercise machine.

Mother is caught up in the new do-it-yourself craze. She is apparently remodeling the basement, using a food mixer for stirring paint. It is unclear whether this is silly (as Father thinks) or clever. She suggests to Father that she should be paid for her work.

Mother:	*If you hired a man to do this, wouldn't you pay him?*
Father:	*Of course, dear.*
Mother:	*Then I should get equal pay.*
Father:	*Heh! Heh! Heh! Heh! We might negotiate something later on.*
Mother:	*When?*

A cuckoo clock goes off. The bird sings, "Now is the best time."

Father: *You stay out of this.*

On this note we move on. This time Father asks us to sing along. Some in the audience, obeying a robot, do so.

It's the 1980s — New Year's Eve. We now see where the theme song's teleology has been leading us.

Life is a prize. Enjoy every minute.
Open your eyes and watch how you win it.

This is a very fancy, open suburban house, presumably in southern California. [63] The kitchen is big and is filled with modern appliances, including the free-standing stove behind which Father is making his ham and eggs. Mother sits at a table in front of a computer. In the living room Grandma and Grandpa are watching the New Year's celebrations at WDW on the big-screen TV while they talk to the rest of the family. Jane holds an electric guitar. Son — now eighteen or so and a real Valley Guy — sits at the breakfast bar in a jogging suit. Sport is still Sport, perhaps Sport V. This is a pretty yuppie family, surrounded by electronic devices.

Grandpa is asked to reminisce.

Grandpa: *The good old days were good, all right. But I'll tell ya', we*
                spent those good old days just taking care of essentials.
Grandma: *We really have a lot to celebrate.*
Father: *. . . the whole quality of our lives.*

Now the son jumps in.

Son: *The world is getting more complex . . . but it is more exciting, too.*
                Today we have so many more choices. [64]

Here is the Disney litany — "more . . . more . . . more."

Mother: *I think that's the best part.*
Son: *Today they're bringing good things to life that weren't even*
                dreamed of a generation ago.

This, in a world of excitement and choice, is the GE message — "we bring good things to life" — inserted in what might seem like a normal, unreflective sentence. To a U.S. audience, of course, this line jumps out like a screeching cat. You'd think GE would be embarrassed at being so blatant.

Sport: *Arf! Arf!*
Father: *See, even Sport's enthusiastic about the future.*

This time Mother asks us to sing along. As we turn toward the exit, the song segues into a pop soprano version. Shadows and lasers are projected on a curtain before us as we make our final turn.

Now is the time.
Now is the best time.
Be it a time of joy or strife.
There's so much to cheer for,
We're glad you're here . . .
For it's the best time of your life.

Male Voice: Thank you and have a happy new day.
Now we are ready for Future World Distory.

5

More Distory: Mostly EPCOT Center

Corporate desire to fudge the past combined with Disney's ability to spruce it up promotes a sense of history as a pleasantly nostalgic memory, now so completely transcended by the modern corporate order as to be completely irrelevant to contemporary life.
                                                                                    —Mike Wallace [1]

EPCOT Center opened in October 1982, eleven years after the Magic Kingdom. As we shall see length in the following two chapters, Walt Disney's original intent for EPCOT was changed entirely by Corporate Disney. Walt had conceived of this project as an experimental attempt to deal with the "problems of the cities" by building a high-technological residential utopia. By the time the decision was made, some years after Walt's death, to go ahead with the project, EPCOT had been reconceived as a two-part theme park — a kind of permanent World's Fair — rather than a functioning live-in city.

EPCOT Center was a huge, expensive undertaking. During its construction in the late 1970s, it was the largest private construction project in the world. To help pay the way, Disney formed partnerships with such giant corporations as AT&T, Exxon, Kodak, Kraft Foods, and General Motors for the pavilions in Future World and with national tourist boards and foreign national companies for those in World Showcase.

Corporate EPCOT was envisioned as a tourist magnet that would tap different demographic categories than did the Magic Kingdom — both an older, more traveled crowd and young adults without children. As Wallace puts it, EPCOT Center's target was "yuppies instead of mouseketeers." [2] The park was designed to mix education with entertainment. The education would be about science, corporate-controlled technology, and international travel. The entertainment would include audioanimatronic shows, films, and international restaurants and shops.

By the late 1970s, however, the sensibilities of EPCOT Center's projected audience had changed from what could have been expected twenty or even ten years earlier. The 1960s and 1970s had had a significant impact on popular historical and political consciousness (as the 1980s would have on popular health and ecological issues). Visitors could be assumed to be more sophisticated than in the past and more cynical, especially with regard to major U.S. corporations. By signing on with the project, the latter became engaged in both advertising [3] and image-repair work. [4]

The tone of the stories told at EPCOT Center, then, is a bit different from that of those told at the Magic Kingdom. First, it is more transparently pedagogical. Second, the EPCOT Center stories generally have much longer time spans than those elsewhere at WDW, including those required by the presentation of geological evolution. Third, many of the corporate stories here acknowledge that there have been some problems in the past. Although none of these problems were caused by the corporations themselves, "we" nonetheless have and can overcome them by "acting wisely." Acting wisely generally means acquiescing to the corporate-controlled technological fix, including especially the colonization of space.

Although all of the Future World attractions except Journey into Imagination have historical components, I focus here on the two with the most extensive reliance on historical stories — AT&T's Spaceship Earth and the ride portion of GM's World of Motion. As a counterpoint to Liberty Square's Hall of Presidents, I also describe here the American Adventure, the U.S. pavilion in World Showcase. This requires a small introductory side tour to Tomorrowland's *American Journeys*.

There is a central contradiction in Disney's presentation of history — that is especially evident at EPCOT. The larger historical stories are obviously made up. Whether they invoke nostalgia, as at the Magic Kingdom, or string together selectively chosen historical icons in the interests of the corporate story, the histories are shallow pastiche. We ride past a scene, trying to take it in for ten to fifteen seconds, jump a thousand years, and spin to another tableau. Many of the scenes are cute and cleverly whimsical, undercutting any attempt to take the past seriously. This is schlock history — a fake real product.

Yet as always, the attention to detail is overwhelming. The tiniest bits and pieces of the sets are constructed with a passion for authenticity — an authenticity that escapes all but the most detail-oriented and knowledgeable visitors. For example, there is an early scene in Spaceship Earth — AT&T's history of communication technologies — in which a pharaoh of the New Kingdom of Egypt is dictating a letter to his scribe. According to Birnbaum, this dictation is excerpted from an actual letter received by an agent of a ruler of this period.[5] It is as if a forest — any forest — is chosen cavalierly to represent the idea of a place and time, and then infinite energy is directed toward the scrutiny of each leaf and each piece of bark on each tree.

Each scene, then, allows a visitor to be seduced by its gross iconic anatomy, its humor, and the claims to authenticity made by the details. The more we know and the closer we look (and the more times we repeat the ride), the more we might be hustled — and the more we are pleased, entranced, and rewarded for our knowledge and attention. It is authenticity inside inauthenticity. On whatever level we take the ride — the details, the iconic scenes, the appreciation of audioanimatronic technology, or the bricolage as a whole — we confront the corporate view of history. Swamped with the constant noise of details, we glide past the splices where the silences of Distory have been edited out.

Spaceship Earth

The great golf ball of Spaceship Earth towers over the entrance to EPCOT Center. It is 164 feet in diameter and, resting on its pedestal, 180 feet high — as high as Cinderella's Castle and Space Mountain. But those end in spires (as does Big Thunder Mountain). In its seeming massiveness, Spaceship Earth *looms*, telling us on the ground about the power of science and technology we will find behind it. Spaceship Earth is the architectural signature of EPCOT Center and, perhaps, for all of WDW. Birnbaum notes that on a clear day, it is visible to air travelers flying down both coasts of Florida.[6]

In its curved lines of pyramidic paneling, the globe points to Buckminster Fuller's geodesic domes, and its construction principles are similar. This is a full globe, however, and not a dome; thus, Disney has christened it a "geosphere." Birnbaum has the specifications.

> Weighing 1 million pounds, measuring 164 feet in diameter and 180 feet in height, and encompassing 2,200,000 cubic feet of space, this geosphere is held aloft by 6 legs supported by pylons sunk 100 feet into the ground. The distinctive sheen of its covering derives from a sort of quarter-inch-thick sandwich made of 2 anodized aluminum faces and a polyethylene core. This sheath is made up of 954 triangular panels, not all of equal size or shape.[7]

The silver sheath shines brightly during the day as the sun flares off its facets. At night it forms an excellent reflective surface for the spinning globe projected on it by lasers following the IllumiNations laser, light, and fireworks show.

Four wide paths lead from the entrance turnstiles past a large central area planted in green leaf and flowers. The paths converge around a fountain in the middle of which is a large plastic tripod with the EPCOT logo — five interlocking circles with a stylized globe in the middle. At night the tripod is lit from below by colored lights.

The paths diverge again as they approach the entrance to Spaceship Earth, moving around its base toward Earth Station behind it. To the right is Camera Center, where film may be purchased and cameras rented. To the left are the Gateway souvenir shop and the stroller and wheelchair rental center. Dead ahead is the ramp leading up into the bowels of the now-giant ball.

The guiding metaphor — earth as a spaceship travelling self-contained through the universe — suggests that we might find some evidence inside of the ecological reasoning that originally gave rise to the phrase Spaceship Earth. Maybe we'll learn something about the interconnections between living and non-living forms or about the limited supplies that can travel together in a spaceship. But *n-o-o-o-o!* Instead we are shown AT&T's history of communication, planned with the advice of Ray Bradbury, among others, and guided by the voice of Walter Cronkite.

Although the central questions purportedly posed by the ride — Who are we? Where have we come from? Where are we going? — are portentous, if trite, the ride itself has nothing to do with them; they are invoked merely as ritual. Spaceship Earth only takes us from cave painting to neon lights and computer graphics.

We enter our Time Machine vehicle for a spiraling trip to the top of the geosphere. We begin in darkness. The feel is clammy, the smell musty. As we climb, Cronkite talks to us from speakers placed behind our heads.

> *For eons the planet has drifted as a spaceship through the universe. And for a brief moment we have been its passengers. Yet in that time we have made tremendous progress in our ability to record and share knowledge. So let's turn back 40,000 years to the dawn of recorded history, as we trace the path of communication from its earliest beginnings to the promise of the future.*

We begin with two central Disney themes — progress and the promise of the future. Because this is AT&T's show, "our" progress (tremendous at that) is measured in information technologies.[8] As we climb, images of Cro-Magnon hunters and mammoths are projected overhead as distorted ghosts. Two more themes are voiced.

> *We have reached the dawn of recorded time. An age when mammoth creatures roamed the land. But with spoken language, the ancient hunters learned to work together and meet the challenges of this hostile world.*

Throughout Future World the world — nature — is hostile, dangerous, and powerful; but as with all difficulties, this hostility is merely another "challenge" in the great competition of life. If "we" can subdue hostile nature, through language and other means that allow "us" to work together, "we" can receive the gifts nature holds for "us." The Disney stance toward the natural world is adversarial, although tinged with nostalgia.

We reach our first tableau. Audioanimatronic Cro-Magnon figures paint animal effigies on a cave wall. Then in the Egyptian temple scene, an attendant (who looks like a movie version of a eunuch) fans the queen while Pharaoh dictates to his scribe. The wall behind the throne is filled with newly invented hieroglyphs.

In a scene set in the ninth century B.C.E.,[9] Phoenician traders settle shipping accounts as one keeps the tally in the newly invented alphabet. Now the written word, available to the common people, begins to travel across the land.

We are on to Greece and a masked actor speaking lines from Sophocles's *Oedipus Rex*.[10] Then it's Rome. Two soldiers converse frontstage. A boy holds a white horse in the background. A ghostlike charioteer rides to the hills in the distance, lit with nighttime fires. But Glorious Rome, with its

long-distance network that carried laws and tidings over a far-reaching empire . . . falls victim to the flames of EX-CESS. [The air is smoky and acrid.]

Ages of knowledge are lost or forgotten in the ashes . . . . But all is not lost, for Islamic and Jewish scholars continued to preserve ancient wisdom in noble libraries. In their travels they record knowledge and share their findings with cultures East and West.

We see the Jewish scholars in their library to the left, and on the right we pass four Muslims sitting on the ground around a tenth-century quadrant.[11] A medieval scene shows two monks copying manuscripts by candlelight. The second monk has fallen asleep and is snoring. We can see his robotic chest expand with each breath.

Now comes the Renaissance and its communication centerpiece, Gutenberg's printing press. We see a master reading to two students, a painter, a sculptor, and two musicians. Again Disney's penchant for detail is noteworthy: "The type on Johann Gutenberg's press actually moves, and the page that the celebrated 15th-century printer is examining is a replica of one from a Bible in the collection of (Los Angeles's) Huntington Library. In the Renaissance scene, the book being read is Virgil's *Aeneid*; the musical instruments in that scene are a lute and a *lyra da braccio*, both replicas of period pieces."[12] Cronkite again.

The Renaissance — a time of renewed interest in the worlds of poetry and music, science, philosophy, and art. Behold the majesty of the Sistine Chapel!

Here the exigencies of myth and ride design suddenly subvert Disney's microveracity. Although it is now clear that Michelangelo stood on his scaffold to paint Pope Julius II's ceiling, he is shown here in the traditional supine position. For dramatic effect, as the ride curves away to the right, Michelangelo is also shown as being left-handed.[13]

Having visited the Renaissance, we jump to the twentieth century.

On a wave of inspiration we sail into a bold new era, an age of astounding invention and ever-increasing progress in communications.

A large, loud printing press is on the left; beyond it is a newsboy shouting, "Extra! Extra! New York Daily!" To the right is a telegraph operator taking dictation. The scenes come fast and furious, signaling the acceleration in communication enterprise — telephone operators, a radio station recording booth, a family watching shows from the Golden Age of television, film clips and movie marquees.

> *Instant communication creates an ever-increasing flow of facts and figures. To manage this growing storehouse of information, we invent the computer, a revolutionary tool made practical by the tiny transistor.*

We pass the messy room of a boy working at his personal computer, then a woman's (his mother?) computer-equipped home office, then find ourselves facing the large electronic maps of AT&T's network operation room. Lights flash across the maps as we see how telephone calls are routed.

> *Today we're merging the technologies of communication and computers to store, process, and share information . . . and we're creating a vast electronic network stretching from our homes to the reaches of space.*

We enter a tunnel with neon tubes of light flashing on and off, and then suddenly we reach the climax of the ride.

> *We have entered a wondrous new age — the Age of Information . . . a time of new promise and new hope for ourselves and our Spaceship Earth.*

Wondering what AT&T has to do with new hopes for ourselves and our planet, we flow into the planetarium at the top of the geosphere. Overhead, against a night background of "stars" (projected by a Disney special-effects "star ball" [14]) is a representation of earth as if seen from space. Out of the blue, this is Spaceship Earth — a sight we have seen before in astronauts' photography and will see often in the future, for our future is in space. Turning for our descent from the top of the globe, we pass people working in space on various pieces of large equipment.

The ride has now run out of conceptual gas, but we still have to descend back to the exit. We travel backward at a steep angle, surrounded by neon lights and blue-tipped fiber-optic cables and accompanied by a song about Tomorrow's Child.

> *Yes, Tomorrow's Child, embodying our hopes and dreams for the future — a future made possible by the Information Age. The technologies of this new era will extend our reach and expand the capabilities of the human mind and help us shape a better tomorrow.*

Images of Tomorrow's Child — playing among computer chips, strands of DNA, and chemical formulas — light our way. As the ride comes to its end, our grandfatherly guide sends us off with our testamentary mandate.

> *Now is the time of unprecedented choice and opportunity. So let us explore and question and understand. Let us learn from our past and meet the challenges of the future. Let us go forth and fulfill our destiny on Spaceship Earth.*

As we exit into Earth Station, we go forth to fulfill our *immediate* destiny by making lunch reservations at the bank of two-way video monitors at the far end, for our hunger shall multiply. Nor is it fruitful to think of destiny on an empty stomach.

World of Motion

At the southeastern corner of Future World is the stainless-steel wheel of General Motors's (GM) World of Motion. Lying on its side, this wheel is 318 feet in diameter and 60 feet high. [15] Inside are the World of Motion ride and the Transcenter. My attention at present is on the ride. I'll discuss the Transcenter — a set of exhibits about automobile design, robotics, and the internal combustion engine, as well as a GM showroom — in a chapter 17.

The structure of the ride is similar to that of Spaceship Earth. The audience passes by audioanimatronicated scenes that tell GM's history of transportation. The tone here, however, is different — consistently whimsical rather than earnestly portentous.

Inside the wheel the line moves beneath speakers across which zoom the sounds of speeding cars. The ride vehicles resemble the seats of a four-door sedan. Spiraling through an open — and sometimes pleasantly breezy — space cut out from the front of the wheel, riders move toward the first tableau. As we do so, we learn GM's theme: "When it comes to transportation, it's always fun to be free."

Freedom is movement and freedom is fun, nothing particularly deep and responsible — just fun. This fun is available through the purchase of a personal automobile, which, of course, is not free. As the "It's Fun to Be Free" ("to go anywhere, with never a care") song surrounds us, our male tour guide takes us through a history of transportation.

We begin once again with Cro-Magnon, this time a family whose members blow on their painfully reddened feet.

> *Throughout the ages we have searched for freedom to move from one place to another. In the beginning, of course, there was foot-power; but with our first wandering steps, we quickly discovered the need to improve our basic transportation. After years of stumbling around, we launch a new idea, our first safe highway — water.*

Here is an Egyptian lad floating on a reed raft in a papyrus swamp, pseudo-menaced by a robot Nile crocodile.

> *Our animal friends give us new freedom — and we test-drive many new models.*

To the right is a congeries of friendly, giving animals — an ox, a camel, an elephant, a zebra, and an ostrich — each with a rider. Above them is a magic carpet, complete with rider and magic vase. At the end of this scene, the owners of a very overloaded donkey offer "gold" pieces to a Semitic-looking innkeeper, who shakes his head. There is no room at the inn.

The wheel is invented. A Middle Eastern potentate smiles approvingly at a bearded man rotating a wheel in front of him. Behind the successful inventor are wannabees with square and triangular offerings.

Next is a chariot outlet where a Roman car dealer is trying to sell used chariots — their prices marked down in Roman numerals — to a senatorial couple — the bald, fat member of which sports a head wreath. Near the entrance to the dealership, a blushing young woman stands with her prize — the latest-model centaur.

> *With our new-found freedom, empires expand, cultures flourish, trade and commerce grow. . . . With proud new ships, we sail forth in search of new worlds, undaunted by age-old myths and silly superstitions.*

As a map shows ships sailing off the end of a flat earth, a robot mariner stares through his spyglass into the eye of a sea monster.

Now comes the Renaissance. To AT&T the Renaissance meant art, literature, and music. To General Motors it is the time of invention and engineering. Here we see Leonardo da Vinci's studio. A very pouty Mona Lisa is being ignored while Leonardo and an apprentice fiddle with the artificial wings of a personal flying machine.

Passing a bewigged man with pigs, chickens, and goats rising in a balloon over the roofs of Paris, we enter the Age of Steam. Near a Mississippi riverboat at night, a Huck Finn-ish lad fishes while a black boy plays the banjo. Later we will see another black musician. To General Motors, apparently, black men were born to strum.

> *Beyond the Mississippi, passengers enjoy the scenic West, with the freedom and adventure of the open road.*

We pass a wagon train, circled against an Indian attack. Arrows protrude from wagon wheels and men's hats. A Wells Fargo stagecoach is stopped by a smoke-snorting bull. A better way to travel is by train.

> *Another kind of horse arrives, a steam-powered horse, bringing fast, dependable, safe travel to the new frontier.*

The one we see, however, is being robbed. Tenderfoot passengers stand with their hands up as a thief requests their valuables. At the caboose a shaking conductor hands down the strongbox. Watching all of this from a bluff, dressed in white and with the glowing heart of a good guy, is a useless sheriff.

Next comes the bicycle. In a park filled with bicyclists, one man is attacked by a dog. Another has fallen off into a pig's mud wallow. A third — a unicyclist — dazzles a damsel with his style as her date looks on, displeased.

> *The call of the open road brings us a new wonder — a carriage without a horse. Yet, with the horseless carriage, we thunder full-speed into the twentieth century.*

We pass an oily-smelling garage where a mechanic cranks an engine. On the other side is a horse that stares at this new horseless carriage with bulging eyes. Straight ahead is the ride's climactic scene — the first traffic jam.

We are in the city. A terrified white horse is at an intersection surrounded by a red car, a double-decker city bus, and an ice truck. The horse has knocked over his cart, sending cartons of chickens crashing to the street. Vegetables are strewn everywhere. Audioanimatronic figures stand or sit around as horns honk. One pops out of an open manhole. Two boys chip away at the ice on the back of the truck. A bowler-hatted policeman stands with arms folded, glowering but doing nothing to help the farmer try to get his horse moving again. This is a very complicated and clever scene.

We pass through it on a Sunday drive to a picnic in the country. Behind a billboard advertising an air show lurks a menacing patrolman on a motorcycle. At the air show, the dashing aviator with his flappers smiles for the photographer.

On our way back to the present, we see shiny, spiffed-up GM automobiles — from the 1930s, 1940s, 1950s, and 1960s. [16] Each is filled with riders. In one — carrying college students to a football game — is another black stringman.

The finale contains the speed rooms and the City of the Future. In the speed rooms, our ride vehicles enter large tunnels on the walls of which are projected 70-millimeter scenes that simulate a fast-moving ride experience. We speed down country roads, airboat through swamps, and ice sail. Our car shakes slightly, and wind is blown at us from hidden fans to give the illusion of rapid movement.

We are through the present and are suddenly turning around the City of the Future. It is dark. The buildings look like tall, skinny phallic symbols. Phosphorescent "vehicles," lit by black light, move through the air. As the ride ends, we step onto the moving sidewalk and drift down the ramp to the Transcenter. Now that we have seen how much fun it is to be free, we can see how GM engineers will make our corporate future even more fun.

We have made one transition from the Magic Kingdom to EPCOT Center, to histories transnational corporations can live with. The connecting link ran through GE's Carousel of Progress. Now I want to follow another link — the mythological U.S. history that leads from Frontierland and Liberty Square (especially the Hall of Presidents) to the American Adventure in World Showcase. The pointer for this transition is also found in Tomorrowland — in the CircleVision 360 film *American Journeys*. There we will find the telos of U.S. Distory.

The Telos of U.S. Distory

What then is the American, this new man? . . . He is an American, who, leaving behind him all his ancient prejudices and manners, receives new ones from the new mode of life he has embraced, the new government he obeys, and the new rank he holds. He has become an American by being received in the broad lap of our great Alma Mater. Here individuals of all races are melted into a new race of man, whose labors and posterity will one day cause great changes in the world. Americans are the western pilgrims.

—Hector St. John de Crevecoeur [17]

De Crevecoeur was a precurser not only of de Tocqueville, whose 1830s study of American character has become suitably famous, but also of Frederick Jackson Turner. Ever since its language was publicly appropriated by John F. Kennedy, Turner's "frontier thesis" has entered into U.S. cultural consciousness. "New frontiers" — necessary because the old ones are closed — are reported everywhere at WDW.

Richard J. Ellis and Alun Munslow have argued that "the Turner thesis has a double status: a modern myth simultaneously constituting itself as an historical narrative." [18] To see what they mean, let's look briefly at the thesis itself.

Turner's claims must be placed in the larger context of American Edenic themes. In seventeenth-century European eyes, America was a wilderness, untouched except by Indians — themselves seen as wild parts of nature. Puritan Englishmen in particular might turn this land into a garden — a new Eden. They would be both justified and successful if they kept their covenant with a God who had promised them protection. This would be a new land, shaped and tamed by its Protestant husbandmen. [19]

Other themes spoke of civil and political life. John Winthrop began with his "city on the hill." The American Revolution and its ensuing political structures and documents were encoded as fulfillments of covenental promises. Having been "invented," as Gary Wills puts it, [20] through the Declaration of Independence, the United States became what Seymour Martin Lipset would later call "the first new nation." [21]

De Crevecoeur and de Tocqueville were among the first to ask, "What effect has the environment — both political and physical — had on the formation of American character?" The latter wrote some years after the Louisiana Purchase, when vast new territory of different climates and topography had become available for white U.S. settlement. Given these and other additions to U.S. territory, David Potter would later characterize Americans as "people of plenty." [22]

Turner advanced his frontier thesis in 1893: "The existence of an area of free land, its continuous recession and the advance of American settlement westward explain American development." [23]

The moving frontier allowed a "perennial rebirth" of U.S. social institutions. Its expansionist milieu, Turner argued, created a new American character — the independent pioneer-hero.

That coarseness and strength combined with acuteness; that practical, inventive turn of mind, quick to find expedients; that masterful grasp of material things, lacking in the artistic but powerful to effect great ends; that restless, nervous energy; that dominant individualism, working for good and for evil; and withal that buoyancy and exuberance which comes with freedom — these are the traits of the frontier, or traits called out elsewhere because of the existence of the frontier. [24]

For Turner the pioneer acted under the determining constraints of the frontier; but out of this interaction — especially the fact that the frontier moved — Americans developed an entrepreneurial individualism that characterizes the U.S. *mentalité*.

Drawing on Hayden White, Ellis and Munslow note that Turner has constructed a "Romantic emplotment and an Anarchist ideological implication" for his story. [25] What happens in Distory is that the romance is underlined and the anarchy defused through humor and nostalgization. The tension between anarcho-pragmatism and mechanical geographic determinism in Turner is resolved by making the "I" into a "we" and the "we" into a corporation, whose scientists will undo the determinism. Disney transforms the pioneer into the inventor.

An important implication of Turner's thesis, as he made clear, was the problem of what would happen to his version of American character now that the frontier had been closed and the land filled up. Around him cities were growing (including slums) as the stream of eastern and southern European migrants flowed on. Factories were going up as the beginnings of corporate America assaulted the agrarian mode of an American Eden. As we see in the American Adventure, Teddy Roosevelt will soon be asked to rescue pieces of the frontier from human onslaught.

Turner's response was denial: "He would be a rash prophet who would assert that the expansive character of American life has now entirely ceased. Movement has been its dominant fact, and, unless this training has no effect upon a people, the American energy will continually demand a wider field for its exercise. . . . There is not a tabula rasa." [26] According to Ellis and Munslow, Turner proposed the myth that "the 'dominant individualism' which is definitively American exists — potentially eternal — and must be defended. The thesis thus constantly seeks to distill a timeless uniqueness for America which conflicts with its own assertion of historical processes as socially determining." [27]

A hundred years later, Turner's myth is enshrined at WDW, but with a bit of whistling in the dark, for a constantly recurring theme — coming near the end of both *American Journeys* and the American Adventure — is escape to outer space. This is especially true at Future World. It seems that the problems of the 1970s and 1980s exacerbated the fantasy of escape. It is as if Disney's imagineers are saying, "The frontier is closed. The land is filling up. Let me out of here!"

The ideological message is that space is the new frontier, and only if "we" feed all our resources toward its "conquering" will "we" be able to retain entrepreneurial individualism that is our characteristic right as Americans. This plays better at Lake Buena Vista than it does in Youngstown, Harlan County, and Liberty City.

With Turner in mind, then, let's take an American Journey and have an American Adventure.

An American Journey

These Disney versions have now themselves become a special mode of first-hand experience in the repertoire of the great national shared experience.

--David M. Johnson [28]

Tomorrowland's CircleVision 360 *American Journeys* shows us the current result of Disney's U.S. history. It is a geographical tour in which the spectacular landscapes of the frontier play an important part — now, of course, in re-creation. Turner's U.S. individualism has been supplemented by countless further immigrants, including non-Europeans. Americans live in cities, bustle about building things, and take breaks in the wilderness, at ball games, and listening to music. But lest we forget our heritage as we ski down the slopes, let's remember the New England seaman, the pioneers in their wagon trains, Abe Lincoln, and the Havasupai. As we fly by Mount St. Helens (two days after the eruption), let us also remember that the frontier landscape is an independent material force.

American Journeys was made with a 700-pound rig holding nine cameras that together shot 360 degrees of film. The audience stands leaning against the railings surrounded by the film.

As this twenty-one-minute film unfolds, the various themes are carried both by the accompanying music and the strategic use of voice types and accents. These voices and accents — a folksy Henry Fonda type for the western wagon train opener; understated New England, New Orleans, and native American accents for the appropriate scenes; Royal Dano again as Abe Lincoln — are U.S. archetypes. They are the kind of U.S. culture that most Americans know but don't know they know. Disney is brilliant at this kind of seamless evocation.

Unlike the Hall of Presidents and the American Adventure, this fast-paced montage begins in the West. An opening canyon flyby is followed by a reenactment of a wagon train's descent through rocky foothills to the Great Basin. The Henry Fonda voice recalls Turner.

All Americans have shared a common dream.

And the dream is that there is something here in this vast, unspoiled land for everyone.

Those first American journeys took many years and many lives.

But the journey and the dream live on.

What really brought people to the West were promises of space for productive activity — for farms, business, gold and silver mines, and the like. For some, such as the Mormons, the West presented a chance to set up a planned ideological community away from the persecutions of the East and the Midwest. For others it provided an opportunity to escape the human crush of eastern and European cities or the famines and ecological disasters of northwestern Europe.

American Journeys, however, is a travelogue aimed at the contemporary traveler, so its opening scenes present the romance of the physical West — a snowy Rocky Mountain with tiny climbers on top, the Oregon-Northern California coast, the hills of southern Wyoming, Utah's canyonlands, and back to the coast — with mountains tumbling down to the sea.

With the land so diverse and seemingly endless, it's no wonder people came from around the world to this new place they called America.

The prologue complete, we return to the East, to New York Harbor and the Statue of Liberty. We are standing on a ferry boat with an immigrant family. A man with an accent speaks. Perhaps he is Italian.

I am proud to be an American. Even before I come here I dream of being in America. People come to America. America. She has so much to offer.

We see a New York City montage as the nine screens break up into separate images. Here is the diversity of iconic ethnic types in the city. From their ethnic emblems it does not appear as if they are melting, although their presentation together suggests that Disney means to say that they are. The theme is drawn together with a picture of the U.N. building as the screens rejoin for a parting nighttime glance at the city skyline from across the East River.

Now it's on to New England, as the travelogue moves north to south, east to west. The film's next theme is our heritage. We are in Connecticut, watching a woodcarver at Mystic Seaport. A woman speaks.

Up here in New England you've gotta sometimes remind yourself it's the twentieth century. We were raised with the heritage of the sea. There's no denying that. And it's the dedication of our craftsmen that keeps all these old traditions alive. Our traditions are kind of like a bond between generations.

After a snowy night on a small New England town common, we are off to the nation's capital. It's the mall at daybreak. A John Huston voice begins.

Some of our traditions are not very old, really. As a nation, we haven't been at this very long. But we created new traditions uniquely ours. The Library of Congress is a treasure house of our collected knowledge, saving it for future generations without turning our backs on the past. We must always remember that the world closely watches what Abraham Lincoln called our experiment in popular government.

Now "Lincoln" speaks, as the film takes us to his monument at night.

Most governments have been based on the denial of equal rights. Ours began by affirming those rights. Men will pass away, but those principles will live, and live forever.

But not without sacrifice, this American dream, as we see across the river at Arlington National Cemetery.

One tradition for which such sacrifice has been made is our uniquely American music. Past an 1820 covered bridge on the Pemigewasset River, the film moves to a bluegrass festival in Norris, Tennessee.[29] Again the screen splits as we see fiddlers, a jew's harpist, and a clogger.

Through a silent bayou we come to the French Quarter of New Orleans and the jazz at Preservation Hall. The musical interlude ends as Dixieland music accompanies us up the Mississippi on a sternwheeler and on toward the plains.

As reapers harvest a wheat farm, a farmer tells us,

> *It's really something when you think of it. These days there's darn few of us left on the farm. But you know, we [still] have . . . a good jump on the rest of the world.*

This is the only evidence in the travelogue that the United States has a Great Plains. As far as the film is concerned, there is no U.S. Midwest. Perhaps Indiana has no culture.

Lest we think about farm debt and agribusiness, we are swept immediately onto a steam-powered train in the Rockies. "Henry Fonda" tells us,

> *Those early journeys across the Rockies took a special kind of courage. Nowadays we see these rugged mountains as a challenge of a different kind.*

A flyover shows the obligatory ski scene. We are now into the sports and vacation travel part of our U.S. heritage. Every travelogue we see at WDW, except for the *Wonders of China* in World Showcase, has a ski scene. It appears to be obligatory.

We see balloons wafting over canyonland buttes, a Southwest native American rodeo (Indians as cowboys — "What used to be a day's work is now a sport"), white water rafting down the Colorado (with a white guy and a black guy in front of the raft). Here the camera rig is on one of the rafts. As it bucks and pitches, so does the audience. At day's end we join an upscale campfire dinner. But lest we forget, we are taken to the gentle pools and waterfalls at the bottom of the Grand Canyon, where a Havasupai man reminds us,

> *The history of this land goes back before anyone was here. For over 600 years, my people have lived in the Grand Canyon.*

Now the film underlines the "forces-of-nature" theme with Carlsbad Cavern, the Mount St. Helens visit ("a constant reminder of how small we really are"), and north to Alaska (dogsleds and the Columbia Glacier), where another native voice makes an indirect claim to precedence.

> *It has been said that thousands of years ago my ancestors came to Alaska across the great ice bridge.*

Back we go to California, past Yosemite's Half Dome, the redwoods and sequoias, to civilization. We see San Francisco and the Golden Gate Bridge from the hills across the strait, and gliding under the bridge with the sailboats, we are plunked down between first and second bases at Dodger

Stadium. The Dodgers are ahead of the Pirates 2-1 in the bottom of the fourth. On the beach is an amazing sand castle. "Fonda" speaks.

> *Americans have always known how to have a good time together. They may know how to work together, too.*

The "work together" part has three scenes, one civilian and two military. A tall building is being constructed in a northwest city, perhaps Seattle. The audience is up in the air with hard-hatted supervisors. It's on to an aircraft carrier and then to Cape Canaveral for a launch of the Space Shuttle Columbia in happier times.

From Florida it's off to Honolulu, where the camera rig has been placed in an outrigger canoe heading for the beach. A Hawaiian woman advertises,

> *In Hawaii we say "aloha" — welcome. The beauty of these islands is yours to share.*

Then it's back six time zones to Florida for an undersea reef visit.

The movement from east to west has stopped. We are now in the logic of the centrifuge, spinning through the final collage, past iconic emblems of the United States as "God Bless America" rises from hum to song.

> *The land . . . the people . . . the traditions. We are a nation of nations . . . people from all over the world, drawn here by different dreams. We all share a common love for this land we call . . . America.*

Now mountains, the northwest coast, the Golden Gate Bridge, the Statue of Liberty and Ellis Island, the Rockies, Mt. Rushmore, back to the Statue of Liberty at night, with fireworks in the background. Differences are obliterated in the swirl. Whew! We are wasted. Then silence . . . and the hostess hoping we have enjoyed our *American Journeys*.

So this is where the American Adventure has led — to music, tradition, and the frontier, packaged as commodity, to outdoor recreation, to the space program. Perhaps we should go to World Showcase and see once again how we got here.

The Generic American Adventure

> With its deep-seated patriotism and acknowledgement of the contributions of all men, The American Adventure stands as the unification of World Showcase. [30]

The American Adventure is the most complicated attraction at World Showcase, both technically and ideologically. By 1982 (and the opening of EPCOT Center) popular consciousness required that public history contain at least some allusions to the conflicts in the country's past. Wallace cites a Disney briefing pamphlet for employees: "We couldn't ignore certain major issues that questioned our nation's stand on human liberty and justice." [31]

The sponsors — Coca-Cola and American Express — agreed. A Coca-Cola spokesman told Wallace, "The warts-and-all perspective is appreciated by most visitors because our country is not perfect and they know it." [32]

The design problem for Disney and its partners was how to point to conflict and yet domesticate it under the aegis of patriotic corporate boosterism. The thematic solution was to turn historical difficulties into opportunities in disguise. Andrea Stulman Dennett suggests that the difficulties were selected with a kind of fill-in-the-blank attitude because the tail that wagged this dog was the issue of technical form.

> *How* the story is told was struggled over for years before the content was ever discussed. Once it was determined that the story was to be told in a "magic theater" type of setting as opposed to a ride-through, the dramatic text, the historical elements, were selected. The repercussion of this fill-in-the-blank attitude is that history is almost non-existent in this production. Characters are icons and historical events have been fabricated, symbolically mythologized, and compressed into vignettes. [33]

Dennett also notes that the final script was approved by the Disney Quality Control Committee.

Yet the result is curiously ambiguous, for the public *has* forced changes on Disney. People *do* leave the show commenting on Frederick Douglass, Susan B. Anthony, Chief Joseph, and John Muir. Perhaps they believe they have seen something contemporary and progressive when they have seen only small breaks in the web of Disney's Pollyanna history. But however tamed, these breaks — like those in the evolution stories and in the ecological discourse at The Land's *Symbiosis* movie — are real.

The American Adventure takes place in a large Georgian building at the far end of Showcase Lagoon. It is the central pavilion of World Showcase and lines up with Spaceship Earth to form the thematic and architectural backbone of EPCOT Center.

We enter the open lobby, perhaps to the sounds of the excellent a capella singing group The Voices of Liberty. The group is in colonial dress as it sings American folk classics ("Skip to My Lou," "Oh, Susanna," and similar songs) for the preshow. The crowd gathers around the fifty-starred circle in the center of the rotunda floor. Around us are paintings and, to the left, a display of Declaration of Independence-signing paraphernalia. [34] On the walls are eleven quotations meant to tap the theme and get us in the republican mood while we wait. [35]

Doors open and we enter a corridor that leads to the Hall of Flags, where an escalator takes us up, past the forty-four flags that have been flown over parts or all of the United States to the balcony and theater entrance. Again doors open and we enter the one thousand-seat theater.

Running down the walls on both sides of the theater are the Spirit of America statues. Embodied by an iconic image of an "American type," each is meant to represent Disney's version of an important national characteristic. To the right in descending order are the Spirit of Adventure (sea captain), the Spirit of Self-Reliance (farmer), the Spirit of Knowledge (female teacher), the Spirit of Pioneering (aviator), the Spirit of Heritage (Indian maiden), and the Spirit of Freedom (pilgrim). To the left are the Spirit of Discovery (mountain man), the Spirit of Compassion (female nurse), the Spirit of Independence (minuteman), the Spirit of Tomorrow (mother), the Spirit of Innovation (George Washington Carver), and the Spirit of Individualism (cowboy). Compassion, heritage, knowledge, and tommorow are presented as women; the rest are men. There is one black American and one native American. It's an ecumenical crowd, gendered as one might expect.

The twenty-nine-minute show — "a hundred-yard dash capturing the spirit of the country at specific moments in time" [36] — takes place on a stage that is actually an open pit behind mock-stage fronting. The sets and robot cast rise into this space from below. Behind it is a seventy-two-foot-wide rear projection screen on which the passage of time will be indexed.

The audioanimatronic technology is extraordinary. Benjamin Franklin — the first Disney robot to "walk" — climbs the last few steps to the garret where Jefferson is slaving over the Declaration of Independence. Even more impressive is the machinery that moves the sets around.

> Underneath the entire theater is a movable carriage device that designers have dubbed "the war wagon," measuring 65-by-35-by-14 feet and weighing 175 tons. The basement that supports "the war wagon" is itself supported by pilings driven approximately 300 feet into the ground; it carries 10 different sets and during the performance rolls forward or backward to position the appropriate set underneath the stage at the appropriate time. Also, because the height of the space underneath the theater is relatively limited, the sets themselves were specially designed to allow certain sections to contract telescopically as proved necessary. These operations are computer controlled. [37]

The curtain rises and we see at centerstage audioanimatronic figures of Benjamin Franklin (the Spirit of the Eighteenth Century) and Mark Twain (the Spirit of the Nineteenth Century). They will be our guides for this adventure. [38] These two quintessential American storytellers sit flanking a small table. Twain's rocking chair squeaks. Smoke rises from his glowing cigar. Franklin and Twain banter like talk-show hosts, showing mutual admiration tinged with a slight edge of verbal competition. Quoting John Steinbeck, Franklin begins.

> *Hope and fear created this land. We built America and the process made us Americans — a new breed, rooted in all races, stained and tinted with all colors . . . a steaming ethnic anarchy. Then, in a bit of time, we became more alike than we were different . . . a new society . . . fitted by our very thoughts for greatness.*

Franklin asks Twain if he recognizes "those inspiring words from one of America's great writers." The latter responds that he doesn't remember having written them. To Franklin, Steinbeck has "learned the same spirit as the Founding Fathers themselves."

When Twain calls Franklin "the proud elder statesman," Franklin replies,

> *Mr. Twain, pride is one of our national passions. Even those who overcome it are proud of their humility.*

Twain again, "I was born humble. Fortunately, it wore off."

Our cohosts now take us into the story. Franklin begins.

> *It started when dreams and visions of a new world were shrouded in the myths and legends of an old world. Finally, through those early myths of uncertainty sailed the first great adventurers.*

The themes are set out: the interaction between human activity and the environment that produced Turner's American character, the melting pot, the new society destined for greatness, national pride, the dreams and visions of a new world versus the myths and legends of the old, and the great adventure — with Englishmen rather than native Americans, Spaniards, or Vikings as the first adventurers.

As paintings of the Mayflower at sea fill the screen, a sea chanty tells of the voyage and the first hard winter in Plymouth. Further paintings of the harsh New England winter, with its suffering and death, bring us to Franklin's words about challenge, struggle, and the untamed wilderness.

> *Yes, far from welcoming the early settlers, this land severely challenged them. It was a struggle for survival that gained but a tiny toehold in a vast untamed wilderness.*

Now we jump 140 years.

> *In the decades that followed, a new challenge began to emerge. They [Americans] were growing more and more apart from the mother country. Passion began to govern and she never governs wisely.* (Emphasis added)

The paintings show that we are in a colonial city in the 1760s. England has imposed new taxes to support the fight on the frontier against the French and their native American allies. A royal proclamation is read; opposition is shouted; tea is dumped in Boston Harbor. Finally, says Franklin, the time had come to speak with one voice in a Declaration of Independence.

Scene 2 shows Franklin's visit to the paper-strewn room where Jefferson is penning the Declaration of Independence, complaining that John Adams should have written it. Jefferson is sick of being a "prisoner" in the attic.

> *Dr. Franklin, while you slept soundly through the meeting this afternoon, we did manage to justify separation.*

As Jefferson begins to read the declaration, the attic set is replaced by paintings of the preparation for war. An optimistic song about what a delight it is "to march and fight along the Freedom Trail" brings us to the next scene — Valley Forge.

It is night. Two freezing, threadbare soldiers stand at the left front of the stage. Fans blow air through their clothes to simulate a bitter winter wind, the sound of which whooshes through the speaker system. As they bemoan their situation, a robot George Washington sits at right rear on a robot horse, gravely sharing their fate.

We see more paintings and hear the rest of the song as the war moves on to its conclusion. Franklin speaks.

> *In the end, we the people prevailed, and achieved perhaps our greatest dream. Thirteen very different colonies became the United States of America. And we were free — an entire nation of dreamers and doers.*

Dreamers and doers! That's what we are. This is Disney's central image of U.S. character, which is echoed throughout WDW; the American — the pragmatic, inventive entrepreneur, seeking freedom to go his or her own way, to make and sell her or his own inventions. Sometimes he or she must join with others to overcome a challenge, but this is necessary only to remove some institutional fetter that binds her or his independence. And where might this simple dreaming and doing be exercised? Take a guess.

> *Twain: Westward bound, Dr. Franklin, to new frontiers!*

But out in these new frontiers, something strange happens to the story. After the inspirational reading of the seventeenth and eighteenth centuries, the tone changes. Disney, Coca-Cola, and American Express begin to play to the increasing sophistication of their audience. Here come the warts. We see paintings of the pioneer move west — a woman behind a plow, men panning for gold. Then Mark Twain introduces the new look.

> *Yessir, Dr. Franklin. You founding fathers gave us a pretty good start, don't you know .... We still had some things to learn the hard way. Seems a whole bunch of folks found out "We the People" didn't yet mean all the people. Folks like Frederick Douglass.*

The problem of slavery is introduced and, underlying it, of U.S. racism. A Frederick Douglass robot poles a small boat across the Mississippi. His boat moves out from the right almost half way across the stage, and then retreats. As it does so, the swampy river background painted on the screen also moves, giving the illusion that Douglass is moving along even when his set is going backward. It is dark. Douglass's lantern flickers.

> Douglass: *Even against the cricket's song here, along Mark Twain's*
> *beloved Mississippi, I hear the rattle of chains and the crack*
> *of the whip.*

Referring to Harriet Beecher Stowe's *Uncle Tom's Cabin*, Douglass claims that anti-slavery

> *is no longer a thing to be prevented. It has grown too abundant to be snuffed out . . . like a lantern.*

The next scene takes us to the studio where Matthew Brady's famous photograph of a family about to be split by the Civil War was taken. Brady stands behind his photography contraption while the family poses. The brothers argue.

> Brother 1: *We only wanted freedom, not war.*
> Brother 2: *Listen to my abolitionist brother.*

Brother 1:	*Johnny Reb!*
Pa:	*Quiet, boys. You're going to ruin Ma's birthday.*
Ma:	*No. No. Nothing can ruin today. We're all together. That's what counts.*

But, of course, the Civil War happens. Photographs are shown on the screen. The song "Two Brothers" is sung, and at the end we return to the Brady photograph, with one brother's face — the dead Johnny Reb — dramatically removed. Apparently the Civil War was pretty much a family tragedy.

Twain: *At last the terrible Civil War ended. The time had come to rebuild. . . . And new immigrants would help us do it. From around the world they came. A thousand noble currents . . . all pouring into one.*[39] *It seems there was a new dawn coming.*

The photo montage of immigrants melting away together is suddenly interrupted. In a startling breach of the audience's expectations, we are reminded of one of the truly ugly blotches on the U.S. story of freedom, dreaming, and doing. Now with a peal of thunder we see a sunset rather than a "new dawn."

Chief Joseph of the Nez Perces rises to the stage. Having been chased from the Wallowa Valley in Oregon into Montana by General Miles's army, Chief Joseph surrendered in the most quoted of all American Indian speeches. Its tag line is reproduced here at the end of the robot chief's speech.

Enough! Enough of your words.
Let your new dawn lead to the final sunset on my peoples' suffering.
When I think of our condition, my heart is sick.
I see men of my own race treated as outlaws, or shot down like animals.
I pray that all of us may be brothers, with one country around us, and one government for all.
From where the sun now stands, I will fight no more.
Forever.

The real Chief Joseph *did* say the last lines of this speech. The rest about brotherhood and government is Disney. With good reason, Chief Joseph was considerably more bitter and certainly less sanguine than is represented here.[40] Twain's response is to cast Chief Joseph as only a sad memory,

     reminding us once again of our long, painful journey to the frontiers of human liberty.

This is gibberish. "We" are reminded about "our" painful journey. Chief Joseph's people, many of them dead, serve as Others in a comment on "our" condition. What "the frontiers of human liberty" means here is beyond me, and I'm sure it would be quite beyond Samuel Clemens. It is a ritual incantation that denies the truth of the history to which it has just alluded. It is rich white peoples' ideology.

Chief Joseph is a downer. The next dramatic move is antidotal, and it boosts us back into the stream of progress. We are at the 1876 Philadelphia Centennial Exposition — a celebration of invention and industry.

Twain: *We came a long way in our first century, and like Susan B. Anthony, we're still speaking out.*

Although Susan B. Anthony stumps for women's rights — quoting Thomas Edison of all people ("Discontent is the first necessity of progress") — the script deflates her by introducing her with the commercial tag for Virginia Slims cigarettes. All we're missing is the "baby."

Alexander Graham Bell and Andrew Carnegie stand at exposition booths praising progress, Tom Edison, Corliss's steam engine, Otis's elevators, and themselves in Scottish accents. At a podium on the left, Twain banters with "the proud Scots," pooh-poohing Carnegie's plans for a new concert hall in New York.

Twain: *Oh, Carnegie Hall, eh . . . it'll never last. Now, libraries . . . Andy, that's a swell idea.*

The words spring out in a rush as everybody chimes the themes.

Bell: *It's an age of ideas.*

Carnegie: *An age of innovation.*

Anthony: *A dawn for new awareness.*

Twain: *A time to challenge the frontiers of a new century.*

The new century brings a montage of invention — cartoons of zippers, vaccuum cleaners, trolley cars, and airplanes, each in a little frame. But again we hear a countervoice. This one is aimed at the ecological-mindedness of Disney's current audience. Teddy Roosevelt stands at the edge of a precipice in Yosemite as a robot John Muir warns him that all this growth threatens the natural beauty of the United States. Muir suggests that Roosevelt should set aside wild places such as Yosemite as national parks.

Twain: *Ready or not, we were thrust into the role of World Leader.*

Thus is World War I introduced. We see a film clip of a U.S. ace pilot going after a German plane and then jump a decade to Charles Lindbergh's flight. This again is the high before a fall, as Disney's sine-curve history continues.

The fall is the Great Depression. An FDR robot tells us not to fear fear itself in a broadcast heard by four rural men on the porch of a country gas station. In what Wallace calls a familiar spate of "implausible retrospective integration,"[41] two men are black and two white. Red eighteen-cents-a-gallon gasoline sits unsold in the pump, and one of the black men strums a guitar and sings "Brother, Can You Spare a Dime?" There is still hope. Perhaps someone will drive out from the city to buy gas and apples from the basket in front.

As the sound moves from the porch radio to the right of the stage, a Will Rogers figure, spinning a lasso, wryly bemoans the lack of U.S. military preparedness — and, sure enough, FDR announces the attack on Pearl

Harbor. World War II is represented by two Rosie the Riveters working to repair a ship in a naval shipyard, hoping the guys will be home soon. One disappears up into the ceiling as the set descends.

The play now shifts in style, as the rest of the American Adventure is told in a filmed montage of thirty-five iconic people and events. Entitled "The Golden Dream," this is the *People Magazine* style of history — big pictures floating past a background of clouds and few words. Here, says Wallace, "history becomes popular culture." [42] Most of the words are found in the song sung during this part of the show. [43]

The people shown are an ecumenical collection, suggesting that almost any ethnic, racial (except Asian), or gender group (except gay males [44]) can produce a celebrity. [45] There are seven women, two children, five black people, one Mexican-American, six war-related scenes, five scenes about music, and five about sports. There are three pictures of the space program, three scientists (including an anthropologist), six actors and actresses (double-counting Frank Sinatra and Elvis), two presidents, and two presidents' wives. There are Walt Disney and Norman Rockwell.

Note especially that Disney had trouble with the Vietnam War period. Initially, this war was skipped completely. [46] When complaints about this omission were voiced, a single picture of a helicopter taking off in Vietnam was added. Wallace reports that a Disney designer told him, "I searched for a long time for a photograph of an antiwar demonstration that would be optimistic, but I never found one." [47]

In the coda, we return to audioanimatronics. Franklin and Twain stand in the crown of the Statue of Liberty as the sun rises behind them, echoing Franklin's famous words about the "birth of America" as a sunrise. With a warning-challenge from Steinbeck, the ever-optimistic Franklin robot foresees that "the American Adventure will continue."

There are a lot of silences in this Distory — as there are in the other historical Disney stories. At WDW history is meant to be packaged as entertainment, which is fully in keeping with the commodification of history in the U.S. cultural marketplace. What makes the American Adventure different from Disney's other historical dramas is that presentation of the warts draws attention to the historical amnesia elsewhere at WDW.

Visitors leave the theater with the notion that here, at least, Disney has not whitewashed the past as much as it usually does. After all, we have seen Frederick Douglass, Chief Joseph, and Susan B. Anthony. We have heard Dr. King say, "I have a dream." But, of course, we have really not seen everything. There aren't many working people in the American Adventure, and there is little about the institutional and class nature of contemporary conflict.

We are still — and ought to remain — beholden to the dreamers and doers who Disney tells us have been such a quintessential part of our national experience. *They* are the subjects of history. We ought to let them go ahead and do what they tell us at Future World would be good for us, especially now that they're confessing a little bit. Then the American Adventure will continue.

Our Walt Disney World adventure will also continue, but like Ben Franklin and Mark Twain, I must now take us back to the beginning.

6

Go East, Young Mouse

One of the things I've learned from Disneyland is to control the environment. Without that we get blamed for the things that someone else does. When they come here they're coming because of an integrity that we've established over the years, and they drive for hundreds of miles and the little hotels on the fringe jump their rates three times. I've seen it happen and I just can't take it because, I mean, it reflects on us.

—Walt Disney [1]

In ten years a quarter of the nation's population had made its way to Disneyland. . . . Of the riches that poured in, $273 million went to Disneyland, but another $555 million was spent outside its gates — just outside them.

—Richard Schickel [2]

By the early 1960s, Walt Disney Productions was in pretty good financial shape. Much of the corporate debt had been paid off. The transition from expensive animation to live feature films was almost complete.[3] The Eisenhower years of postwar consolidation were over.

Walt turned sixty on December 5, 1961. His vision had been vindicated. He had won most of the awards he was going to receive, from Oscars to honorary doctoral degrees. He was among the most famous people in the world and was lauded as a centerpiece of U.S. cultural production. By all accounts, he had become increasingly bored.

According to Joe Fowler, who would later be in charge of building Walt Disney World, inquiries about the prospects of building Disney theme parks had come from various parts of the country. [4] Developers in St. Louis, for instance, sought an indoor Disney park for a planned riverside project. E. Card Walker, later president of Walt Disney Productions, told Edward L. Prizer that Walt Disney and other corporate planners began to think seriously about such a project somewhere in the country in 1960-1961. [5]

As the search for a project site gained momentum, issues were clarified. Disneyland had been built near a large population center, with a captive audience from which repeat business could be generated. However many visitors might come from elsewhere, the local and regional populations could keep the place going. Such was indeed the case, but this left untapped populations in the rest of the country, especially east of the Mississippi River.

In the East and Midwest, however, most large concentrations of population were in cold enough climates that outdoor amusement activities had to be seasonal. The southern California weather allowed Disneyland to flourish year-round. Disney considered St. Louis, Niagara Falls, Baltimore, Washington, D.C., and other northern locales but soon turned its focus to the warmer Southeast.

Because of the distribution of population in the Southeast, however, a theme park site of any magnitude would have to rely on drawing visitors from elsewhere. It would have to be a destination site to which people would travel by automobile or public conveyance and around which visitors would organize an entire vacation. By 1964 the search had settled on Florida, a state in which tourism was already a major industry.

Initially interested in Ocala, Disney commissioned studies of existing and potential traffic flow throughout the state. The Florida coasts were eliminated, according to Joe Potter, because the beaches would provide too much natural competition for Disney activities. [6] Walt wanted to be in the middle of the state. As Card Walker said, "Walt's thesis is that we should be in the middle of the state where we could get two cracks at them, once when they were coming down and once when they were going back." [7]

The Orlando area was attractive for three reasons. First, it was near the intersections of a number of existing federal and state highway systems. I-4 passed through the area from Tampa Bay on Florida's Gulf Coast to Daytona Beach on the Atlantic. This highway — part of what would later be called "the golden girdle" by central Floridians and "the wall" by southeast Florida tourist interests — would connect Orlando with three other major highway systems.

At Daytona, I-4 intersects with I-95 (and U.S. 1), the main north-south artery on the East Coast. Vacation traffic from Richmond, Virginia, to Portland, Maine, and Montreal would have federal highway access all the way to Orlando. Just west of the city I-4, meets the Florida Turnpike, tapping into two more vehicular funnels. To the north, the Turnpike connects with road systems coming south from the Midwest and east from the

Louisiana-Texas Gulf Coast area. Eventually, I-75 would form the major artery for the former and I-10 for the latter. To the south, the Turnpike runs to Florida's Gold Coast — the populous and growing Palm Beach-Ft. Lauderdale-Miami megalopolis. Miami is also an international air travel gateway to Latin America, the Caribbean, and Europe.

The second reason the area was attractive was that Orlando was growing. Martin Marietta had opened a plant south of town in the mid-1950s, becoming central Florida's largest industrial employer. A new technological institute (later the University of Central Florida) had opened west of town, in large part to service the space age technological complex at Cape Kennedy. Orlando was clearly on the make.

As John Rothchild puts it, Florida had always been "up for grabs." [8] In a political climate in which the developer is king, Disney could certainly assume that his own kingdom would be welcomed with all the concessions open-armed local boosterism and the commerce-driven legislative process might afford.

Third, although Orlando itself was growing, the country around it was still pretty sleepy. Small towns, orange groves, pasturage for cattle, and a lot of swamp and scrub forest basically made up the rest of Orange and Osceola counties. A lot of the land was still relatively wild. Twenty miles southwest of downtown Orlando, large areas of land could be had, if the Company were clever, at very low cost.

The Mystery Industry

In the spring of 1964 began the cloak-and-dagger days of what the local newspapers called "the mystery industry." [9] The Disney strategy was to purchase land and land options straddling I-4 and the Orange-Osceola county line in the name of dummy corporations set up in Miami. Local real estate and banking agents were kept in the dark about the purchaser; they were told only that the land acquisitions would lead to one of the most important things ever to happen to central Florida.

The first large parcel — 8,380 acres of swamp and brush — was purchased from state senator Ira Bronson in October 1964, at a price of $107 an acre. [10] Disney's plan was to obtain options on the largest pieces of land and then to buy up smaller parcels, many of them held by owners elsewhere: "Many of these people had never seen the land they owned. Some tracts had been purchased from the old Mungar Land Co. back in 1911 and passed on to the heirs of the buyers. One man came out from the Midwest and hired a surveyor to locate the property in a Jeep. The terrain was so wild he could not get closer than half a mile." [11] Once the smaller parcels were picked up, options were called on the larger tracts. [12]

Disney people in California called the project Compass East, and all mail
to Florida and back was routed through a post office box in Kansas City.
Most of the transactions were handled in cash, thus eliminating part of a
potentially enormous paper trail. Obviously, secrecy was important to
Disney in order to keep land speculation from taking hold before the
acreage was under control. In achieving this, Disney got some assistance
from the major local paper, the *Orlando Sentinal Star*. Billy Dial, who was
practicing law at the time, said in an interview with *Orlando-Land* some
years later,

> The problem was that they had some pieces of property that they had not
> been able to secure — what we call "ins." They were inside the parameters of
> the general property. One was a piece of grove property. They said they
> couldn't afford any leaks as to who this was until they could get their ducks
> in a row.

> Well, I took them down and introduced them to Mr. (Martin) Andersen,
> who was then publisher of the paper, and he agreed to cooperate by not
> publishing any iffy stories, that type of thing. We knew the first time we
> recorded some deeds, the fat would be in the fire. Everybody would be
> looking and guessing who it was. [13]

The first newspaper account, coupled with a warning against "individual speculations," was not published until May 4, 1965, the day after
the Bronson sale (and one other) was recorded at the office of the Osceola
County clerk. [14] From May on the rumors about the "mystery industry"
grew. With Cape Kennedy nearby, many rumors centered around space and
aircraft technology. McDonnell Aircraft, North American, Republic Aviation, Douglas Aviation, and Lockheed were all mentioned, either singly or
in consortia. [15] Volkswagen, Chrysler, and Ford also surfaced as potential
neighbors. Disney's name popped up, but it was discarded in a May 20
Sentinel article.

> There has been one consistent rumor that the land is being purchased for
> a second East Coast Disneyland attraction, but little credence is given this in
> view of the fact that Walt Disney himself, in a recent statement to the Orlando
> Sentinel while on a visit to Cape Kennedy, said he was spending $50 million
> to expand his California attraction and had neither the time nor the talent to
> look for a second venture. In short, Mr. Disney said he already had his hands
> full. [16]

Just three days later, in an editorial that was strange indeed, the *Sentinel*
confessed to its agreement not to publicize the mystery land transactions
and, further, admitted that it had helped the buyers "pick up 35 acres they
wanted and needed." [17] On May 28, the *Evening Star* published a story that
detailed forty-seven transactions made by an Orlando brokerage firm
(Florida Ranch Lands, Inc.). These transactions covered 27,258 acres purchased for $5,018,770 — an average price of less than $200 an acre. [18]

As the summer wore on, rumors continued to build. By the middle of
June, the names Rockefeller and Howard Hughes had been added to the

list. The Manned Orbiting Laboratory Project surfaced in July. Disney's name rose and fell with regularity. Californians sneaked in and out of the swamps near what is now Lake Buena Vista,[19] but the secret was kept until October, when a local reporter — Emily Bavar — broke the story after an interview with Walt Disney in California.[20] On October 25, Governor Hayden Burns announced that Walt Disney Productions was coming to Florida.

On October 24, one day before the official announcement, the *Sentinel* published an editorial that characterized the beyond-open-arms relationship that would hold between Disney and the local forces of greed and development. "Walt Disney to Wave His Magic Wand over Us" showed that Disney's inflated rhetoric was eminently contagious. The beginning of this editorial gives the flavor of the early days of Orlando's Disneyfication.

> The Magic Wand of Walt Disney will soon wave over Orlando and Central Florida to create a fabulous entertainment mecca for millions in this prosperous land of citrus and electronics.
>
> The results will be fantastic.
>
> Orlando will become the greatest tourist city in the world. What area can hope to compete with the Moonport at Cape Kennedy backed up by the crowning creation of Walt Disney who will turn 30,000 acres into a land of fun and fantasy as much out of this world as the astronauts zooming among the stars of a distant galaxy.
>
> The magic of this modern Merlin will touch us all here in this promised land of prosperity. Every inch of land should be worth two or three times its value of yesterday; every business from the peanut stand to the department store will bloom, and professional and service people will move into a new era of activity.[21]

Well, you get the picture.

Three questions need to be answered. What exactly was Disney planning to do on these 27,400 acres? What legal empowerments did the Company need in Florida in order to do what it intended? What was the response of the local citizenry as the Disney plans unfolded? Many things were happening at once, but let me take them one at a time.

During the rest of 1965 and on through 1966, as Disney engaged in the political lobbying necessary to get its enabling proposals through the state legislature, communications about the Company's plans were vague. There was talk about an experimental community. There were various reports about the amount of money Disney would invest in its project. The creation of a theme park similar to the one at Disneyland had been announced, but the rest was pretty speculative.

On December 15, 1966, Walt Disney died of lung cancer. Confusion and doubt spread, both at Disney headquarters in Burbank and in central Florida. Although Walt's brother, Roy, had issued a public statement that Walt's plans would continue to move ahead, considerable skepticism remained. The creative genius, after all, was gone.

Walt's Plan

On February 2, 1967, less than two months after Walt's death, Walt
Disney Productions held a press conference in Winter Haven to which they
invited the governor, the state cabinet, state legislators, local mavens, and
the press. At this event Disney laid out its plans for Disney World. According to the Company's own news release,

> Basic elements of the proposed development include a new amusement
> park similar to the world-famous Disneyland in California; a series of theme
> motels surrounding and compatible to the theme park development; outdoor
> sports centers for golf, tennis, boating, camping, and other recreational ac-
> tivities which will take advantage of and preserve the natural beauty of the
> area; an Industrial Park covering about 1,000 acres, planned as a "showplace
> to the world of American industry"; a Jet Airport of the Future offering service
> to private and executive planes, commercial charters, and freight carriers; an
> Entrance Complex to receive and service the millions of visitors expected
> annually; and an Experimental Prototype Community of Tomorrow, planned
> for 20,000 permanent residents. [22]

The centerpiece of this presentation was the last film that Walt Disney
made, an eerie twenty-five-minute piece made shortly before his death in
which he outlined his vision for the Florida development. Among the most
important of his films, it deserves quotation at some length.

> Here in Florida . . . we have something special we never enjoyed at
> Disneyland — the blessing of size. There's enough land here to hold all the
> ideas and plans we can possibly imagine.
>
> Here in Florida, of course, there will be another amusement park similar
> in size and many other ways to the one in California. We're now developing
> a master plan that encompasses the theme park and all the facilities around
> it that will serve the tourist — hotels, motels, and a variety of recreation
> activities. In fact, this area alone will be five times the size of Disneyland in
> California. . . . But the most exciting and by far the most important part of our
> Florida project — in fact the heart of everything we'll be doing in Disney
> World — will be our Experimental Prototype Community of Tomorrow! We
> call it EPCOT.
>
> (This model city . . . will) take its cue from the new ideas and new
> technologies that are now emerging from the creative centers of American
> industry.
>
> It will be a community of tomorrow that will never be completed, but will
> always be introducing and testing and demonstrating new materials and
> systems. And EPCOT will always be a showcase to the world for the ingenuity
> and imagination of American free enterprise.
>
> (I don't believe there's a challenge anywhere in the world that's more
> important to people everywhere than finding solutions to the problems of our
> cities. But where do we begin?) Well, we're convinced that we must start with

the public need. And the need is not just for curing old ills of old cities, or even just building a whole new shiny city. We think the need is for starting from scratch on virgin land like this, and building a special kind of community.

So that's what EPCOT is — an experimental prototype community that will always be in a state of becoming. It will never cease to be a living blueprint of the future, where people actually live a life they can't find anywhere else.

Everything in EPCOT will be dedicated to the happiness of the people who live here and work here . . . and to those who come here from all around the world to visit our living showcase.

A project like this is so vast in scope it will take the cooperation of many people to make it a reality! You people here in Florida have one of the key roles to play in making EPCOT come to life. In fact, it's really up to you whether this project gets off the ground at all . . . .

We must have the flexibility in Disney World to keep pace with tomorrow's world. We must have the freedom to work in cooperation with American industry, and to make decisions based on standards of performance.

If we have this kind of freedom, I'm confident we can create a world showcase for American free enterprise that will bring new industry to the state of Florida from all over the country.

I believe we can build a community here that more people will talk about and come to look at than any other area in this world.

I'm sure this Experimental Prototype Community of Tomorrow can influence the future of city living for generations to come. [23]

Where did this vision come from? And what happened to it as Walt Disney turned into Corporate Disney after his death?

According to Leonard Mosley, Disney was obsessed with his plans for EPCOT during his last year of life. [24] EPCOT would be the culmination of a life that led from illustrator to animator to moviemaker to global fame as the voice of childhood and filmmaker laureate of the United States. As educator, sage, and prophet, he would now take the next classical step in male public life by becoming a social planner and futurist philosopher.

The cities were the problem. The utopian plan was not to fix them but to start over. Buoyed by the positive critical response to Disneyland of such people as architecture critic Peter Blake and "new city" urban designer James Rouse, Disney envisioned an enormously risky project — a technological utopia set down in the swamps of Florida. [25] I look further at the idea of a technological utopia in Chapter 11, but here let us take a provisional look at Walt Disney's approach to utopia.

Michael Harrington has suggested that EPCOT links two contradictory aspects of Disney's heritage. [26] Harrington reminds us that Disney was the son of a turn-of-the-century socialist. In his Marceline, Missouri, days, Elias Disney "tried to organize the local farmers into an American Society of Equity that would focus their hatreds of the middlemen and the railroads.

He voted for Debs and he read the *Appeal to Reason*, the famous radical paper published in Kansas and reaching a mass audience of the Left." [27]

The U.S. socialist tradition, Harrington points out, contains sentiments about the underdog and about social justice;[28] but it also contains another strain — the "warmhearted, futuristic authoritarianism" found in Edward Bellamy's *Looking Backward*. In a book much read by radicals of Elias Disney's generation, Bellamy presented "a neat, rational, crisis-free society with distributional justice — and without any visible democratic noise, conflict, or argument." [29]

Disney's description of the future Experimental Prototype Community of Tomorrow seems to bring this Bellamy strand of social planning together with Disney's obvious faith in "free enterprise" and the "wisdom" of U.S. corporations. As Disney further describes EPCOT,[30]

> It will be a planned, controlled community, a showcase for American industry and research, schools, cultural and educational opportunities. In EPCOT there will be no slum areas because we won't let them develop. There will be no landowners and therefore no voting control. People will rent houses instead of buying them, and at modest rentals. There will be no retirees. Everyone must be employed. One of our requirements is that people who live in EPCOT must keep it alive. [31]

Disney's last year was difficult. Although the cancer diagnosis was not made until early fall, he was in a lot of pain through much of 1966. Closeted in a secret room at the Burbank studio, Walt worked out the details for his city of tomorrow. He had always been interested in science and technology and now became fixated on medical technology. Leonard Mosley reports that Disney asked Joe Potter and Marvin Davis "to get out a report on the newest medical discoveries in repairing failing human bodies and the prolonging of life." [32] At this time Walt learned about experiments in cryogenesis — the freeze-drying of human bodies, which would be resuscitated sometime in the future when medical science supposedly will have found a way to fix whatever the body died from. [33]

After his diagnosis, he worried not only about himself but about the future of the entire Disney organization, especially the plans for EPCOT. He constantly pushed his people about the EPCOT development. He wanted EPCOT to go on as he had dreamed it but was driven by the thought that no one *could* continue the project correctly. Presciently, he suspected that no one *would* carry it out, that his brother Roy — "good, reliable, dull, unimaginative, and above all, a moneyman" [34] — would be interested only in profit, not in dreams. His major worry about cryogenesis was that "to be brutally frank, could it be guaranteed, in fact, that he could be *brought back in time* to rectify the mistakes his successors would almost certainly start making at EPCOT the moment he was dead." [35]

After Walt's death his plans were, in fact, scrapped. EPCOT was changed from a quasiutopian city to a kind of world's fair — a combination of industrial exhibits and foreign national pavilions. The post-Walt Disney EPCOT became a theme park rather than a social experiment. The Vacation Kingdom carried Walt's name, but it might more appropriately be called Roy Disney World.

Walt's twisted spirit still hangs over the corporation. People still ask, "What would Walt say?" as part of the rhetoric of their own present corporate maneuvering. They sometimes speak of him in the present tense, as if he had just stepped out for a while. In a bizarre turn, one that underscores the anxiety and paranoia of his last days, Walt made a series of films to be shown after his death. I will let Jack Martin, Orange County commissioner in 1970, describe them.

> When Dick [Nunis] was younger Walt used to hold monthly conferences with his executive officers. They'd all sit around the table and Walt would say, "Now, next year we want to be sure this gets done." Or "Last year we said such and such would get done; Joe [Potter] or Dick [Nunis], how's your schedule on that?"

> Well, apparently he realized his plans and dreams would outlive him so he called in a camera crew and set up some empty chairs. What he did was to hold conferences right through the 1980s. I think it's once a month these fellows sit down and view the film. And there's Walt Disney saying, "Bob, this is October, 1976. You remember we were going to do this or that. Are you sure it's underway now?" I think that demonstrates his remarkable attention to detail. [36]

The Birth of Reedy Creek

The second major question about the early days of WDW is "What did Disney want from the state?" The first dose of reality for citizens of the greater Orlando area came only eight days after Governor Burns's announcement of Disney's arrival in Florida. On November 2, 1965, Florida voters turned down a $300 million state road bond issue. [37] Although Disney needs had little to do with the voters' decision, it became clear from the Company's surprised response that a number of public costs would be associated with Disney's development. In particular, battles over the funding of public highways — access roads for construction, for employees, and later for tourists and other visitors — would be an enduring theme in the relations between Disney and central Florida.

From the fall of 1965 until the next biennial meeting of the Florida state legislature in 1967, Disney lobbied for a political package unique to the state. The Company requested an independent governing district free from interference from local county agencies. [38] The clearest statement of what Disney requested is found in an *Orlando-Land* article.

> Three proposed acts totalling 481 pages were presented to legislators. They would define the authority of the Reedy Creek Improvement District, a

quasi-governmental entity with far-ranging powers to regulate water management, fire protection, wild-life, roads and bridges, zoning and building codes within the Disney property. It would have power to tax and issue bonds, and would be run by its own governing body.

The legislation would set up two municipalities, Bay Lake on the north and Reedy Creek [now Lake Buena Vista] on the east, with their own city charters. [39]

In addition, "Disney insisted on provisions for state regulation of trademarks [to protect its many characters and insignia] and detailed licensing procedures." [40]

Publicly, Disney people masked their passion for complete control over their political and economic environments with arguments based on the size and nature of the project. First, development and construction of the project would take place in many areas simultaneously and would enter the bailiwicks of a number of different county and state agencies. Disney argued that its integrated plan would be unworkable if it continually had to seek permits from different administrative authorities. Especially important was control over water, which Disney planned to affect significantly with its drainage canals. In general, Florida's ecology is such that the drainage district is the most significant geographical administrative unit. Thus, legislative designation as a drainage (later improvement) district was crucial to Disney designs.

Second, the Company wanted control over zoning and building codes. Whatever else it might be, WDW was a land development project. Its shape would be fundamentally dependent on its powers to zone at will. Furthermore, because a central part of the plan involved the use of technology —) much of it experimental —) Disney wanted the freedom to try new materials and new techniques without having to go through cumbersome county certification processes. Disney has always claimed, with justification, that its building codes are significantly stronger than state and local codes.

Control over local taxation and governance obviously mean what they say — control. Disney's carrots were the jobs, money, and tourists it would bring to the greater Orlando area as well as the promise to fund its own internal roads, bridges, sewage systems, and fire protection services. Disney also planned to put in place significant wildlife protection policies. The stick, of course, was the threat that the Company would go elsewhere. A Disney spokesman was quoted early in this process of negotiation: "We are not asking for a blank check. But many of our problems get down to a county level. When we put on a show here . . . both counties [Orange and Osceola] will see the revenues we will bring in. But it is darned important to us that no one adopt the attitude, 'We've got the Golden Goose, let's wring its neck.'" [41]

The initial local response to Disney's November 1965, announcement about its planned development — at least the response that made it into the local newspapers — was overwhelmingly positive. The language of this response was that of sheer economic boosterism. Orlando *Sentinel* headlines the next day read:

"Disney Tells of 100 Million Dollar Project"

"Walt Disney to Build World's Best Tourist Attraction in Mid-Florida"

"Disney Boom Impact Likened to Space Age" [42]

Yet even at the beginning, in a refrain that has continued to the present, Orange and Osceola county officials felt slighted by the Company. They felt considerably more put upon when Disney revealed its plan to bypass the counties entirely as administrative districts by appealing directly to the state legislature for designation as an autonomous political unit.

The maneuvering over the proposed new municipal corporation went relatively slowly from the Disney point of view, as it did for those waiting in the land speculation wings. Like "boomers" at the Oklahoma border, most were waiting for a final decision as to whether or not Disney would stay in Florida because Disney's most powerful bargaining chip was the threat to go elsewhere.

There were three main partisans in the legislative battle: Disney, the economic growth boosters, and those who were politically worried. Disney's argument was, first, that it needed administrative freedom to do what it wanted and to keep on doing it. Along with Walt Disney's February 2, 1967, postmortem filmed announcement of the plan for EPCOT, Donn B. Tatum (then vice-president and administrative assistant to the president of Walt Disney Productions) said in an official news release:

> This (proposed) act is, in essence, a composite of special assessment, improving and taxing districts already provided for under existing Florida laws, each of which provides for a separate and independent district under separate governing bodies. The proposed Act will have the effect of combining services these districts perform within a single District under a single governing body. . . .
>
> The Act clarifies the District's authority to perform work of drainage, flood and pest control; amplifies the District's authority to build and maintain roadways, utility and sewer systems, to provide and administer a public transportation system, police and fire protection, airport and parking facilities, and to regulate and administer land use and planning within the District limits. . . .
>
> By far the most voluminous section of the Act deals with the District's authority to issue bonds to finance improvements necessary to perform the services this District will be authorized to perform. . . .
>
> In serving the needs of those residing here, our Experimental Prototype Community of Tomorrow must utilize the technological advances of American industry as they continually develop. . . . To take advantage of these

technological breakthroughs, the operating agency must have flexibility — the flexibility to assume that EPCOT will always be a showcase of the future. [43]

Second, Disney would clearly bring a great deal of money into the area if it were allowed to do what it wanted. The growth boomers licked their collective chops. As the bargaining process moved along, local papers were filled with large numbers of speculative dollars, and the local population and state legislators were publicly lobbied.

The tone was set by Governor Claude R. Kirk, Jr., at the February 2, 1965, announcement of Disney's plans. Summarizing an independent — but quick — study of the project, Kirk claimed that

> During its initial construction and first ten years of operation, Disney World will directly generate $6.6 billion in measurable economic benefits for the State of Florida as a whole. . . . Of this $6.6 billion estimate, $3.978 billion will result from expenditures by new tourists attracted to the State by Disney World. Another $2.261 billion of this total represents payrolls for new jobs created, and approximately $414 million represents monies to be spent for construction materials and equipment. [44]

In fact, all of the future calculations — whether of monies to be generated by Disney and the speculative projects it triggered or the number of tourists, visitors, and newcomers moving into the area — were underestimated. Local people had little idea of the size of the tiger whose tail they were about to grab.

Disney's third selling point was the promise that it would finance all the costs of its internal infrastructure. At the announcement meeting, Donn Tatum said, "The landowners will be relying on their own financial resources to provide the services frequently imposed upon existing governmental agencies in other newly developed areas." [45] News release no. 3, however, underlined the fact, for those who were paying attention, that this promise pertained to development *within* Disney boundaries. This release noted that Disney officials had requested that the state construct two interchanges — one involving I-4 — and add highway lanes to I-4 and State Road 530 (later U.S. 192). This and other future road building would add significantly to the state and county costs of hosting Disney.

Nonetheless, Disney boosters filled the newspapers with numbers, scenarios, and other arguments. They worked to generate support for pushing the legislative process along. Even other local amusement park owners got on the bandwagon, reasoning that a Disney park would bring more visitors to the area who would spill over into their parks.

There were two kinds of worriers — those who said central Floridians didn't know what they were getting into, and those who warned that the unprecedented governmental powers Disney was requesting would someday constrain the authority of Orange and Osceola counties. [46] A sample of the first type was made public only three days after the big announcement in an editorial by Martin Andersen in the *Sentinel*.

> The Man in the Engine Toots, Toots, Toots:
> What Say We Back in the Caboose?

> What impact rides the caboose of Disney's spectacular world for Central Florida?

> Everybody has told us what Disney plans to do for us. Nobody has said anything about what we plan to do for ourselves after Disney gets here. . . .

> This business about the billions [in] money for new jobs, homes, taxes, retail sales and so forth and so on is so astounding that it will take two years for many of us to comprehend the impact of Disney's arrival. . . .

> Some of our elected leaders and many ordinary citizens should be doing some cogitating. . . .

> You cannot dump 50,000 tourists a day into this community along with 50,000 new jobs and build 40,000 new homes without putting somebody out of joint. . . .

> Disney has taught us that, knowing the facts of life as to what is to come, we should plan for the great confrontation . . . . If we are forewarned of what is to come, we will prepare for this startling growth. This is our responsibility today as citizens. We must think no little thoughts . . . and we must make no little plans. [47]

As we shall see, speculative planning was considerably more energetic than social and political planning.

Don Rider voiced the second worry in a March 16, 1967, *Sentinel* article, "Disney World Being Built on Political Foundation."

> The question arises — at least it did among legislators at last Saturday's local hearing — if Disney World could be a 42-square-mile globe excised from the tax rolls of Orange and Osceola Counties, with all sorts of immunities from state and county regulations. . . .

> The District of Reedy Creek is unlike any other political entity in Florida, and yet Disney's lawyers can say it would have no powers that cannot be found in other special districts in Florida. . . .

> "We'll take their city charter — either one of them," Orlando City Attorney John A. Baker said with unconcealed envy. [48]

In May 1967, Disney's bills passed through the Florida house and senate with only one dissenting vote, and a signing ceremony was set for May 12. [49] An hour after the signing, the state road board met and voted to divert about $5 million of its funds over the next five years to build highways near Disney World. Disney's political heft was already being felt. "Disneylaw" [50] had come to central Florida.

The Reedy Creek Improvement District — which crosses county borders — is governed by a board of supervisors made up of people outside of but friendly to the Company. The two municipalities of Bay Lake and Lake Buena Vista are officially governed by those elected by the few permanent residents who live in trailers in each of the communities, almost all of whom are Disney employees. Administrative crossovers between Reedy Creek and the two towns make them all function as one unit under the eagis of WALT DISNEY WORLD CO., the division that runs the entire project. Thus

Disney's Vacation Kingdom straddles two towns and a drainage district whose charters, in fact, make it more of an actual kingdom than any other administrative district in the state of Florida.

Early Plans

By the end of 1967, Disney's stock prices had tripled, work had begun on remaking the great swamp, and the land speculation boom was on. Even before the signing of the Disney legislation — even before Walt Disney's death — work had begun on water management on the property. A former Army Corps of Engineers honcho, Major General William E. (Joe) Potter, was in charge. Disney had met Joe Potter, who was also a former governor of the Panama Canal Zone, at the New York World's Fair, where Potter had been an assistant to Robert Moses. After Disney's scathing reaction to his first arrow-straight canal, Potter designed the rest of the WDW canals to meander across the property like rivers. [51]

Disney also brought Admiral Joe Fowler, who had run the construction of Disneyland, out of retirement as a senior vice-president of engineering and construction for "the world's biggest private construction project." [52] Although much of this part of our story — the building of the infrastructure at WDW — is discussed in Chapter 10, three important elements will be mentioned here: financing, the master labor contract, and the plan and schedule.

In early 1968, Disney easily sold out two convertible bond issues that totaled $90 million to finance the major construction at WDW. [53] The Company also arranged a $50 million revolving line of credit with the Bank of America and a group of Florida banks. The bond issues were retired in 1970 as Disney stock continued to climb. Because Disney spent $230 million of its own money on the project, by early 1971 — with WDW 85 percent complete — the project was almost debt-free. [54]

By mid-1971, commercial companies were still lining up to become part of WDW. As an "advertising associate," a chosen company could pay an annual fee for the use of the Disney name and characters. For another $40,000 or so a year plus $35,000 in construction costs, a company could lease space in a shared building to sell or promote its product. For $100,000 plus $250,000 in construction costs, it could have its own building.

> To some two dozen major corporations ranging in size from jelly maker J. M. Smucker Co. to U.S. Steel Corp., the operation is "Promotionland." Each is putting up a sizable amount of money to sell its product to the throngs of visitors and to use the Disney name and trademarked characters in advertising. . . . Most of the companies that have begged Disney to let them participate realize that they have as much chance of making a profit on their investment as Captain Hook has of defeating Peter Pan. [55]

For the chance of symbolically linking the company brand name to Disney's in front of the expected millions of visitors — and at about the cost of sponsoring a two-hour special on television, however — many corporations were willing to chalk up the costs of operation to the advertising budget.

In February 1969 — through its main contractor, Allen Contracting — Disney negotiated a master labor agreement with eighteen building trade unions, which ensured labor peace until the opening of the Magic Kingdom. With a no-strike, no-lockout clause, this agreement provided for expedited grievance procedures and binding arbitration. Although pay scales were lower than elsewhere in Florida, Disney's agreement to use mostly union workers was important to labor in the state. Ned Brown, manager of the Central Florida Chapter of Associated General Contractors, said, "This area has lagged for many years. Until Disney came along, this area was largely unorganized as far as unions are concerned." [56]

Once the drainage system was under control, the massive job of building the Magic Kingdom began in earnest. The opening had been announced for October 1971. By the end of 1969, construction was going on throughout what would be the Magic Kingdom and the first two hotels. Coordination of this work was critical. Prizer gives us the flavor of this activity. Describing a visit to the "staff shop" one year before opening day, he writes:

> Fluorescent lights glare on hundreds of craftsmen hard at work in rooms the size of football fields. The air reverberates with the screech of saws and rattle of hammers. There is a strong odor of paint and chemicals and sawdust. Seven bare and twisted trees (designed for the Haunted Mansion) stretch their branches toward us. Sections of a Victorian cornice for the Emporium lie on the floor. These fiberglass stalks of bamboo — looking altogether real — will go into the Polynesian Hotel. I stop to admire an exquisite clock. It will go into the railroad station tower, I'm told.
>
> All around me I am seeing the making of the pieces which will fit together to create the Magic Kingdom. Hundreds of thousands of individual pieces. Perhaps millions. Created out of wood and rock and plastic and fiberglass and metal. Meticulously designed and crafted.
>
> You wonder how they will ever find their way to their proper place in the vast complex that is taking shape outside. . . .
>
> [Bud Washo, staff shop supervisor] reaches in a cabinet and pulls out a yard-wide roll of paper. He spreads it on a drafting board. With unconcealed pride, he exclaims, "This is the master timetable. It includes every step in the theme park schedule for two years." . . .
>
> Here is every minute detail in order of execution, thought out and planned by those anonymous WED [57] "Imagineers" 3,000 miles across the continent, many of whom had never even seen Florida.
>
> Along one wall of the office is a file of project blueprints sent east from California. One set for the Cinderella Castle, one for the Railroad station and so on. For some projects, exquisite scale models have been put together by WED.

"As soon as we get the authorization, we set up a job board for a project and go to work," Bud says. "We have a complete material takeoff. We decide what will work best. We're always researching new materials. We've never been given anything we couldn't make. This department ends up with the most miscellaneous group of things you can imagine. We're making ancient stone for the Cinderella Castle, coral rock and shipwrecks for the submarine ride, animal hides, boat canopies. . . . Oh well, you name it."

What it amounts to is, first, building solid steel and concrete structures (strong enough to resist hurricanes) and then applying exterior and interior "costumes" that turn the basic building into a town hall or a Colonial tavern or a South Seas ceremonial house or an ancient Asian ruins. Then installing the marvelous Audio-Animatronic figures from California (for the shows). Then planting masses of trees and shrubs and flowers appropriate to the theme of each area.

Add locomotives from the Yucatan, monorails from Orlando's Martin Marietta plant, boats from Tampa Bay, a skyride from Switzerland, a carousel from Detroit and this and that from everywhere.

Sprinkle liberally with Disney men and women in costumes to match the "costumes" on the building.

And you have Walt Disney World! [58]

And Orlando?

Meanwhile, "sleepy Orlando" [59] was waking up. Having grown steadily but slowly during the 1950s and 1960s, Orlando and its surrounding counties now entered into a scramble for which they were not well prepared. Disney predicted that its first year attendance would be 10 million visitors. Although these numbers promised an economic bonanza to the area, they also promised to overload roads and hotel facilities.

Boosters pointed to such civic assets as the new airport on the southern city limits, the new university, and the Naval Training Station. The area's largest employer, Martin Marietta, had cut back severely in the wake of the aerospace crunch that had affected the money flow from Cape Kennedy, but this would be nearly offset by the number of new construction jobs Disney World would bring. Looking beyond the immediate present, some could see the potential for developing a region of high-tech industry drawn to central Florida by promises of low labor costs and lifestyle considerations. Disney would be the catalyst.

Land within five miles of the Disney property was bought and sold. Prices skyrocketed. Realizing that most visitors to WDW would come by automobile, oil companies jumped into the search for suitable properties. Marathon Oil Co. paid $155,000 for a one-acre lot for a filling station near the main entrance to the Disney property.

Hotel and housing developments sprung up everywhere. Insurance and banking institutions built office buildings in downtown Orlando. From all accounts, it was pretty chaotic. Many worried that WDW was too far away from population centers to draw the same number of visitors as its park in California. In response Disney pointed to the 500,000 visitors — far more than expected — who had come to its preview center during 1970 and to the 175 conventions that had been booked into its hotels a year before the park opened. [60]

Disney was clearly in for the long run. Although many local people focused on the park for its own sake, wondering if the number of projected visitors would support the economic madness overtaking them, Roy Disney put the park in perspective. In an interview with the *New York Times* in late 1970, Disney said, "The big difference between this and Disneyland in California is that this is a real estate venture for us. . . . The amusement park is just a catalyst that will draw other investments here." [61]

As land values around the park soared, property owners began to complain, especially in Osceola County. In the fall of 1970, the first break came in the relations between Disney and local politicians when the Osceola County Tax Adjustment Board increased the assessed value on 10,500 acres of Disney land, doubling the tax assessment. [62]

By 1971 a number of local people were taking a second look at Disney. Although those who provided tourist services would benefit from the park, and although Disney would continue to generate new jobs, the average citizen of Osceola, Orange, and Seminole counties would be faced with costlier homes, higher prices, crowded schools and roads, and eventually higher taxes to pay for the services required by a rapidly growing population. [63]

Further, Disney was not going to provide a lot of direct help. One situation in particular gives a flavor of Disney's attitude toward Orange County in the early days. The *Sentinel Star* called it "the saga of State Road 535." [64] Paul Pickett, Orange County commissioner at the time, tells the story.

> An 18-foot-wide, twisting road designed to carry citrus fruit from grove to market, what was then a country road was designated by Disney as the access route for its thousands of employees.
>
> "I told them that was ridiculous," Pickett said. "They said, 'That was your problem' . . . and when were we going to widen it?"
>
> Disney devised an unusual public relations campaign to make its point about the road: Employees composed a jingle called "Can You Arrive Alive on 535?" [65] and urged disc jockeys to play it. They cranked out bumper stickers that read "Arrive Alive on 535?" (and erected a billboard reading "Congratulations, You Arrived Alive on 535" [66]). The campaign bombed. But the road was taken over by the state. [67]

Matt Walsh reports, "The stalemate broke one weekend after two tractor-trailer rigs got stuck in the mud on the service road. Disney officials went to Pickett's office on a Monday morning and asked him how much it would cost to pave the road. He told them $40,000, and that afternoon Disney officials returned with a $40,000 check." [68]

On NBC's "Monitor," on August 13, 1983, Pickett responded to a Lloyd Dobbins question about the saga.

> They [Disney] took the position that anything within the boundaries of their property was their responsibility and starting about three inches outside the boundaries of their property was the county's responsibility. So, when they decided to use little county roads as entrance roads for their eleven or twelve thousand employees and we told them that there was no way those little roads could handle their employees, I was assured that that was outside their property and that was my problem; if the roads wouldn't handle the traffic then go build some better roads. [69]

Elsewhere Pickett claimed that Disney cost the county $8.25 million in 1971 alone in start-up expenses, [70] and $12-14 million in all [71] before the park opened in October 1971: "That much expense was added in services of all kinds. The only place we could get $8.25 million was to pull it off scheduled projects. We moved 'em back a few years. Some still haven't gotten done. It was grossly unfair to taxpayers in Orange County." [72]

Some of the county's new problems, especially in Orlando itself, stemmed from the flood of transient families drawn to the city to look for work. Relief agencies, police departments, the court system, and other municipal agencies requested additional budgetary relief. Disney was hiring — "auditioning," in company parlance — for all the jobs that needed to be filled once the park opened; but with the large number of applicants — 30,000 to 40,000 inquiries by the end of March 1970 [73] — Disney could afford to be very selective. Once hired, the good-looking, short-haired boys and unmadeup girls were "Disneyfied" at Disney World University, "where rose-colored glasses are part of the curriculum." [74]

By all accounts, the last few months before the October 1, 1971, opening were pure madness. All the projects on the master schedule were coming to completion. Right to the end, landscaping was being done, some jury-rigged at the last moment. The opening was covered as a major world news story by *Look, Life, Time, Newsweek, Paris Match, Epoca, Esquire, Forbes,* and *Business Week.* At the end of October, WDW was introduced in a ninety-minute NBC television special.

The opening day crowd was smaller than expected; in fact attendance was relatively low throughout October and most of November. Some of the naysayers felt vindicated in their belief that the goose might not lay a golden egg after all. Although they were nervous, Disney officials felt some relief. The Magic Kingdom was open, and its shakedown problems could be handled without the difficulties of capacity attendance. After Thanksgiving, however, the crowds hit 251,000 in one four-day period. The Disney machine was up and running. Central Florida was, in fact, going to become Fantasyland.

7

Let's Make a Deal

By the conventional wisdom, mighty mice, flying elephants, Snow White and Happy, Grumpy, Sneezy and Dopey — all these were fantasy, escapism from reality. It's a question of whether they are any less real, any more fantastic than the intercontinental missiles, poisoned air . . . and scraps from the moon. This is the age of fantasy, however you look at it, but Disney's fantasy wasn't lethal. People are saying we'll never see his like again.

—Eric Severeid [1]

They want to take you by the jeans, turn you upside down and shake till all your spare change comes loose.

—Rod Caborn [2]

In autumn of 1971, as the great mousetrap sprung open in central Florida, many Americans were looking for a Lancelot. "Sleepy" Orlando awoke to a country deeply divided. The preceding five years had seen a wing of the civil rights movement match the militance of white America with a turn to black power. The keynote events in this period of U.S. racism were the urban riots of 1965-1967, the assassination of Martin Luther King in 1968, the Attica massacre of 1970, and George Wallace's surprisingly successful run for the presidency in 1968. Like King, Robert Kennedy was also murdered, bringing to three the assassination total of major U.S. figures in the mid-1960s.

The counterculture, with its anarchic attack on white Protestant American values and institutions, was scaring the bejeezus out of mainstream Americans. With its music, its clothes (and lack of same), its hair, its pseudo-Eastern religious touches, and most of all its marijuana and LSD, this movement attacked U.S. institutions — both church and state — as being philistine and irrelevant. A central tactic was guerrilla theater, such as the Yippie dumping of dollar bills from the balcony of the New York Stock Exchange. The Woodstock generation reached its apogee as Disney was digging in its swamp.

The women's movement had risen, putting into serious question the micropolitics of the family, sex discrimination in the workplace, and especially the locus of control over biological reproduction. *Roe vs. Wade* was only a few years off.

The student movement, Students for a Democratic Society (SDS), and the New Left had sprung up to attack the U.S. form of capitalism and state power just as similar movements had arisen in western and central Europe. By the end of the 1960s, violence and anger had escalated. The state had unmasked its violence at the 1968 Democratic National Convention in Chicago, and SDS had splintered into a number of offshoots, among them the Weathermen.[3]

All of these developments were bracketed by the central crisis of the time — the war in Vietnam. Here was the terrible violence of the American empire — an undeclared war fought primarily by the "underprivileged" of the United States against the soldiers and civilians of an Asian land in the name of morally corrupt regimes both here and there and shown to us every night on television. The United States split in two — its cities, towns, communities, and families. A president was driven from office. Students were killed at Kent State and Jackson State universities. It was as though an entire generation at once — both those who escaped going to war and those who went only to discover that their military superiors were duplicitous and crazy — discovered that their elders had lied.

On the other side were those who believed deeply that protesters of all sorts were treasonous and were enemies of the American way. "Make love, not war" slogans were opposed by "America, love it or leave it." In the middle were millions of confused people, threatened by those who opposed the government but increasingly wondering as the body bags returned home if there were not something fundamentally wrong going on.

Eight months before the break-in at the Watergate, the Magic Kingdom opened its gates. This was fantasy, not politics, in a park full of kids with short hair who were trained to treat customers as guests.

The First Years

Opening in October, the worst Florida tourist month, the Magic Kingdom got off to a slow start. Much of it, in fact, was not ready. Little of Tomorrowland was open. The initial shakedown cruise lasted until Thanksgiving, when attendance began to soar. Disney had severely underestimated the need for food facilities, transportation from the parking lot to park gates, and camping spaces at Fort Wilderness, and each of these problems received immediate attention.[4] By the end of the first fiscal year, Disney counted 10,712,991 admissions, exceeding its projections, and recorded $139 million in gross revenues.[5]

Reviews of the park were overwhelmingly favorable in both mass and special interest media. The response of urban planners, architects, and engineers was particularly important. These people found the combination of high technology in the park infrastructure — the computerized control network, monorail, trash disposal setup, and use of underground corridors to shunt sewer, water, and electric lines as well as people and materials — and the symbolic architecture (designed to present the *idea* of a structure rather than the structure itself) to be worth serious study.

The impact of the park's first year on Walt Disney Productions may best be seen in the following figures. 1971 Company revenues rose 87 percent by the end of fiscal 1972 ($175,611,000 to $328,830,000), net income per stock share grew 51 percent ($2.03 to $2.90), and stockholders' equity rose 44 percent ($318,464,000 to $460,619,000). As stockholders' shares outstanding grew by only 8 percent (13,176,580 to 14,273,805), these gains clearly were not diluted. Although working capital was down 43 percent, the significantly larger long-term liabilities were almost halved. Not all of these differences can be attributed to WDW but the success of WDW's first year was helping Walt Disney Productions pay its own way.[6]

What about Orlando and the rest of Florida? Three recurring themes reemerged during WDW's first year of business. First, development continued to burgeon outside Disney boundaries. Tourist-oriented facilities such as hotels, motels, and shopping centers were under construction everywhere. Land prices skyrocketed. Pieces of land that had sold for $100,000 a few years earlier now traded hands for $300,000.[7] By early 1972 around twenty thousand new hotel and motel units were under construction,[8] resulting in six thousand construction jobs. Banks were getting richer financing this construction.

Second, central Florida had to take the bad with the good. The Salvation Army's transient lodge and other local facilities were swamped by itinerant workers, some with families, who flooded into the area looking for jobs.[9] Existing roads were overloaded. Residential housing was severely inadequate, especially for construction workers and for the relatively low-paid employees of Disney's park. Housing needs began to spread into Seminole County towns, putting pressure on their existing infrastructures.

Land speculation fueled a rise in property taxes. Not only were retirees on fixed incomes squeezed, but so were the area's farmers and ranchers. Many owners were forced to sell out due to rising tax assessments on citrus and cattle lands. According to a 1972 report of the Florida Department of Agriculture and Consumer Services, "In the peak year of 1967, Orange County showed 68,005 acres in citrus trees. At the last survey, that figure had declined to 60,551 acres — and it is still dropping. Seminole County in the same period had declined from 13,418 citrus acres to 10,952 acres and Osceola County had plunged from 19,363 acres to 17,589." [10] Paul Pickett, chairman of the Orlando County Commission and spokesperson for the rural parts of the county, opined, "Disney World would be great if it were in Miami." [11]

South Floridians probably would have agreed with Pickett because, third, the impact of Disney on tourism to the rest of the state was beginning to be felt. As Marjorie Green reported,

> Recently released statistics by the State Department of Commerce revealed that 10.8 percent of the visitors arriving in Florida by automobile during October were heading to the Orlando area. The previous October it had only drawn 3.7 percent.
>
> In the same period, Dade County and its Miami Beach resort area dropped sharply from 10 to 7.7 percent. Tourist figures also dipped somewhat for St. Petersburg when 12.4 headed into the area as opposed to 13.6 the previous year. [12]

Thus were felt the beginnings of what would later be called "the great wall" and "the golden girdle."

By the middle of its first year, WDW had moved to the top of the list of U.S. travel destinations of interest to international travelers, according to the U.S. Department of Commerce. [13] The impact of all this activity on Orlando is best summarized in Table 7.1 — the city's economic indicators chart.

TABLE 7.1 Orlando Economic Indicators (1971-1972)[a]

1. Sales activity	1971—$105,278,345 1972—$147,744,407	up 40%
2. Employed (nonfarm)	1971—151,800 1972—170,000	up 12%
3. Building permits	1971—$17.28 million 1972—$39.92 million	up 131%
4. Telephones in service	1971—263,316 1972—302,056	up 15%
5. Auto sales	1971—2,367 1972—3,305	up 40%
6. Airline boardings (McCoy)	1971—51,889 1972—113,717	up 119%
7. Air freight (outgoing)	1971—887,286 1972—1,214,335	up 37%
8. Real estate sales	1971—$44.57 million 1972—$39.84 million	down 11%[b]
9. Gasoline sales (gals.)	1971—21.12 million 1972—23.58 million	*up 12%*
10. Daily I-4 traffic (at Gore exit)	1971—61,480 1972—82,460	up 34%

[a]Disney's reporting year runs from October 1 through September 30.

[b]"Real estate sales were down 11 percent . . . mainly because of 'last-hour' speculations last year before the October 1 opening of Walt Disney World." Leonard

E. Zehnder, *Florida's Disney World: Promises and Problems* (Tallahassee: The Peninsular Publishing Company, 1975), p. 266.

Sources: Adapted from Dick Marlowe, "Area Indicators Chart Upward Economic Course," *Orlando Sentinel*, September 3, 1972. Also cited in Zehnder, *Florida's Disney World*, pp. 267-268.

Somebody was making a buck.

These three themes continued during the 1972-1973 reporting year. Growing pains spread outward as Orlando became the fastest-growing metropolitan area in the country.[14] By September 9, 1973, the area had jumped to eighth on the list of the world's top twenty cities in hotel room count, sandwiched between Las Vegas and Honolulu.[15] This glut of hotel rooms resulted in severe overbuilding. In May 1973, the area's occupancy rate fell to 50 percent, and a number of projects went under.[16]

Orlando suburbs were beset with problems of growth. Quiet Altamonte Springs tripled in size from 4,391 residents in 1968 to 13,000-plus in 1973.[17] Bills for service — schools, sewage, and water systems — grew as inadequate systems began to be upgraded. As Paul Pickett said in a *National Geographic* article, "Unless he is a land speculator, owns a bank or sells insurance . . . the average taxpayer around here not only has had zero profit from this tremendous growth — he is paying for it."[18]

Disney had brought money into the area: $110 million in payroll salaries, $28 million in state taxes, and over $100 million in local purchases for goods and services during the park's first two years.[19] By mid-1973, Osceola and Orange counties ranked first and fifth, respectively, in the state in increased sales tax collections,[20] but arguments were made that these revenues were not worth the problems brought by Disney's presence.

The Magic Kingdom continued to flourish. As the Disney 1973 annual report stated, "Revenues [from WDW] increased 21% to $168,162,000 which came from the following areas: admissions, including recreation, $62,182,000; merchandise sales, $36,702,000; food sales, $40,207,000; lodging revenues, $22,443,000; lessee and other rentals, $5,386,000; and other revenues, $1,242,000. All operating divisions contributed to the increased profitability of the project."[21] As Zehnder points out, "It is significant to note that Disney's combined food and lodging sales of $62,650,000 exceeded admissions by $460,000; an indication that Walt Disney World is in the hotel and restaurant business just as deeply as in the amusement park business — without even considering hotel gift shop sales."[22]

Although I deal with the importance of merchandising in the next chapter, let me underscore here the point that the Walt Disney Company had changed considerably from the studio and Disneyland days. By the early 1970s, Disney had become a land development and food and lodging company. It wasn't until the arrival of Frank Wells and Michael Eisner in the mid-1980s that the film divisions again began to carry their own weight.

Finally, lest we forget the surreal nature of WDW, it was here in 1973 that Richard M. Nixon — the real one, not the robot at the Hall of Presidents — responded to the Watergate impeachment proceedings by telling a convention of Associated Press managing editors, "I am no crook."

The Rest of the 1970s

In the fall of 1973, the real world intervened. The Mideast war led to an OPEC oil embargo of the Western nations. Although the United States in general was jolted by this move, the tourist industry — especially those parts of it that depended on automobile transportation of their customers — was particularly threatened. Florida was hurt, as tourism dropped off significantly by the end of 1973. It became clear that the state's economic dependence on tourism made it particularly vulnerable to global political stress.

Stock prices of many Florida corporations fell precipitously. The Florida Banks' Index dropped 19 percent in November 1973.[23] By January 1974, the hotel and construction industries were in trouble. At a January 9, 1974, meeting of the Florida Hotel and Motel Association, officials warned,

> The nation's energy scare has brought a 25 percent decline in tourism and the threat of lay-offs in the state's largest industry, which employs an estimated 600,000 workers. The financial hard times pose a very serious threat that owners of new multi-million-dollar hotels will face foreclosure if tourist income continues to plummet. . . .
>
> Because so many who have built new hotels and motels at extremely high rates of interest are experiencing low occupancy rates, the income from rooms doesn't even meet the principle payments and in some cases not even the interest.[24]

Disney retrenched. Lights in the Magic Kingdom were cut back, and 630 employees were laid off.[25] As Walt Disney Productions stock plummeted,[26] the WDW operation staff made two moves. First, it set up an operations room. As Robert C. Allen, then-chairman of the Walt Disney World Operating Committee, told Edward Prizer in 1981,

> We asked ourselves, "Can we penetrate the Florida market more? Can we reduce costs?" We made a chart that outlined our operations at various levels of attendance. We told management that's our game plan. We had to lay off employees, but we actually learned to operate our business better. . . .
>
> We monitor the number of autos entering the state. . . . All our planning is keyed to anticipated attendance. We know what to expect as soon as we get a count of cars crossing the border into the state. Since the energy crisis, we've learned to respond quickly to new situations.[27]

Second, the Company pushed forward its plans for diversification, designating nine thousand acres of Florida land for raising cattle and growing commercial hard wood timber for paper products.[28] Donn B. Tatum explained the breadth of Walt Disney Production's capabilities for dealing with economic flux.

> There are many strings in our bow. Sometimes I feel the understandable preoccupation with Walt Disney World has tended to overshadow this important fact. We are in a position to adjust the emphasis in our activities coincidentally with the changes in direction of the economy.
>
> We can and will augment our motion picture and television effort. . . .
>
> We can and will expand in the field of outdoor recreation. . . .
>
> We can and undoubtedly will pursue very seriously the possibilities of development abroad. . . .
>
> We have a future in transportation through our broad experience and knowledge of that subject as developed in our various people-moving and other transportation systems.[29]

The crisis deepened in the winter of 1974. Florida tourism was off 22 percent.[30] WDW attendance was down 17.2 percent.[31] By March 1975, however, larger state allocations of gasoline had begun to alleviate the situation. By April, after the lifting of the oil embargo, conditions were on the rebound. The oil crisis was over, but there was little grace time before the 1974-1975 recession.

Central Florida suffered with the rest of the nation as inflation and unemployment rose and the recession deepened. In greater Orlando, plant, warehouse, and office space was empty. Apartments and condominiums were vacant. Orlando responded with the Great Orlando Property Sale, organized by the Chamber of Commerce Committee of 200.

> Everything in town [is] 10 percent off — warehouses, offices, condominiums, land. Take your pick. The campaign was so far out, so audacious, that it caught the attention of the media all across the nation and made headlines everywhere.
>
> Inquiries poured in from Bangor to San Diego. Although there was never any reliable tally of how many actual sales were made, the Great Sale focussed attention as never before on the glowing potential of the Orlando area and laid the groundwork for the new cycle of growth that ultimately started.[32]

Ironically, as the country was mired in economic pain, WDW flourished — especially as gasoline supplies again grew. As if to escape reality, people flocked to the fantasy of Disney's world. The park set attendance records. Airline boardings at the Orlando airport were up 14 percent. Amtrak passenger traffic increased similarly.[33] By Easter vacation 1975, WDW had hauled greater Orlando out of the doldrums. Hotels and motels were full, and the flow of visitors continued to grow.[34]

In retrospect, Edward Prizer marks the turn toward local optimism by two highly symbolic opening ceremonies at WDW. The first, in January 1975, was RCA's Space Mountain, with astronauts Jim Irwin, Gordon

Cooper, and Scott Carpenter taking the first ride. [35] The second, in early spring 1975 — amid tuxedos, evening gowns, champagne, and Glenn Miller music — was the Lake Buena Vista Shopping Center (later Walt Disney World Shopping Village; currently, Disney Village Marketplace). [36]

In summer 1975, Disney announced the next phase of the corporate plan — the launching of EPCOT. At a news conference at the Contemporary Hotel, the Disney brass presented a preview of the plan. As Prizer reports, Card Walker addressed the audience.

> Walt's concept was truly international in scope, and in the years immediately before his death it became his major interest and concern. In planning the entire Florida project, everything was considered as an eventual part of the master plan of EPCOT.
>
> The first phase has been the recreational community — the Magic Kingdom, the hotels and lakes and campground — which has played host to more than 40,000,000 in less than four years. Now we are launching the second phase of Walt's ideas: the scientific, industrial, communication, world-cooperation aspects of EPCOT. [37]

Then a preview film of EPCOT was shown, depicting the permanent world's fair embodied by World Showcase and the industrial display of products in Future World. Prizer reports, "What we saw in the film shown at the news conference was something entirely different from the concept that had struck [*sic*] in the public mind from Walt Disney's generalized comments. This was not to be a city where people lived and worked in a climate-controlled environment under a massive dome. Instead it was to be a showplace where people came to see and learn." [38]

Although Disney people claimed "we are doing exactly what we talked about when Walt was alive," [39] it was clear that EPCOT was going to be quite different from what people outside the company thought Disney had said it would be. It became an Experimental Prototype Commercial of Tomorrow.

This new plan regalvanized metropolitan Orlando, probably far more than if Disney's original conception had been carried out. Banks began to lend development money again. Other tourist attractions — such as Sea World, Circus World, and Tampa's Busch Gardens — expanded. Commercial and residential building accelerated. Downtown Orlando began to revitalize its city center. The rest of the 1970s, the Carter years, were a boom time. When Ronald Reagan asked in 1980 if people were better off than they had been four years before, a lot of central Floridians — who would have voted for Reagan anyway — could say "yes."

An overview of Disney's first ten years — October 1, 1971, through September 30, 1981 — shows nearly continuous growth in all relevant aspects of the park's performance. [40] The Magic Kingdom opened with thirty-five major attractions, and new ones have been added at the rate of more than one per year. They include: CircleVision 360 (1971), If You Had

Wings (1972), Walt Disney Story (1973), Tom Sawyer's Island (1973), Plaza Swan Boats (1973), Pirates of the Caribbean (1973), StarJets (1974), Space Mountain (1975), GE Carousel of Progress (1975), WEDway People Mover (1975), Main Street Electrical Parade (1977), and Big Thunder Mountain Railroad (1980).

At the same time attractions were being added to the Magic Kingdom, additions were being planned elsewhere on the property. They include: Fort Wilderness Campground and Tri-Circle-D Ranch (1971),[41] Golf Resort Hotel (1973),[42] Pioneer Hall (1974), Discovery Island (1974), Walt Disney World Village (1975), River Country (1976), Empress Lily Riverboat Restaurant (1977), and Walt Disney World Conference Center (1980).

In the first decade, more than 126 million people passed through the gates of WDW — almost double Walt Disney's own projection of 65 million. Its first-year attendance of over 10 million people put WDW ahead of the United Kingdom, Austria, and West Germany as a vacation attraction. The single-day record for attendance, set on December 31, 1980, was 92,969.[43]

Yearly attendance and WDW revenues for the years 1972-1980 are shown in Table 7.2.

TABLE 7.2 Attendance and Revenues (1972-1980)

Year	Guests[a]	Revenues[b]
1972	10.7	$140.0
1973	11.6	$171.5
1974	10.0	$186.8
1975	12.5	$236.3
1976	13.1	$275.4
1977	13.1	$300.5
1978	14.1	$345.6
1979	13.8	$389.6
1980	13.8	$433.4

[a]Attendance in millions.

[b]Revenues in millions.

Source: This table is adapted from Patricia Bellew, "EPCOT: One Year and Counting," *Business Monday, Miami Herald,* September 28, 1981. p. 1.

In 1981, WDW hosted over 1,262,000 foreign visitors, distributed as follows (in thousands): [44] Canada, 625 (Ontario, 488; Quebec, 100; all others, 37); Europe, 402 (United Kingdom, 229; West Germany, 64; France, 31; Sweden, 14; Spain, 12; Switzerland, 12; the Netherlands, 12; Ireland, 7; Belgium, 5; Italy, 5; Finland, 2; Austria, 2; Norway, 2; Denmark, 2; Portugal, 1; all others, 2); South America, 164 (Brazil, 49; Venezuela, 44; Argentina, 35; Colombia, 22; Panama, 5; all others, 9). In addition, visitors came from Mexico (14), Asia (14), Africa (7), Oceania (6), the West Indies (5), and the Middle East (5).

Table 7.3 shows the financial growth record of Walt Disney Productions for the period 1976-1980.

TABLE 7.3 Five-Year Financial Growth Record (1976-1980) (in million $)

	1980	1979	1978	1977	1976
Revenues					
Entertainment and	643,380	571,079	508,444	445,165	401,613
recreation	(21.5%)	(22.1%)	(20.8%)	(20.7%)	(n.a.)
Motion pictures	161,380	134,785	152,135	118,058	119,113
	(33.0%)	(29.8%)	(35.6%)	(39.1%)	(n.a.)
Consumer products	109,725	90,909	80,564	66,602	63,150
and other	(51.0%)	(49.3%)	(46.5%)	(47.0%)	(n.a.)
Total	914,485	796,773	741,143	629,825	583,876
Net income	135,186	113,788	98,385	81,947	74,599
Earnings per share	4.16	3.51	3.04	2.53	2.30
Cash dividends per share	.72	.48	.32	.14	.12

Sources: This table is adapted from "Wall Street Report," *Television/Radio Age*, March 9, 1981. The percentages in parentheses are gross profit margin figures for four of the years. They are taken from "Disney (Walt) Prod.," *Value Line*, May 23, 1980.

Note the growing importance of the consumer products division. Over the five-year period shown in Table 7.3, consumer products revenues increased by 74 percent. Its gross profit margins were also considerably larger than those of the other two divisions. For the year ending September 30, 1981, Disney's current assets stood at $457.8 million, its current liabilities at $191.6 million, and its long-term debt at $161.9 million;[45] but as we'll soon see, with its movie division not pulling its weight, Walt Disney Productions was heading for trouble.

Disney's Effect on Orlando in the 1970s

What about greater Orlando — Orange, Osceola and Seminole counties? Frances Novak-Branch has produced the best study of the overall effect of Disney on central Florida during Disney's first ten years,[46] and I will stick close to her findings.[47]

The population of the three-county area grew from 453,270 to 700,055 during the decade — a rate of 54.5 percent.[48] During the previous decade there had been a 34.3 percent increase in population, so the rate grew significantly.[49] Population in Florida as a whole increased 43.6 percent during the 1970s, whereas that of the United States grew by only 11.1 percent.[50] The population coming to central Florida was younger than that of the state as a whole, with more arrivals of working age and fewer retirees than in the rest of Florida.[51]

Employment in the three-county area rose 119 percent in the decade — from 114,174 to 250,287.[52] Perhaps 50,000 of these jobs are attributable to Disney.[53] Disney was the second-largest employer in the area in 1981, with a normal complement of 11,000 workers (8,000 full-time and 7,000 part-time workers, computed as sharing 3,000 jobs). Only the U.S. Naval Training Center, with 16,150, had more employees.[54] Florida and the United States saw employment rise 66 percent and 30.7 percent, respectively, during the 1970s. In greater Orlando retail trade employment was up 119.7 percent, with the subcategory of drinking and eating places up 230.6 percent.[55] In general, local service area income rose some 11.11 percent, more than double the state's 5.4 percent and the country's 4.28 percent.[56]

Yet although total service industry income rose, the mean real per capita income declined 6 percent from 1970 to 1980.[57] More people were being employed but at lower service industry wages. Compounding this was a decrease in contract construction, manufacturing, and retail trade real per capita incomes.[58] Overall indicators were up; personal indicators were down.

Although overall unemployment grew in the greater Orlando area from 3.8 percent in 1970 to 5.8 percent in 1980, it was still lower than the national figures of 4.9 percent and 7.1 percent. [59] In comparison with the rest of the state (2.9 percent in 1970 and 5.9 percent in 1980), the three-county area had caught up in its proportion of employed. Many of these new workers were women and teenagers, working for lower-than-average wages. Thus, median family income rose, and real incomes increased (although median real incomes decreased among those employed) as more workers were employed. [60]

Tourism indicators were obviously up. [61] Perhaps the most amazing of these was the change in arrivals by airplane during the decade from 103,423 in 1970 to 2,273,000 in 1980 — a 2,098.8 percent increase. [62] Automobile traffic rose 433.4 percent, compared with a state increase of 10.5 percent. [63] No wonder south Floridians complained about the "great wall." Although Florida's tourism rose 46.1 percent in the 1970s, greater Orlando's was up 648.3 percent. [64]

To get a sense of what these numbers mean, let me quote from Novak-Branch's discussion of Disney World's comparative status as an international tourist attraction. Remember that these data antedate EPCOT Center and the Disney-MGM Studios.

> In its first year of opening . . . Disney World . . . became more popular as a vacation spot than the Great Smokey Mountains National Park which drew 7 million visitors; Gettysburg with 5.2 million visitors; and Yellowstone with 2.4 million visitors. . . .
>
> Among international tourist attractions, Disney World was ranked sixth, falling behind Spain, Italy, France, Canada, and the United States, as a tourist destination. . . .
>
> After nearly 10 years, in early 1981, Disney World had had over 126 million visitors, placing Central Florida among the top tourist attractions in the world, surpassing the Eiffel Tower, Taj Majal, Tower of London, Egyptian pyramids, and Disneyland, in the total recorded attendance. . . .
>
> In 1980, with 13 million to 14 million visitors annually, Disney World received 1.4 million or 10 percent of the foreign visitors to the United States. [65]

These tourists spent money. Note the following changes in expenditures over the decade: park admissions up 57.6 percent in real dollars (to $921 million); restaurants up 140.9 percent (to 4.9 billion current [1981] dollars); hotels, motels, and apartment housing up 83.2 percent; filling stations up 273.6 percent (to $7 billion). [66] Disney World received more than $14 billion in tourist-related expenses during the first ten years. [67]

Novak-Branch estimates that tourist expenditures (and the unusual increase in population) attributable to WDW accounted for 11.5 percent of the total increase in sales and use tax revenues to the state and 61 percent of the increase in gasoline taxes. [68] These effects were partly, but by no means fully, offset by the expenditures — law enforcement, highways, education, and public welfare — required by the influx of permanent and transient people. As this is Florida, it's no surprise that the first category of expenditure received considerably more attention than the last three.

When Novak-Branch develops her investment multiplier to see what impact Disney has had on the greater Orlando area, she finds that the multiplier is approximately 1.1 — surprisingly low.[69] First, she suggests that there has been a greater increase in employment than in incomes.[70] Thus, mean per capita income has not risen commensurate with overall investment. Second, she reminds us that WDW is owned by California investors; thus, there is what she calls a "profit leakage" to California.[71] "This has kept Florida from experiencing the full impact of the Disney World multiplier."[72] This profit leakage was important to Walt Disney Productions because the movie business was lousy.

The Battle for Disney

EPCOT Center's first six months after its October 1, 1982, opening were spectacular. Crowds were larger than anticipated;[73] but by the last quarter of 1983, the rush was over and attendance began to drop. This was dangerous for Walt Disney Productions because in 1983 the theme parks represented 87 percent of the Company's earnings.[74]

The main problems were in the movie division. First, the animation department had been decimated in 1979 when Don Bluth led a number of other disaffected animators out of the company. Disney's annual film production had always been small; Bluth's defection made it even smaller.

Second, annual movie output was low at Disney because of its mania for control. Disney seldom used independent producers who might come to a project with their own ideas. Further, Disney shunned outside investors.[75] Thus, using its own money, the Company was unable or unwilling to make a lot of movies.

This made the success of any particular movie crucial, and the studio had not been doing well. In order to preserve its homey image, Disney insisted on turning out its traditional cute, bland, sentimental product. This raised the third problem, which was that the movie audience had changed. The public was willing to bring its children to rereleases of Disney animated classics, but it was not enamored of the studio's new releases. In 1981 and 1982, Disney wrote off $21 million for *Something Wicked This Way Comes*, $10.5 million for *Night Crossing*, $10.4 million for *Tron*, and $6.8 million for *The Watcher in the Woods*.[76] The only bright spot was the rerelease of *The Fox and the Hound*, which did $50 million in film rentals in 1981.[77]

Walt's son-in-law, Ron Miller, who had become president of Walt Disney Productions in 1980, continued to push for the production of more contemporary movies. He was opposed by older Disney hands, such as E. Card Walker and Dick Nunis, head of the theme park division. Nunis was joined by James Jimirro, head of the Disney Channel — the cable television service started in 1983 — in worrying that more modern movies might sully the Company's reputation for niceness and thus threaten its bailiwicks.[78]

Miller's plan was to establish a second production label to make movies to appeal to a changed public. A market research study commissioned by Disney clinched the issue.

> The resulting report established that Walt Disney Productions was the only motion picture studio with name recognition: It meant a movie for children. One nineteen-year-old queried in the study said he "wouldn't be caught dead" going to a Disney movie because he would be laughed at by his peers. However, he said, he looked forward to the day when, older and married, he would take his own children to Disney movies.[79]

Touchstone Films, the new distribution label (with its connection to Disney originally somewhat muted), opened its first movie, *Splash*, in March 1984. Showing a bit more of Darryl Hannah than Walt Disney might have approved, the PG-rated *Splash* was a major success. Touchstone Films would help lead the Disney renaissance.

In addition to the U.S. parks and the movies, two other elements of the Disney package need to be mentioned — the Cable Channel and Tokyo Disneyland. By 1983 "The Wonderful World of Disney" was no longer in regular production. Network television revenues had fallen from $44.4 million in 1982 to $27.9 million a year later.[80] The Company had started a pay-TV cable channel in April 1983, but the subscriber growth rates were much slower than expected.

Also in April 1983, Tokyo Disneyland opened to strong attendance. Although Disney has no equity involvement in this project, the Company gets a 10 percent royalty on admissions and 5 percent on food and merchandise. Royalties for 1983 were around $10 million.[81]

By early 1984, financial analysts around the country were hinting at the possibility of a takeover of Walt Disney Productions.[82] Stock prices were down. Attendance at the parks had fallen off, perhaps because of a particularly cold winter in Florida. Movie production was on the rise, but this was only in its early stages. Disney also had two large assets to tempt a corporate raider — the thousands of acres of undeveloped land in central Florida and the Disney film library, which Walt Disney and those who followed him had refused to sell.

The temptation was there, and in the spring of 1984 the bait was taken. The result of "the battle for Disney" was a major transition into the present form of Walt Disney Productions (as of 1986, the Walt Disney Company) and WDW — the world of Michael Eisner.

The story is told well and completely by John Taylor in *Storming the Magic Kingdom*, so I will just present the bare bones of the tale.[83] The public beginning of the saga may be marked as March 9, 1984, when two things happened. First, Roy E. Disney — Roy O. Disney's son and Walt's nephew — resigned from the board of directors of Walt Disney Productions. Roy E.

had disagreed for some time with other members of the board over the direction of the Company.

At particular issue was Roy's belief that the movie division needed a severe philosophical overhaul in order to reenter the contemporary world. A month later, on April 11, Roy announced that he had increased his holdings in the Company from 2.7 percent to 4 percent, and rumors circulated that he was part of an outside takeover.

Second, on March 9 Saul Steinberg began to buy Disney stock. Steinberg, chairman of Reliance Group Holdings, had a track record of successful greenmail. A ubiquitous recent feature of late capitalism, greenmail is the selling of stock bought as part of a threat to take over a company back to the company at a premium. The Disney story contains greenmail, arbitragers, "shark repellent," a "white knight," and all the other paraphernalia of postmodern corporate finance. With Steinberg buying stock, Disney was clearly "in play."

On March 28, Disney announced that it had extended its line of credit from $400 million to $1.3 billion in a first effort to respond to the threat of a hostile takeover. Steinberg's shares continued to grow from 6.3 percent of the Company's shares as of March 29, 7.3 percent by April 3, 8.3 percent by April 10, to 9.3 percent by April 13. By May 1, Steinberg's stake was up to 12.1 percent, and he had filed with the Securities and Exchange Commission, stating his intention to purchase up to 25 percent of the company.

Although Steinberg had not yet announced a takeover — he would not do so until late May — Disney management finally made a move to respond to the threat. On May 18, Disney announced that it would acquire Arvida Corporation for $200 million in Disney stock.

This acquisition had a number of implications. First, it signified Disney's intent to pay serious attention to the development of its Florida property. Arvida was primarily a land development company, with a series of recent successes behind it. Second, the acquisition of Arvida diluted Disney's general shareholdings, spreading ownership more widely and making a takeover more difficult.

Third, and perhaps most important, the purchase of Arvida brought the Bass brothers of Fort Worth into the action as "white knights." In December 1983, Arvida had been bought from the Penn Central Corporation by a combination of Arvida managers and the Basses. [84] By trading Disney stock for ownership in Arvida, Disney transferred a large bundle of shares to the Basses. The question of what they would do was not answered for a while. [85]

On the same day that Disney announced its intent to purchase Arvida, Steinberg received notification that the federal government would not block his purchase of up to 49.9 percent of Disney stock. In the next week, 15 percent of Disney stock — more than 5 million shares — changed hands. The arbitragers were in. Michael Milkin was involved. On May 25, Steinberg announced that he might be considering a takeover, and four days later he said he would try to oust the Disney board of directors.

On June, 6 the board tried some shark repellent, announcing plans to buy Gibson Greeting Cards — owners of licensing rights to Garfield the Cat and Big Bird — for $345 million in Disney stock. This purchase would further dilute shareholdings.

On June 9, Steinberg made a tender offer for Disney at $67.50 for 49 percent of the outstanding shares — $72.50 if Disney would agree to stop the Gibson deal. Before shareholders had a chance to decide whether to sell their shares at this price, on June 9 Disney made Steinberg a counteroffer of $70.83 a share for his shares. When he took it, a profit of $31.7 million plus $28 million for "out-of-pocket" expenses, the greenmail was over.

Stockholders were furious, some because they had not been offered Steinberg's price and some because the buyout left Disney in a very precarious position with at least $500 million in new debt. Others were also furious. Steinberg had indicated that, on taking control of Disney, he would break up the company by selling off the movie division and various other parts of Disney holdings. Response to this was vehement (and not without anti-Semitism), for many people felt Steinberg was attacking a public U.S. symbol. Robert Knight spoke for this viewpoint.

It is part of a disquieting trend in American industry — takeover and liquidation, which . . . aims to "kill the company and get the cash."

While Steinberg and his ilk are making millions by threatening to tear down what took years to build, Disney and other creative institutions still are developing ideas, tangible products — and jobs.

Steinberg apparently thought nothing of dissolving an American original, a monument to ingenuity and quality. His attitude is beyond cavalier.

Breaking up Disney to cash in on its assets would be on the order of smashing a Tiffany vase to get at the penny that fell inside. [86]

Greenmail was under scrutiny in the U.S. Congress. Then-Representative Timothy E. Wirth had introduced legislation that would prohibit corporations from paying a buyout premium to shareholders of more than 3 percent unless the majority of holders approved. [87]

Yet for all the furor, Disney was still vulnerable. Roy E. Disney was still buying shares. Ivan Boesky owned more than a million shares. By summer 1974, another run on Disney was underway, led this time by Irwin Jacobs of Minneapolis. The story again is best told by John Taylor, so I will just relate the various upshots.

By the fall of 1984, the Basses had bought out Jacobs's shares, which added to their own, made them (at just over 24 percent) the largest shareholders in Disney. [88] The Gibson Card deal had been dropped. Roy E. Disney was back on the Board. Ron Miller had resigned as president. On September 23, Frank Wells, formerly of Warner Brothers, had been hired as president of Walt Disney Productions, and Michael Eisner, president of

Paramount Pictures, had become Disney CEO. The two of them would lead Disney's renaissance.

The film background of Eisner and Wells suggested that Disney would refocus its energy on moviemaking, but this direction took an interesting turn when Disney announced in July 1985 that it would build a $300 million movie studio and tour attraction at WDW in collaboration with MGM Studios. This was to be part of phase one of a three-stage plan to use Arvida's expertise to develop more of the Florida land.[89] John Taylor described the plan in a report of a mid-October discussion with Disney officials.

> Over the next 30 years, the company will pour billions of dollars into Walt Disney World to build an experimental city twice the size of Manhattan that features a movie studio, Disney's two theme parks — Epcot Center and the Magic Kingdom — numerous hotels, as many as 20,000 residential units to be marketed as time-share apartments, a massive state-of-the-art research and high-technology center and single- and multifamily homes for as many as 50,000 full-time residents.[90]

This looks vaguely like a return to Walt Disney's fantasy, but the governmental difficulties — the "one-man-one-vote" problem — remained. As Michael Eisner said in responding to questions, "Walt wasn't against people voting; he just didn't want them hanging their dirty laundry out. . . . I don't agree. I don't disagree."[91]

Right!

The Recovery

Although Disney argued that the Disney-MGM Studios, which opened in May 1989, had been on the planning board for years, many — including MCA, the parent corporation of Universal Studios — castigated Disney's planned park as a "spoiler attraction." Although the same would be said of the Living Seas at EPCOT Center (a potential threat to Sea World), Typhoon Lagoon (a threat to Wet 'N' Wild), and Pleasure Island (a threat to Church Street Station in downtown Orlando),[92] the Disney-MGM Studios park was particularly galling for Universal.

> MCA's indignation also appears to be fueled by the fact that the Basses — solicited in 1981 as potential partners in the MCA project — had access to its plans, including marketing studies showing that a Universal Tour might damage tourist enthusiasm for both Epcot and the Magic Kingdom. The Basses declined to back the project but formed a joint venture with MCA to acquire part of an Orlando company with land holdings near the proposed studio. That partnership was dissolved shortly before the Basses became involved with Disney . . . leading MCA officials to feel "a bit like jilted lovers."[93]

By the summer of 1989, the $500 million Disney-MGM Studios had opened,[94] as had Typhoon Lagoon and Pleasure Island. The latter in particular, a night spot near Walt Disney Village with themed nightclubs and a number of restaurants, is part of Disney's strategy to fill a void to enable it to compete as a top convention destination.[95] The Grand Floridian Resort Hotel and the Caribbean Beach Resort were open, with the latter offering lodging at lower-than-normal on-site Disney prices. Tokyo Disneyland was bringing in more than 14 million visitors a year,[96] and Euro Disneyland near Paris was under construction, set to open in spring 1992.[97]

Set about twenty miles east of Paris amid the beet fields of Marne-la-Vallée, Euro Disneyland has not developed without opposition. Some French intellectuals have dubbed it "a cultural Chernobyl".[98] However, local opinion polls taken shortly after the announcement of the new park showed that 85 percent of the respondents favored the development — perhaps because of the expected thirty thousand jobs.[99]

In contrast to its Tokyo Disneyland decision to opt for licensing fees and a percentage of revenues instead of ownership interest — a decision Disney found to be a costly mistake — the Company has a legal maximum 49 percent stake in Euro Disneyland. This move has already paid off on paper, as Disney's original 86 million shares in Euro Disneyland have jumped from $1.90 to $22 each. When the park opens, Disney will receive 10 percent of the admission fees and 5 percent of the food and merchandise revenues (these are the same as its Tokyo cuts) as well as the return on its ownership shares. Disney has put up only $160 million of its own money; the rest has come from other investors, special partnerships, and the French government.[100]

Stephen Greenhouse notes that 17 million people live within a two-hour drive of the park, 41 million within a four-hour drive, 109 million within a six-hour drive (including those who will come through the Chunnel), and 310 million within a two-hour flight. This is a lot of potential customers, some of whom have already made a portion of the 2.7 million visits to WDW by Europeans in 1990 alone.

As far as movies are concerned, Disney raised its yearly output. Stars such as Bette Midler and Robin Williams were signed to multifilm contracts. The Touchstone label hit with *Splash, Down and Out in Beverly Hills* ($62.0 million), *Ruthless People* ($71.5), *Outrageous Fortune* ($53.0), *The Color of Money* ($52.3), *Three Men and a Baby* ($168.0), *Good Morning Vietnam* ($124.0), *Cocktail* ($77.0), *Stakeout* ($65.7), *Beaches* ($55.0),[101] *The Dead Poets Society,* and *Honey, I Shrunk the Kids.* The 3-D *Captain E-O* — a collaboration among Francis Ford Coppola, George Lucas, and Michael Jackson — opened at EPCOT Center's Journey into Imagination. In 1989 and 1990, Disney hit big with *The Littlest Mermaid, Dick Tracy,* and *Pretty Woman.*

Animated features returned with *The Great Mouse Detective, Oliver and Company,* and especially the very successful *Who Framed Roger Rabbit?*

($153.0 million), which introduced a major new character to the Disney pantheon. In very un-Disney-like fashion, Eisner and Wells funded these films through limited partnerships, thus risking other peoples' money. In 1988, with 19.4 percent of the nation's ticket sales, Disney rode to the top spot in the box office standings for the first time in history. [102]

The normal seven-year schedule for the rerelease of animated feature-length movies was shortened to five years. [103] Overseas distribution, run through the Company's Buena Vista International subsidiary, had grown in importance. For the first time, Disney released around two hundred titles from its film library for sale on video cassettes. On network television, Disney developed "The Golden Girls" and "The Gummi Bears." The Disney (Cable) Channel turned the corner. In 1988 the Company purchased VHF station KCAL-TV, a commercial television station in Los Angeles. In the summer of 1990, *Arachnophobia* opened as the first product of Disney's new Hollywood Pictures film unit. [104]

For the first time, Disney began national advertising campaigns designed to lure tourists from fifty key cities in the Northeast, Midwest, and South. [105] The imagineering department at WED was contracted to outside clients to create special exhibits. The Company began to sell original animated stills (now available at the Studio Tour). Upscale Disney-character clothes began to appear in boutiques.

In the summer of 1986, fear of international terrorism, deregulated air fares, and relatively cheap gasoline brought record attendance. That winter Disney stock prices soared, and the corporation made a 4-for-1 split. [106] Four shares were now trading at $50 each — split from $200 a share — less than two years after Saul Steinberg had been bought off for $70.83 a share. [107]

In order to reflect the spread of Disney interests, in early 1987 Walt Disney Productions was renamed The Walt Disney Company. Disney had learned what it needed to know from Arvida and sold the company in 1987. [108] In early 1987, Delta Airlines replaced Eastern as the "official airline" of WDW. Michael Eisner, the most highly compensated CEO in the United States, could now agree with Frank Wells when he said "the sun never sets on the Delta-Disney empire." [109]

Orlando: 1986-1990

What about Orlando, the local part of the empire? By the end of 1986, the population of metropolitan Orlando was approaching one million — more than double what it had been when the Magic Kingdom opened in 1971. Between 1980 and 1985, Orlando had become the tenth-most-active housing market in the country. Office space and retail sales doubled, the latter reaching $1.7 billion a year. [110] Even the fast-food market was booming: "Managers of everything from burger to fried-chicken chains said their

No. 1 stores nationwide, by sales volume, are in the International Drive area, the tourist strip near Disney and 12 miles south of downtown Orlando." [111]

"Sleepy" Orlando had awakened. Joining Martin Marietta, Harcourt-Brace-Jovanovich, and Tupperware, General Electric, United Technologies, Litton, Parks Jaggers Aerospace, Westinghouse, Stromberg Carlson Corporation, and Harris Corporation opened high-tech divisions in Orlando. Local boosters, clearly giving Disney its due as a catalyst, nonetheless claimed that Orlando would have grown anyway, if more slowly. [112] "The Sun Belt is the top growth section in the country and the pivotal state is Florida. . . . Orlando is the hub. . . . It's the only major city in Florida with 360 degrees to grow. Miami, Jacksonville, Tampa/St. Petersburg are all hemmed in by the ocean. . . . Major industry was destined to come to Orlando." [113]

However, despite Disney's payments of $60 million annually in property, sales, and resort taxes and its weekly payroll of $5 million, [114] many local citizens had decided that "it's not easy living with the Mouse." [115] Much of the argument was summed up by Matt Walsh, who claimed the hiring of Wells and Eisner had brought a new aggressiveness to Disney. Walsh cited four problems in particular: the jamming up of Orlando's transportation system; the unaffordability of housing in Orlando or near WDW caused by rising prices and the low wage rates of Disney and other tourism-related jobs; the perceived lack of Disney's participation as a citizen in the local community; and Disney's new strategy for dominating and controlling visitors at the expense of non-Disney hotels and attractions.

The powers given to the Reedy Creek Improvement District by the state of Florida exempt it from the impact fees paid by other developers to offset the costs of roads and other governmental services. With the development of hotel complexes and shopping centers on Disney property, local officials became incensed at Company practices. "It's one thing for Disney to build Cinderella's castle," [said] Orange County Commissioner Linda W. Chapin. "It's another for Disney to build shopping centers." [116]

Disney had not supported an Orange County planners' attempt to get federal funding for a light-rail system to connect Orlando International Airport with WDW and International Drive, Orlando's main hotel area. Although Disney questioned the need and financial feasibility of the project, local people felt Disney did not want the train to run through its property. [117]

By the spring of 1989, there were rumors that Disney might build such a train after all. On September 28, 1989, the Company announced that it would allow the proposed Maglev (magnetic levitation) train to deliver passengers to a piece of undeveloped land three miles south of EPCOT, near the intersection of I-4 and U.S. 192. Although spokespeople for the International Drive business interests were dismayed that the proposed line would pass them by, Osceola County interests near the proposed site were pleased. They began to talk of a bullet train linking Tampa, Orlando, and Miami with an Osceola County-WDW station.[118]

In the summer of 1989, the Walt Disney Company and Orange County reached an understanding by which Disney agreed to contribute around $16 million for improvements to county roads. The county wanted $32 million, and Disney originally offered nothing. Disney gained one important thing with this compromise: It included an agreement that Orange County would not challenge in court Disney's special right to be exempt from government rule.[119]

Disney acknowledged the housing problem. Walsh quotes Rick Bernhardt, Orlando's planning director in 1986, as saying, "but they don't feel like it's their problem. Their contention is it's a private market situation. The city's contention is it's a problem — period — and anything Disney can do will be appreciated."[120]

Disney had consistently fought attempts by other local interests to legalize a resort tax to pay for the desperately needed improvements in local infrastructure.[121] Disney officials rarely served on Orange County advisory boards, and Disney had been accused of being the "magic kingdom of aloof."[122] An *Orlando Sentinel* article in early 1985 claimed Disney had considered building its own monorail to the Orlando airport, thus "isolating itself from the surrounding tourist community."[123] As the *Sentinel* later put it, "The unmistakable conclusion is that Disney isn't involved with local governments because Disney doesn't need anything from them."[124]

In 1990 Disney and Orange County continued their squabble over the issue of tax-exempt bonds. As Andrew Holleran reports,

> Every year Florida makes available to various regions of the state . . . the authority to issue tax-exempt bonds ($663 million this year) to help these regions build sewage systems, low-cost housing, and manufacturing plants. The bonds are awarded on a first-come, first-served basis. Reedy Creek submitted its 1990 application on January 2nd, two days before Orange County. . . . Not only did Reedy Creek get permission to issue $57.7 million in tax-exempt bonds to pay for an expansion of its sewage system . . . but it also won a lottery that put it first in line to receive as much as $47 million on July 1st, when unused bond allocations revert to the state.[125]

By virtue of its efficiency, Disney garnered bonds that would otherwise have been available to Orange, Osceola, Seminole, Lake, Brevard, and Volusia counties — a share it refused to relinquish when asked.[126]

In fairness to Disney, however, we might note that the company is forced to deal with expectations that it has created in part through its public image production. Dianna Morgan, WDW's director of public relations in 1986, told Walsh that her office received sixty to eighty requests a day for visits by Disney characters, parade participation, full stage productions, money, free tickets, and similar items. Morgan claimed Disney and its employees contributed around $900,000 annually to local charity interests — half in cash, half in services. The company also sponsors a program to bring terminally ill children and their families to WDW, picking up the costs for tickets to its attractions. [127]

As for the suspected attempts by Disney to lure visitors at the expense of other local attractions, I have noted the new Disney "spoiler" attractions. According to Phil Williams, Philip F. Wood and Harry W. Collison, Jr., of the Real Estate Consortium of Winter Park claimed that

> Disney has an elaborate plan to increase attendance by overbuilding the luxury hotel market on its property and, as a result, forcing hotels away from Disney World to lower their prices substantially to remain competitive.
>
> The goal: making a trip to Walt Disney World more possible for lower income families.
>
> That won't hurt Disney hotels . . . because tourists will always be willing to pay premium prices for lodging close to the attraction. [128]

Disney people respond by saying essentially, "Well, that's how free enterprise works." [129]

"We've always had the goal of being a complete and total destination resort," Disney spokesman Charles Ridgway said. "That implies we will provide entertainment so guests don't have to go anywhere else to enjoy themselves."

"It's not only in our interest, but it's also in the interest of the guests," added Michael Eisner, chairman and chief executive officer of The Walt Disney Co. "Any time we can keep them from getting in a car, especially at night, it's to their advantage." [130]

Altruism at its finest!

With the opening of its Studio Tour, Disney changed its ticket policies. Its three-day Passport disappeared, replaced by four- and five-day tickets. The average tourist stayed in central Florida for five days, so even the four-day pass left other central Florida attractions to scramble for a share of the fifth day. Sidney Sheinberg, president of Universal Studio's parent company, asked the *Orlando Sentinel*, "Do you really want a little mouse to become a ravenous rat?" [131] The words of Wayne Bachard, a tourist from New Hampshire, suggest that Sheinberg's fears are not misplaced. "We went to the parks, we played golf, we rented boats, we went swimming. We did anything we could have wanted to do and we never left Disney World. It's unbelievable." [132]

Having had a brief look at the history of Disney in Florida, we need one more piece of the economic picture before we move on. The business of Disney is business. As Walt Disney was once quoted in *The Wall Street Journal* as having said, "Dream, diversify — and never miss an angle." [133]

One crucial piece of Disney's world of commodification consists of the merchandise it sells throughout the globe, but especially at WDW. The consumer products division, with its souvenirs and other traveling corporate symbols, is central to the spread of the empire. In the next chapter, I take a look at the organization of merchandising at Disney and WDW.

8

Marketing the Magic Mall

I'm going to Disney World

—Orel Hershiser, Gretchen Elizabeth Carlson, Joe Dumars,
Joe Montana, the Chicago Bulls, and so on

Please Waste

—words on WDW trash bins

The Walt Disney Company has a lot of marketing tasks. It sells itself as a whole — its subsidiary companies and divisions, its theme parks, its movies, its character-based merchandise,[1] and all the other items available at its theme park malls. Recently the Company has begun to open Disney Stores retail outlets and has opened its first independent restaurant — Mickey's Kitchen — in southern California.[2] Disney has entered into complex relationships with a lot of businesses and large, powerful corporations whose names, products, and ideologies are part of the combined sell at WDW.

In its self-descriptions, Disney talks a lot about its "Disney synergy."[3]

The continued success of the Disney organization requires the perpetuation of a delicate balance of functions. Every function is dependent upon other functions. All are interdependent. None stands alone. We have the parent company that branches out into subsidiary companies, divisions, departments, and other functions; and though we're diversified, each subsidiary is related to the same corporate product . . . "The Finest in Family Entertainment." This is what we call the Disney Synergy.[4]

In this training literature, Disney presents a structural chart that shows the interlock among its various parts. To give some idea of this corporate model, I have extracted the relations between WDW and some of the other activities carried out by The Walt Disney Company. Entitled "Disney Teamwork," the original chart is centered around the Walt Disney Studio, but I will relable it "Disney Interlocks" (Table 8.1) and recenter it around WDW.[5] In the full chart, relations among all the other activities are also presented.

TABLE 8.1 Disney Interlocks

Walt Disney Studio	⟹	produces promo material		WDW
	⟹	plugs park in films		
		plugs motion pictures	⟸	
		keeps characters before public	⟸	
		provides show settings	⟸	
Disneyland	⟹	advertise each other	⟸	WDW
TV	⟹	promotes future projects		WDW
	⟹	promotes park		
		source for show material	⟸	
Merchandise	⟹	promotes through toys and similar products	⟸	WDW
licensing	⟹	provides sales outlet in major market		
		provides additional sales outlet	⟸	
		source of new products	⟸	
		turns exhibitors into licensees	⟸	
WED[a]	⟹	provides audioanimatronics		WDW

	⇒	imagineers and designs attractions		
		showcase for design talent	⇐	
		proving ground for future projects	⇐	
		master plans future projects	⇐	
MAPO[b]	⇒	fabricates mechanical systems		WDW
16mm 8mm		source materials for	⇐	WDW
Educational media		provides customers for	⇐	WDW
Music	⇒	feeds theme music for		WDW
		feeds ideas for albums	⇐	
Publications	⇒	promotes park		WDW
		provides sales outlet	⇐	
		source material for	⇐	
Comic strips	⇒	showcase for characters		WDW
Magic Kingdom Club	⇒	communicates with customers		WDW
Celebrity Sports Center		trains manpower [*sic*] for	⇐	WDW
Future projects		trains manpower [*sic*] for	⇐	WDW

[a]WED, for W(alt) E(lias) D(isney), is the company's planning and engineering division. This is where the imagineers hang out.

[b]MAPO stands for MA(ry) PO(ppins).

Source: This chart is adapted from "The Disney Management Style," an unpublished training manual. It predates Touchstone Pictures and the Disney-MGM Studios. Connections between these and WDW are new and complicated. See "The Disney Management Style" (Walt Disney Productions, n.d.).

This is obviously the most molar of models, but the structure of inter-connections among Disney's many divisions is replicated throughout the system. Table 8.2 presents an alphabetical sampling of Disney's constituent subcompanies and related entities drawn from the Company's 1982 publication, *The World-Wide Disney Team*.[6] To this list I must add those corporate entities concerned with Touchstone and Hollywood Pictures, Tokyo Disneyland, Euro Disneyland, the Disney-MGM Studio Tour, and similar entities.[7]

TABLE 8.2 Disney's Constituent Subcompanies (1982)

Buena Vista Construction Company

  • in-house construction for The Walt Disney Company, Buena Vista Distribution Company, Inc.

Buena Vista Distribution Company, Inc.

  • markets films, television shows and music inside the United States and Canada.

Buena Vista Interiors

  • provides interior design expertise, both in-house and externally.

Buena Vista International, Inc.

  • markets properties outside the United States and Canada, including educational movies and souvenir merchandise.

Buena Vista Realty, Inc.

  • provides real estate services in Florida; leases and manages townhouses.

Character merchandising[a]

  • licenses use of Disney characters for merchandise, comic books, magazines. Oversees direct mail merchandising, motion picture and television promotional tie-ins.

Cities of Bay Lake and Lake Buena Vista

  • cities chartered by the state of Florida to perform municipal functions within Reedy Creek Improvement District.

DISNEYLAND

  • the California park.

Lake Buena Vista Communities, Inc.

  • owns, plans, and develops real estate within the city of Lake Buena Vista. This includes vacation homes, townhouses, hotels, the Lake Buena Vista Club, Disney Shopping Village, a golf course, a tennis center and the Orange Vista Hospital.

Madeira Land Company, Inc., and Ranch and Grove Holding Corporation

- two of the land-holding companies for the Florida project.

The Magic Kingdom Club

- nationwide employee recreational program that provides exclusive Disney values and benefits.

MAPO

- named for the movie *Mary Poppins*, MAPO fabricates, assembles, and tests prototype systems and components for WED-designed entertainment attractions, including all audioanimatronic figures.

Reedy Creek Improvement District

- a public corporation of the state of Florida empowered to perform land reclamation services, furnish utilities, administer building codes, and provide fire protection.

Reedy Creek Utilities Company, Inc.

- supplies utilities to WDW; operates the Central Energy Plant, the Automatic Vaccuum Collection System, and the Waste Water Treatment Plant; and supplies water and natural gas to the property.

Theme Fabrication Company

- produces costumes for Disneyland and WDW.

United National Operating Company

- leases and operates the merchandise shops in the Hotel Plaza hotels in Lake Buena Vista and the various shops in the Disneyland Hotel in Anaheim, California.

The Vineland Agency, Inc.

- offers insurance to Walt Disney Company, its subsidiaries, their employees, and the general public.

Vista Advertising

- buys air time and print space and prepares copy for Walt Disney Company related advertising.

Vista-United Telecommunications System

- a partnership between Walt Disney Company and the Florida Telephone Corporation; provides telephone services to the property.

Walt Disney Attractions Entertainment Division

- division of Buena Vista Distributing Company, Inc., responsible for special events that happen outside the theme parks, such as half-time shows at the Super Bowl.

Walt Disney Music Company (ASCAP) and Wonderland Music Company, Inc. (BMI)

- responsible for publishing and promoting Disney music.

Walt Disney Productions (now Walt Disney Company)

- the parent company.

Walt Disney Telecommunications and Non-Theatrical Company

- handles the 16millimeter film rental market, video sales and rentals, pay television, and educational audiovisual materials.

Walt Disney Travel Company, Inc.

- travel agency for the public, members of the Magic Kingdom Club, and employees of Walt Disney Productions.

Walt Disney World Company

- the legal entity which controls Walt Disney World Vacation Resort.

Walt Disney World Village (Disney Shopping Village)

- owned and operated by Lake Buena Vista Company, this is the shopping mall in Lake Buena Vista.

WED Enterprises

- the master planning, design, and engineering arm of Walt Disney Company. Developed overall plan for theme parks.

WED Transportation Services, Inc.

- division of Buena Vista Distribution Company, Inc. Plans, designs, constructs, and operates transportation systems within the theme parks; and consults with cities, airports, and shopping centers in the planning of short-range mass transportation systems.

---

[a]In 1987 Disney greatly expanded the scope of its mail order catalogs by purchasing Childcraft Educational Corporation from Grolier Publishers.

Source: Adapted from *The World-Wide Disney Team* (Walt Disney Productions, 1982).

All of this organizational apparatus — and all of these companies and divisions — intertwine to produce and market Disney. By 1990 the Walt Disney Company included the following subsidiaries: Buena Vista Home Video, Buena Vista International, Inc., Buena Vista Pictures Distribution, Inc., Buena Vista Television, Childcraft Educational Corporation, The Disney Channel, Disney Development Company, The Disney Stores, Inc., EDL Holding Company, KHJ-TV, Inc., Lake Buena Vista Communities, Inc., Reedy Creek Energy Services, Inc., Walt Disney Imagineering, Walt Disney Pictures and Television, Walt Disney World Company, and WCO Parent Corporation.[8]

To give the reader a feeling for Disney's marketing activities, I briefly outline some different kinds of marketing: movies and their fallout, WDW as a whole, and merchandise in the parks. To flesh out my description of the marketing of merchandise as a whole, I present some examples of the kinds of merchandising patterns found at Disney. In the next chapter I take a walk down Main Street USA, the merchandise center of Disney's great mall.

The major vehicle for Disney's transgenerational seductions is the animated feature film. Purloined and Disneyfied, the tales told in Disney's animations have become important icons of U.S. conservative postmodern culture. They are unique carriers of a powerful nostalgia parents often feel compelled to share with their children. Because Walt Disney had the prescience to retain control over the corporate film archives — even during the most difficult financial moments — Disney is able to orchestrate the rerelease of its classic films to maximum benefit.

Until recently, when home movie rentals changed the rules of the game and the interval was shortened somewhat, Disney practice had been to release a film every seven years. Walt Disney considered this the optimal interval. The films would not become stale through overexposure, and in seven years a sizable new cohort of children would have come of age to be incorporated into Disney's vast market. [9]

Prerelease and postrelease strategies are similar for both the rerelease of Disney classics and the marketing of new Disney, Touchstone, and Hollywood films. [10] Prior to a film's theatrical release, Disney employs its "unique 'Total Marketing' concepts" [11] to create countless impressions of the film for the viewing public. [12] Advertisements, books, games, puzzles, toys, and clothing based on the movie's characters are manufactured and put on sale. Comic book strips appear in newspapers. Songs and music, especially familiar songs from the animated classics, are sent to stores and radio stations. The radio stations at WDW announce the rereleases as promotions appear at the parks. Corporations with which Disney has commercial ties incorporate promotions into their own activities.

Disney's great advantage is that it has a presold audience, an audience generated in part by the integrated postrelease activities that followed the film the last time around. The film's various spinoffs — merchandised in their own right — point back to the films themselves, the parks, and the company as a whole in an endless round of self-referential coadvertisements.

For training purposes, Disney cites the example of *Snow White*. [13] The production of the film (first released in 1937) was merely the first step in the generation of Disney-Snow White products.

"Whistle While You Work," "Heigh Ho," "Some Day My Prince Will Come," "I'm Wishing," and all the other songs have sold millions of records over the years. Books, comics, games, toys and other merchandise based on

Snow White have sold millions of units. Millions of people have enjoyed the Disneyland attraction reliving Snow White's Adventures, and an untold multitude of people have marvelled at the ice shows and stage shows in which characters from Snow White have appeared around the world. This is the Disney Diversity in action. [14]

When we realize that every Disney commodity, large or small, enters into this kind of integrated marketing machine, we can see the enormous synergy that results from merchandise functioning simultaneously as commodity and advertisement.

Arching over all of these commodities — tying them together and constraining their form and content — is the model of what a Disney "product" ought to be. The Company's enormous success is based on what Disney people call "public trust" and what Pierre Bourdieu calls "symbolic capital." [15] For Bourdieu, symbolic capital consists of culturally appropriate intangibles — such as honor, integrity, age, esteem, trust, and goodwill — that may be gathered, stored, and used as tools to generate tangible capital. [16]

Disney is militantly aware that its existence depends on continually convincing the public that its product is unique and that its symbolic capital is earned and praiseworthy. [17] As any of its products, images, or interfaces with the public may potentially crack the façade, intense control is maintained over the quality of products, the use of trademarks, [18] and the on-site behavior of employees.

For Disney to perform as a central icon of the American way (and to generate revenue in doing so), the Company needs to mask its interest in control and in the strategic commercial use of its public trust. In the wonderfully shallow postmodern oxymoron, "the Disney business philosophies," [19] Disney translates its commercial needs into abstract cultural categories whose positive connotations will appeal to everybody. Thus, Disney does not offer materials and experiences that will make a profit but offers integrity, uniqueness, quality, wholesomeness, value, friendliness, timelessness, and universality. At the parks, where most people confront the Company face-to-face, these materials and experiences are offered by smiling people who, whatever their position in the Disney hierarchy, wear name tags that show only their first names. Bob and Sally are just like we wish the people back home were — informal, friendly, and helpful. Gee, what a nice bunch of folks! [20]

At the same time, we are convinced that we don't want to know what goes on behind the scenes. That would spoil the magic. For all of our curiosity, Disney has taught us to rein ourselves in voluntarily. If we want to see the Disney version of the back stage, let us go to the Studio Tour.

Marketing the Parks

One interesting twist on the "Disney-is-different" theme is found in the marketing of the theme parks. Until the arrival of Frank Wells and Michael Eisner in 1984, Disneyland and WDW stood outside the crass commercial fray because the Company did not advertise them in the "normal" way. The parks were not profaned by commercials; they were above that. [21]

Disney had relied traditionally on self-referential coadvertising and on word of mouth. [22] This practice allowed the company to get by with virtually no separate advertising budget. By the mid-1970s, Disney had invented what Thomas R. Elrod, director of marketing, called the "Tom Sawyer" approach to marketing: [23] Get the other guys to do it by convincing them that it's a good deal. Right through the opening of EPCOT Center, Disney piggy-backed on the promotions of its corporate associates — or "participants," as Disney calls them.

The first substantial example of the Tom Sawyer method began in 1975 with target marketing. [24] Developed in conjunction with Eastern Airlines, target marketing involved a promotion in which a local radio station in a targeted city ran a contest in which the winning prizes were all-expense-paid trips to WDW. These promotions included many of the following: a six-week radio blitz to acquaint the listening audience with WDW; use of a primary retail outlet (often Sears) as the only "point of entry" for the contest; [25] a visit to the city by Disney characters for a publicity kickoff and party; a declaration by the city's mayor of "Walt Disney week"; and showing Disney movies at local theaters. In such a campaign, Disney, Eastern Airlines, the local retail outlet, local movie theaters, the participating radio station, and the city government all promote themselves and each other.

As the opening of EPCOT Center approached, Tom Sawyerism expanded. In 1983 Thomas R. Elrod explained Disney's EPCOT campaign.

> We started with a very clear marketing objective. . . . Perhaps it was idealistic, but we decided that by opening day, October 1, 1982, we wanted every man, woman and child in the United States to have at least heard the word EPCOT; not necessarily to know what it was, but to have at least heard the name and to be able to associate it with Walt Disney World in Florida.
>
> And we wanted to do that . . . without spending any media dollars at all. [26]

What Disney did was rely on the independent promotions of the corporations — Kraft, GM, Eastern, and others — that had given a collective $300 million to Disney in order to associate themselves with Disney symbols and the Disney image. Elrod's EPCOT campaign culminated in a twenty-four-page magazine supplement jointly funded by Disney, Kodak, Eastern, Sperry Univac, Coca-Cola, American Express, Days Inn, and Sea World. [27] This advertisement ran in *Newsweek, Time, Life, People, Food & Wine,* and *Travel and Leisure,* and was carried in the seat pockets of Eastern planes throughout December 1982.

Although Disney spent few dollars on directly placed advertisements, Elrod reports that significant monies were spent to encourage editorial coverage. This has always been company practice — to elevate Disney above crass advertising by convincing the mass media to cover Disney events as news. [28] Press support, satellite uplinks, and especially the offer of free junkets have provided the Company with a massive stream of good press. [29] In recent years, Disney has changed its approach to advertising. Although continuing its use of print inserts and supplements, the Company has also greatly expanded its use of radio and television in getting its messages before the public. Because of Disney culture, including its need for control over symbolic information, these advertisements have been placed by Vista Advertising (an in-house arm of the creative support division) rather than by an exo-Disney company. [30] By 1986 Vista Advertising had become one of the largest in-house agencies in the United States.

Media blitzes have accompanied the accelerated openings of new Disney theme parks — the Disney-MGM Studios, Typhoon Lagoon, Pleasure Island [31] — as well as theater releases of new Touchstone and Hollywood pictures. In fact, there has been some critical backlash about the ubiquity and taste of Disney's marketing methods. Alice Hinkle complains that Disney ads suggest that family problems — often presented as the neglect of children caused by parental job harassment — will be solved by a trip to WDW. [32] Anyone who refuses this "obvious" solution deserves our opprobrium. Hinkle's comments are accompanied by a cartoon showing Mickey Mouse holding a sign that reads "Take a vacation . . . OR ELSE!"

More recently, others (including myself) have been driven nuts by what *The Nation* calls "Disney trippers." [33] These are the contest winners whose first public act after victory is to face the television camera and say, "I'm going to Disney World/land." Although this plague has been visited on us especially by sports figures, it has shown up elsewhere. Concerning the 1988 Miss America contest, *The Nation* reports Tom Elrod's explanation given on "CBS This Morning."

> Taking no chances, Disney contacted every Miss America contestant at the Atlantic City pageant last month and told each one that if she won, a producer and film crew would be on the runway ready to record her spontaneous answer to the question, "You've just been crowned Miss America. What are you going to do next?" All she had to do was answer with the magic words about the Magic Kingdom and she would awake, like Snow White after the prince's kiss, in a commercial. Two actually: one for Disney World, another for Disneyland. They were on the television networks less than twenty-four hours after the cameras rolled. [34]

The Nation's tongue-in-cheek response to this campaign was ambiguous, suggesting how difficult it is to think about Disney in black-and-white terms: "Regarding payment for the promotion, Elrod told his CBS host,

Harry Smith, that 'it's a lot less than you might think.' This is only just. It seems to us that only Scrooge McDuck would want serious money to shill for the Disney amusement havens." [35]

Disney Merchandising

Disney markets the company, the movies, and the parks; but it also sells merchandise. As noted in the previous chapter, the revenue from this merchandise is substantial. Here are some figures to remind us. From 1972 to 1981, merchandise sales at WDW more than tripled, increasing from $29.3 million to $121.5 million. [36] By 1978 visitors to WDW were spending more on merchandise than on food, and customer merchandise expenditures were approaching the figure for admissions and rides. In 1982 Suzy Hagstrom estimated WDW's annual sales per square foot at $784 — 5 1/2 times the $140 per square foot average at a shopping mall of comparative size. [37] With EPCOT open, the yearly sales figure rose to $178,791,000 for the fiscal year ending September 30, 1983. [38] "With those sales, they would either be the number four or number five department store chain in Florida behind Burdines, Jordan Marsh, Maas Brothers, and maybe JByrons." [39] By 1990 consumer products revenues had risen to $573.8 million. [40]

We need to ask three questions about this merchandising: What does Disney sell at WDW? How does Disney sell it? Where is it sold? I'll begin with the first question.

Disney sells an enormous range of items at WDW, from Magic Kingdom pencils and Mickey Mouse ears to hand-crafted swords from Spain and other items in the five-figure range. What has surprised many people is the quantity of retailing that is not specifically park-related. People buy not only logo tee-shirts, stuffed Figments, and collectibles but also kitchen items, crafts, flowers and plants, apparel, and designer fashions. [41] The Shopping Village and the resort hotels all contain stores with items easily available outside the parks. World Showcase is designed as an international mall, where nationally themed merchandise found by Disney buyers and specialties offered by foreign participating companies are part of the show.

A number of reasons might be suggested for this non-Disney buying at WDW. First, a good bit of retailing takes place at the Disney Village Marketplace, where area manager-buyer Raye McMullin estimated that 25 percent of the village customers are locals rather than tourists. [42] Such people are presumably doing normal shopping with a Disney kick. Second, as Gershman notes, many of the items sold at WDW are weather-related: hats, sunglasses, rain coats, umbrellas, shorts, tee-shirts, swim wear, and the like. [43] Disney merchandisers are continually delighted by visitors' lack of foresight.

Primarily, however, these purchases are the result of impulse. As Tony Schroeder, merchandise manager for WDW in 1981, told Lynn Trexler, "People don't come here to shop, but to be entertained. And they want to take home a piece of the show — be it mouse ears or something from the Contemporary Woman. We try to satisfy their desires — not their needs. People are more impulsive here." [44] As Gershman puts it, [45] "Once inside the Magic Kingdom, it is the grown-ups who relax, who drop their guards and become childlike. They buy everything in sight, shoving off much of it on their kids, wearing some of it and stashing some of it as gifts for others . . . the adults themselves lose control over not only the purse strings but their very sense of self. [46]

For all the designer swimsuits it sells, Disney's bread and butter is character merchandise. Whether sold in its parks or elsewhere, Disney character items are not produced by the company but are sold under the arrangement called licensed product merchandising (LPM). [47] Basically, through LPM Disney "rents" the character to a manufacturer for a fee. [48] Through short-term agreements to produce trademark items (usually for one year but sometimes even less), Disney licenses manufacturers to produce commodities that feature its characters, stories, and songs. [49] Because of Disney quality control interests, the company must continually approve each type of item before it leases its name. [50] For items sold at its parks, Disney receives not only its contracted royalties but also its own retailing mark up. [51] In 1982 Disney had agreements with 165 licensees, [52] a figure that has grown substantially since then. This merchandising does not include that done by the participating corporations whose presences grace the parks for a fee.

A good place to begin to see how Disney orchestrates its sales is in its 1982 EPCOT Center training manual, *Merchandise*. Here employees are introduced to what Disney calls "the merchandise experience." They are told that "Merchandise is an extension of the total guest experience. . . . Each of our guests will most likely want to take with them a memento, a representation of what EPCOT Center is. That's at the core of our merchandising philosophy. It ensures that the EPCOT Center Experience will be a lasting one." [53]

This merchandise is themed — presented as part of the show by being put into an appropriate setting. Thus, each outlet carries material associated with the attractions that surround it. [54] This is particularly true of the shops in World Showcase, which are filled with imported items chosen to depict national crafts and products representative of the various countries. One or two Disney buyers are assigned to each country and contract for all the various merchandise categories.

The store planning and production design unit is responsible for developing the merchandising environment. This includes not only setting a mood for a particular outlet but also planning stock rooms, counter and cash register space, merchandise mix, and traffic flow. All Disney shops are simulacra — shells covered both inside and out with symbolic architecture and design. World Showcase in particular fills each pavilion with a synthesis of design styles. As its *Merchandise* training manual states, "World Showcase represents what people would expect to find on their travels rather than what they actually will see in a given country's shops." [55]

Interior design — case lining, wall finishes, custom carpet, floor, drapery, and furniture styles and colors — is central. Interior materials must not only enhance the merchandise experience, but they must be durable and childproof. Sprinklers, air ducts, speakers, and functional lighting are camouflaged. Although functional lighting does the major illuminating, character lighting — kerosene lamps, chandeliers, and other "ideas of light" — plays to the store's theme.

Display design is also important. Window displays incorporate merchandise, fixtures, and props that both advertise commercial items and enhance — often whimsically — the "authenticity" of the store. Even bag design, which is separate for each theme park but complementary in color and form, is part of the show. "The better we are at presenting the merchandise in an entertaining way, the more we sell. That's what it boils down to. Most of our merchandise is theatrically staged to sell. The more different we are than anybody else, the more exciting it is for the customers, the more they want to buy." [56]

Clerks in themed costumes — called "hosts" and "hostesses" — are told that they are ambassadors of happiness, hope, optimism, and good will. They are expected to help "our audience . . . feel good about the merchandise experience, themselves and the future." [57] Part of this assistance, a stroke of marketing genius on Disney's part, is the package delivery service at EPCOT. [58] Customers can have their purchases from any shop in the park taken to a guest service storage area at the park entrance. Instead of lugging bags around, thus inhibiting further purchases (and purchases of large, ungainly items), visitors can pick up all their stuff at one time as they leave. Guest service employees make approximately hourly rounds to all the stores as they trundle the merchandise to the pickup site.

Sometimes, unfortunately, customers need a little spur to recharge themselves for what Hugh Dalziel Duncan calls "the drama of shopping." [59] *Florida Trend* reports that "at Disney World the piped-in music picks up gradually in the afternoon, just when people are starting to get tired, to try and stimulate a second wind." [60]

Imagining the piped-in music, we will soon take a tour of Main Street USA. First, however, I'd like briefly to describe a sample of different marketing endeavors — candy, flowers, Coca-Cola, and the Arribas Brothers glassblowing, cutting, and engraving business. I also make some preliminary remarks about Disney's relations with sponsoring corporations and other participating groups. I return to this topic in my later discussion of science and technology.

An article in *Candy Wholesaler* perfectly describes the Disney strategy of placing commodities in such a position that one has to buy something to participate in the show.

> You're in the middle of one of the most famous amusement resorts in the world. Everything around you is full of fun and fantasy. A castle straight out of a fairy tale beckons you onward. Characters you've known since childhood's cartoon-filled Saturday afternoons at the movies suddenly come to life and mingle with the hordes of visitors wandering from shop to show. You join them in a stroll down a street that would fit right into turn-of-the-century America and stop in at an old-fashioned confectionery shop for a snack . . . but what you buy is more than just another candy bar. You purchase a piece of the scenery, and become in the process an integral part of the production at Walt Disney World's Magic Kingdom in Orlando, Fla. [61]

Candy, thus, is not a convenience. It is part of the show, and we participate only through purchase. Candy is there, in part, to lend verisimilitude to the false-front real stores. It is both commodity and prop. Because the illusion would be spoiled if visitors could buy the same candy at WDW that they do in the supermarket back home, most candy is bought in bulk and packaged at the parks. [62] Mickey Mouse lollipops, Goofy Goof balls, and the like, are sold in twenty-one sales locations in the Magic Kingdom alone; but four sales areas in the Magic Kingdom are devoted primarily to candy.

Each of these, of course, is appropriately themed. Main Street USA, the shopping hub of the Magic Kingdom, has two candy stores — Main Street Confectionery, with its pink-and-white interior and a glassed-in work display that shows employees making peanut brittle, and Market House, a turn-of-the-century general store, with a pot-bellied stove and the only loose bulk candy counter in the Magic Kingdom.

In Fantasyland, just beyond Cinderella's Castle, is Royal Candy, a fairy-tale-like open stall with candy and some other Disney paraphernalia. Finally, a vendor dressed as a pirate works the wooden vendor's cart in Caribbean Plaza, selling boxed and bagged candies out of wooden boxes and barrels. [63]

Candy is meant to be consumed on the premises as a snack (along with popcorn and ice cream), but it is also meant to be taken home as a souvenir — a cleverly packaged part of the scenery. The bulk of it, therefore, is designed to be unmeltable.

After a bit of candy — or after a few hours of walking around in the Florida heat — people get thirsty. Coca-Cola is waiting for them. [64] Coke's-red-and white cups are everywhere (except on the ground). Although the only areas specifically sponsored by Coca-Cola are the Refreshment Center on Main Street and the American Adventure in World Showcase — cosponsored with American Express — Coke or its fellow corporate soft drinks (Diet Coke and Sprite) are sold at most of the food outlets at WDW.

In addition to the obvious fountain sales and the corporate goodwill leached from Disney's charisma, Coca-Cola gains in two other ways by its presence at the park. First, like the other big companies at WDW, Coca-Cola has access to the special guest relations services available through Disney's corporate communications department.[65] Customers, employees, and other guests of the Coca-Cola Company and its various U.S. and foreign subsidiaries are given the VIP treatment at the parks. This may include special itineraries, hotel and restaurant reservations (including prime tables at dinner shows), and deliveries of Coke to hotel rooms.

Second, WDW provides Coca-Cola with a testing ground for fountain dispensing systems. In particular, Tomorrowland Terrace at the Magic Kingdom has given Coke one of the highest-volume fountain locations in the world — with four fountain points, each with fourteen valves.[66] In conjunction with Disney, Coke developed a compressed-air pumping system powerful enough to pump syrup from fifty-four-gallon drums, thus eliminating the frequent changing of five-gallon containers.

A different and more indirect marketing pattern may be seen when we look at flowers and plants at WDW. Disney's retail operation is Walt Disney World Florist, set up in 1971 by Ray Budd initially as a floral service for Disney hotel guests.[67] By 1983 the operation — located then on the second floor of the Contemporary Resort Hotel (and in a corner under the Magic Kingdom) — had thirty employees to handle design, sales, delivery, and secretarial functions. By that time, Walt Disney World Florist was responsible for any perishable items retailed on the property, including fruit, wine, and cheese for gourmet baskets.

Many of the flower shop's customers are other Disney units. The gourmet baskets, for instance, are contracted in large batches by the WDW sales division for hotel convention guests. The largest client for flowers is the convention entertainment arm of the WDW entertainment division, which regularly requests themed flower centerpieces for banquet shows. Corporate VIP lounges, especially in Future World, and World Showcase restaurants are standing customers.

Walt Disney World Flowers serves two other groups. Day visitors purchase a significant number of plants — including topiaries — especially at the flower shop in the Marketplace. Many of these are shipped by Disney, some even direct from the nursery by Disney vendors. The largest group of customers, however, is Disney employees, who can benefit from economies of scale on a cash-and-carry basis. The WDW employee relations division also has a standing policy of delivering flower arrangements or dish gardens to any full-time company employee forced to spend time in a local hospital. Because employees live away from WDW, this service is subcontracted out to local florists.

Walt Disney World Florist gets its flowers from a number of sources. Some are flown in from California; some come from South America and Holland. Most, however, come from local wholesalers — especially those a few miles up the road at Apopka, home of the Florida Foliage Association and self-dubbed "indoor foliage capital of the world." Ray Budd says, "Give the visitor something he can't get elsewhere. This may include alstroemeria, tulips, daffodils, larkspur, gerbera daisies, freesia, or whatever. We want our guests to leave here feeling they got good value for their money and not feeling ripped off in any way, shape or form." [68]

My fourth example concerns retailing by one of the few companies that is a lessee rather than merely a participant. The Arribas Brothers operate a number of glassblowing, cutting, and engraving outlets scattered throughout the parks. [69] They staff and operate these outlets themselves, paying Disney a percentage of their gross revenues. Having started with Disney in 1967 at Disneyland, the Arribas Brothers followed the company to Florida and on to Tokyo Disneyland.

The Arribas family was originally from La Coruna, Spain, but migrated to the United States in the early 1960s. In 1983, thirty-one family members were employed in the Disney enterprise. Although the Disney parks are their only retail outlets, they have ridden the coattails well. In 1967, their gross sales were $220,000; by 1983, annual gross sales had risen to over $5 million. Sold at Crystal Arts on Main Street, La Princessa de Crystal in Caribbean Plaza, Artesanias Mexicanas in World Showcase, and Crystal Arts and EUROSPAIN at the Disney Village Marketplace, Arribas Brothers' products come from their own plants and artisans as well as from other European and U.S. companies. Each Disney outlet features glassblowing and carving demonstrations, and one can purchase just-cooled flamingos, palm trees, and drinking mugs with Uncle Pat's name carved on them.

Candy, Coca-Cola, flowers, and glassblowing — we will find all of these on Main Street USA, but throughout WDW we see many more corporate products and corporate logos. Before we head for Main Street, I present a partial list of participants and sponsors at WDW (I do not include here the many companies associated with World Showcase): American Express Company; American Telephone and Telegraph Company; Arribas Brothers; The Coca-Cola Company; Colombian Coffee Growers; Coppertone; Del Monte Corporation; Delta Airlines; Dole; Eastman Kodak Company; Edison Electric Institute; Elgin National Industries, Inc. (Bradley Time Division); Exxon Corporation; Fleetwood Enterprises, Inc.; Florida Citrus Commission; Frito-Lay, Inc.; Gaines Foods, Inc.; General Electric Company; General Motors Corporation; Gerber Products Company; Gibson Greeting Cards, Inc.; The Goodyear Tire and Rubber Company;

Greyhound Lines, Inc.; Hallmark Cards, Inc.; Hormel; Hunt-Wesson Foods (Orville Redenbacher popping corn); The J. M. Smucker Company; Kikkoman International, Inc.; Kitchens of Sara Lee; Kraft; Lever Brothers Company (Mrs. Butterworth's syrup); Lorus Watches; M & Ms; McDonnell Douglas Corporation; Monsanto Company; National Car Rental; Nestlé (including Toll House cookies); Oscar Meyer and Company, Inc.; Polaroid Corporation; RCA Corporation; Rubio Artists Company; Sealtest Ice Cream; See's Candies; SONY; Sperry Univac (now UNISYS); Sun Banks of Florida, Inc.; Tenneco West (Sun Giant products); United Technologies; Western Publishing, Inc.; and Wise Foods.

Now we're ready for Main Street USA.

9

The Price Is Right: Main Street USA and Hollywood Boulevard

While there are many "carrots" at Disney World, there is only one exit. At the end of a long day, everybody files past Main Street USA.

—Florida Trend [1]

Main Street USA

Heading toward shore on the ferry boat from the Ticket and Transportation Center (TTC) or gliding into the Magic Kingdom station on the monorail, the visitor faces the second-most-important visual marker at the Magic Kingdom.[2] The red brick Victorian train station for the Walt Disney World Railroad — maybe with a train tooting to exchange passengers — rises up over the entrance gates and the two tunnels that lead into the park.

In front of the station, sloping down from the tracks, is the head of Mickey Mouse, planted in bright flowers and surrounded by green grass. On the station walls — under the gray shingled roof with its grill work, clock, flagpole, and weathervane — are signs that indicate the name of the place (The Magic Kingdom), the population, and the elevation.

The WDW Railroad consists of four Baldwin diesel fuel-burning steam locomotives acquired from the United Railways of Yucatan in 1969 and rebuilt at the Tampa shipyards.[3] Each engine pulls a set of open bench cars modeled after Narraganset-type street cars. The railway makes a mile-and-a-half clockwise loop — stopping at the Main Street Station, Frontierland, and Mickey's Starland — and defines the perimeter of the Magic Kingdom. The red locomotives are named the Roy O. Disney, the Walter E. Disney, the Roger E. Broggie,[4] and the Lilly Belle.[5]

Main Street USA — a fantasy, fairy-tale version of a U.S. town at the end of the nineteenth century — sets the tone for the Magic Kingdom. It is the funnel through which everyone must pass to get in and to get out. Thus, it carries a metasymbolic burden, not only serving itself but also bringing visitors into the appropriate conceptual and emotional orientations.

The idea of the small town has come to function in U.S. culture as the home of nostalgia for a pre-urban Anglo-America. It is the place where harrassed people in a dangerous, impersonal, and unfriendly world can symbolically locate friendship, order, intimacy, innocence. As Richard V. Francaviglia puts it,

> The small town . . . is a repository of American longings. When translated into the realm of popular culture, it becomes one of the most significant symbols of the American ethos. It is tied to sacred icons which simplify and symbolize behavior and institutional structure, e.g., the virginal white kiosk where patriotic oratory flows out across a village green under the American flag, surrounded by town hall and the familiar façades of Main Street storefronts.[6]

But real main streets circa 1880-1910 were pretty messy. They were unpaved, muddy, or dusty, depending on the weather. Commercial buildings covered with signs and advertisements were built right out to the street. If anything lined the sidewalks, it was bare, functional telegraph poles rather than the leafy elms we carry in our imaginations.

This was not the small town Walt Disney chose to remember. His version — first at Disneyland and then at WDW — was a romanticized, idealized, architecturally controlled main street with no "other side of the tracks." There would be only pleasant buildings here — an ice cream parlor, an apothecary shop, a theater, a candy store.

Whether or not he based this concept on his boyhood home of Marcelline, Missouri, Walt took a more direct hand in designing Main Street USA than he did any other parts of his parks. His favorite spot in Disneyland was his small apartment over the Town Square fire station, from which he could watch visitors' reactions when they first saw Town Square.[7]

Disney's Main Street is a pedestrian's environment. All but novelty vehicles are banned from the street. The buildings are covered with busy Victorian façades, more consistently so than in the actual midwestern towns of the time. With its wrought iron, bay windows, imitation gaslights, pastels, Main Street USA is "picture-pretty."[8]

The space is shaped like a dog bone,[9] with Main Street USA itself forming the connection between Town Square and the bulbous Plaza-Hub. Behind the Plaza is Cinderella's Castle, the visual magnet that draws visitors down Main Street USA and deeper into the Magic Kingdom.

Town Square bustles with activity. [10] Past the old-fashioned red popcorn cart at the entrance, we see a town green with benches, leafy trees, lawns, and flowers bordered by iron grillwork and a flag pole — all surrounded by a square of pavement. This is the turnaround loop for the novelty vehicles and horse-drawn carriage that takes visitors to the Hub. In the morning, the Walt Disney World Marching Band might give a concert on the green. At the end of the afternoon, the Flag Retreat takes place — complete with small band, color guard, and white homing pigeons (heading for their loft behind Cinderella's Castle).

1890-1910 was a time when towns in the United States blossomed, towns based on burgeoning technology — the telegraph, electricity, mechanical horsepower — and on a kind of standardization of style. Town Square and Main Street USA are a fantasy distillation of this style, which Francaviglia calls "an architectural overstatement." [11]

Surrounding Town Square are buildings that represent some of the key institutions of U.S. life — a city hall, a bank, a railroad station, an emporium. [12] These institutions introduce the visitor to the liminal timelessness of the Magic Kingdom, because in this transition zone, they all perform some version of the function they would have performed at the turn of the century.

At the southwest corner of Town Square is the red brick Sun Bank, which provides check cashing, cash advances on credit cards, and foreign currency-changing services. Just north of the bank is City Hall. Built right on the square, this yellow brick building — with its white portico and trim, balcony, cupola, and clock, [13] — has the most intricate façade on the square. At the first floor counter, visitors can get general information about the Magic Kingdom as well as weekly schedules of live entertainment throughout the park. The lost-and-found department is here in City Hall, as are Walt Disney Merchandise mail order catalogs. [14]

Beyond a courtyard that leads to public restrooms, in the northwest corner, is the firehouse of Engine Company 71. [15] This red brick building, with its bell tower and campanile, contains a small late-nineteenth-century firehouse exhibit, which includes the fire engine passenger vehicle when it is not in use. Just beyond the firehouse, at the very corner of the square, is the gate through which the daily character parade begins its march through the Magic Kingdom.

On the east side of Town Square — to the right as we come through the train station tunnels — are the Hospitality House and the Town Square Café. The former houses Walt Disney and Disney Studio memorabilia. There are Oscars, photographs, paintings, letters, posters, and explanations of major Disney projects, such as the nature films and the making of *Fantasia*. Here is Disneyana Collectibles, selling what it says. Here also are two 260-seat theaters showing *The Walt Disney Story*. This twenty-three-minute movie tells the standard company story of Walt's journey from Marcelline to Orlando. Much of it is narrated by Walt Disney himself.

The film includes such clips as Walt's television announcement of the EPCOT Project and Walt riding around in his backyard train. From time to time, *The Walt Disney Story* is preempted by WDW specials, such as previews of the Studio Tour. This out-of-the-way, well air-conditioned theater is often nearly empty. The hosts and hostesses, who don't have too much to do, are especially solicitous. It's a good place to go on a hot afternoon. [16]

On the northeast corner of the square sits Tony's Town Square Café, with its logo picture of Lady and the Tramp. This table-service restaurant, with an outdoor terazzo-tiled patio, is full of curlicued woodwork and polished brass. It is supposed to be reminiscent of New Orleans. [17]

Looking down Main Street at night toward Cinderella's Castle and its towering spires, we see a panorama of light. Here are the twinkle of lights in the trees of the Plaza in the distance, the fake gaslights, the marquees, and most of all the lights that outline the roofs and balconies on both sides of Main Street. This is not quite like Copenhagen's Tivoli Gardens — an original inspiration for Disney's park-building activity — because here all the lights are white, outlining the Victorian filigree without multicolor distraction. [18]

Main Street proper contains four buildings, each with multiple façades. Each structure is divided internally into different shops, all internally connected. At the west corner of Town Square and Main Street is the Emporium, another landmark Disney building. Faced in pink brick, with its overhanging roof and cupola at the corner buttressed by pairs of very skinny columns, the Emporium is the biggest store on Main Street. Here we find display after display of Disney character mementos, toys, clothing, books, records, and decorative gifts. Main Street is open one hour earlier than the rest of the Magic Kingdom and stays open one hour later. At the end of the day, the Emporium is packed with visitors in shopping frenzy.

At the north end of the Emporium is one of the two side streets that make Main Street seem longer than it really is. Here is the flower market, packed with colorful blossoms, both real and silk. A favorite picture spot, the flower market contains benches, flower wagons, and other props for photographic poses. The façades in this cul-de-sac are narrow and of different styles and are painted with different, contrasting colors. This gives the illusion that lots is going on here — far more activity and variety than the space might normally warrant. Flowers can be bought here at the Greenhouse — silk ones to be stored in the lockers under the train station or real ones (and topiaries) to be sent to the kennel at the TTC where a plant-sitter will take care of them until they are retrieved. [19]

In the Emporium building, facing the back end of the flower market, is the Harmony Barber Shop. In that old-fashioned setting, one can actually get a shave and a haircut as well as buy nostalgic shaving items such as mustache cups. Here also is where the Dapper Dans, an old-time barber-shop quartet, retreat after their periodic concerts out on Main Street.

North of this side street is another building that contains three shops, a snack bar, and the penny arcade. Disney Clothiers, Ltd., sells character fashions and accessories in a more relaxed and upscale way than does the Emporium. The dark House of Magic provides what it says — magic tricks, puzzles, books, gag items, and monster masks. Main Street Bookstore, presented by Western Publishing Company, sells cards and stationery. At the corner is Coca-Cola's red-and-white Refreshment Corner, with hot dogs, Cokes, and coffee. The Refreshment Corner's sidewalk tables and awnings spread out into the Plaza, where customers are entertained by a costumed pianist playing ragtime and other piano tunes on the upright piano on the porch.

Semicircling around the Refreshment Corner is the Penny Arcade. This space contains both modern electronic games and a number of authentic antiques, including strength tests and a Kiss-O-Meter. Of special interest is a set of early Mute-o-scopes and Cail-o-scopes — moving pictures made up of stacks of pictures on a roller that can be turned to flip the pictures and animate the stories. [20]

West of the Refreshment Center (on the way to Adventureland), with entrances on the Plaza rather than on Main Street proper, are the Magic Kingdom Baby Center, the First Aid Center, and the Crystal Palace. Staffed by a registered nurse, the First Aid Center can deal with minor emergencies — the most common of which, according to Steve Birnbaum, is sunburn. [21]

The Baby Care Center exemplifies Disney's utopian attention to detail and to the needs of some of its visitors; here (and at the EPCOT Baby Care Center) are feeding rooms, high chairs, and facilities for warming bottles and changing diapers. Baby paraphernalia, formula, pacifiers, and baby food (Gerber's) are on sale here. There are also special name tags for children — to wear in case one gets lost — and a lost children's logbook, where parents can check with Disney employees to see if a lost child has been found (and is being entertained) elsewhere in the park. [22]

Behind the flower-bedecked sidewalks, facing the Plaza and the bridge to Adventureland is the Crystal Palace. This cafeteria (sponsored by the Colombian Coffee Growers) is the essence of Disney Victoriana. Modeled after a number of similar buildings, one of which still stands in San Francisco's Golden Gate Park, the Crystal Palace gestures especially to Joseph Paxton's Hyde Park building built for London's 1851 Crystal Palace Exhibition. With its gaslights, indoor palms, decorative grillwork, white wickerwork and glass dome, the Crystal Palace is reminiscent of exotic late-nineteenth-century European herbaria and other indoor gardens.

At the northeast end of Main Street, on the way to Tomorrowland's Plaza Pavilion, is the Plaza Restaurant. Like the Refreshment Corner across the street, this table-service restaurant has an outdoor patio, including a space between the sidewalk and the canal that flows around the Plaza. This patio overlooked the loading dock for the Swan Boats when they were still in operation.

Turning back up Main Street toward Town Square, we find on our left (or east) Sealtest's Plaza Ice Cream Parlor and the Main Street Bake Shop. Heading toward Center Street, we pass the Shadow Box, where employees of Rubio Artists create and frame silhouettes while we wait, and the Arribas Brothers' Crystal Arts.

The cul-de-sac on this side of Main Street is a bit less busy than the flower market across the way. Perhaps this is because the mobs from the Emporium do not flow into it. The dark Main Street Market House, with its pegged oak floors and wood paneling, offers pipe and tobacco products and candy along with its other gifts. In the courtyard is the Main Street Hot Dog Wagon and, further on, the entrance to Disney & Co., a logo-merchandise store.

The final — southeast — quadrant of Main Street contains four stores and the Main Street Cinema. From north to south these include Uptown Jewelers (jewelry, Hummel figurines and other china, clocks, and Lorus watches), the cinema, the pink-and-white Main Street Confectionery (See's Candies) — where "cast members" make candy behind a big picture window — the Kodak Camera Center, and the Chapeau. The Camera Center sells (and processes) film, cameras, and video accessories. It also rents cameras and Camcorders by the day for a small charge (and a large deposit). In a corner of the shop, visitors can put on Victorian costumes and have souvenir pictures taken on the faked rear end of a nineteenth-century caboose. The Chapeau, which faces Town Square Café, sells hats and Mouseketeer ears — the latter available for monogramming.

Main Street Cinema is an air-conditioned heaven. Often quite empty, this is a place to cool off and relax in front of six small movie screens that show Disney cartoons and other classic films of the silent screen era. The featured film is *Steamboat Willie*, Mickey Mouse's 1928 film debut.

To enter Town Square and walk the springy asphalt of Main Street is to enter a cinematic Disney street scene complete with balloons, popcorn vendors, a barber shop quartet, and the various vehicles that loop around the dog bone. Birnbaum claims that with all the activity going on, the merchandise to see, and the detail to notice,[23] the average visitor takes forty minutes to get from one end of Main Street to the other.[24]

Among the strange payoffs of slow travel are taking in the names and titles painted on the second-story windows. These commemorate many of the people involved in producing the Magic Kingdom, blending names and whimsical titles to form a who's who of Main Street.

Over the Shadow Box is

**The Original
Dick Nunis
Gym
Night Manager**

Elsewhere we see:

**Sailmaker & Sailing Lessons
Roy E. Disney**

*

**Dr. Card Walker
Licensed Psychiatrist and Justice of the Peace**

*

the Pseudonym Real Estate Dev. co. [25]	**Roy Davis President Bob Price Vice-President Bob Foster Travel Rep.**

*

**Iwerks-Iwerks
Stereoscopes
Cameras**

*

**Buena Vista
Magic Lantern Slides**

*

Burbank House of Graphics

*

M. T. Lott Real Estate Investments "A Friend in Deeds Is a Friend Indeed" Donn Tatum President	**Auditors & Bookkeepers Legal Associates Props & Scenic Backdrops**

The colorful if inefficient vehicles include a horseless carriage, a jitney, an omnibus, a fire engine, and a horse-drawn trolley. The latter is pulled by plastic-shod Belgian and Percheron draft horses, which work two or three hours a day, three or four days a week. [26] The rest of the time the horses may be seen in the horse barn at Fort Wilderness.

Although Main Street is the main mall — the inescapable funnel — many other clusters of stores are spread throughout WDW. Adventureland has two clusters — Adventureland Bazaar (six shops) and Caribbean Plaza (six shops). Frontierland has six shops. Fantasyland and Liberty Square have eight each. Tomorrowland, with a paltry four stores, is the most commercially undeveloped section of the Magic Kingdom — perhaps signifying that in the future we will all shop by mail and through television catalogs.

As we see in Chapter 12, World Showcase is also designed as a multi-themed mall, with each pavilion dressed in culturally appropriate retail ventures. In Disney eyes authenticity is to be found in shopping, the central travel experience. History, architecture, and culture are meant to be costumes, to dress up the show. [27]

The largest shop in EPCOT Center, however, is in Future World. Here Centorium (Central Emporium, perhaps?) covers half a building in Communicore East, with EPCOT and Disney character memorabilia as well as state-of-the-art electronic items on the second-floor balcony.

Hollywood Boulevard

At the Disney-MGM Studios, most of the stores are clustered on Hollywood Boulevard. [28] Leading from Crossroads of the World to the Chinese Theater, Hollywood Boulevard is an echo of Main Street USA. But rather than McKinley-era America, Hollywood Boulevard takes us from the art deco of the 1930s to the Populuxe [29] of the 1950s. Here are tall, skinny palm trees rather than the leaves of Main Street. Here also are characters — the newsboy, the actress, the director, talent scouts, gossip columnists, the young would-be movie star with her cardboard suitcase — wandering about, interacting with visitors and giving the boulevard a fake verisimilitude.

Behind the entrance plaza, with its aqua-and-white lighting, is a California variation of Town Square. [30] No lawn here, with its benches and trees; no city hall, bank, or fire station. This is a world of different dreams. This square is paved. In the middle — forming the central sight line with the Chinese Theater — is Crossroads of the World, with its vertical white poles supporting a silver globe with Mickey on top. Crossroads of the World sells souvenirs, rain gear, sundries, and sunglasses and also dispenses information and guide books.

To the left of Crossroads of the World, instead of City Hall and the bank, is Hollywood Boulevard's own strange equivalent — Sid Cahuenga's ONE-OF-A-KIND. The only "original" house left on the boulevard, Sid's (with Sid and a friend sometimes sitting on the front porch) now sells Hollywood collectibles — movie posters, antiques, and curios. Colored lights edge the roof of this open wooden bungalo, the only pre-art deco Hollywood building around. Next to Sid's is one of those signs that shows the distance from Hollywood to a number of U.S. cities. [31]

Across the square is Oscar's Classic Car Souvenirs, a 1930s gas station with red pumps showing Mohave Oil Company gas for 34 cents a gallon. [32] Along with selling car souvenirs, gag license plates, and the like, the gas station also fronts for Oscar's Super Service, where strollers and wheelchairs can be rented and infant products and lockers are available.

Although City Hall has been replaced by Sid Cahuenga's and the Hospitality House by Oscar's, Town Square's Emporium is reincarnated as Mickey's of Hollywood, and the Camera Center, on the same corner as it is on Main Street, is now the Darkroom. We have moved some forty years from Walt Disney's Main Street to Michael's Hollywood Boulevard. Except for the Emporium — and the timeless metastatement of the camera store — the civic institutions of late-nineteenth-century township America have been replaced by a curio shop and a gas station, the town flag pole and bandstand by a newspaper kiosk. The weighty impersonality of these institutions has flattened out into the simulated informality of the first name — Sid's, Oscar's, Mickey's. We have entered the new world of pretend equality and "intimate strangers" [33] brought by the movies, radio, and television.

The theme of Hollywood Boulevard, as it is elsewhere at the Disney-MGM Studios, is fame. It is Andy Warhol-land, where for a small price, everybody can take home a marker of public celebrity. The crowd may be small, but we each get our fifteen minutes.

The boulevard has three venues where we can splice our talents into carefully controlled scripts and take away the results for posterity. At Cover Story we can have our picture taken and dubbed onto the cover of a national mass circulation magazine. Just up the street, past Celebrity 5 & 10 (clothes, posters, jewelry) and the candies of Sweet Success, is Calling Dick Tracy (née Pacific Electric Pictures). Talent scouts fish the street, looking for wannabes (or friends to volunteer them) to "star" in their own home video version of a Hollywood movie. In front of the crowds that wander in and out of the building, customers read their lines on one of the stage sets. For a price, they take the tapes home to document what might have been.

The third celebrity activity requires some talent. Across the Boulevard from Pacific Electric Pictures is Sights and Sounds, where visitors can record their own music videos. The playlists available — in pop, standard, and country — are inoffensive enough that many visitors won't recognize (and thus know the words to) many of the tunes. But if you *do* know the words, you can record in a ministudio with windows that face the street and your image on overhead TV monitors.

Lakeside News (comic books) and Keystone Clothiers share the building with Sights and Sounds. They open out onto Echo Park and face Echo Lake. Behind Mickey of Hollywood's, also facing Echo Lake, is the Hollywood and Vine Restaurant. This 1930s art deco cafeteria — with its huge stylized maps of greater Hollywood — serves salads, sandwiches, seafood, steaks, and ribs.

Beyond Pacific Electric Pictures and the Theater of the Stars (stage show — currently offering both a history of movie music and *Dick Tracy* musical revue) are Starring Rolls (muffins, cookies, pastries, and coffee) and the Hollywood Brown Derby. This copy of the Los Angeles original — complete with brown derby roof facade — is the most elegant restaurant at the park. The walls of the foyer and the balcony that surround the sunken central room are covered with copies of the original Brown Derby star caricatures.

The Plaza at the end of Hollywood Boulevard is very different from the Plaza at the Magic Kingdom. Like Crossroads Square, it is mostly concrete pavement. The few trees only vaguely frame the entrance to the Chinese Theater and the Great Movie Ride.

The Mall Register

Before we leave the political economy of WDW, it is appropriate to take one more look at the collective Disney shopping experience. Thus, in Table 9.1 I present a list of stores at WDW as of summer 1991. This does not include restaurants, which I discuss in Chapter 18.

Table 9.1 Walt Disney World Shops (Summer, 1991)

MAGIC KINGDOM (55)
Main Street USA (16)

Newsstand	Kodak Camera Center
Emporium	Main Street Confectionery
Harmony Barber Shop	Uptown Jewelers
Disney Clothiers	Ltd.
House of Magic	Main Street Market House
Main Street Bookstores	The Shadow Box
The Chapeau	Crystal Arts
The Greenhouse	Disneyana Collectibles

Adventureland (12)

    Adventureland Bazaar (6)
    Zanzibar Shell Company
    Elephant Tales
    Traders of Timbuctu
    Tiki Tropic Shop
    Colonel Hathi's Safari Club
    Bwana Bob's

Caribbean Plaza (6)
House of Treasure
The Golden Galleon
Plaza del Sol Caribe
Lafitte's Portrait Deck
La Princesa de Crystal
Crow's Nest

Frontierland (6)

    Frontierland Trading Post
    Tricornered Hat Shoppe
    Frontier Woodcarving

Bearly Country
Big Al's
Brier Patch

Liberty Square (8)

    Olde World Antiques
    Silversmith
    Heritage House
    The Courtyard

Ichabod's Landing
The Yankee Trader
Silhouette Cart
Parasol Cart

Fantasyland (8)

    The Mad Hatter
    Tinkerbell Toy Shop
    The King's Gallery
    Mickey's Christmas Carol

The AristoCats
Royal Candy Shoppe
Kodak Kiosk
Nemo's Niche

Tomorrowland (5)

    Mickey's Mart
    Skyway Station Shop
    Film and Glow Kiosk

The Space Port
Space Place

EPCOT CENTER (65)
Future World (9)
    Entrance Plaza Gift Shop

    Gateway Gifts

    Camera Center,
    Centorium
    The Living Sea Shop

Communicore West Shop (at the
    Robot Show)
Cameras and Film (Journey (into
    Imagination)

Broccoli and Co. (The Land)
Well and Goods Limited (Wonders
    of Life)

World Showcase (56)
  World Showcase Lagoon (2)
  Disney Traders   Port of Entry

Mexico (4)
  Plaza de Los Amigos   La Familia Fashions
  Artesanias Mexicanas   El Ranchito del Norte

Norway (1)
  The Puffin's Roost

China (1)
  Yong Feng Shangdian

Germany (9)
  Sussigkeiten   Volkskunst
  Weinkeller   Der Bücherwurm
  Glas und Porzellan   Der Teddybar
  Die Weinachts Ecke   Kunstarbeit in Kristall
  Germany Cart

Italy (5)
  Delizie Italiane   Il Bel Cristallo
  La Gemma Elegante   La Bottega Italiana
  Italy Cart

The American Adventure (3)
  Heritage Manor Gifts   Hammered Dulcimer Cart
  American Adventure Cart

Japan (2)
  Mitsukoshi Department Store   Mitsukoshi Kiosk

Morocco (8)
  Casablanca Carpets   Tangier Traders
  Jewels of the Sahara   The Brass Bazaar
  Fashions from Fez   Medina Arts
  Marketplace in the Medina   Berber Oasis

France (8)
Plume et Palette
Tout Pour Le Gourmet
Guerlain Boutique
La Signature

La Maison du Vin
Galerie des Halles
Art Fest
France Cart

International Gateway (2)
Showcase Gifts

World Traveler

United Kingdom (7)
The Tea Caddy
The Magic of Wales
The Queen's Table
Pringle of Scotland

Lords and Ladies
The Toy Soldier
U.K. Cart

Canada (4)
Northwest Mercantile
The Trading Post

Wood Cart
La Boutique des Provinces

DISNEY-MGM STUDIOS (22)
Hollywood Boulevard (13)
Oscar's Classic Car Souvenirs
Sid Cahuenga's ONE-OF-A-KIND
Crossroads of the World
Movieland Memorabilia
Mickey's of Hollywood
Keystone Clothiers
The Darkroom

Cover Story
Celebrity 5 & 10
Lakeside News
Sweet Success
Calling Dick Tracy
Sights and Sounds

Lakeside Circle (1)
Golden Age Souvenirs

Backlot Annex (3)
Indiana Jones Adventure Outpost
Endor Vendors

Indiana Jones Cart

Backstage Studio Tour (4)
The Disney Studio Store
The Muppet Store

The Loony Bin
Fototoons

Animation Tour (1)
   Animation Gallery

HOTELS (29)
Fort Wilderness (2)
   Meadow Trading Post

Settlement Trading Post

Contemporary Resort (6)
   Fantasia Shop
   Concourse Sundries and Spirits
   Contemporary Woman

Contemporary Man
Kingdom Jewels
Bay View Gifts

Polynesian Village Resort (7)
   News from Civilization
   Crusoe and Son
   Polynesian Princess
   Kanaka Kids

Outrigger's Cove
Trader Jack's Grog Hut
Village Gifts and Sundries

Grand Floridian Beach Resort (4)
   Summer Lace
   Sandy Cove

Commander Porter's
M Mouse Mercantile

Disney Inn (2)
   The Pro Shop

Gifts and Sundries

Swan (1)
   Disney Cabanas

Dolphin (4)
   Daisy's Garden
   Brittany Jewel

Indulgences
Signatures of Fashion

Beach Club (1)
   Atlantic Wear and Wardrobe
      Emporium

Yacht Club (1)
   Fittings and Fairings Clothes and
      Notions

Caribbean Beach Resort (1)

Calypso Trading Post (at Old Port Royale)

DISNEY VILLAGE MARKETPLACE (20)

Mickey's Character Shop

Mickey and Co.

You and Me Kid

Christmas Chalet

Personal Message

Crystal Arts

Great Southern Country Craft Co.

Lillie Langtry's Old-Fashioned Photo Studio

EUROSPAIN

Sir Edward's Haberdasher

Conched Out

Candy Shoppe

Board Stiff

Country Address

Resort Wear Unlimited

24 KT Precious Adornments

Team Mickey's Athletic Club

Village Spirits

Windjammer Deck Shop

Gourmet Pantry

TYPHOON LAGOON (2)

Hammerhead Fred's Dive Shop

Singapore Sal's Saleable Salvage

PLEASURE ISLAND (11)

Avigator's

The Island Depot

Hammer and Fire

YesterEars

Suspended Animation

SuperStar Studios

The Mouse House

Changing Attitudes

Doodles

D-Zertz

Front Page

10

The Grounds: Spatial Infrastructure

If you are driving northeast on Interstate 4 toward Orlando and are momentarily inattentive to highway exit signs, you can drive through a fair portion of Walt Disney World without knowing it. The highway is flanked by everglades scrub and forest, part of which is included in the Walt Disney World conservation area.

If you *are* attentive and exit at State Road 192, the overhead signs will direct you to the multilane highway into the woods toward the Magic Kingdom. Just beyond the first big bend of this well-manicured highway is a roadside sign directing you to turn to 1190 AM on your radio dial for Walt Disney World information.

From a small transmitter hidden in the woods, the day's operating hours for the Magic Kingdom, EPCOT Center, and the Disney-MGM Studios; parking and ticket information; special event announcements; and ads for Disney motion picture rereleases are broadcast in continuous loops, with cycles calibrated to the average speed of automobiles on the entrance road. You are still about five miles away from the Magic Kingdom parking lot and maybe seven miles from Cinderella's Castle, but you are already in Disney's hands.

The pure numbers are important in understanding the scope of Walt Disney World: 27,433 acres — 43 square miles — is about the size of San Francisco and twice as big as Manhattan.[1] This is a lot of land for a corporation to own east of the Mississippi. Yet I think an appreciation of the immensity of Disney's holdings — although by no means total comprehension — is best had by those who have seen Disneyland in California. There is no seven-mile entry road in Anaheim. There are no woods in Disneyland, no radio stations, no Seven Seas Lagoon. When you park your car, you're there. There's no EPCOT Center or River Country, no Golf Resort or Disney Village Marketplace — certainly no Discovery Island or experimental farm.

As we have seen, the purchase of this Florida land and the strategy by which it was effected were undertaken while Walt Disney was still alive. It is clear that control over such a vast territory would obviate the problem of unorganized development in the immediate environs of whatever themed areas the company might construct. Thus, Walt and his successors would not have to look at the kinds of commercial developments that surround Disneyland either as eyesores or as profit-making operations out of their purview. The areas outside the boundaries of Walt Disney World have fed significantly from the Disney enterprise, but the corporation has maintained a significantly larger handle on hotel and restaurant revenues than it has in Anaheim.

Although aesthetics and the protection of Disney symbolic capital may be easily connected with corporate profits, there is another strain of thinking that provided a powerful impetus for the development of Walt Disney World. It was also conceived as a utopian model of microregional planning. Many analysts have written, pro and con, about the utopian form of Disney's urban planning; but they generally have focused on design elements within the Magic Kingdom and EPCOT Center. I wish to situate the theme parks in the larger context of Disney's 27,433 acres. Many of the responses visitors and critics have to Walt Disney World assume a brilliantly constructed spatial infrastructure.

When Walt Disney Productions won the political battle in the Florida legislature that resulted in the designation of the land as the Reedy Creek Improvement District, the way was opened for an extraordinary transformation of central Florida swamp and scrub. The logistics were staggering, and the speed and coordination with which they were carried out required planning and organization much like the ideal type of Louis Mumford's "megamachine."

Mumford invented the notion of the megamachine to describe large work forces that are differentiated in function and coordinated to perform massive tasks. "To call these collective entities machines is no play on words. If a machine be defined . . . as a combination of resistant parts, each specialized in function, operating under human control, to transmit motion and to perform work, then the labor machine was a real machine."[2]

Mumford's earliest example of the megamachine was the work force that built the Great Pyramid of Cheops at Giza. He argues that such immense task forces have been resuscitated in the twentieth century through the techniques of modern management. The building of Walt Disney World seems to be an example. In passing, note that the Mexico Showcase in EPCOT Center contains two partial pyramids, as does Future World's Journey into Imagination.[3]

The first major planning problem for the corporation concerned the ecology of the land it had purchased. The area was defined by two existing drainage channels — Reedy Creek and Bonnet Creek — with a ridge of high ground between them.[4] Whereas Bonnet Creek emptied into Bay Lake, Reedy Creek ended in a sizable swamp. Throughout the entire area, the water table rested right at (or very near to) the land surface.

Much of this land — 75 percent, according to Peter Blake — was normally under water during the central Florida summer. At best, during the dry season, a quarter of the land would be inundated. Around 7,500 acres of the property, including the wettest land, were set aside as a conservation area. Much of the rest was transformed by the construction of a technologically sophisticated drainage system designed "to keep three-fourths of WDW dry, year round, without unduly lowering the water table and thus adversely affecting the total ecology of the area."[5]

The original plan, which started in 1967, called for the dredging and construction of forty miles of canals (later increased to fifty-five miles).[6] The canals have been landscaped to look like natural streams. Water flow is controlled by double-ballasted automatic floating gates. Since the late 1970s, water flow in Walt Disney World has been monitored by a satellite in stationary orbit over the equator, using radio telemetry and electronic sensors to measure the level, flow rate, and chemistry of park waters.[7]

Water was everywhere in the Reedy Creek Improvement District; thus, Walt Disney World was going to have an overall aquatic theme. The 450-acre Bay Lake, however, was not suitable for Disney purposes. The lake was drained, the bottom scoured, and the dirty water replaced with clean water. Just west of Bay Lake lay a low, wet area that was put to use by extending the aquatic theme there from Bay Lake. Thus, the Seven Seas Lagoon was dug. This man-made lake covers around two hundred acres, contains three islands, and has an average depth of ten feet.[8] Connected to Bay Lake by a unique water bridge — an aqueduct-type structure that passes over the road to the Contemporary Hotel and beyond — Seven Seas Lagoon could now serve as a focal point for the themed resort hotels and the Magic Kingdom itself. Water is everywhere at Walt Disney World, designed and controlled to perform an array of functions. It itself is a major theme.

Although the long entrance drive into Walt Disney World provides intimations of Disney space, the highway is closed in by forest. It winds ahead toward the Magic Kingdom and EPCOT Center parking lots, which are enormous but, after all, are just parking lots — blacktop and painted lines. At these lots the transition begins from automobile life to a pedestrian and public conveyance world. The transportation tramride from Chip 'n'

Dale or Daisy to the ticket booth, the dash to find the shortest line, the pileup at the entrance gate — each move brings a further constriction of space in the interests of border access control.

For first-time visitors, passage through the entrance gate signifies that we are now finally there; but this is somewhat of a false start. This is only the Ticket and Transportation Center (TTC). We have two choices — left to the ferry boat or straight ahead to the monorail. Most people choose the latter. The massive platform, with its entrance ramp close ahead, conceals all views of what is beyond. Jostled by crowds, we are herded to the waiting area. Because the Magic Kingdom Monorail loads from the left side, as we wait for it we face out across the track to the EPCOT Center Monorail. Through the concrete we can see the forest. If we are lucky, strategically clever, or have a WDW veteran as a guide, we get on the line to the right in each two-line loading stall; that way we will ride forward. The monorail arrives and unloads. We enter, sit down, and pull away from the station.

Suddenly, the view opens up. Immediately on the left, beyond the manicured grass and topiary, is Seven Seas Lagoon. Across it are the Polynesian Village and Grand Floridian Resorts. Ahead in the distance we can see the spire of Cinderella's Castle and the top of Space Mountain. Soon, to the right, Bay Lake comes into view. Our transition into Disney's world is marked by water and by our passage through the womb-like lobby of the Contemporary Resort Hotel — a passage Conrad Kottak suggests symbolizes rebirth.[9]

At Walt Disney World, water serves to open up space. Bay Lake and Seven Seas Lagoon as well as Lake Buena Vista and EPCOT Center's World Showcase Lagoon, although not particularly large, loom so in a pedestrian's world. They form a counterpoint to Disney's cinematic blocking of space and provide an opportunity for the use of middle-distance perspective.

The most telling example of the use of water to create perspective is World Showcase Lagoon, the creation of which also illustrates the Mumfordian megamachine scale of the Walt Disney World infrastructure.[10] Geological test borings at the EPCOT site showed that the low-lying area near its center was a typical central Florida sinkhole — full, because of its age, of organic soil and underlain by sand. Because organic soil will not support weight, construction plans were changed, and much of this sinkhole became World Showcase Lagoon.

Up to fifteen feet of muck was dredged in some parts of the sinkhole by draglines, land-hauling equipment, and a massive dredge taken apart and reassembled at the site in a flooded slip. Sand was layered over the lagoon floor to compress the unstable soil below. Two "root islands" — areas of tangled stumps and roots that could not be removed — were buried under twenty-seven feet of sand, which sank them below the bottom. An eight thousand-foot reinforced concrete bulkhead completed the construction.

In all, reports the *Engineering News-Record*, 5 million cubic yards of earth were moved.

The result, World Showcase Lagoon, is the body of water around which the eleven World Showcase pavilions are ranged. From any side of the lagoon, one can look across the water to the architectural signatures of national pavilions on the other side. The 1.3-mile promenade that circles the lagoon opens up further space for visual and pedestrian use.

At Walt Disney World, water is not only used to construct space and perspective. It also acts, in a number of different forms, as borders, boundaries, transportation channels, recycled wastewater filters, elements of architectural design, swimming, boating, and fishing media, water hazards at the Disney Inn golf courses, and wish-laden coin depositories.

The digging of Seven Seas Lagoon dovetailed with two other engineering requisites. First, the earth dredged from the lagoon — some 8 million cubic yards — could be used to give contour to the surrounding flat land. Because the Disney "show" would extend beyond the various theme park borders, the amount of back stage intrusion needed to be controlled. Thus, many of the land contours were constructed as berms in order to hide maintenance and cast parking areas as well as some of the public roads. These sodded and landscaped berms form boundaries between front stage and back stage.

The second and most important use of the lagoon earth was as fill to build up the construction sites for the resort hotels and the Magic Kingdom itself. Because the latter was designed as a utopian pedestrian space, all but themed vehicles were to be kept out. Guest automobiles could be parked beyond the Ticket and Transportation Center and cast vehicles beyond the berms and back walls. However, the Magic Kingdom required delivery and maintenance vehicles on a continual basis as well as storage and utility areas. Further, the internal theming of the park required that cast members have access to particular areas without having to pass incongruously through others. What the Magic Kingdom needed was a basement.

Because the site was already at the water table, the basement would have to be at ground level. The lagoon landfill was used to build up the site to fourteen feet to give room for the extensive "underground" storage, utility, and transportation network ("utilidors," in Disneyspeak).

EPCOT Center is on the first floor. Because its area is about six times larger than that of the Magic Kingdom, there was sufficient space to build World Showcase pavilions back from the lagoon on recovered fill. Employee access to these areas could be effected from behind the pavilions, shut off from sight by walls, plantings, and berms. Future World pavilions, also reached from behind, are widely separated and contain many of their own storage areas. Even though there are fewer costumed "characters" at EPCOT Center, those that are there — a kimono-clad Minnie Mouse at the

Japan Showcase, for instance — as well as cast members clad in national costumes need not travel through inappropriate themed areas.

One important part of EPCOT Center that is underground is the computer center, placed twenty feet below grade in Communicore East.[11] This area is kept dry by sixteen pumps, which hold the water table below the spread footings. The pumps were judged to be more cost-effective than below-grade construction strong enough to resist hydrostatic pressure.

Before venturing further inside the gates of Walt Disney World's various entertainment venues, we need to look at three other elements of Disney's infrastructure. One — transportation — bridges space. Another — the waste disposal system and sewage treatment apparatus — aestheticizes and conserves space. The energy plant supplies power for Walt Disney World machines. Additional parts of the infrastructure — coordination of the distribution of goods and services, especially the crucial use of computers in performing coordination and informational functions — and further comments on landscaping will be treated elsewhere.

Transportation

One of the most important utopian aspects of Walt Disney World is its pedestrianism. People leave their cars in the parking lots or are discharged from tour buses at the TTC. Although it is possible to walk on some of the paved roads, especially those near the resort hotels and Fort Wilderness Campground, most of the distances between venues are too great to allow for strolling. Thus, the Company must provide "external" conveyances to transport large numbers of people from place to place.

The transportation system is also one of Disney's major mechanisms of social control. Walt Disney World is divided into front stages and back stages. There is public space into which people can go and public space people can see (from certain planned angles) but not enter. Although interdicted space inside the parks is marked off by unobtrusive doors, some labeled "Hosts and Hostesses Only," external space has no intrusive "keep off the grass" signs. Yet people on foot, especially in the large numbers that visit Walt Disney World, are hard to police. One's apparent ability to wander freely *within* the parks and hotels (except through closed doors) is set off and bounded by the difficulties of doing so *outside* park boundaries.

From the moment people enter the parking lots, they are channeled toward the transportation system and its staging areas. Those who — in a burst of manic, if guilty, freedom — walk across the grass may find that they have blundered into a shallow, mucky, well-camouflaged drainage ditch. Their reemergence into public space will be marked by a telltale calf-high mudline. They are usually cured of such disorderly behavior.

The transportation system, then, is a crucial part of the Walt Disney World infrastructure. Again we see that apparent freedom Disney-style is embedded in a larger system of nearly total control. Yet, as always, control is gently masked, in Huxleyan fashion, by turning up the volume of sensory information. We are distracted, entertained, pointed toward the topiary outside the monorail window and away from the fact that we are traveling in a narrow path in a vehicle that we can't leave until allowed to do so. External transportation media have "destinations" — places we are fated to go but in the most engaging way possible.

There are four basic external transportation media at Walt Disney World — trams, buses, watercraft of various sorts, and the monorail system. Except for those early arrivers who manage to park their cars near enough to the park entrance gates to walk, the open auto park trams form the outer link of the Disney system. We have been directed to turn on our radios and directed to our parking space by uniformed attendants. Now we are directed — again with the utmost courtesy — to sit back, to refrain from smoking, and to hold on to our belongings. With the "we're clear!" signal, the natural gas-powered tram moves us through whatever breeze is available to the ticket center. The Magic Kingdom trams — which are capable of carrying up to 210 passengers each — are designed to move as many as 12,000 people per hour in each direction. [12]

Particularly welcome at the end of a day on foot, the tram ride back to the parking lot is also for most people the penultimate place for Walt Disney World-controlled information. Tram attendants direct visitors to the Disney Car Care Center for gas, oil, and minor repairs and alert them to the parking lot security and battery service patrols. The last bits of information are available on Walt Disney World radio during the drive out. The circle is closed.

Although the Disney trams are the most open of the external conveyances, I have not found any record of litigation brought against the Company by visitors who have fallen out en route. Disney discipline and the civility it generates seem already in place during the transition by tram.

The second component of the external transit system (and the first in this series to require proof of park or transportation ticket purchase) consists of the buses that tie together the various Disney venues. Although most visitors move from the TTC to the Magic Kingdom by monorail or ferry and from the former to EPCOT Center by monorail, and although Discovery Island must be reached by watercraft, [13] other routes are dependent on bus (or car) transportation. [14]

There are a number of different bus routes in Walt Disney World, each one signaled semaphorically by a flag and color combination affixed to the appropriate bus. In various ways, the bus routes connect the TTC and EPCOT Center with the other Disney venues, including the Disney-MGM Studios, Fort Wilderness, Typhoon Lagoon, Disney Village Marketplace,

Pleasure Island, Walt Disney World Village Resort Villas, and Walt Disney World Hotel Plaza. As always, Disney personnel are available at the main stops to direct the intelligence-impaired to the correct bus. [15]

To a far greater extent than is the case with trams and buses, watercraft and the monorail *are* part of the show. Watercraft provide the Walt Disney World publicity department with one of its wonderful moments of silly Disneyspeak hyperbole. Adding its conveyances at various rides in the Magic Kingdom and EPCOT Center to the ferry boats and other watercraft that ply the Seven Seas Lagoon, Bay Lake, Lake Buena Vista, World Showcase Lagoon, and various WDW canals, Disney people like to boast that Walt Disney World has the fifth-largest navy in the world. Relying on the 20,000 Leagues Under the Sea ride, they also claim the fifth-largest submarine fleet. If ever one wanted to see a trivialization of military power and an argument for entertaining ourselves to death, Disney boat talk is it.

Three six hundred passenger ferry boats move visitors from the TTC to the Magic Kingdom and back. Although it is slower than the monorail, the ferry is more direct. One heads out across Seven Seas Lagoon with Cinderella's Castle directly in front. Less crowded than the monorail, the ferries also have room in which to move during the trip — the only external vehicles that do.

Water launches provide transportation from the Magic Kingdom, Polynesian Village, and Contemporary Hotel to Fort Wilderness and Discovery Island — and from the Studios to the EPCOT hotels. The first two of these routes pass over the water bridge that connects Seven Seas Lagoon and Bay Lake. These bodies of water are the spaces with the highest possibility of chaos at Walt Disney World; in addition to the ferries and launches, the lakes are often full of small speed boats (Water Sprites), sailboats, pontoon boats, pedal boats, water ski boats, and outrigger canoes — all available for rent at park marinas. Canoes in the canals at Fort Wilderness, canopy boats on Lake Buena Vista, fishing boats used for the Fort Wilderness fishing expeditions, and World Showcase water taxis complete the boating picture. Noel Perrin has argued that contrary to Walt Disney World's image as being environmentally concerned, many of these watercraft — especially the Water Sprites — add gasoline to Disney lake waters. [16]

The fourth major component of the Walt Disney World external transportation system is the Altweg Mark IV monorail. The system at present contains three loops: from the TTC to EPCOT Center and back, a counterclockwise loop from the TTC to the Magic Kingdom, and a clockwise route that stops at the Magic Kingdom and the three resort hotels on Seven Seas Lagoon. The most dramatic of these is the second loop, which passes without warning through the Contemporary Hotel high above its lobby floor. Because the monorail system (like the WEDway People Mover) is a major part of WDW's utopian urban planning design, it is worth spending some time on its specifications and capabilities.

The Magic Kingdom loops — together approximately seven miles long — use five- or six-car trains capable of transporting a total of ten thousand people per hour.[17] Trains are controlled manually, with an electric backup system that reduces power if train passes a stop signal. Loading efficiency is maintained by a "flow-through protocol"[18] by which passengers exit one side of the car as others enter from the opposite side. Engineered to attain speeds of up to 45 miles per hour,[19] the cars are carpeted, air-conditioned, and, filled with Disney-voice taped information. Recently, Disney has added new, larger cars on line. These cars have fewer seats and — like subway cars — rely on space for standees. The tradeoff is more passengers per car against the necessity for some — who are hot, tired, and cranky — to stand. What we have is a loss of civility in the interest of efficiency. A harbinger, perhaps?

The trains run on rubber tires over a twenty-six inch-wide beam and are powered by electricity fed by a bar beneath each beam.[20] The Magic Kingdom beams, reinforced concrete and steel wrapped around a styrofoam core, were cast in Oregon and trucked to central Florida. The EPCOT extension boasts a cast-in-place substructure for reasons both of cost and safety. Support structures — 404 beams and 327 piers cast in a number of forms depending on the contour of the land — are set on pile because of soil and water conditions.[21] Disney people tout the technology of the monorail construction, especially the flexible-form on-site beam casting, as being cost-efficient for grade-separated urban transit systems.

They also claim cost-efficiency for operating expenses. In 1981, according to Dan Wascoe, Jr., Disney publications claimed a "reliability of 99.9 percent and operating expenses of less than 8 cents per passenger mile, with no major injuries."[22] No doubt, even given the large amount of what Dick Weidenbeck — the general manager of WED Transportation Systems in 1983 — called "meeters and greeters,"[23] costs are held down by nonunion wages.

Waste Disposal

With 30 million annual visitors and a cast of thousands, WDW generates a lot of trash. A central aspect of Disney's utopian utilization of space is cleanliness, so collection and disposal of this trash are crucial to WDW's control of the environment. The waste disposal system has a number of components, many of them experimental. These components have remained in operation insofar as they have been cost-effective.

The system starts — especially inside the parks — with the constant vigilance of low-paid, costumed street sweepers, each with a broom and long-handled dustpan. These people continually patrol the streets and other public places, sweeping up cigarette butts, popcorn, and any other items carelessly dropped by visitors. The street life of such detritus is extremely short. This cleaning process is facilitated by a corporate decision not to sell difficult-to-clean items inside the parks. There is no chewing gum in utopia.

The jury is still out as to whether this constant cleaning affects the behavior of Disney visitors. Disney people as well as a number of reporters have argued that whether through suggestability or shame, people are trained at WDW in the civility of trash can use. This is hard to measure. As any visitor can see, people do use these themed trash collectors as well as the large ashtrays outside attraction entrances. But it is also possible that many visitors, knowing their refuse will soon disappear, have little compunction — and perhaps an odd sense of freedom from guilt — about dropping things here and there.

Disney employees take the bagged refuse from the trash cans at regular intervals and feed it into the well-protected intake mouths of a Swedish-designed pneumatic garbage system (called AVAC for automatic vaccuum). Capable of handling fifty tons of refuse daily, the underground system moves garbage at sixty miles an hour to a central compaction plant. Once collected, this solid waste material is trucked to a wet-area landfill outside Reedy Creek boundaries under a program conducted for the Environmental Protection Agency. [24]

A number of experiments carried out at WDW pertain to waste disposal. Some involve solid waste, others wastewater. [25] Since the opening of the Magic Kingdom, Disney had operated a modern incinerator with scrubbers to clean its own stack emissions. In September 1981, Disney began testing a solid waste energy conversion (SWEC) facility. Sponsored partially by the U.S. Department of Energy, the plant used blast furnace technology to produce energy from municipal refuse. Capable of reducing one hundred tons of solid waste per day, the SWEC facility burned garbage at high temperatures and further burned the resulting combustible gas to power a boiler. The steam was supposed to drive part of WDW's air-conditioning system. The entire plant was intended to turn a liability into an asset, leaving WDW with only 3 to 5 percent of the original waste volume — and that in a form of glassy black granular slag which is useful as building material. In early 1983, the facility was shut down because it was less cost-efficient than landfill, especially combined with a fall in the price of the oil used to power the systems the plant's steam would have handled.

The wastewater treatment system consists of four components — a sewage treatment plant, the Living Filter Tree Farm, the Water Hyacinth Project, and the WDW canals into which treated water flows. [26] The sewage treatment plant uses the activated sludge process, relying on bacteria and air to break down organic matter. Waste water passes through both primary and secondary settling tanks prior to chlorination and discharge into WDW canals.

Although standards at the facility exceed those required by the state of Florida, there is some question as to whether WDW is releasing excess waste material into its canal system and thus polluting downstream lakes. The Reedy Creek Improvement District has successfully fought to persuade the state Department of Environmental Regulation (DER) to deny local utility systems permits to discharge wastewater into Reedy Creek. In April, 1986 Ted McKim, sanitary engineer and Reedy Creek spokesman, defended the permit allocation and the DER's strict controls. "We produce a very high-quality effluent," he told *Orlando Sentinel* reporter Katherine Long. Although this may be true, complaints from residents on downstream lakes have led the DER and the Florida Game and Fresh Water Fish Commission to take a deeper look at the situation.

Between 5 and 10 percent of the treated effluent is syphoned off and used to spray-irrigate 148 acres of ornamental trees and shrubs at the Living Filter Tree Farm. These plants use nutrients in the wastewater for part of their growth processes, thus acting as a tertiary filter to the water before it returns to the water table. The tree farm also provides a testing ground for new WDW plants.

The newest part of the system is the experimental Water Hyacinth Project. This project is a paradigm case of the way the corporation operates at WDW. It is a joint project, involving the private and public sectors, aimed first at testing the use of a noxious, space-eating plant to treat wastewater and second, at developing practical, marketable uses for such plants.

The list of participants exemplifies Disney's way of sharing costs for the development of technologies. [27] Basic funding for the project came from the Environmental Protection Agency's Research Aquatic Branch. Further contributions were made by WED Enterprises, Boyle Engineering Corporation, United Gas Pipelines, the Gas Research Institute, the Solar Energy Research Institute, Aquamarine Corporation, and the Reedy Creek Improvement District. The advisory board for the project includes members from each of the contributors as well as from various state regulatory agencies, the University of Florida, the University of Arizona, and NASA.

The project is based in a facility that contains three channels into which water in various stages of treatment may be fed from the water sewage treatment plant. Water hyacinths in different arrays are placed in these channels to test how much organic and suspended material may be filtered by their floating roots or absorbed into the plants themselves. The project claims that 90 percent of these materials can be removed, thus meeting EPA secondary water treatment standards.

The project has made a number of attempts to discover what to do with the harvested hyacinths. Although the plants are high in protein, they have not been successful as animal feed. The costs are high, and the animals tried so far don't seem to like the stuff. Drying the plants appeared to be too energy-intensive. Composting chopped hyacinth seems practical, at least for the extensive landscaping needs of WDW itself. One prospective use for the hyacinth is as feed stock for an anaerobic digester for methane production.

Disney people suggest that an integrated water hyacinth project, although land-intensive, would be feasible for small municipalities that lack the technology or funds available for more costly energy-intensive secondary sewage treatment facilities. [28] Whether Disney would market any of the technological components is left unspecified.

The Energy Plant

The final piece of WDW infrastructure I introduce here is the energy plant. I have more to say about energy and the computer system that runs it later in Chapters 17 and 18, but here I'll take a first pass at it. [29]

The first thing to understand about energy at WDW is that it is provided by the Reedy Creek Utilities Company (RCUC). The supplier and the users are subsidiaries of the same parent organization — the Walt Disney Company. Thus, there are possibilities for both joint energy-use goals and creative accounting. Energy policy and conservation have been coordinated since 1974, when the Energy Management Committee was formed in response to the energy crunch. This committee — which includes representatives from the maintenance, engineering, and utilities Departments, along with operating personnel from the theme parks, Lake Buena Vista communities, and the resorts — has had a good deal of range in implementing energy projects.

The RCUC maintains nine utility systems (including those that collect and dispose of sewage and solid waste described above). The RCUC generates and distributes high-voltage electricity, hot and chilled water, compressed air, fuel oil, natural gas, and drinking water. Twenty-five percent of the electricity, all of the hot water, and most of the chilled water used for air-conditioning are produced by the computer-controlled and monitored Central Energy Plant. This plant includes cogeneration facilities that recycle waste heat from the jet engines that drive the turbines to produce hot and chilled water. The RCUC claims a 70 percent efficiency in its use of nonpolluting fuel. Further cost savings are effected by the computer control that prompts the system according to park use cycles. The remainder of WDW energy needs is met by the purchase of external electricity.

Although WDW makes some use of solar energy — especially at RCUC headquarters and at the Energy Pavilion in Future World — Noel Perrin argues that even at midday, such solar facilities generate only two-tenths of a percent of what WDW consumes. To him, "Disney World seems designed to maximize energy consumption." [30]

How much power does it take to run Walt Disney World? In 1984, Perrin claimed,

> A little more than five times as much as it takes to run Nantucket Island. At a typical moment, Nantucket is using about six million watts to heat houses, light streets, run beer coolers, do whatever Nantucketers do with electricity. At a similar moment, Disney World is using about thirty million watts to run the monorail, air-condition the hotels (and the kennels, where visitors must deposit any pets they bring), power the robots. A lot of watts. To put it in another context, the Hawaii Electric Light Company and Maine Public Service use only about twice that much to supply power to a goodly share of their respective states (Disney World: 257 million kilowatt hours per year; Hawaii Electric Light: 447 million kilowatt hours per year; Maine Public Services: 553 million kilowatt hours per year). [31]

Aside from externally supplied electricity, which externalizes pollution, most of the Disney generators are powered by natural gas. What happens if natural gas becomes scarce or prohibitively expensive? As Perrin points out, "Part of the deal with Florida is that the amusement park has the authority to own and operate a nuclear reactor." [32]

Some utopia, eh?

11

Utopia and Urban Planning

The truth of the matter is the only new towns of any significance built in America since World War II are Disneyland in Anaheim, California, and Disney World in Orlando, Florida. Both are "new," both are "towns" and both are staggeringly successful.

—Peter Blake [1]

The trouble with Walt Disney World is that it doesn't smell.

—D.L. [2]

The previous chapter's description of some of the WDW infrastructure readies us to enter the theme park gates. Here we encounter two related issues of central importance to the Disney project. The conjunction of these issues — utopia and urban planning — is marked in much of the critical literature on WDW. The utopian comments tend to be directed toward EPCOT Center, which originally was conceived as a "city of the future," whereas most of the remarks about urban design — ironically — focus on the Magic Kingdom. All in all, said Charles Moore, "the whole thing is a marvel of technology applied to mass psychology . . . one of the most intelligently conceived pieces of architecture in America. [3]

Much is made, clearly, out of what people claim to see as the utopian (or sometimes antiutopian [4]) aspects of WDW. These claims take many forms, because each, in hallowed tradition, opposes some elements of the Vacation Kingdom to practices found elsewhere in the United States. Many of these outside practices are disvalued in favor of Disney arrangements. Although it is true that leisure activities — games, theater, cinema, reading, television, concerts, sports, even visits to amusement parks — are meant to give one a momentary break from the routine of everyday life, WDW, which presents all of these leisure forms, gathers and concentrates oppositions to normal experiences. Much of what Disney sells to its visitors as commodified experience resonates strongly with the visitors' real desires. As Robert Venturi claimed, "Disney is nearer to what people really want than anything architects have ever given them.[5]

WDW's simulations include many that belong to no place most people know.[6] These are not just the bizarre notions of cleaned-up history or the U.S.-touristic presentation of the non-U.S. world. The *form* of one's experience at WDW is different. There are no overhead utility lines. Except for the novelty vehicles, there are no cars, trucks, buses, bicycles, or motorcycles inside the theme park boundaries. The Magic Kingdom and EPCOT Center are pedestrian worlds.

One of the most palpable things at WDW is the lack of fear — not just fear of moving vehicles (except, perhaps, at Space Mountain) but fear of other people. Visitors remark that one can walk Disney's streets without fear of being attacked, hurt, or robbed. Even at night, under lights often surprisingly subdued, people seem unafraid. Although WDW is clearly a haven only to those who can afford its fees, there is nonetheless an attractive civility available to those with the requisite amount of money. People talk to each other, even if only to ask, "Where ya from?" The civility is real and mostly welcomed. People are rarely aware of the security forces around them — some wearing cast garb, others dressed as tourists. The place is clean. There are no drunks, no panhandlers. There is little rowdiness.

This civility is also maintained by the thousands of Disney University-trained WDW workers — smiling, well-coiffed, clean, and unbejeweled, almost a parody of a rural American notion of "nice kids" — who attend to visitors in one way or another. Although the blandness of their studied "have a nice day"-ism and the unremitting corniness of their patter can make one long for some astringency, such behavior serves to "cool out" enormous crowds of people who have come together in the same — often hot — place with time constraints and, by late afternoon, cranky children.[7]

One aspect of WDW is particularly utopian. This concerns planning for disabled guests. Special services, devices, and modes of access are available to the hearing-impaired, the sight-impaired, and those in wheelchairs. These services are more extensive at the more recently built EPCOT Center than they are at the Magic Kingdom, but they are still exemplary at the latter.[8]

For the hearing-impaired, EPCOT Center offers personal translator units that amplify the audio portions of various presentations. A sign language interpreter can be arranged with advanced notice. Throughout both theme parks there are public telephones with amplified handsets. Sight-impaired visitors can obtain complementary tape cassettes and portable tape re- corders to assist them. Among the features of these tapes are explanations of the smells simulated at various venues. Leader dogs are allowed at most locations inside the parks, although some rides — Mission to Mars and Space Mountain, for instance — are "not recommended" for the dogs. At Space Mountain and at Big Thunder Mountain Railroad, a sight-impaired person may request that a host or hostess go along for the ride.

Wheelchairs are ubiquitous at WDW; most are rented by visitors at the entrance to the parks. Close-in parking is available for nonambulatory guests. Once inside the parks, such guests find ramps, appropriate restroom facilities, wheelchair-height public telephones, special ares for parade watching, and access procedures for many shows, rides, and res- taurants. Some locations (although only three in EPCOT Center) are acces- sible only to those who can walk short distances. The *Guidebook* clearly points out which attractions are accessible in which manner. It also suggests that because of an almost imperceptible incline at the Magic Kingdom, wheelchair guests might best begin their visit in Tomorrowland and roll counterclockwise to Adventureland. In general, and contrary to much of the real world, the disabled are made welcome at WDW.[9]

WDW, especially the Magic Kingdom, has appealed to many recent urban planners, particularly those who espouse the romantic tradition of Louis Mumford. Walt Disney's overall design for EPCOT Center is reminis- cent of Ebenezer Howard's cellular "garden city" approach to urban design.[10] Howard argued for cities of approximately thirty-two thousand persons that covered six thousand acres with high-density cores sur- rounded by a greenbelt and with a varied industrial, commercial, and social life. These cities would to be divided into wards, or neighborhoods — each with its own balanced public life — and would be connected by rapid transit to other such cities. Each city would have a specialized range of facilities and resources such that a group of connected cities would be able to provide the full range of urban amenities no one city could support by itself.

Strained in part through Mumford's theoretical sieve, such ideas find a voice today in much of the literature on the planning of sustainable postin- dustrial cities. The important aspects of such concepts are scale, com- munity, sustainable resources, and the organization of service infrastructure.

Mumford's interests, centered as always on the quality of life, were in the planned arrangement of urban spaces so as to generate variable but coherent urban social life. In *The City in History,* he drew out the implica- tions of various kinds of organic urban development — especially in the different types of medieval cities — for such social planning.[11] In his urban model, "The basic cell of the city is the domestic and neighborhood unit; the city itself must be planned as a related cluster of such units, wards, or quarters, differentiated according to function and defined further by appropriate architectural treatment." [12]

What was crucial to Mumford were the wards, each self-contained and marked off from others by some consistent, perhaps architectural theme. Unlike Haussmann's Paris or L'Enfant's Washington, D.C., broad, martial avenues would not be found in Mumford's cellular city. Streets would meander, opening up around corners into public spaces in which street life would surprise us but remain intimate.

These Mumfordian notions are realized in parodic form at the Magic Kingdom (and at its precurser in California), just as Ebenezer Howard's macrocity planning underlies EPCOT Center. EPCOT Center, however — especially Future World — is quite un-Mumfordian. Corporate Disney has made it into the simulation of a technological utopia. Both the Magic Kingdom and EPCOT Center are parodies of urban planning, in part because no one lives there. The daily populations that fill these urban spaces often approximate those suggested by Howard's and Mumford's senses of scale; but they are transients. Michael Harrington suggests that Disney's city is actually a Potemkin village: "Technological Disney World is encapsulated within the invisible structure of a corporate utopia . . . Control. That is the key to Disney World and the future it envisions. . . . Disney World is a sort of man-made moon, an extraterrestrial, unpopulated Space. A Potempkin village." [13]

People-Moving: Layout, Lines, and Loading

Perhaps the most remarked-on element of utopian management at WDW concerns the organization of human movement inside park boundaries. Those who have been there talk with some ambivalence about lines, line management, and line lore. Enormously sophisticated procedures must be used to move transients, rather than denizens, around urban spaces. Transients need to be kept on the move. At this, Disney planners are geniuses.

Many elements are involved in the organization of internal traffic flow at the theme parks. Among them are the design of public spaces, the use of vehicles — both inside and outside the various attractions — and the organization of access to rides and shows. This last element includes everybody's favorite WDW topic — lines.

I restrict myself here to those design issues that pertain to crowd flow. As it is at any amusement park, the Disney strategy is to disperse people as widely as possible and to keep them moving. Although the various venues attempt to implement this strategy in different ways, one overriding assumption guides Disney planning. John Hench, then-senior vice-president of WED Enterprise, summed up this assumption in a 1982 interview with the *Philadelphia Inquirer*. "Decision-making is very fatiguing," he said. "Relating things that are unrelated is fatiguing . . . if you start wandering from one thing to another, not quite knowing what you want to see, you will wear yourself out." [14]

Disney park designers have taken it on themselves to combat this fatigue factor. Once beyond the ticket booths, most customers entertain the illusion of free choice as to where to go and what to do, an illusion abetted by the "one-ticket-for-everything" policy that eliminates the starting-and-stopping cost-benefit analyses a limited number of separate attraction tickets used to evoke before the policy was changed. Yet WDW's various cinematic designs determine, however gently, the range of decisions to be made at any one moment.

The layout of EPCOT Center is based on extensive study of guests' behavior at Disneyland and the Magic Kingdom and on computer modeling of decision-making and traffic flow. "This," says the *Philadelphia Enquirer*, "is the most severely edited of environments." [15] EPCOT Center is to the Magic Kingdom as Corporate Disney is to Walt Disney. Where the Magic Kingdom generates sentimentality and nostalgia, EPCOT Center — especially the Future World section customers first confront — represents corporate power and explicit technological domination of the earth. These two parks present different but internally consistent variations on the basic Disney themes for people-moving.

The Magic Kingdom is laid out like an immense lollipop. The stem — which leads from Town Square with its commons, bright green park benches, manicured trees, and central flagpole, to the Plaza — is Main Street USA. Everyone travels Main Street twice because it's the only way in or out. The street is lined with 1890s small-town, Victorian façades, behind which are internally connected stores of various kinds. Approximately halfway down Main Street USA is a cross street that ends in flower-filled cul-de-sacs. People can move down Main Street USA through the shops or on the pavement.

There is a lot of activity on Main Street USA. Along with the stores are various novelty vehicles, some horse-drawn, that travel the lollipop stem. A barbershop quartet sings at regular intervals at the street's one intersection. People stop to read the signs on the truncated second-story windows. Here people mosey, meander, and linger — especially on their way out of the park. The false-front façades engage pedestrians by providing an idealized, romantic continuity of experience — a fantasy of "innocent," small-town America with no jails, no bars, no other side of the tracks. [16] Building on their Disneyland experience, WDW planners made the Magic Kingdom's Main Street considerably wider to facilitate travel around clumps of loiterers.

Beyond the Plaza, near the center of the lollipop candy, soars Cinderella's Castle — the architectural signature of the Magic Kingdom. The castle and the landscaped Plaza in front of it are "visual magnets" [17] that draw visitors further into the park. Disney uses such magnets throughout WDW to move people along. During the Christmas season, an enormous Christmas tree in Depot Square leads people out of the Magic Kingdom. As Walt Disney himself put it with his usual consummate elegance, "You've got to have a weenie at the end of every street."

Streets radiate clockwise from the Plaza to Adventureland, Liberty Square, Fantasyland, and Tomorrowland. Frontierland cannot be reached directly but only through Adventureland or Liberty Square. Each path takes visitors across or alongside water, which forms the boundary between Main Street USA and the various "lands."

Once inside the lands, perspective closes down. Streets are no longer straight and uniform. They meander in planned disorderliness, alternating relatively closed spaces with busy plazas that contain attractions, shops, and food-dispensing places. Each plaza has a subtheme and focal points that draw the pedestrian on. Rounding a corner one confronts a new subtheme with new visual characteristics.

At four places (Caribbean Plaza [Adventureland]-Frontierland, Adventureland-Frontierland/Liberty Square, Liberty Square-Fantasyland, and the Plaza-Fantasyland), boundaries between the lands are marked by porticoes at which a transition is made to a new major theme. Because Liberty Square and Frontierland share the same historical metatheme, a clear transition is not needed. Further, they share the same central focus, as they range around the wide canal that surrounds Tom Sawyer's Island and carries the Disney river boats. Even here, as vistas open up, there is still a strong sense of intimate street life.

The one exception to Disney's medieval urban design, and the one that seems to jar most people, is Tomorrowland. Here the Magic Kingdom theme of time as space breaks down into an inconsistency of vision. There is little feeling of intimacy in Tomorrowland. Except for the cluster of attractions on the entrance street from the Plaza, the other attractions are just scattered around the concrete. Some attempt has been made to tie Tomorrowland together by way of the WEDway People Mover, which visits most of the venues. In a way, such a tour seems consistent with the overall feel of Tomorrowland, for here pedestrianism breaks down. Here the cinematic structure of the Magic Kingdom is badly edited.

There is no porticoed entrance from Fantasyland to Tomorrowland. We just sort of slide past 20,000 Leagues Under the Sea and there we are, expecting tomorrow and finding ourselves at The Grand Prix Raceway. Beyond that sit concrete buildings and the Star Jets that look like something from the 1950s. If Tomorrowland has any theme except a "default" theme — that which the rest of the Magic Kingdom does not represent — it is the corporate theme because here is where corporate sponsorship of attractions is most intrusive. In this way as well as its lack of intimacy Tomorrowland points toward Future World.

However transitional and out of place Tomorrowland may be, it contains one of the major Magic Kingdom magnets. Space Mountain sits at the back edge of Tomorrowland, as far away from Main Street USA as one can get in that part of the park and still remain inside the Walt Disney Railroad tracks. Most of the major attractions at the Magic Kingdom have been placed at intervals around the perimeter of the park. Visitors are spread out by design and must keep moving around the edge if they are to see everything.

Lines

People *do* stop to see some things, and when they do they stand in lines. The Magic Kingdom has forty-one attractions (and thirty-five restaurants and fast-food locales). These attractions range in duration from one-and-a-half minutes for Dumbo, the Flying Elephant, to thirty minutes-plus at the Diamond Horseshoe Jamboree.[18] Each is a potential clog point in the circulation of customers. Depending on the time of year, day of the week, and time of day, these clog points grow and shrink. Much of the information about WDW presented in commercial guidebooks concerns strategies for minimizing the amount of time spent in line while maximizing access to attractions. Much of the lore picked up by veteran visitors consists of such strategies.[19] Those who have actively sought to contend with crowd circulation tactics and who have produced and refined plans are rewarded with a sense of "being in the know." Throughout the day at WDW, one hears people claiming to be in the know by giving advice to others about what to see and when and how to see it. Yet however much lore one knows and however efficient and refined one's plan, there are still lines.

Lines are perhaps the only existing Hobbesian solution to the problem of social order. At least in those places where lines are normal ways of distributing people over services, people have rationally agreed to follow rules they don't particularly like in order to keep life from being short, nasty, and brutish. In the United States, the concept of the line is not based only on principles of order, propriety, and efficiency but also on the democratic principle that lacking an appointment, people should have access to services based on time of arrival at the service point. First come, first served. This deeply held principle holds that all people are inherently equal in the service situation. Status, strength, connections, and similar factors should not move one to the front. One should wait one's turn, ordered only by an impersonal temporal ranking.

Although most of us agree in principle that lines are a good idea, there is a tension between social reason and our individual desires to be entitled, at least for the moment. We are impatient and wish to justify an attempt to cut through the red tape or perhaps just move to the front without justification, like celebrities whose ability to do that a part of us envies.

This is not a perfect world. People *do* cut in line. They save places for fifteen others, who join them as they get to the counter. They dump twenty-one items in front of the ten-items-or-less checkout cashier. We have many cultural rules about lines, each of which has a moral aspect. These rules tell us how to feel in such situations and what we might reasonably do. They tell us what excuses are acceptable and how to make or avoid eye contact with others. Lines are arenas for both civility and potential chaos. They are also the one central experience all visitors to WDW share.

Disney lines are marvels of length and human engineering. No matter how successfully visitors are distributed around WDW, there are still enough lines for everybody to complain about — especially in Fantasyland, where there are some pretty small rewards at the end of the line. There are five basic elements in Disney line practice: (1) the hidden line, (2) the illusion of progress, (3) sensory entertainment, (4) cooling the line, and (5) loading and unloading the attractions.

The Hidden Line

You are in Adventureland. Ahead is the Florida Citrus Growers' Enchanted Tiki Room. To the left is the Jungle Cruise. Neither has a line, as far as you can tell. Although the Jungle Cruise has a "30-minute wait from this point" sign out front, the people you can see in line seem well ahead of it. So you head left, turn a few corners, and find the real line snaking back and forth endlessly as it inches its way to the loading dock. Well, you're there now, and the deeper you go the more time you have invested, and the harder it is to get out of the line and go somewhere else. [20]

Had you gone to the Enchanted Tiki Room, you would have found yourself lined up in rows behind balustrades, waiting for the "preshow" to begin. You might have passed through this part of Adventureland and gone straight to the Pirates of the Caribbean. Again, no apparent lines. Yet inside the fort, you would have been faced with a series of short dungeon-like corridors, each narrower than the one before, as you funneled down-slope. Once in the hidden line at the Jungle Cruise, you could have seen the loading point. Here at Pirates of the Caribbean you don't know where you are or how many corridors lie ahead.

Space Mountain also has a hidden corridor inside its shell. Yet if you go there forty-five minutes before closing on a busy day, you might see an enormous line outside of people waiting to get in. The irony is that there is no hidden line inside. The crowd is held outside to discourage others from queuing up. At the appropriate moment the line is released, people walk directly to the space cars, and the attraction closes on time.

These are the three basic forms of lines at WDW — the open snake, the preshow balustrade, and the inside corridor. Other arrangements, such as the hidden indoor snake at Future World's Journey into Imagination, are combinations of these patterns.

Disney lines gradually narrow as they funnel visitors from the open spaces outside the attractions to the loading points. Thus, the potential for space jumping is eliminated. The last decision point for those who have chosen to enter any attraction comes in those situations in which there are two lines. Many lines have two loading points with a line leading to each one. Some of these — Space Mountain, Mr. Toad's Wild Ride, and Snow White's Scary Adventure — have mirrored tracks. Two similar but not identical versions of the ride are laid out side by side. In his guide to WDW, Stephen Birnbaum suggests that the lines on the left are usually shorter. He doesn't know why. I don't, either.

The Illusion of Progress

The Disney version of psychological manipulation reaches its apogee in its organization of line movement. Once people are committed, their impatience is partially pacified by evidence of progress. "This line's moving pretty well," people say to each other, sounding like serious connoisseurs. Except for some of the theater attractions and restaurants, the lines *do* move. The most interesting lines, and one of the few situations in which Disney secrets are shown to the public, are the open snakes. These are complex mazes formed by narrow post and rope channels. Throughout the day attendants vary the arrangement of the maze by opening and closing channels, depending on crowd flow. Enough channels are always open to preserve a measurable sense of forward movement.

This movement, together with the openness of the maze, encourages tolerance in another way. As people snake back and forth, they repeatedly see others in the contiguous channels. Eye contact can be made — not just the fleeting glance that is usual in the normal busy urban scene, but several contacts can be made. Brief conversations can take place, especially with or about the many children in line. Information can be offered and stories told about other lines. Faces change as people move on, turn, and repass each other. Based on the shared experience of queuing up, social solidarity is formed. As Jim Fitzgerald writes, "New friendships are continually renewed. Headed south, you come face-to-face with the same people you saw a few minutes earlier when you were headed north. After several meetings, it seems natural to ask how they've been, and why they never write, not even a postcard." [21] Disney people-engineers have discovered that if you can keep people moving back and forth in a line, they will entertain and police themselves.

Sensory Entertainment

People watching is not enough for some. It is certainly not enough for Disney. A relentless sensory and informational assault surrounds Disney lines. As transition zones from the outside to the inside, line — and other waiting — environments must set the tone for each of their attractions. Although architectural façades are advertisements for what lies behind them, line environments are the preambles. They both distract and instruct.

Visual distractions always surround Disney lines. A few — such as the semiserious, semimuseum exhibits at The Living Seas — are instructive in the obvious sense. Some (Horizons) set the theme for the attraction with simulated functional messages. Still others (It's a Small World) use colorful, stylized visual montages. At the two rollercoaster rides — Big Thunder Mountain and Space Mountain — the lines pass through spaces where people can see significant portions of the ride layout. Such views are available at the least threatening of rides — Cinderella's Golden Carousel, Dumbo, the Flying Elephant, and the Mad Tea Party in Fantasyland — and at the most threatening ones. Views of the latter give visitors a lot of information and a chance to back out.

Many waiting zones exude whimsy. The silly gravestones at the Haunted Mansion and the signposts at Mr. Toad's Wild Ride distract and entertain. Visitors play the game of guessing which dwarf name they will get on their car at Snow White's Scary Adventure or which truly stupidly named boat they will ride in at the Jungle Cruise — Irrawaddy Irma, Nile Nellie, Amazon Annie, and the like.

Along with visuals, Disney planners also use sound and texture — often all three together. Many attractions have musical signatures, the refrains of which are repeated over and over — sometimes, as at It's a Small World, ad nauseam. Others, especially those with inside corridor lines, have tone-setting nonmusical sound tracks, such as the departure announcements at Horizons or the vehicle noises passing overhead at World of Motion.

As one approaches the loading point at many rides, especially those with open-snake lines, one begins to hear the ongoing patter of the attendants. Much of this is filled with carefully scripted cornball humor, aimed in part at masking the necessary directions that get people into conveyances. Although the freshness of these spiels is lost through repetition, one gets the feeling that unbearably bored by their own endless recycling of the script, the attendants try to test and stretch the limits of allowable talk with spontaneous repartee.

Although all Disney lines have ropes, chains, or metal, wood, or naugahyde-covered railings to touch, the most tactile entry corridors are in the Pirates of the Caribbean. Inside the pavilion a path leads gently down between the narrowing walls of a simulated fortress. The place is dark; the air is cold and clammy. You can run your hands along the walls, stopping every so often to peer through window grates into dungeons and storerooms. The sensory envelope here is nearly complete.

Cooling the Line

Central Florida is debilitatingly hot much of the year. The mean high temperature from April through October is eighty-two degrees Farenheit or above. The mean lows in the summer months remain in the seventies. It is also humid, especially in the rainy summer and early autumn. Lines bring people together, adding body heat to the potential sources of claustrophobia. Indoor attractions can be air-conditioned, although, as we saw earlier, at considerable expense. [22] Outdoor areas, especially line areas, present problems that are not so easily controlled. Yet lines must be cooled, or visitors will become sick.

Other than internal air-conditioning systems, there are four basic elements to WDW visitor cooling. First, all Disney lines pass eventually into areas covered by awnings or roofs. Only in the longest, slowest-moving lines does one have to remain in the sun or rain for too long a time. Second, the roofs provide anchorage for overhead fans that circulate air in localized but appreciable spaces. Third, water fountains are placed at regular intervals so people can replace lost fluids. Finally, air curtains are used where possible. These are sheets of cooled air, driven under high pressure. They are placed especially at entrances to attractions that require wide entry points at which doors cannot be used to retain the internal conditioned air. These curtains introduce visitors to the attraction and keep most of the internal cooled air inside.

Loading and Unloading

The entire queuing apparatus, and thus a good deal of the emotional management of Disney customers, depends on the efficiency of the loading and unloading process. This process works differently depending on the structure of the attraction. Basically, WDW offers rides and theater productions. There are a number of museum displays — especially in World Showcase (China, Mexico, Japan, and Morocco) — but these are separate shows with museum queuing rules. The Swiss Family Island Treehouse is a walk-through attraction. Future World contains a number of areas — the World of Motion's Transcenter, the Image Works in Journey into Imagination, and the various displays in The Living Seas, CommuniCore East, and CommuniCore West — with scattered, mill-around exhibits. The latter four areas include handson displays with their own special queuing practices.

Rides. In *The Unofficial Guide to Walt Disney World*, Bob Sehlinger and John Finley classify rides as continuous, interval, or cycle loaders. [23] Each creates its own patterns of people-moving. Continuous loaders never stop.[24] Ride vehicles continue around their track as if it were a conveyor belt. These rides require moving sidewalks for both loading and unloading. Once visitors are through the turnstile, attendants sort parties into manageable numbers and direct them to the moving sidewalks and the appropriate vehicles. Continuous loaders require constant vigilance on the part of attendants.[25] Only when there are no lines is inattention possible. These rides also require automatic manipulation of vehicle doors and retainer bars as well as recorded safety message loops, many of which are placed in speakers inside the vehicles.

As long as enough vehicles are on the track, continuous loaders move lines the fastest. This is one of the lessons Disney planners learned from the Magic Kingdom, where only four attractions — the Haunted Mansion, Peter Pan's Flight, the WEDway People Mover, and Dreamflight — are continuous loaders. All the rides in EPCOT Center except Listen to the Land (in The Land), El Rio del Tiempo (in the Mexico Showcase), and the Maelstrom (in the Norway Showcase) load visitors this way.

At interval loaders, vehicles are unloaded, filled, and started through the ride at regular intervals. Eight of WDW's ten water rides are interval loaders (the exceptions are the Tom Sawyer Island Rafts and the Liberty Square Riverboat), as are the roller coasters, the Skyway, the Grand Prix Raceway, the Snow White and Mr. Toad rides in Fantasyland, and the Great Movie Ride and Backstage Studio Tour at the Disney-MGM Studios. Only three of the ten water rides — Listen to the Land, El Rio del Tiempo, and the Maelstrom — are in EPCOT Center.

Some of these rides, such as Space Mountain and Pirates of the Caribbean, load and unload from the same side of the vehicle, which is stopped, unloaded, and then moved forward to the loading area to be refilled. Others are flow-through loaders (as is the Monorail). Visitors "step out to the left, please," as others simultaneously enter from the other side. The vehicle is then moved up to a staging area where it is held until the preset interval has passed and the previous vehicle is sufficiently out of the way. Alerted by a simple, multicolored computer display, ride attendants release cars and monitor the ride.

Although continuous loaders have a somewhat higher hourly capacity, many interval loaders are still efficient at moving crowds through the attractions. Many of the boat rides as well as the multicar Big Thunder Mountain Railroad carry a good number of people per trip. Those such as the Fantasyland rides, which carry few people per vehicle, are significantly slower. In general, the speed of line movement depends on the number of vehicles in use and the length of the interval, each potentially calibrated to the size of the crowd. At rides such as 20,000 Leagues Under the Sea, space severely limits the number of vehicles, and even at maximal efficiency, flow-through is chronically slow. The vehicle and interval parameters at all interval loaders are bounded for reasons of safety and aesthetics. Some rides need more space between vehicles than others in order for their full effect to be felt.

Visitors who *really* like to wait in line for a small payoff would do well to patronize cycle loaders. These are rides that come to a complete stop, unload, load, and begin again. While the ride is underway, the line doesn't move at all. There are six cycle loaders at WDW, all at the Magic Kingdom. Four of them — Cinderella's Golden Carousel, Dumbo, the Flying Elephant, the Mad Tea Party, and the Star Jets — are the kinds of rides one might find at a traditional amusement park. The first two in particular appeal especially to the youngest visitors.

As Sehlinger and Finley note, "cycle time" is set by "ride time" [plus] "load time." [26] Because load time is relatively long at these rides, lines can only be kept moving by shortening ride time. These rides, all under two minutes long, are the shortest at WDW. Nonetheless, cycle rides have by far the lowest hourly capacities of any Disney attractions.

The remaining two cycle rides are interesting because they lead the visitor away from the maddening crowds. Although the Tom Sawyer Island Rafts load slowly, they lead to Tom Sawyer's Island in the middle of the Rivers of America. This island, especially Cardiff Hill, is one of Disney's oases where one can find a few moments' peace. Aunt Polly's is the least-crowded restaurant at the Magic Kingdom, a place from which to watch the rest of the world go by. Because children can't get off the island without taking a return raft, this is also a spot where visitors can somewhat relax parental vigilance

The longest ride at the Magic Kingdom, comparable in length to the generally longer rides at EPCOT Center, is the Liberty Square Riverboat. The ride cycle here is twenty-four minutes, including a sixteen-minute voyage around Tom Sawyer's Island. [27] The riverboat also offers a place to rest as well as relief from hot pavement and Florida heat on its often breezy upper deck.

Theaters. WDW theater shows present an additional set of problems for Disney people-movers because there is one extra stage to the loading process. Instead of leading directly to the attraction, theater lines lead to a holding area in which people wait until the previous show is over. The front of the line moves through an entrance in which photoelectric lights are placed to count automatically the number of visitors who have entered the holding area. Each side of the entrance has two light sources, which are slightly separated horizontally. Depending on which light beam is interrupted first, the computerized counter can register whether someone is entering or leaving the waiting area. When the crowd has matched theater capacity, an attendant stops the line.

Theater lines move continually unless the crowd is large enough to fill the holding area. For people in line, especially for popular shows such as the Country Bear Jamboree, the question is, "Will we get inside (and into the air-conditioning) for the next show?" Hopes rise and fall as people clog up the entrance for various reasons and then move on. When the waiting room fills up, the line stops.

At the Magic Kingdom, with the exception of Mission to Mars, it is difficult to tell how long it is until the next show. Mission to Mars and a number of theaters at EPCOT Center have clocks that count down the number of minutes until the show doors open. If the holding areas are not filled, this information often allows visitors to fill waiting time with other activities.

Some Disney attractions — for example, the Tropical Serenade (Enchanted Tiki Room), Mission to Mars, and *American Journeys* in the Magic Kingdom; Future World's Universe of Energy, Cranium Command (Wonders of Life), Backstage Magic (Communicore East), and Magic Eye Theater: *Captain E-O* (Journey into Imagination); and the Great Movie Ride in the Disney-MGM Studios) — employ preshows to pacify those waiting for the show. These shows range from the semiaudible robot bird spiel at the Enchanted Tiki Room to the eight-minute artistic and engineering marvel at Universe of Energy and the film clips at the Great Movie Ride.

With the announcement that the theater doors are about to open, people start to implement their seating strategies. Many bring normal cinema tactics with them as they jostle toward the front in order — they think — to get the best seats. Disney veterans hang back, knowing, first, that all seats at Disney theaters are pretty good and, second, that one can insinuate oneself into the middle of a crowd and get center seats because visitors are directed to "please move all the way down the aisles, filling in all the empty seats."

Every Disney theater crowd has two kinds of sociopaths, each of which makes things unpleasant for those around them but neither of which can be stopped. Some people stop and sit in the middle seats, forcing others to stumble past them. Others ignore the attendant's request to refrain from flash photography, thus annoying and sometimes momentarily blinding others in the theater. In the face of such uncivil "me-firstism," one sometimes wishes for even more corporate control over human activity.

At the end of the show, visitors are directed to the exit doors as the next group enters. Exit hallways lead directly outside. The walls, often covered by durable carpeting, are unadorned so that people have nothing to catch their eyes as they exit. Efficient as they are, Disney's theater shows move as many people through per hour as the fastest rides.

EPCOT and Utopia

Whereas the Magic Kingdom beckons visitors into its various lands by leading them down Main Street USA, EPCOT Center has a very different feel. The huge polyhedral Spaceship Earth, EPCOT's signature structure, seems to *block* peoples' access to whatever lies beyond.

EPCOT Center is the essence of Corporate Disney. What had been envisioned by Walt Disney himself as a living city of the future, organized by ever-changing experimental technology, has instead become a kind of permanent World's Fair, with its industrial expositions and national pavilions. Whereas the Magic Kingdom seems intimate — with its relatively narrow streets, busy façades, and open-air restaurants — the Future World part of EPCOT Center especially is massive and impersonal.

Hidden behind Spaceship Earth are nine widely spaced buildings constructed in the Disney version of monumental architecture. CommuniCore East and CommuniCore West[28] face each other at the center of Future World. Constructed in arcs supposedly reminiscent of St. Peter's Square, these buildings surround the central fountain and border the pavement that leads to World Showcase.[29] Behind the CommuniCores, forming one loop of the figure eight that defines EPCOT Center, are seven scattered pavilions — Universe of Energy, Wonders of Life, Horizons, and World of Motion on the left; The Living Seas, The Land, and Journey into Imagination on the right.

Vistas at Future World are severely edited. From any vantage point one can see, through and around the landscaping, only a small number of pavilions other than Spaceship Earth. The CommuniCores cut the space, blocking the view from one side of Future World to the other. At any point a first-time visitor is presented with just two possible directions to take. One moves along barely conscious of making decisions. At pavilion exits, especially those in the CommuniCores, views of other pavilions are framed by trees that block out alternative views and point the visitor in a particular direction.

Future World is not unrelieved Le Corbusier. Landscaping catches the eye. Fountains relieve the concrete, especially the whimsical "jumping" fountains outside Journey into Imagination. Still it is a visual treat to approach World Showcase Lagoon and get one's first glimpse of the international pavilions of World Showcase. Here the view opens up, for the point is to be able to see all the pavilions spread out around the lake. At the far center, at the other end of the EPCOT axis from Spaceship Earth, sits the American Adventure. A 1.3-mile promenade circles the lagoon, passing the pastiche architecture of the eleven pavilions. Visitors are again required to choose which of two directions to move around World Showcase, although here there are time-consuming but foot-conserving shortcuts in the two motor launches that traverse the lake and the double-decker buses that ply the route.

Because much of the critical discussion of EPCOT Center has focused on its utopian aspects, I will pause to consider this issue. EPCOT Center *is* a kind of diluted utopia, a pseudoutopia reminiscent of the kind Howard P. Segal has described as "technological utopias." [30]

Segal has written about a genre of U.S. futurist fiction the most important examples of which spanned the fifty years between 1883 and 1933. The theme of this fiction was technological utopia, and some of its classic examples were Edward Bellamy's *Looking Backward* (1888) and King Camp Gillette's *The Human Drift* (1894). Each of the twenty-five novels Segal treats argues for a vision of the future in which technology would be the main motivating force. Although the shared characteristics of these utopias are found at WDW in general, Future World is very much an advertisement for a technological utopian organization of the future. As it taps into certain real utopian interests of its visitors, WDW also harkens back eerily to those older imaginative worlds. [31]

Segal describes eleven major themes shared by these authors. First,

> The difference between their utopias and the present was not qualitative but quantitative: They multiplied what they saw as the outstanding contemporary trend and predicted the greater and greater advance and spread of technology. . . . The utopians were not blind to the problems technological advance might cause, such as unemployment or boredom. They simply were confident that those problems were temporary and that advancing technology would solve mankind's major chronic problems, which they took to be material — scarcity, hunger, disease, war, and so forth. They assumed that technology would solve other, more recent and more psychological problems as well: nervousness, rudeness, aggression, crowding, and social disorder in particular. [32]

We shall see that the Disney presentation of technology at Future World, orchestrated in partnership with the sponsoring corporations, sells the confidence projected by these utopian authors. We shall also see why the corporate vision of the future is quantitative rather than qualitative. As the section on lines, people-moving, and crowd control suggested, Disney planners are very sophisticated in attacking the problems of aggression and social disorder.

Second, "[Utopian] Society is not . . . to be a mass of sooting smokestacks, clanging machines, and teeming streets. The dirt, noise, and chaos that accompanied industrialization in the real world are to give way to perfect cleanliness, efficiency, quiet, and harmony." [33] Technology is to be tamed in these future worlds, just as it is presented and enacted at Walt Disney World.

Third, nature also is to be domesticated. "Wind, water, and other natural resources will be harnessed — into electricity above all, its supreme cleanliness and quiet befitting its supreme power. The mastery of nature is regarded as the fulfillment of man's destiny, the beginning of a new epoch for mankind, and the elevation of man to a status only slightly short of omnipotence." [34] This theme is evident not only in WDW's artificial lakes, water bridge, landfill construction, berms, and landscaping but is also presented as an explicit argument for the future in Universe of Energy and The Land.

Fourth, well-spaced roads, walkways, and bridges are to be constructed so as to avoid pedestrian and vehicular overcrowding. Avenues are to be smooth and clean. As we have seen, Disney has built such an environment by placing the Magic Kingdom over infrastructural corridors and by placing access roads to EPCOT Center outside the park boundaries.

Fifth, agriculture is to be organized in technical fashion. Gillette writes that in his city of the future, agriculture "is an integral part of the producing machine, and the producing machine must be a unit. . . . Agriculture, like industry, when reduced to its lowest terms, is a problem of applied mathematics and engineering." [35] Clearly EPCOT Center could not feed its workers and customers on the proceeds of its fields alone. Yet it does provide some of its restaurants with fruits and vegetables from the experimental fields associated with The Land pavilion.

The image of agriculture's future presented at The Land and at Horizons is one of hard-path engineering, with water engineering, fertilizer delivery systems, and robots (Horizons). As an inhabitant of Chauncy Thomas's *The Crystal Button: Or Adventures of Paul Prognosis in the Forty-Ninth Century* (1891) says, "Horticulture has supplanted agriculture, and every acre is studied and stimulated to do what it can best do." [36]

Sixth, the various parts of utopia are to be connected by electric-powered communication and transportation systems. This utopian aspect has been significantly realized at WDW, with its fiber-optic telephone system, computer control system, WorldKey Information System, monorail system, and — as a commercial prototype — WEDway PeopleMover. Trams, buses, watercraft, and the Walt Disney World Railroad rely on nonelectric sources of energy, as does the Central Energy Plant itself. As in most depictions of utopia, the externalities of energy production at WDW are elided.

Seventh, in the technological utopia, homes and offices will be filled with new mechanical and electric devices, many of them normal and taken for granted today. Air-conditioners, vaccuum cleaners, electric clothes washers and dryers, refrigerators, dishwashers, ranges, garbage disposals, phonographs, razors, and the like were to fill the home. As King Camp Gillette put it, these inventions would free people "from all the annoyances of housekeeping . . . everything [would be designed] for [all the] comfort, economy, convenience, and freedom from care that a Corporate Intelligence could think of." [37]

Although no lived-in homes are found in EPCOT Center or in the Magic Kingdom, the entire hidden operation is based on technological devices and the organization of work, information, and service delivery they make possible. From the solar-powered air-conditioning at WED offices to the computer-controlled robot shows and sensory envelopes at EPCOT Center and on to the central kitchen and its machines, which make thousands of hamburgers and salads each day for delivery to the various food outlets, WDW makes use of a great number of such technological devices.

At the Magic Kingdom's Carousel of Progress and at its companion exhibit at EPCOT Center — Horizons — Disney and General Electric present advertisements for electric-based pseudoutopian homes. Here we have corporate intelligence at work. The Carousel of Progress presents an inordinately silly and self-serving set of tableaux, sandwiched between an unctuous and annoying musical refrain, that purports to show how electricity has brought "progress" to the home during the twentieth century. The final scene shows how we would live if we were white, rich, and residing in California.

Horizons shows an equally silly group of scenes that depict views of the future from Jules Verne to the 1950s. Here the serious and earnest nature of technological utopias is completely bowdlerized. We are led not to the present but to versions of the future in which our domestic options apparently will be confined to a high-tech city, a California valley given over to robotic and chemical-intensive agriculture, a large structure under the sea (with a fancy restaurant), and a space colony. In each case, as the soundtrack tells us, the surroundings will be there for "our" use, convenience, and entertainment.

Eighth, technological devices will fill the workplace, bringing what the utopians considered to be improved working conditions. Segal notes that his writers were quite vague about work conditions. Suffice it to say here that other than food service and the vast amount of what Arlie Russell Hochschild calls "emotional labor," [38] work is hidden. The machinery is underground, behind walls, or comes out only at night.

Ninth is the weather. Again I quote Segal.

> Utopia's climate is as pleasant, and nearly as uniform, as everything else — again, the achievement of technology. Excessively hot regions have been cooled and excessively cool ones warmed; excessively wet ones have been made drier and excessively dry ones wetter . . . . The utopians have been able to dredge, rechannel, and even create rivers and lakes; to irrigate deserts, heat the soil, flatten mountains, and clear the land; and to erect huge domes to capture and preserve sunlight. Declares [Albert Waldo] Howard [author of *The Multimillionaire*, 1895], "We have absolute control of the weather." [39]

We saw earlier how the Walt Disney Company did rework the land and produce rivers and lakes. The central Florida climate is another story. Yet Disney's use of air cooling has mitigated at least some of the problem of excessive heat.[40] Walt Disney's original fantastic conception of EPCOT Center included a dome to cover the entire city in hopes of gaining as much control over the weather as he wanted over everything else.

Without Walt's dome, rain is as difficult to deal with as the heat. Yet even rain provides an opportunity for clever confusion between the simulated and the real. I was sitting on top of a Mike Fink Keelboat one afternoon when it began to drizzle. The attendant assured us that there was no problem. "This isn't real rain," he said. "It's fake rain, brought to you through the magic of Walt Disney."

Tenth, efficiency is central to Segal's utopian dreamers. Schemes for organizing production, transportation, and the distribution of goods and services are extended to other realms of social life, such as education and government. The latter especially is to be engineered by technical experts because "expertise, not popularity, is what good government requires."[41] As Harold Albert Loeb explains, "Administration in a technocracy has to do with material factors which are subject to measurement. Therefore, popular voting can be largely dispensed with. It is stupid deciding an issue by vote or opinion when a yardstick can be used."[42]

From the centralized kitchens at the Magic Kingdom and the ubiquitous street cleaners to the huge inventory of shades of paint kept on hand by the paint department, WDW is engineered for efficiency. Artistic and other planning is also organized on technocratic efficiency principles. As we have seen, such planners are called imagineers in Disney-speak.

The state of Florida requires that some minimal number of people must live in the Lake Buena Vista-Reedy Creek Improvement District in order to fill mandated governmental requirements. The small number of official residents are employees of the Walt Disney Company. Thus, the minimal legal representational requirements of government can be efficiently performed by the same people who work at, plan, or administer Walt Disney World.

Eleventh, the technological utopians were not only interested in machinelike efficiency: They wanted to couple this efficiency with self-control on the part of the citizens of utopia. As technology is to be used to achieve control over nature, so people would be led to gain control over human nature — that is, over themselves. Utopian citizens were to conform — in dress, in bodily appearance, in food, in abstinence from vice, in family structure, in public mien, and in morality in general.

In the first decades at California's Disneyland, dress and hair codes were enforced. Over time, and especially at WDW, the early blatant controls over public deportment were relaxed and were replaced by a more subtle style of behavior engineering. The Disney price structure, the cleanliness, the theme-uniformed security personnel and other employees combine — even given the availability of alcohol at EPCOT Center and the Disney-MGM Studios — to produce a pleasant pseudoutopian middle-class experience. Forms of antisocial behavior — such as the persistent taking of other peoples' rented wheelchairs and the anarchonarcissistic use of flash photography at indoor theater shows — are infinitely less upsetting and terrifying than those encountered in the real world.

These eleven characteristics suggest that WDW is reminiscent of the arrangements described in the U.S. technological utopian literature. However, Segal reminds us that there are genuine and false utopias. The former aim at radical and comprehensive improvements in the preutopian conditions of life and are characterized by a deep seriousness of purpose. False utopias "manifest only a portion of this attitude, if any. They frequently serve simply as means of escape from the real world; genuine utopias actively seek to make the real world a better place." [43] Walt Disney World seems a false utopia, conservatively "bridging rather than widening the gap between the real and the ideal worlds by demonstrating their relative proximity." [44]

Glitches

Two problem areas detract somewhat from WDW's utopian image. The first concerns crime. There is some shoplifting by visitors at Disney stores. Thus, many of the three hundred or so security personnel perform their activities dressed as guests. [45] Although shoplifting is an aggravation to the Company, far worse for public relations are hotel theft, purse snatching, and automobile burglaries and vandalism in the Disney parking lots. It is difficult to find data on the incidence of these crimes at WDW. In 1981 a Disney spokesman claimed, "Our security measures and efficiency have been improved over the last few years and . . . our guests are better protected than in most other hotels in the country." [46]

As for automobile burglaries, an Orange County deputy said, "We may get 9 or 12 of them a day." [47] One's sense is that the Disney people do the best they can under trying circumstances. We might also note that 35 percent of the items lost in the theme parks — including sunglasses, Cabbage Patch dolls, and false teeth — get returned to their owners by the lost and found department. [48]

The second problem area concerns issues of the safety of employees and visitors. Employee health and safety are supervised jointly by the safety inspection department — charged with maintaining WDW's "industrial hygiene program" — and the training department, Disney University, which stresses safety as well as job skills. [49] Beyond normal job requirements, WDW must deal with situations unique to cast members dressed as Mickey Mouse, Pluto, and other Disney characters. The costumes are hot and clumsy. Children often pummel characters they equate with the indestructible cartoon characters seen on television. Employees dressed as the Seven Dwarfs need special training. Their costumes do not have arm openings, and they have a particular problem protecting themselves from injuries. For instance, they cannot reach out to break a fall.

The Company takes considerable pains to protect its customers from harm and has an enviable safety record. Yet accidents do occur.[50] Although the corporation does not disclose the annual number of injuries to visitors at WDW, between fifty and one hundred personal injury lawsuits are filed against Disney each year.[51] The Company has been very successful in its own defense.

The studied solicitousness Disney employees are trained to evince at the scene of a problem settles many complaints. Such things as free tickets are accepted as recompense by aggrieved visitors. When presented with a lawsuit, however, Disney is notoriously hard-nosed. Settlements are hard to come by.[52] Disney lawyers press for summary judgments.[53] If such attempts are denied or overruled, jury trials are overwhelmingly decided in Disney's favor.[54] Clean-cut, polite Disney witnesses testify before juries made up of people already positively disposed toward Disney, most of whom have had a good time at the parks and many of whom have friends and relatives who are or have been Disney employees. Although Disney's legal staff does its utmost to protect the corporate image, we might consider that fewer than a hundred lawsuits from over twenty-five million visits to WDW is a pretty utopian figure.

12

Kungaloosh! The Theme Park World

It is the middle class that systematically scavenges the earth for new experiences to be woven into a collective, touristic version of other people and other places.

--Dean MacCannell [1]

Around the world in thirty minutes.

--CNN Headline News

Walt Disney World is a pilgrimage center. Yet as Alexander Moore has suggested, the Vacation Kingdom is not so much a religious center as it is a center of "grand play." [2] Moore argues that play and ritual share important characteristics: "Both are symbolic, transcendant, or 'make-believe,' both allay anxieties and prepare the organism to act; both are related to changes of interaction rates over daily, yearly, and generational cycles, and to interaction across population boundaries." [3]

Many writers have seen the pilgrimage as a "rite of passage," embodying the three phases of separation, transition (or liminality), and reincorporation outlined in Arnold Van Gennep's classic work. [4] "The pilgrims leave their homes; their journey to the pilgrimage center is one long separation from their ordinary lives. They enter the sacred precincts; their stay is the phase of transition. They leave on a return journey of reincorporation into their ordinary world, accomplished at their welcome home." [5]

Walt Disney World is the "sacred precincts" for the visitors' playful pilgrimage. One's passage through the various gates and barriers leads over the threshhold into liminal space. Conrad Kottak suggests that the extended process by which one enters the Magic Kingdom is itself a minirite of passage, signified — as one passes by monorail through the womb-like Grand Concourse of the Contemporary Resort Hotel — by the symbolism of birth associated with the rite's phase of reincorporation. [6]

Once inside the theme park boundaries, pilgrims find both the "communitas" and "antistructure" Victor Turner has recognized in pilgrimages and rites of passages. [7] The liminal phase of a rite of passage is a "time out of time" — a sacred and sometimes dangerous period in which one has left the normal world and is in a situation quite opposed to it. Those who share liminality undergo a heightened sense of shared experience. Without the normal markers of status from the normal world, pilgrims are "reduced to a human common denominator in perfect equality." [8] Turner calls this shared state "communitas." At WDW guests dress in informal vacation clothes. Children and adults mingle, the latter often acting more childlike than the former. People talk to and eat with strangers, offer advice, and commiserate about the heat and lines.

As in many liminal states, these visitors share communitas in a situation that possesses antistructure. Within liminal phases of the ritual process, role reversals and fantasies may occur. Such antistructures, fueled by liminality and communitas, may build to an intensity that — at carnival or Mardi Gras — escapes the ritual boundaries. Such potential calls for the routinization and supervision of liminality. At WDW the antistructure is the attraction. Animals are portrayed as people. People are portrayed by robots. Ghosts dance. Children make family decisions. The Magic Kingdom is a simulated opposition to the world outside; but it exists as benign liminality only because the environment is controlled, the civility constructed. Although the ostensible activity at WDW is play,

> Certain secular, symbolic themes are taken with deadly seriousness . . . Main Street America of the 1890s; Lincoln, culture hero of that America; the triumph of technology over death; and the inevitability of progress and space travel, to name a few. . . .
>
> To engage in these metaphors, visitors must engage in industrial motion, the orderly movement of many persons in time with machines, all measured and synchronized against the clock. This obedient, orderly, measured and managed movement is the genuflection — ritual motion — of members of a mass industrial society. Such motions, and the electronic nature of the amusements the crowds move through, lead one to suspect that the true North American civil religion is not the bland multi-denominational cult of God the Father . . . but rather an exciting cult of technology and industrial order, and one that is partaken overtly as edifying play. [9]

As pilgrims, visitors travel to a ritual center in which they are enveloped "in the dim region where art, magic, and religion meet and overlap"; where they meet what Gregory Bateson calls "the metaphor that is meant." [10] They return from their hajj, slides and souvenirs in tow, blessed by the Mouse and taught by General Motors that "it's fun to be free."

People come to Walt Disney World as pilgrims but also as tourists — sightseers in search of experience. In its normal sense, the activity of touring includes leaving home to travel and experience at least the illusion of being somewhere else. Perhaps one goes where there are famous things to see — some natural, some marked by history or a canonical aesthetic. Or one may go to experience another culture. [11]

Generally, tourism is an industry organized around localized profit and national strategies for raising foreign exchange. The industry is maintained by making available in an organized fashion access to attractions. Many of the attractions are constructed as shows that offer the illusion of authenticity to those with little prior knowledge of local customs (or to those whose information is the result of carefully marketed caricatures). The cynically presented "native dances" and other tourist-oriented ceremonies of much of the tribal world offer such a sop to tourist ignorance.

As Dean MacCannell emphasizes, those in the know reproach tourists "for being satisfied with superficial experiences of other people and other places." [12] Fearful of exposure as one who has had an inauthentic experience, one may feel what MacCannell calls "touristic shame." As the success of Lindblad Tours and similar organizations proves, the rich may enter into the exotic tour competition, pushing farther out from the normal tourist world in search of an experience that in all likelihood will be yet another artificial performance. As MacCannell puts it, "Increasingly, pure experience, which leaves no material trace, is manufactured and sold like a commodity." [13]

WDW is a particular kind of touristic place — a "spurious attraction . . . built from scratch to be a tourist attraction." [14] Yet its very commercial transparency eliminates touristic shame. Traveling around World Showcase, the visitor encounters simulacra of the touristic world — second-order artificiality. World Showcase is full of the kinds of differentiations a tourist seeks, but with a twist. As the middle class "scavenges the earth for new experiences," [15] it does so at at WDW, too; but here the differentiations are simultaneous. One can go around the world in eighty minutes, passing one brilliant simulation of a sacred sight after another — each fronting for the commercial activities behind it. From an Aztec pyramid one can see the Eiffel Tower. As MacCannell writes of the real world of the tourist, "The differentiations *are* the attractions." [16]

Rather than causing vertigo, World Showcase seduces many into a delighted acceptance of cognitive and sensory overload. The joy of recognizing major touristic icons — the Piazza San Marco, the quintessential Japanese pagoda, a Canadian totem pole — almost overcomes the confusion of decontextualization. Freed from touristic shame, we stroll into the

Disney world — enveloped by its cartography — ready for another highly structured cinematic media message.

Cultural Geography

When the Disney people talk about making a Main Street USA "as it should have been," they are not just referring to main street. This notion of "as it should be" is extended to WDW's depiction of the rest of the world. There are no references to Eastern Europe here. Except for the dolls that point to these places in It's a Small World, there are no references to the Soviet Union and few to Africa, India, or South America. Only recently, at the Kingdom of Morocco Showcase in EPCOT Center, are any asides made to the Arab world, and even the Marrakesh Restaurant is sold in a quintessentially American way.

This restaurant initially had some difficulty drawing customers. Visitors tend not to know what North African food is like. Its management took to sending shills, sometimes Americans, out to the promenade to advertise and hustle potential diners.[17] In October 1986, I overheard the following spiel given by an American woman in Moroccan garb in front of the pavilion.

> People don't understand Morocco. Don't know anything about it. It's a shame. You know, of all these countries around here [pointing to the German, Italian, Japanese, French, and United Kingdom Showcases], Morocco has been our longest true ally. We've fought wars with all these other people. We've killed their boys. They've killed our boys. Only Morocco [shaking her head in mock disgust]. People don't know about Morocco. You should try it.

Unlike its understanding of history and science, the corporate Disney view of geography is not significantly different from Walt Disney's own understanding. This view resonates with a citizenry whose average member cannot place Belgium on a map of the world. If there is anything to be learned by this average citizen about geography — cultural, political, or otherwise — WDW will teach it.

Adventureland

The main locus of geographical and cultural information is the World Showcase part of EPCOT Center. Yet there is a lot to be learned about Disney's packaging of the world elsewhere in WDW. The Magic Kingdom contains geography of the 1950s, a time before the boom in tourism took many Americans to exotic parts of the world previously (except for World War II soldiers) beyond their ken.

To most Americans, exotica means the tropics — whether jungle or desert. What people know about these places, to the continual dismay of geographers and anthropologists, is not only very little, but it is constructed by years of imbibing extreme caricatures (usually racist) brewed by various popular media. Disney's imagineers are masters of caricature. They draw on and reinforce U.S. folk images of the tropics, visiting every possible cliché.

Adventureland is the geographical pièce de résistance of the Magic Kingdom. Once over the bridge that leads from the Hub to Adventureland, a visitor is engulfed by the pseudoexotic. The first portion of Adventureland, from Kikkoman's Adventureland Veranda restaurant to the border of the Caribbean Plaza, is a potpourri of various tropical styles — architectural, horticultural, and others. It is a fantasyland of ersatz strangeness (although perhaps not so strange for Floridians). The shops are called Zanzibar Shell Company, Colonel Hathi's Safari Club,[18] Tiki Tropic Shop, Elephant Tales, Traders of Timbuctu, and Bwana Bob's. The fast-food places are the Adventureland Veranda, Aloha Isle, the Sunshine Tree Terrace, and the Oasis. Through the Magic Kingdom sound system, one hears parrots squawk, drums beat — and every so often, in the distance — a cannon shot. Here we visit the cartoon history of colonialism and empire.

The core of Adventureland is the Jungle Cruise, a bricolage within a bricolage within a bricolage. As do most of the attractions in the Magic Kingdom, this one takes us to another time — a more entertaining time than the present.

We board a launch named Mongala Millie, Amazon Annie, Rutshuru Ruby, Nile Nellie, Irrawaddy Irma, Orinoco Ida, or Congo Connie (all female names, most with diminutive endings) for a trip through an impossible array of tropical scenes — the Nile Valley, the African savannah, the rain forest of the Amazon, and a southeast Asian jungle complete with a crumbling, python-filled temple. This is the most heavily planted area of WDW. It is a horticulturalist's delight or nightmare, depending on how one feels about the juxtaposed planting of trees, shrubs, and bushes from very disparate parts of the world. Because many of these plants are highly sensitive to cold temperatures, concealed gas-fired heaters and electric fans are scattered throughout the attraction to pump hot air when the temperature falls below thirty-seven degrees Farenheit.[19]

In addition to horticulture, the Jungle Cruise has three other subthemes. The first is corniness. The launch is led by male guides in khaki outfits and bush hats, whose pun-filled script has changed little over the years. The script is harmless and, as when a guide silently points out some of his favorite plants, slightly clever, except when it connects with one of the other two subthemes.

The second subthemes is "cute" colonial racism. With the exception of one white explorer escaping a robot rhinoceros (and followed up a pole by four blacks in fezzes), all of the human characters in the Jungle Cruise are people of color. Some of these are characterized in terms of mock threats to visitors; others are incompetent sillies. All are caricatures that, in the interests of "normal fun" might reinforce visitors' notions of exotic (and colorful) others. This possibility connects with the third subtheme — animalism.

As in totemic societies, animals steal the show at WDW. The most memorable characters on the Jungle Cruise are simulated elephants, hippopotami, gorillas, and snakes. In this sense the ride parallels the practice of those Americans who can afford it — who travel to exotic parts of the world to see, in the most comfortable manner possible, the animals rather than the people. Here we have a middle-class version for those who don't mind being crowded together on shared seat cushions.

The gorillas have captured an explorer's hut and turned over his jeep, and one is trying on a pith helmet as the upturned jeep wheels spin. The hippos and elephants "menace" the launch but are shot with cap pistols or otherwise barely avoided. As in the rest of the Magic Kingdom, animals repeat the secular Sun Belt model of the relations between husbands and wives. The guide points out one large robot elephant who is afraid of only one thing in the world — his wife. Finally, as the launch rounds the last bend in the river, the guide warns us that we are entering the most dangerous part of our journey, the return to "civilization."

This is a "fun" way to do geography. As *Walt Disney World*, the commemorative Disney volume, puts it, "The *Jungle Cruise* is a favorite of armchair explorers, because it compresses weeks of safari travel into ten minutes of fun, without mosquitos, monsoons or misadventures." [20] The Jungle Cruise is one of the most visited attractions at the Magic Kingdom.

This ride is flanked by the Swiss Family Island Treehouse and the Tiki Room. The former is a re-creation of the set of the Disney movie *Swiss Family Robinson*, [21] invoking an unspecified Pacific island. This treehouse is built on one of the most extraordinary structures at WDW. The giant banyan, called by Disney people *Disneyodendron eximus* (extraordinary Disney tree), weighs over 200 tons. It has concrete roots that descend 42 feet and a 90-foot crown covered with 800,000 vinyl leaves and flowers set on 600 branches, which drip with Spanish moss. Much of the trunk has a green patina painted to look like lichen. Unlike the Jungle Cruise, there are no natives here. In fact, there are no people at all — only the house structure and the artifacts it contains.

The treehouse consists of five spaces, three of them enclosed, connected by ladder steps with fake bamboo railings. The Swiss family Robinson seems to have been extraordinarily fortunate, for despite their shipwreck they are well-provisioned with manufactured items. The treehouse contains mirrors, lamps, quilts, pewter mugs, barrels with and without spigots (some of which actually contain fire extinguishers), plates, quill pens, and other salvaged items. Other things have been fashioned or discovered on the island. The sink in the bathroom area is made of a giant clam shell, the stove of stone. In the kitchen are sacks of food, a hanging slab of meat, peppers, onions, grapes, bananas, lemons — a collection of foodstuffs probably available only in a supermarket. [22] The entire structure is serviced by an ingenious water delivery system made of ropes, pulleys, wheels, and hollowed-out pieces of bamboo.

The treehouse plays off of the Disney transformation of the Wyss transformation of the Robinson Crusoe story. Defoe's hero is also shipwrecked on an unnamed tropical island. His story describes how a mid-seventeenth-century Englishman methodically creates an English existence in a state of nature. *Robinson Crusoe* was written as a moral tale about a Protestant's response to necessity and the importance of character in a situation in which extensive social support is unavailable. [23]

Over the years since Defoe wrote about Crusoe, the meaning of that unnamed tropical island has changed in European and U.S. folk culture. Especially by way of Gauguin, Michener stories, such movies as *South Pacific* and *Mutiny on the Bounty*, and (by the mid-twentieth century) the touristic marketing of Polynesian islands (particularly the Hawaiian chain), the Pacific has become not a place to deal with if stranded but a place to which to escape. [24] It has been reconstructed in the interests of tourism as the antithesis of modern urban life — a place where the only noises are bird songs and the wind whirring through the palms, where fruit falls off the trees and normal clothes aren't necessary. The Swiss Family Island Treehouse reproduces this mythology. This particular paradise apparently requires defending, for the first landing takes us past cannon and cannon-balls. The treehouse is also a fortress.

Directly across from the Jungle Cruise is the entrance to the second Polynesian attraction in Adventureland — the thatch-covered Tropical Serenade (Enchanted Tiki Birds). The entrance is set in a structure with ascending thatch-covered rooms — each diminishing in size and height until the top is reached. This is an excellent example of Disney's use of perspective. This show was Disney's first audioanimatronic endeavor, and was first presented at Disneyland in the early 1960s. It is also the only show in Adventureland clearly sponsored by a corporate group — in this case, the Florida Citrus Growers. It is also the only one with a preshow.

Inside the Tiki Room, a very slow beginning leads the overhead show through a series of musical skits to a thunderstorm and fake volcano explosion crescendo. These skits are performed through lip-synching with the sound track by robot birds, flowers, masked figures over false windows, and stylized faces on vertical beams scattered around the back of the room (the tikis). The masters of ceremonies are four parrots — French, Irish, German, and Mexican — in the styles of Bing Crosby, Maurice Chevalier, and Jimmy Durante, who introduce the exotic creatures around them. Even though there are no people in this Polynesia, the show still smells metaphorically of colonialism — of Europeans (even the Irish) directing exotics. The one breach occurs when a chorus of French cancan birds descends over the magical fountain in the middle to the obvious delight of the masters of ceremonies.

Near the far end of Adventureland, one makes the transition to the Caribbean Plaza. This is a completely cleaned-up version of the eighteenth-century Spanish Caribbean. It is full of happy fountains — Fuenta de la Fortuna, Fuente Cielo Azul, Fuente del Arbolito, La Fuente Serena. The shops are named to evoke a tame version of the Spanish Main — the Golden Galleon, Plaza del Sol Caribe, La Princesa de Crystal, the House of Treasure, the Crow's Nest, and Lafitte's Portrait Deck, where one can have a picture taken in pirate garb on the fake foredeck of a fake galleon. The sets mix a number of Spanish colonial styles, all tied together by the grillwork on the second-story balconies. In the midst of this scenery, near the Fuente de la Fortuna, is an intrusion from the British Empire — the steel drum band, J. P. and the Silver Stars.

The core of the Caribbean Plaza is the Pirates of the Caribbean, in which all of the characters are audioanimatronic robots. This ride is basically about the burning and pillaging of a nameless Caribbean port. This port is inhabited mostly by women. Two colonial soldiers are tied up in the treasure room, and one merchant is repeatedly dunked in a well — presumably to force him to give up his secrets — but the rest of the port's denizens are women and animals. These pirates are a jolly lot. They sing, drink, gambol with pigs, revel among treasure, and chase women. They are "positive outlaws" who make the idea of pillage fun.

Technically, Pirates of the Caribbean is exquisitely realized. Animals move. The fires are convincing. One pirate sitting on a bridge over the waterway has simulated hair on his leg. Yet masked by the fun, the story told is not so pleasant. In addition to destruction and perhaps torture, one of the central messages — however cutely presented — is about rape. At the middle of the ride, next to an auction of young women, is a scene in which the motif of pirate chasing after luscious young woman is repeated twice. In an attempt to take the edge off this message, there is a further vignette in which a fat port woman chases an elderly, chubby pirate. It's a sexist joke and a joke about fat people. [25] People in the launch laugh.

At the end of the ride, the boat passes a scene in which a number of pirates behind bars in a burning jail attempt to entice a robot dog into giving them the keys in its mouth. This is a cute scene. It is the one we are most supposed to remember most as we think about the ride. It mitigates the story of destruction we have just seen. This softening of the message is also effected by the musical theme — "Yo ho, yo ho, a pirate's life for me" — in which pirates are equated with children just having fun.

The ride empties out into the shop-filled Galeria de la Fuente. Out past a cactus garden and through the arched Paseo de la Flores lies the Tex-Mex cactus of Pecos Bill's Café and Frontierland.

Although other pieces of geographical information are scattered throughout the Magic Kingdom, geography is a major theme in Adventureland. This is fantasy geography in which signs of exotica are thrown together in an undifferentiated way. We don't recognize a particular representation as we do in World Showcase. Instead we move about surrounded by symbols and artifacts that produce a sense of "places like that" one sees in old airline ads. There is no specific "real world" place here, only a Populuxe Polynesia that draws meaning from our folk images of the tropics.

Interlude One: The Polynesian Village Resort Hotel

The tropical geography theme is carried outside the Magic Kingdom by the Polynesian Village Resort Hotel, the Adventureland of Disney hotels. [26] Here is another version of the touristic South Pacific (without the sailors). This complex has an out-of-the-way feel. Its outer buildings are oriented toward Seven Seas Lagoon, with its two stretches of white sand beach and a close view of the nightly Electric Water Pageant. Inner courtyards contain two swimming pools, one a free-form affair with waterfall and waterslide. Paths meander among the scattered buildings. At night these paths are lit by knee-high lights, preserving a kind of romantic tropical darkness. The paths provide another example of Disney attention to evocative design: They are full of bubble holes, as if made of natural volcanic lava. Every so often there is an embedded pile of pebbles, as if they had been rolled in by the sea.

Two or three stories high, the guest buildings are built as ersatz Pacific longhouses. Each has a name to invoke somebody's idea of the South Pacific — Tahiti, Fiji, Pago Pago, Tonga, Bora Bora, Oahu, Bali Hai, and so on. The central building, which contains the customer service area and most of the restaurants, bars, and shops, [27] is the Great Ceremonial House. This building is connected to the monorail by a wooden walkway on the second floor. Unlike the Contemporary Hotel, the monorail here is out of the way, its bustle removed from the tropical ambience. The lobby of the Great Ceremonial House is filled with a three-story-high miniature tropical rain forest, complete with volcanic rocks, waterfall, coconut palms, ferns, orchids, banana trees, and other tropical and subtropical plants.

At the TTC end of the complex are the Tangaroa Terrace Restaurant and Moana Mickey's Fun Hut, an electronic game room. At the other end, past the marina, is Luau Cove. Accompanied by indifferent food, the Polynesian Revue dancers put on nightly shows for the tourists. Birnbaum claims that "the performers' dancing is some of the most authentic this side of Hawaii's well-respected Polynesian Cultural Center — where many of the WDW dancers have studied." [28] This is authentic tourist dancing rather than authentic dancing or inauthentic tourist dancing. Again, into this hotel called "village," surrealism creeps.

Interlude Two: Typhoon Lagoon

A furious storm once roared 'cross the sea;
Catching ships in its path, helpless to flee;
Instead of a certain and watery doom;
The winds swept them here to Typhoon Lagoon!

So says the roadside sign on the way in. Typhoon Lagoon is Disney's newest water park. [29] At fifty-six acres, it is four times larger than River Country. [30] As with Pleasure Island, Typhoon Lagoon has a central conceit. According to the story, a typhoon hit a small lagoon village some years ago, toppling trees, knocking over buildings, and dumping Miss Tilly — a shrimp boat out of Safen Sound, Florida — on top of Mt. Mayday. [31] Every few minutes, with a siren's roar, the Miss Tilly shoots a geyser of water from her smokestack in a fit of mechanical pique. "Debris" is strewn around the lagoon, left in place as the villagers rebuild their shacks amid the mess. Parts of the lagoon look like Gilligan's Island after a visit from Marmaduke.

Typhoon Lagoon has two 214-foot speed slides — Humunga Kowabunga — each with a 51-foot drop, and three twisting body flumes (Stern Burner, Rudder Buster, and Jib Jammer). Across the lagoon are raft rides. Two of these — Mayday Falls and Keelhaul Falls — are for single tube riders. The third, Gangplank Falls, fits groups of up to four into 6 1/2-foot-wide tubes. Ketchakiddie Creek has scaled-down slides, waterfalls, and minitube rides for those under four feet tall.

Shark Reef, complete with harmless bonnethead and nurse sharks, provides an opportunity to borrow some park equipment for a quick snorkel. Tropical fish surround a reef built around a sunken tanker whose portholes form observation points for nonsnorklers.

The park's centerpiece is Typhoon Lagoon itself, a 2 1/2-acre swimming pool surrounded by white sand, beach chairs, and thatch shelters. At the far end are the water chambers that form a wave machine capable of generating 4 1/2-foot waves — large enough, were there not lemming-like crowds, for body surfing. The equipment also generates crosshatch waves that intercept each other at almost ninety degree angles, jouncing swimmers around as they try to figure out the rhythm. The timid hide out in two smaller tidal pools, Blustery Bay and Whitecap Cove.

Surrounding the lagoon is Castaway Creek, around which visitors may slowly float in inner tubes. The waterway passes by and through caves, waterfalls, and various pieces of debris left by the storm. Leaning Palms and Typhoon Tilly's Galley and Grog serve simple fast food, and Singapore Sal's sells themed merchandise.

This park comes complete with changing rooms, towel rental, coin lockers, tube rental, a first aid station, and lots of lifeguards.

Interlude Three: The Adventurers Club

The most cluttered concentration of Disney's cultural geography is found in one of WDW's newest and most entertaining settings — the Adventurers Club on Pleasure Island. Sitting next to the Disney Village Marketplace, the six-acre manmade Pleasure Island is Disney's new (1989) night club area.

According to legend, this "recently unearthed" island once belonged to Merriweather Adam Pleasure, a nineteenth-century ship merchant.[32] Having developed Pleasure's Canvas and Sailmaking, Inc., and the island community around it, Pleasure turned everything over to his sons while he adventured around the world until 1939, when he was lost at sea. His lazy sons let the island fall into complete neglect until the intrepid Disney corporate planners stumbled across it while dining at the Empress Lilly. Redeveloped, the island now holds a nightly New Year's Eve Party as well as six or seven nightclubs, eleven shops, three restaurants (plus the three on the Empress Lilly), and two dessert shops. No doubt, Merriweather would be proud.

The captain's stuff, collected on his many travels, is on display at the Adventurers Club, styled as a turn-of-the-century British safari club (with modern bar). Here, as the sign at the entrance tells us, we "explore the unknown, discover the impossible." Both upstairs on the balcony and downstairs, the walls are utterly packed with masks, photos, books, statues, and fake animal heads — including the dreaded drooling "yakoose."[33] In the middle of the Main Salon is a fig-leafed statue of Zeus, with rod and creel, fishing. Up in the far right corner, often asleep, is the colonel, the head of security. In his red uniform of the Raj and brilliantly manipulated, when awake, by a puppeteer behind him, this dummy opens the evening show with audience repartee. Sometimes he speaks to the large stone Burmese goddess head on the opposite wall.

Milling among the guests are the club staff[34] — Graves, the cavernous butler; the French maid; Marcel, the gorilla, who dusts furniture and guests; and members of the club. Visitors find themselves conversing with people who turn out to be Camilia Perkins, the President of the Club; world-renowned ichthyologist, Professor Otis T. Wrenn; Hathaway Brown (a terrible pilot); Fletcher Hodges, the club curator; Mendora, the femme fatale; or Emil Bleehall, the nerd from Sandusky, Ohio. Club members give "lectures" in the Mask and Treasure Rooms, and twice each night new members are inducted into the club — taught the club song and secret hand gestures. Visitors also learn the Adventurers Club greeting, "Kungaloosh!" which is heard throughout the park when a club tee-shirt is spotted.

Every hour or so, the wood-paneled library is opened. Visitors move into this separate room, with its own bar, where various club events take place. Here the audience watches the "Serial Thriller Radio Broadcast (Tales of the Adventurers Club)" and "The Balderdash Cup Competition," featuring Emil Bleehall and his Marching Pigeon Corps (including Rodin, the five hundred-pound pigeon).

The whimsical, corny, but thoroughly entertaining Adventurers Club forms a conceptual bridge between the world of empire at Adventureland and that of international commerce at World Showcase.

World Showcase

World Showcase presents a significantly different approach to geography. The World Showcase at EPCOT is where Disney presents its real fake geography. Arranged more or less cheek by jowl around World Showcase Lagoon are pavilions that represent the United States and ten other friendly nations — Mexico, Norway, China, Germany, Italy, Japan, Morocco, France, the United Kingdom, and Canada.

Conceived as a kind of permanent World's Fair, World Showcase presents a geography that is far more cultural and commercial than the fantasies of Adventureland. This is synecdoche heaven. Each pavilion is a compromise between Disney conceptions and those of the participating countries and foreign corporations. The result is a depiction of the "spirit" of those nations, built of symbols recognizable to most visitors. The France Showcase has its scaled-down Eiffel Tower, the Japanese Showcase its pagoda.[35] The craftwork — much of it performed by natives of the participating countries — is extraordinary.

Inside each pavilion are shops and restaurants that serve some form of the national cuisine. Some have movie presentations, some museum areas. Mexico and Norway have rides. This juxtaposition of national styles is mildly disorienting. The move from Mexico to Norway to China to Germany is a bit strange. After spending an afternoon in World Showcase, one begins to talk about Italy and Canada rather than showcases. "Let's have lunch in Japan and dinner in England," I heard one person say. The souvenir book, *Walt Disney World*, introduces World Showcase thus: "It would take a lifetime of vacations to explore the many countries of the world. For travellers to EPCOT Center's World Showcase, however, the dream of world travel comes true."[36]

This kind of world travel is considerably easier to undertake than the real thing. One hits the highlights — such as the façade pyramid at the Mexico Showcase — the things one might expect to see in actual world travel. One does not hit the lowlights. There are no beggars in World Showcase. There are no shots to get. The streets are clean. Not only are there lines that move smoothly, there *are* lines. Showcase staff — shop clerks, waiters and waitresses, entertainers — speak English, although with traces of their own quaint accents. One hears appropriate themed music, sees appropriate street people, eats appropriate food. Those who collect the illusions of foreign experiences can collect many in one day.

Many Disney guests bring experience in the foreign countries depicted here. For them there is the joy of recognition and the activation of memory. Especially in the movies, one hears whispers: "That's Victoria!" or "I skied there once." Sometimes it's criticism: "The souk doesn't look like that!" In these cases, there is active participation on the part of visitors. They are engaged in their tour, bringing to bear experience and information. Some have the opportunity to feel superior, "in the know," about these lands. They can gain symbolic credit as experts by critiquing Disney's representations.

Other visitors do not have much experience with other cultures. For them World Showcase is exotic and strange but not particularly threatening. I suspect they carry away from World Showcase the message that the real nations of the world are essentially theme parks — World Showcase pavilions writ large.[37] The world to them is made up of quaint people speaking quaint languages, living in old buildings, having nice days.

Many of the pavilions in World Showcase represent other times as well as other places. The countries are depicted in a truncated, idealized fashion. For many pavilions, the icons of idealization are those of the past. Yet these idealizations and icons are precisely the distilled versions of cultural geography the participating countries highlight in the interest of their own tourist trades.

Mexico Showcase

Traveling clockwise around World Showcase Lagoon from the World Showcase Plaza, one comes first to Mexico.[38] Except for La Cantina de San Angel and the El Ranchito del Norte store — to the right between the Promenade and the Lagoon — the Mexico Showcase is entirely enclosed. The signature symbol of Mexico, visible from nearly all points around the lagoon, is the Meso-American-style pyramid fronting that forms the pavilion entrance.

This pyramid is an amalgam of elements familiar to many who have toured Mexico's archaeological sites. Its general style is Formative Mayan, a period that ended in approximately A.D. 300. Protruding from the side walls of the building behind the pyramid are the serpent head representations of the Aztec god Quetzalcoatl. In front of the priests' steps up the front of the pavilion is a wide carved stela that hides the fixture that lights the pyramid at night.

Flanking this stela are entrances to the pyramid, which houses a small museum that currently (1991) contains an exhibit entitled "Reign of Glory — A Celebration of Mexico's Pre-Columbian Arts." [39] The exit at the far end, under a large Aztec sun stone and flanked by two carved Toltecs, is the Plaza de Los Amigos, the major part of the showcase.

The entrance is higher than the plaza, with steps running down to the right and left. This is not a typical Mexican plaza, but it is perhaps the most romantic of all the World Showcase venues. It is twilight, and the dark blue sky covers a market hung with piñatas. On either side of the central mercado are tourist shops that sell sombreros, pottery, serapes, carvings, and similar wares. Above the shops are foreshortened colonial-style second stories, with balconies bordered by wrought iron railings and covered with silk flowers.

Beyond the market is the San Angel Inn, slightly sunken and set off from the public space by a waist-high wall. As with some other World Showcase restaurants, this one is a branch of a restaurant of repute in the sponsoring country. Thus, we have a kind of pseudoauthenticity surrounded by an iconic representation of a "tourable" country in a part of an amusement park that itself has become a shrine of sorts.

Behind the restaurant lies the waterway that forms the beginning of the Rio de Tiempo (River of Time) ride as well as a smaller, internally lit and highlighted version of the pyramid signature that fronts the pavilion. This ride traverses what its designers term "the Three Cultures of Mexico" — the pre-Columbian, the Spanish colonial, and modern Mexico.

The story is told through the medium of dance. After floating past the restaurant and pyramid, one enters a section of the ride in which pre-Columbian Meso-America is symbolized by slides and film clips of stylized dances performed by dancers dressed as Aztec priests and temple maidens. The gorier part of Aztec history is missing — silenced in favor of images of richness and splendor. The stylization of this portion of the ride matches that of the pre-Columbian art.

The colonial period of Mexican history is no less stylized. Thematically cross-tied with the happy puppet children of It's a Small World in Fantasyland, Rio de Tiempo focuses both on children celebrating an eternal All Souls' Day fiesta and on puppet adults dancing their mechanical circles, clothed in various colonial outfits and uniforms. As are those of the earlier period, the clothes that represent colonial times are quite authentic. This part of the ride seems like passing quickly through a happy museum in which the mannequins move.

From the colonial segment we glide past an almost art deco representation of modern Mexico City at night. The walls around us are painted with phosphorescent outlines of skyscrapers, theaters and cafés. A marquee announces Cantinflas, a name those of middle age and beyond might recognize as quintessentially Mexican. Simulated fireworks flash overhead. The map at the ride's end and the narrator suggest that we visit Mexico soon. Out on the Promenade, the Marimba Mayalandia or the Mariachi Cobre entertains the passing crowd. The latter band, originally from Tucson, has a significant local following. [40]

Norway Showcase

The next showcase is Norway. WDW is one of the few imaginable places where this juxtaposition might be made. It seems as reasonable as the transition from Canada to the United Kingdom or from the latter to France one makes traversing the promenade counter-clockwise. At WDW the move from Mexico to Norway or from Norway to the Peoples' Republic of China on the other side seems normal, unremarkable. It is the passage from one piece of cultural geography packaged as commodity to another. Mexico and Norway are just more themes. Each is as quaint as the other.

The contiguities in World Showcase are a major part of the message. The pavilions are meant to be taken at least semiliterally. They are meant to strike chords that encourage tourism or at least the purchase of souvenirs and other merchandise. But at a deeper level, the arrangement of places is quite serious and literal. The national pavilions in World Showcase are completely decontextualized except as a quasirandom group that represents some of the important U.S. allies arranged around a small body of water. The arrangement is successful, in part because Americans have learned to think of geography — if at all — in terms of a vague sort of politics that sorts out present allies from present enemies. [41] For most people, this geography contains little history. That is why the shill at the Morocco Showcase has to tell visitors about the history of friendly relations between the United States and the Kingdom of Morocco.

The Norway pavilion presents the most complete touristic mélange on Showcase Lagoon. Here are history, architecture, commerce, and industry, forest, city, and sea as well as the most popular ride in World Showcase. At the front left of the cobblestone town square — and thus serving as our introduction to the pavilion as we move around the lagoon from Mexico — is a freestanding replica of a medieval Norwegian *stavekirke*. Thirty wooden stave churches remain in Norway out of at least 750 that were built after Christianity was introduced into the country around the year 1000. [42] This one is styled after the Gol Church of Hallingdal (c. 1200), which has been moved to the Norsk Folkemuseum at Bygdoy, Oslo. [43] The third and fourth of its six levels of roofs and eaves are surmounted by carved dragon heads, recalling the prow of a Viking longboat. The vertical roof shingles and intricately carved doors are signatures of medieval Norwegian architecture.

Inside the church is "To the Ends of the Earth — The Polar Quest of Fridtjof Nansen and Roald Amundsen."[44] In a juxtaposition within a juxtaposition, the extraordinary carved doors have Yale locks.

Beyond the stave church is the Kringla Bakeri og Kafé, which sells pastries and open-faced sandwiches. The back patio of the café is covered by a typical rural sod roof. Young Norwegians often sit at the back left table serenading customers — sometimes with Norwegian drinking songs, sometimes with bad U.S. rock and roll. Formal entertainment is provided in front of the bakery by the Snaustrinda and Valhalla folk musicians and singers.

Continuing on through the square past the rustic pool, we come to the Puffin's Roost (curios and collectibles) and The Fjording (china, pewter). These connected shops sit behind façades that recall the Hanseatic buildings of Bergen's Bryggen. The dark red-and-orange façades lead us to the waterfall that "threatens" riders on the Maelstrom. As customers stand in line in the square waiting for their turn on this ride, they can watch passenger-laden Viking boats as they almost go over the falls.

The right side of the pavilion is formed by the Restaurant Akershus, which advertises a Royal Norwegian buffet. This multicourse smorgasbord is housed in a copy of the Akershus Castle — a fourteenth-century stronghold that still dominates Oslo's harbor. The façade of this building is replicated stone — big stone, little stone, solid stone, crumbling stone — that counterpoints the wooden façades on the left side of the pavilion and the urban plastered walls that stretch along the back of the square from the waterfall to the castle. Part of the restaurant is styled after the Olav Hall in the Akershus, with red-and-gold wallpaper standing in for the painted walls of the original.[45]

At the back of the square is the entrance to the Maelstrom and, to its left, the Norwegian tourist bureau office, which catches visitors as they leave the Maelstrom and funnels them into the stores. The plaster front of this section contains replicas of the large iron butterfly studs that can still be seen on old urban Scandinavian buildings.[46]

The centerpiece of the Norway Showcase is the Maelstrom and the dramatic five-minute film that follows. The Maelstrom is a boat ride through Norway's past and folklore and on to the North Sea, the country's current source of industrial wealth. We begin with a line that often stretches well out into the square. This fast-moving line takes us through corridors to an inside snake that leads to the imitation Viking longboats that are our ride vehicles. The foyer contains two large murals. On the right wall as we enter is a large map, "Milestones in Norwegian Exploration," making sure we know about Leif Ericson as well as the extensive travels of the Vikings to the south and east. On the opposite wall is a mural with fifteen scenes that represent modern Norway.

We enter the boat — maneuvering to the front right if we want to get wet — and begin to ride upward through a dark hall. Suddenly, a beam of light shines at us down the slope, emanating from a single simulated eye that shines from the face of a Viking warrior. "Many have passed this way before," says the eye. We are told that to understand Norway, we must "look to the spirit of the seafarer." The boat crests, and we pass through three Viking scenes — a blond woman with braids standing near a cottage, men unloading a boat, and a Viking man blowing a horn to call across a fjord. As we soon see, however, Norway is not only Viking, sea, and fjord.

Crashing through a door, we enter the forest — home of the trolls. Three particularly ugly ones rise before us, asking how we dare enter their realm. Throwing sparking troll dust at us — effected by the twinkling of tiny overhead lights — they threaten to make us "disappear...disappear." Our boat has now been turned around, and we continue our voyage backward. Now we move rapidly through a maelstrom into the arctic north, past puffins and massive rearing polar bears and on into Geiranger Fjord.

As the boat is about to go backward over the waterfall we saw from the town square outside, a one-eyed troll in the shape of a gnarly tree trunk reverses our boat again, and we plunge forward down a chute and splash into the North Sea. Past a deep sea oil-drilling rig, our boat moves through a night storm until, through another door, we are deposited into a peaceful, dark coastal village. Here we wait until called into the theater.

It is night in a fishing village such as one might find on the southeast coast. Sailboats, rowboats, nets, floats, and traps sit in the harbor. Thirteen simulated little buildings — homes and commercial enterprises — surround the small square in which we wait. On the building walls and windows are names and logos of various Norwegian companies — Royal Viking Line, Norway Foods, Frionor, Den Norske Creditbank, Seimer-Sande, and similar enterprises. It is peaceful here, a quiet interlude between the North Sea storm and the sudden, dramatic loudness of the film to follow.

The small blue theater holds padded benches with slim fan-shaped wood slat backs — very Scandinavian contemporary. The short Scandinavian Air System-sponsored film is driven by sound and image. A young boy stares up at the Oseberg Ship at Oslo's Viking Ships Museum. Suddenly, with startlingly loud sounds, we are at the edge of a Viking village as men rush past us down to the sea to set sail. Then, with even more noise, we watch a helicopter land on a North Sea oil platform. Sledgehammers fall. Industrial flame shoots out. The film then quiets as we are led, with gentle background music, through a visual montage — contemporary fisherman in a quiet village, a woman with a cane walking down a cobbled street, an electrical lineman at work, a Norwegian Tom Sawyer dozing while children paint his fence, a ski jump, a sailboat, a suburban family at a backyard table, a farmer and child on a tractor, boys at a swimming hole, a parade in Oslo before the royal family on a national holiday, an office scene, ballerinas, a sledding scene, fashion models ready for work, businessmen, technicians, a school visit to Oslo's Edvard Munch Museum, cross-country skiing, a horse-drawn sled, and finally — after returning to the boy at the museum who is gently touching the ship — a fjord.

The voice-over is short, simple, poetic.

To know this land's heart and soul . . .
to discover its spirit.
Norway . . . Norway.
It was born in challenge . . .
in a thousand years
of challenging the sea.
It's a spirit that knows
a quiet sense of timelessness.
Our spirit lives in daring.
It lives in our traditions.
Our spirit lives in our people.
Our spirit lives in our people.

Thus imbued, we head for China.

China Showcase

From the piercing exuberance of the Mexican mariachi and the excitement of Norway's Maelstrom, we gear down abruptly at the entrance to the China Showcase. Here the rhythm is different. With the lagoon on our right, we turn to face the ceremonial gate behind which stands a replication of Beijing's Temple of Heaven and the three-tiered blue roof of the Hall of Prayer for Good Harvests. To the right, through the ceremonial gate, lie quiet pools and a garden. Chinese music, soothing and calm, plays softly through hidden loudspeakers.

The central experience of the showcase is the CircleVision 360 film *Wonders of China: Land of Beauty, Land of Time*. This film, made by the Disney people in close and strictly monitored partnership with the China Film Co-Production Company (a subsidiary of the People's Republic of China's [PRC] Ministry of Culture), is the most politically complex movie production at WDW. The footage was shot in 1981-1982 during the early days of Deng Xiaoping's "opening to the West." Due to political and strategic sensitivity, some of the earlier scenes were filmed by Chinese crews, with the Disney people not allowed off the ground.

How does the PRC portray itself to people who, for the most part, know little more than bits of information about U.S.-style Chinese food, the Great Wall, Mao Tse Tung, the "yellow peril," and the revolt in Tienanmen Square? Like other films in World Showcase — in France, Canada and Norway — *Wonders of China* takes us through a set of scenes that depict a selected version of nature, cities, rural life, famous sights, faces, and the seasons. There is, mercifully, no obligatory ski scene in this film. Because China is less familiar to us than the other countries, however, we need special help with sight markers.

Our tour is conducted by an actor who portrays Li Bai, an eighth-century Chinese poet. [47] He takes us to the high plains of Mongolia, the Great Buddha of Leshan, Shanghai, Hangzhou and its morning tai-chi exercises, the Shilin Stone Forest in Yunnan, Kweilin, and the Reed Flute Cave below. Li Bai shows us the Yangtze River, explaining that one-tenth of the world's population lives in its drainage basin. He shows us Suzhou on the Grand Canal, a city Marco Polo called "the Venice of the East." In possibly the only critique of Euro-American ethnocentrism at WDW, Li Bai slyly mentions that if he had gone to Venice, perhaps he would have called it "the Suzhou of the West."

Li Bai takes us not only to the portion of the Great Wall we might be familiar with through travelogues, but to its beginning in the western desert and its end at the eastern sea. Two of the most spectacular sights, both of potential political interest, are handled gingerly. These are the Potola at Lhasa in Tibet and the Forbidden City in Beijing. Each is presented in a touristic belt-notching fashion in which the most highlighted information concerns the number of rooms in each. Li Bai leaves us with a poem of return and exits through a filmed door over the real one by which the audience will leave.

Wonders of China is a spectacular movie, fully deserving of the usual applause at its end. It is beautiful, informative, and — in keeping with its theme — poetic. It engages the audience, teaching its members something they did not know, or filling out with elegant images the information and experiences some viewers might have had. *Wonders of China* is an example of WDW at its best.

The film exits into the Bountiful Harvest, the largest shopping area in WDW. In addition to the silk, jade, and porcelain articles, and the usual knickknacks, the Bountiful Harvest employs calligraphers who for a small price ($5 in 1988), will draw a souvenir.

Separated from the waiting hall for *Wonders of China* by a set of windows is the House of the Whispering Willows, which houses a small museum with rotating exhibits from the PRC. [48] The displays in this museum, as in Mexico's presentation of the colonial period, remind us that modern nations enlist the past — especially the prerevolutionary and colonial past — in the political and commercial interests of the present.

The Lotus Blossom Café and the Nine Dragons Restaurant serve tourist versions of the food of China. The latter offers a range of regional cuisines — Human, Mandarin, Szechwan, Kiangche, and Cantonese — in rooms decorated in brown, red, and gold.

On the way out of the showcase, the visitor passes again by the ponds and garden. Perhaps a street artist, silently making birds out of pliable toffee, has gathered a crowd around him or her near the pavilion gate. Stepping out onto the promenade, one leaves the China envelope with a jolt.

Let us walk to the canal bridge just beyond the China Showcase — the canal through which afternoon entertainments on the lagoon are staged — and look around us. To the immediate right we see the Chinese ceremonial gate from which we have just come; beyond it are the roofs of Norway and the Mexican pyramid. Off in the distance to the right lie the totem poles of Canada and the gabled rooftops of the United Kingdom. To the left rises Germany's castle, and next to it the Campanile from the Piazza San Marco in Venice. Directly across the lagoon, side by side, are the Georgian façade of the American Adventure, the Nara Pagoda of Japan, Morocco's towering minaret, and France's Eiffel Tower. Jarringly, the postmodern dolphins, swans, shells, and roof lines of the EPCOT hotels clutter the sky behind the Eiffel Tower, making a complete mess of the visual field.

Plying the lagoon from Germany-Italy and Morocco-France to World Showcase Plaza are water taxis. Behind us a London-style double-decker bus passes over the bridge on which we are standing.

This is truly a strange kind of geography, especially at night when IllumiNations outlines the pavilion roofs with white light bulbs. Stepping into a showcase, we are enveloped by a seamless web of national bricolage. Sights, sounds, accents, plantings, use of water, and even pavements are perfectly themed. We disappear for a while into a foreign land. It is a powerful illusion of travel — easy travel, for the bathrooms are clean, the water is good, and we can leave without going through customs. Stepping out onto the Promenade, we are reminded us that WDW has packaged entire countries for consumption. We learn to think of other nations as theme parks.

Germany Showcase

The German Showcase — nine shops, a biergarden, and the Sommerfest patio restaurant set around a central plaza — is a geographically fantastic potpourri. It is designed to resemble a "typical" German town, but its elements come from many places and from more than one century. Der Bücherwurm [49] is modeled after a merchant's hall in Freiburg. The façade of the Biergarten is reminiscent of Bavaria. The castle is modeled after the Eltz Castle on the Mosel. [50] In the center of St. Georgesplatz is a statue of St. George himself, sitting atop his pedestal slaying the dragon. Behind St. George is the glockenspiel that marks the hour.

The Biergarten Restaurant presents a "continuing Oktoberfest," complete with alpenhorns and the chicken dance. Representing the plaza of sixteenth-century Rothenburg, this restaurant — like Mexico's San Angel Inn — conveys the indoor illusion of enormous space. It contains no movie and no ride (as of 1991), and the German message is carried by architecture, commerce, folk music, and *gemütlichkeit*. Accordian players and a brass band roam the plaza. Shoppers and wine tasters from the Weinkeller might notice most of the Hapsburg emperors carved on the façade of Der Bücherwurm. Emperor Maxmillian, carved on the original merchants hall in Freiburg, was omitted here in the interests of space. [51]

Italy Showcase

The Italy Showcase is next door, a pretty easy transition. From fairy tale, lederhosened Germany, it is only a few steps to Venice. Here are the Campanile, the Doge's Palace, statues of St. Mark and his lion companion on separate pedestals, and gondolas tied to barber shop poles. Some of these — especially the gondolas — are clear synechdochical signs not only for Venice but for all of Italy, much as the Eiffel Tower stands for both Paris and France. Other signs, such as St. Mark and the Campanile, require more special experience on the part of visitors.

The colors around the Piazza San Marco are pink, white, and umber — buildings in the sun. Atop the Campanile the angel is plated in gold leaf. Behind the back wall stand Italian cypress trees and Florida slash pines, which replace utransplantable Italian pines. To the back right is a fountain with a statue of Neptune, modeled after Bernini, as its centerpiece.

Here again is the ubiquitous Disney attention to detail. The statue of the Doge, who was never allowed to go bareheaded, shows him with a cap on so that should he remove his hat, his head would still be covered. The building to the right of the plaza is depicted with bricks showing in places where the plaster has fallen off the walls. This simulated aging gives the building the appearance of "sanitized squalor." [52]

In the center of the Piazza, behind the Campanile, is a raised platform on which the Teatro di Bologna players put on fifteen-minute improvisations, drawing in members of the audience as sacrificial bit players. This interaction between players and audience, which is found throughout World Showcase, is considerably more intelligent and less crass than the scripted routines in the Magic Kingdom. Members of the audience are picked on but not terribly manipulated. No one here says, "I said aloha!" or "howdy!" forcing an embarrassed response.

The restaurant at this showcase is Alfredo's, a branch of the famous restaurant in Rome operated by the original fettucine Alfredo Alfredo. The restaurant walls are covered with *tromp l'oeil* paintings, and at dinner the waiters periodically "break into song."

The American Adventure

The architectural pivot of World Showcase is the large three-story building that houses the American Adventure. With Spaceship Earth at the other
end, this structure forms the anchor of the axis that binds all of EPCOT
Center together. As I have said much about this presentation earlier, I will
be brief here. Set back from the Promenade behind a fountain flanked by
trees, this Georgian building is faced with real hand-made bricks. Its side
cupolas are echoed by the camouflaged design of the sound system that
flanks the stage at the American Gardens Theater by the Shore. This
outdoor theater swings out into Showcase Lagoon and is the site of the most
highly featured World Showcase live entertainment.

At the left side of the American Adventure is the fast-food Liberty Inn,
with its hot dogs and fried chicken. On the right side sits Heritage Manor
Gifts, which sells Americana, and beyond it, a relatively peaceful formal
rose garden. The central cupola holds the only clock visible from most parts
of the Promenade. The place is almost timeless.

Japan Showcase

As the commemorative EPCOT Center volume tells us, the Japan Showcase is characterized by Disney versions of "grace, refinement, serenity,
formality, taste, proportion, decorum, delicacy."[53] The Disney people are
not suggesting commerce and technological facility but art, landscaping,
and other elements of the exotic harmony Americans have vaguely come
to understand as the flip side of Japan, Inc. And grace and harmony *are*
here.

The Japan Showcase has a number of architectural signatures. The
entranceway from Showcase Lagoon is marked by a vermillion torii — a
ceremonial gate in calligraphic form. Such gates are found throughout
Japan at entrances to important shrines. This one is reminiscent of the
Itsukushine Shrine in Hiroshima Bay.

Across the Promenade, ranged with asymmetrical tension around the
concrete courtyard, are the other major elements of the showcase. These are
divided into three sociological themes. To the left are culture, religion, and
aesthetics. At the center are politics and history; to the right, commerce.

The five-story pagoda to the left of the showcase entrance was modeled
after the seventh-century Haryuji temple in Mara. Its five stages represent
the fundamental elements of the classical Buddhist universe — earth,
water, fire, wind, and sky. The eighty-three-foot-high structure is topped
by a spire (*sorin*) that containing nine rings, each with its own wind chimes.
At the very top of the spire is a stylized water flame (topped by a lightning
rod).[54] At night the pagoda is internally lit, with diffused light emanating
from each of its stories.

The original design for this pagoda, based on photographs of popular pagodas in Japan, apparently showed too strong a Chinese influence. Japanese advisers suggested that the design be changed to reflect more traditional Japanese sensibilities — less color and ornamentation and simpler lines. The WDW pagoda is a result of these changes.

The pagoda's first story contains the backstage room from which Kanto Abare Daiko — a drum group from Tokyo whose rhythms can be heard throughout World Showcase — and other performers emerge to entertain showcase crowds. Among the performers are a kimono-clad Minnie Mouse and Masaji Teresawa, the "fantasy dreammaker," who shapes small animal sculptures out of toffee for onlookers — a traditional art called *amesaiku*.[55]

Behind the pagoda is a Japanese garden. Here streams slide over waterfalls toward a small pond filled with *koi*-fish at appropriate times of the year. Foot bridges pass over the streams at several places, offering different vantages of the garden. Rocks (brought from North Carolina and Georgia), pebbles, water, a bamboo half tube noisemaker, trees (few indigenous to Japan), flowers and other plants, and lanterns are arranged to provide another of WDW's surprising peaceful spaces just steps away from the crowds.

A small tea house, representing a scaled-down version of the sixteenth-century Katsura Imperial Summer Palace in Kyoto, sits at the back edge of the garden. Complete with umbrellas, sliding screens, and lanterns, this is the Yakitori House — a fast-food restaurant that specializes in skewered beef and chicken fare. People can take their saki or plum wine out into the garden for a moment of rest.

The back end of the showcase is filled with a structure — the White Egret Castle — modeled after the Shirasegijo, which overlooks the city of Himeji. This fortress recalls the warlike nature of feudal Japan. A narrow entry castle filled with large "bronze" statues leads across a moat to the main fortress. Plans call for filling the castle with a pavilion show that will present a Disneyfied Japanese history. Presently this space houses the Bijutsu-Kan Gallery, which recently featured an exhibit called "Feather on the Wind — the Art of Kites." It now holds "Echoes Through Time," a mixed-media show about women artists.

To the right of the showcase we come to commerce. The simulated Shishinden (A.D. 794 Hall of Ceremonies from the Gosho Imperial Palace complex in Kyoto) houses the money-making parts of this venue. On the first floor is the Mitsukoshi Department Store, which contains the Japanese version of whatever is sold elsewhere at WDW. Above the store the Mitsukoshi Restaurant serves tempura at the small Tempura Kiku and stir-fried dishes at the Teppanaki Dining Room. Some Americans recognize the latter as Benihana-style cooking. Finally, strange as it seems, you can get sashimi at WDW. The Matsu No Ma Lounge — which also offers a wide view of Showcase Lagoon — serves Disney's best sashimi plate.

Kingdom of Morocco Showcase

We go from sashimi to bastilla.[56] From Japan to Morocco is one of the odder transitions at World Showcase. Japan, however misunderstood in the interests of U.S. propaganda, is a country much on the minds of many visitors. Morocco is hardly misunderstood. As we saw in the shill's rhetoric at the beginning of this chapter, Morocco doesn't even exist for most Americans. Well, maybe those of a certain age remember the map at the beginning of *Casablanca* or have some vague recollection of the desert and the French Foreign Legion. A few may even know the place Crosby, Stills, and Nash's "Marrakesh Express" is supposed to be about. At the Morocco Showcase, the Disney people have their best opportunity to create a national caricature that will define a country for millions who know nothing else about it.

As the lettering on the left entrance tower proclaims (the only such lettering at World Showcase), Morocco is a kingdom. It is also an Islamic country. As such it carries quite a burden at WDW, for U.S. views of this world religion are not generous. The mere presentation of Morocco at World Showcase is progressive given U.S. cultural politics.

This showcase evokes the desert. Many of its buildings are treated to look like reddish sandstone. Others are covered with tan plasterwork, and some are carved to look like brick. The Moroccan signature is a replication of the Koutoubia Minaret in Marrakesh. This structure introduces the intricate decorative motifs that characterize Islamic art and architecture. Moroccan artisans were engaged at the showcase to produce its carved plaster designs, terra-cotta tile work, and carved wood. In front of the showcase, drawing from World Showcase Lagoon, is a working water wheel that intricately shuttles water to a series of gardens that front the promenade.

As are many Moroccan cities, the showcase is divided into a *ville nouvelle* (new city)[57] and a Medina (old city). The former, which fronts the promenade, contains an open courtyard that is the site of regular presentations of tourist-oriented Moroccan music and dance. To the left is the Royal Gallery, which contains exhibits of silver work, traditional musical instruments, pottery, costumes, and embroidery. To the right is the Center of Tourism with its continuous slide show and Air Moroc desk.

Entering the narrow, winding streets of the simulated souk, one passes through a replica of the Bab Boujouloud Gate from Fez. The leather smells here make the souk the olefactorily richest area of World Showcase. Here stores are named, in typical Disney alliteration, with what seem like every exotic North African label visitors might know — Casablanca Carpets, Jewels of the Sahara, Tangier Traders, Medina Arts, the Brass Bazaar, Fashions from Fez, Berber Oasis, and Marketplace in the Medina. As usual, the alliteration undercuts any seriousness of presentation and reminds us that merchandising is fun.

At the very back of the showcase, the lane takes us to the Marrakesh Restaurant, where waiters in *djellaba* (long robes) and *babouche* (pointed slippers) serve Americanized versions of Moroccan cuisine. Diners are entertained with live music and, to the embarrassment of some (and the joy of others), a belly dancer.

It is not clear what impressions people take away from the Kingdom of Morocco Showcase, but at least they know the simulation exists.

France Showcase

Although our tour of World Showcase has taken a clockwise route, this showcase is best approached from the other direction. The space between the United Kingdom and France contains the International Gateway entrance from the EPCOT hotels; but the gateway building, with its World Traveler and Showcase Gifts shops, is out of French sight lines from the Promenade. So, rounding a slight bend to the right, one approaches France face-on. The effect is one of the strongest at World Showcase — a tourist's pastiche of Parisian clichés.

Three-story buildings with simulated stone facings and copper and slate mansard roofs surround La Promenade, the showcase's main boulevard. Chimney pots adorn the roofs. Two fountains lead to the central Palais du Cinema, behind which rises a scaled-down version of the Eiffel Tower (created from Gustav Eiffel's original blueprints and complete with tiny elevators and beacon lights). The use of forced perspective is quite successful here. [58] This is the Paris of La Belle Epoque, the "beautiful age" at the end of the nineteenth century.

To reach France from the United Kingdom, one crosses over an offshoot of Showcase Lagoon that forms a canal bordering the showcase on the right. The bridge is a miniature Pont des Arts that, before it was removed, used to pass across the Seine from the Louvre to the Left Bank. To the right, between buildings and the canal, is a small park. Filled with Lombardy poplars, this hint of the Bois de Boulogne was apparently inspired by Georges Seurat's "A Sunday Afternoon on the Island of La Grande Jatte." A twelve-foot-high kiosk, portrait artists with their umbrellas ranged along the lagoon, mimes, a beret-topped strolling trio with accordian, and an outdoor café (Au Petit Café) clutter the forespace of visitors' expectations.

Bordering the right of La Promenade are two upscale Parisian stores — Plume et Palette and La Signature — separated by an arcade with an art nouveau-style façade like many entrances to the Paris metro. To the left are the outdoor café, the keystone restaurant Les Chefs de France, and above it the Bistro de Paris with its red neon sign, which is lit at night. Les Chefs de France is a touristic collector's item, for it is run — more or less — by three of France's most famous chefs — Paul Bocuse, Roger Vergé, and Gaston Le Notre. [59] Food critics have been uniformly disappointed by this restaurant, but for most visitors — whether they know who these chefs are or not — the price is right. This restaurant is one of the earliest to be reserved each day.

To the back left of the showcase is La Petite Rue, a narrow lane that offers a simulation of a village in provincial France. With Barton and Guestier's La Maison du Vin and Tout Pour Le Gourmet on one side and the Boulangerie Patisserie on the other, La Petite Rue leads to the Gallerie des Halles — a token of the iron-and-glass-ceilinged market torn down in Paris some years ago. Among other things, this space collects visitors as they leave the Palais du Cinema.

As do the China and Canada showcases, France offers a movie. Unlike the others, which are CircleVision 360 films, France's *Impressions de France* is shown in a 350-seat theater on five 27 1/2-foot-wide by 21-foot-high screens. This is a film about landmarks, with some scenes of village life thrown in to complete the travelogue. Mont St. Michel, Versailles, Loire Valley chateaux, Cannes, and the French Alps with its obligatory ski scene are included, as are the Seine near Notre Dame and the Eiffel Tower. Rural and town scenes include grape picking, a village flower market and pastry shop, and the celebration of a Brêton wedding.

Counterposed to these scenes is the subtheme of movement — the ski scenes, bicyclists roaring down a country road, an antique automobile race, and a hot air balloon outing about which the narrator quotes Baudelaire on French character. The French Tourist Bureau wants us to know that France has Culture with a capital C. Along with the Baudelaire; the castles, palaces, and other architectural exemplars; and the elegant narration, *Impressions de France* is distinctive in its use of classical music. The music of Offenbach, Saint-Saëns, Debussy, and Satie fills the film's sound track. Especially impressive are the coupling of Satie's *Trois Gymnopédies* with an Alps scene and the use of Offenbach's *Organ Symphony* as a camera rapidly ascends the Eiffel Tower, dramatically presenting Paris below. The latter effect is beyond what even Roland Barthes imagined.[60]

The United Kingdom Showcase

This showcase highlights domestic architecture. Its subtheme reminds us that the United Kingdom has often been called a nation of shopkeepers. Although this showcase offers no movie or ride, there is a good deal of intellectual payoff for those who know something about southeast English architecture and interior design. There is little here of the industrial mid-lands, the north of England, or Cornwall and the southwest.[61] Wales and Scotland are represented essentially by shops — the Magic of Wales and Pringle of Scotland, respectively — although their heraldic crests are visible, along with those of England and Northern Ireland, on the façade of the Toy Soldier facing the lagoon. This is really the England Showcase.

The homey centerpiece of this showcase is the Rose and Crown Pub, the only World Showcase table-service restaurant that sits directly on the lagoon. This building is a paradigm of the showcase's blending of exterior façades and its attention to interior design. Externally, the pub façade presents three separate styles — an early rural cottage, a Tudor tavern, and an 1890s late Victorian bar. The interior recapitulates the same progression of styles.

Whereas the Rose and Crown (with its motto *Otium Cum Dignitate* — Leisure with Dignity) dismembers one's sense of time, the view up High Street accelerates the process. This is a museum view of architectural styles, except that instead of each being shown in its own decontextualized exhibit, they are all recontextualized by a time-bending juxtaposition into a sentimental essence of England.

To the left up High Street, past the sun dial, is Disney's depiction of Anne Hathaway's sixteenth-century Cotswold cottage, half timbered and with a plastic broom-bristle thatched roof that fits Florida's fire regulations. Housing the Tea Caddy (Twinings teas), this cottage leads to the Magic of Wales, which is contained in a fake-four-story structure with a cantilevered Tudor front that hangs out over the street. A pre-Georgian plaster façade (the Queen's Table-Royal Daulton China) and a formal Palladian exterior lead to Britannia Square — a small green with its Hyde Park gazebo and statue of Shakespeare. Behind the High Street shops is another of WDW's quiet spaces — a small village court that contains an herb garden tucked away in the bend of the building and that is faced with its own independent set of façades.

On the right side of Britannia Square is a set of residential late Georgian row houses, connected by a railed balcony, which completes a nostalgic cliché of touristic London. This space houses Pringle of Scotland, with its woolens and tartans. Returning down Tudor Lane and High Street, one passes more façades that lead back to the Toy Soldier and the Promenade. His Lordship — a men's gift shop — simulates a baronial setting, with heraldic trappings, a Jacobean room, and a small Great Hall.

On the right corner are the two façades of the Toy Soldier (which has a Through the Looking Glass chess set for sale for $8,000). Facing High Street is the simulated stone front of a late-sixteenth-century Scottish manor, with round turrets and a stepped gable parapet inspired, according to Birnbaum, by Abbotsford Manor where Sir Walter Scott wrote many of his novels. [62] The promenade side resembles the old red brick part of Henry VIII's Hampton Court, with its turrets and crenellation.

Exiting past the Cockney Pearly Band or the Renaissance Players, we come to yet another small park flanked by scarlet London telephone booths. By now, I guess, visitors are supposed to be humming, "England swings like a pendulum do."

Canada Showcase

"Americans think of Canada as a wooded country full of Eskimos and Indians. This pavilion feeds that image." So says a busboy at Le Cellier, the restaurant at the Canada Showcase. [63] Among other things, this showcase offers an opportunity to assess Disney designers' default mode, which is brought into play when no national government agency or sponsoring corporation participates in the planning.

According to Jim White, the Canadian government (through its Ministry of External Affairs) declined to spend the $10 to $15 million in start up costs and the yearly $1 million maintenance fees demanded by EPCOT officials. [64] He goes on, laying bare motives for participation: "Sounds typically Canadian, eh? Here's a chance to reach some millions of money-spending tourists (they've traveled as far as EPCOT to spend their dollars, haven't they?) to convince them to visit Canada on their next holiday. And what do we do? Nothing." [65] Canadian critics then go on to complain about the showcase's cultural clichés — the totem poles, [66] the woodsy "hoser image," the "true-north-strong-and-free" theme [67] — and about the Disney version of regional Canadian cuisine. [68]

To the continual dismay of Canadians in general, most Americans cannot conceive of Canada as a separate nation with its own culture and traditions: It is just sort of the cold part of America. Exotica may be noted — the red-coated Mounties, for instance — but Americans still wonder why some Canadians speak French. If Canada surprises us, it is usually because some black athlete — Ferguson Jenkins, Grant Fuhr, or Reuben Mayes — turns out to be Canadian.

Disney presents exactly the caricatures of Canada Americans expect, and it is this caricature — not Robertson Davies, the gouvernor general, or Toronto's *real* food — that draws the tourist dollar. Whatever might be meant by the "Saskatchewan" entrée at Le Cellier [69] — chicken and meat-ball stew — the buffet-style restaurant is the most successful restaurant at World Showcase in terms of customer turnover. Considering only commercial purposes, perhaps the Ministry of External Affairs was right: It could rely on Disney designers to construct the appropriate touristic clichés. The advertising is free.

The major theme of the Canada Showcase is the great outdoors, both wilderness and garden. The subtheme is sports. Although cities are represented, especially in the CircleVision 360 film *O Canada*, they are usually presented as encased in nature. Toronto is approached with a camera shot that lifts from the woods at its edge. The first view of Montreal is presented from the air over Mount Royal with the St. Lawrence River in the background. Vancouver, which is surrounded by nature, is shown from the water. Even the Hotel du Canada, the main showcase building — a simulation of Ottawa's French Gothic Chateau Laurier — has a Canadian Rocky Mountain behind it.

As with the France Showcase, Canada is best approached counterclock-wise because the garden sits at its Future World side. Victoria Gardens recalls Butchart Gardens just north of Victoria. Deodar cedars replace Canadian hemlocks and the firs are Fraser firs from North Carolina, but because red maples are native to the entire eastern portion of North America, it was possible to transplant a large specimen from a nearby Florida swamp. Many of the garden annuals — such as cineraria, geraniums, and begonias — are rare transplants to Florida. Added to the indigenous local flora, these flowers produce an ambience quite reminis-cent of Butchart Gardens. [70]

Beyond the garden, the Hotel du Canada (which houses La Boutique des Provinces with its pottery, jewelry, and silks), and a house with a stone façade like many in Ontario, we come to the wilderness and the commer-cialized signs of its inhabitants. The tone is set by large fake boulders on the lagoon side of the Promenade, out of which come Gordon Lightfoot music and retractable light fixtures for nighttime parades.

The courtyard of the showcase, on the lower level before one climbs the steps to the Hotel du Canada and civilization, represents the Canadian West. Totem poles ring the courtyard. Those most frequently touched are made of wood; the others are simulated wood. Bordered on the left side by the Northwest Coast Indian-Style Trading Post and the Northwest Mercan-tile shop and designed to invoke the frontiersmen — English and French trappers, loggers, prospectors, and traders — this courtyard gives us the usual picture of exotic aboriginal artifacts and the white men who came to "tame" the wilderness. Here is where the Maple Leaf Brass — "hosers" all — and the Caledonia Bagpipe Band entertain visitors.

To the left of the pavilion entrance is a small stand of conifers that illustrates another example of Disney planning. The problem with conifers, as Richard R. Beard notes, is that they grow. [71] If allowed to do so naturally, they would destroy the forced perspective scale of the Hotel du Canada and the mountain behind it. Three of the trees, then, are fakes. As Beard writes,

> EPCOT designers sent a crew to Eugene, Oregon, where loggers took them into the forest. There they selected one eighty-foot beauty and had it cut down. One of the craftsmen made a mold of the tree from which a perfect replica was cast. Two trees of the exact texture and color of the original were built, one forty-eight feet high, the other forty feet, and destined to remain so. A third, with a trunk three-and-a-half feet in diameter, the same size as the totem pole, has had its growth stunted, as if by a stroke of lightning, before it could tower too high. [72]

At the back of the showcase sits the mountain. Steps from the Quebec lane in front of the hotel and the "wooden" path along the stream from Victoria Gardens meet (almost) at salmonless Salmon Island. Here one has a close — and wet — view of the waterfall and the pond into which it drops.

Beyond the pond and under the mountain is the entrance to Moosehead Mine and *O Canada*. This "mine," with its simulated rocks, shoring, and Klondike equipment and staffed by Canadians in red-and-black Pendletons, is the waiting area for the film. *O Canada* shows cities, natural wonders, and — above all — sports and recreation. As we have seen, many of the city scenes are encased in nature. We are taken to Quebec City, Montreal, Toronto, Ottawa, Vancouver, and Victoria. Nature is missing only at a Tiger-Cat game in Hamilton, in a Montreal street and the Cathedral de Notre Dame, in the military scenes in Ottawa, and in the bagpipe scene in Halifax. Even the view above the top of the Canadian National building in Toronto turns toward vast Lake Ontario.

We are surrounded by Canada geese and caribou and by slides of moose, bear, elk, and other wildlife. We are taken to the arctic north and to Banff National Park. In and out of this wilderness there are sports — hockey, skating, bobsledding, boating, fishing, a dogsled race, a wagon race at the Calgary Stampede, and the aforementioned football game. The maritime sailing scene, with Gordon Lightfoot singing about "the Bluenose," epitomizes Canadian sports. Oh yes, they ski in Canada, too.

As with all Disney films, both the content and the media are the message. Although part of our attention is drawn to the images around us, part is noticing the technology involved in their making. The 360-degree nine-camera setup seems more foregrounded in this presentation than it does in the similarly made *Wonders of China*. Many of the shots here call attention to their virtuosity in a way the more contemplative China film does not. *O Canada* has by far the least insipid musical theme at EPCOT Center, a duet sung in French and English that actually has something to do with its subject other than commercial sloganeering.

So?

Other than the small national flags for sale at each showcase, what do we take away from Walt Disney's Potemkin village? First, we have some differences. Most showcases present a signatory temporal theme. Mexico's pyramids, Norway's stave church and Akershus, Japan's medieval pagoda and fortress, and France's bel époque structures highlight particular periods of national history. The United Kingdom, Germany, and Canada showcases present a determined architectural collage of different moments of their traditions. Morocco and China (and perhaps Italy) are timeless, emphasizing particular versions of culture and place rather than history per se.

The showcases stress different arts. Mexico builds on dance; Norway, folklore; China, poetry; Italy, opera and theater; France, music; the United Kingdom, architecture; Germany, folk music. Japan shows its landscaping, Morocco its carving and tile work, Canada its sports. Each offers a simplified example of what tourists expect its culinary arts to be.

Each showcase is wrapped in its sensory envelope, consistently themed from its national muzak and street shows to the accents and costumes of its staff — many of them part of WDW's World Fellowship program. The detail is extraordinary. "You may be proud of yourself for noticing something," says a Disney spokesman, "but somebody thought to put it there." And people *do* notice things, from the fake underbricks of Italy and the fake barnacles on the Japanese *torii* to the horticultural efforts throughout World Showcase. All these detailed differences make it difficult to see the forest for the trees.

To see the forest we must look across Showcase Lagoon, especially at night when the IllumiNations show lights up showcase outlines. From this vantage the details blur. World Showcase looks like a pop-up play set of national icons — a pastiche of façades juxtaposed as if a giant had dumped out a sack containing simulacra of less controversial U.S. allies. "Give us thirty minutes," claims CNN Headline News, "and we'll give you the world." So in a day, around one promenade and without Ted Turner, World Showcase presents its version of the same gift.

Yet there is no news, only commercials. These are wonderful commercials, showing distinctive kinds of caricatures and supported by samples of merchandise further promised. Our tailored experiences have entertained us. There is no real history here, only historical items and nostalgia purloined in the interest of fun and commerce. There are no politics, no tragedy, no poverty. We have come to this simulation — left the real world with its real time — for precisely that reason. We are tired and sensorily stuffed, joyful in the knowledge that they don't ski in China and in the feeling that, to paraphrase Henry Ford, "context is bunk."

13

Cinema, Music, Fantasy

It's crazy as hell out there. There has arisen from this mess a strange form of comfort with artifice and falsehood. . . . There may be an actual preference for the unreal.
--Joel Achenbach[1]

"He's old, mom," says the little kid sitting behind me as Ben Franklin creaks up the stairs into Thomas Jefferson's garret. Jefferson is working by candlelight on the umpteenth draft of the Preamble to the U.S. Declaration of Independence. Crumpled papers are strewn around the floor. Smoke rises from the candle. Dirty plates, with the remains of Jefferson's dinner, sit next to the desk.

Franklin has just been talking to Mark Twain. Pretty soon, when the business with Jefferson is finished, George Washington will turn up on his horse, and then, by God, Frederick Douglass will row across a river.

This is part of the show at the American Adventure in World Showcase. At the end — after the stirring music has filled the ear and the sun set over the Statue of Liberty — the audience applauds, loudly and enthusiastically. What it claps for — the people, the horse, Chief Joseph, Will Rogers, and Rosie the Riveter — are robots. The only living part of the show is the attendant who tells us to move all the way down the row and to take our belongings as we leave.

People applaud for a lot of things at WDW that aren't real — well, not real in the sort of picky, naive sense a correspondence theory of truth might lead to. For the robots *are* real — sort of. The clothes and wigs are "authentic." Some of the things the robots seem to say were actually said (or written) by the real people the robots are pretending to be. The characters the robots are supposed to represent are fake in a number of interesting ways. The story they tell is made up. People clap anyway, although it's tricky trying to figure out what they are applauding.

The Disney strategy is to juxtapose the real and the fantastic, surrounding us with this mix until it becomes difficult to tell which is which. A kind of euphoric disorientation is supposed to set in as we progressively accept the Disney definition of things. We are asked to submit to a willful suspension of disbelief in the ostensible interest of a complete entertainment experience.

Frederic Jameson has argued that something like this euphoric disorientation is a characteristic symptom of people's experience of postmodern culture. [2] It's a kind of giddiness that sets in when the normal parameters people use to define reality become occluded in various ways. Joel Achenbach calls the results of this process "creeping surrealism...an imperfect term...meant to describe a general fear that everyone has experienced at one time or another, the fear that *nothing is real anymore.*" [3]

In this part of the book, I argue that the postmodern United States — in which everything, including experience, nature and the unconscious, has become commodified — has creepingly become surrealist. Simulations — models of things that don't exist in reality — abound in advertising and politics. As Achenbach notes, people may still be able to tell the difference between reality and artifice, but increasingly they don't care which is which. They write letters to the characters on *St. Elsewhere* asking for help with their medical problems.

> People are confused. Alienated from nature, liberated from such primordial responsibilities as the growing of food, the making of clothes, the construction of shelter, people in the late 20th Century have entered a revolutionary phase in which they passively accept a cartoon version of reality that is projected upon them by an overwhelming assortment of unrealiable, distortive and sometimes diabolical media. It's crazy as hell out there. There has arisen from this mess a strange form of *comfort* with artifice and falsehood. . . . There may be an actual preference for the unreal. [4]

Begging the question for now, I will discuss postmodern culture in the United States in Chapter 15. There I attend to some of the social and critical theory that has recently been used in explanating the present world. I first describe the Disney use of art and fantasy at WDW. Suffice it to say here that vinyl leaves on a concrete tree and conversations between Ben Franklin and Mark Twain sound like creeping surrealism to me.

The Real and the Fake

Because it seems to me that the Disney plan is to juxtapose the real and the fake, we might start with these as axiomatic categories in approaching WDW. There are, undeniably, real things there — the undeveloped scrub forest, the various park structures, the climate. The food is real; so are the lines, the visitors, the conveyances, the ticket counters, and the utility corridors. The whole point of any amusement park, however, is to entice visitors with things and events that are not real and not normal. Otherwise, why would anybody make the effort and spend the money to go to one?

The genius of Disney, obviously, is in the artifice; but this artifice is extremely complicated. The lines between the real and the fake are systematically blurred. For instance, there are real birds at WDW. They fly in and out of the park, perch on trees, and scrounge food at outdoor restaurants.[5] They have adapted to life in this new city. Their chatter, chirp, and whistle seem normal. Yet bird sounds also come from branches on which no birds sit. These are recorded sounds played through hidden speakers. Now, it's clear that the storefronts on Main Street USA are false, but it's not so clear about the birds.

Disney's relentless presentation of the fake as real is often charming. Each time we discover this artifice — especially subtle examples such as the vinyl leaves, the phony exposed bricks at the Italian Showcase, and the concrete trees at "Canada" — we are amazed at the cleverness. Yet this amazement chips away at our confidence that we can make discriminations. How many fake things have become real for us? And as Achenbach might ask, does it matter that we might not be able to tell the difference?

As the fake becomes real, space opens up for the real to become fake. "This is not *real* rain," we are told, as what seems like real rain begins to fall on us in our Mike Fink Keelboat. "It is brought to you through the magic of Walt Disney." This is a postmodern cultural experience not unlike the strange stories we are told in commercials or by governmental officials. The form of Disney illusions parallels that of those we are used to at home. At WDW we know we will be surrounded by fantasy. We have paid for it; yet many things slip by as reality, because Disney simulations articulate with the fantasies of middle-class America. Umberto Eco places these ontological confusions in the realm of "hyperreality . . . where the American imagination demands the real thing and, to attain it, must fabricate the absolute fake."[6]

The concepts of real and fake, however, are too blunt to capture the subtleties of Disney simulations. At WDW things are not just real or fake but real real, fake real, real fake, and fake fake. I want merely to circle around these metaphysical categories of representation. Let me suggest some examples.

The real birds and the climate are real real; so is the limestone geology that underlies WDW. Hunger, thirst, crowds, trash, and sewage are real real.

These are often elements of nature, and they are the parameters with which Disney must work. The Disney project requires that these elements be transformed or brought under as much control as possible. In my discussion of spatial infrastructure, urban planning, and utopia in Chapters 10 and 11, I described WDW techniques for dealing with the real world. As we have seen, these technical procedures are sophisticated and efficacious.

Fake fake things at WDW are the stuff of fantasy and commerce. These are representations of things the Walt Disney Company has invented or purloined. Many of them, such as the Veggie Combo dolls from the Kitchen Kabaret, are marketed as souvenirs. [7] Others, such as the mermaid in 20,000 Leagues Under the Sea, are fantasy elements of various attractions.

Among the most important fake fakes are the live cast members dressed as Disney characters who populate the Magic Kingdom. Here, in an ironic phrase, "Disney characters come alive" to greet and mingle with the crowd. Most of these characters were borrowed from literature and turned into animated versions by Disney movie productions. These characters are now embodied by real people in costume earning hourly wages. The most important character, of course, is Mickey Mouse, invented by Walt Disney himself and given a kingdom in Florida. As an animated character, Mickey is a real fake; As portrayed by a cast member, he is a fake fake. As children know, this fake fake is more real than the real fake. Just listen to them cry, "Look, its *really* Mickey!"

Most of the messages at WDW are carried by the fake real, the real fake, and the dialectical movement between the two. Disney presents real fakes, countless numbers of them, and runs its audience past and through them at high speed. The result is not merely the blunting of visitors' powers of discrimination and the blurring of boundaries between reality and artifice: It is, more important, a transformation of the real fake into the fake real. What is presented is fantasy but, especially at EPCOT Center, fantasy that is often to be taken as true. We are given simulations of various orders — models of things that don't exist that we are to see as real. The "ideological seams" [8] are tightly drawn and marked by the message that after all, this is just play.

The process works because the artistry of the real fakes is brilliant. Whether it is the false turn-of-the-century façades on Main Street USA, the collapsing seat cushions at the Mission to Mars, the Caribbean reef aquarium at The Living Seas, the pagoda at the Japan Showcase, the Indiana Jones Epic Stunt Spectacular at the Disney-MGM Studios, or the ubiquitous audioanimatronic robots throughout WDW, the skill and control of the artifice are stunning. We know objects are ersatz because for we are in World Showcase, not Paris. But the fakes are authentic in the way (we have been taught) only Disney can make them. Wandering through Liberty Square is a real experience, although this may be disputed by the staff at Colonial Williamsburg. [9]

The crucial concern is: How do many of us come to believe Disney's authentic simulations represent realities? For most people, riding through the Haunted Mansion is a relatively benign experience. We don't think of the ghosts as real ghosts. It's not so clear, however, how we are to understand the raping and pillaging in Pirates of the Caribbean. The guidebooks all tell us that the ride is zany and that we will be amused. Well, yes and no.

The shift from the real fake to the fake real is positively dangerous, however, when we look at the images of the past and future shown to us by the corporations of Future World. The future here requires us to place ourselves in the hands of "benign" corporate leaders who control the technology that will help us fulfill our dreams of "conquering new frontiers." Here we are asked to take our soma.

These issues of the representation of history, visions of the future, and the selling of the idea of technology as neutral salvation occupy us elsewhere in this book. Here I discuss Disney artistry. How do the presentations at WDW work? How are fantasy and rhetoric used to construct Disney's real fakes?

Animated Myth

The artistic roots of Disney are found in the movies. Whatever the source of Disney stories — fairy tales, novels, music (as in the case of *Fantasia*), or purely independent invention — they were transformed in the interest of cinematic presentation. The core of the Disney Studio's work for many years was animation — the birth source of Mickey, Donald, Goofy, and all the other characters that have colonized the globe. In the mid-1940s, live animation — the combination of live actors and animated characters mixed together on the screen — generated such classics as *Song of the South* and later *Mary Poppins*.

As the drawing power of feature-length animation waned, as television brought the animated short into the home, and as the expenses of animation soared, Disney turned to fully live feature films. Later, with the invention of CircleVision 360, the wraparound pseudodocumentary travelogue became possible. All of these cinematic styles as well as the 3-D techniques of *Captain E-O* are found at WDW.[10]

The organizational principles at WDW are cinematic. Attractions, lands, and worlds are put together in acts and scenes. We are led step-by-step through Disneyfied stories, whether in single attractions or in larger areas of the parks. Even in the most extended presentations — those that seem most like theater — the scenes are cinematically short.

One must understand WDW as a carefully edited place. Elements are included or left out through editorial decisions. We are pointed in particular directions and away from others by the scene structure. Sometimes the control is obvious, sometimes not, because there are varying rhythms of autonomy at the parks.

Rides are the most constrictive attractions. We are strapped into a conveyance and sent passively through a story. The cars or boats move past tableaux that often surround us. We face forward or look to the side. Many cars have high backs and eye-restricting sides. They spin and turn, pointing us toward the next scene and away from anything that might spoil the illusion. They frame our view as we ride past in the dark. Exits to vehicle storage areas are camouflaged. Only with a glitch in the ride is our attention drawn to escape routes and the possibility of leaving the ride. Yet leaving a stalled ride leads to disappointment, not the exhiliration of escape.

Although we cannot walk out of a "bad" ride, we can walk out of a "bad" theater show. We are strapped in only by our patience, sense of civility, and viewing location. Theater shows must captivate both adults and children lest disruptions occur. For instance, the *Tropical Serenade* in Adventureland is a problem. One of the oldest and slowest-paced shows at WDW, this attraction is plagued by visitors — especially teenagers — who regularly walk out, opening the exit door to the outside sunlight and thus interrupting the illusion.

Released from our confinement — whether ride or show (preceded by a line) — we head for a concession stand. Here during intermission between shows we are offered food, drink, and Disney souvenirs that refer to the experience we have just had. Our need for autonomy is directed toward impulse buying. That, of course, is much of the point.

But it is not all of the point. The stories themselves have content, and WDW as a whole tells cinematic metastories in which each attraction becomes a scene in a larger production. Our rhythms of autonomy and carefully organized openings for choice are orchestrated to let the metastories seep into us as if by osmosis.

What kind of movies are we in at WDW? Let me begin where Walt Disney began — with animation — because much of the Magic Kingdom and some of EPCOT Center consist of cartoons. Animation is far more demanding than many people imagine. The technical process is extremely labor-intensive; and because this is highly skilled labor, animation is costly. [11]

Artistically, animation presents a distinctive set of problems. Further, Disney's intended audience — children and whatever adults they might inveigle into accompanying them to the theater — had special requirements of its own. These problems have to do with story line, character development, and mood and style.

Story lines must tack between the simplicity and clarity required by a child audience and the difficulties of sustaining people's attention through an entire feature-length cartoon. The solutions to these requirements resulted in a method Richard Schickel has called "Disneyfication." [12] Many of the studio's animated features retell classic stories to which children may already have had access. Snow White, Cinderella, Peter Pan, and Pinocchio, among others, exist as available fairy tales. In appropriating these tales for commercial purposes, Disney imposes a number of changes on the material. To understand these changes, a brief excursion into mythology is needed; some simple notions about how myth works illuminate the function of fairy tales.

In *The Social Construction of Reality*, Peter L. Berger and Thomas Luckmann suggest that mythology is one of the types of conceptual machinery that acts to support a social group's "universe-maintaining symbolic system." [13] In the anthropological literature, there are two basic theories about how this works. The first, associated with the name Bronislaw Malinowski, says that myth forms a "cultural charter," which a society's members use to direct and interpret their social rules and behavior. The second theory, presented by Claude Lévi-Strauss, is that myth acts to mask and cover over actual contradictions in the institutional structure of society. These contradictions are worked out in myth and thus do not have to be worked out in structure-based social action.

I think myth performs both of these functions but in a particular consistent order. That is, myth masks contradiction and then, as ideology, acts as a charter for understanding and policy. For example, except in times of national crisis, federal policies that affect employment, family support, and child care have been predicated on the idea that a husband is the only worker. Yet this myth covers up the fact that great numbers of women have worked outside the U.S. home for over a hundred and sixty years (at least since textile mills came to Massachusetts in the 1830s) and that a great number of U.S. families have had single women (never married, divorced, or widowed) as the sole source of material support. As more and more women enter the work force, it becomes more difficult for this particular myth to mask the contradiction and chart policy.

Will Wright further highlights the cognitive function of myths for the people to whom they are told as he stresses that both the structure of myth and its story help people think through contradictions in their social world by displacing those contradictions into metaphor, at the same time identifying and resolving them in ways that help people live with paradox. "When the story is a myth and the characters represent social types or principles in a structure of oppositions, then the narrative structure offers a model of social action by presenting identifiable social types and showing how they interact. The receivers of the myth learn how to act by recognizing their own situation in it and observing how it is resolved." [14]

The fairy tales and children's stories Disney has animated include these mythic features. Children are taught charter-like precepts about truth and falsehood (*Pinocchio*), jealousy (*Snow White*), and physiognomic differences

(*Dumbo*). Messages such as these are obviously pedagogical. They are dramatically and viscerally underlined.

Cognitive lessons about contradiction are a bit less obvious. Many such lessons are appropriate to the particular historical circumstances that surround their production. Stories about princes, princesses, commoners, pirates, disease, and death arise from social and medical worlds that may no longer exist. The stories persist either by becoming sentimental and nostalgic anachronisms — encapsulated as timeless members of the fairy tale canon — or by changing in ways that speak to new circumstances. [15]

Twentieth-century efforts to tame the harshness found in many fairy tales mask the harshness found in many children's actual lives behind a putative sentimental niceness. At the same time, contradictions such as those embodied in the Oedipus complex or class conflict are metaphorically displaced onto animal characters. In *The Three Little Pigs*, for example, the "law of nature" is thwarted by the Protestant ethic.

Fairy tales and myths do not only act cognitively: Their power may also be deeply felt emotionally. Fairy tales are prime evidence that an analytical separation between cognitions and emotions is ontologically inappropriate. We might better speak of "cogmotions." Bruno Bettelheim, among others, has written extensively about the psychodynamic functions of fairy tales. [16] He suggests that fairy tales provide a forum in which deep and troubling human contradictions might be felt through, especially by children. By confronting the stories in fairy tales — many of them concerning punishment, death, revenge, vindication, greed, envy, love, and hate — children can emotionally discharge strong feelings without threatening their normal, everyday lives.

For instance, parents are often split metaphorically into good and bad characters in stories that contain punishment for the latter. Often such punishments are quite horrible, as with the demise of the wicked queen in *Snow White*. These exaggerated punishments, perhaps wish fulfilling on the unconscious level, provide what Bettelheim considers a relatively safe fantasy for the displacement of children's real anger.

Bettelheim argues that in the interest of psychodynamic health, such stories are very useful. He further suggests that removing the violence and sadness from such tales in the interest of protecting young minds from disturbing information does children a disservice. Smoothing out the emotional highs and lows eliminates vehicles for displacement at a time when such vehicles are needed.

Disney animation retells and creates children's stories in the interest of commerce. These productions aim not so much at the cogmotive functions of these stories as ends but rather as means to sell theater tickets. Frederic Jameson's suggestion that one of the hallmarks of late capitalism is the commodification of the unconscious is particularly apposite to Disney products.

Disney's story lines contain a characteristic mixture of smoothing out and emotional punching, a mixture Richard Schickel has described as gratuitous and manipulative. We must remember, first, that the popular sources of Disney's works become "properties" in the hands of the studio. Once James Barrie's *Peter Pan* or Lewis Carroll's *Alice in Wonderland* is appropriated, it becomes available for Disneyfication. [17]

In the attempt to turn fairy tales and children's stories into commercial animation, Disney faced some central dilemmas about time. Fairy tales tend to be short. We hear them in a limited period of time. They are appropriate, perhaps, to the length of an animated short. Expanding a fairy tale to feature-film length allows and requires considerable creative liberties. Stories must be stretched and filled in. As Disney animators and story men were advised ad nauseum, nothing should reach the screen that does not advance the story line in some way. Busy elements that might distract the audience from the tale, no matter how technically or artistically interesting were to be eliminated. Much of Disney's intended audience, after all, was not expected to have much of an attention span.

The classical children's story presents a different version of the time problem. Written to be heard or read in small chunks, such literature is episodic. Characters appear in a series of vignettes loosely tied together by such metathemes as a journey, a dream, or an attempt to return home. Although the animation of fairy tales leads to the invention of episodes, children's novels are too long for this. They must be trimmed. The need for shortening allows Disney considerable editorial license. [18]

In seeking to retain an audience for an hour-and-a-half, Disney chose story strategies that contained what Edmund Wilson called "an infallible formula to provoke [the audience's] automatic responses." [19] Walt Disney always understood that any show needed to contain periodic rewards for its viewers. Yet his brand of folk psychology led him to believe that such rewards — especially vengeance and vindication — would be most subjectively effective if they followed moments of deep sadness and tragedy. When his stories swing from emotional neutrality — filled with sentimental cuteness and simulated warmth — to emotional intensity, they do so with a vengeance. This emotional manipulation is especially strong in movies such as *Dumbo* and *Bambi*, whose main characters are animals. As Schickel notes, "There was one subartistic current of criticism that has plagued all of Disney's animated films. That was the claim that the film was too violent, too frightening, for children." [20]

There is a good deal of cruelty in many Disney films. We might ask whether the fear such cruelty taps in its audience is Bettelheim's psychodynamically salutory fear, Wilson's automatic response, or simply gratuitous. Although there is some evidence for all three interpretations, I think the last two are the more salient.

Walt Disney claimed to believe something similar to what Bettelheim later argued: that it was good for children to be frightened so that later joy might be heightened. But why heighten joy? Bettelheim was not interested in the happy resolution of fairy tales but in the symbolic presentation of difficult and dangerous psychosocial contradictions. The fear that resulted from such stories was healthy, much more so than the potential fear generated by real life. Disney's joy was used to sell movie tickets and, incidentally, to support the merchandising of the characters who elicited that joy. "It is the business of art," writes Schickel, "to expand consciousness, while it is the business of mass communications to reduce it." [21] Wilson's infallible formula for automatic response is a marketing ploy.

We might still say that Disney was Bettelheimian, even if the end of the emotional roller coaster was commercial. Yet curiously, Disney pulled his punches just at the point where his folk psychology might have made sense. Schickel writes, "Wild things and wild behavior were often made comprehensible by converting them into cuteness, mystery was explained with a joke, and terror was resolved by a musical cue or a distinct averting of the camera's eye from the natural process." [22]

Unpleasantness is pointed out but ultimately glossed over by a last-minute manipulation under the pseudoguise of protecting young sensibilities. The extent to which Disney people consider this to be a normal procedure that is barely, if at all, in need of justification can only lead to queasiness. These tugs at the heartstrings lead beyond sentimentality — perhaps even beyond commercialism.

Schickel calls the animated cartoon "that primitive theater of cruelty" [23] and "a compulsive's delight." [24] Animation easily lends itself to certain kinds of exaggerated slapstick — "a cartoon character could take a great fall, break into a dozen pieces and be put back together, no harm done, with a few strokes of an animator's pen, thus conventionalizing and therefore deemotionalizing sadism." [25]

Cartoon cruelty, especially to animal characters, need not have consequences. It may thus, and in many Disney movies did, seem gratuitous — just a way of having fun. Yet when questioned about the deeper, darker aspects of his cartoons, Disney never confessed. As Schickel writes, "Barely on familiar terms with his own — not to mention anyone else's — subconscious mind, he rejected all interpretations of the work which extended beyond what is actually shown." [26]

What is actually shown is often something that happens to animals. With the exception of feature films such as *Snow White, Cinderella, Pinocchio,* and *The Sword in the Stone,* Disney's important characters are animals. Even these films contain major animal characters. Disney's short cartoons almost always have animal stars.

From *Aesop's Fables* on, animals have been used in western folk traditions as anthropomorphic vehicles for human attitudes, foibles, and personalities. The Disney oeuvre extends this practice, adding to it a slick sentimentality that is passed off as appropriate to "family entertainment." Schickel writes, "Disney blended a citified sentiment about dumb creatures with his practical acceptance of the harshness and blunt humor of the farm." [27] Further, viewing Disney films, "Audiences could easily feel simultaneously affectionate and superior to [animals]." [28]

Although they could be bathed in bathos, as they were in *Dumbo* and *Bambi*, or be perky and bouncy, animals could also be used to develop sharper-edged ongoing personalities. The most famous — the putative monarch of the two Magic Kingdoms — is Mickey Mouse, but Donald Duck, Goofy, Pluto, and others have developed their own systematic personae.

Mickey began his career as a rather cruel mouse, a perpetrator of pranks, and a general troublemaker. Over the years, perhaps scared by his role as the sorceror's apprentice in *Fantasia*, Mickey has mellowed considerably. Now he is the nonjudgmental king of sweetness, master of ceremonies, and smoother of the water in his realm. Curiously, as Stephen Jay Gould has shown, Mickey's physical form has changed over the years. [29] His body and features have become more rounded and less pointed. As his character changed, Mickey's illustrators marked the changes by neotenizing him. Whether consciously or not, they followed classical rules of physical development, reversing them as Mickey became more childlike and less threatening.

Animated human characters have always presented more difficulties than do animals. The problem with lead characters such as Cinderella, Snow White, and even Mowgli is to make them interesting. The most interesting human Disney characters have always been secondary ones. Captain Hook, Smee, the Seven Dwarfs, and various types of witches and crones are amenable to caricature in a way Disney's sweet heroines and heroes are not. The latter come to life most successfully not in animation but as embodied by live actors at the theme parks.

One of the significant absences in Disney's panoply of characters is the role of the mother. No one except Dumbo seems to have one, and she, like Bambi's mother, is bathetically removed from the story. [30] Mothers are divided into good and bad surrogates, good witches and bad ones — the former loving and helpful, the latter punished for their misdeeds. Among the bad ones are stepmothers, who boost their own unpleasant children and are jealous of their stepdaughters.

Kay Stone has some interesting things to say about Walt Disney's fictional women. [31] The stories Disney chose to animate — especially "Sleeping Beauty" and "Snow White" from the Grimm brothers and Perrault's "Cinderella" — are filled with bland, passive heroines. Their villains are all female. Stone writes,

Walt Disney is responsible not only for amplifying the stereotype of good versus bad women suggested by the children's books based on the Grimms, he must also be criticized for his portrayal of a cloying fantasy world filled with cute little beings existing among pretty flowers and singing animals. . . . Heroes succeed because they act, not because they are. . . . Heroines are not allowed any defects, nor are they required to develop, since they are already perfect. [32]

One wonders why this treatment of animals and women has been so successful. Animals and such distinctive humanoids as Snow White's dwarfs are clearly excellent vehicles for cartoon character development. We remember Donald's and Dopey's quirks long after we have forgotten much of the films in which they are found. Other human characters present the problem that unlike live action films in which actors and actresses have their own independent personae, training, and acting skills to bring to bear on their various roles, cartoon humans must be constructed entirely out of the projective skills of the animators. One cannot anthropomorphize Cinderella or Gepetto in the same way that one can Kaa, the python in *The Jungle Book*. Captain Hook and the witches can be given memorable signatures through exaggeration, but the "nice girls" are different.

Yet for generations of U.S. children (as well as those elsewhere), fantasy has been redefined as a genre with precisely the "magical" characteristics and "pixie dust" Disney has offered. Behind this pixie dust are pretty, sweet, bland heroines — with a touch of sexless sexiness [33] — klutzy villains, and adorable animals. Even as Disney's animated feature films became less popular and the studio turned to equally bland live films, the classical animated animal characters remained central icons of U.S. fantasy culture. They just changed residence to Disneyland and the Magic Kingdom.

Animation and the 3-D extensions of its capabilities and requirements define much of WDW, but especially the Magic Kingdom. The Disney strategy is to place its customers in the middle of a series of animated scenes so they become part of the show. This technique draws from the studio's combined animated live films, *Song of the South* and *Mary Poppins*; but Disney's animation has been extended at the parks in a number of important ways through the coupling of normal animation concepts with computerized robotics. The invention of audioanimatronics such as the Jefferson and Franklin robots mentioned at the beginning of this chapter, has led to a qualitatively different kind of simulation. I return to the "tronics" part of these robots later, but for now let me say a few things about the "audio" part. [34]

Voices

Sound is central to both animation and the show at WDW.[35] In both, the style, texture, and synchronization of voice with animation perform constructive and rhetorical tasks. The feedback relation between an actor's voice-over and the development of a particular character was crucial to Disney films. Some of these voices — Mickey's, Pluto's, and especially Donald's — became Disney signatures, recognizable in their own right as corporate audiologos. Amplified by sound systems, these voices are highly evident at WDW.

Many voices at WDW are used rhetorically as devices for telling Disney's metastory. First, Disney makes use of voices familiar to us from the public world. When Walter Cronkite speaks to us in our cars at Spaceship Earth, telling us that nature is hostile but that through corporate-controlled technology we can face the new frontiers of a better day, his familiar grandfatherly voice seductively lends credence to the spiel. When the American Adventure tells of expansion to the west, it sounds like Henry Fonda doing the talking. As Lincoln at the Hall of Presidents, Royal Dano does a pretty good Walter Brennan. These and other voices are used partly because they have become associated with particular characters or communication genres in U.S. culture and partly because they have become accepted as icons of trustworthiness.

Second, some Disney voices are recognizable only to the cognoscenti as belonging to particular people. These are the clear, melifluous, Standard American English voices — mostly male — that have come to be known generally as Disney voices.[36] We hear them in the monorail, on the park radio channels, and in the rides. They tell us to "step out to the right," to "take small children by the hand," and to "remember our personal belongings." They welcome us, reassure us, and tell us what we are not supposed to do — almost always with a "please."

Women's voices are far less evident at the Magic Kingdom than they are at EPCOT Center. As pleasant and "accentless"[37] as the men, disembodied women are evident at the Magic Kingdom mostly when rides malfunction. Male voices tell us that the ride has temporarily stopped (sometimes due to malfunction but usually in order to load handicapped visitors into ride vehicles), reassuring us that Disney knows about our motionless plight. A female voice tells us that our ride is about to continue, letting us know that our hearts can begin to beat again.

Women's voices are more in evidence at EPCOT, reflecting slightly the changes in women's public status since the Magic Kingdom was built. Although "mother" reprises her Carousel of Progress role in Horizons, she at least gets equal — if ditzy — time in the car speakers. A woman stars in the Backstage Magic computer revue, albeit as a secretary, and a Susan B. Anthony robot turns up at the American Adventure. Perhaps the most adult example of a woman's voice is found at The Living Seas, where a woman narrates the short opening film on the beginnings of the earth's oceans.

Third, there are the live voices. Attraction attendants, mostly young, are hired from the surrounding communities. Here is our chance to hear the soft drawl of central Florida. Most of the spiels are tightly scripted, and, as is especially evident in the pre- and post-theater show announcements, some attempt has been made to instill the earnest, mechanical, misplaced-emphasis style of elocution that increasingly characterizes U.S. public service speech.

At World Showcase (and to a limited extent at the Polynesian Village Resort) we hear different accents. Crucial to its cosmopolitan pastiche are the sounds of the nations represented around World Showcase Lagoon. Consistent with national themes, attendants with the appropriate accents are hired to deal with the public. Many of these cast members[38] come to WDW by way of the International Fellowship Program, which brings foreign nationals to Florida for a year or so for jobs and training.

Other live voices belong to the many musical performers scattered throughout WDW. These include the barbershop quartet on Main Street USA (the Dapper Dans); the bands at Tomorrowland Terrace; the steel drum band at Caribbean Plaza (J. P. and the Silver Stars); the Diamond Horseshoe Jamboree and various resort hotel shows; the Kids of the Kingdom (performing in Cinderella's Castle's forecourt and the Tomorrowland Theater); and the various groups who perform at the American Gardens Theater by the Shore in World Showcase, the open-air theater on Hollywood Boulevard, and the nightclubs on Pleasure Island. World Showcase presents a number of nationally themed musical groups at regular intervals as well as the a capella Voices of Liberty at the American Adventure. Much of the music at WDW is performed by winners of periodic national auditions, who are chosen for yearly professional internships.

One group from which we will not hear the human voice is made up of the various Disney characters who roam WDW in costume. Here the illusion of animation come to life is not to be spoiled by inappropriate vocalization. Mickey Mouse costumes are often worn by young women, whose voices would ruin the effect. If these characters need to be heard, their recorded voices blare out over park sound systems.[39]

Music

Music is an integral aural component of Disney films and of the show at WDW. Frank Thomas and Ollie Johnston report on the increasingly sophisticated techniques by which musical scores have been attached to animation.[40] Such techniques have included the invention of a musical notation that coordinates a score with the movement of photographed animated frames. The music for the most part has been determinedly middlebrow — even the passages chosen for *Fantasia*. Most Disney music has been unmemorable, although a few songs — "When You Wish upon a Star" (*Pinocchio*), "Whistle While You Work" (*Snow White*), "Zip-a-Dee Doo Dah" (*Song of the South*), and "Some Day My Prince Will Come" (*Cinderella*) — have become U.S. classics. [41] Each of these songs has become a signature not just for the film in which it appeared but for Disney sensibilities in general.

Many attractions at WDW have musical signatures. Although they differ somewhat in style in the various theme parks, they perform a similar set of rhetorical functions. Most of the show music at the Magic Kingdom is infantilizing. The themes suggest that adults performing nefarious and violent activities, as at the Pirates of the Caribbean, are just like children whose mommies and daddies will tuck them into bed after their adventures. The ghosts and goblins at the Haunted Mansion are not to be taken seriously; the possibilities of supernatural terror are punctuated with humor and general silliness. [42] The theme from It's a Small World presents "a world of laughter" in which fractious adults do not exist. Although initially separated by continents, child dolls join together in the last room — dressed in white — in a sentimental internationalism.

All of the tunes at the Magic Kingdom are inoffensive, even cute, at first hearing. They are sufficiently short, however, that one can hear them many times at a given attraction. "It's a Small World" can be heard throughout the entrance area. Even though its volume has been significantly curtailed, it is nonetheless reminiscent of the proverbial water torture. Like obnoxious commercial jingles from other media, Magic Kingdom tunes are difficult to get out of one's head. With them, Disney succeeds in capturing a portion of customers' cognitive space.

Disney music and sound effects pervade the parks, adding their cacophony to the massive assault on visitors' senses. Compartmentalization and decontextualization ride in tandem, provided by the themed experiential "envelopes" through which customers are led. These envelopes are like scenes in a movie into the middle of which visitors are inserted. Until we leave one scene for the next, we are surrounded by multivalent Disney effects.

The use of music at EPCOT Center is different from the childlike fantasies evoked by the music in the Magic Kingdom. Especially at Future World, EPCOT's music is that of a world of corporations. In keeping with its monumental architecture, Future World greets us with monumental music. Beyond the entrance, as we head for the giant golf ball of Spaceship Earth, hidden speakers blare the theme from the American Adventure — rhetorically tying together the two disparate parts of EPCOT Center. This music, reminiscent of "Fanfare for the Common Man," is meant to charge up the visitor, to set an expansive, celebratory tone for the EPCOT experience. It is quite unlike the localizing, small-scale public music of the Magic Kingdom.

This monumental music gives way throughout the rest of Future World's public spaces to Disney muzak — a major sign of the corporate world — emanating from camouflaged speakers throughout the landscaping. This muzak forms a pervasive undertone to our meander, presumably performing the unobtrusively relaxing or charging up function muzak claims as one of its raisons d'être.

Inside most Future World pavilions, music has a different purpose. Here it is clearly ideological, as the insipid signature tunes present a message that defines the world in the interest of sponsoring corporations. These songs appropriate general U.S. cultural desiderata — fun, freedom, creativity — and associate their fulfillment with the commercial products purveyed by the sponsor.

In the World of Motion, for example, the General Motors ditty tells us that "it's fun to be free." This song weaves its way through a ride that presents GM's version of the history of transportation — a history that leads teleologically to four wheels and the internal combustion engine. Other forms of transportation are presented as amusing and cute, but as Mike Wallace points out, each one leads to some sort of mishap.[43] GM denatures freedom, redefining it as the ability to travel the open road in one's own automobile — presumably a GM product.

AT&T's Spaceship Earth presents its history of communication and the corporation's "solutions" to "challenges" — spoken of in terms of "we" and "us" — not in the interests of corporate profits but in those of "Tomorrow's Child." As the song tells us, tomorrow's child is going to have an exciting, communicative future.

General Electric's Horizons doesn't have a theme song, but it does have a signature slogan — "if we can dream it, we can do it." This echo of U.S. pragmatic optimism also uses the rhetorical "we" as it lines us up behind the corporate planners. We don't miss a theme song here, however, because "This Is the Best Time of Your Life" is still ringing in our ears from GE's Carousel of Progress in Tomorrowland. At least at Horizons we are not asked to sing along.[44]

Kodak's Journey into Imagination and Kraft's The Land present more than one type of music.[45] The former begins with an audioanimatronic ride, throughout which the Dreamfinder sings the pavilion's theme song. This song, "Imagination," is in the Magic Kingdom genre — the only one like it at EPCOT.

The middle part of this attraction provides one of EPCOT's hands-on exhibits — Image Works. Here visitors can wander through a number of different setups in which, within the technical limits programmed into each, they may "create" their own art. Included are a few areas in which, by stepping on portions of the floor lit with different hues or moving their hands over certain marked display areas, people can create patterns of musical sounds. Given the control under which people spend much of their time at WDW and the ensuing passivity, the Image Works is quite liberating. It is illuminating to watch parents, eager to move on to the next part of the pavilion — the 3-D Michael Jackson movie — try to drag recalcitrant children away from the musical and drawing apparatuses, with which the children are having a good deal of fun.

Captain E-O, the Michael Jackson movie, is distinctive at WDW for a number of reasons.[46] First, this is the only film at WDW the creative direction of which has been contracted out to non-Disney Hollywood people. The film stars Michael Jackson, who is responsible for the musical direction and the choreography. It costars Angelica Huston as the evil empress freed by Jackson's music. The film was produced by Francis Ford Coppola and directed by George Lucas. These are all non-Disney heavy hitters, although Jackson's bizarre affinity with the Disney corporation makes him less non-Disney than the others.[47]

Second, *Captain E-O* is a three-Dimensional film, produced with a technology that has not been notably effective with the public recently. Disney Studio 3-D technology is state of the art — even more sophisticated than the earlier offering, *Magic Journeys*. Playing off Lucas's *Star Wars* trilogy, *Captain E-O* features Disneyfied versions of the puppet-like and fantasy-costumed characters that filled Lucas's earlier movies. Lavender plastic glasses are distributed to the audience for viewing, some of which end up as souvenirs. As with all such movies, the audience responds with the appropriate "oohs" and "aahs" as characters appear to leave the screen and intrude on peoples' personal space.

Third, Michael Jackson's music, played without decibilic restraint, is meant to appeal to a demographic category of potential visitors not well tapped by the Magic Kingdom or the rest of EPCOT Center. In a bland New Age muzak version, this kind of upbeat music has spread into the various shows put on throughout WDW, especially the Magic Kingdom Fantasy Parades. Everything sounds like an electronic cousin of Mannheim Steamroller's "Good King Wenceslas." Accompanied by a somewhat-more-than-cheerleader sexiness and a mini-skirted "rocking" Minnie Mouse, the Kids of the Kingdom and their music are part of Disney's modernization campaign.

The Land also has different kinds of music, including, I think, both Future World's most clever and most pernicious musical offerings. I discuss this pavilion extensively in Chapter 16, but here let me note a few things about the music. The Kitchen Kabaret tells its story with a very entertaining set of allusions to musical styles and performers of the 1930s, 1940s, and early 1950s. There is a payoff here to those — older parents and grandparents — who bring knowledge of those times with them.

Symbiosis is the most elegant film at Future World. Taking its theme from René Dubos and accompanied by a dramatic, grand orchestral score, *Symbiosis* is filled with stunning visual imagery as it describes various relations between humans and nature.

The bologna in this sandwich is Listen to the Land, a boat ride through a series of demonstration hothouses that purports to show us the agriculture of the future. The tune sung at the beginning and end of this ride is a paradigm of corporate ideology and mystification. The exhibits show how agricultural high technology, much of it beyond the means of nonindustrial farmers, will transform the way "we" grow our crops. The land is to be manipulated, tricked, and beaten into submission, told what to be, and certainly not listened to. Pretending to contain the kind of ecological understanding that might carry over from *Symbiosis*, the signature tune tells us to "listen to the land." This message is clearly the opposite of that conveyed by the exhibits. Few visitors seem to note the contradiction.

The cinematic structure, architectural style, and uses of music in World Showcase are somewhat different from those of Future World. As I discussed World Showcase in the previous chapter, let me now return to the Magic Kingdom and WDW's original land of make-believe: Fantasyland. Following this tour, I take a look at the Disney-MGM Studios, where the entire focus is on cinematic art.

14

Fantasyland and the
Disney-MGM Studios

All the horses are white, Disney spokespeople will tell you, because all the riders are good guys.

—Steve Birnbaum [1]

Fantasyland

If any icon other than Mickey Mouse represents the carefully constructed eternal childhood Disney offers to the market, it is Cinderella's Castle in Fantasyland. [2] Rising 180 feet in the air on the north side of the Plaza, this structure embodies much of what the Magic Kingdom is about. With its many spires and its filigree, this fantasy is a composite design that draws from Mad King Ludwig's castle at Neuschwanstein in Bavaria and the gothic architectural designs of twelfth- and thirteenth-century France and their transformations by Disney artists into the generic fantasies of Disney animation. [3]

Inside and below this architectural shell is a series of levels on which Magic Kingdom functions are performed. At the top, a cable runs from the castle across the Plaza. On those nights when the park stays open long after dark, an acrobat dressed as Tinkerbell slides down the cable, bathed in a spotlight. This illusion of flight, along with the Disney fireworks display, caps the presentation at the Magic Kingdom. [4]

Inside the central spire are a broadcast room, security rooms, an elevator, and a small apartment — built to be used by the Disney family in the same way as was Walt Disney's apartment over the City Hall on Disneyland's Main Street. Apparently, no one has ever stayed here, and the space has been used as a storeroom and a changing room for various Tinkerbells.

Beneath the apartment is King Stefan's Banquet Hall. Named for Sleeping Beauty's father, this restaurant — with its high ceiling, stained glass windows, pewter mugs, and medieval courtly dressed waitpersons — looks appropriate for King Stefan, although what Sleeping Beauty's father would be doing in Cinderella's Castle, I don't know.[5]

Below the restaurant, on what most people take to be ground level, is a series of spaces. In the middle is the arch tunnel that forms the entrance to Fantasyland from the Plaza. Part of this tunnel is blocked off during shows in the castle forecourt because it forms the entrance for the characters, dancers and musicians. Large glass mosaics that show well-known parts of the Cinderella story line the walls.

To the right of this entrance as we face the castle is the staging area for the shows. Behind it on the Fantasyland side is the high-ceilinged, dark, and bare waiting area for King Stefan's, from which people are moved to the restaurant by way of a spiral stone staircase or in a camouflaged elevator.[6] To the left of the entrance is the King's Gallery, a shop that sells themed gifts such as clocks, chess sets, and jewelry. Under the castle are utility corridors through which people and materials move out of the sight of Disney's guests. Cinderella's Castle is a summary statement for all of WDW, containing as it does fantasy, food, communication, and commerce: "Beyond the castle drawbridge is the land that Walt Disney called a 'timeless land of entertainment.' This is Fantasyland, dedicated to all those children, young and old, who believe that dreams really can come true."[7]

On the far side of the castle, Fantasyland is divided into four quadrants, which center on Cinderella's Golden Carousel and Dumbo, the Flying Elephant. The southwest quadrant provides a good example of Disney's multiuse structural planning. As can be seen from the Skyway,[8] this quadrant contains approximately half of one large building, the other half of which, including The Hall of the Presidents and the Columbia Harbour House restaurant, is in Liberty Square.[9]

Fantasyland is a children's land par excellence. Here are the tamest Disney's rides and, given Walt Disney's vision of fantasy, some of the scariest for children. Everything is done up in fairy tale German-Swiss façades and bright colors. Steve Birnbaum suggests that this "land" is "reminiscent of a king's castle's courtyard during a particularly lively fair."[10] This idealized fantasy fair, however, like much of the modern United States, is paved.

In the southwest quadrant, which is made up of the building shared with Liberty Square, are six venues — two attractions, one snack bar, and three shops — all faced in variations on the theme. Directly northwest of Cinderella's Castle — just beyond the wonderful little Cinderella Fountain

(La Fountaine de Cendrillon) is the Tinkerbell Toy Shop, which sells Disney merchandise for children. Beyond it is the largest space in the quadrant, Fantasyland Theater. The original show here, *The Mickey Mouse Review*, has been replaced by a 3-D movie. This film, *Magic Journeys*, was the original 3-D film at WDW; it was shown at Journey into Imagination in EPCOT Center until it was displaced by *Captain E-O* in April 1986.

The 70-millimeter *Magic Journeys* is filmed as a child's daydream, built around circus toys come to life and sandwiched between opening and closing scenes of children running through a meadow beneath apple blossoms that seem almost to touch one's nose. Our hero is a cute nordic blond, accompanied by the classical U.S. ideological fantasy group of cinematic kids — a black and an Asian but no Italian from Brooklyn.

Next come the Mad Hatter and Disneyana Collectibles, each selling what its name says. In between the latter and Peter Pan's Flight, adjacent to the passage to Liberty Square, is the Troubadour Tavern with its snacks and soft drinks.

Sentimental sucker that I am for nighttime views of cities from the sky, Peter Pan's Flight is my favorite part of Fantasyland. Birnbaum suggests that I am not alone [11]. This ride is based on Disney's 1953 animation of James Barrie's story about the boy who refused to grow up. Customers enter small replicas of Captain Hook's sailing ship two or three at a time. These vehicles ride on a rail at the entrance but, in a nice bit of special effect, are transferred to an overhead cable as the car rises to fly through the Darling's bedroom and out into the night over "London." Constructed in rapidly diminishing scale, this idealized London contains the appropriate icons — the Thames, London Bridge, Big Ben, the Tower of London. Small, twinkling lights, including those that represent cars moving down the streets, slide below as our vehicle heads for Never-Never Land.

The remainder of the ride features Disney's traditional insipidity as we pass by coquettish, nippleless mermaids, Princess Tiger-Lily and other stylized Indians, and the plank walking and other scenes from the movie. Captain Hook and Mister Smee — both found in costume on the streets of Fantasyland — pass beneath us, as does the ticking crocodile. As we exit, the crocodile is trying to eat one of the robot Captain Hooks.

The "pixie dust" with which Tinkerbell sprinkles Wendy, John, and Michael in the animation has become a central corporate metaphor. On the one hand, it is used to speak of the transformation by which ordinary material objects (including people) become rhetorically set apart through magical contamination as special, even sacred. Disney, of course, claims a monopoly on pixie dust. As newly hired workers become cast members, they are constrained to share in the transubstantiation brought about by this charismatic, if imaginary, substance. Sometimes the metaphorical vaccination does not take. [12]

The northwest quadrant of Fantasyland contains three venues — two rides and a restaurant. Across the street from the entrance to Peter Pan's Flight is the station for the Skyway, the aerial tram to Tomorrowland. The simple gondolas pass in two legs (coming to the ground near the Grand Prix Raceway) high over Fantasyland to the Tomorrowland station. This is the highest point visitors can reach inside the Magic Kingdom, except perhaps inside Space Mountain. From the air we can see the shallow pond of 20,000 Leagues Under the Sea, the various spires of Fantasyland, and some of the aforementioned roofs and backstage areas. The Skyway boards in a simulated Swiss chalet, semihidden from the street. The attendants wear leiderhosen. The line here is always longer than it is at the Tomorrowland end.

Directly to the right of the Skyway entrance is It's a Small World. Under a façade outlined with small white lights and covered with stylized heraldry, the entrance ramps lead down inside the ride pavilion to a boat launching area. On the back wall are more lights as well as photographs of children in "native" costume. Moving down the ramp, we are introduced to what many visitors feel is WDW's most maddening tune (mercifully only in the instrumental version — we hear the words and children's voices further inside). This song — "It's a Small World After All" — is interspersed with pop culture national musical icons such as "Hava Nageela" and "The Mexican Hat Dance."

The water in the canal at the loading point, like almost all artificially contained water at WDW, covers coins of various denominations (a surprising number are not pennies) thrown by visitors (one presumes) as a ritual response to anything that looks like a fountain. If wishes can be said to come true at Fantasyland, this magical enhancement would seem to be superfluous. We are told such coins are gathered up each night after closing hours by Disney cleanup crews. We are not told what happens to them or whether any are left as seed coins for the following day.

The original It's a Small World was created at the behest of the Pepsi-Cola Company for the 1964-1965 New York World's Fair. In its sunny southern California brand of simulated ecumenism, this attraction seems the natal home of U.S. "have a nice day"-ism. Hidden behind the animatronic children dressed in native garb is the kind of geography lesson we visited in Chapter 12.

Touristic icons are gathered together in large rooms through which boatloads of visitors pass. As the ride progresses, we glide through Europe before heading for more exotic parts of the globe. Rooms that depict the latter seem put together as textbook examples of what Edward W. Said has described as "Orientalism." [13] They are presented as undifferentiated symbols of Southern Hemisphere locales.

We begin in Western Europe — Scandinavia (skaters), England (Big Ben and Beefeaters), France (the Eiffel Tower and cancan dancers), Scotland (kilts and bagpipes), Ireland (green leprechauns), the Netherlands (windmills), Spain (Don Quixote and Sancho Panza), and on to Germany (dolls in lederhosen), Switzerland (clocks), and Italy (gondolas). The national markers are obvious, both in form and color — totemically exaggerated for ease of recognition. Eastern Europe does not exist in this small world.

The transition from room 1 to room 2, the more-or-less Asia room, goes through Greece (the Acropolis), which is represented on both sides of the barrier. India (Taj Mahal) is followed by Thailand (temple and dancers), Arabia (veils), Russia (cossacks), Japan (kimonos), and China (peasants and ox carts).

Africa fills the next room. The continent seems to consist of Egypt (Sphinx and pyramid) and an undifferentiated sub-Saharan Africa filled with a rain forest, elephants, giraffes, and a laughing hyena. This is precisely the image most Americans have of Africa, an image aided and abetted by the national bureaus of tourism of those countries that still have large animals. The children here have chocolate-brown skin and kinky black hair but, curiously, have the same facial features as their pale counterparts in the European room. Disney's homogenization (also quite evident in the Asia, Latin America, and Pacific rooms) suggests that all children do or should look alike — except for their native costumes and skin color — just like Euro-Americans.

Room 4 takes us through Latin America and the Caribbean. We begin, oddly enough, with Antarctica, home of the penguin. This placement of Antarctica presumably validates the territorial claims of Argentina and Chile. Mexico, Central America, and the islands provide markets, festivals, and other celebrations. Whereas we are invited to Europe, Asia, and Africa by touristic sites, animals, and folk culture, here the children beckon us to the market. From highland Latin America, we ride into the tropical rain forest, with monkeys and silly Disney snakes.

Room 5 shows the Pacific — Polynesian surfers, hula dancers and Easter Island statues, Melanesian masks and drums (all Melanesians wear masks), and Australia with its koalas, boomerangs, and aboriginal kids. Again each society is suggested by touristic icons.

Room 6 — decorated in white, blues, and art deco lavender — is the last room. Here is a fantasy World's Fair scene with hot air balloons, a roller coaster, a river boat, and a carousel. The child puppets here, still in native costume, are all dressed in white. [14] Mixed into a kind of Disney United Nations, this room suggests — not without reason — that children don't have much interest in competition, strife, and war. Even in its homogenized sameness, the white room presents a salutary fantasy, a kind of harmonious world community as white Californians might define it. The sentimentality clearly remains silent about poverty, starvation, and violence to the young, but it would be daft to suggest that Disney represent such realities. [15]

This ride is a mechanical counterworld to the real world visitors are spending money to escape for a time. It is a world not only without strife but without adults. It is mild, bland, clever, and cute — a building block in a "community of memory" that customers may want to share — a community without sin, evil, or violence. It would be nice if some of the puppets interacted with each other, but that's not in the program. Communities of memory are built on sameness, not difference.

The exit from It's a Small World is flanked by a semiecumenical goodbye, with words written in — among other languages, Italian, German, Hebrew, French, Chinese, Japanese, Spanish, Arabic, Hawaiian, English, and Swedish.

Completing the northwest quadrant are the Swiss chalet-style Pinocchio Village Haus, with its hamburgers and fried chicken surrounded by scenes and characters from Pinocchio's story, the Fantasyland Pretzel Wagon, the Tournament Tent snack bar, and the Fantasy Faire. Disney characters perform a musical revue at the latter that is aimed especially at children.

The northeast quadrant contains only one attraction — 20,000 Leagues Under the Sea, which is based on the 1954 Disney live action rendition of Jules Verne's fantasy classic. Copied from the movie, Captain Nemo's thirty-eight-passenger submarines are designed as undersea monsters, with headlights that appear like bulging eyes when they head under water for the trip to Vulcania. A claustrophobic's delight, these vessels are entered after a wait in one of the slowest lines at the Magic Kingdom. The line passes by large simulated volcanic rocks, presumably the kind that would have been found in Vulcania. Birnbaum reports that the ceiling of the basement below had to be specially reinforced in order to support the southern magnolia and Senegal date palm that bring some shade to the entrance area.[16]

20,000 Leagues Under the Sea has an effect reminiscent of the "elevator" illusion at the Haunted Mansion and The Living Seas — the illusion of substantial vertical movement, carried out by a trompe l'oeil in a small space. The boats travel clockwise on a track that allows them to descend just enough to bring the portal windows below the water surface. Simulated shells, starfish, barnacles, and other tidal pool life line the pool walls on either side. As the submarine begins its fantasy journey — signaled by recorded crew voices — bubbles fly past the portholes, giving the illusion of downward motion. The boat takes us, so the captain's narration says, to the bottom of the sea — past Atlantis, a sea serpent and giant squid, a mermaid (with nipples), a shipwreck, under the North Pole, and on to Vulcania. From the waiting line, we can see the submarines disappear into a Disney cave where these effects are staged.

As we float into Vulcania we are treated to a standard Disney story element — sudden harmless, fake peril — in this case, a volcanic eruption that causes the "crew" to make an emergency escape. This is how we can tell the ride is almost over. The same theme occurs at Mission to Mars. The tide pool representations we see as we approach the dock are considerably more effective than the effects seen during the heart of the ride. As usual, Disney planners, artists, and craftspeople are more successful at constructing the fake real than they are the fake fake. Only when the technology of representation approaches that of the audioanimatronic figures at the Hall of Presidents and Pirates of the Caribbean does it become dazzling rather than silly. It is, of course, the dazzle that masks many of the deepest Disney messages about truth and fantasy.

The southeast quadrant of Fantasyland contains a single building with two attractions, three snack bars, and three shops. Just east of the quadrant — on the way to Tomorrowland, are the free-standing Nemo's Niche (film, stuffed toys, and information) and the Mad Tea Party. The latter is basically a souped-up carnival ride in which visitors ride decorated spinning "tea cups" based on those at the Mad Hatter's un-birthday party in the animated *Alice in Wonderland*. This ride is enlivened by a simulated drunken dormouse who pops up every so often from the teapot in the center of the platform.

On the southeast side of the quadrant's one building is the Enchanted Grove, a snack bar that serves citrus drinks and citrus-whirl soft-serve. Walking counterclockwise we come to Mr. Toad's Wild Ride. Ultimately derived from Kenneth Graham's *The Wind in the Willows*, this ride has been filtered through Disney's 1949 animation, *The Adventures of Ichabod and Mr. Toad*. Here Mr. Toad has traded the deed to his mansion to the weasels for a stolen automobile. In small cars named for characters in the story (Cyril, MacBadger, and the like), customers careen through one of two back-to-back tracks as they simulate Mr. Toad's vehicular adventures.

The cars zoom through rooms where black light illuminates neon paint, chased by the police past scenes from the mansion and jail and into a barn filled with chickens. The climactic moment threatens riders with pretend annihilation by a railroad locomotive, a simple but clever effect. This is one of the two rides in Fantasyland (Snow White's Scary Adventure is the other[17]) that warns parents that the ride may be too "intense" for young children. The tableau at the loading point — with its character pictures and signs pointing to Cheshire, Not So Shire, Worcestershire, and Toad in the Hole — is a classic example of WDW whimsy.

Next to this attraction, as we work our way back toward the castle, are the Round Table soft-serve ice cream bar, Gurgi's Munchies and Crunchies (sandwiches, soft drinks, and chicken nuggets), and the Royal Candy Shoppe. Facing the carousel is the entrance to Snow White's (Scary) Adventure. Parents are also warned about the intensity of this attraction, a ride that points to Disney's first (1937) feature-length animation. Reminiscent of Mr. Toad's Wild Ride, visitors here ride through scenes from the Disney-Grimm Brothers story. Wicked witches, with their red apples and cackle, jump out at the car as it twists along its track in the dark. In the final scene, one of them dumps a simulated boulder down on us, accompanied by the sudden stars of cartoon concussion. The cars here are named for the Seven Dwarfs, reminding us again about Bashful and what's-his-name. It is a mark of Disney's place in U.S. culture that the 1988 Democratic campaign joke, "More Americans can name the Seven Dwarfs than the seven primary contenders," made reasonable sense at the time. [18]

Beyond Snow White, almost completing the circle, are two more shops — the AristoCats toy and gift store and Mickey's Christmas Carol, a year-round purveyor of Christmas paraphernalia. In the center of Fantasyland Plaza are two rides for children whose distant cousins may be found at any traditional amusement park. Yet here, both Dumbo, the Flying Elephant and especially Cinderella's Golden Carousel show the extra effort and attention to detail the Magic Kingdom calls for.

Dumbo is the simplest and shortest ride at the Magic Kingdom. We sit inside cars wrapped up as Dumbo from Disney's 1941 movie. The cars ride up and down and travel in a circle. At the center of the arms that hold the cars sits Timothy Mouse, Dumbo's agent in the film.

Finally, there is Cinderella's Golden Carousel, which — as Birnbaum tells us — has its own story: "This carousel, discovered at the now-defunct Maplewood, New Jersey, Olympic Park, was built for the Detroit Palace Garden Park (also long gone) by Italian-born wood-carvers of the Philadelphia Toboggan Company back in 1917, toward the end of the golden-century of carousel-building that began around 1825." [19] The original horses were stripped and repainted, and their legs were repositioned to simulate energetic movement. Eighteen separate scenes from the Cinderella story were hand painted on the wooden canopy above the horses. All the white horses are decorated differently. Further, "The band organ, which plays favorite music from Disney studios (such as the Oscar-winning 'When You Wish upon a Star,' 'Zip-a-Dee-Doo-Dah,' and 'Chim-Chim-Cheree'), was made in one of Italy's most famous factories." [20]

Not counting Main Street USA service establishments, Fantasyland has the largest number of venues in the Magic Kingdom. This includes the largest number of attractions as well as the most restaurants and snack bars. [21] Further, Fantasyland has the second-largest percentage of venues that are attractions (39 percent) and the second-smallest number that are shops (32 percent). The rides here may be quick and small, but the mix between entertainment and commerce is not bad.

Other areas in WDW ought to be included under the rubric of fantasy: the Haunted Mansion in Liberty Square, Mickey's Starland, Journey into Imagination in EPCOT's Future World (the ride here is the closest anything at EPCOT Center comes to achieving the more old-fashioned tone of the

Magic Kingdom), the Disney-MGM Studios, and the new Swan and Dolphin hotels. The Haunted Mansion sits on a bend of the Rivers of America at the northern end of Liberty Square. Built in the style of an eighteenth-century Hudson River Valley Dutch manor house — albeit with a Disney bat on its weather vane — this attraction evokes the imaginative world of Washington Irving's Rip Van Winkle, Ichabod Crane, and the Headless Horseman. Under a dark green awning, the queue curves to the right around a wall toward the graveyard and the entrance foyer. Shrieks emanate from hidden speakers. On the plaza in front of the entrance a pale, dour character actress dressed to look like a demure Elvira, mistress of the dark, is sometimes found. She is available for photographs but, as usual at WDW, not for conversation. The graveyard contains headstones, each with a piece of doggerel so silly as to work effectively as a preshow.

As the doors open, severely dressed and demeanored hosts and hostesses usher us into a dark, wood-paneled, polygonal foyer, through a sliding door, and into the slightly lit portrait gallery. The door closes and a deep bass voice, dripping puns, speaks to us of the mansion's ghostly denizens. As it does, one of Disney's most successful effects occurs. The picture-covered walls around the waist-high wood paneling begin to stretch, giving us the illusion that the floor holding us is moving downward. [22] As the walls stretch, the bottom halves of the portraits emerge into view — each with a silly story to tell. This silliness dispels the spookiness of the low lighting, the apparent sinking of the floor, and the sonority of the recorded spiel. Suddenly the lights go off, thunder crashes, and lightning illuminates a body hanging in the attic overhead. More doors open, and we are sent to our "doom buggies" for the ride through and "around" the Haunted Mansion.

This is a noisy ride, filled with the sounds of putative ghosts attempting to escape from locked rooms and caskets. Down the hall past the library we go — past a beating heart, a lively suit of armor, the head of a fortune teller in a crystal ball, a number of ravens, a mummy, and a rodent of unusual size. Among the high points is the banquet hall in which the ride's best effect takes place. Ghostly dancers, projected through glass from below the car track, seem to twirl before us as shadow hands play the piano.

Serenaded by a trio of "happy spooks," we enter the graveyard, which is guarded by a decrepit robot watchman and his quivering robot dog. This cemetery contains the appropriate collection of would-be escapees, most suggested by coffin lids raised by skeletal hands and the like. We exit past a mirror where, through another projection, our "doom buggy" turns into a bullet car and we pick up a dufus ghost. The announcer tells us that the Haunted Mansion contains 999 ghosts, ghouls, and gobblins — "but there's room for one more."

Mickey's Starland

In October 1988, Disney opened a new "land" at the Magic Kingdom. Tucked into a three-acre plot next to the northeast corner of Fantasyland is Mickey's Starland. Originally christened Mickey's Birthdayland, this area is aimed at children and was built to celebrate Mickey's sixty years in show business.[23] Meant as a temporary display, the renamed land appears to have achieved permanence. Its provenance, however, has left it with a kind of transient tone — cardboard and tents — that is somewhat out of keeping with the rest of the Magic Kingdom. This feeling is especially noticeable if, as Magic Kingdom announcements suggest, visitors arrive by way of the Walt Disney World Railroad.

As the train nears Duckburg Station, we see the party tents and then the light blue and white of the station itself. We are now in Duckburg — "a town that's everything it's quacked up to be." This is a colorful place. The striped tents loom behind the town. To the right, behind a small green with a gazebo, is the residential section. To the left is the children's playground and, beyond it, the Duckburg shops. Straight ahead down Duckburg Blvd. is Coot Common with its theater, bank, and county courthouse. This is all a cartoon version of Town Square on Main Street USA.

The welcoming sign announces, "Population 'bill'ions and still growing." Below it is the list of civic organizations: the Benevolent Protectors of the Gosling (BPOG), the Mystic Order of the Mallard, the Sewing and Tatting Circle (Daisy Duck, President), and the Billionaire's Club (Scrooge McDuck, President).

If we head to the right from the station, down Barks and Nash,[24] we come to Quackfaster Circle, where Barks and Nash intersects with Hyperion Blvd.[25] Turning left on Hyperion, we are now on Duckburg's main street. Two brightly colored house façades lead us to Mickey's place on the corner of Coot Square.

Mickey is clearly the major citizen. His is the only establishment built to more-or-less normal scale. The shops farther up Hyperion are all scaled-down, toy versions built for children that emphasize the cartoon fantasy nature of their proprietors. Mickey's house, on the other hand, suggests that he is real — like us, albeit with an odd physiognomy.

Behind the white picket fence is Mickey's car, sporting a "Mik 'N' Min" license plate. The yellow garage, with its blue door and red shingle roof, matches the house next to it. The house has four rooms, in none of which Mickey seems to be at the moment.

First is Mickey's bedroom. Pictures of Walt, Minnie, and the original Mouseketeers are on the wall. To the right is a "Mousechusetts" pennant.[26] The living room contains a green couch, a player piano (with "Steamboat

Willie" sheet music), and a painting of Mickey as Grandma Moses ("Grandma Mouses"). The fireplace andirons have mouse ears. On top of the TV, which is showing Disney film clips, is a picture of Mickey on Santa's knee. Past an easy chair with doilies and a footstool, we find ourselves at Mickey's study.

Again there is detail — scrapbooks, medals, copies of *Variety*, a baseball signed by Pluto, comic books, a record player and records, an oversized set of keys, and another picture of Walt Disney. What looks like a real letter envelope, sent by an actual human being, sits on the desk. Behind us, covered with fruit wallpaper, is Mickey's kitchen. There is a teapot with boiling water on the stove, but no Mickey.

Out in the back yard are a little lawn mower and the path that leads past the homes of Mickey's coterie — the S.S. Donald Duck, Goofy's shack, Gyro's house with Box #12 on the mailbox and a satellite dish on the roof, and Daisy's little pink cottage. Then we are inside the purple-and-white tent for the preshow to Mickey's Magical TV World, a review that hucksters Disney's television fare. The show stars characters from "Ducktales," "Rescue Rangers," and the "Gummi Bears." The show over, we are disgorged out the "entrance" to the Duck County Courthouse into Coot Square.

To our right, past Feather Federal Savings (1928), is the yellow-and-white tent of the Hollywood Theater, where children can go backstage to Mickey's dressing room and have their pictures taken with the star. In the center of Coot Square is Cornelius Coot Commons, surrounding a statue of old C.C. himself dressed as a pilgrim and holding an ear of corn (an appropriate vegetable) in his hand.

On up Hyperion we go, past the children's park on the left with its waist-high (to an adult) Mousekemaze, Mickey's Treehouse, and Minnie's Doll House. Here also is Grandma Duck's farm, including a barn and pens full of baby animals.

On our right is Duckburg's commercial center — small, pastel façades on the stoops of which sitting adults look huge. Here are Goofy's Clip Joint (a barbershop),[27] D. Duck's candy store, Minnie's Dress Shop, H D & L Toys, the Duckburg News, Daisy's Café, and the Duck County School. At the intersection of Hyperion, Tailfeather Trail, and Cornhusker Lane, we begin the walk out of Mickey's Birthdayland. On the left are topiary — pigs at a flower trough and Snow White and the Seven Dwarfs. On we go, back to the reality of Fantasyland.

Journey into Imagination

Another piece of fantasy is found in EPCOT Center. Here the Company introduced its first new fictional character in years. Figment (of Imagination), a small purple dragon with horns, is invented by the Dreamfinder —

our Victorian host at Journey into Imagination. This pavilion contains Disney's clearest advertisements for political and philosophical idealism. As the commemorative EPCOT Center volume puts it,

> The human imagination is one of the most powerful and mysterious forces in the universe. Although no one really understands the process of imagination, it is the wellspring of creativity. Our ability to imagine and create is the source of all our achievement and progress. . . . Journey into Imagination uses the Disney tools of magic, fantasy and enchantment to remind us that all of our accomplishments begin with ideas. [28] . . . Journey into Imagination demonstrates that we need only learn to unlock imagination and use the elements that surround us to find new solutions to the problems and challenges of tomorrow. [29]

The pavilion is formed by two truncated pyramids faced with triangles of glass in a tubed aluminum frame. The gardens to the left of the two entrances hold a number of whimsical Disney fountains, all of which draw their share of attention. The Jellyfish Fountains shoot streams of water that break off, leaving jellyfish-like shapes falling through the air. At the Upside Down Waterfall, water is propelled upward over a dam to a pool. What appears to be the most popular fountain is the Serpentine (or "Leap-Frog") Fountain. Here electronically controlled squirts of water shoot from planter to planter, at one point passing over a path in the middle.

The north entrance to the pyramids leads to the pavilion ride and the Image Works. The Journey into Imagination ride begins with a visit with the red-bearded Dreamfinder in his Jules Verne-like flying vaccuum cleaner. As the Dreamfinder's contraption sucks up elements to be used by the imagination, colors and shapes are projected on the rear wall, and we are introduced to the pavilion theme song and to Figment. The stage and cars sit on a plate that moves clockwise. Here the set is small enough to rotate on one plate, unlike the stationary sets of the rotating Carousel of Progress in Tomorrowland.

The circle completed, we head for the Dreamport where the basic building blocks of imagination are stored. These are elements to be used, the ride shows us, in the visual arts, literature, the performing arts, and science and technology. Among other things, this ride is a playful primer on the relationships between form and content. In a delightful excursion through the theory of logical types, this ride is full of colorful, iridescent words that do what they say. "Tremble" trembles; "flash" flashes; "avalanche" almost avalanches.

Each of the arts is represented by its creative building blocks, dealt with in a mock-serious way by the Dreamfinder and in a rambunctious, "childlike" way by Figment. At the end of the arts segment, as the Dreamfinder's "But what about science?" echoes around us, we enter the first of the final two loops. Images of Disney science — sped-up pictures of flowers opening and other natural processes as well as colorful spinning images of stylized geometric patterns (computer circuits, molecular chains, and similar patterns) — are projected on the screens around us as the Dreamfinder lectures from the middle of the loop. He holds his pointing baton like a magic wand.

Lest we leave on any semblance of serious discourse, we pass to Figment's loop. Here we see cartoons of the little purple dragon at his most imaginative and childlike. He lifts weights, climbs mountains, conducts an orchestra, captains a ship. He dresses as Superman and a as a cowboy. He is rich. As we finish the ride, our own pictures are flashed in front of us, taken earlier by flash photography. This is one of a number of places in WDW where people are shown their own images.

A staircase spiraling around an elevator then leads us to one of the most popular parts of Future World: the hands-on Image Works. Something interesting happens here, for this is one of the few places where Disney's control over our progress through its realm is attenuated. Children (and others) can spend as much time as they wish here, doing electronic art and orchestrating various kinds of music. We can potentially spend the entire day here. Many people remark on the sense of freedom they feel at the Image Works, as if they have momentarily escaped the corporate organizational clutches. For some, however, this is a scene of anxiousness and conflict. At the entrance is a clock that shows the amount of time left before the next showing of the pavilion's third attraction — the 3-D Michael Jackson movie, *Captain E-O*. As the numbers dwindle, tugs-of-war begin. Children are told to hurry up and, in some cases, are dragged protesting away from their knobs and screens.

The Disney-MGM Studios

Disney-MGM Studios gives everybody some time in the limelight; if nobody puts you on stage, you can always cut your own record or make the cover of Newsweek. And if you crave a glimpse of an actual movie star instead of a man in a mouse suit, be content with what you do see. The real Brown Derby is gone, and movie stars today aren't so different from everybody else. Robert Redford raises horses on his ranch in Utah; Paul Newman sells popcorn and lemonade. Stick with the illusion. Even in Hollywood's heyday, that was always the rule.

—William J. Sertl[30]

The Backlot Annex

The 135-acre Disney-MGM Studios theme park is built around a very extensive work display.[31] It is in part a work display display. Here we are shown how Disney constructs its cinematic effects — how it produces its real fakes, its fake reals, and its fake fakes. We are let in on some of the secrets — secrets carefully kept from us at the Magic Kingdom and much of

EPCOT Center.[32] We are shown actual people at work — drawing cartoons, rehearsing shows, making costumes. Here we confront the real Americana, the sophisticated simulations of the media that as Mark Crispin Miller tells us, "box us in" to mass-mediated culture.[33] This is where the real late-twentieth-century Fantasyland is produced.

The levels of logical typing and cross-reference are very complicated here — complicated enough to disuade me from attempting an impossible "deep reading" of this theme park. However, I present a surface description and suggest some elements of the cultural palimpsest we find at the studios.

An initial example. In the Backlot Annex is the Indiana Jones Epic Stunt Spectacular. Here Disney presents a forty-five-minute show that reenacts a number of the stunts from *Raiders of the Lost Ark* (1979) — the first Steven Spielberg-Indiana Jones movie. Spectators sit in a two thousand-seat stadium facing an expanse of concrete on which wheeled stage sets and other large props are moved about as the scenes change. Indy falls through the stadium roof, stopped by his safety rope before he splats on the concrete. He runs through the sharpened punji sticks as they pop up from the ground and escapes the massive rolling boulder in the cave. He and Marian escape pursuing "Arabs" across the roofs of stage set buildings. There are gunfights. Marian is kidnapped by the Nazis, whose truck overturns and burns. The munitions dump explodes. Finally comes the airplane scene where, as in the movie, Indy lures his attacker into the whirling propeller blades.

In the show we see the spectacular effects, the explosions, and the fires. Between the scenes we watch the personnel involved in moviemaking pretend to do their work — the first and second unit directors, the prop people, sound and camera technicians, script people, and the casting director, who has drawn people out of the audience to participate in crowd scenes (including one fake audience member who is actually part of the real cast).

To the audience, much of this is familiar. Most audience members have seen the movie and recognize the scenes. Most have seen enough movies or television shows about making movies to have some idea about how directors and script people are supposed to be presented. People clap, shout, and oooh and aaah.

Let me peel away a few of the layers. *Raiders of the Lost Ark* is a movie that tells a story the elements of which point apocryphal arrows in many directions — at Nazis, Arabs, archaeologists, expatriate bar owners, and at all the stories that orbit around the Holy Grail. Actors play the various characters in the screenplay, especially Harrison Ford and Karen Allen, with their half-submerged connections to other characters in other movies. For the physically dangerous parts of the filming, stunt people stand in to take the falls for the actors (although we know Ford does a lot of his own stunts). Further, thanks to television and especially to Lee Majors's series,

The Fall Guy, many of us know something about the mass-mediated image of stunt people.

At the Indiana Jones Epic Stunt Spectacular, we find actors and actresses who portray the stunt people who portrayed the characters in the movie. [34] Actors portray the directors, cinematographers, stagehands, and other personnel. We have replications of the technical effects — the explosions and the punji sticks. The scenes are taken out of the film, gathered together, and relabeled to highlight their technical virtuosity.

Before the show officially opened in the summer of 1989, visitors to the studios were invited to attend rehearsals — much shorter versions in which one or two stunts were practiced. Personnel were dressed the way an audience might expect them to be dressed at a rehearsal. The question at the time was, "How much of the rehearsal activity — with its mistakes, its repetitions, and its shop talk — was staged?" If any parts were — and it is hard to believe that they were not — what we had were rehearsals staged by actors who portrayed stunt people who portrayed actors in a very postmodern adventure movie.

To the right of the stunt show is the Backlot Express fast-food restaurant. Styling itself as "A Warehouse of Good Eating" — specializing in "Custom Built Meals" — the Backlot Express sells build-your-own hamburgers in a building that suggests a craft shop at a movie studio. The building looks like a warehouse, if not a factory, with corrugated iron walls and pipes running across the roof. Inside, the walls and free-standing cabinets are filled with props, sculpture, and models, construction and painting tools, and the like. The paint shop section has paint slopped over the floor and tables.

Star Tours, sponsored by M & M, completes the Backlot Annex. This is the counterpart to a popular ride at Disneyland (and is similar to the Body Wars ride in EPCOT's Wonders of Life). Visitors ride in forty-person flight simulators with bouncing, jumbling motion synchronized with a film at the front that is full of special effects. The show simulates a very screwed-up ride to Endor, the planet of the Ewoks in George Lucas's *Return of the Jedi* (1983). Piloted by an incompetent rookie, this Star-Speeder takes us out the wrong exit from the mother ship — zooming past Endor, through giant ice meteors and laser battles, down the canyons of the Death Star just like Luke Skywalker, and finally back home. Along the way we are shaken and jounced, protected by seat belts from everything but motion sickness. Apparently this has been a shopping trip because the exit, past the "droid and baggage claim" sign, leads us to the bunker-like Endor Vendors and its "Star Wars" souvenirs.

The entrance line to Star Tours winds by an At-At (the giant mastodon-like mechanical monsters that attack the *Star Wars* heroes on Endor) and past large cutoff tree shells that represent the redwoods of northern California where the Ewok village scenes in *Return of the Jedi* were filmed. [35] The shells hold spotlights that illuminate the "mountain" façade that covers the ride building. Above the line is a simulated Ewok tree village with its thick rope structures and paths. Inside the building we pass through a repair hanger where C3PO and R2D2 are repairing space craft, including one Star-Speeder 3000 with laser bullet damage. We line up next to one of the six simulators, watch a video that shows another tour group (including Chewbacca and Ewoks going home) buckling its safety belts, and then put ourselves in the rookie pilot's hands.

Lakeside Circle

Between the Backstage Annex and Hollywood Boulevard is Echo Lake, surrounded by Lakeside Circle with its distinctively television theme. Lakeside Circle contains four food and drink stops, two attractions, and one shop. Walking from Hollywood Boulevard past the Hollywood and Vine Café ("Cafeteria of the Stars"), we come to Echo Lake. Off to the right, near the intersection of Echo Park Drive and Sunset Plaza, is an old, decrepit tramp steamer — the S. S. Down the Hatch — which contains Min and Bill's Dockside Diner. To the front and left of the ship is a pile of wooden shipping crates addressed to Rick Blaine in Casablanca. This walk-up snack bar, with its Santa Monica Submarine and San Pedro Pasta, points to the 1950s and 1960s genre of "island" television shows, such as "Gilligan's Island" and "McHale's Navy." In the midst of all the corporate hoopla at WDW, Min and Bill's reminds us of the small-time mom-and-pop establishments of the past, when small businesses might have been called by peoples' first names. It also echoes Disney's practice of having all its personnel wear first-name name tags, furthering the illusion that this huge corporation is still just Min and Bill's writ large.

The entire Hollywood Boulevard side of Lakeside Circle has this 1950s pseudo-gemütlichkeit tone. Further down Echo Lake to the left is an example of "California crazy" architecture[36] — a big dinosaur whose side opens into an ice cream counter. This is Gertie's Ice Cream of Extinction.

Across the street from Gertie's, sharing a building (and kitchen) with the Hollywood and Vine Café, are the Tune In Lounge and '50s Prime Time Café. The façade of the café depicts a two-story 1930s art deco apartment such as one might find in Miami's South Beach or in Roman Polanski's *Chinatown* Los Angeles. The cream-colored walls lead up to a second-story balcony with mustard trim and surrounded by aqua ship's railings. Tropical plants and plastic flamingos sit on the balcony.

Inside, the restaurant is divided into a number of rooms that look like slightly bigger versions of Beaver Cleaver's mom's kitchen. This is pure 1950s Populuxe.[37] The formica tables have boomerang wedges in their surface design. The salt and pepper shakers are porcelain cows and pigs. There are coloring books and crayons for the kids. Jello molds hang on the walls. Each booth has visual access to round-cornered 1950s television sets, which show continuous food clips from "I Love Lucy," "The Honeymooners," "Our Miss Brooks," and other early sitcoms. The menu has meat loaf and gravy, s'mores, and a peanut butter and jelly milkshake. "Mom" is cooking back in the kitchen, and she will be real pleased, the waitperson tells us, to hear that we have ordered a salad.

The Tune In Lounge next door is the living room (with bar), full of couches that face the same TV shows. Its façade is recessed, slightly hidden, except at night when the neon sign is on.

Sharing the same building across Echo Lake are the Monster Sound Show and Superstar Television, both sponsored by Sony. The first, topped by a transmission tower with the neon logo for Station SFX,[38] brings the audience into a theater in which the stage has been turned into a Foley pit.[39] To the right of the stage is a glassed-in room with sound technicians and computerized wall and console equipment (filled, as usual, with dramatically lit buttons). Members of the audience have been chosen as "Foley artists." They sit or stand on stage in front of the sound effects paraphernalia, some with earphones connecting them to the sound technicians. A brief haunted house comedy film, starring Chevy Chase and Martin Short, is shown on a screen behind the stage. Then the ever-effervescent master of ceremonies tells a little about Foley artistry and announces the opportunity for the volunteers to become Foley artists.

The film is shown again — without sound this time — and on cues from the sound technicians, the volunteers rattle, punch, turn, and poke the stage equipment. By this time the audience is a little like repeat attendees at *The Rocky Horror Picture Show*, so when asked to yell "Look Out!" everyone comes in on cue. Finally, the film is shown a third time — now with the out-of-sync volunteers' sound effects added.

When the show ends we leave the theater by way of SoundWorks, a hands-on exhibit of special sound effects gadgets. At SoundWorks is Soundsations, a set of booths with earphones in which we can experience "3-dimensional sound."[40] The technical effects of Soundsations are among the most extraordinary at the studios.

Nestled in a corner of the Monster Sound Show is Golden Age Souvenirs, a small shop with items from the "Golden Age" of radio and television. Continuing to the right of the Monster Sound Show we come to Superstar Television, with its rounded Hollywood deco spire. This, too, is an audience participation show. As we wait for the show, we stand in an open-sided foyer that slopes down to a small stage in front. Overhead are rows of Sony televisions on which Barbara Walters, Alan Alda, Jim McKay, Harry Anderson, and others take us on a tour of TV programming through the years. We end in the future, as usual with robots. A voice then comes on with the ironic meta-lie, "We now return control of our television set to you." A master of ceremonies-casting director comes on stage to cast members of the audience for parts in the upcoming show. That done, we enter the one thousand-seat theater.

On the large stage are a number of sets. Volunteers in costume enter the sets one scene at a time, say the lines printed on the prompters in front of them, and are spliced by "blue screen" techniques into scenes from famous television shows. [41] Overhead monitors show the results to the audience. The audience thus sees the stage work — the rushing around of cameras, directors, prompters, and other personnel from set to set — as well as the results of the splicing. [42] When audience "applause" signs are raised, the audience applauds and cameras pan out into the crowd. By the end of the show, visitors have learned something about television techniques; and some, as Andy Warhol predicted, have been famous for fifteen minutes.

The Great Movie Ride

At the end of Hollywood Boulevard, past the shops and the Theater of the Stars and through Sunset Plaza, [43] is the great front of the Chinese Theater — "a full-scale replica of the façade of Hollywood's premier movie palace." [44] The courtyard at the entrance contains the beginnings of a set of hand- and footprints impressed into the concrete, just as at Grauman's original (although with Disney characters and stars). This entrance is a false front, for the building it advertises is cantilevered off to the left at a forty-five degree angle to parallel the studio's production bungalows. The actual entrance is at the right side of the false front and lines up with the orientation of the building rather than the façade. Bordering the theater's left side is the concourse that leads to the studio where the revived "Let's Make a Deal" is produced. Visitors form the audience for the daily tapings of this show.

Inside the building is the Great Movie Ride, which reminds us of the MGM part of the theme park. The entrance line snakes through a replica of Grauman's gaudy foyer, past ornate Chinese screens and urns, under arches, past red pillars and painted walls. Display cases hold artifacts from some of the movies featured on the ride — the piano from Rick's American Bar in *Casablanca*, Dorothy's ruby slippers from *The Wizard of Oz*, space suits from *Alien*.

Turning a corner, we enter the preshow room where the snake continues as a screen in front shows clips from classic MGM movies. The clips are calibrated so we barely enter the second round before we are let through a door and onto the ride vehicle — reminiscent of the moving theater at the Universe of Energy at EPCOT Center. On the wall is a mural of the Hollywood Hills at sunset. As the vehicle moves under the brightly lit entrance marquee, the Great Movie Ride begins.

We pass through a series of stage sets that depict iconic moments of famous U.S. movies. Each tableau contains audioanimatronic figures that bear an uncanny resemblance to the stars. We hear their voices on the sound track. Beginning with the musical, a Busby Berkeley chorus line leads us to Gene Kelly "singing in the rain." The commemorative souvenir book claims, "The spirit is so contagious, the music so alive, you'll feel like singing and dancing down the nearest rainy street you can find!" [45]

Well, pilgrim, maybe.

From Gene Kelly we move on to Dick van Dyke and Julie Andrews on the London rooftops in *Mary Poppins*. Then the tone changes as we enter the dark nighttime city of Jimmy Cagney's *Public Enemy* — with orders whispered through a doorway and gangsters in a black car. Gunfire erupts, and perhaps a live "gangster" gets rid of the guide and takes over the tram. Here, or alternatively a couple of scenes down the ride, Disney presents a new dramatic effect. A live actor emerges from the scene and commandeers the vehicle, "kidnapping" the audience. The original guide runs off.

We head on, past Clint Eastwood and John Wayne — telling some pilgrim that he probably oughtn't to go where he's planning to go — and into a Western town where a bank robbery erupts. The safe is blown, "searing" us with heat. If our guide made it through the city, here's where a bank robber hijacks us. [46]

Now we head into the smoky caverns of the Nostromo, past Sigourney Weaver-Officer Ripley and on to be slimed by an "Alien." From space it's on to the Wall of Souls from *Indiana Jones and the Temple of Doom*. A jewel glows on the balcony wall. As our hijacker runs up the stairs to grab the stone, the curse strikes. A shrouded priest struggles with the robber, and in a puff of smoke, the latter turns into a skeleton. Down the stairs runs the ex-priest, our original guide, who now escorts us to Tarzan's jungle. Tarzan swings by on a vine; Jane rides an elephant; Cheeta chatters.

Our African safari moves north, to the tarmac of Casablanca's airport, where a very large-headed Bogey is seeing Ingrid Bergman to her plane. Next comes the munchkins' village from *The Wizard of Oz*, where we and Margaret Hamilton are surrounded by robot munchkins. As we follow Dorothy and company down the Yellow Brick Road toward the Emerald City, we enter the grand finale of the Great Movie Ride — a three-minute film tribute to Hollywood. Accompanied by Sensaround, this montage contains iconic snippets of over ninety famous films. Almost all the Hollywood greats are here somewhere. Then we are out of our tram and off to look for a rainy street.

The Studio Tours

To the right of Sunset Plaza, through the blue-tiled arched gate of the Disney-MGM Studios, is the smaller plaza that leads into movieland. Here we find the two tours, the Backstage Studio Tour and, to its right, the

Animation Tour. Here also are the Soundstage Restaurant and, above its far wall, the Catwalk Bar.

The central dining area of the restaurant is framed by the fake walls of the hotel lobby from the Touchstone film *Big Business*. At the back are separate serving counters that dispense pizza, sandwiches, pasta, soup, and salad. Stairs to the right and left lead to the Catwalk Bar, its dark walls lined with props and lighting paraphernalia. In front of the restaurant, just as on Hollywood Boulevard, the garbage cans read "Keep our City Clean."

To take the Animation Tour we enter a holding room (with an alcove on the left) that contains display cases showing original Disney animation at various stages of the filmmaking process. This is the Disney Animation Collection. Jack's beanstalk is here, as are animated sequential drawings, layouts and backgrounds, cel setups, and, in a central case, some of Disney's many Oscars. Through the back window are Mickey and the magic brooms from *The Sorcerer's Apprentice* in topiary.

Having moved into a small theater, we are shown *Back to Neverland*, an eight-minute film — part live action, part animation, part live animation — which gives an overview of the animation process.[47] The film stars bemused, live Walter Cronkite and Robin Williams, who is turned into one of "the lost boys" (in a blanket sleeper with feet) to illustrate the process and commune with Captain Hook. Here we see Michael Eisner's hand rather than that of Walt Disney, for Robin is his usual anarchic postmodern self. "Whee!" he says, having been turned momentarily into Mickey Mouse. "I'm a corporate symbol." The film is packed with Williams's rapid-fire cross-references to movies and television shows. "You bet your hook," he answers the good captain at one point.

At the film's end we begin our actual tour through the animation studio, conducted by Walter and Robin as they appear on the video monitors over glassed-in parts of the production area. With brief descriptions from our "guides," we watch as studio employees go about their work. As we catch brief glimpses of the various departments, our pace is set by the short length of the descriptions. We need to clear out of the way of the group following us.

The tour covers ten departments, at each of which Robin is placed in some peril.[48]

1. *Story*. Where characters and their adventures are developed.

2. *Animation*. The first step in bringing Disney characters to life.

3. *Clean up*. The animators' drawings are cleaned and detailed.

4. *Effects*. Where lightning, fire, rain, and other effects are developed.

5. *Backgrounds*. Here, artists create the painted "sets" on which animated characters act.

6. *Photocopying process*. Where the animators' drawings are transferred from paper to plastic cels.

7. *Paint lab.* Paints are mixed to create the exact colors needed for every character and scene.

8. *Inking and printing.* Cels receive the finishing touches in this area.

9. *Animation camera.* Where cels are photographed one at a time to create the illusion of life.

10. *Editing.* Where scenes are joined together to create the final movie we see in our neighborhood theater.

A final turn brings us to a set of monitors on which we see various animators talking about how they do their work. The theme here is that animators are "actors" who must get inside their characters through movement, noisemaking, and other strange kinds of "empathy" to get the characters to "act." The souvenir pamphlet tells us, "None of them owns a magic wand — but they can make a two-dimensional drawing seem as real and alive as the person sitting next to you." [49]

The tour ends with another short film, a retrospective of classic Disney animation shown in the Disney Classics Theater. We exit through the Animation Gallery, where limited edition reproductions and original Disney animation cels are on sale.

Past the Studio Store is the Muppet Store and the entrance to *Here Come the Muppets.* Using live actors in costume, this revue stars Kermit the Frog, Fozzy Bear, Bean Bunny (a new character invented for the show), Gonzo, Miss Piggy, and Dr. Teeth and the Electric Mayhem Band. The music includes "Personality" (Miss Piggy), "Make 'Em Laugh," and Kermit's classic, "It's Not Easy Being Green." The ensemble closes with "The Heart of Rock 'n' Roll" and "Shout."

The centerpiece of the Disney-MGM Studios is the Backstage Studio Tour. Past the Screen Extras, a wandering saxophone band, we enter the line that snakes toward the tour shuttle. Overhead are video monitors on which familiar movie and television stars talk about the history of the Disney Studios. Gauged to take two hours, the tour has a lot of parts. We begin in the red tour shuttle, entering as the side nearest us raises up and out like the wing of a large bug. The intrepid slide all the way across to the left-side seats, where they will get the fullest effects of Catastrophe Canyon.

The tour begins modestly, looping back around to the left past production bungalows labeled with building numbers and the names of the shows currently being produced therein. The shuttle passes between one of these buildings and a line of topiary and plants to the right, all stored for use on the various sets. Off to the right is the Earful Tower — the water tank with mouse ears that is the architectural signature for the entire theme park. Here our guide, in front with a microphone, imparts some typical Disney information — perhaps the hat size of the tower.

The shuttle enters the Production Center tunnel. Here we pass along the outside of the building, looking through glass windows at the costuming area, where employees design, make, and store costumes and wigs.[50] Cases in the tunnel display outfits from Disney and MGM movies. The shuttle passes the camera, lighting, and prop rooms, presented with hyperbolic Disney-talk, and on to the scenic shop where sets are built.

Out in the open again we enter the back lot. The shuttle rides down the studio's residential street. On both sides are perfectly coiffed house fronts, built in a number of regional middle-class American suburban styles — including the one shown at the beginning of "The Golden Girls." On the right is the "house" from *The Love Bug* movies, with a mechanical "Herbie" revving and leaping at the shuttle like a chained dog. The last house on the left looks lived in; it is ready for filming with toys in the yard and a frisbee on the roof.

Turning right from the residential street, the shuttle passes around the end of a canal and heads to Catastrophe Canyon. We go by the "bone yard," where various decrepit vehicles — boats, parts of an airplane — are set, all jumbled up as if deposited by some giant kid. These movie vehicles include jeeps from the 4077 M*A*S*H unit.

From this vantage point, we can see across to the "backs" of the houses on the residential street. It is clear that we saw only the façades of what would be filmed as real houses, because here we see the unpainted wood and support struts of the façades, which are built and painted only enough to have their fronts filmed.

The Backstage Tour follows a consistent pattern. We are shown an effect and then taken behind it to see how it was made. For most of us, the divulging of the secrets of the fake real does not keep us from accepting the illusions created the next time we turn on the television set or see a movie. We have a double whammy here. The effects are cleverly done (for example, the frisbee on the roof), and the craft and technology that go into them can be appreciated on their own level. The latter are presented as quite functional and seemingly unadorned, although clearly these work displays are also "shows."

The front-to-back transition is nicely shown at Catastrophe Canyon. The shuttle approaches a desert mountain. We pass through a chain-link fence that holds a warning sign and enter onto a track going to the left of a desert oil-drilling scene. We are told that this is a back lot set, although nothing is being filmed there at the moment. Behind telephone poles strung with wire are a small rocker-arm oil rig, storage tanks, and a Mohave oil truck sitting precariously on the side of the hill. Large gulleys flank the central oil tanks. We are in an open-sided tunnel, protected to the right and above. This is a stage set for the show we are about to be part of.

Suddenly, in simulation of an earthquake, the track we are on begins to rock the shuttle from side to side. Poles fall down. Oil tanks explode with surprising heat. The truck starts to slide toward us. Now rain falls, and sudden torrents of water wash down the gulleys as we are threatened by a flash flood. From the roof over our heads, more water flows as the flood reaches its climax. Then everything stops. The fires go out. The water flows into channels beneath us. The "catastrophe" is over. Splashed and semi-seared, we move off the track and around the back to see how the scene was produced.

What we see from the back is a large scaffold covered with dun-painted wire mesh sprayed with thin concrete, all looking like papier-mâché. Pipes are everywhere, color coded to show us which ones hold water, which gas, and which compressed air to drive the water cannons. Our guide tells us how high the water cannons can shoot (in case we have any Bull Connor fantasies, I guess). It is the biggest mechanical apparatus we see on the tour, and it is quite impressive.

Having escaped "total catastrophe," as the souvenir book puts it, we head back down the street to a second back lot. Here the false fronts represent a New York City street. We enter this back lot by way of a town square. On the left is a two-sided church — one side represents a small-town church, the other an urban church. The square holds a replica of the Washington Square arch, which can be removed to suggest a city other than New York.

The set — New York Street — continues past the square for two more "blocks," cut by an oblique cross street (8th Avenue). At the end of the main street are façades painted in forced perspective of New York City skyscrapers, including the Empire State and Chrysler buildings (and the Hotel Puilly). The effect is to give the set an extended trompe l'oeil illusion of size. These façades can also be removed to de-New York the set, for the other vaguely timeless false fronts could represent any northeastern or midwestern city during the last fifty years.

The shuttle passes a drug store, a bank, and a dingy stone office building (containing McDonald and Co., Brokers) with its directory in the entrance alcove. [51] There are the Plaza Hotel, Desjardins Clothing Store, the Nouveau Museum of Contemporary Art, Smith Bros. (appliances), the Venture Travel Agency, and Raymond's Chevrolet. Many of the windows are city dirty. Walls have graffiti. On New York Street are a yellow Empire cab and a blue-and-white "Battery Park" Metro Transit Authority bus. A look in the window of the New York Street News [52] shows, in addition to the expected tobacco, paperback books (*Raiders of the Lost Ark*, Shirley Conran's *Lace*, Robert B. Parker's *Stalking a Seahorse*, and Robin Cook's *Fever*, among others) and magazines (including *Glamour* right next to a *Harvard International Review*). It's not clear who shops here.

On the right arm of 8th Avenue are city apartment buildings with stoops, an optometrist, and a locksmith. This street has been painted in bright cartoon colors as part of the Dick Tracy hype. When the movie opened in 1990, a brief cop-robber scene was enacted here for shuttle passengers. The other arm leads to Toon Park and, at Monahan's Freight Company, the belching Dipmobile that threatened Roger Rabbit and the other Toons. On the street sit the red trolley and Bob Hoskins's beat-up jalopy.

The shuttle drops us off at Backstage Plaza. Here are the Loony Bin — a store filled with Toon Town paraphernalia, toys, and gag items — and the patio of the Studio Catering Company, a snack-food counter restaurant (with churros). From this patio visitors have a good view of the backs of the New York Street façades. Off to the side is a little park with a statue of the mermaid from *Splash*.

Between the Studio Catering Company snack shop and New York Street is the Honey, I Shrunk the Kids Adventure Zone. This is a replica of the movie set with twenty-foot-high stalks of grass, giant cheerios, a huge, leaking hose, and a climbing net. This is a high-concept kids' playground — full of nooks and crannies, all overcrowded.

From Backstage Plaza visitors have a number of options. They can stroll down parts of New York Street, looking in store windows and generally noticing the detail of the façades. From the street there is an exit to the Backlot Annex and Star Tours. Visitors can go back to the shuttle station for an uneventful ride back to the tour entrance. The intrepid, willing to risk warning and derision, can slink back past the production bungalows. The main attraction continues, however, with a guided walking tour back through a different part of the production facilities.

To take this tour, we walk past the *Bladerunner*'s police car and the Cadillac from *Tin Men*, and wait for our guide, entertained meanwhile by Goldie Hawn and Rick Moranis on the overhead monitors. Eventually we are taken to the Water Effects Tank.

Two things happen here. First, at the far end of the tank sits a model of the USS *Tennessee*, which was used in filming the television mini-series *The Winds of War*. Special-effects technicians set off a tiny sea war in front of us. "Cannon shells" splash in the water. We are then shown what the results look like when they are enlarged and run on the monitors overhead.

Second, an audience volunteer is dressed in a yellow slicker and led to the mock pilot house of a tugboat, where he or she is told to hang on to the steering wheel. Painted on the wall behind is a cyclorama depicting a storm cloud sky. The boat is rocked and the "sea captain" doused with water to simulate an ocean storm. Again we see the composite results overhead.

The audience is led into the building and on to the Special Effects Workshop, crammed with giant ants and other special-effects props. Here we are shown how one-frame-at-a-time filming and matte painting are used to create special-effects illusions. On the Special Effects Shooting Stage, more volunteers are brought into the show. This is the room for "blue screen" shooting. The volunteers are placed on a large prop — the giant bee from *Honey, I Shrunk the Kids* — and told to hang on and scream as the bee is swung back and forth. All of this is filmed against a blue screen behind them. This tape is then mixed with footage from the movie, filling in the blue screen background space. The results put the volunteers into the scene.

Before we leave the room, there is a witty piece of cross-reference — another example of how much this movie studio show is about television. Gene Siskel and Roger Ebert appear on the screen in their normal balcony set and give a short critique of the film clip. They don't like the scene much, but they both give thumbs up to the actors.

Now we enter the soundstage area. In a short film, Warren Beatty shows us how indoor soundstage filming works. It is night. As Dick Tracy, Beatty enters a diner, does a short bit, and then exits. Rain and snow fall. Then we see three soundstages, viewing them from windows high above. One contains the set for "The Mickey Mouse Club." The Cosby "family" does the explanatory honors here. Next we see another short film, *The Lottery*, starring Bette Midler as a New York piano teacher whose winning lottery ticket is swiped and, after a couple of minutes of slapstick adventure, returned by a pigeon.

As we enter the postproduction part of the tour, we see how this film was put together. We have already seen the outdoor sets — they are found on the New York Street. We pass by the indoor sets — the piano teacher's room, the subway turnstile, and the sawed-off simulated subway that threatens to run Midler down. In the postproduction editing bay we see how the physical stunts, with stand-ins, were done and edited. George Lucas demonstrates some of the editing techniques used in Luke Skywalker's laser sword fight with Darth Vader. Here we get our first glimpse of the importance of computer technology in filmmaking.

Now it's on to the audio editing rooms, where we are shown how music and sound effects are added and dialogue edited. On the monitors Mel Gibson and Pee Wee Herman exchange voices as part of the demonstration.

Our final stop is the Walt Disney Theater to see a sneak preview of an upcoming Disney or Touchstone movie. Introducing these previews is a film clip that shows Michael Eisner at his postmodern best. He is sitting in his office welcoming us to the studio when Mickey Mouse enters. They chat. Suddenly, Eisner looks at his Mickey Mouse watch and announces that the preview is about to begin. Mickey looks at *his* watch, which shows Michael Eisner's face. Off they go.

On the way to the theater, they gather all sorts of characters to join them — Disney workers, costumed characters, and cartoon figures (including a closetful of brooms from *The Sorcerer's Apprentice*). As they sit down to see the preview, a disruption is caused by Chernaborg, the devil from the *Night on Bald Mountain* section of *Fantasia*. Eisner reprimands him and receives an abject apology: "Sorry, Mister Eisner. It won't happen again." This is the postmodern essence of Michael Eisner's Walt Disney Company.[53]

Fantastic Hotels

Some new additions have been made since 1988 to Disney's presentation of fantasy. Five new hotels have opened[54] — the sprawling, Edwardian Grand Floridian on Seven Seas Lagoon and the four EPCOT Center hotels.

The Grand Floridian, which opened in 1988, points to such late-nineteenth-century grand hotels as the Royal Poinciana in Palm Beach (which has burned down). With turrets, towers, white board walls and red shingle roofs, gingerbread trim, verandas, wicker, and ceiling fans (not to mention the English tea service in the Grand Floridian Café and the afternoon big band on the Grand Lobby balcony), this hotel reeks of nostalgia.

The Swan and Dolphin hotels southeast of EPCOT Center present a different look: They are "serious" architecture. Spurred by Michael Eisner, Disney has become one of the most active corporate patrons of contemporary architecture in the United States. As Gary Delshon writes,

> Some are comparing the company's impact on the art of building to the effect corporate clients such as IBM and Johnson Wax had when they commissioned pioneering works of modernism in the 1960s and 1970s.
>
> Last spring, the New York Times said, "No company has ever tried to market serious architecture to the masses the way Disney is now doing." That is why, whatever the buildings turn out to be, there can be no doubt that Disney is a force to be reckoned with in the last decade of the 20th century — a corporate patron like no other, past or present.[55]

Well, Michael Graves's postmodern Dolphin and Swan hotels turned out to be pretty interesting. Topped by eponymous creatures, the two hotels face each other across a small lagoon and are connected by an awning-covered walkway. The twenty-six-story, 1,509-room Dolphin looms over the World Showcase roof line. Halfway up the front, nestled below the pyramidic roof, is a clam shell waterfall, which flows down through five shell basins to a fountain where four dolphins hold up a fifty-four-foot clam shell. The red-tan stucco façade is painted with banana leaves growing out of a trellis. The barrel-roofed, 758-room Swan — painted the same base color and with a shell fountain on the roof complementing the swan — has aqua waves flowing around *its* façade.

Inside, the lobby of the Swan is reminiscent of a Victorian conservatory. Painted parrots sit on chandeliers under ceilings designed to echo the carpets. A tent motif recurs throughout the Dolphin, harking back to the tented lobby. According to Beth Dunlop, "Graves . . . said he carried two simultaneous images as he designed — one of a thousand proctologists checking into the Dolphin at once; the other of a six year old child arriving at the hotel for the first time. . . . 'It had to be not too jokey for the proctologists, and not too serious for the six and eight year olds. . . . Still, I wanted everything to give a little smile.'" [56]

Completing the new EPCOT Center hotels, A. M. Stern's 634-room Yacht Club and 580-room Beach Club represent a turn-of-the-century New England yacht club blended with a middle-Atlantic beach club. [57] They are at once more representational and less fantastic than the Grand Floridian. These physically connected hotels share Stormalong Bay — a free-form swimming pool-"lagoon" complete with hot tubs and a beached treasure ship from which a small body flume begins.

How are we to think of all this fantasy; this art, architecture, cinema, and music? Is Disney fantasy really contained by Fantasyland and the Disney-MGM Studios, with a few spillovers? How does Disney fantasy relate to the world outside WDW, the world we usually live in? Is the world under the rule of commodities "fantastic?" Let us now look at one set of answers.

15

Consumption and Culture Theory

The spectacle is not a collection of images, but a social relation among people, mediated by images . . . the spectacle is the main production of present-day society.

—Guy Debord[1]

Creeping Surrealism and Simulacra

Postmodern culture is anchored in the breakdown of the signifying chain. The referential functions of normal, everyday language have been shattered and the signifier disconnected from the signified. Orwell wrote about one type of referential dismemberment, a relatively straightforward kind based on naked repression and lexical control. But the postmodern world is not Orwellian. It is Huxleyan — and the fortunes of signs, symbols, and human meaning have taken a different form.

Joel Achenbach characterizes this turn as "creeping surrealism" — the general fear, brought about by the manipulation of narrative and public discourse, that "nothing is real anymore."[2] His introductory example of what people have come to understand as normal is taken from the back of a package of Pepperidge Farm "Nantucket" chocolate chunk cookies: "Only the bakers of Pepperidge Farm could pack so much scrumptious personality into classic American cookies. . . . They added a heaping measure of fuss and bother. That meant making each cookie one of a kind, with an individual personality all its own. So they gave them rugged, irregular

shapes, just as if someone had lovingly shaped each cookie by hand."
Achenbach comments:

> Each sentence lacks credibility, starting with "Only the bakers of Pep-
> peridge Farm," etc., an absurd lie that, as trained consumers, we let pass.
> Beyond the quicksands of the language there are several levels of untruth:
> First, there's the Humble Down-Home Multinational Corporation affectation.
> Pepperidge Farm is a huge company that is itself owned by Campbell's, the
> world's largest soup company, yet it pretends these cookies are virtual
> Mom-and-Pop numbers. Fine. We can live with that. At least they don't claim
> that elves bake them in a brick oven in a hollow tree (as Keebler does).
>
> What is more disturbing is that they have clearly designed a machine that
> makes cookies that look like a human being made them. And then —
> astonishingly — they confess the fakery right there on the back of the bag.[3]

Not only has the line between reality and fiction become attenuated in the
United States, but, says Achenbach, "Americans . . . no longer think the
distinction matters . . . lies have been raised to an art form in this country,
information manipulated so delicately, so craftily, with such unparalled
virtuosity, that you can no longer tell the genuine from the fake,[4] the
virtuous from the profane."[5]

Further, people take a certain comfort in artifice.[6] They celebrate the
weddings of television characters, watch "Peoples' Court," and pay attention to videos of airplane attendants explaining safety features while ignor-
ing live announcements. As Umberto Eco has suggested, "The American
imagination demands the real thing and, to attain it, must fabricate the
absolute fake."[7] Life, art, and fantasy become intertwined, and all three are
increasingly the products of market researchers and corporate planners.
Fantasy goes on the market, as the last remaining vestige of uncommodified
life — the unconscious — is brought into the market system.

Creeping surrealism is a useful beginning for the present project, but we
need to go further because as an artistic and philosophical movement,
surrealism was anchored in reality. It merely claimed that there were special
moments in which the banal might be seen as extraordinary. Jean Baudrillard and Frederic Jameson have presented ways of thinking about the status
of reality in the modern world that let us see how far beyond surrealism
we have come.[8] Let me present one version of their argument and then
unpack it.

In "Postmodernism, or the Cultural Logic of Late Capitalism," Frederic
Jameson refers to Plato's notion of the simulacrum — "the identical copy
for which no original has ever existed."[9] Jameson uses the simulacrum to
describe the "pseudoevents" and "spectacles" of our time — a time "with
a whole historically original consumers' appetite for a world transformed
into sheer images of itself."[10] Not only have we been led to "image addic-
tion" through pseudoevents — themselves formed of historical,
geographical, and fantastical pastiche — but these images have "become
the final form of commodity reification."[11]

Baudrillard chases the disappearance of referential reason (the "liquidation of all referentials" [12]) into what he calls the "hyperreal." This is a world in which "illusion is no longer possible because the real is no longer possible." [13] For Baudrillard, reality has been effaced by the substitution of signs of the real for the real itself: "The simulacra is never that which conceals the truth — it is the truth which conceals that there is none — the simulacrum is true." [14] "This state is effected, he argues, through "the orders of simulacra. . . . The first-order simulacrum never abolished difference. It supposed an always detectable alteration between semblance and reality. . . . The second-order simulacrum simplifies the problem by the absorption of the appearance, or by the liquidation of the real, whichever." [15]

There is, finally, a third order of simulacra, in which, like a helium-filled Mickey Mouse balloon, we are let go into the hyperreal. Here, "Only affiliation to the model makes sense, and nothing flows any longer according to its end, but proceeds from the models, the 'signifier of reference,' which is a kind of anterior finality and the only resemblance there is." [16]

Here we confront not Gregor Samsa but an audioanimatronic cockroach. We live in an "'esthetic' hallucination of reality." [17] For Baudrillard, then, everyday life has been captured by the signs and sign systems generated to represent it. We relate to the models as if they were reality. In his argument, California's Disneyland functions as "an imaginary effect concealing that reality no more exists outside than inside the bounds of the artificial perimeter." [18]

Baudrillard's signs and models seem to be autonomous. He shares with many structural and poststructural thinkers — especially the deconstructionists he claims to oppose — the notion that the human subject has been deposed as an interesting ontological category. Decentered and fractionated, this subject is now merely an epiphenomenal effect of the semiotic juggernaut. Although his descriptions of the hyperreal and its simulacra are reasonably accurate, his concept of the necessary autonomy (and thus "deconstructive undecidability") of the models is a symptom of the ills of postmodern culture in late capitalism rather than a useful etiology. [19]

Have *actual* human beings been decentered and fractionated — or is this just a convenient model, available for deployment in intellectual "model wars?" My answer to the first clause, with some caveats, is yes. Actual human beings have been and are being decentered and fractionated, especially in the United States. Furthermore, simulacra and the hyperreal are being forcibly exported around the world as the U.S. way of life and death. Living in a rich country, trained to expect an ever-increasing set of entitlements, and led to embody those entitlements not in any civic notions of the social good but in private accumulations of what George Carlin calls "stuff," Americans insistently implicate themselves in this process.

They can, for the good of their own and other species, transform this process, but it will not be easy. To think about this and to see why Huxley and not Orwell was right we need to dwell on the vehicle for this process — the commodity. This discussion will lead us from Baudrillard back to Jameson and eventually to WDW.

Commodity Aesthetics

The classical description of the commodity is found in volume 1 of Karl Marx's *Capital*: "A commodity is, in the first place, an object outside us, a thing that by its properties satisfies human wants of some sort or another." [20] Marx argues that both ontologically and historically, objects are produced initially with the sole purpose of realizing their value in use. Tools are made to be used in the local group for digging roots, hunting, making clothes, making other tools, and similar functions. As people's wants grow through time, production expands and aesthetic considerations come into play. The interest in and motivation for productive activity — including the invention of stories, paintings, and songs — remain attached to the quality and direct usefulness of the product.

In the complicated course of time, a new motivation for production developed. By the mid-1800s in Marx's Eurocentric world, production for exchange had achieved hegemony. Objects were now being made with their use value only secondarily in mind. The primary purpose of production, Marx argued, had become exchange value: Things were made to be sold for money. Once the purchase had been made, the manufacturer had completed his or her business and was essentially uninterested in how the product was used or whether it was used at all. The primary interest in production for exchange value is quantity (or in monopolistic situations, control over quantity) rather than quality. With the advent of mass production, the quantity of products was vastly increased.

For exchange value to be realized, however, purchasers at the end of whatever circulation path the product might take must be convinced of the product's use value. [21] Whether the product is presented as a solution to an actually existing human need or as the answer to a fantasy one created by marketing activity, the product must insinuate itself into consciousness as an "object of desire." [22]

As Adrian Forty has written, the original device for convincing purchasers that an object would be useful for something was the design of the object itself. Although some design considerations had to do with the functional capabilities of the product, much of the interest was directed at attaching aspects of the objects — their form, size, and color, for instance — to positively valued cultural symbols. Although quality was invoked as a central argument to convince purchasers of the use value of the product, the use of this argument became increasingly rhetorical as design began to carry the burden of sales.

In Chapter 3, I discussed the crisis of overproduction in the United States at the end of the nineteenth century and the consequent invention of the "consumer." Countless products entered an expanding market. Commodities produced for exchange value filled newly invented market niches. Manufacturing companies competed, often brutally, over the quantity of sales of similar products that became increasingly indistinguishable in quality. The burden of convincing the public that each of these similar products had a singular and particular use value shifted from design to packaging. Advertising, which had previously consisted of densely packed functional information, took over as the engine of discourse-producing packaging. [23]

The questions were, How do we convince people that they need this stuff, and how do we differentiate our product from qualitatively similar ones so we can sell a lot of ours? As we remember from Chapter 3, we are dealing with "possessive individuals" — people who have internalized the ideological model of human nature that underpins bourgeois democracy in a market system. In presenting this model, C. B. McPherson pointed out that unfettered proprietors of their own person and capabilities faced the problem of making themselves attractive to the labor marketplace. [24] Those without capital must compete with one another for jobs — hawking their credentials, training, and experience in the fight for gainful employment.

In *Nixon Agonistes*, Gary Wills reminds us that the liberal tradition further extends the project of individual self-construction. [25] In this tradition, our lifelong job becomes the development of our self. We tinker, polish, learn, grow, develop character, gain status, and the like. In the United States, this model has taken on a powerful, moral meaning. It is taught to us through many avenues of public discourse as a natural duty for which we may claim entitlement to natural rights. Among these natural rights for modern-day Americans is the right to consume. Anticonsumption arguments must battle against the additional weight of this new "natural rights" entitlement.

This right (and its attendant needs) has developed in large part out of the commodity market system and the need to convince people that products produced for exchange value actually have use value. A person whose central existential problem is self-creation needs certain tools to work with. Ironically, because the marker of successful self-development is public ratification, the tools themselves increasingly become those of symbolic packaging. This is especially true in a mobile, middle-class society with careerist patterns that extract people from local communities and from each other.

In the United States, the exercise of freedom has been squished into the terrain of economic choices. For those who *can* manage the wherewithall to make some of them, these choices merely pertain to ranges of commodities we are trained to see as objects of desire. How do we move from use value to desire?

In *Captains of Consciousness* and *Channels of Desire*, Stuart and Elizabeth Ewen help us understand this process.[26] In these studies of the history of advertising, the Ewens argue convincingly that twentieth-century advertising discourse is founded in lack, envy, resentment, and fear. Such rhetoric is meant to convince us that we do not have some object we desperately need in order to continue our project of self-production. Perhaps public ratification that our project is going well will come from the purchase and display of the advertised product.[27]

We are told stories about how those who have the product are succeeding, whereas those who don't have it are left out, shamed, and avoided. Our agonistic task is made increasingly more difficult as we are pulled into a world of simulacra in which lack proliferates. The range of problems we didn't know we had — halitosis, ring around the collar — expands endlessly. We find we have been left out of the Pepsi Generation, Marlboro Country, or the Coors Silver Bullet Bar. We are terrified by insurance companies, tire manufacturers, even sellers of household cleaning products. Without commodities we have no friends, no lovers. Our families fall apart.

We are directed to *feel* bad if we don't have the commodities that solve the problems we're told we have. We need eternal vigilance to keep a handle on things because we have been taught that feeling bad is the worst thing that can happen to us. In a perverse anti-Calvinism, feeling bad becomes a public sign of zits on the soul.

From the marketing point of view, there are three central problems. First is the development and selling of new products. Second is the expansion of markets for existing kinds of products. Here one is in competition with producers of other kinds of products — soft drinks versus iced tea or, for that matter, health and shelter — for peoples' money. Third, there is competition within commodity niches among essentially similar products that must somehow be differentiated from each other to survive in the marketplace.

Each of these problems requires the creation of desire. People must be convinced that products have use value. Products proliferate and the market expands through the creation of new commodity niches. Life spaces free of the commodity form are colonized, much as cancer cells colonize the body. Territories of desire that have already been brought into the marketplace are subdivided so that where one "need" existed before, now there are many. General circumstances are broken down into special circumstances. We no longer merely try to get rid of headache pain, for instance; we must now do it differently at night than we do it in the morning.

As our circumstances are multiplied by fractionation, so our bodies are parsed into constituent and subconstituent pieces — each of which must be polished, groomed, and controlled if we are to continue successfully with our project of self-creation. Our bodies become divided into smaller and smaller pieces in a continual commercial anatomy lesson. We learn not only that anatomy is not destiny after all but that we have a moral responsibility to try to overcome whatever cards the genetic code has dealt us. Not to "be all that we can be," with the help of commodity technology, is to abdicate our rights as free Americans.

As we are to take responsibility for all the pieces of what used to be — in our primitive preconsumer consciousness — our integral body, so we are to assume moral responsibility for the things around us. Our clothes, furniture, front yards, automobiles, and our food and drink all become potential sources of guilt, shame, and moral triumph.

In its relentless expansion, the realm of commodities differentiates the human world into smaller and smaller commodity niches. Each niche creates a reified need, something new to which we now have to attend. When our attention has been captured, the need niche and its commodity solution survive until the public is satiated or further differentiation begins.

The rhetorical process by which commodity niches are created is somewhat different from that which regulates competition within each niche because within established niches, competition takes place among commodities that are virtually identical in material composition. Thus, marketing discourse must differentiate products in the language of form rather than content.

W. F. Haug has described this language of form as "commodity aesthetics." [28] Design, packaging, and advertising must be presented to appeal to something other than people's sense of function: The competition here is over people's attention. Advertising rhetoric needs to be constructed so as to intrude into consumers' minds, to colonize mental space with metaphorical neon signs. Territory controlled inside people's minds is to be translated into market shares.

The project of commodity aesthetics, then, is military. Advertising is organized in campaigns. The activity bespeaks its own violence. Tactics are semiotic. The way into peoples' minds is through the practical manipulation of symbols and other elements of cultural meaning. Most of these symbols are clearly embedded in cultural scripts — stories that present human situations we are to take as problematic. Many of these scripts are meant to make us feel bad. We are told our bodies are ugly (but they would look better in Calvin Klein jeans). We miss our family and friends (but we can "reach out and touch someone"). Our family is a mess (but it would come together around Campbell's soups). We are in dire need of sexual attention (choose an ad). We are growing old.

Other scripts appeal to envy and resentment, telling us what beer to drink, what car to buy (and how to knock people off the ladder to success), what credit cards to carry in order to feel like "we are somebody." Some, such as insurance company ads, appeal to naked fear. The rhetoric of advertising becomes organized not around the intrinsic qualities of a commodity but on the connotations of characteristics in the social world. Ads present symbols of the social world to show us what we lack, counting on induced desire for the symbols themselves.[29] As Jameson points out, images become the final form of commodity reification.[30]

The point is to capture our attention. If it takes banging on our heads, that will be done. If it takes appeals to cuteness and nostalgia, we'll see some, especially on television. Even if it takes poking fun at the product advertised, any and every attention grabber will be tried.

But there is more. Advertising does not merely create specific needs through the invention of pseudosolutions to human problems. The bulk of advertising is now seen on television, a communication medium that crosses family boundaries into almost all U.S. homes. Competition for space inside the heads of viewers has honed the creativity of producers of televised commercials to the extent that they have surpassed that of producers of the "real" programs. Corporate stories must be told in thirty-second bursts — stories compelling enough that they can be referred to in even shorter edited versions. Commercials become ongoing serials. They must capture viewers' attention in the face of cable and satellite-dish technologies that present increasing possibilities for the attack on attention. Remote control devices with channel-changing and muting capabilities allow viewers to "graze" up and down the dial — to "zap" immediately any image that does not instantaneously capture their attention.

Disconnected commercials are often at the mercy of those that form part of an ongoing saga in which characters reappear in a series of different stories. Some of these characters — Spuds McKenzie, Joe Isuzu, Clara Peller ("Where's the beef?") — become cultural icons whose ontological status is blurred. Commercials refer hermetically to competitors' commercials. Many of them — Bartles and James, Blue Diamond Almonds — poke fun at their own truth value. Creeping surrealism is continually reproduced and expanded by commercial simulacra competing for the attention of image-addicted U.S. couch potatoes. Yet these messages make us laugh. They *do* entertain us. They often entertain us more than the programs in which they are embedded.[31]

Neil Postman suggests that commercials and television shows have converged in form and content. Shows become commercials. Ongoing commercial story lines become television series; it's just that the former have shorter episodes. This convergence is also true, he argues, of so-called "nonfiction" television[32] — news shows, documentaries, and the like.

Everything becomes marketing. Game shows are clearly commercials: The beauty is in their nakedness.

Messages on television, transparently commercial or not, are edited into shorter and shorter cuts that pass in front of us faster and faster. Both commercials and transitions are accompanied by music. As the editing gets faster and faster, the use of music grows. Senses are assaulted as the battle over our attention escalates. We pay what little attention we do to information only if it is entertaining.

It has been argued that these blips of information, presented as discrete packets in disconnected series (a war story followed by a liver transplant story followed by a toothpaste commercial followed by a promo for a network "docudrama" on surrogate motherhood), are isomorphic to the structure of the world of commodities. This world exists as a megabanquet of individual, discrete items screaming for our attention, connected not to each other (or to their social patterns of production) but to the images and fantasies presented in the stories about them. Thus, it has been said, the structures of public discourse and of the world of commodities are parallel. As a Weberian might say, they have an "elective affinity" for each other, each reinforcing the other in a positive feedback loop.

The truth, of course, is that they are not parallel: They are one and the same. Like the ads we see on television, public discourse is a commodity. As Max Headroom showed us, it is full of "blipverts" — advertisements so short as to be subliminal. Public discourse is made of commodities that refer to other commodities. It is all a hermetic circle in which editing becomes the central theme of our lives.

What does it mean to lead a severely edited life? First, the mere velocity of the scenes flashing constantly past us makes us jittery. It interferes with temporal continuity in our lives. Second, the speed of these images means that increasingly, more of them can be put in front of us in the same period of time. We can be overwhelmed by the quantity of images. Speed and quantity deprive us of the ability to compare messages, to reflect on them so as to tell what is important. Everything is presented as if it were the same weight and size. This is profoundly disorienting.

Third, the competition to hold our attention must become frantic because the commercial process has taught us a further "natural" entitlement — the right not to be bored. Not only must we be amused, as Postman argues, but we have come to require that all public discourse be entertaining. If it is not, we will zap it.

Fourth, the content of these images — including what is called the "news" — increasingly consists of simulacra made to sell audiences to advertisers. News, docudramas, and commercial references follow each other with ever-increasing speed. Life imitates art, which imitates life, which imitates commercial message, which imitates commercially edited versions of life. Truth and lie become indistinguishable. This confusion itself becomes entertaining and is explicitly invoked as an advertising ploy. Presidential candidates, television anchor people, and sports stars are crafted by media image consultants to be their own advertising — commercials for themselves. [33]

Achenbach suggests one response we might make to this environment. His creeping surrealism leads us to disassociation in which an understanding of the difference between reality and falsehood doesn't matter. We may be able to tell the difference, but we don't care. What results is the kind of boundless cynicism George Felton sees in his college classroom.

> We've all seen the people in brand-name advertising: young, energetic types, apparently jobless but laughing and alive, having more fun than we're having, swaying to the beat of some driving tune, all brought to us, fast, with plenty of jump cuts, by Levi 501s, Chevrolet, Michelin or Nike. It seems seductive, but as the commercial goes by my students are not being asked to accept any overt arguments or propositions. They don't have to make any commitments; they don't have to listen closely; most important, they don't have to believe anyone. And the only thing better, it appears, is to get them to laugh at the idea that anyone could even try. [34]

Felton does not go far enough because he believes commercials are neutral about commitment. In *Culture Against Man*, Jules Henry argues that advertisement is by no means neutral. [35] For Henry, the central commercial metamessage is against commitment. We are asked to betray the products we have been using faithfully, to switch to a newer one that is more glamorous, tougher, more closely associated with the symbolic characteristics we still lack. As commodification spreads itself into personal, social, and political relations, it becomes a driving force in the national crisis of commitment.

Jameson describes the characteristic emotional tone of postmodern life as a "strange compensatory decorative exhiliration." [36] All of our themes are captured in this phrase. The emotionally shallow nature of exhiliration appropriately codes a world presented to us cynically and ironically. The stream of commodities and commercial messages, some camouflaged as news, surrounds us like toxic air and water. Without ironic distance, we gasp for air.

All this rapid de- and recontextualization has cognitive affects as well. Jameson claims postmodern culture is characterized by a breakdown of the signifying chain — the relation that exists, following de Saussure, between the signified and the signifier. The commodification process uncouples signs and symbols from their conceptual referents, allowing them to float free in a chaotic world of their own. Symbols and images are captured by the cartographers of public discourse, pumped up like balloons, and reattached to new referents in the interest of economic and political rhetoric. Truth is not obscured so much as rendered irrelevant. History is annihilated, captured totally by the spin-doctors of market forces.

Deflective Attention

In order to suggest what happens to our minds because of all this — how we can be led to Jameson's "strange compensatory decorative exhiliration" — I want to describe some simple ideas about the relationship among symbols, the signifying chain, and consciousness. For this I borrow C. O. Evans's idea of "deflective attention."

Evans distinguishes between "symbolic consciousness" and "nonsymbolic consciousness." [37] His colleague Edward Henderson characterizes the former as detachment, the latter as immersion. [38] Symbolic and nonsymbolic consciousness are alternate and opposed states, defined by Evans in terms of what is happening to attention. Three things can happen to attention: It can be absorbed, deflected, or unordered through distraction.

Evans suggests that deflective attention is the normal human state in the symbolic world. Signifier and signified are tied by a process in which focus on a sign causes us to deflect our attention to the concept signified: "Our attention passes from the sign we see to the thought of what the sign means: Attention is deflected from sense experience of sign to thought of the thing signified . . . subjects report that the sign has meaning." [39] A good sign, he argues, is one that does not call attention to itself but remains in unprojected consciousness, directing us transparently to the thought signified in projected consciousness: "A symbolic A(lternate) S(tate) of C(onsciousness) is one in which all attention is symbolic action: That is to say, it is an ASC in which each experience of an event itself causes attention to switch to another event, and in turn that experience of an event further causes attention to switch to another event in an endless concatenation of attention deflections." [40]

These attention deflections — from signifier to signified to signifier to signified — create meaning, an ongoing world of symbolic consciousness. Each experience of an event "will depend on both the mental set of the person having the experience, and his perception of the setting of the experience." [41]

But suppose attention deflection is inhibited? What happens if the connection between signifier and signified becomes unplugged? This is precisely what Evans is interested in; he is trying to describe the alternate state of consciousness that results when the sign function of an event is missing. When this happens, he argues, "perception is thrown back upon the object itself." [42] This causes our notion of setting to disappear, and "with the loss of setting goes loss of mental set, and with the loss of mental set goes the loss of deflective attention." [43] Without deflection, attention is absorbed. [44]

The state of consciousness that results is nonsymbolic, "a consciousness the significance of which is that it has no significance." [45] Evans claims this is the state of consciousness sought by various kinds of mysticism. Through the paradoxes of the Zen koan, the repetition of a meaningless (and thus metaphor-breaking) mantra, and other such techniques, mystical practices inhibit deflective attention. As attention is absorbed, experience of the self vanishes: "Reality testing and ego functions cease." [46] Evans quotes the Zen sage Te-Shan: "Only when you have no thing in your mind and no mind in things are you vacant and spiritual, empty and marvelous." [47]

Evans is attempting to give a psychophilosophical justification for the mystical practices in meditation that lead to absorptive attention and thus, perhaps, to nirvana. He is tracing what may happen when the sign disappears. He gives us clues, however, to a state of consciousness that he mentions but then ignores. There are two kinds of nonsymbolic alternate states of consciousness: "[1] a nonsymbolic ASC of a subject who totally lacked a symbolic ASC; [2] a nonsymbolic ASC of a subject who has the capacity for symbolic ASCs but who at the time was suspending the operation deflection." [48] Evans focuses on the latter state, in which the subject "has the capacity" for attention deflection but suspends it by overriding the sign. I want to suggest that in a world of simulacra — of creeping surrealism — the object rather than the sign disappears. "The experience of an event is neither in unprojected consciousness nor in projected consciousness when nothing else is going on over and above the experience of events. As experience is taking place, that is all, and the subject is not aware that he is experiencing events, or even that he is experiencing." [49]

The break between signifier and signified remains, but the result is disordered rather than absorbed attention. In the realm of commodity Zen the subjects increasingly lack the capacity to suspend attention deflection: It is already done for them. They enter the hyperreal world of sound bites and become, as Te-Shan says, "vacant and spiritual, empty and marvellous." [50]

But *cui bono*, this nirvana?

Culture Redux

Commercial images have colonized our public discourse. As shared public symbols, they have become the hegemonic cultural form of our time. The makers of commercial images manipulate and invent tradition. Their power to lead us into commodity Zen is derived from the depth and intimacy with which they commingle with everyday culture. Our attempts to live meaningful, honorable, and good lives are thought through and practiced within the taken-for-granted matrix of commodities. To understand further the naturalization of the commodity form, I now return to the concepts of "culture."

In Chapter 2, I proposed a very general sense of culture — the anthropological notion of culture as a more-or-less shared set of public symbols people use to understand and create their lives. I suggested that culture was like a set of maps people refer to in navigating the territory of their everyday social world. Any group that could control the production of these maps — through unnatural selection (dampening the distribution of other maps) and the like — would benefit from people behaving "properly" in the normal course of events.

This anthropological sense of culture is relatively new. In *Keywords*, Raymond Williams suggests that the modern sense of this concept begins with Johann Herder's *Ideas on the Philosophy of the History of Mankind* (1784-1791).[51] For Herder, the intimate semantic tie between "culture" and "civilization" was blatantly ideological (as we would call it today), representing the teleological thinking of late-eighteenth-century Europe: "Men of all quarters of the globe, who have perished over the ages, you have not merely lived solely to manure the earth with your ashes, so that at the end of time your posterity should be made happy by European culture. The very thought of a superior European culture is a blatant insult to the majesty of Nature."[52]

Herder thought we needed to uncouple this tie and speak of cultures in the plural — each one specific and rich in itself. Although Herder made room at the human table for non-Europeans, he retained two aspects of the concept of culture that continued to have important ramifications. First, although there now were many cultures, each was still considered in a kind of undifferentiated global sense. The mores and customs of a particular group were thought to be shared completely by all its members. Boundaries could be drawn both conceptually and politically around societies as they were brought under colonial control one by one and as they were ranked on the evolutionary developmental charts of Klemm, Morgan, and Tylor.

Second, Herder's national and traditional cultures were defined by their "spirit." This "spirit of the folk" became available repeatedly as an organizing tool for romantic and nationalistic movements. Culture became idealist and ineffable. This ineffability has had a number of effects because although people might feel some sense of local or national identity, it is often difficult to tell what constitutes this sense of local similarity. As we have discovered, mores and the belief systems that underly them are contested terrain.

The "democratization" of culture set in motion successful nineteenth-century attempts to capture part of the territory of spirit by those who retained their attachment to European civilization. Drawing on the earliest meaning of culture as the process of cultivation, the concept of high Culture — Culture with a capital C — was developed. This Culture was self-consciously aesthetic and avowedly elitist. It required training and taste. As

Collins has put it, this Culture was conceived as a kind of "Grand Hotel . . . a totalizable system that somehow orchestrates all cultural production and reception according to one master system." [53]

The rich and cultured could separate themselves from the masses and their folk cultures — not directly through their riches but indirectly by virtue of the free time for cultivation their class position afforded. They and their minions, from Matthew Arnold through T. S. Eliot to Allan Bloom, could claim to be the last defense of civilization before the hordish onslaught. [54]

Andreas Huyssen has written about the split between high and low culture as "the great divide." [55] As I argued in Chapter 3, following Daniel Bell, this division is dependent on the uncoupling of the sphere of culture from the economic system. Huyssen writes, "This differentiation of spheres . . . was actually the historical prerequisite for the twin establishment of a sphere of high autonomous art and a sphere of mass culture." [56]

But this division was not simple; within each stream were conflicting currents. Within high culture the split was between classical systems of representation and a new "modernism," which struggled against both high tradition and the contaminating influence of everyday life and its mass culture. Huyssen's ideal type characterization of modernist art is worth quoting in its entirety.

- The work is autonomous and totally separate from the realm of mass culture and everyday life.

- It is self-referential, self-conscious, frequently ironic, ambiguous, and rigorously experimental.

- It is the expression of a purely individual consciousness rather than of a Zeitgeist or collective state of mind.

- Its experimental nature makes it analogous to science, and like science it produces and carries knowledge.

- Modernist literature since Flaubert is a persistent exploration of and encounter with language. Modernist painting since Manet is an equally persistent elaboration of the medium itself: the flatness of the canvas, the structuring of notation, paints and paintbrush, the problem of the frame.

- The major premise of the modernist artwork is the rejection of all classical systems of representation, the effacement of "content," the erasure of subjectivity and authorial voice, the repudiation of likeness and verisimilitude, the exorcism of any demand for realism of whatever kind.

- Only by fortifying its boundaries, by maintaining its purity and autonomy, and by avoiding any contamination with mass culture and with the signifying systems of everyday life can the artwork maintain its adversarial stance: adversary to the bourgeois culture of everyday life as well as adversary to mass culture and entertainment, which are seen as the primary forms of bourgeois cultural articulation. [57]

Since the last quarter of the nineteenth century, art, literature, music, and architecture have all been insulated from everyday life. Such connections as were made, as Cecelia Tichi suggests in *Shifting Gears,* often drew on the design and function of machines such as the dynamo before which Henry Adams swooned at the Chicago Exposition.[58] High aesthetic experience may have spoken to the intellect and emotions of an insulated modernist elite, but its transformatory power over most people was limited to the massive — even sublime — nature of architecture.

But what about mass culture, folk culture, popular culture — the various typifications of the "low" tradition? Modernism finds its decline in the rise of the power of this mass culture and the use of that culture to postmodern effects. Among these effects is the galloping metastasism of the process of commodification. I turn again to Huyssen.

> 20th-century Capitalism has "reunified" economy and culture by subsum-
> ing the cultural under the economic, by reorganizing the body of cultural
> meanings and symbolic significations to fit the logic of the commodity.
> Especially with the help of the new technological media of reproduction and
> dissemination, monopoly capital has succeeded in swallowing up all forms
> of older popular cultures, in homogenizing all and any local or regional
> discourse, and in stifling by co-option any energy resistance to the rule of the
> commodity.... Cultural entities typical of the style of the culture industry are
> no longer *also* commodities, they are commodities through and through.[59]

This "swallowing up all forms of older popular culture" is not the only form of commodity subsumption, for high art as well — as Christie's and Andy Warhol with his Campbell Soup Can screens have shown us — is just another form of merchandise. However, it is the former to which we now attend.

Folk, popular, and mass culture are various terms that have been used to describe "low" culture. Each of these labels codes a process as well as content. "Folk" is a label attributed by nonfolk people to traditional activities in which people, usually rural people, engage in relatively unself-conscious ways. Art, music, and particularly crafts of various kinds embody much of folk culture. These activities, especially music,[60] arise out of ongoing work situations and the normal vicissitudes of life. People themselves didn't call what they did folk; it was just normal life. For whatever reasons of solidarity and yearning, the label "folk" was applied from outside. The often ironic effect of this categorization was the drawing of conceptual boundaries around certain activities, reifying and recontextualizing them. Thus domesticated, chunks of folk art could enter the market to be sold as tokens of nostalgia, quaintness, and craftspersonship (itself an item of nostalgia). Folk traditions joined the rest of U.S. culture as something for sale.

Popular culture and mass culture, larger streams than folk culture, have become confusing and difficult concepts. Neither is Culture with a capital C, but they differ in different ways. Since the early days of the Frankfurt School, mass culture has carried a perjorative connotation. Adorno and

Horkheimer used it as their image for a seamless world of understandings shared, sheeplike, by the "masses." For the early Frankfurters, these understandings were nothing but ideology imposed on a passive populace in the interest of politics and commerce.

Although the pessimism of their critique led many practitioners to withdraw back into the world of Art with a capital A, the idea of mass culture remains useful. It "draws our attention to what has happened to symbolic forms in various stages of their industrial production and distribution." [61]

Popular culture is a more recent invention. It has been a very contentious idea, a center of much argument about the content and social functions of popular cultural forms. Wilfred Fluck has outlined four approaches to popular culture.

First is the kind of pessimistic cultural criticism — focused on the high art-low art dichotomy — associated with the Frankfurt School-type theorists mentioned above. Second is the response to this criticism associated with the rise of popular culture studies in the United States. As Fluck describes this stance,

> In a gesture [that is] merely the result of an inversion of "high" cultural criticism it automatically grants an authentic and democratic essence to popular culture which seems to entirely disregard the culture industry's influence on shaping and deforming popular cultural forms for its own financial interests . . . the new movement mainly idealizes [popular fictions] as a mirror-image of a nation, as a "voice of the people." [62]

Salutary as an antidote, the pendulum here swings uselessly far.

The third and fourth approaches to popular culture, which deal particularly with social functions, are considerably more useful. Focusing respectively on ideological manipulation and on the economic functions of popular culture as a form of commodity production, these versions correctly point to the deformation of peoples' thoughts and desires in the interests of political control and commerce.

Particularly important to these critiques is the influence of mass media on cultural forms. Some, such as Leo Lowenthal, argue that mass-mediated popular culture *reflects* political-economic structures. [63] Others (Paul Lazersfield and Robert Merton) talk about *channeling*. C. Wright Mills says media *cause* particular beliefs and behaviors. These approaches are all useful in drawing our attention to the existence of the culture industry and its central place in bourgeois cultural hegemony. Yet they remain too simple, too linear, too automatic, too "top-down" in their assumptions of human passivity. Popular cultural forms *are* often pleasurable. They entertain. They exercise our abilities to think, feel, and remember. In many cases they are relatively resistant to deformation; they are robust and hard to domesticate.

Even as popular cultural forms become commodified, they speak to people's real life situations. As Huyssen puts it, "In general, consumption satisfies needs, and even though human needs can be distorted to an amazing degree, every need contains a smaller or larger kernel of authenticity. The question to be asked is how this kernel can be utilized and fulfilled." [64] W. F. Haug goes further.

> Manipulation could only be effective if it somehow latched on to the "objective interests" of those being manipulated . . . while pursuing their interests. Even manipulative phenomena must "speak the language of real needs" — they must express real needs even in an alienated or estranged mode, if they are to inscribe themselves in the domain of subjective sensuality . . . where real needs are "experienced." [65]

Popular culture enjoys at least some relative autonomy as a body of activity with significance to peoples' actual needs. [66] But, as both Huyssen and Haug suggest, the modern world is rife with distortion and manipulation. The activities whose logic requires the capture and control of popular culture are organized into two overlapping sets of institutions — the culture industry and the mass media. Each of these constructs products for the market but in slightly different ways. The former, like the Walt Disney Company, constructs stories in which to embed the solutions to human needs claimed for their products. The latter, except for explicit advertisements, builds its narratives so as to mask the identity of its product — the audience itself, to which it hopes to appeal. The two realms divide the labor of bringing all things into the market and protecting the resultant division of spoils. The stories and other narratives draw on popular culture and because the media enter every home, invent it, as Disney does with its various characters. As we saw above in the discussion of commodification, design, and advertisement, ersatz needs and commodified solutions are constantly being inserted into our minds. Even if we catch some, many slip through.

Ours has become a mass-mediated culture in which relations between the institutional order and human consciousness are not direct. They are mediated by the representations of the mass media. Although it is clear that the institutional order has the power to represent itself to our consciousness — the media are, after all, owned by corporations that are part of the ruling order — it is also clear that power is not undifferentiated. [67] Media shift in importance as people exercise the options brought by technological change. People stop reading newspapers (although they buy them for the coupons). They switch from radio to television. Within a particular medium, patterns of consumption change. *USA Today* becomes a success. Television viewers switch from network to cable television then use their zappers to "graze."

The reality of these activities joins the ideology of commerce to produce the mystifying oxymoron of consumer sovereignty. As all this apparent choice is hypostasized and our gaze is focused on popular culture, something deeper is going on because underlying popular culture, folk culture, high culture, low culture, and the other cultures is anthropological culture. I return in a brief echo to the argument of Chapter 2 — to Berger and Luckmann's "symbolic universe" and to maps and territories.

As we focus on what map we want to buy, the colorful one or the topographical one, we hardly think that we are acting in a market context. If we have the money, we can buy the map. We hardly think of other ways maps might be distributed. We hardly wonder why anybody would make those maps or why what is on them is on them. Socialized into a particular institutional order, we live in a symbolic universe — with its gods, kinfolk, and property — we understand as correct reality. What would the world be like without Mickey Mouse? It's nearly inconceivable.

As long as we act in terms of our shared symbolic universe, life — even if difficult — is explainable. Further, we will not threaten those who control the goodies. As long as we believe the "consumer" is a correct ontological category, we will enact the metaphorical digestion of the market. To control the cartographic enterprise (and thus the information by which we travel through the territory) requires both positive acts — the drawing of new maps and new symbols for the legend — and the policing activities I have called "unnatural selection."

What is important is that along with "deep" maps, there is "deep" territory. Whatever the choices we may be making from the postmodern smorgasbord of late capitalism, we are headed for a commodity nirvana in which differentiation will be everywhere and thus nowhere.

> In postmodernism . . . everyone has learned to consume culture through television and the other mass media, so a rationale is no longer necessary. You look at advertising billboards and collages of things because they are there in external reality. The whole matter of how you justify to yourself the time of consuming culture disappears: You are no longer even aware of consuming it. Everything is culture, the culture of the commodity. [68]

A Postmodernism of Reaction

Focusing on California's Disneyland, Michael R. Real has argued that the "Disney universe" embodies a kind of morality play. [69] He suggests that Disney productions summarize the spirit and worldview of the contemporary middle-class United States in the same way Dante summarized those of the medieval European world. Using a standard definition of the traditional morality play as "a dramatized allegory in which the abstract virtues and vices (like Mercy, Conscience, Perseverance, and Shame) appear in a personified form, the good and the bad usually being engaged in a struggle for the soul of man," [70] Real writes that "both [Disney and Dante] idealize fundamental characteristics into utopian worlds of absolutes." [71]

Far more complicated than Disneyland, WDW carries a more complex set of moral meanings. Further, within a metamap of shared moral meanings, there are significant differences between the allegories of the Magic Kingdom and those of EPCOT Center. Although Walt Disney always thought of himself as an entrepreneur and an entertainer, in his later years he acquired the labels of moral educator and urban planner as well. The theme parks especially would use entertainment to "spread a patriotic American's idealized vision of nation and world, of the past, the present, and the future."[72]

Disneyland and its Magic Kingdom clone lead visitors through scenes that depict happiness, innocence, industriousness, resourcefulness — all watered-down versions of morality play virtues but nonetheless appropriate to a "have a nice day" America. These minivirtues are found in a quasiutopian context of cleanliness, friendliness (studied though it may be), safeness, and relative efficiency. These positive characteristics — the Disney version of family entertainment — triumph both narratively and literally over meanness, anger, rudeness, idleness, slovenliness, and critical thinking.

Underlying all of these characteristics is a worldview that presents an idealized United States as heaven (with Mickey Mouse as Beatrice leading all of us Dantes to Cinderella's Castle). History is decoration. Colonialism was fun, the colonized cute (but a little stupid). How nice if they could all be like us — with kids, a dog, and General Electric appliances — in a world whose only problems are avoiding Captain Hook, the witch's apple, and the Toad Hall weasels.

But Walt died, and Corporate Disney built EPCOT Center. The stories here are about technology, corporations, nature as a storeroom full of "gifts" for us, and foreign lands as theme parks. It is an Experimental Prototype Commercial of Tomorrow rather than an Experimental Prototype Community of Tomorrow. Walt's technological utopia became a mall.

Rebelling against modernism, Disney attempted to return to an idealized, carny-less past; but his use of technology, proliferation of niches, and wonderful simulations have instead become perfect icons of a "postmodernism of reaction,"[73] with history as pastiche, geography as façade, fantasy as property, and sensual experience as commodity.

16

Nature's "Gifts": Land, Garden, Sea

Disney World is nothing if not homage to the Mickey Mouse that lurks in each one of us, an advertisement written to the Genuine Imitation. It is a tribute to the lifelike. As opposed to, say, the live.

—Ellen Goodman[1]

Walt Disney spent much of his life creating a world of fantasy, filled with characters that have become America's cultural icons. Through his live action theater and television films and at his theme parks, Disney also invented a U.S. history that made conventional optimism meaningless. These fantasies and histories contributed to the commodification of experience by which Walt Disney Productions earned its keep.

With EPCOT, Walt became an urban and social planner. This turn to the future was motivated partly by his critique of contemporary society — what he called "the problem of the cities" — and partly by his faith in the wonders of technology and engineering. As we have seen, Walt's fantasy was to jury-rig the future into a technological utopia.

He was a tinkerer. His orientation to technology was not that of a theoretical scientist but that of a practical engineer. A company tinkerer would become an "imagineer" — an imaginative designer of futurist solutions to theatrical and infrastructural problems.

With Walt's death EPCOT became something else — a permanent World's Fair that is part technological exposition, part international mall.[2] The technological exposition became Future World — filled perhaps with vernacular architectural flourishes but built to heroic scale. Instead of the medieval fair at the Magic Kingdom — with its closed vistas, twisty streets, and collaborative street life — Future World would be a Disney version of Le Corbusier's modernist Chandrigar.

Many critics have remarked that Future World is emotionally flat. As at Tomorrowland in the Magic Kingdom, the Company's imagination deserted it when it came to depicting the future. "Tomorrow" is invoked — both at Tomorrowland and at Future World — through a futurist style that speaks more about the present than the future. A central irony at WDW is that history and geography — the past and the elsewhere — are represented in postmodern idiom whereas the future lags behind, depicted in the futurist style of modernism.

There is an interesting contradiction at Future World. Disney's shows about science, technology, and the future are primarily corporate ideology. They are intended to convince us to put our lives — and our descendants' lives — into the hands of transnational corporate planners and the technological systems they wish to control. These systems, however, can only be hinted at in the various futuristic dramas of Future World. Because participating corporations have little interest in giving away strategic secrets, the technology we do see is not particularly new. The future is only hinted at, whereas many of the stories told at Future World are about the past.

The texts of Future World were written by Disney but with the collaboration of other corporate storytellers. Because the corporations intend to present themselves as qualified and logical purveyors of the future, they need to underpin their claims to authority and control with reasonable credibility. Basing these claims on science and technology, Exxon, United Technologies, and the others needed to tell stories that would make sense to their relatively well-educated customers. Thus, EPCOT's little dramas tell us about evolution, pregnancy, and other relatively secular processes. Norman Rockwell, yes; Oral Roberts, no.

Undergirding the show at WDW, however, is an infrastructure based on state-of-the-art technological systems. Here's where the utopian stuff really is. Earlier I looked at the transportation, trash disposal, sewage treatment systems, and other parts of the spatial infrastructure at WDW. Here and in the following chapters, I will consider another batch of technologies — the computer control systems, fiber optic communication, the WorldKey video disc system, the organization of food delivery, and the light and sound technologies — as we work our way to and through Future World.

Customers are shown science-technology-engineering future dramas in an environment that has been "improved" with top-flight technology — technology that is much more interesting than that portrayed in the content of the shows. Disney's infrastructural technology holds a range of promises for human life — possibilities for egalitarian community as well as authoritarian control and management.

My discussion of the science and technology actually used at WDW, as well as the ideological and propagandist arguments for centralized corporationist engineering and the technological fix, will require a small detour into the philosophy of technology. I spend some time in the next chapter with Langdon Winner and Albert Borgmann as I try to ferret out the messages Disney is pushing. My entry into these issues, however, will be by way of Disney's depiction of nature.

Human life exists only as human groups come to some terms with the physical environments in which they find themselves. The variegated history of the species is one of adjustment and transformation — the first when necessary, the second when possible. These processes are constrained by the level of technology available to groups of people at any one time and by the internal and external power relations by which people are distributed across the environment.

Relations between human groups and nature are also structured by shared systems of anthropological culture. Here is where we find the deeply learned maps that tell us where and what nature is, where its boundaries are, and where we fit in. Legitimated by mythology, theology, philosophy, science, or other types of discourse, these cultural maps attempt to wrap human groups in taken-for-granted ontologies and epistemologies that solve the nature-culture problem. Here is where the battle takes place between those who would make such maps timeless and metaphysical and those who claim them as historical and contingent.

For some, human life is part of the natural world. Nature is immanent in human and other life systems. Connections among parts of this world — including human groups — are ecological, systemic, and nonlineal — full of feedback loops. Natural species are part of a nonhierarchical web of life. For others, human life is transcendent, not immanent. It exists alone and beyond other parts of the natural world — whether animate or not — as the pinnacle of existence in the universe.

This transcendent stance has been central to the Western European tradition, at least since the recording of the Book of Genesis. What William Leiss has called "the domination of nature" remains the authoritative tradition of the Western and modern worlds.[3] Recently, however, there have been significant challenges to this worldview by the growing voices of immanence. The oppositional list grows daily: ecologists; healthists; vegetarians; defenders of the natural world — greens, Earth Firsters, animal rights folk — those fighting chemical dumping, acid rain, oil spills, carcinogenic food additives, and pesticides; antinuclear, small is beautiful, appropriate technology people; ozone layer supporters; and localists, regionalists, populists, anarchists, and other bottom-up organizers.

A major corporation itself, the Walt Disney Company obviously has a stake in this conflict over political ontology. What it does as a business is possible only because of transcendent control over its local environment. Its corporate partners at WDW rely on Disney to help naturalize the transcendence that maintains their own power and market position. Disney's task, especially at Future World, is deeply metaphysical: It is to capture time, and thus annihilate it, by seducing its audience into willing complicity with corporate authority and control. Let Exxon and AT&T do it, and all will be well.

I want, then, to suggest some things about Disney and nature. I take a look at the messages presented at Horizons, The Land, and The Living Seas at Future World. As with the other major areas of interest examined so far, Disney tells stories that propose a particular set of relations among human beings, corporations, and the natural world. At The Land, Horizons, and The Living Seas in particular, Future World shows us a nature with contradictory aspects. It is harsh and hostile on the one hand, an adversary to be conquered with engineering and will. If so controlled, we will find that nature is full of "gifts" for us that are ready for the taking. The environment is like a wild horse — to be broken, tamed, and ridden where we will. The wranglers who help fulfill the utilitarian dream and who protect us from the hooves are corporate scientists and technicians.

At the Wonders of Life, we take a further step. Here the central metaphor is war. Teenage executive homunculi act as cranium commandos, driving us like tanks through a day at junior high school, overcoming the "natural" wildness of our hormones and other biochemicals. Should we get sick, miniaturized health personnel are sent to fight body wars on the battlefields inside us.

In the Disney spirit, I will enter the grounds of nature, science, technology, and the future through the tao of General Electric. The appropriate path from the past to the future leads from GE's Carousel of Progress to its spiritual clone at Future World — Horizons.

Horizons

On the east side of Future World, bounded by GM's World of Motion on the south and Metropolitan Life's Wonders of Life to the north, is the gem-shaped building that houses Horizons. In a show that points to the other pavilions around it, Horizons acts as Future World's table of contents. Here the robot couple from the Carousel of Progress guides us through a futurist retrospective and on past a set of stages that portray four different scenarios for upper-middle-class life in the future. These scenes are built around the various family members, all of whom seem to have had pretty good life prospects.

The theme of Horizons is "if we can dream it, we can do it." Here again Disney sleight of word captures the first-person plural. Who knows who the "we" who "dream it" might be, but we certainly recognize the corporate "we" who will "do it." Included in this latter "we," Disney would have us understand, are the kinds of people we see represented here by Horizon's robots, in whom we might wish to recognize ourselves.

As Walt Disney originally envisioned EPCOT, his utopia would escape the urban predicament by avoiding it. The new cities would have no slums, no homeless, certainly no drug problem. They would be pretty, white cities — Anglo middle-class technological utopias. The motto at Horizons might lead us to think that technology and engineering are all that are at stake in Disney's imaginative vision of the future. We might keep in mind that "if we can dream it, we can do it" encodes social and demographic engineering as well.

We enter the pavilion through Future Port, with its destination announcements, and head to an inside snake past holographic images of space. This is not the most popular attraction at Future World, so the line is usually pretty short. Suspended from an overhead track, ride vehicles seat four. Visitors sit side by side on hard plastic as the cars scuttle through the show. In front — currently darkened — are panels that depict three of the scenes we will soon see. We will be asked later to "vote" for which of those sites we might wish to "visit."

Before entering the future at WDW, it is obligatory that we visit the whimsical past. As at Spaceship Earth, World of Motion, Universe of Energy, and similar venues, we so begin. Talking in our ears through vehicle speakers, Mother and Father — transposed from the Carousel of Progress — start us off "looking back at tomorrow." We glide past theater marquees with American moderne graphics and simulated neon. Showing at the Bijou and the Nickelodeon are *La Voyage Dans La Lune* and *Looking Back at Tomorrow*, respectively. Drawings in the style of the French artist Albert Robida depict nineteenth-century images of the Paris of the future — Paris of the 1950s, with its subways and fish-shaped dirigible taxis. [4]

In a cutaway we see an audioanimatronic Jules Verne — accompanied by a flying dog and chicken — sail through weightless space in a plushly upholstered, bullet-shaped Victorian rocket. We see film clips of science fiction versions of the future taken from such films as Fritz Lang's *Metropolis* (1926) and *Woman in the Moon* (1928) and Woody Allen's *Sleeper* (1973). [5]

It's on to the Populuxe of the 1950s — phosphorescent paint, black light, hula hoops, drive-in restaurants — the future of the Jetsons. Mother reminds Father, "We always thought the future would be kind of fun." These cardboard futures give way to a household scene that parodies the 1930s futurology of the mechanical house. As a robot butler in black tie vacuums near the window, an audioanimatronic Grandpa (perhaps Cousin Orville?) sits in a mechanized barber chair. Overhead is a sun lamp.

Grandpa's shoes are being buffed by an apparatus at the foot of the chair. Upstairs a television is on.

In the kitchen is the pièce de résistance. Here a shiny, round, metal kitchen robot is destroying his surroundings. In chef's hat and scarf with a medal of distinction hanging down his round body, the robot is frantically cleaning up after a meal. Mechanical arms holding a broom and wash rags are everywhere as the robot spins around, overwhelmed and out of control. Dishes are piled up at the sink behind him. Some are smashed on the floor near a puddle of spilled milk.

From this parody of the domestic future, we enter the Omnisphere and its high-tech cinematography.

> Here we are confronted with two Omni-Max screens, each eight stories high and eight stories wide. Screens like these are already in use elsewhere, but at EPCOT Center for the first time every viewer will be placed at the vantage point or "optimum spot," at the center of the screen. This will give the impression of being completely surrounded by film, creating a mysterious and awesome environment. It is the perfect medium to engulf us in the wonders of modern science and technology.[6]

On the screens an Omnifax 70-millimeter projection system shows a series of "microphotography, super macro-photography and underwater footage."[7] Among the scenes we see are a space shuttle launch, a growing crystal, and a flight over Manhattan that segues into a "flight" over a city-like magnified computer chip. We see a DNA chain, a thermal land scan, and animated sequences of a space colony. As Richard R. Beard writes, this segment of the ride deals with the present — "tomorrow's horizons today" — bridging the silly past views of the future and the cities of the future upcoming.[8]

Moving on to a future that is "just around the corner," we ride past "tomorrow's windows." Here we see four sets that represent the Disney-GE version of the future. It is an introduction to the "incessant optimism" at EPCOT.[9]

The metatheme at Horizons is the youthful nuclear family, which apparently will endure into the twenty-first century. Mother and Father, now grandparents, are still youthful and seemingly healthy. They sit in an elegant apartment with a picture window that looks out on Nova Cite, another of Disney's Moholy Nagy-like futurist cities. Father is playing a piece of self-composed "music" on what sounds like a theremin. He calls it a "symphosizer." The barking dog — perhaps Sport X from the Carousel of Progress — is not amused.

Mother sits at the huge wraparound sofa at the right, talking to one of her daughters, whose shrunken image is projected in a holographic televiewer. They are planning a child's birthday party, to which everyone will come by image. The daughter speaks from the desert robotic farm we see next. Transportation systems — including the magnetic levitation (or mag-lev) cars we see out the window and various space craft — and communication systems (such as the holographic viewer in this set) will enable people to transcend space. They will do so, however, in a world without much fashion design. The jumpsuits everybody wears are pretty boring. [10]

We turn another corner and enter the desert. This is Mesa Verde, a high energy use robotic farm. Mother's college-educated daughter stands in a semienclosed plastic pod with a video screen and a computer terminal. A "smellitzer," or scent cannon, sprays the air with essence of orange blossom. On the circular bench surface are simulated genetically engineered fruits and vegetables. The daughter talks to both Mother and her husband, who warns her of an impending storm.

In front of the command pod stretch long rectangular irrigated plots filled with industrial plants, all tended by machine. Robotic land vehicles collect produce, which is transferred to hovercraft and flown to wherever plants will be flown in the future. The daughter's one-person air vehicle sits next to the control pod.

Daughter and her family live nearby, next to a desert pool with a robot frog in it. A cat fishes for whatever. We pass the electronic kitchen where Husband and Son are working on a birthday cake. Wraparound windows and a "glassed-in" roof open the kitchen to the desert view.

Mesa Verde is our introduction to Disney's notions about industrial farming in the future — robots, high energy use, genetic engineering, and hardly any people. Mesa Verde gives us a macroscopic view of such an operation. It points directly to the microview of farming-gardening-to-be that we will visit soon at The Land.

An audioanimatronic granddaughter is in the home communication center. She is supposed to be doing her homework on the computer behind her but is talking to her boyfriend on the videophone, warning him not to be late for the party. He is repairing a small "solo sub" in a workshop in the Sea Castle, a floating city in the Pacific Ocean.

The transition to the Sea Castle is cleverly made. We see the robot granddaughter talking to her boyfriend on the screen. Then we ride past the submarine repair shop where Boyfriend is talking to Granddaughter on the screen. As Mesa Verde points to The Land, so Sea Castle gestures toward The Living Seas.

We glide by an undersea restaurant, peeping in through the windows at two well-dressed black women at one table and a male Anglo, looking at a menu, at another. An Asian mother and daughter peer out a window at us. All have Anglo hairdos. These seem to be the only simulated people in the show not wearing jumpsuits.

Beyond the restaurant is an undersea staging area where three children are being taught to scuba dive. This is Disney's most efficient presentation of implausible integration. There are five living beings here: a red-headed

Anglo boy, a blond girl, a black boy, a female Asian diving instructor, and a seal.

The children will presumably take underwater trips to the kelp farm — "seaweed," Mother says in our ear before Father corrects her — and the mining operations. Both of these are full of robots, just like the farm. Curiously, we will see more humans and fewer robots in the ensuing space set. Here Mother presents the sea as nature's storehouse, full of "gifts for us" — a place where "we've found a lot of good things."

We'll also find "good things" in space, we are told, as we head toward the space colony Brava Centauri. We pass a scene of audioanimatronic astronauts assembling a satellite in space. Then we are in the center of a spherical space colony, revolving to simulate gravity. Roads, houses, lakes, even greenery are visible in the distance. According to Beard, EPCOT designers created a miniature set and then photographed it from the center. [11]

Space will be full of zero gravity and nuclear families. Passing an upside-down cycling machine with a screen in front of it showing sights of earth, we enter a nearby docking port. A newly arrived family faces the peril of zero gravity. Mom calls to her young son, who has forgotten to put on his magnetic shoes. He floats through the air holding the leash of his upside-down dog. Overhead, Dad retrieves a flying teddy bear. Next door another grandmother-type is growing giant industrial crystals in the zero gravity. Suddenly we are back on earth, where the extended family has gathered for the birthday party — some live, some in holographic projection.

For its finale, Horizons offers its passengers a high-speed "ride" to one of three future habitats — Mesa Verde, Sea Castle, or Brava Centauri. The touch-sensitive panels in front of each passenger light up with pictures of these destinations. Passengers are advised that they can "vote" for their destination by pressing the appropriate picture on the panel. "Majority rules" (although there seems to be room for ties). The default mode appears to be the desert, because that's where we go when no buttons are pushed.

For the thirty-second, ride our car tilts backward and vibrates. We are shown fast-moving close-up visuals of travel to our destination. Screens drop into place to shield us from the films of the cars next to us. The effect is like a small, intimate version of the speed rooms at World of Motion and Dreamflight.

Our ride over, we debark at FuturePort. Let us now cross Future World through the CommuniCores, to The Land and pick up Disney's stories about nature, the environment, and agriculture.

The Land

At six acres, The Land is the largest pavilion at EPCOT Center. It is reached by a wide sloping walkway from the center of CommuniCore West, bordered by geometrically arranged ornamental plants. Inside we will be asked to "listen to the land," but the plantings already suggest that the land is going to be yelled at some. In The Land we see highly technological gardening and, in fact, very little land.

The pavilion resembles a huge polyhedral glass greenhouse with a crown on top. Spreading out from the central glass tower, crisscrossed by metal girders, are the walls (ochre in front to match the walkway) of the various greenhouses that have been incorporated into the attraction. The entrance is flanked by mosaics that depict stylized geological crosssections of the earth. This is the most expansive entrance at Future World.

The Land is sponsored by Kraft Foods, one of the world's largest purveyors of processed eating materials. The story Kraft and Disney claim to tell is about human relationships with nature and the land — especially those that center on food and subsistence. Customers are shown simulations and films of the world's different ecotypes, from harsh to lush. We see how humans have interacted with their environment, making creative agricultural adjustments in order to stay alive. We take a boat or a walking tour through working greenhouses developed to test controlled-environment agriculture (CEA) techniques and "exotic" and underused plants suitable for marginal ecological niches. A major theme at The Land is that extensive use of technology in agriculture and animal spousery is not new but is a long-time part of the human heritage: Thus, a future of *corporate-controlled* technology is an appropriate next step. It's o.k. Trust "us."

Kraft-Disney claim the model is one of "partnership" based on symbiosis — the synergistic codependence between people and the land. To introduce this theme, pavilion designers have turned to the biologist-ecologist-philosopher René Dubos, whose words grace a plaque at the entranceway.

> Symbiotic relationships mean creative partnerships. The earth is to be seen neither as an ecosystem to be preserved unchanged, nor as a quarry to be exploited for selfish and short-range economic reasons, but as a garden to be cultivated for the development of its own possibilities of the human adventure. The goal of this relationship is not the maintenance of the status quo but the emergence of new phenomena and new values.

Kraft is clearer about how this symbiosis will work. In its souvenir pamphlet "Listen to the Land," Kraft notes the place of business in this symbiosis. We also get a clearer look at the real, utilitarian rather than symbiotic relationship intended by the corporation. People are to "use" the environment effectively, however else they may dwell in it.

The Land, presented by Kraft, is the only show in the world designed around food production and agricultural research. The pavilion was created to foster a spirit of hope based on sound accomplishment and to illustrate that while no one has all the answers, the future is bright because there are alternatives to present techniques and unlimited opportunities. . . . The pavilion represents Kraft's faith in and commitment to a future in which people and business can flourish in a creative and confident environment. . . . The Land is a unique demonstration of peoples' effective use of their environment and their provisions for future generations. [12]

I think The Land is the most ideologically interesting venue at Future World. Here visitors see practices that *do* point to one kind of utopian future. We see a film that suggests that ecological mistakes were made in the past but that the potential for healing praxis still exists. Each of these ambiguous presentations has a potentially progressive edge to it, especially for the ecologically minded middle-class gardener. Those "of an age" will also be entertained by one of the cleverest audioanimatronic shows at WDW. The Kitchen Kabaret takes us back to the pre-rock-and-roll U.S. musical tradition in an entertaining parody set to teach us that Kraft products are good for us.

We begin, as we enter the building, with a balcony overview of the Farmer's Market. Above is the soaring roof, painted in blues and white — a cartoon sky covering the fairgrounds below. Up and behind us a skylight brings in the sun. Three "hot air balloons" (representing food groups) rise and fall over the large white, blue, and earth-brown fountain in the middle of the lower level. Stairs and escalators at the far end — in front of the entrances to *Symbiosis* and the Land Grille Room — lead down to the plaza.

Directly below us are the eight-counter service stands that make up the Farmer's Market. Each counter serves a specialty marked by a brightly colored advertising façade. [13] The stalls are connected to one another by an open hallway in the back so personnel and supplies can be quickly transferred from stall to stall. In front are plastic tables surmounted by umbrella covers. The plaza looks like a collection of toy mushrooms.

Across the plaza on the balcony is the Land Grille Room, a revolving restaurant that serves regional U.S. specialties. [14] As customers sit in "velvet"-upholstered, wood-trimmed booths, the restaurant cycles through scenes from the Listen to the Land ride below. Small planters on the tables hold seedlings of economically important U.S. crops — corn, wheat, soybeans — and blurbs about the productivity of U.S. farms. The menu contains a list of Kraft products and an advertisement for "free enterprise." [15]

The Listen to the Land ride was designed both for its own riders and for patrons of the restaurant above. Thus, there are effects that can only be seen from the Land Grille Room. Riders go through each scene only once unless they take the ride again. The restaurant revolves slowly enough so diners may see boats pass a particular scene many times. This enables them to see patterns that escape boat passengers. Beard notes,

> There are animation effects that are tripped off by photoelectric sensors reacting to the boats' progress. In the rain forest, for example, the arrival of the boats triggers the monkeys and birds into a higher level of activity. Their sounds become louder as well, so that it seems to the people in the restaurant that the boats have actually alarmed them. . . . As the boats approach, the rain comes down harder, and when they reach the desert the sandstorm kicks up higher, changing the color of the sun. [16]

Beard also notes that the speed of revolution varies during the day — faster at breakfast, slower at dinner when people linger — so each meal takes approximately one revolution.

Symbiosis

At the right rear of the balcony level is the entrance to the five hundred-seat Harvest Theater and The Land's visually stunning film, *Symbiosis*. [17]

Nothing in the universe exists alone.

Every drop of water,

> *every human being,*
> *all creatures in the web of life,*
> *and all ideas in the web of knowledge*

are part of an immense, evolving, dynamic whole,

as old —

> *and as young —*

as the universe itself.

So intones the narrator at the beginning of this eighteen-minute wide-screen film. *Symbiosis* purports to tell the story of the relationship between human groups and the environments in which they must seek their subsistence. In particular, the film focuses on technology and technological systems and their impacts on food production. [18] Disney claims that this relation is one of "partnership" — not between people and people but between people and the land. As the film shows, this partnership has been threatened from time to time by technological forces — disembodied rather than incarnate in the institutions that benefited from the use of those forces. Thus, as we'll see, no one in particular is at fault for environmental degradation, just "us" all together. What makes *Symbiosis* distinctive at Future World, however, is the critique it gives of human action.

With the spread of ecological consciousness throughout mainstream U.S. culture in the 1980s, this story could not be avoided in any treatment of food and agriculture; but it needed to be told in such a way that visitors would be led away from the social impact of the family farm crisis (and thus away from a glance at agribusiness, banking, farm loan policies, and the like). Thus, Kraft's film points us toward *technologies* as purveyors of problems and solutions to the food crisis. Specific scenes portray peoples' ingenuity in adapting nature to their needs. [19]

We begin with nature sublime — desert, arctic tundra, fjord; no people, no animals, just nature, beautiful, harsh, and raw. Into this nature, brought by extraordinary dramatic photography, come living things. First are the birds — ducks, geese, flamingos — thousands of them in flocks that fill the sky. We are in East Africa with elephants and giraffes striding past the sun.

Suddenly, in an anthropological strike, humans are added. These are low-tech humans — Maasai, Lapp reindeer herders, Innuit on a dog sled, net fishers. We are meant to understand these and other simple ecological adaptations as Dubos's "creative partnerships," allowing "humans generation after generation to pursue a way of life that sustained them without upsetting the balance of their natural environment." [20]

The illogical leap about which anthropologists seem unable to disabuse the public — that simple may be directly equated with ancestral — is evoked, as the first groups of people we see are technologically romanticized.

> In ancient times, humans were less likely to do damage to nature. This was largely so for two reasons. First, there were relatively few people competing for land and resources. Second, the technology used was simple and not really capable of changing the natural world to any great extent. As *Symbiosis* shows, however, developing civilizations brought changes that often served to harm the environment. [21]

We now see a classic image that represents the confrontation between the romanticized noble savage and the crushing onslaught of modern megatechnology. A single native American in costume sits stoically on his horse on top of a desert mesa. [22] In a rapid shift, the camera flies past the warrior until suddenly we see that the mesa stands next to a massive dam — modern engineering at its most heroic.

The narrator now suggests that those who argue that the dangers of nature-transforming technology are a curse of modernity are misspeaking the problem. It is not technology that is at fault but the patterns of usage of such technology, for technology is old, not new. [23]

Symbiosis shows an Egyptian pyramid, a Roman aqueduct in southern France, and the stone ruins of Macchu Pichu — all presumably salutary architecture. These projects lead us thematically back to the food problem, which was solved thousands of years ago in Luzon, the Philippines, by large-scale Ifugao rice field terracing. In these scenes we see how one population ingeniously altered the land in an agricultural system that has remained functional for over three thousand years.

The contemporary world requires new solutions to the food problem because a shot of a busy Hong Kong street shows that there are a lot of us now. We must travel, the film tells us, from Ifugao rice terraces to the

International Rice Institute (also in the Philippines) where agriculture science will save us as we are forced to rely on increasingly marginal land.

Land and technology are two of the central themes of *Symbiosis*. The third is water — sometimes too little, sometimes too much. Again we are led from traditional solutions to modern technologies. In a land with too little water, Egyptian fellahin water fields with a screw pump. Israeli desert water techniques — based on computerized drip irrigation — suggest a capitally intensive solution to desert agriculture, as does the circle watering of the U.S. Plains.

Sometimes there is too much water. We "fly" low over a stretch of calm water, aiming toward a dam-like wall in the near distance. Suddenly over the wall we are in the polders of Holland, filled with windmills and small farms salvaged from the sea. A quick visit to a project mock-up shows us how the dam and dike systems of the Delta project in southwestern Holland are planned and tested.

We are now warned, however, about the dangers of the human enthusiasm for technology because the "onslaught of technological man" has caused the natural world deep trauma. The film shows us the High Plains dust bowl of the 1930s, floods, and industrial waste in rivers and lakes. We are almost told about acid rain.

Disney and Kraft acknowledge what everybody knows. They could not expect to be taken seriously without reference to the contemporary assault on nature; but they are not about to tell it like it is publicly and lay the responsibility at the doorsteps of the corporations, banks, and industries that have led the way in this attack. Instead the culprit is abstracted and generalized to technological man — all of us (including, I suppose, women).

"We" have tamed the wilderness with "our" mechanized equipment and chemical fertilizers — no doubt invented, jury-rigged, and put together in our very own individual workshops in our spare time. The result is that the land has blown away, the forests have been logged out, and the waters are polluted.

As in all Disney films, we have seen despair. Now it's time for Disney hope (Dhope?). Governments and scientists are working hard to reverse the damage caused by private industry. We see the Thames, Lake Constance, and Oregon's Willamette River all being brought back to life — "for our use." The Black Forest of Bavaria, forests of Sweden, and the Pacific Northwest are claimed as being saved. We are shown forest burning and replanting, both done at state expense after private logging has clear-cut public lands.

We are led back to farming. The narrator lists the major problems: pesticides, lack of storage and transportation, bad planning and the destruction of land and rivers, and pollutants in the rain. This is a very different tone from that of the Magic Kingdom — this serious naming of bad things. It is for many people a dramatic surprise, coming from Disney.

The narrator now calls for a "second agricultural revolution." Its aim, says Wendy Murphy, "is to restore the old partnership between people and the earth, and to make this partnership work through the use of new methods of scientific farming." [24]

Intercropping, fallowing, and no-till plowing will be joined by high-tech irrigation to bring a New Age technological solution to the agricultural difficulties caused by technological man. "We have the power," the narrator claims, stirring us to follow the new technological lead. "We need the will." [25]

Listen to the Land

Down below our theater is the entrance to Listen to the Land, Disney-Kraft's boat ride through the greenhouses in which the new methods of scientific farming are demonstrated for New Age gardeners. Here we see small test versions of the agricultural procedures shown at Horizons' Mesa Verde desert farm. Let's descend.

Listen to the Land is Disney's paean to controlled-environment agriculture. Visitors take a 13 1/2-minute boat ride through experimental greenhouses designed to show a vision of the computerized gardening of the future. The godfather and chief designer of this "brave new garden" [26] is Merle Jensen, a research horticulturalist from the Environmental Research Laboratory at the University of Arizona. [27] Speaking about the design and development of the prototype growing system at The Land, Jensen says, "We can grow the World's required food if all nations and people work together, sharing new ideas in the development of food systems for the future. It is our goal that the land Pavilion set the stage for this cooperation, plus stimulate and challenge the spectator to meet the needs of tomorrow's agriculture today." [28]

Before reaching the greenhouses, however, the roofed-over twenty-person boats take visitors past six preliminary scenes, setting the stage for the wonders to come. With our scintillating and sometimes understandable [29] live guide at the microphone, we enter the "Symphony of the Seed" — a giant multicolored plasticoid collection of tubes and swirls our guide tells us is about "GERmiNAtion and PHOtoSYNthesis." Beard describes what this opening set is supposed to portray.

> The "Symphony of the Seed" [is] conceived as a reminder that all life on Earth is based on the miracle of the green plant. It features projected illusions of seeds germinating, plants growing, fluids flowing, sun caressing, flowers opening, and fruits ripening. This lyrical illustration of a plant's life cycle is accompanied only by the sounds of the earth and the gentle lyrics of "Listen to the Land." [30]

What these "gentle lyrics" do, however, is point to the first of two huge ironies at The Land. The ride and song are called Listen to the Land, but the content of what we are shown suggests that future gardening will talk (perhaps shout) rather than listen to the land. High-tech future agriculture will involve significant manipulation to go along with what we are shown here as blending. The blending we see later is not natural but is the result of clear — if sometimes traditional — human activity.

The second irony is that what we are to listen to is surely not "the land" because there is virtually no land at The Land. We are to listen to richly fertilized growing solution — the medium in which many of the crops are grown. One can sympathize, however, with the lyricist's difficulty in fitting this medium into the song.

From the acrylic Symphony, riders pass to the first of three sets, which represent climate zones — biomes — that have presented humans with subsistence marginality. These sets represent the tropical rain forest, the desert, and the prairie — the dioramas we visited from above while noshing at the Land Grille.

Each set contains an interpreted multisensory theme, complete — where appropriate — with audioanimatronic animals. At the tropical rain forest, birds chirp and monkeys chatter. The air, filled with "rainfall" that actually falls on the roof of the boat, is hot and dank. The forest of fake plants is luxuriant. The "smellitzer" aroma cannon creates the edge of a heart of darkness atmosphere.

The desert — with its sand, cactus, dry heat, and sand storm — is bleak. Projected on the rear wall, the sun turns from white to yellow to red as the storms blow past. On the prairie, wild grasses blow in the wind. Robot bison (including a calf) graze, and prairie dogs pop from the ground. In the distance a lightning storm sets the prairie on fire, stirring up a cloud of locusts.

Here on the American plains, a "natural midstation between tropic and desert climates,"[31] is where mechanization opened vast territories to grain farming. The boat passes a re-creation of a turn-of-the-century midwestern farm — complete with trees and tree swing, windmill, scarecrow, pumpkins, chickens, pigs, and a robot dog on the porch. Then the boat turns into the Barn Theater.

This structure is filled with small vintage farm tools. On the walls are screens showing film clips of the history of the family farm. The theme is mechanization — efficiency on larger scales. Huge combines and other equipment stalk the fields. The disappearance of the family farm passes barely remarked. "Agriculture is becoming more scientific rather than a way of life," says the narrator in bland passing, as if large-scale farm technology were not a way of life.

Before passing into the experimental greenhouses where we will see the technologies that will make farming in the tropics and desert profitable,[32] let me note that the floral artistry at Listen to the Land is, as usual at WDW, utterly brilliant. All these indoor plants — the tropical leaves and prairie grasses — look quite real. Let me turn to Steve Birnbaum for comment. [33]

> As fantastic and unreal as they appear, the plants on view in the experimental greenhouses are all living. In contrast, those in the biomes (ecological communities) were manufactured in Disney studios out of flexible, lightweight plastic that simulates the cellulose found in real trees. The trunks and branches were molded from live specimens; the majestic sycamore in the farmhouse's front yard, for example, duplicates one that stands outside a Burbank, California, car wash. Hundreds of thousands of polyethylene leaves, made in Hong Kong, were snapped on. These are fire retardant, as are the blades of grass, which are made of glass fibers implanted into rubber mats. In the South American rain forest scene, the water on the leaves and trunks is supplied by a special drip system that provides a constant flow of moisture. [34]

From the difficulties of food production in the tropics, desert, and prairie, we ride again into the Disney version of hope for the future. The working greenhouses of The Land take visitors past agricultural experiments that focus on CEA, integrated aquaculture, gardening in space, and the development of "the untapped agricultural potential of the tropics and the desert." [35] Crops are selected for the show — and we must remember that this is also a show "based on present or potential importance to agriculture, including home gardening, and seasonal adaptability to the greenhouse environments." [36] Let's follow the tour and return later to a general description of what is going on here through an extended interview with Dr. Henry A. Robitaille, agricultural manager of The Land.

First is the Tropics House. Here we see crops native to Africa, Southeast Asia, South America, and the southern United States — rice, cassava, sugarcane, cocoyam, bananas, pineapples, [37] ground nuts (peanuts), corn, vanilla orchids, cacao trees, coconuts, and peach palms. Featured is the winged bean from Papua New Guinea, a superplant all parts of which are edible. [38] Also introduced is the practice of intercropping, both to conserve space and to complement natural biochemical plant needs.

Next we enter the aquacell, its roof covered in red to reduce visual stimulation and stress in the fish kept here. The boat track splits two sets of raceways filled with channel catfish, paddlefish, tilapia, and freshwater shrimp. [39] Aquatubes at the end contain American eels, more tilapia, and whatever else rotates through the system.

> The Land's Aquacell uses a circulating water system with four shallow tanks, two each of 5,000 and 8,000 gallons, and six cylindrical 200-gallon acryllic tubes. Filtration equipment in an adjacent building cleans, oxygenates and maintains the recirculating water's desired temperature. This technology, called "closed system intensive culture," produces high yields while conserving water and land. Although yields can exceed 100 times those possible from earthen ponds, this intensive aquaculture requires more capital, energy and technical expertise. [40]

The Desert House displays drought-resistant grains such as sorghum and millet as well as other potentially important plants — guayule (a source of rubber), *Euphorbia latyris* (a source of transportation fuel), the buffalo gourd, jojoba (lubricating oil), and the rapid-growing *Leucaena* tree, a source of wood (used especially for cooking fuel) that is actually a member of the legume family.[41] Also on display are triticale (a wheat-rye cross that produces high yields in poor soil) and amaranth, the seeds of which are a source of flour.

Highlights of the Desert Greenhouse include the computer-controlled irrigation and fertilization systems. Plastic tubes buried in the sand carry water and nutrients to each plant. Cotton plants are watered by drip irrigation. Salt-tolerant halophytes are part of the experiment. Not only can these plants (many of which are edible) be produced in salty desert soil, but because potentially they can be irrigated by seawater, they would open up the world's desert coastlines to agricultural food production.

The Production House highlights controlled environment agriculture. Here we see hydroponic gardening — lettuce being grown on floating plastic foam flats, its roots soaking in water that contains minerals and nutrients for optimal growth. Strings rise from rock wool slabs to the plastic sheet roofs. Making use of vertical space, tomato plants are trained to grow up the strings. Fans draw air across wet paper pads for summer cooling.

In the Creative House, plants dispense with the ground altogether. Peppers are carried on belts with their roots hanging in the air. The belts aeroponically rotate the roots through a spray that contains water and nutrients. Lettuce grows on vertical A-frames. Much of the activity in the Creative House is cosponsored by NASA, which is seeking efficient, space-conserving ways to grow food to cut down on the amount of food carried on extensive personnel journeys. The hit of the show is eight-foot drums, their walls covered with lettuce plants, spinning around a central light source to simulate gravity.

In an extended interview with the *Jacksonville (Illinois) Journal-Courier*, Henry A. Robitaille, Agricultural Manager of The Land, explained the Disney/Kraft view of what happens here.

> As the name suggests, Controlled-Environment Agriculture is a general term for agriculture in a situation which provides some degree of environmental control. The ultimate controlled environment would also allow for precise control over temperature, air movement, quantity and quality of light, atmospheric composition and other parameters.
>
> At The Land, we[42] grow crops in greenhouses that enable us to heat in winter, cool through evaporative cooling in summer, and provide wind protection throughout the year. The greenhouses enable us to remain open to guests regardless of prevailing weather conditions.
>
> Through trickle irrigation, we provide plants with a concentrated fertilizer solution. Computers monitor temperature, relative humidity, light and leaf

surface moisture. In the Creative Area, we introduce mechanical refrigeration — an additional level of environmental control. . . .

We have a system that injects a concentrated, complete fertilizer solution into the irrigation water to provide the right amount of nitrogen, phosphorus, potassium, calcium, magnesium, manganese, sulfur, iron, boron, molybdinium, zinc, copper, and chloride for the plants. The plant support medium is primarily sand but also includes floating plastic boards, conveyors and spinning drums. Sand provides good aeration and drainage, ease of cultivation, and a good background for showcasing the crops. [43]

In addition to the agricultural displays, much research is carried on behind the scenes, especially in biotechnology — tissue cultures [44] and genetic engineering. As noted, agriculture has been computerized; computers monitor relative humidity, temperature, sunlight intensity, and other environmental parameters. In 1989, a new biotechnology laboratory was added at the end of the ride. Here visitors can see beakers and vials in a room full of white scientific equipment.

Integrated pest management is a crucial part of the experimental work at The Land. Here's Robitaille again.

We use integrated pest management (IPM), which is a decision-making approach to agricultural production that considers a variety of techniques to maintain pest populations below damaging levels.

The first consideration is exclusion; and every effort is made to slow the entry of pests through sanitation, screening, etc. [45] "Scouting" is also important; careful examination of each planting at least weekly is necessary to thoroughly understand plant conditions. The presence of low numbers may not warrant application of a control.

When pests do reach damaging levels, we consider several types of control measures: biological — releasing predatory insects; [46] mechanical — yellow sticky tapes that catch leafminers and white flies; physical — heat sterilization of the sand; [47] cultural — selecting plant cultivars that are disease or insect resistant whenever available; and chemical — using necessary and appropriate pesticides. [48]

The Land also offers a walking tour through the display greenhouses, guided by the professional staff. This tour is packed with gardeners — some curious, some competitive, who beat others on the head with their gardening expertise. [49] Visitors seem to forget the claim Kraft and Disney are making that these agricultural procedures will be able to feed millions. They seem not to notice that the capital costs of this computerized agronomy are beyond most of us. Although this gardening looks as if it might abet decentralization, we know that Kraft (and we suspect Disney as well) is certainly allied with agribusiness, not with the small farmer. The entire show here — the biome dioramas (especially the family farm scene), the tomatoes crawling up strings to the roof supports, the insipid theme song — is meant to glide visitors into computerized, robotic industrial farming, leaving us with nostalgia for the family farm and a sense of wonder at the clever New Age gardeners.

Peg Boyles writes eloquently about the uneasiness that can be felt in the face of this "brave new garden."

> I found these displays intriguing and terrifying. For what these artificial gardens lacked were ordinary people, folks like you and me with dirt under their fingernails and blisters on their palms. These greenhouses were tended by technicians with clipboards in charge of gauges, valves and flow-meters. Gone was the imperfect natural world, with its winds, rains, plagues of insects, hailstorms, unseasonable frosts and marginal soils.
>
> Most visitors are terribly impressed, oohing and aahing. The specter of starvation and hunger seemed far away, perhaps banished, along with the frosts and insects.
>
> I wonder if any of those visitors really believed that people could and would develop ways to feed themselves if they had access to land and efficient tools. I wonder if the visibly impressed tourists sharing my boat considered the capital and operating costs of these climate-controlled glass houses, magnified to the vast scale that alone could justify this means of growing food. I wondered if they were getting the message — surely intended — that nature no longer provides an ample balance of resources for feeding the planet, and that food production surely is too complex and too sophisticated for ordinary folks like us and should be left to the technocrats. [50]

These are the scary corporate-academic agricultural technologists who, in the words of Brian Tokar, are "engineering the future of life." [51] Further, Hope Shand has written,

> Higher-yielding food crops and faster-growing trees, however, do not in themselves address world hunger. Dramatic changes in agricultural production and trade worldwide will accompany these advances. These changes threaten to further concentrate economic power in the hands of transnational corporations, increase the dependence of Third World farmers on imported technologies, and put at risk the biological diversity of the planet. [52]

Issues of biotechnology, genetic engineering, biological growth hormones, and the like, are political issues people must take up as persons and as citizens. Kraft-Disney would have us believe they are merely technical issues whose positive valuation nobody would reasonably question. Visitors are gee-whizzed into a fundamental misunderstanding of what is going on. We are not "listening to the land," we are yelling at it, splicing it, and recombining it so it will twirl around and grow in space.

The Kitchen Kabaret

The Kitchen Kabaret is a vaudeville-style musical revue performed by an audioanimatronic cast of foods. This is the vegetoid part of EPCOT Center. [53] We wait for the show in an anteroom that simulates a 1930s theater side street, flanked by posters hyping the cast. The doors open, and we follow the jazz sounds under a lit marquee and into the plush red "velvet" 250-seat art deco theater. With the guidance of the Kraft Nutrition Advisory Council [54] — whatever that might be — the thirteen-minute show claims to teach its audience about nutrition. We see robotic skits taking place on a large kitchen stage set; these are meant to alert us to the "four main food groups" that should be represented in our daily diet — the milk and cheese group; the cereal and grain group; the meat, poultry, fish, and bean group; and the fruit and vegetable group. Alas, no Butterfinger group. The robotic foods sing, play musical instruments, and indulge in unbearably corny puns in a show that resembles in tone the Country Bear Jamboree.

This is a very clever show — in my opinion, it is among the highlights of EPCOT Center. It is clever enough to make us forget that the Kraft label and familiar Kraft forms are in evidence only in the house band that opens and closes the show. The Kitchen Krackpots is a condiment band. A smiling jar of mayonnaise plays beet and tuna can drums. A jar of barbecue sauce plucks a whisk base fiddle. There is a parmesan cheese guitar player, a mustard jar on saxophone, and "salsa" playing a matchbook piano. Although Kraft made its name selling condiments (and Velveeta "cheese"), the audience is meant to take away the notion that the company is interested in nutrition beyond only the ketchup-is-a-vegetable kind.

The revue has four acts sandwiched between an opening and a grand finale. The opener and closer feature the Kitchen Crackpots and our hostess, Bonnie Appetit. The robot Ms. Appetit has stepped out of a Marabal Morgan fantasy. She is a true Stepford wife in showgirl leotard, blue tuxedo jacket, net stockings, high heels, and apron. After a song about beating the "mealtime blues," Bonnie directs the audience to the giant refrigerator on the left where Mr. Dairy Goods and his Stars of the Milky Way continue the show.

The show's guiding conceit now becomes evident. Each set of characters will sing or tell its story in a parody of actual entertainers or obvious vaudeville types. This is a delight for many of the adults in the audience who are old enough to recognize the clever references. Mr. Dairy Goods is a bug-eyed milk carton with a pencil-thin mustache and a smarmy baritone crooner's voice. He holds a radio mike with the call letters KOW as he introduces his ladies from the refrigerator, who are all dolled up like Ziegfield showgirls. Miss Cheese is clearly Mae West; Miss Yogurt, Marlene Dietrich; Miss Ice Cream, Pearl Bailey. Because this is "vaudeville," we need some risqué gestures, so Miss Ice Cream promises, "I've got a *double* scoop for you."

On the right side of the stage, sitting coquettishly on the shelf, are the Cereal Sisters — "stars of stage, screen, and spatula" — Rennie Rice, Connie Corn, and (shudder) Mairzy Oats. Accompanied by a piece-of-toast trumpet player in shades — the Boogie-Woogie Bakery Boy, the Toast of the Town — the cereals do an Andrews Sisters number.

Scene Three has the vaudeville patter as straight man Mr. Hamm sets up Mr. Eggz in a series of execrable puns. They sit on top of a large stylized gas range at the right of the stage. Fat Mr. Hamm — with watch chain and stiff collar — vainly tries to keep his dignity in the face of the jaunty wisecracks of his buddy — with his bow tie, straw boater, cane, spindly legs, and constant eyebrow-raising smirk.

Scene Four is a tribute to the tropical-Latin jazz combos of the 1940s and 1950s. At stage center is the Colander Combo — mustachioed Tomato and Eggplant in ruffled jackets surrounding tall, skinny Sr. Broccoli, with his pink-rimmed sunglasses. The latter, pace George Bush, has become one of the merchandising stars of EPCOT as a stuffed doll. Behind and to the left of the Colander Combo are the Fiesta Fruit — three bananas, two mangoes, an apple, and a pineapple in a wicker basket — who accompany the combo in the show-stopping "Veggie, Veggie, Fruit, Fruit."

Everyone returns for the finale and its signature song about eating right. Bonnie Appetit, what a mom! We then exit past the Broccoli & Co. gift and memento stand on our way to the Farmer's Market and its scientifically planned menus.

The Living Seas

Consider, if you will, the recipe for making an ocean. Combine 1,750 tons of steel with 20,000 cubic yards of concrete. Install 549,000 pounds of acrylic windows throughout the seabase. Collect and transport 4,000 marine animals. Introduce them to six million gallons of water and 2,000 tons of chemicals ranging from salt to lithium. Stir slowly, adding equal parts of technology and humanity. And there you have it — man's greatest attempt to recreate a natural environment.[55]

Out the door, down the slope, and to the left, we move from land to sea. Here at The Living Seas is the world's largest fish tank.[56] Sponsored by United Technologies with a $90 million investment, this oceanographic display is meant to "sort of trick you into learning by providing a grand assault on the senses."[57]

This is, by intent, the most educational of Future World's offerings.[58] The pavilion contains a museum display, two film shows, six extensive "modules" — with information, displays, and aquarial fauna — and the central aquarium. There's a wave tank, a kelp tank, and a floor-to-ceiling diver lockout chamber. Let's begin at the beginning.

At the entrance to the building is a simulated tidal pool, complete with the rhythmic sound of crashing surf. The façade is painted to suggest layered waves breaking onto the rocky beach. Just inside the building is an extended mural that illustrates the history of diving. From Alexander the Great's diving bell through sketches of undersea breathing devices by Leonardo da Vinci to primitive submarines, Sir Edmund Halley's diving bell, and Charles William Beebe's bathysphere, we are treated to a Distory of diving. Physical models of actual early diving suits are joined by a suit from Disney's *20,000 Leagues Under the Sea* and an eleven-foot model of the submarine *Nautilus*. All these pictures and displays flank the line as it esses slightly upward to the preshow theater.

Here we see the first of two films, a 2 1/2-minute, 360 degree multimedia presentation about early divers and ocean research. The film devolves into an advertisement for United Technologies — "high technology is the common denominator of all we do" — reminding us who is to be our mediator with the sea. The exuberant rhetoric is meant to sweep us away as it constructs an image of adventure in new frontiers.

We begin, as always in Disney's version of nature, with the unknown — in this case the mysterious ocean. Into this realm come "courageous pioneers" with "insatiable curiosity" and (thank goodness!) "engineering skills." These courageous, curious engineer-pioneers "faced challenges." But "with new knowledge we built new tools. . . . Each advance in technology brought about the opportunity to explore further and learn more, transforming vision, curiosity, and wonder into practical knowledge."

These orientations soon lead to Western utilitarianism because the sea is really to be seen as little more than a storehouse of potential economic goods for human appropriation.

> The sea is a resource . . . a realm shrouded in mystery, yet possessing enormous potential for humanity. . . . And United Technologies is proud to play a new role . . . committing the technology we create today to the exploration of new frontiers tomorrow.

It seems even Disney and United Technologies realized that this corporate pragmatism is a bit too flagrant because visitors pass immediately to a second theater — this one with seats — for a seven-minute film about the critical role of the oceans in planetary history. *The Sea* is dramatic and poetic. It is the only film at EPCOT Center narrated by a woman, whose elegant stage elocution draws us into the cosmological story. We see here in the birth of the oceans and the beginnings of organic life a clear story about evolution. This secular tale — progressive to many, anathema to some — is a pervasive metatheme at Future World.

The film takes us to the ocean depths, to "an endless night darker than the darkest night on land . . . amid raging storms and fiery underwater volcanos, mountain ranges that dwarf the Himalayas, and gorges four times deeper than the Grand Canyon." Here are "life forms that have astonished biologists by finding the means for their survival not in photosynthesis and the sun but in the chemicals of the earth itself."

This undersea world, "where we've spent more time than on the surface of the moon," is sitting there, "waiting for our discovery" — passing the time, one supposes, like Vladimir and Estragon. While these seas wait, they "conceal" knowledge and "hold" resources, all of which "we" and our technology will soon search out and take. "We" will use these gifts to make whatever we can in industrial processes and the circulation and consumption of commodities that result in enough effluvia and garbage to turn the living seas into something else entirely. Having "listen(ed) to the land" next door to The Living Seas, here we are taught to whistle in the dark.

With heavy breathlessness, we are invited into

... a future of amazing technological creativity
... a future of incredible adventure and discovery
... a future of remarkable awareness and
understanding. [59]
We welcome you now to take the first steps into
  that future.
We welcome you to The Living Seas.
We welcome you to Sea Base Alpha.

The "descent" to Sea Base Alpha — a futuristic research station somewhere on the ocean floor (and thematically cross-linked to Horizons) — is made by means of "descent hydrolators" whose effect is a kind of cross between the Haunted Mansion and 20,000 Leagues under the Sea. The special effects — bubbles rising upward past "coral" rocks outside the window, level indicators, lights and a sound track, shaking of the elevator — simulate a rapid descent deep to the sea floor. We have traveled two inches.

Leaving the hydrolator, visitors — "aquanuts," as Disney calls them — enter continuously loading "sea cabs" for a three-minute ride to Sea Base Concourse. This is our introduction to the aquarium that contains the Caribbean Coral Reef, one of the most extraordinary engineering marvels at WDW. The ride passes through concrete and acrylic tunnels in the center of a 197-foot-diameter, 185,000-square-foot, 28-foot-deep reinforced concrete tank of synthetic seawater. [60]

This tank holds 5.7 million gallons of water and over 200 varieties of sea life, from crabs to sharks, scattered around a simulated Caribbean coral reef. [61] This aquarium (the largest in the world as of 1986) is the brainchild of Kym Murphy, corporate manager of marine technology for the Walt Disney Company and director of The Living Seas. [62] Murphy had created an underwater filming environment for the Columbia Pictures version of Peter Benchley's *The Deep* by cutting a giant aquarium into a plateau of rock and coral in Bermuda, coating it with polyurethane, and filling it with water and creatures from the adjoining Atlantic.

Murphy's reef at The Living Seas is made mostly of fiberglass, silicones, and urethanes. It was constructed by Richard Rush, whose company copied corals purchased and gathered (by permit) for models in the Bahamas. [63] It is apparently real enough to fool such coral eaters as parrotfish, so Murphy has invented a recipe for "coral cookies" that enables such fish to get their nutrients without eating fiberglass. [64] The rest of the fish must be well fed or, presumably, they would eat each other. So, "every day 600 pounds of enriched clams, scallops, shrimp, and restaurant grade frozen fish are on the menu for Living Seas inhabitants. Vitamins are usually injected or implanted. Shrimp, however, are allowed to swim in a vitamin solution before entering the tank. Divers distribute the food and sometimes feed fish by hand." [65]

The seawater is synthetic, made with a special recipe to ensure that the final water quality equals that of natural seawater. [66] Because artificial seawater is expensive — the first filling cost over $400,000 — it is reused, thus requiring an extensive filtering and recycling water treatment facility.

The coral reef tank is not alone. Before looking at the exhibits at Sea Base Alpha, let me borrow a description of the physical plant at The Living Seas from Philip Gatsoulis and associates.

> In addition to the 5.7 million gal. main tank, Walt Disney Imagineering and James M. Montgomery (Consulting Engineers, Inc., Pasadena, Calif.) designed several secondary exhibits that are included in the main facility, including a 120,000 gal. dolphin performing tank, two 30,000 gal. dolphin holding tanks, a 4,400 gal. seal pool, a 3,500 gal. sea lion pool, a 7,200 gal. kelp tank, a 12,850 gal. predator tank, and a 4,250 gal. Pacific coral reef tank, and various other isolation and smaller exhibition tanks. [67]

Sea Base Alpha is meant to represent a prototype undersea research facility. It has two levels — connected by escalator — ranged around one large arc of the Sea Base Concourse. Six display rooms, called modules, open off this arc. The concourse contains three displays. First is a twenty-four-foot-long glass tank with a wave machine designed to demonstrate wave action on a sandy beach. People gather around this tank, talking and explaining things to each other. Second is a full-range model of the Deep Rover, a one-person submersible vehicle. Deep Rover is suspended from the concourse mezzanine.

The concourse centerpiece is the twenty-two-foot ceiling-to-floor diver lockout chamber (the Scuba Tube) through which visitors can see divers enter and exit the main tank. This acrylic, illuminated tube takes sixty seconds to fill with four thousand gallons of water and forty-two seconds to drain. [68] Divers can be heard communicating to support technicians through a wireless radio in their face masks. Upon exiting the tube on the concourse level, divers describe the equipment and answer questions from the audience.

On the concourse floor, Module 1A is the Ocean Ecosystems exhibit. Here is the Seabase Challenge, a set of menu-driven interactive filmstrips with questions for visitors to answer. The questions and answers include blurbs on Surtsey, the Bay of Fundy, El Niño, icebergs, and manganese nodules. Module 1A contains a number of acrylic tubes — with the 7,200-gallon kelp tank in the middle — and presents exhibits about camouflage, symbiosis (clownfish and sea remora), and bioluminescence. There is a simulated Pacific coral lagoon — with an attendant biologist to answer questions — a predator tank (Nassau grouper, moray eel, barracuda), Sea Watch (films of sea otters, underwater archaeology, octopuses, and a whale shark), and displays on filter feeders ("Filter Feeders: A Fine Mesh"), zooplankton ("Zooplankton: A Floating Zoo"), phytoplankton, and "The Web of Life: Not a Fast-Food Chain."

The theme of Module 1D is undersea exploration. Here is Jason, an audioanimatronic version of a deep-sea robot.[69] With film clips, Jason describes atmospheric dive systems such as the submersible Alvin and Deep Rover and the deep-dive JIM suit. Nearby are cutaway models of this suit, where visitors can slip inside and try to manipulate the underwater grasping tools. Here also is a cartoon about human physiology and its requirements vis-à-vis deep-sea diving.

Earth systems is the subject of Module 1C. Here Disney and United Technologies tell their stories about land and sea relationships. "Oceanography from Space," "Anatomy of the Sea," and "What on Earth?" bracket *An Animated Atlas of the World*. This cartoon, starring Atlas, presents a geological history of earth. We see maps of sea floor spreading, maps of winds and currents, Pangeia, continental drift, and earthquakes. Here is science, natural laws, uniformitarianism, and above all, evolution. The immanence of the cartoon is announced by cleverly translating current time into geological time — "5.9 billion years 'til showtime . . . 2.1 billion years."[70]

Module 1B is the underwater viewing station for the Marine Mammal Tank, which extends up to the second floor as Module 2B. Atlantic and bottlenose dolphins, sea lions, manatees, divers, and Chae — the paddling dog — can be seen here through eight-and-a-half-inch acrylic windows — some convex, some concave for differential viewing. Video monitors around the tank flash over- and underwater images. Upstairs in Module 2B we are above the waterline across the tank from the platform from which researchers interact with their charges. In 1986 Gretchen Jacobs, a marine mammals research module trainer, told *Reader's Digest*, "It's basically a communication-research program that allows dolphins to control their environment through their own vocalizations. Aided by an underwater computer that distinguishes the sounds, researchers hope to decipher their meaning. Then when a dolphin wants, say, the lights turned off or music on, its request will be granted."[71]

Also on the observation level (level 2) is Module 2A, Ocean Resources. The exhibits here describe "harvestable resources of the ocean — from minerals to fish."[72] Here is a mariculture display — an operational hatchery with quahogs, oysters, redfish, pompano, Caribbean king crab, clownfish, sea urchin, and attendant researcher. There are films about "current" events, another interactive Sea Watch (clips of dolphins and cuttlefish), and a display about commercial minerals found on the ocean floor. Visitors are introduced to the importance of mining rights secured through the posting of an Exclusive Economic Zone.[73]

The pièce de résistance of the second level is the Observation Module. A tunnel with acrylic windows takes visitors into the center of the Caribbean Coral Reef. Beneath us we see the Sea Cab tunnel. The simulated reef stretches on all sides. Fish, divers (including, from time to time, Mickey Mouse in custom wetsuit[74]), and submersibles float through the reef.

From the Sea Base Concourse, hydrolators return us the two inches to the surface. Turning around the pavilion to the left, visitors reach the entrance to the Coral Reef Restaurant. Specializing in fish, the restaurant seats customers in front of four large windows that form part of the Caribbean Coral Reef tank. As we eat we watch the fish we have just seen from the Observation Module. The food is pretty good, but eating it seems like cannibalism.

Disney's Gardens

Walt Disney had wanted a green park — everything green — for he recalled the cold winters of his childhood in the east and opined that Disneyland must be eternal spring.
                                                             —Derek Walker[74]

I can not leave the WDW approach to nature without consideration of Disney's treatment of flora and fauna on the property. In earlier chapters I have written about lakes, canals, wildlife preservation areas, tree farms, and architectural landscaping in general. Here I say a few things about the ubiquitous gardens at the parks and about Discovery Island, Disney's zoological park.

Pace to Leo Marx, what we have here are gardens in the machine. In *The Machine in the Garden*, Marx traced the importance of the pastoral idea in U.S. history.[76] Into the seventeenth-century wilderness of North America came Englishmen primed to transform the American wilds into an European garden — cleared, planted, and under human control. Two centuries later, both wilderness and garden were invaded by the machines of science and industry, engendering a cultural crisis in U.S. intellectual history.

Another century-and-a-quarter later, the process was inverted in central Florida, after the Disney megamachine rolled into the swamp and scrub southwest of Orlando. The architectural, commercial, fantastic, high-technological machines that make up WDW were to be domesticated and softened — surrounded with themed, fresh, ever-changing gardens[77] all meant to augment and enhance the show. By 1986 the horticultural establishment was substantial — nine huge greenhouses and over three hundred gardeners in the complex (not including the golf courses), planting almost half a million square feet of annuals in EPCOT alone.[78]

Each garden is themed to bring consistent staging to the show. Flowers in World Showcase — pink, white, and blue for Italy; pastels for France; bright reds and whites (and a rose garden) for the United States — accent the pavilions. Trees are carefully chosen and pruned to invoke national flora — camphor trees in Mexico, cypress in Italy, evergreens in Canada. If exactly correct trees are unavailable, either because of federal importation laws or for climatic reasons, substitutes are cleverly made. One weeping mulberry tree was trucked from New Jersey for the China Showcase. Disney's own tree farm has supplied thousands of plants to the parks. [79]

As is everything else at WDW, the watering system for all these trees, shrubs, flowers, and grasses is computerized. The underground irrigation system at EPCOT consists of over six hundred valves, each of which controlls an area studded with sprinklers. Timers and moisture sensors are programmed to turn the water on and off, monitoring the supplemental effects of rainfall. [80] The plants are all inventoried by computer so proper care can be maintained.

Full treatment of Disney's stunning horticulture is beyond the scope of this study. The best description, including discussion and extensive photographs, is found in *Gardens of the Walt Disney World Resort.* [81] This book suggests the following ten-category typology of WDW's gardens: flower gardens for all seasons; gardens in the rough; gardens of yesteryear; old world gardens; gardens found within gardens; gardens of the exotic; interior gardens; gardens with a purpose; gardens of tomorrow; and gardens of fantasy. Together with Birnbaum's guidebook, *Gardens* is indispensable for gaining an appreciation of WDW.

Discovery Island

Just off the southeast shore of Bay Lake is Discovery Island, Disney's eleven-acre zoological park (sponsored by Gaines Foods). Accessible by boat from the Magic Kingdom, the Contemporary Resort, and Fort Wilderness, Discovery Island is an accredited member of the American Association of Parks and Aquariums. [82] The island has been designated a species manager for the scarlet ibis and a sanctuary for the brown pelican and other avian life. [83]

Originally, Discovery Island was to have had a Treasure Island theme. Before WDW opened, the flat, scrubby island was cleared of vegetation and remade, like everything else, in Disney fashion. Here again is Birnbaum.

> They cleared the vegetation, brought in 15,000 cubic yards of sandy soil, and added 500 tons each of boulders and trees. They built hills, carved out lagoons, sowed grass seed, and planted 20 types of palm trees, 10 species of bamboo, and dozens upon dozens of other plants from Argentina, Bolivia, the Canary Islands, China, Costa Rica, Formosa, the Himalayas, India, Japan, Peru, South Africa, Trinidad, and other nations around the world. Then they

added winding paths, built aviaries and filled them with birds, and added a few props to carry through the Treasure Island theme. A wrecked ship salvaged from off the coast of Florida was installed on the beach, and a Jolly Roger hung from the lookout post. [84]

According to the Discovery Island brochure, the island now holds over 90 species of animals and 250 species of plants. Visitors leave the Thirsty Perch near the boat slip for a walk along the pathways. The forty-five minute walk — with no dawdling — passes caged birds and various free-ranging animals. The trek passes through Avian Way, which at nearly an acre is one of the largest walk-through aviaries in the world. Here is where the scarlet ibis stay, along with rare white peacocks, muntjac deer, and the not-so-rare African crowned cranes. The walk passes pools, rivulets, and a waterfall. [85]

Among the free-ranging fauna are peacocks, Patagonian cavies — a member of the guinea pig family — and the wonderfully bizarre brush turkey that spends its time kicking forest trash backward onto an ever-growing nest.

> Nesting season provides the setting for an amazing display of nature's wonder. The Brush Turkeys, natives of Australia, create a large mound of brush and leaves, six to eight feet high and 20 feet in diameter. The female digs a hole under the mound and lays her eggs. The male keeps the temperature of the nest constant by adding or taking away leaves. Measurements on the Island have found that the nest temperature varies no more than a degree from its 92 degrees optimal temperature. [86]

Customers can also see macaws and cockatoos at the Discovery Island Bird Show as well as trumpeter swans, hornbills, kookaburras, sandhill and Demoiselle cranes, white neck ravens, snowy egrets, great blue herons, Florida alligators, Caribbean flamingos, Galapagos tortoises (weighing up to five hundred pounds), and two caged primates — the golden lion tamarin and ring-tail lemur.

A few injured southern bald eagles, unable to survive on their own, are given sanctuary here, as are a number of injured brown pelicans. The latter were severely threatened throughout Florida by the use of DDT until the state banned its use as a pesticide in 1965. The bird is now making a comeback. [87]

Not so lucky was the dusky seaside sparrow, the last of which were housed on the island in a last-ditch effort to avoid extinction of the species. Unfortunately, the project failed, as the last sparrow died in 1988.

In recent years, Discovery Island has been visited by one seemingly unsolvable plague. Large migratory birds, especially vultures, have discovered the sanctuary. Defecating on benches and park walkways, these disruptive birds triggered Disney vengeance. [88] Although the birds are protected by federal and state migratory bird laws, employees trapped, confined, and killed a number of them according to criminal charges filed against the company. [89] Disney pleaded guilty to one charge of violating the federal Migratory Bird Treaty Act and was fined $10,000.[90] Employees were reassigned.

A summer 1990 visit to Flamingo Lagoon revealed an army of black vultures filling the trees and the beach. An attendant, carefully trying to feed only the flamingos, admitted that the workers were trying to discourage the vultures by not feeding them. It didn't seem to be working.

One can sympathize with Disney's plight because this is probably the largest concentration of vultures east of the Mississippi, and they are not attractive birds. Furthermore, the island is an important avian sanctuary in which the Company is doing good and important conservationist work. Yet Disney has become such a target for local abuse (a bed of its own making in many ways) that lots of people take the side of the vulture against the Mouse.

17

Tomorrow and the Future

With EPCOT, Disney is marrying an international exposition to an industrial trade show, sending the happy couple off in a shower of technologically sophisticated amusements to set up housekeeping in an immense shopping mall.

—J. Tevere MacFadyen[1]

EPCOT is the world's biggest trade show.

—Jennifer Allen[2]

Part of Walt Disney's original intent was to make EPCOT Center a demonstration of the utopian efficacy of science and applied technology in solving the "problems of the cities." The engineering of technological infrastructure would be combined with strict admissions policies and firm political control to form an experimental city that would be efficient, entertaining, and civil. This city would use the best technology U.S. free market industry could develop for Disney's imaginative social experiment. EPCOT would be ever-changing — marching in tandem with engineering progress.

Walt was a tinkerer, the first imagineer. Engineering problem solving was the fun part — that is, solving problems in the interest of a larger vision such as making a movie or building a ride. His notion of social life in the future was also of a life amenable to such tinkering.

As EPCOT Center turned from a residential experiment to a permanent world's fair after Walt's death, the direction of influence was inverted.

Future World became a showcase for transnational corporations. Under Disney's mouse ears, AT&T, Exxon, General Motors, and the rest could buff up their corporate images — diverting attention away from oil spills, plant closings, military contracts, and other corporate mayhem. They could tell stories in which problems were overcome with the hard-path technological fix of corporate-controlled science.

The corporations were no longer merely called in to help produce WDW, but symbiotically WDW became the umbrella under which the transnationals could sell their own ideas about high technology. These advertisements — for the sponsoring corporations and their science and technology — form the show at Tomorrowland and Future World. As Martin Sklar told Jennifer Allen, "Industry has lost credibility with the public, the government has lost credibility, but people still have faith in Mickey Mouse and Donald Duck."[3]

The stories told at Future World are secular, produced by Disney in collaboration with corporate scientists and managers. They contain interesting modern elements — stories about evolution, recovery of the environment, and sex education. These stories are calculated to match the sophistication of many park visitors. Their effect in the early-1980s was to drive Christian fundamentalists to what was then Jim Bakker's Heritage Park. Like much else at WDW, Future World is not simple.

Further, the depictions of science and technology at Future World are encased in the applied technologies of WDW itself — transportation, energy, computer, theatrical, and food technologies. To describe science and technology at WDW requires analysis of both the show and its messages and of the technological organization that makes the show possible. We have seen some discussion of this in earlier chapters about spatial infrastructure, but I add to it in the next two chapters. Before continuing, however, I make some general remarks about science, technology, and the sociocultural world. In particular I visit some issues in the philosophy of technology brought to our attention by Langdon Winner and Albert Borgmann.

Philosophy of Technology

Today we can examine the interconnected systems of manufacturing, communications, transportation, and the like that have arisen during the past two centuries and appreciate how they form de facto a constitution of sorts, the constitution of a sociotechnical order.
—Langdon Winner[4]

In *The Whale and the Reactor: A Search for Limits in an Age of High Technology*, Langdon Winner asks a number of thoughtful questions about the place and moral standing of technology in the modern world. Clearly, technology and technological systems have been hallmarks of human existence since *Australopithecus*. What Winner explores is the question of whether there is something qualitatively new about contemporary technology, something dangerous we all may miss because of what he calls our "technological somnambulism."[5] "Everyday life," he argues, "is continuously transformed by the mediating role of technological devices [which work together] as a powerful force acting to reshape [human] activity and its meaning."[6]

We have come to live — to borrow from Wittgenstein — a technological "form of life" in which technology has become as unremarked as the air we breathe.[7] These technological systems are intimately implicated in the distribution of commodities and useful things that is part of the promise of democracy.[8]

However, technologies bring with them side effects about which we, as citizens and as human beings, ought to make choices. "In the technical realm," Winner writes, "we repeatedly enter into a series of social contracts, the terms of which are revealed only after the signing."[9] Among these terms is the organization of social life: "The construction of a technical system that involves human beings as operating parts brings a reconstruction of social roles and relationships. Often this is a result of a new system's own operating requirements: It simply will not work unless human behavior changes to suit its form and process."[10]

Winner asks us to pay attention to large-scale technological systems, to ask "where and how have innovations in science and technology begun to alter the very conditions of life."[11] For Winner, technologies have politics. They often "appear to require or be strongly compatible with particular kinds of political relationships."[12] This is especially so given that we live in a world of "ongoing social process[es] in which scientific knowledge, technological invention, and corporate profit reinforce each other in deeply entrenched patterns, patterns that bear the unmistakable stamp of political and economic power."[13]

Reminding us of Louis Mumford's distinction between "man-centered" and "system-centered" technologies, Winner argues that many technologies have a distinctly political cast.[14] They may call for centralized control or decentralized distribution. They may be egalitarian or inegalitarian, repressive or liberating. Winner notes that "attempts to justify strong authority on the basis of supposedly necessary conditions of technical practice have an ancient history . . . as a society adopted increasingly complicated technical systems as its material basis, the prospects for authoritarian ways of life could be greatly enhanced."[15]

Winner lists five important tendencies of current technological systems, tendencies toward

1. control over events from a single center or a small number of centers

2. increase in the most efficient or most effective size of organized human associations
3. hierarchical authority
4. large, centralized, hierarchically arranged sociotechnical systems crowding out and eliminating other varieties of
   human activity
5. ways large sociotechnical organizations exercise power to
   control the social and political influences that ostensibly
   control them. [16]

We might keep these tendencies in mind as we continue our visit to Future
World, especially as we confront the high tech and the hype, because Future
World is an advertisement for the idea of high-tech systems and their form
of technological fix. It is an embodiment of Winner's example of the
propagandistic list.

> Long lists of specific services spell out the utopian promise of this new age:
> interactive television, electronic funds transfer, computer-aided instruction,
> customized news service, electronic magazines, electronic mail, computer
> teleconferencing, on-line stock market and weather reports, computerized
> Yellow Pages, shopping via home computer, and so forth. All of this is
> supposed to add up to a cultural renaissance. [17]

In *Technology and the Character of Contemporary Life: A Philosophical Inquiry*,
Albert Borgmann leads us further into considerations about technology. [18]
Whereas Langdon Winner worries about the macropolitics of technological
systems, Borgmann directs inquiry toward philosophical and psychological
aspects of the relation between people and technology. He, too, connects
technology with liberal democracy: "Technological culture is the largely
unspoken but pivotal issue of liberal democracy. Without modern technology, the liberal program of freedom, equality, and self-realization is un-
realizable." [19]

This freedom is based on a Baconian-Cartesian desire to dominate nature,
not so much in the interests of exploitation as in those of disburdenment and
liberation: "The desire to dominate does not just spring from a lust of power,
from sheer human imperialism. It is from the start connected with the aim
of liberating humanity from disease, hunger, and toil, and the enriching of
life with learning, art, and athletics." [20] However, "the initial genuine feats
of liberation appear to be continuous with the procurement of frivolous
comfort." [21] Borgmann describes the path down which we have traveled
from disburdenment to frivolity. Liberation and enrichment have been made
possible over the last few centuries as technological devices have become
increasingly available. By available, Borgmann means such devices and the
commodities [22] they produce must be "instantaneous, ubiquitous, safe and
easy." [23] In answer to these requirements, the machinery of such devices
retreats into anonymity. [24] It becomes concealed and unfamiliar as the ends
become prominent and available. Eventually the device becomes stand-
ardized, mobil, discardable, carefree, and light.

But along the way, Borgmann argues, something important happens as an unintended consequence of the spread of technology and its devices. As he puts it, "the depth of things is dissolved" as previous contexts and social worlds fall away. People become consumers: "It is merely a matter of scientific and textual sophistication, so it seems, to produce by electronic stimulation, for instance, an experience of the wilderness which has all the intensity and nuances of the real experience." [25]

Advertising, as Boorstin suggested, becomes the rhetoric of our time. Human life becomes shallow and lived on the surface as experience is attenuated. The relations between labor and consumption become disengaged. [26] "Improved productivity," writes Borgmann, "entails the degradation of work and greater consumption leads to more distraction. Thus in an advanced industrial country, a policy of economic growth promotes mindless labor and mindless leisure." [27] He continues, "What distinguishes technological life is not surliness but its division into surfaces, rough or pleasant, and concealed, inaccessible substructures." [28]

We lead, then, divided, decomposed lives. Given its deep, unremarkable hegemony, [29] "Technology is seldom offered as a choice, i.e., as a way of life that we are asked to prefer over others, but is promoted as a basis for choice. . . . As long as technology as a whole is generally sanctioned, there is no need or possibility to adopt responsibility for this or that part of technology." [30]

Borgmann calls for a reform *of* the device paradigm of technology, not reform *within* that paradigm. Such reform includes a return to deictic discourse — plain talk rather than euphemistic, scientific, or political babble. It includes a turn from the shallow consumption produced by the surface commodities of ease to a deep engagement with "focal things" in committed "focal practices" — a turn from the "standard of living" to the "quality of life." [31]

Future World offers its visitors a consistent vision of a world in which the hard-path technological fix is the answer to the challenge of maintaining and enhancing the standard of living of Americans and of transnational corporations. As such, it commits many of the acts Winner and Borgmann ask us to think about. Disney's ideological task here is to "turn abstract ideas into personal experience . . . through dramatization [to] interpret past, present and future." [32]

In "To the Disney Station," Michael Harrington describes this task: "Disney World is going to 'communicate' ideas and ban controversy and ideology at the same time. . . . The communicators will be big businesses, and they will present themselves, not as profit maximizers, but as problem solvers. Only their 'objective' solutions will conceal a highly controversial, very partisan corporate self-interest." [33] Nowhere is the control of discourse clearer than at Exxon's Universe of Energy. Exxon's in-house journal, *Profile*, quite unself-consciously describes the process.

Exxon employees worked with Disney writers and producers on some 40 drafts of the script over nearly four years. Their goal was to make sure the content is balanced and includes the points that the Company hopes to communicate to the public. Explains Ames Smith, Public Affairs coordinator for the project, "We want people to realize that energy is an important part of daily life, that there are satisfactory solutions to our present energy problems, and that as a large, diversified supplier of energy, Exxon can help solve some of those problems." [34]

Harrington reminds us of the provenance of some of those problems: "It was Exxon and associated companies that, with the help of enormous direct aid and indirect subsidies from the government, made the nation dependent on Middle Eastern oil and refused to develop the very technologies [35] that it will now present in Disney World. . . . One might as well have the homesteaders' exhibit organized by the cattle rustlers." [36]

Before we run further aground at Exxon, however, let us weave our way back for a moment to the Magic Kingdom because the prologue to Disney's science and technology of the future is found at Tomorrowland.

Tomorrowland

Disney's depiction of the future begins in "concreteland" — otherwise known as Tomorrowland. Here the space-time continuum at the Magic Kingdom bumps up against a moving target. The result in my opinion is the least successful of the themed lands at WDW. Just as we often have today's view of yesterday at Future World, here we have yesterday's view of tomorrow.

Open spaces covered in concrete are anchored at the far end of Tomorrowland by the 180-foot-high white steel-and-concrete cone of Space Mountain. Scattered around the concrete are the round wheel of the Carousel of Progress, the Saturn rocket spire of the StarJets, the functional Skyway tower, and the Tomorrowland Theater. Flanking the street from Fantasyland is the Grand Prix Raceway, across from the shell that contains the Tomorrowland Terrace and other shops and restaurants. Directly from the hub is the street that goes past Mission to Mars, *American Journeys,* and Dreamflight. Snaking overhead is the futurist ribbon of the WEDway PeopleMover, tying Tomorrowland together above the concrete. Most of Tomorrowland is built around transportation — automobiles, airplanes, space craft, rockets, and the WEDway PeopleMover. Disney's imagination about the future is pretty much limited here to graphics, neon, and vehicles.

The dearth of trees — mostly palms scattered here and there — renders the space stark. Buildings and other structures rise up separate from one another, dominated by the massive Space Mountain, which is three hundred feet in diameter. The architectural tone is more Future World than

Magic Kingdom. It is the future of old science fiction movies, when the dominant tone was the stark white of a bright sun on flat concrete buildings.

From the hub the architectural look is softened by green grass, trees and shrubs (even if futuristically pruned), and the canal that surrounds the plaza. One waterfall complements the pastel geometric designs of the Plaza Pavilion, a restaurant with its own Jetson-like spires. Another falls more peacefully near the polyhedral patio of Tomorrowland Terrace.

Rising as a counterpoint to Space Mountain beyond the eastern boundary of the Magic Kingdom is the Contemporary Resort Hotel. This fifteen-story concrete A-frame straddles the monorail, which passes through its fourth-floor concourse. Its bulky monumental architecture — like hurricane-proof south Florida state buildings — argues that Disney is better at designing history, geography, and fantasy than at rendering the present or the future. [37]

In keeping with the space-eating monumentalism, three of the seven paths branching off from Main Street and the plaza lead into Tomorrowland. The first sets off to the right at the end of Main Street between the Plaza Restaurant and the sidewalk café tables that flank the canal. This path takes us into the Plaza Pavilion, which serves pan pizzas and other Italian fare. Outdoor tables face the canal, which is dotted here and there with willows and guarded by a topiary sea serpent.

Continuing through the restaurant, visitors join the "main street" of Tomorrowland as it passes from the plaza to the right between the two central structures. Sharing the Plaza Pavilion shell are the CircleVision 360 *American Journeys* and Dreamflight, Delta Airlines' replacement for If You Had Wings. [38]

One of the curious things about Tomorrowland is that most of its attractions are not about the future. With the possible exception of the WEDway PeopleMover and the bland Mission to Mars — retooled in 1975 from Flight to the Moon — *none* of it is prescient. Even the WEDway PeopleMover has been commercially realized since 1981 at Houston International Airport.

As at Future World, the stories here are about the past — so much so that I presented *American Journeys* and the Carousel of Progress in my history chapters. Delta's Dreamflight might have joined them were it not for the futuristic graphics in the speed rooms that gave me an excuse to save it for the present context.

According to Steve Birnbaum, Dreamflight is meant to be "a whimsical look at the adventures and romance of flight — as seen through the eyes of a child." [39] Perhaps this is why there is so little continuity.

The entrance takes us through Gate 3 and along a ramp flanked with neon piping. Ahead are continuous-loading vehicles passing alongside a mural of the Delta Air Service, Inc., which is part of a 1930s-1940s airfield. The 4 1/2-minute ride begins as we visit a large "pop-up book" depicting the early days of flight. Here are woods, farms, a country fair with an air show and flying daredevils. Airplane rides are offered at $3, $4, and $5. A cow with binoculars watches the scene. The audience rides into a "barn" through which one unlucky barnstormer has crashed.

Next is a film segment that shows live air stunts at a northwest air show, performed by Col. J. Franklin's daredevil airplane. Wing walkers slice through ribbons upside down as our cars head for the M-130 Flying Boat that will take us around the world. [40]

We are in San Francisco on August 30, 1937. The Golden Gate Bridge is off in the distance. It is sunrise at Gate 2. We pass a globe of the earth and the announcement of our 9:00 A.M. Global Clipper flight #801 to Tokyo and Paris. Riding through a cross section of the airplane's elegant dining room, set with tablecloths and silverware, we emerge at a Japanese temple and garden, where — strangely — an American is taking a picture of a Japanese couple.

Turning a corner, we are in Paris on the Rue des Rêves at sunset. Here are the Café Montmartres, L'Hôtel Dauphin, the Café des Artistes, a *boucherie*, a *chappelerie*, the Escargot Café, and Les Fleurs de Paris flower shop.

We've seen Paris. Now we cruise the graphics part of Dreamflight — three segments, each more spectacular than the last. First we ride into a "real" jet engine. Special effects create the illusion that the turbine is rotating around us. Second is a speed room in which a 70-millimeter film clip shows us zooming down a simulated mountain-flanked desert runway and flying past canyons into space. The third segment contains what I feel are the best graphics at WDW. We fly through a city of the future, off into space once again, and back to earth and the city. The computer-enhanced modeling is superb. This segment alone makes Dreamflight worthwhile: The technology is amazing. As the ride ends, we pass another pop-up story book whose pages turn from New York City to a pot pourri page of European urban icons.

To the right of the exit from Dreamflight is the Tomorrowland Theater, an outdoor stage for the regularly scheduled Disney character-Kids of the Kingdom musical stage shows. Across the street is Mission to Mars, which shares its building with (from south to north) the Space Port gift shop, the Lunching Pad (a purveyor of salads and health foods — one of the few places at the Magic Kingdom to get sprouts), Mickey's Mart (Disney merchandise — sponsored by Coppertone sun-care products), and the Tomorrowland Terrace ("hosted" by Coca-Cola). This last is the largest fast-food spot in the Magic Kingdom. It contains a stage where pop music bands and Louis Armstrong impersonators entertain diners.

Sponsored by McDonnell Douglas, Mission to Mars follows a visit to Mission Control with a simulated space flight to Mars and a tour of Mariner Valley and Olympic Mons volcano. Our audioanimatronic director at Mission Control, Bob Johnson — a dead ringer for Father at the Carousel of Progress — explains some of the activities monitored on banks of screens behind him. Visitors stand in parallel lines facing Bob, his screens, and red-lit computers peopled by other Disney robots. Wall clocks tell us the time in Tokyo, New York, Honolulu, and Moscow.

As men's voices in Mission Control-speak crackle over the speakers, Director Bob shows us space station-based solar research, zero-g metalwork and crystal growing, and heavy equipment being manipulated by somersaulting weightless astronauts. His spiel is interrupted by an all-out alert and a gull crash landing on the runway.

We are led into our "space craft" for Flight 295 to Mars. This craft is a round theater with seats rising in banks from a screen in the center of the floor. Overhead is another circular screen. On the walls are further screens, on which will be projected films simulating travel just above the Martian surface.

In the major effect, our seats shake and collapse as air is drained from the seat cushions. It is as if we are being pressed down by the gravitational force that accompanies takeoff. Sub-audible sound waves make the theater shudder as the "booster rockets" kick us into space. A "hyperspace jump" to Mars orbit is accompanied by colorful light effects shown on the upper and lower screens.

Our tour of Mars includes a talk on canals, winds, and the atmosphere given by (the voice of) Third Officer Collins. Unmanned rocket ships send back pictures of Mariner 9 ("3,000 miles long, 10 times bigger than the Grand Canyon back home") and Olympus Mons ("the biggest volcano in the universe . . . 370 miles long at the base and about 25,000 feet high at the tip . . . the floor is about 50 miles across").

Our tour is interrupted by an emergency, a meteorite shower that sends lights blazing, sirens screaming, and our ship — in a panic — back to earth. As we land, we see the landing target emerge out of the earthscape as it shrinks down below us. The craft rattles to a halt, and we exit on the hot central Florida concrete.

In the middle of this concrete rises the StarJets, Tomorrowland's version of Dumbo, the Flying Elephant. This is a simple "carny" ride. Visitors ascend the red elevator to a platform from which rises a mock Saturn rocket. Around the rocket are "jet" cars that circle the rocket at the end of arms. The main thrills here are the height at which the pods spin and the inward tilt and illusion of the possible danger of falling out.

Almost as bland and even less futuristic is the Grand Prix Raceway on the northeast side of the street from Fantasyland. Four 2,260-foot-long tracks guide small but noisy gasoline-powered cars through a looping track underneath the Skyway. At seven miles per hour maximum speed, the trip takes about four minutes. Drivers enter from a bridge that crosses the roadway, which feeds them to a starting line with drag strip accoutrements.

Birnbaum reports that these cars — with rack-and-pinion steering and disc brakes — cost about $6,000 each.[41] The design of the tracks obviates much of the need to pay attention to the sophisticated steering mechanism. For some reason, this ride always has a substantial line.

Two attractions at Tomorrowland are about themselves rather than about something else. The Skyway is an aerial cable car that transports customers from Tomorrowland to Fantasyland.[42] The ride takes five minutes and makes a dogleg turn, coming to earth to change direction on the far side of the Grand Prix Raceway.[43] The cars are made in Bern, Switzerland, and shipped to Orlando.[44]

The WEDway[45] PeopleMover is slightly different because it represents a transportation technology the Company has developed and put on the market. In 1981, a PeopleMover began service at the Houston International Airport. In Tomorrowland the PeopleMover track winds overhead through most of the buildings — a ribbon that ties them together. Entering the ride from a centrally located platform,[46] customers traverse a circular moving sidewalk to the five-car open trains. Because these cars travel at about ten miles an hour, customers can catch a nice breeze on a hot day as they preview the Tomorrowland attractions.

The PeopleMover is operated by a linear induction motor that has no moving parts. Our voice guide — a self-styled "commuter computer" emanating from overhead speakers — tells us that there are more than six hundred electromagnets embedded in the track to pull us along, slow us down, and speed us up. Disney claims the linear induction motor uses little power and thus emits no pollution.

The PeopleMover reminds us of an important sinister element of Disney's utopia. The commuter computer warns visitors that "you will be under surveillance: Please remain seated." Customers often have their pictures taken at WDW. Sometimes, as at Journey into Imagination, they find this out later in the ride; sometimes, as at Superstar Television, they volunteer; sometimes, as on the PeopleMover, they are told the cameras are on them and they'd better behave. One of the tradeoffs of a safe, clean, civil visit to WDW is that visitors become — innocuously and bit by bit — more accustomed to surveillance. It's one thing when a bank or grocery store puts us on television. It is perhaps another thing when Mickey does. Here's where we might remember Winston Smith.

Riders are also surveilled at Space Mountain, Tomorrowland's feature attraction.[47] This is a roller coaster-type ride dressed out to simulate a high-speed trip through space. Inside a 180-foot-high truncated conical shell with rocket-like spires,[48] support scaffolding holds two tracks[49] on which small "rocket ships" with riders are jerked around and plummeted in deep space darkness. Shooting stars and meteors are simulated with flashing lights, mirrored globes, and projections onto the ceiling. The cars are lined with glow-in-the-dark chartreuse dashes, which flash about over-head as screams waft down to those in the queue.

The line begins outside the entrance at a sign telling visitors how much older they will be when they get to the front. Another prominent sign at the door — like the ones at Big Thunder Mountain Railroad, Star Tours, and Body Wars — warns riders that have heart conditions, motion sickness, or neck or back problems or that are pregnant, young, or short. The line then snakes into the darkness, past holographic displays and photographs of the laughing astronauts who took the inaugural ride when the attraction opened. Potential riders suddenly enter an open, dark staging area. "Rock-ets" fly high above, dipping and darting in chartreuse flashes to disem-bodied shrieks. There is an escape door for those who suddenly discover discretion.

At the front of the line, survivors are strapped tightly into the cars and told to bid their glasses, purses, and false teeth adieu. Then around a corner and up the slope to the top we go, past costumed Disney employees in a control room filled with closed-circuit video monitors. The 2-minute-38-second-ride[50] ends in deceleration through a tunnel with flashing lights.

The exit from Space Mountain traps people on a moving sidewalk that climbs past "RYCA 1/Dream of a New World." This is a display with robot figures playing with electronic media in the future (having tamed a "hostile planet" and built a city on pods). Again, visitors are videoed by RCA Broadcasting Systems and shown on monitors as they rise toward the exit and their "chicken" friends and families.

We can't leave Space Mountain and Tomorrowland without some statis-tics from Birnbaum: "The mountain itself — which occupies a 10-acre site and contains 4,508,500 cubic feet, enough to accommodate a small skyscraper — is composed of 72 pre-stressed concrete beams cast nearby, then hoisted into place by mammoth cranes. Each rib weighs 74 tons, and measures 117 feet in length and, in width, 4 feet at the top and 13 feet at the bottom."[51]

Future World

Universe of Energy

Just east of the CommuniCores, Universe of Energy is housed in what seems at its entrance to be a truncated pyramid lying on its side and sloping down to the south. The building is actually an asymmetrical pentagon, with one of its apexes extending to an accentuated point at the front. The point itself is a separated, free-standing six-story-high triangle, covered with mirrors to reflect the blue water of the pool in front of it (and the yellow flowers at its border). At the front of the pool, standing on the blue tiles that show through the clear water, is the upside-down pyramid sign with red lettering that names the pavilion.

The sloping front roof is covered with 80,000 three-inch wafer-shaped solar collectors, diagonally arranged in 2,200 panels — two acres in all. [52] These panels convert sunlight directly into electricity — 77 kilowatts of current in peak sunlight conditions — to help run the "moving theater" of the ride inside. [53]

The sides of the building hold six vertical panels each, shading from yellow at the back to dark orange at the truncated front, which is mirrored just like the separated triangle before it. [54] To the right, a line of southern live oaks is pruned to parallel the roof as it slants up to the right.

This building gleams. It radiates light and mirrored color out past the green grass islands and palm trees and the pink coral paths. The pavilion is meant to suggest the dynamism of energy in constant flow.

Visitors enter the building to stand in a long rectangular lobby and await the preshow, which its creator, the Czech filmmaker Emile Radok, calls a "kinetic mosaic." [55] The fourteen-by-ninety-foot projection surface consists of one hundred triangular sections, set to rotate horizontally in various patterns as the film progresses. Each triangle has two panels coated with a reflective white surface and one panel coated with nonreflective black. As directed by the show's computer, the panels can be set flat or rotated ninety degrees so that a point of the triangle faces the audience. Each panel has a servomotor that receives messages from the master computer and can be independently positioned.

Five projectors produce rapidly changing images on the "screen." The film is continuous, so the rotating panels and the black-and-white surfaces seem like a three-dimensional kaleidoscope capable of infinite patterns. One set of images, a sunset with rapidly growing shadows cast by the protruding triangles, is stunning.

Multiple images from this "living mosaic" [56] dance across the screen. As the narrator tells us about the conservation of energy, we are shown how energy is stored in different forms — nuclear, chemical, electrical, mechanical, heat, and light energy. Each is depicted with vivid kaleidoscopic images as the "power clicks" of the constantly changing screen join the dynamic sound track. [57]

Humans appear in the story, and we realize that once again we are being told a history. Here is more of the Future World metastory about utilitarian human control over nature.

> *Through the genius of the human mind came the realization that energy could be harnessed. . . . Energy locked* [58] *in the earth's vast forests was put to use. Fire became both friend and tool. The unbridled winds were captured. The falls of mighty rivers were tapped.*

Energy is construed as a living thing, locked away awaiting rescue — a friend[59] or perhaps a horse unconsciously seeking the bridling human touch.

Although people got by for centuries with fire, water, and wind, it was not until the discovery of fossil fuels that humanity really got going.

> *Then only a little while ago, we learned to use the energy locked in fossil fuels . . . in coal . . . in oil . . . and natural gas . . . the energy from these fuels has dramatically advanced civilization.* [60]

These, however, are nonrenewable resources, and "sooner or later, present resources will not be sufficient for the world's energy needs. Only by understanding energy in its various forms — the universe of energy — can we build a transition to a better tomorrow." [61]

We will see and hear Exxon's message about this understanding and this "transition to a better tomorrow" a little later in the show; but now, as the attraction's theme song — "Energy, You Make the World Go 'Round" — fills the sound track, we enter Theater I and the next phase of our journey. This theater is filled with what appear to be two banks of seats flanking the center aisle, but a further look shows that each bank is divided in three. These are Disney's "traveling theater" cars — six in each cluster — that carry visitors through the show. These cars rotate, separate, and recombine, led along a guide wire that is only 1/8-inch thick. Because the vehicles are partially powered by the solar power system, Disney announces that its audience is "riding on sunshine." [62]

When filled, the theater rotates 180 degrees to the right to face the wall over the entrance doors (and the exit doors, as we find out later). The entire theater rises on a giant turntable that floats on a thin cushion of air as it turns. The wall is now covered with three movie screens forming one huge screen 155 feet wide by 32 feet high. Here the audience sees the largest piece of animation ever done[63] — a cartoon story about the creation of fossil fuels. [64]

The film begins as lightning strikes a dank, primeval forest, thus beginning the chemical reactions that form organic molecules and — eventually — life. Sunlight is absorbed by microscopic plants in the sea, which are eaten by tiny sea animals. The latter die, fall to the ocean floor, and are turned into oil and gas by millions of years of pressure, heat, and bacterial action. [65]

On land, plant life dies and — covered by layers of sand and mud — is transformed under pressure from peat into coal. The screen is filled with huge strange insects, exotic plants, dinosaurs, and volcanos. This is the Age of Dinosaurs, into which we are about to enter.

As the theater rotates back ninety degrees to the left, the curtain rises, and we are invited to "come with us now and experience a few moments of that dark and mysterious past." The moving theater moves forward into the main sensory shock of the Universe of Energy. Past robot millipedes much larger than they need to be, the theater moves forward and stops in the middle of a scene from the Age of Dinosaurs. The temperature is suddenly warm, the air close and dank. The room is filled with fog. We are in a swamp — the kind in which plants and animals decay into deposits of fossil fuel.[66] Smellitzers work overtime, filling the space with a musky, musty swamp odor. A loud sound track emits squeaks and grunts.

Ahead past giant dragonflies is a group of brontosauruses (or whatever they are called these days), munching quietly away audioanimatronically at swamp grass, water dripping from their jaws. Behind them, painted scenes embody the age.

Now the moving theater comes apart, as its six component cars uncouple and head — one after another — into the dark carboniferous forest. We are delighted that brontosauruses are vegetarians. Richard R. Beard describes the flora.

> This is probably the best primeval diorama ever built. The designs even used fossil references to make the foliage as authentic as possible. Indeed, page after poster-size page of blueprints indicates a painstaking effort at authenticity, right down to the leaf-scar patterns and needle clusters of the smallest sapling in the farthest clump of trees.

> The ride traverses 275 million years and lasts only five minutes — though for the impressionable, the echo could last a lifetime. Here in the dim and eerie setting of prehistory, we encounter the slithery sabalites, the towering araucari-oxylons, the squat and sinister bjuvia — and these are only the plants![67]

The cars glide past robot pteranodons, a dimetrodon- edaphosaurus,[68] and an elasmosaurus that looks like another of Disney's silly fantasy sea monsters. A sudden simulated rainstorm brings a duck-billed trachodon down to the water.

Now we come to the end of the age. Overhead a robot Tyrannosaurus Rex battles an armored stegasaurus on a teetering rock.[69] With the smell of sulfur and the sound of thunder, volcanos erupt. "Molten lava" slides down toward the water and our vehicles.[70] Suddenly, we pass through a curtain of mist and enter the darkness of Theater II.[71]

Here is the EPCOT Energy Information Center. The moving theater is reassembled to face three screens, each thirty feet high and seventy-four feet long, wrapping around the audience for 220 degrees. To our right is a set of geographical displays, lit up to show Exxon's version of energy sources, needs, and uses. There is a live Disney person here, sitting at a lit display podium at right front. Behind us, sneaking around in the darkness, an employee is trying to fix the door.

In Theater II, visitors see the main cinematic presentation. In a twelve-minute movie that fills the visual space and that uses window insets on the screen to make specific story points, Exxon makes its main pedagogical pitch.[72]

This is a film about the contemporary world, about the "toil, sweat, and ingenuity required to obtain energy." [73] Exxon obviously wants to lead us to fossil fuels [74] — and to the nuclear fuels in which Exxon, GE, and United Technologies have direct or indirect financial interests [75] — but we start out with some rhetorical sleight of hand designed to draw our attention elsewhere.

The film begins with what is called an "alternative energy source" — something a bit flaky and not mainstream, reasonable, or efficient. This source is the sun. The opening image shows the gleam of hundreds of solar panels standing in the California desert. "It's out there," the narrator tells us, "everywhere . . . much of the time pouring down on us like an endless rain. Sometime in the next century its immense power may be economically harvested, and sunlight itself will become one of the real keys to the universe of energy."

The crucial variable, Exxon suggests, is expense. "We" can't yet "harvest" sunlight "economically." The big energy breakthroughs will all have to do with corporate economic feasibility. Until then, we will be dependent on sources of energy such as they are. This is the centralization of technology Langdon Winner argues is deeply political.

One of the present sources of energy is oil. The film moves from the solar desert of California to the Arabian peninsula, where a pipeline carries petroleum across the sands to refineries near the sea. But this supply is not inexhaustible, and it is "uncertain." [76]

Given the global demand for energy, which continues to increase, "we" must "continue to conserve and extend today's energy sources and develop a broad mix of alternatives for the future. [After all] the world can't simply park its cars and turn off its lights until that day."

The tour of "old" energy sources — oil and coal — takes the audience from the Middle East to satellite scanning in space to a drilling platform in the North Sea. Oil exploration and recovery "must" continue into increasingly difficult places. The recovered oil must then be transported. The film takes to the air, following part of the trans-Alaska pipeline from Prudhoe Bay to Port Valdez. Pipeline and tanker spills are unmentioned. [77]

But even as these frontiers are explored, new technologies are being developed that one day may economically provide energy in the form of synthetic gas and liquids. [78]

Synthetic oil from Alberta tar sands (mined in the snow with huge equipment), western U.S. oil shale, even the "pesky, river-clogging . . . water hyacinth," grains, recycled wastes, and other biomass resources, are to be pursued in the search for synthetic energy.

Coal is still perhaps the most abundant fossil fuel. We see film of underground miners, including women, cutting into a coal seam with powerful digging machines. The enormous downside of industrial coal recovery and use is glided over with language that mentions no health issues, [79] and pretends that corporations have always — out of the goodness of their souls — reclaimed strip mined land and used scrubbers to clean up plant emissions. Accompanied by dramatic imagery, the audience is reminded of geothermal steam power, of wind, wave, tide, and waterfall.

Then comes the plug for nuclear energy. It's so safe that everybody's using it.

> *Chicago, for example, gets more than half of its electric power from nuclear plants. And around the world, France, Germany, Japan and many other nations are continuing to develop nuclear power as part of their energy bridge to the future.*

The audience is told that some countries are moving ahead with breeder reactors — fusion reactors that create fuel as they operate. We are told that within two decades, a quarter of the world's electricity will "probably" be derived from nuclear power. [80]

> *Unlimited electric power for tomorrow. Is it a fantasy? A pipedream? Scientists at Princeton and other research centers don't think so as they inch toward the process of the stars.*

The film now returns to the beginning, to solar energy "already in limited use." The audience is told of the solar panels on the pavilion roof and told that it has been "riding on sunshine." Then, before the compulsory advertisement for NASA — as everywhere else in WDW, a Cape Canaveral rocket launch — the audience is treated to a typical piece of Disney show summation.

> *In our ever-changing world, the road to tomorrow's energy is indeed long, complex, and challenging. It demands the development and wise use of today's energy resources. It calls for practical and affordable new sources for tomorrow and it will require the combined efforts of science, industry, government, and the public. Then we will indeed bridge to the future — to a world which one day will harness the entire universe of energy.*

With a left swivel of 120 degrees or so, the audience returns to Theater I. A new song, "The Universe of Energy," is sung as the curtains rise to reveal the mirror-covered side walls. A computer-animated reprise of the show flashes around us in laser-like light. As a drawing in front of us shows a little girl growing up to be an astronaut (presumably to "challenge" the future in space), we are told that if these scenes of laser prosperity are to continue, "we" the public need to cooperate with industry and government. [81] We can start by picking up our personal belongings and leaving through the exit doors behind us.

The Energy Exchange

Just west of the Universe of Energy, we return to CommuniCore East — the crescent building that, along with CommuniCore West, curves around Future World Plaza to form the hub of Future World. CommuniCore is short for Community Core, a Disney-speak attempt to draw on the connotations of the word community. The CommuniCores are a focus of the next chapter, but now I need to make one incursion into this space because here is the Energy Exchange, Exxon's hands-on informational exhibit.

South of Backstage Magic and across the aisle from the Stargate Restaurant, Energy Exchange is an open display area filled with materials, machines, games, films, and demonstrations designed to continue the public's education about the corporate hard-path version of energy. We walk down a ramp that curves around a large mobile of interlocking wheels and gears. Once on the floor under a mock-up of an oil-searching satellite, visitors are confronted with an array of materials — all available to be touched, seen, or heard.

There is a thirty thousand-pound piece of Colorado oil shale that contains, so the sign says, five hundred gallons of kerogen. There is a large model of a deep sea drilling platform and a huge strip mining shovel that has become a small theater. To the back is a neon coil that reaches up toward the ceiling and is lit with different colors, each representing the proportion of the world's coal reserves held by the major coal mining nations. There is an exhibit that shows how oil wells are drilled, from discovery and drilling to pumping out and processing. Visitors also learn about dealing with blowouts. This exhibit includes a collection of drills and bits to show how the process works.

Energy Exchange contains Future World's most concentrated mix of pedagogical entertainment. There is a series of small theaters and other film clip displays. These programs discuss hydroelectric power, wind energy, geothermal energy, biomass, synthetic fuels, oil and natural gas reserves and mining, nuclear energy, and coal mining. There are films about offshore oil platforms, undersea drilling, and producing oil and natural gas in the arctic.

Each program carries part of the economist message. The film on hydro energy, for example, tells us, "Now that other fuel sources for generating electricity are growing more costly, the country is taking a new look at the many dams and sites once considered too small to make economic sense." The wind energy narrator says, "The rising price of [fossil] fuels in the 1970s made the idea of wind energy interesting again." And from the biomass film, "Due to rising costs of other fuels, researchers are now looking for processes to convert biomass [82] into fuels we can use for transportation and a wider range of industries."

Sometimes the cost is worth it. The film on surface mining of coal tells us the land is *always* fixed up afterwards

> *After mining, the earth is replaced and topsoil spread. Then the seeds of plants and grasses are mixed with mulch and sprayed evenly. Soon the land will have the same appearance as it did before the coal was removed. In fact, it may even be more productive.*

The films are attended by displays that expand the lesson. Some of these are serious; others are fun because, as Douglas tells us, "the operative approach is that learning can be fun. Play is, in fact, a particularly effective way to convey knowledge about a subject as complex as energy." [83]

Some of the play is meant to show visitors how insignificant human energy capabilities are in comparison with centralized energy sources. A bicycling machine tells us how many days of steady pumping it would take to produce the energy — measured in horsepower — derived from one gallon of gasoline. At another display we turn a hand crank that lights up a 100-watt bulb. We are told that a week of crank turning would generate one dollar's worth of electricity.

Such play puts the cost of energy into exact perspective. The message is that we're pretty puny and not very cost-effective light bulb lighters (however many of us it might take to change one). [84]

The wind energy display — with DOE-NASA, Evertech, or GE branded on the equipment — stresses the commercial use of wind power. The solar display describes active and passive solar systems and reminds us (a bit hyperbolically) that solar energy "helps power EPCOT Center." [85] To illustrate voltaic cell energy, visitors are instructed to use their hands to stop light from reaching a spinning wheel. A further display has information about saving energy in the home.

The nuclear energy display includes a simulated reactor core, with control rods customers can manipulate, as well as a radiation counter to check the clock and antique glassware provided nearby. There is information about the nuclear fuel cycle (including land reclamation and waste management) and a map that shows the worldwide use of nuclear plants. If Belgium, France, and Finland use nuclear power, it must be safe. [86]

Because this is Exxon, the oil and natural gas displays are extensive. We are told that because finding oil is difficult, in order to "meet the challenge . . . incentives are necessary to make exploration worthwhile, especially in the depths and in the harsh environments where the search now goes on."

Although arctic drilling into the frozen ground of the permafrost is extraordinarily complicated, the environment is especially difficult in the ocean, thus requiring some of the most sophisticated equipment and technology known to many. Oil platforms, floating rigs, and the newer guyed rigs — designed for operations beyond 2,500 feet of water depth — are shown on film. We are told many oil platforms have become new artificial reefs, drawing entire ecosystems to their structures. The sea life under the platforms in the Santa Barbara Channel is apparently particularly prolific. Gawrsh, they're so nice for fish we ought to have more of them!

The synthetic fuels exhibit, near the Canadian shale, gives Exxon another opportunity to assure us that nature will be protected.

> *Sophisticated control systems and engineering design will ensure protection of the air, water, land, and people. . . . Concern for the environment is an integral part of all energy projects, and restoration of any disturbed land is an important element of synthetic fuels plant operations.*

The central message Exxon and Disney want us to carry away from Energy Exchange (and the Universe of Energy) is found in "Energy Perspectives," the crucial overarching discussion.

> *Right now in the United States domestic energy supply and demand are out of balance . . . our supplies of oil . . . are less than the demand, while our coal resources are greater . . . what can we do to bring supply and demand back into balance?*
>
> *First, we must use all energy more efficiently.*
>
> *Second, we must use other energy sources . . . coal, uranium, solar power.*
>
> *Third . . . because we will continue to need liquid fuel, especially for transportation, [we must] increase domestic oil production to reduce reliance on imports.* [87]

Can we meet the challenge of the new frontier of energy needs? You bet! If we can dream it, we can do it! But because it's fun to be free, let's go back to GM's World of Motion and look at the internal combustion engine and its need for liquid fuel. Who knows, maybe we'll find Roger.

GM's Transcenter

> *Most of the exhibits start with the Dawn of Civilization so you can get a clear picture of how miserable everybody was before we had large corporations such as General Motors.*
> —Dave Barry [88]

I previously described the ride at GM's World of Motion, a ride that begins, as Dave Barry notes, with the Dawn of Civilization. This whimsical "history" of transportation disgorges its passengers into the second hemisphere of the pavilion, the Transcenter — a 33,000-square-foot exhibit area "that demonstrates how close we already are to a future dreamed up long ago by science fiction writers." [89] Actually, what we find are futurist engineering exhibits, two propaganda shows, and a General Motors showroom filled with cars without sticker prices.

Customers begin with Aerotest, a display that shows how automotive design is improved by wind tunnel tests and computer modeling. At the right edge of Aerotest, visitors can hear the spiel that advertises *The Bird and the Robot.* In this show, an audioanimatronic Groucho-Marxian toucan, complete with cigar and bow tie, introduces to the audience his protégé — an industrial robot making its "debut" in show business. The Bird runs the robot, Tiger, through his paces — showing how clever, cute, and useful industrial robots can be. The Bird quells Tiger's attempted revolt, thus suggesting to the crowd that unlike Dr. Frankenstein's monster, industrial robots can always be controlled. The message is that it will be wonderful when industrial robots take over all the unpleasant factory jobs.

There is no mention of what might happen to human workers displaced by these robots. As many of us have seen — in the documentary film *What's Good for General Motors,* [90] in Michael Moore's film *Roger and Me,* and in a good-sized body of published literature on General Motors — this is a company with less than zero social conscience and no sense of moral responsibility. *The Bird and the Robot* is a nice piece of propaganda for such a company. [91]

So, in another way, is *The Water Engine*. This is a cartoon, shown on a set of video screens, in which various characters argue for their version of the engine of the future. A mustachioed cowboy (who looks as though he might be Rusty Jones's uncle) stumps for the internal combustion engine — saying more or less that he believes in free competition but that until a better engine comes along (which he'll be the first to buy), he's stickin' with his old faithful. [92] Other engines — the coal-fired turbine, the battery-electric, the magnetic levitation, the flywheel, the hybrid flywheel-turbine, the hybrid turbine-electric, and the horse (*Equus Cheapus*) — are all spoken for. The dramatic climax comes when a Peter Lorre character pumps up his hydrogen-powered "water engine," which explodes across the screens as the other characters dive for cover. The message, as GM's neighbor Exxon would be the first to applaud, is that the internal combustion engine is best.

On the way to the Dreamer's Workshop, Concept 2000 presents information on internal automotive design — seats, upholstery, and the like. Visitors are shown a GM vehicle torture test as well as displays about seat belts, electronic power systems and other components, and the use of microprocessors. We see a film clip on the factory of the future — people in sterile uniforms and industrial robots. The central tool in all of this is computer-aided design (CAD). This CAD technology has been used to design prototype models for an enormous aerotruck, undersea vehicles, an off-road touring bus, and various mag-lev or hovercraft, including a Hovair train and an air-supported hovercraft hotel.

The two main creations on view at the Dreamer's Workshop are the Aero 2000 and the Lean Machine. The former is a front wheel drive subcompact with a three-cylinder turbocharged 68 horsepower diesel engine. [93] Its features include voice command computer operation, radar-activated brakes, an instrument panel display with computerized map, and a communications system that can be linked to a satellite.

The three-wheeled Lean Machine is a single-person, motorcycle-like, all-weather vehicle with a pedal-operated tilting capacity for cornering. [94] The rider sits in a clear fiberglass compartment with controls contained in handlebars. An automatic transmission is connected to a rear-mounted 38-horsepower engine (advertised at 200 miles per gallon). The upper and lower units operate independently, the upper part swiveling so the rider can lean into a turn while the lower unit stays upright. [95]

Near the exit is the showroom and the General Motors Information Center. The former — called Concept to Reality — is what GM people call a "contemporary vehicle salon." [96] Here visitors climb in and out of sample cars and trucks. The Information Center is peopled by a GM representative, "eager" to answer questions. It's not Roger.

Wonders of Life

We need to visit one other pavilion in Future World before ending our tour in the CommuniCores. Thematically, Wonders of Life might have fit better with my earlier discussion of nature; but its high-technology hands-on presentation suggests that aligning it with energy and motion is not inappropriate.

In between the Universe of Energy and Horizons is the newest pavilion at Future World, Metropolitan Life's Wonders of Life. Housed in a 100,000-square-foot golden geodesic dome,[97] its entrance sits just up the hill to the east of the CommuniCores.[98] Out front is a 72-foot-tall[99] steel mock-up of a DNA molecule. Visitors walk under an arch built with triangular pipe forms. The arch ends in fountains that contains what look like bubbling-over lab beakers.

Inside, the pavilion is designed as a rural fairground — Fitness Fairgrounds. Colorful tents and awnings roof exhibits and shows scattered about the "field." A giant mobile swings overhead. This bucolic scene evokes nostalgia for days gone by. But slowly, as we traverse the pavilion and find out what else it has to offer, nostalgia begins to darken.

Off to the side are two attractions — Body Wars and Cranium Command — that encase health and life in the metaphors of war. Life is a battle, medicine is military, the body a war zone. Bit by bit the feeling grows that we are in a 1940s Hollywood movie, having a last summer picnic on the sunny fairgrounds before sending the boys off to war. If we can visualize the lines waiting to get into the shows as troop trains, the fantasy is complete. First the fair, then the combat.

The fairgrounds are full of activity. Ahead of us as we enter is a little open theater with benches. Here is *Goofy about Health*, an eight-minute cartoon[100] that traces Goofy's transformation from an unhealthy slob to an organic, nonsmoking, nondrinking, exercising, nonstressed, health-conscious hound.

Past the new Goofy to the right is another small theater in which, with audience participation, the Anacomical Players perform semiscripted improvisational theater skits about health and nutrition. Unlike the improv in World Showcase, these skits often are not very funny. A third theater — to which I will return — presents Disney's risky fourteen-minute film, *The Making of Me*. This film takes a curious character — played by Martin Short — back in time to see how he came into existence. The journey involves some Disneyfied sex education for its audience.

The fairground contains many hands-on activities. The Sensory Funhouse tests the senses. Visitors feel hidden things and try to guess what they are. They see optical illusions. There is a state-of-the-art aural exhibit, which uses the same technology as that at Soundsations in the Disney-MGM Studios' Monster Sound Show.

Visitors can ride wondercycles — stationary bicycles with video screens that enable riders to simulate passages down Main Street at Disneyland and in the Rose Bowl Parade. These computerized bikes continuously record pedaling speed and distance traveled on the screens.

Near the bikes is the Met Lifestyle Review, where customers can answer an interactive questionnaire on the monitors that, in a very gross way, leads to a simple analysis of the subject's healthstyle. "Stop smoking," it says. "Eat less."

It doesn't send us to Coach's Corner, but here we are anyway. In this screened-in area, guests — usually children — are videotaped swinging a golf club, a tennis racquet, or a baseball bat. Disney "coaches" — athletic-looking young employees — punch a simple instruction into the computer console, and a video of Nancy Lopez, Chris Evert, or Gary Carter appears on the overhead screens. Depending on what the "coach" punched in, the pros give us a short bit of advice about how to improve our swing. This, I'm afraid, is not personalized service.

Three further venues round out Fitness Fairgrounds. Between the exits from Body Wars and Cranium Command, Frontiers of Medicine presents a serious display of current developments in medicine and allied fields. Well and Goods, which sells athletic wear and health-related materials, is the pavilion store. Deserts and Things offers fruit topping-smothered waffles and frozen yogurt.

To the left of the entrance to Fitness Fairgrounds is Body Wars. The premise of this ride is that we are to be miniaturized inside a special body probe by a private medical research company. We will be sent into a human body to pick up a research scientist who is studying the body's response to a wooden splinter in the volunteer's finger.

We walk through Dermatropic Purification Station 1 (a pulsing blue arch). Overhead are video screens on which MET (miniaturized exploration technologies — the same initials as Met Life, our "host corporation") spokespeople tell us about miniaturization. Beyond the red arch at Dermatropic Purification Station 2, we line up in front of our travel pod. More video directions, then we enter a theater vehicle just like the ones at Star Tours in the Disney-MGM Studios. [101]

Piloted by Tim Matheson, the craft will jounce and bounce us as it rocks and jumps its way through the trip. Visitors were already warned at the entrance to stay away if they have back problems, a heart condition, or a propensity to motion sickness. Thus, the fasten your seat belt order is not unexpected. [102]

The trip starts reasonably smoothly. Our ship is miniaturized, and we are sent into the index finger of the splintered volunteer, where the doctor is monitoring white cell reaction. [103] The splinter looks like the broken spar of a tall ship. Suddenly, there is a problem. Attacked by microphages, the doctor is pulled into a capillary and begins to shoot through the bloodstream toward the heart and lungs.

Guided by Matheson, we follow — leaping and darting after the doctor — shot forward by the powerful pulse of the heartbeats. We are staying too long. Mission Control warns that we are running out of power. With little power left, we catch up with the doctor. Riding a pulse beat to the brain, the pod crosses the blood-brain barrier, where Matheson attempts to steal exit power from a firing brain synapse. It works, and we escape. The pod stops, the doors open, and we unbuckle and stumble out the exit, gagging all the way.

The Making of Me is EPCOT Center's *Back to the Future*. Our hero, played by Martin Short, travels back in time to see how his parents "got together" and decided to have a child — him. We begin with his mother as a child in *her* mother's room. Time passes, and there's Dad (also Martin Short) in a high school classroom. At college, Mom and Dad meet at a dance. While the Big Band plays, Mom and Dad find each other, their eyes locking over the shoulders of their respective dates.

Marriage is followed by the fun of young adulthood — water skiing and dancing the tango. Mom and Dad are on the living room couch. They are looking at a photo album when suddenly they get the desire to have a child. There is a segue to the bedroom where the camera pans from the bed, up the wallpaper, to the roof, where Martin Short is rooting for himself.

The movie now becomes a cartoon. There is a sperm race from the "city limits," where the sperm enters the body through the fallopian tube, to a seductive young Wilma Flintstone-like egg wearing an apron with a target on it. The egg has a clock, which ticks on as stupid sperm rush past, falling over the edge until one strikes home.

Now pregnant, Mom and Dad leave a theater full of smokers. We see film of fetal development, which shows the fetus with fingers at six months and open eyes at seven months. Now, in an extraordinary departure from normal Disney practice, the audience (duly warned at the entrance about the mature nature of the film) sees footage of an actual birth, filmed over the mother's shoulder. Thus, bloody, blue "Martin Short" is born. *The Making of Me* closes the circle, as Martin Short's daughter recapitulates the opening scene in her mother's room.

This is an interesting, contradictory film. Since the mid-1980s, Disney has sought to broaden the demographic base of its market. Under the Touchstone label, the studio has produced films aimed at an adult audience — normal films in the current marketplace but certainly more risky than the traditional Disney fare. *The Making of Me* continues this trend. It is aimed at a contemporary secular audience. Adults-parents are generically warned about its contents, but there are no age limitations for viewing.

Like "birds and bees" stories, the sex education here is minimal. A camera pan leads to a cartoon. Blue animated sperm race at yellow eggs with aprons. This is not too progressive. Jesse Helms presumably would not want to see the birth footage, although he probably would be delighted with the fetal scenes — perhaps with a different script. Yet Short's parents choose to try to get pregnant. They live something of a yuppie life beforehand, but — although contraception is never mentioned — they seem to have taken control of their reproductive life. Having children in a nuclear family is good, at least for the main character, but so is family planning. It is good that although *The Making of Me* has a competitive race — run by a bunch of pretty dumb sperm — there's no combat here. It's a nice change from the wars around it.

The nearby Cranium Command gives us a chance to get yelled at by Robin Williams. Williams does the voice for General Knowledge, a cartoon curmudgeon whose job it is to train and oversee cranium commandos as they learn to pilot human brains. In my opinion, this eighteen-minute show (fourteen minutes for the main show, four for the preshow cartoon) is, as of mid-1990, Disney's cleverest show at Future World. Infused with a Monty Python tone and "Saturday Night Live" personnel, Cranium Command is crammed with postmodern double entendres and witty references to the characters of current mass-mediated culture.

Our hero is Buzzy, a boy with chubby cheeks and thick-rimmed glasses who resembles the boy in the Mr. Peabody cartoons. Stumbling in late to General Knowledge's orientation lecture on evolution and the brain, Buzzy gets his first threat. Screwups are assigned to the brains of squid, lungfish, talk show hosts, and chickens.

"From Command Center in the cortex, you will run the whole thing," shouts General knowledge, as recruits in pilot outfits are taken to a factory filled with heads and brains. A young woman is assigned to pilot a nuclear scientist; a boy goes to a football hero. A worker unloads a carton labeled "Zits — one gross." Candy bars and other things are poured into heads, which are then screwed onto bodies and sent — like Delta Dreamflights — to the runway for takeoff. Buzzy (and we as well) is placed in the cranium of the most difficult vehicle of all — a twelve-year-old boy named Bobby.

We enter the main two hundred-seat theater. On a chair high in front sits Buzzy, now an audioanimatronic figure in earphones. We are inside Bobby's skull. It's dark, a little like the Nostromo. Buzzy is behind Bobby's nose, in the cortex. Screens to right and left are Bobby's eyes, through which we see the outside world as he sees it. A round screen at the top shows the brain; one at the bottom shows the heart, stomach, and adrenal gland. All these characters are played by television-movie actors, appropriately cast.[104] They will argue, plead, fight, advise, scream, and the like, as Buzzy tries to coordinate their functions to get through a day at school. Along the way, Bobby falls in love and gets in a food fight. Chaos reigns before Buzzy gets things under control.

Bobby is jarred awake by his alarm, skips breakfast, runs to school (chased by a dog), meets the new girl — who is precociously tarted up — tries to protect her from two bullies, and gets in the food fight. Madness escalates as Buzzy loses control. Body part-characters shout for attention from the screen. At the height of the fight, Bobby is called to the principal's office. Charles Grodin convinces Buzzy-Bobby to tell the truth. The principal, Herbert Hardcase, lets him off the hook. So does General Knowledge, who takes his chicken away, muttering, "This chicken doesn't need a brain; he's going into politics." Bobby gets a kiss on the cheek from the new girl and makes an informal mall date.

It is not clear what we are to learn from this contemporary popular culture test, except to stop and count to ten once in a while. If there's a homunculus in my brain, I hope it's not Buzzy.

Glittering Gizmos

Instead of educating or inspiring those in its audience, EPCOT distracts them with sleight of hand. It is a high-tech fun house filled with costumed mannequins, glittering gizmos and special effects . . . it ignores serious technological questions that confront America as the 20th century draws to a close.

—Peter Larson [105]

Exxon and General Motors in particular have presented the kinds of arguments for the technological fix Langdon Winner warned us about in *The Whale and the Reactor*. They have attempted through their fascinating gizmos and special effects to convince us to remain in our "technological somnambulism," to ignore the side effects of the technological realm. At Future World, Disney argues in favor of large-scale technological systems in which "scientific knowledge, technological invention and corporate profit reinforce each other." [106] These meta-advertisements try to convince us subtly that Winner's five tendencies of current technological systems — single centers, increased size, hierarchy, political control, and the crowding out of other activity — are benign side effects of our way of meeting the challenge of the future and its new frontiers.

Albert Borgmann tells us that the domination of nature — which we looked at in the previous chapter, but which is also a theme of Wonders of Life and its military models — has led us from disburdenment to frivolity. For Borgmann, as for Frederic Jameson, Jean Baudrillard, and other thinkers I discussed in my chapters about postmodernism, the "depth of things is dissolved." Human life becomes shallow, divided, decomposed, lived on the surface. Where others argue that this is a matter of culture and commodity, Borgmann suggests it is a result of modern technological systems themselves. Such systems have had severe unintended consequences. Previous social contexts for human activity have often fallen away. People become merely consumers, advertising the rhetoric of our times. Borgmann suggests a studied return to the engagement with "focal things" — deep but simple things-in-themselves (nature, craft, and the like) — in committed "focal practice."

Future World presents the counterargument. It is a place of absorbing surface frivolity and corporate propaganda. As John Rothchild writes,

> EPCOT is a showcase for futuristic prototypes, but it is more than entertainment. It is a showcase for a belief, a holy land of engineered progress. It purports to be educational, but it inspires awe, not curiosity — and the sponsors are the beneficiaries. One can niggle from now until the next century about how it fails to deliver what its name promises, but one is left with the fact that it will attract 23 million people this year. [107]

Not all of those people will be enthralled. Some will turn their backs on Disney altogether. But others will find nowhere else to go in this postmodern, commodified world but back to Disney in another form — to the nostalgia sold at the Magic Kingdom. Beverly Beckham speaks for many in her response to EPCOT Center.

> But I don't want reality. I want fantasy. I want to park my car in Chip and Dale, not Communications. I want to hear "When You Wish upon a Star" and "Winnie the Pooh" filter through speakers as I meander about a land teeming with smiling adults and children. I want to visit worlds where pirate ships sail and Davy Crocket [sic] roams and where a wooden puppet who is much loved can become a real boy and bring happiness to an old man.
>
> I don't want my dreams dissected and my illusions explained. EPCOT does this, throwing back the curtain on the wizard as he manipulates his panel of lights. EPCOT shows us things as they are and as they will be, not as we would like them to be. Which, I suppose, is laudable. After all, we live in a real world. And yet . . . [108]

18

ComputiCore: Computers, Parades, Lunch

The function of EPCOT is to excite people to potentials, and to be as accurate as possible . . . not to educate fully, of course, but to be on the rim of educating, so that when you leave, your life is changed forever.

—Ray Bradbury[1]

Whereas Mickey and Figment are WDW heroes of the past and present, the most important characters for Disney's vision of the future are the Bird and I/O — the little burst of electronic light that assists our tour guide at EPCOT Computer Central's Backstage Magic. Short for input/output, I/O's task is to help assuage visitors' fears of computational future shock. Here in one of the most computerized civilian installations in the world, Disney planners worry openly about their ideological task. In all of the commemorative literature about WDW, computerization is the sole topic that recognizes human fears. *Walt Disney World* tells us,

The future holds an exciting and limitless array of possibilities for the improvement of human life. As with any sudden or technological change, anxieties can occur. People are unsure about these changes, or feel intimidated by futuristic, seemingly complex systems.

CommuniCore offers us the opportunity to deal with advanced technology on an individual level. The exhibits are aimed at making us feel comfortable with computers and other implements of high technology. . . .

Computer wizards bring backstage "on stage" every day in the Backstage Magic show. . . . In the process, these mysterious machines become a little less intimidating and a little more familiar.[2]

I/O is a squeaky-cute "sorcerer's apprentice" — an assistant to the back stage computer wizards who bring us Disney's show. These same magical machines, in the hands of (perhaps) different wizards, will bring us the living theater concocted by Disney's corporate comrades-in-arms. The calming story here, as elsewhere in Future World, is aimed at the adults in the audience.[3] Many children already know something about computers.

Working out of the CommuniCores, I again look at parallel processes. I briefly describe Disney's infrastructural use of computational and communicational technologies. I also describe the ways in which these technological systems become part of the show, thus performing the ideological task of dampening future shock. Along with computerization and information systems — including fiber optics and interactive video discs — I look at some other kinds of technology and at robotics, theatrical staging, and food systems.

CommuniCores

From the air, the CommuniCores together resemble a giant lobster claw reaching north to grab Earth Station and the Great Golf Ball. The central fountain has been stored back at the claw's hinge. These two crescent-shaped claw buildings — CommuniCore East and West — were built at the center of Future World. Surrounding an open plaza with the fountain at its center, this was to be the Communi(ty) Core. Perhaps nothing underlines Disney's newspeak marketing cynicism so much as the use of the word "community" here. The outer ring of pavilions that surrounds the CommuniCores is, with the exception of a few fish, a hinterland of robots.

Each CommuniCore consists of two buildings, separated by a central crosswalk but covered by a single roof. Access to the pavilions of the outer ring is by way of these buildings. At the far (south) end, the plaza gives way to the wide mallway to World Showcase.

When the entrance gates to EPCOT Center open at 8:30 A.M. or so, visitors face another thirty minutes before they can get beyond the northern halves of the CommuniCores and out into the rest of the park. This is one of the more interesting times of the EPCOT day, when the expertise and special knowledge of WDW veterans orchestrate elegant strategies around bewildered rookies.

From all gates, people dash up the Entrance Plaza, past the fountain with its tall plasticine slabs and park logo, and up along the sides of Spaceship Earth. Unless they are staying at a WDW hotel or are members of a special category of guest, visitors will have to make lunch and dinner reservations for the restaurants in World Showcase (as well as the Land Grille and the Coral Reef Restaurant) at Earth Station, tucked underneath the back of Spaceship Earth.

Here, in front of a large open space partly filled with plastic benches, is a bank of video monitors lining the south wall. At the east entrance is the Guest Relations Service Desk, where visitors find general information as well as the *Entertainment Show Schedule*, which is printed weekly and lists the theater and street shows at each pavilion. Around the perimeter of the room, above the doors, are screens on which are shown stylized advertisements for the park's attractions. At the north end of Earth Station is the exit from the Spaceship Earth ride. When the park opens, veterans will send guests off to ride Spaceship Earth while they go directly to the reservation line.

The line snakes to an attendant, dressed in what looks like plaid fox hunting garb, who directs us to a video monitor. The line passes a sign that lists the restaurants and the state of reservation availability. During high seasons, the reservation line grows geometrically in the first half hour, and restaurants are often fully booked by 10:00. Directed forward to a monitor, customers make their reservations by talking to a uniformed human being through two-way cameras. Sitting behind the wall, reservation agents book seatings through a computer system, which then prints the relevant information on the video screen. Visitors are introduced to both Disney's computerization and the interactive video network that is evident throughout EPCOT.

East of Earth Station in CommuniCore East is EPCOT Computer Central, where visitors can pass the time until the rest of the park opens at 9:00. Beyond EPCOT Computer Central is the Stargate Restaurant, where breakfast (including pizza omelettes) is served. Directly across the central aisle — behind a fourteen-foot lucite sphere — is the TravelPort, presented by American Express. [4]

The TravelPort contains a set of booths — "vacation stations" — with touch-sensitive video screens. Video disc slide shows are available on a menu guests may peruse to "preview" various vacation sites. Touristic attractions and lodging and dining information are stored in the presentation. An American Express travel service office sits in the corner with an agent who provides a limited range of travel services.

Let me pause here to describe a little of WDW's touch sensitivity. Disney calls its customer communication system the WorldKey Information Service. Built by Disney World and Bell Labs engineers, WorldKey is designed to answer the thousands of questions asked daily by park customers. The system integrates computers, microelectronics, television, laser video discs, touch-sensitive screens, and fiber optic transmission in a user-friendly, menu-driven information service.

Scattered throughout EPCOT Center are two-way television terminals that can communicate in English and Spanish. By touching the screen in various spots as directed, a viewer activates the menu of information retrieved from a video disc player at Computer Central. The players are queued by VAX computers, which route information from the disc players to the monitors. Visitors pursue this information by following directions about where to touch the screen sensitively as they work their way through subdirectories.[5] Information is shown on the screen, accompanied by a Disney character narration that includes an animated character called Bit, who tells visitors how to work the system.[6] If need be, live attendants can be accessed, just as they are at Earth Station, for a two-way television discussion.

AT&T calls this its Ariel (Automatic Retrieval of Information E-Lectronically) system. The EPCOT version is the first large-scale test of this technology. Jack Hollahan quotes Bell's EPCOT project director, Bruce Stresser, who suggests that this information retrieval system would be valuable to

> shopping centers, airports, and even museums, when previewing a vast collection, of which only a small part can be displayed at any one time. Our systems here at EPCOT are experimental, but they will be used extensively in the future by all sorts of businesses and institutions. The Bell System is at EPCOT to demonstrate to a broad audience our leadership in information age technologies, products and services.[7]

Near the entrance ramp to Backstage Magic — the show that tells about the use of computers at WDW — EPCOT Computer Central contains a number of other "activity islands."[8] Customers visit these while waiting for the park to open and to fill time on the afternoons of second or third days at EPCOT Center, when they've seen all the things they've come to see. Four of these activity islands are built around touch-sensitive interactive computers. The fifth, SMRT-1, is voice-activated.

SMRT-1 is a robot constructed as a purple space boy. Visitors speak to the robot over amplified telephones arranged in a circle around it. They "play" guessing games, including a birthday guess. SMRT-1 asks a question in a synthesized voice. Customers, usually children, respond. SMRT-1 decodes the response and asks further questions until arriving at its answer.

The monitors for the Great American Census Quiz sit under a display that purports to keep up-to-the-minute track of the growing U.S. population. Stepping up to the terminals, visitors choose which quiz to take — On the Farm, Home Sweet Home, the Fifty States, School Days, Communication Line, or Population Clock. Each consists of four multiple choice questions based on the most recent national demographics. Quizzees touch the screen next to their chosen answer. Incorrect answers are accompanied by an obnoxious beep designed to notify those around you that you are an ignorant fool.

The other three sets of games are business-oriented. The Manufactory asks visitors to put together U.S. flags by touching stripes and stars as they appear and then depositing them in their correct places by additional touches. Speed and accuracy are of the essence here, as we get a couple of shots at making a flag. Good and true workers are rewarded with graphic fireworks and digitalized patriotic music. Making a couple of flags is fun. Doing this all day — day after day — probably calls for a different reward structure.

Near the flag game is another that relies on speed and accuracy. In the Get Set Jet Game, customers slide their finger up a screen for sixty seconds, loading passengers and baggage into a jet plane as they pass by on a conveyor belt. Loading is interrupted by simulated maintenance checks, which require momentary inattention to the conveyor belt. Just as the Manufactory showed us how much fun production can be — especially with computers and computer graphics to help — so this seductive game inducts us into the joys of the service industry. Before we know it, we are trying to beat our previous high score.

The last activity here — before we climb the ramp to Backstage Magic — is a little different. At Compute-a-Coaster, customers can design a roller coaster ride by choosing the order in which to arrange the graphics that depict parts of standard coasters — drops, loops, rises, and the like. Orders that are dangerous from an engineering standpoint are disallowed.

This introduction to computer-aided design (CAD) ends with a simulated ride through the coaster the customer has just designed. For many, this is a first introduction to any hands-on knowledge of CAD, a process that through television and the movies, they may already have begun to take for granted without noticing that they have done so. Just another piece of unattended magic.

The entrance to Backstage Magic (originally the Astuter Computer Revue) is a ramp leading up to a balcony that overlooks the computer games. Spaced overhead are monitors on which customers see a short animated preshow. This is a cartoon Distory of computational devices — from fingers, cavemen, and dinosaurs through the abacus, early Turing machines, and holorith cards to the contemporary electronic computer. We are told about Eniac, Univac, the vacuum tube, transistors, circuit boards, integrated circuits, and microchips. Here are inputs and outputs, memory, retrieval, control language, program execution, and hardware and software. This simple shot at demystification is Unisys's attempt at dampening computerphobia.

Our hostess for the show is Julie, a live human being (on film) who, along with her sidekick I/O, introduces visitors to the central EPCOT computer room. I/O is an animated ball of light that squeakingly boings Julie to wherever she needs to be for the show.

The preshow over, visitors file into the showroom, in which they stand in rows facing the window that forms one wall of the computer room. Down below are the computers that, we are told, run EPCOT Center. In front are two half-circle console areas from which instructions can be entered into the system. Disney employees wander in and out, impervious to the visitors.

Julie, I/O, and the other elements of the show — red lights that highlight various parts of the machinery and a "light bridge" that connects the workstations Julie will cross as part of the presentation — are projected on the glass from below the audience, much as the ghosts are projected in the dance scenes at the Haunted Mansion. At the top of the window are the video screens where I/O dwells. A miniaturized Julie down below stands on the consoles and tells the audience about two of the major computer systems that organize the show — the MACS (the monitoring and control system) and ECS (the entertainment control system).

I describe ECS later in this chapter in my discussion of theatrical technology, but here a word about MACS. The monitoring and control system checks the park's crucial maintenance and operating variables — for example, security alarm points, critical bearing temperatures, operation of all freezers and refrigerators, and wastewater lift station levels. [9]

Julie and I/O's show has a number of purposes. First, it is a piece of entertainment with its own script, multimedia vehicles, and theatrical technology. Second, it offers a "behind the scenes" glimpse of a kind of work display. The cybernetic activity here is done by machines, designed and programmed by actual humans who have done the work elsewhere. The few people we see through the window may be monitoring parts of the system or may be acting as if they are doing so. Unlike the animation at the Disney-MGM Studios Animation Tour, these people are not clearly working; but unlike the staff behind the window of the Mission to Mars, at least they're human.

A third purpose of Backstage Magic is ideological. The show is a mock piece of education meant to mitigate computerphobia. The machines — big cabinets, really — are benign. The controls at the consoles seem familiar, with big colored buttons and video monitors. I/O is adorable. In her power suit and tie, the perky Julie suggests that we have real professionals here — friendly but competent and even a bit wide-eyed themselves at the electronic marvels around them.

Fourth, Backstage Magic is an advertisement for Unisys. It all works together — commercial, education, ideology, and entertainment.

Just beyond EPCOT Computer Central are Energy Exchange — visited previously — and to the right the Stargate Restaurant and Beverage Base. While waiting for the rest of the park to open, customers can ingest breakfast at the fast-food Stargate.

This northeast quadrant of the CommuniCores is the only Future World building other than Spaceship Earth and Earth Station open during the 8:30-9:00 A.M. period of liminality. Visitors pile up here — as they do outside the northern half of CommuniCore West — for the 9:00 stampede to the peripheral ring of pavilions. At the appointed hour, we are welcomed over the loudspeaker system by a spokesman for the Disney "family," the automatic doors open, the ropes go down, and the race to Body Wars and Captain E-O is on.

Separated from this quadrant by an arcade is the southern half of CommuniCore East. Here is the largest store in EPCOT Center, the spread-out, two-story .Centorium. With everything in one building, this is Future World's version of the Main Street USA shops. Like those shops, the Centorium is the last place to close as EPCOT shuts down for the night. Here are character merchandise and other souvenirs, tee-shirts, hats, dolls, and similar items. Upstairs, which is reached by way of a glassed-in elevator, are electronic gadgets, tape players, watches, model vehicles, and Mickey's sports clothes collection from Team Mickey.

The final, southernmost space in CommuniCore East is perhaps the scariest part of Future World. Here is the Electronic Forum, "as lively and democratic as Athens's agora and infinitely more efficient." [10] The slightly sunken foyer to the Electronic Forum contains three banks of televisions hanging from the ceiling in 360-degree configurations. Two of the groups show news, sports, business, and weather stations. The third cluster receives Disney news, including information about activities on the property. This is the same news shown on the special local park station available to visitors who stay at Disney hotels.

These monitors receive their signals through the satellite dish stationed outside CommuniCore East, which collects its feed from a Telstar III satellite overhead. Below the sets are smaller screens, recessed in low-set consoles, facing upward. Each is accompanied by a telephone receiver on which one can may dial a number and call up one of the offerings for a private showing with sound. At certain times — late Saturday afternoon in the fall, for example (college football scores) — the telephones are well used.

Behind this hanging information glut is an alcove with monitors through which Disney is conducting a fin de siècle person of the century poll. After eliciting some simple demographics, the program asks participants to pick their choices for the five most important world figures of the twentieth century. The winners will be announced as we approach the millennium. Visitors are given a list of names from which to choose. Freud is on the list; so are Lenin, Mao, Gandhi, King, Henry Ford, Thomas Watson, and James Watson. Visitors can choose Babe Ruth, figures from show business, Ronald Reagan, or that sure winner — Walt Disney.

The main weenie of the Electronic Forum, however, is the Future Choice Theater, where EPCOT's regular ongoing polls are taken. From the anteroom, flanked on the right by a satellite communication display, pollees are led into a theater whose seats are equipped with a bank of push buttons. Visitors are asked to respond to questions put to them by a live smarm in training, who is beginning a broadcasting career, at the podium in front. Responses are made by pushing the appropriate button on the console —

each button corresponding to a multiple choice answer shown on the large monitor in front. Answers are immediately tabulated by computer, and the results of the audience's response distribution are shown on the screen.

Again we begin with demographics. Then the moderator introduces the central theme of the poll, which is focused on some set of current issues about which Disney wants answers — to questions that are "uppermost in peoples' minds at polling time." [11] Disney wants its answers simple. The poll is presented with allusions to democracy and personal empowerment. We are to, "contribute our own opinions on current issues — and actually have someone take notice. . . . The armrest consoles offer a rare opportunity to get a number of things off your chest and into a computer, to compare your views with those of your countrymen (as well as with the opinions of foreign visitors), to make your voice heard, to stand up and be counted — while sitting in a comfortable chair." [12]

The moderator presents a brief scripted account of today's issue, accompanied by film clips and videotapes that feature experts and others. The audience is asked a series of questions that solicit individual opinions, which visitors register by pressing armrest buttons. The results are shown immediately; the tabulation suggests how much work would need to be done to mold the audience into consensus.

Note the themes. We are asked for opinions and feelings. Giving them will allow us catharsis. We will get things off our chests, make ourselves heard, stand up and be counted. Disney suggests that in the normal state of the world, we are small, powerless, unnoticed. Here someone will "actually" take notice. But who is this "somebody?" Richard R. Beard gives us a clue when he says, "The armrest consoles offer a rare opportunity to get a number of things off your chest and *into a computer*" (my italics). [13]

Who is going to listen? A computer. This is not a "rare opportunity" but a normal procedure in the expansion of Orwellian information management. The data are stored in the interests of marketing and government: "It is hoped that the findings may become part of the decision-making process in government, *which sometimes seems so remote*" (my italics). [14] You can't fight City Hall; but maybe they'll listen to your feelings and give you the illusion that they're not so distant, so impersonal — that they "care."

What visitors *can* do is compare themselves anonymously with others in the room — others about whom they know almost nothing. Under limits set by the carefully crafted, innocuous questions and the array of centralist, narrow-band, proferred answers, pollees can see where they fit in a crowd of anonymous people who can afford WDW. [15]

What is perhaps most compelling is that we can "stand up and be counted" by sitting down and pushing buttons. We are told we don't need to work, struggle, or "do something" in order to be somebody, to be empowered, to affect our lives and the world around us. We can do it all sitting down. As good Americans, Disney suggests, we'd rather do it that way; it's convenient to make a revolution sitting down, entertained as couch potatoes.

Maybe the revolution will be televised after all — interactively, of course. We will throw out entire governments, change institutions, declare war, lower taxes, and fight drugs and pornography by collectively and instantaneously responding to centralized power and emotionally charged interactive video referenda. We need not think — there isn't time. We've got to push the response button before the theme music stops. And we can do all the feeling we need in order to "state our opinions" without moving much. But the central question remains: How are they going to get us to turn off "Totally Silly Videos" and Oprah and pay attention?

Across the central plaza with its large circular fountain is CommuniCore West — again two buildings with a roofed-over dividing walkway. The entrance nearest to Earth Station — in the northwest quadrant — brings customers into AT&T's FutureCom. Here the theme is information — gathering, storing, sharing, and disseminating. The overall display has five parts and, in the back left, a small sales area.

Two of the displays are sculptural. Front and center is the art deco *Fountain of Information*. This piece is made up of a collection of informational artifacts and communicational media. Jumbled together are televisions, radios, records, video, laser and audio discs, video information strips, telephones, newspapers, maps, sprays of tape and film, books, magazines, computer printouts, neon signs, yellow traffic lights, other traffic signs and lights, train signals, catalogs, and stock certificates. This is a perfect postmodern jumble — laser discs and train signals — designed with Disney's signature whimsy. This *Fountain of Information* is like a prop from a futuristic Mr. Toad's Wild Ride.

The second sculpture, spread across the left wall, is Walter Einsel's animated *The Age of Information*, which "sets the electronic cottage and the animated office to music." [16] Animated wooden figures move about against the wall, supposedly demonstrating the organizational efficacy of electronics at home, at the office, and on the road. The sculpture looks like a giant version of those incredibly expensive wooden European kids' toys.

In front of this sculpture — indeed, all around the floor — are computers in various configurations, with games and displays available for hands-on activity. Many of these games are more complicated than those at EPCOT Computer Central. Turnaround time is somewhat slower, and the stations are usually occupied, with potential players circling like sharks waiting for an empty screen.

Many of these games deal with the control and transfer of information. Network Control, for example, allows players to simulate the management of the flow of long-distance calls on a map of the United States. Another computer — the Phraser — "speaks" the words customers type out on the keyboard. Because it can only follow standard rules of spelling and pronunciation, this display suggests how far computer researchers are from the production of artificial language. The computer's sound system is capable of mispronouncing words in a number of languages.

On the right side of FutureCom are two shows with live people. Nearest the walkway through CommuniCore West is a twenty-by-thirty-foot representation of the nationwide telecommunication network. This map has a color-coded fiber optic light display of long-distance telephone routes. A Disney-Bell representative gives a periodic spiel about the wonders of AT&T's movement of information. In front of this map is a bank of touch-sensitive monitors on which visitors can call up state-by-state tourist information.

Just beyond this map is another series of monitors that forms part of an exhibit on teleconferencing. While visitors watch themselves on the monitors, filmed by semihidden cameras, a Disney operative sitting behind buffers on a balcony banters desultorily with the crowd.

South of FutureCom are two EPCOT services — EPCOT Outreach and the Teacher Center. The former holds displays of plans and artists' renderings of future pavilions and exhibits. There is a description of the international fellowship program through which foreign students and other youth are brought to EPCOT to work in World Showcase and to attend Walt Disney University. There are also poster and photo scientific displays keyed to the pavilions of Future World — energy, agriculture, transportation, and the other themes. These are keyed to the resource center, which features information such as pamphlets and fact sheets available at a counter in the back.

Behind the counter is the Teacher's Center, a room where educators can get study guides and preview EPCOT Center educational material. This material is part of one of Disney's major product lines. The Company uses its characters and story lines to tell all sorts of "pedagogical" stories [17] — most, as usual, in the interests of the transnational corporation worldview. EPCOT Outreach is completed by a shop that sells children's games and books, Disney character merchandise, and convenience items.

The southwest quadrant of CommuniCore West is split into two parts. The Sunrise Terrace Restaurant architecturally balances the Stargate Restaurant of CommuniCore East. Like the latter, it protrudes out into the plaza, where people can sit at glassed-in tables and watch the fountain and the passing parade. The fast-food place features fried chicken and seafood as well as the expanding collection of Disney salads.

The final section of the CommuniCores sits at the southern end of CommuniCore West. Here is Expo Robotics, part of WDW's extensive advertisement for the deployment of robots and other electronic servomechanisms throughout U.S. industry.

One of the most important ideological tasks Disney performs at its parks is the dampening of human fears about machines that are designed to take over human tasks — especially machines designed to mimic human characteristics. Deep and troubling fears about the escape from human control of artificial human surrogates echo throughout Western culture. From Frankenstein's monster through Kubrick's HAL in *2001: A Space Odyssey* to the various cyborgs of the contemporary cinema, robots and other humaniform inventions have triggered human anxieties. As industry replaces human labor with robots, propaganda needs to be created to justify the resulting job losses. This is one of the things Disney does at WDW.

Disney's most ubiquitous advertisements for robots are the brilliant audioanimatronic figures found throughout the parks. From the Hall of Presidents and Pirates of the Caribbean in the Magic Kingdom through the figures of EPCOT — at World of Motion, Spaceship Earth, Horizons, and the American Adventure — to those of the Great Movie Ride at the Disney-MGM Studios, robots mimic humans all over the place. There are also robot dogs, pigs, horses, buffalo, vultures, monkeys, snakes, elephants, hippos — even pteranodons, brontosauruses, a stegasaurus, and Figments of imagination. Less lifelike but still effective are the dolls of It's a Small World and the birds and flowers of the Tiki Room. Perhaps with robot actors in mind, Paul D. Lehrman notes that "though the system at EPCOT is flexible to a tremendous degree, it allows no room for mistakes attributable to biological entities." [18]

Future World, however, contains some shows whose purpose is more transparently aimed at the relation between robotic labor and industrial and craft tasks. GM's *The Bird and the Robot* at World of Motion explicitly argues that industrial robots ought to take over human manufacturing jobs. [19] A Groucho Marx-like robot toucan leads an industrial robotic arm named Tiger through its paces in a parody of a trained animal act. Part of the message is what a good and accurate worker Tiger is, able to work under miserable conditions. By thwarting a humorous robotic revolt, the Bird suggests to the audience that humans need not worry about the machines taking over.

As does *The Bird and the Robot*, Expo Robotics features relatively ungussied-up industrial robot "arms" in its three displays. The central show is designed to teach its audience about the extraordinary precision of which industrial robots are capable. In the show, tops are spun in various configurations — on the edges of swords, on the tips of batons, and along strands of wire. One spinning top is placed on top of another by a precise electronic arm.

Just as the Bird's protégé is named Tiger in World of Motion, so the robotic arms here are metaphorically brought to life. Some are given names. Pixel is a star performer; others are designated as assistants. Their act is accompanied by mock-dramatic circus music — music that serves, among other things, to coordinate the audience's applause. The male announcer tells us about the machine's capabilities: It is accurate to one ten-thousandth of an inch. The voice thanks us "robot lovers" for coming.

There are two other parts of the show, plus a small shop that sells toys and games that feature artificial intelligence. At the back of the space, industrial robot arms use televideo sensors to draw caricatures of customers. Whether these robots will eventually displace the bereted human artists at the France Showcase or whether the latter will be kept around for their double nostalgia (both French and human) is perhaps up for grabs.

Near the south exit from the building, Team Radius robots airbrush Minnie, Donald, and others onto tee-shirts for sale. Once again, the message is that robots are clever, precise, and fun. They can paint, draw, and balance tops just like circus performers. Above all, they are entertaining and not to be feared.

Show Technology

Sound — announcements telling guests where to park, where to eat, how to get out, or blaring pseudo-ethnic and Korngodlian movie-score music — is everywhere. It emanates from four low-powered AM-radio-transmitter networks and three closed-circuit-TV channels, from hundreds of speakers hidden in the ground and in the outer walls and ceilings of the buildings, and from elaborate multi-channel high-powered sound systems in the pavilions, exhibits, and movie theaters.... If you try to resist the flow of the music, an interesting phenomenon occurs: You suddenly get very, very tired ... battling against the music's inexorable push into Disney's vision of the future is like swimming upstream.

—Paul D. Lehrman [20]

Throughout EPCOT Center, computers control the show by means of the entertainment control system (ECS) and the digital animation control system (DACS), whose machines we saw at Backstage Magic. [21] DACS controls the theater shows, ensuring that all the robots do what they are supposed to do. Each show is controlled by its own computer, and all are monitored by a redundant system of Unisys V77-500 minicomputers.

ECS has been called EPCOT's central nervous system. [22] This is the system that runs the audio and lighting for all the nontheater show events in EPCOT, especially those that take place around World Showcase Promenade. [23] Minicomputers at EPCOT Computer Central communicate through fiber optic data transmission links with microcomputer-based remote interface cabinets (RICs) placed throughout World Showcase. The RICs in turn control lighting, dimmer modules, audio processing equipment, and the functions keyed by the pageant float identification system. Antennas buried in the promenade road surfacing — just as they are on Main Street USA in the Magic Kingdom — activate control functions when triggered. Float and pavilion audio systems, for example, are blended as the parade passes by. Hidden lights, such as those in the fake rocks at the Canada Showcase, are brought into service. [24]

Showcase Promenade is divided into twenty-two pageant zones. When a parade float passes into a zone, the buried antennas read the float's code from the pageant float identification system. Appropriate music and other effects are blended into float and zone audio systems. [25] "Each float carries an FM wireless-receiver and audio-amplifier and speaker system. On top of the building housing American Adventure is an FM-radio transmitter carrying 11 channels of high quality audio, originating from an Ampex 24-track tape deck at EPCOT Central. Each float is designed to receive one channel of the audio signal and play it through its own sound system." [26] Further, "a graphics display terminal at the operations console in Computer Center shows real-time displays of the status of each stage area. A radio communications station allows the operator immediate access to maintenance and entertainment departments if needed." [27]

The most spectacular Disney parade, however, isn't at EPCOT Center; it's at the Magic Kingdom. Here the Main Street Electrical Parade, with its synthesized Baroque hoedown theme music and its character theme floats — covered with light bulbs [28] — travels nightly from Town Square to the end of Frontierland during the summer and Christmas seasons.

The nightly Water Pageant on Seven Seas Lagoon and Bay Lake and World Showcase's laser-based IllumiNations also depend on parade technology. IllumiNations joins the shows at the Magic Kingdom, the Disney-MGM Studios, and Pleasure Island in presenting the world's most spectacular set of nightly fireworks displays.

Food

Disney's technological systems, computer-based and other, affect another crucial part of the show at WDW — food service. As of the end of 1990, Disney was running 161 restaurants and other food and beverage outlets at the Magic Kingdom, EPCOT Center, the Disney-MGM Studios, Typhoon Lagoon, Fort Wilderness and River Country, Pleasure Island and the Disney Village Marketplace, and at the park's nine resort hotels. [29] These restaurants are staffed by chefs and other culinary professionals, by local full- and part-time workers, by "externs" from various East Coast culinary institutes and hotel and restaurant management schools, and — in the case of World Showcase — by young adults from "showcase countries" who are part of the international fellowship program. [30] We have been on World Showcase Promenade to see the parade technology, so let's have lunch here, too.

When EPCOT Center opened in 1982, park planners had guessed that 1,450 restaurant seats in twenty-eight restaurants would suffice to feed their customers.[31] After all, experience at Disneyland and the Magic Kingdom suggested that people would eat and run to get back to park attractions. World Showcase planners were not even sure they could fill the table-service seats they had. At EPCOT's opening, however, it quickly became clear that Disney had seriously underestimated visitors' willingness to experiment with "exotic" food and to spend time at the table enjoying the themed cuisine and restaurant ambience as part of the show. The stopgap Renaissance Faire food tent was erected between the United Kingdom and France showcases, and further restaurants and expansion were planned immediately.

Further, in one of Disney's few lapses of consciousness, meal reservations could only be made at first at the restaurants of World Showcase, which were set around the lagoon at the opposite side of the park from the entrance. Thus, to eat in World Showcase, one had to be fit enough to run the road race to France or Italy when the park opened.[32] A retired couple with arthritis or a mother with a small child would have to eat at the Farmer's Market at The Land or else starve. Within a few months, Disney had opened its reservation service at Earth Station.

Each showcase except the American Adventure, with its hamburger-hot dog-fried chicken food counter, has at least one table-service restaurant.[33] France and Japan have three each. Some — Mexico's San Angel Inn and Italy's L'Originale Alfredo di Roma — are branches of the originals in the home country. The Japanese restaurants are sponsored by Mitsukoshi, Japan's largest department store chain.[34] The French restaurants and the counter-service Boulangerie Patisserie are sponsored jointly by three world-renowned chefs — Paul Bocuse, Roger Vergé, and Gaston Lenôtre. Germany (oom-pah band) and Morocco (Arabian music and a belly dancer) have floor shows. Mexico has its view of the volcano and a distant mariachi band, Italy its singing waiters, and Japan its teppanyaki chefs. All but Italy and Morocco have counter-service eating. This includes Canada's Le Cellier cafeteria and the pub bar food at the United Kingdom's Rose and Crown. In addition, a number of the showcases have snack and beverage carts out on the Promenade. The United Kingdom, for example, offers the Potato and Beverage Cart and a Tea and Pastry Cart. Italy has gelato; Morocco has dessert pastries.

For all its connections with international institutions and chefs, quality control is still centralized in Disney test kitchens under Disney executive chefs. At EPCOT's opening, the job was held by Walter Meyer, a veteran of New York City's Restaurant Associates and the Four Seasons. He had helped open the restaurants at the Polynesian Hotel and the Empress Room aboard the Empress Lilly. Meyer's job included travel and planning, recipe generation, interviewing chefs, setting up taste-testing panels, and organiz-

ing the flow of specialty items and the planting of an herb garden (at The Land) for the national dishes. [35]

Although many of Disney's restaurants have been well received by food critics, [36] those at World Showcase have had a curious response. Disney clearly designed the restaurants to be part of the show. They were built to satisfy a lot of people who will never go to the places they represent. The food is exotic, but not too exotic. The restaurants were also designed to feed a lot more people a lot faster than such restaurants in the home countries. In some cases they are true simulacra — perfect copies of originals that do not exist.

The food critics don't particularly like them — except for the Marrakesh, which seems pleasantly exotic to the regional press. [37] Yet they fill up. People who've traveled talk about the decor and mock-architectural design. Japanese eat in the Teppanyaki Rooms and British in the Rose and Crown. Showcases may be designed with U.S. mass culture in mind, but one finds natives there, too. [38] The secret, says Rob Morse, is to "look at Les Chefs de France not as a restaurant, but as an attraction in an amusement park — something like 'Three-Star Chef World, presented by Michelin.' Then Les Chefs de France doesn't look so bad." [39]

Whatever the critics may think, the public has tempted enough WDW restaurateurs off the property to elicit a Company response. According to Vicki Vaughan, by fall of 1986, restaurateurs associated with four World Showcase pavilions — Mexico, France, Morocco, and Italy — had opened establishments off Disney property. [40]

Local residents had asked Disney management why a way couldn't be devised to let local people into park restaurants without having to pay park entrance fees. Disney's response was that the logistical problems were too great. Disney and the restaurant owners then agreed that new venues could be opened outside the park as long as they were not linked with EPCOT. A Company spokesman said Disney doesn't want to stop the restaurateurs from pursuing other ventures: "We don't ever want to be accused," he said, "of not letting them go after the American dream." Yet Vaughan reports that Disney was about to insist that future contracts forbid EPCOT restaurateurs from opening other venues within fifty miles of WDW.

Another success story, thanks to the central Florida heat and to Disney's relaxation of its ban on alcohol, is beer. The amount of international beer sold at each of the World Showcase pavilions has far exceeded expectations.

Some pavilions sell more beer than others. It just seems natural that the Rose and Crown Pub in the U.K. has a beverage sale ratio of 75 percent beer and 25 percent of everything else. The Bass and Guiness people, who supply the pub, estimated when the pub opened that they'd be lucky to sell a total of 3,500 barrels each year. In 1984, 5,000 kegs rolled empty from the storage facilities of the pub, proving them wrong. [41]

Food Service Technology and Employee Benefits

From the beginning of its foray into theme parks, Disney planned for its food service to be part of the show. An early decision to contract these services out at Disneyland was rescinded in 1965, when Disney bought out the American Broadcasting Company's (ABC) share in the park — including an ABC subsidiary that handled the food. Disney reasoned that autonomous concessionaires would seek profits for their individual units and would cut corners if need be. Disney has always been willing to tolerate lower volume outlets in the interest of the overall presentation. [42]

Like everything else at WDW, what drives food service are economies of scale, technology, and — above all — organization. The heart of the system is the Food Distribution Center (FDC), originally put in place by John Cardone. In 1986 the center consisted of a central 48,000-square-foot kitchen supplemented by a 52,000-square-foot warehouse, a 25,000-square-foot frozen food area, a bakery, a smokehouse for chicken and ribs, and a test kitchen.

According to Jim Armstrong, vice president for food administration, "We provide a support service to restaurants with an amazing variety of ethnic and market-level experience. The makings of those 8,000 menu items require us to supply about 4,000 food products." [43] This facility deals directly with vendors, eliminating the middleperson and saving on costs.

A computerized scale keeps track of items such as wheat, eggs, and sugar that are purchased by weight. [44]

> Tony Geraci, executive chef [in 1982] of [FDC], operates on a stock number system: He orders, receives, and ships out by stock number, while the computer keeps track of what is on hand and what needs to be ordered. In dealing with vendors, Geraci's first concern is the "quality of the product. After that comes service and whether the vendor is large enough to supply the account adequately . . . then price." The food is the best money can buy, and a rigid control system guarantees it is. [45]

Although purchasing and storing supplies in quantity is obviously an aim, this facility also allows for a good deal of pre-preparation of foodstuffs for park restaurants. [46] Meat for the various restaurants is cut to order here daily. Other than meat, restaurants are instructed to keep a day-and-a-half's supply of food on hand. Food orders are turned in by each restaurant early in the morning for processing that day and for delivery that night for the following day's business. [47] These request lists are processed by computer, which allocates orders to the bakery, the sauce area, and other sites.

Hamburger patties are cut. Soups, sauces, and salad dressings are mixed in large stainless steel vats. Salad and cole slaw makings are chopped. Pasta is precooked and poured into huge colanders that drain through floor grills. Liquor also passes through the Food Distribution Center. [48]

A pizza-making machine turns out thousands of seven-inch pizzas at two seconds a pizza — down from 11.9 seconds a pizza when they were made by hand.[49] There are machines that turn out crepes, meatballs, dumplings, and cookies — all watched over by people whose cooking skills consist of pressing buttons.[50]

The bakery makes around 190 items in addition to 21 specialty breads.

> Everything is standardized to assure success. A wall rack in this area, as in other areas of the center, holds plastic-covered recipes followed to the letter to produce consistently good products. . . . In fact employees who measure the ingredients for the bakery are cloistered away from the others to avoid mistakes. "They have a room where they do nothing but scale out ingredients — they're separate, so no one bothers them," [bakery manager Dominic] Robertiello said. Other workers do nothing but mix the ingredients; still others do nothing but finish baked goods.[51]

Visitors to Walt Disney World are not the only consumers of park food. Thousands of salaried and hourly wage workers must be fed daily. Disney managers claim that when employees — pressed from all directions by the public — step back stage for a break, they become guests themselves.

In 1986 the Disney food service operated eleven employee dining areas, hidden away under the Magic Kingdom and behind EPCOT walls.[52] Here cast members and hosts and hostesses can purchase highly subsidized meals in milieus designed to be relaxing rather than purely functional. This treatment of employees combined with a number of other corporate practices keeps the food service (and overall) job turnover rate under 20 percent.

In return for an agreement to abide by the "Disney look,"[53] employees are oriented at Disney University, sprinkled with pixie dust, then allocated directly to their first on-the-job training work site. Disney routinely rotates its long-term employees from job to job, which sometimes requires that they return to the university for further specialty training. It is a company practice to promote from within, so those with any intelligence and energy who find the Disney style congenial can foresee the possibility of moving up the ranks.

Disney also offers its workers in-house recreation opportunities — recreational parks and picnic areas with a swimming pool, tennis courts, and softball fields on Little Lake Bryant — financial and retirement planning assistance, reduced rate travel packages, various in-park discounts, and other benefits of employment.[54] There are family and other special events — including special menus at employee restaurants — and a "cast" newspaper-magazine.

Well, we've been computerized, paraded, and fed by these nice people. The fireworks are over. We've pretty much seen it all. I'm sure you're delighted. You're probably tired. I am — tired and a bit cranky. My back hurts. I've got a headache. It's time to wind things up and head for home.

19

Conclusion: Theses on Disney

They can be forgiven a certain amount of hubris because the laws of reality do not operate here.

—Jennifer Allen[1]

This has been a long day in the Vacation Kingdom — from the rush in the morning through the lines and rides to the late-night fireworks and lasers. This is my last night here this trip. I'm exhausted, trying to see everything one more time. While waiting in Chip and Dale for the courtesy car to come and give me a jump start, I'll take a brief look back.

Images float across my internal video screen. Sounds and smells slide through the soft Florida night in my head. As usual, I have been thoroughly entertained — amused and bemused by craft and whimsy. As usual, I have been thoroughly appalled by corporate ideology and the commodification of culture. As the Terminator says, "I'll be back."

The everyday life of an anthropologist is often weird. Whether or not one cares at all about the burning disciplinary issues and in-house arguments that purport to mark the institutionalized professional, the actual *doing* of anthropology — the being in the field part — is difficult to stop. Once you've turned yourself into a research tool, everything around you becomes culture, data, odd practice, magic, and example. Awash in curious movement and strange conversation, the normal world becomes mysterious and often ludicrous.

Having lived in rural Africa during various times of my life, I find have developed an informal diagnostic for capturing the strangeness of American culture. When confronted with a fake modular car phone, a microwavable "traditional Thanksgiving dinner in a pouch," or the pink Energizer rabbit, I ask myself, "How would I explain this to Emmanuel (a rural Cameroonian friend, forever seventeen years old)?" I can rarely figure out an answer to that question, but I know that when it occurs to me, I have seen or heard something odd. Recently I have been asking myself that question a lot — increasingly in situations those around me have come to take completely for granted.

Walt Disney World is full of such odd things. And although its marinade of nostalgia and sentiment is meant ostensibly to bespeak a kinder, gentler world (the violence in the cartoons aside), the producers have put us into "films" with a bit of an edge. Disney's forest, I think, is ultimately a dangerous one — both for its shape and for the seductions by which we are led to the gingerbread weenies at its core.

Let me try to summarize these woods with a short recap of the way in, through the surrounding valley, followed by a brief series of snapshots taken from above at different heights. Appropriately, this finale will be a little like the "speed rooms" at the end of Delta's Dreamflight.

Mickey, Meet Ludwig

Walt Disney World is to Disneyland as the *Grundrisse* is to Theses on Feuerbach — a behemoth of an entirely different scale but with an unfolded genetic connection. It's Mickey Mouse on steroids. Whereas Disneyland fills a couple of hundred acres and is surrounded by the tick-tack of hotels, motels, and other Orange County, California, effluvia — all out of Disney's direct control — Walt Disney World contains 27,433 acres of central Florida swamp and scrub. This property is about the same size as San Francisco and is twice as big as Manhattan. Merely to reach Main Street USA — the entrance to the Magic Kingdom in the northern part of the property — customers who cross Walt Disney World boundaries must undertake a 4 1/2-mile automobile ride to the parking lot, a tram ride to the Ticket and Transportation Center, and a monorail or ferry boat ride to the Magic Kingdom entrance. Including walking and line times, this liminal transition from outside to inside may take an hour. A child's question "Are we there yet?" cannot easily be answered.

Into this spot of nature, which was secretly purchased by dummy land companies in 1965 at an average price of less than $200 an acre, Disney has built four to seven theme parks (depending on how you count them), a bird sanctuary, ten resort hotels (as of mid-1991), a campground, a shopping village, and the attendant parking lots, roads, and waterways — the latter including a number of artificial lakes. Support buildings — office buildings, construction workshops, central storage facilities, waste treatment facilities, and the central energy plant — dot the scrub, hidden from visitors behind trees, camouflaged walls, and artificial berms and hillocks. Around 7,500 acres are set aside as a wilderness preserve, leaving at present over 16,000 acres for further development.

The flagship theme park at Walt Disney World is the Magic Kingdom, a larger version of Disneyland with essentially the same layout, rides, and theater shows; but those benighted few who think of Disneyland and Walt Disney World as interchangeable are, as we've seen, quite wrong.

Two-and-a-half miles southeast of the Magic Kingdom, hiding behind the great golf ball of Spaceship Earth, is EPCOT Center. If we think of EPCOT as a kind of permanent world's fair, we can think of its hybrid structure as forming one theme park. Like a world's fair, EPCOT has two very different constituents. Future World contains an industrial-technical-science display in pavilions sponsored by huge transnational corporations such as Exxon, AT&T, General Motors, and Kraft Foods. World Showcase, with ten national pavilions ranged around an artificial lake, presents iconic hints of various friendly nations. These presentations center around shops, architecture, and food, although most also have films, rides, or museums. When EPCOT Center was being built from 1979 to 1981, it was the largest construction project in the world.

River Country, a water park near the campground, and Discovery Island, a bird sanctuary administered in partnership with the state of Florida, have been in operation since the 1970s. In 1989 three more theme parks opened. The most extensive is the Disney-MGM Studios — a movie theme park in the art deco Hollywood style of the 1930s, which features a studio tour through Disney's new production facilities. Typhoon Lagoon, another water park, and a nightclub area near the Disney Village Marketplace called Pleasure Island fill out the current fare. Each of these parks opened in direct competition with an existing tourist attraction in the metropolitan Orlando area. Between the theme parks and the resort hotels — which together offer a full complement of land and water sports, shows, and food — Disney is trying to keep tourists on its property for their entire visit to central Florida.

The parks have been enormously successful. In 1988 turnstiles clicked over 26 million times, making Walt Disney World the most visited tourist site in the world other than Spain.

Why is it here, and what does it do? It exists in part because for pure business reasons, Walt Disney wanted to tap into the tourist dollar of Americans living east of the Mississippi River. The California park draws mostly from its immediate surroundings, relying on repeat visits by southern Californians and their visiting kin. Walt Disney originally envisioned a park somewhat like Disneyland — one built in a large metropolitan area that contained a large local constituency. He looked at St. Louis, Niagara Falls, and the Washington, D.C., area but soon realized that the major eastern population centers were in climates cold enough to make any park a seasonal operation.

Looking south for warmth, he was drawn to central Florida — first to Ocala and later to Orlando. The latter had three particular virtues. First, it was near the crossroads of a number of interstate highway trunk routes and the Florida Turnpike. The federal transportation system was already set up to funnel tourists from the Northeast on I-95, from the Midwest on I-75, and from the central-south on I-10. I-4 crossed Florida from Tampa Bay to Daytona Beach. The turnpike would bring patrons north from the West Palm Beach-Ft. Lauderdale-Miami megalopolis.

Second, there was a lot of scrub land southeast of Orlando that was used for little else besides hunting and the desultory pasturing of cattle. If it were done quickly and quietly, a large chunk of this land could be purchased at very low cost.

Third, in the mid-1960s Orlando was a city on the make — ready, like the rest of the state of Florida, to give away the farm in the interests of economic growth. Yet as many have since pointed out, Orlando and Orange and Osceola counties (in which Disney's property would sit) were not politically organized in a sophisticated enough fashion to deal with Disney sharpies.

Unable to control development around Disneyland and despairing especially about the lost revenue garnered by hostelries and restaurants outside park borders from customers drawn to the area through Disney's efforts, Walt Disney insisted on buying enough land to buffer his Florida project from a similar commercial claustrophobia. Such complete control was enhanced tremendously when the Florida state legislature designated the property as the Reedy Creek Improvement District with nearly full municipal powers.

The size of the property also required that Disney think big, because from a movie company with an ancillary amusement park, Disney had suddenly become a land development company as well. As acreage grew, so did Walt Disney's conception of what he called EPCOT — the Experimental Prototype Community of Tomorrow.

Walt had begun his career as a cartoonist. He had expanded into short animated films and had begun a movie company that, in spite of its share of difficulties, had become the most famous studio in the world. He had invented characters that had become U.S. icons. He had won Oscars and honorary degrees. In what would be the last few years of his life, Walt had come to think of himself as an educator, an urban planner, and a technological visionary. Images began to grow of a utopian city of thirty thousand people, perhaps covered by a retractable dome, in which the most modern experimental systems would be put to use to solve the problems of the cities.

The Magic Kingdom would be the magnet to draw people to his city. Future World would evolve into a high-tech industrial park from which ever-changing technologies would emerge. World Showcase would be the shopping mall and urban entertainment area, complete with international food. There would be housing, green belts, a monorail and people-mover transportation system, and sophisticated waste disposal and energy systems. Walt presented his EPCOT plan to the public on his television show shortly before he died on December 15, 1966: "It will be a community of tomorrow that will never be completed, but will always be introducing and testing and demonstrating new materials and systems. And EPCOT will always be a showcase to the world for the ingenuity and imagination of American free enterprise." [2]

With Walt Disney's death things changed. His brother Roy, along with the other corporate officers, decided to go ahead with EPCOT but not as Walt had envisioned it. Because of Florida state voting requirements, which would have given residents voting rights, the Company quickly decided to scrap the residential aspect of EPCOT. It would become a kind of permanent World's Fair rather than a utopian live-in city. Although many think of the Magic Kingdom as Walt Disney's World, EPCOT Center might more appropriately be called Roy Disney World. In the early 1990s, after a decade in which a series of greenmail episodes occurred that led to the hiring of Michael Eisner as CEO of the Walt Disney Company — bringing a return to the corporation's roots in the movies — we might think of the property as Michael Eisner World.

Let me now answer the general question, "What does Walt Disney World do?" I will do so by making a number of suggestions about what goes on there and how WDW articulates with the world outside its borders. These summary points are my "theses on Disney."

Thesis I. Walt Disney World Is a Money-Maker.

The most obvious source of revenue at the parks is admissions. At the entrances to the Magic Kingdom, EPCOT Center, and the Disney-MGM Studios, visitors are offered a choice of one-, four-, or five-day ticket packages. Although the initial outlay for any group that plans to spend more than one day in the parks is substantial, a prorated price for adult customers who stay in the parks during full operating hours for four or five days is not much more than $2 an hour. River Country, Discovery Island, Typhoon Lagoon, and Pleasure Island have separate admissions. Although not unreasonable for many visitors, Disney admissions do form an effective screen against the poor and the not so poor. This is part of Disney's utopian planning.

But the obvious is not the essence. Disney collects parking fees, fees for special programs, and royalties on sales of technological systems developed for Walt Disney World. Its major revenues at the parks, however, come from three other sources — hotels and restaurants, merchandising, and land development. Presently, the largest chunk of Walt Disney World revenues comes from its own on-site hotels and townhouses, payments from non-Disney hotels at the Hotel Plaza, and the numerous restaurants, clubs, and snack bars scattered throughout the property. Whatever else it is, Disney is a food and lodging company.

At its many shops and product stands, the Company sells everything from souvenirs and character merchandise to designer clothes and expensive specially crafted artifacts. From 1972 to 1983, merchandise sales rose from $29 million to $179 million. That's a lot of mouse ears.

Thesis II. Walt Disney World Generates Symbolic Capital for the Rest of Walt Disney Company's Enterprises.

As we know, Disney has interests other than Walt Disney World. In addition to its parks in California, Tokyo, and France, the company makes movies under its Walt Disney, Touchstone, and Hollywood labels; rereleases its animated classics (and has recently begun to sell them for home video systems); runs a cable television channel; leases its studios, equipment, and personnel for movie and television productions by others; and sells educational materials. As Ariel Dorfman and Armand Mattelart note in their excoriation of Disney comic books, the Company has a global reach.[3] Mickey Mouse is arguably the best-known character, human or otherwise, on earth.

Disney's array of products is cross-referential on a massive scale. Character merchandise points to movies. The parks point to merchandise. The television shows point to the parks. The educational materials point to the parks. And so it goes. Each advertises the others in the guise of simply presenting its own products.

The Company has managed to insinuate its characters, stories, and image as a good, clean, fun enterprise into the consciousness of millions around the earth. In doing so, it has become a U.S. icon — enough so that critics of the attempted buyouts in 1984 often accused the perpetrators of being un-American.

All of this good feeling generates revenues, and these revenues in turn become crucially dependent on this good feeling. Millions of visitors personally confront the Company each year at Walt Disney World. Depending on their experience at the property, each of those visitors may become further enmeshed in the web as a lifelong customer of Disney products or may be driven away. The show at Walt Disney World — the rides, the films, the hotel rooms, the food, and especially the cleanliness, orderliness, safety, and the comportment of the park's workers — all forms part of the ambience that generates real income. These elements make and re-create Disney's reputation — a reputation that in turn becomes symbolic capital in Pierre Bourdieu's sense. Disney's reputation for good, clean fun — what it calls family entertainment — brings people to the products from which real capital is generated. Walt Disney World is on the front lines of this campaign.

Thesis III. Walt Disney World Presents a Distillation of One Version of the United States and Its View of the World, a Version Both Mythical and Real.

The parks are constructed like sets of Chinese boxes. Each has an overriding theme but is subdivided into subsidiary parts, each with its own subtheme: Main Street USA, Adventureland, Frontierland, Liberty Square, Fantasyland, Tomorrowland, and Mickey's Starland in the Magic Kingdom; Future World and World Showcase in EPCOT; Hollywood Boulevard, the Backlot Annex, Lakeside Circle, the Backstage Studio Tour, and the Animation Tour at the Disney-MGM Studios. Each of these divisions is "themed" — presented in a consistent architectural, decorative, horticultural, musical, even olefactory tone with rides, shows, restaurants, scenery, and costumed characters coordinated to tell a consistent set of stories.

The structure is cinematic. Visitors are placed in the middle of scenes that unfold in a carefully choreographed manner as they move through them on foot or strapped into Disney's various ride vehicles. The stories within stories are both different and the same. Each tells its own tale; but together they tell metastories about the United States and the world, history and the future, nature, fantasy, and dreams. They are the tales of a secular Sun Belt culture that has appropriated and defanged Franklin, Lincoln, Twain, even Frederick Douglass, Susan B. Anthony, and Chief Joseph; that considers the earth to exist only for human — read American — purposes; and that understands the world as a set of theme parks. Culture is construed as spirit, colonialism and entrepreneurial violence as exotic zaniness, and the Other as child.

Thesis IV. Disney Is the Muse of Corporate America.

The Walt Disney Company speaks for itself at Walt Disney World, marketing its own products and protecting its symbolic capital by encapsulating its customers in seamlessly themed, safe entertainment. But Disney also speaks for the transnational corporations that have joined it — for a substantial fee — to sponsor pavilions, restaurants, and exhibits at the parks. From Toll House cookies and Kikkoman soy sauce to Exxon, AT&T, General Motors, Kraft Foods, and United Technologies, corporations join Disney in telling stories that are entertainingly consistent with their public relations purposes. As Mike Wallace puts it, Disney tells histories the corporations can live with. [4]

Culture and fantasy are timeless. History — in which Cro-Magnon man, Michelangelo, Da Vinci, and Lincoln play considerable parts — was pretty goofy. There were some problems, but they have been fixed by creative spirit. The present is not the result of the past but is the first step toward a future that will be wonderful and exciting if we dare to use our imaginations. The future is another "new frontier," to be lived in space or under the sea eating hydroponic food and surrounded by neon and black light — the Future as Graphics. It will present many "challenges," which we will meet if we entrust ourselves to the corporate scientists, engineers, technologists, and planners. After all, are we not having a good time in the technological utopia of Walt Disney World?

Thesis V. Walt Disney World Is an Epicenter of Decontextualization.

Disney tells its stories by inventing new cultural symbols and appropriating existing ones, decontextualizing them, and reinserting them into its own mythology. Benjamin Franklin and Mark Twain robots talk to each other about the American adventure, in which barely related iconic images are surrounded by the silences of untold historical stories.

Geography is mixed up. The Jungle Cruise in Adventureland connects the Amazon River to the Congo, the Nile, and the Irrawaddy without a break. In World Showcase, the Norway pavilion sits between China and Mexico. Minnie Mouse wanders the Japanese pavilion in her kimono. Leonardo da Vinci is invoked as AT&T's favorite Renaissance man. At the Kitchen Kabaret, Mae West becomes Kraft's Miss Cheese.

Walt Disney World is a bricolage writ large, charming but insidious. By pulling meanings out of their contexts and repackaging them in bounded informational packets, decontextualization makes it difficult for people to maintain a coherent understanding about what is going on. Meanings get all jumbled together — separate in that all are abstracted from their different environments and equal in that their packaging destroys any sense of scale by which they could be measured against each other. Differences are glossed over, and "differences that make a difference," as Gregory Bateson puts it, are neutralized. [5] Disconnected information passes in front of us at high speed. It seems, as the apocryphal phrase about bad history has it, "like one damn thing after another."

Thesis VI. Walt Disney World Is Postmodern.

Whatever Walt Disney's intent, Walt Disney World is a postmodern place — a locus of what Hal Foster has called a "postmodernism of reaction." [6] It is a seemingly endless mélange of discreet, bounded informational packets plopped down next to each other willy-nilly — Liberty next to

Fantasy, Japan next to Morocco. It is so rife with differences and strange borders that the very concept of difference is obliterated. Buildings in the Magic Kingdom contain multiple façades, creating a pastiche of vernacular evocations. EPCOT Center has the massive architecture of Future World and the touristic international iconography of World Showcase. The Disney-MGM Studios is exaggerated art deco Hollywood.

Joel Achenbach writes of "creeping surrealism,"[7] the general fear brought about by the manipulation of narrative and public discourse that nothing is real anymore. The tenor of postmodern times is such, he argues, that even when people *can* tell the difference between the real and the fake, increasingly they do not care. As long as we are amused, Neil Postman might say, it is enough.[8]

Frederic Jameson claims postmodern culture is characterized by a breakdown of the signifying chain — the relation that exists between the signifier and the signified.[9] This is a cognitive result brought on by the rapid and ubiquitous de- and recontextualization of symbols in mass-mediated culture. Cognitive overload sets in, and the referential function of normal language becomes shattered. We respond with what Jameson calls "a strange compensatory decorative exhiliration," which he likens to schizophrenia but which I think is more like a form of meditative bliss. Earlier I called it the bliss of commodity Zen.

Jameson uses Plato's idea of the simulacrum — the identical copy for which no original has ever existed — to describe the "pseudoevents" and spectacles of our time — a time "with a whole historically original consumer's appetite for a world transformed into sheer images of itself."[10] Jean Baudrillard chases the disappearance of referential reason through the "orders of simulacra" into what he calls the "hyperreal" — a world in which "illusion is no longer possible because the real is no longer possible."[11] For Baudrillard, reality has been effaced by the substitution of signs of the real for the real itself. A day spent looking at the fake oysters attached to the torii at the Japan Showcase, counting the vinyl leaves at the Swiss Family Island Treehouse, talking to people at Pleasure Island's Adventurers Club who turn out to be Disney characters, and wondering whether the bird sounds throughout are real or Memorex brings a "strange compensatory decorative exhiliration" indeed.

Thesis VII. Walt Disney World Presents a "Scholastic Program"
for the Naturalization of the Commodity Form.

The world we live in is a world of commodities. Not only our physical survival but our relations with other people and with ourselves are mediated increasingly by the commodity form. Whatever particular items or experiences we gather to build our daily lives, they all come to us more and more through the same process: They are available in, and only in, the market. We can't even do the simple rituals that bind us together without purchasing paraphernalia. The commodity form, assumed and unremarkable, is *the* taken-for-granted hegemonic truth of our times.

Antonio Gramsci describes hegemony as

the permeation throughout civil society . . . of an entire system of values, attitudes, beliefs, morality, etc., that is in one way or another supportive of the established order and the class interests that dominate it . . . to the extent that this prevailing consciousness is internalized by the broad mass, it becomes part of "common sense." . . . For hegemony to assert itself success fully in any society, therefore, it must operate in a dualistic manner: as a "general conception of life" for the masses and as a "scholastic programme." [12]

That is, we must be taught that it is good, reasonable, just, and natural that the means necessary for life are available only through the market. We must be taught the myth of commodity fetishism — that relations among people are to be seen as relations among things. And most important, we must be enmeshed in the field of commodities — a world of discrete packages and disconnected cultural forms, presented in swirls of cross-reference, timeless and fantastic, wherein we are to dwell and seek our salvation.

Walt Disney World sells itself. It sells other Disney products. It sells the messages of its corporate affiliates. But it also teaches us that dreams and experiences are for sale: We need merely give our proxies to the world of commodities and commercial cross-reference.

Thesis VIII. Postmodernism Is Isomorphic to the World of Commodities in Late Capitalism and Walt Disney World Exhibits This Connection.

Following Ernest Mandel, Frederic Jameson has argued that late — or postindustrial — capitalism is the most complete form of capitalism. [13] Under its regime, market relations have spread everywhere — colonizing every available niche in human life, including nature and the unconscious. The model is one of metastasis.

Postmodern cultural forms — in their endless proliferation, their ironic self-reference, their evanescence, and their intimate connection with commercial mass media — have an elective affinity with the field of commodities. They are reflections of each other, collectively sharing the same form.

Examples of this connection are rife at Walt Disney World. When Disney buys tons of sterilized dust from a California supplier to spread around the air-conditioned Haunted Mansion at night to give it the correct dinge, and when Mickey Mouse wears a Michael Eisner watch in the movie preview theater at the Disney-MGM Studios Backstage Tour, the world of commodities and the cultural form of postmodernism have meshed.

Thesis IX. Walt Disney World, Postmodernism,
and the World of Commodities Are Chaotic.

With its themes within themes within themes, Walt Disney World represents the replication of similar patterns at different scales that is characteristic of fractals.[14] Lakes and plazas act as Lorenz attractors. I merely suggest here that the world of commodities, postmodernism, and Walt Disney World can be represented as Mandlebrot sets.

Thesis X. Walt Disney World Is Beguiling, Infinitely Interesting, and Utopian.

The Disney parks are enormously entertaining. As Alexander Moore has suggested, they have become "playful pilgrimage sites" for people from all over the world.[15] The planning, craftwork, art and architecture, staging, and technological engineering are extraordinary. There is something at Walt Disney World to draw out the knowledge and experience of all but its youngest visitors.

But millions of visitors come there for other reasons as well. It is a pedestrian's world. We can walk the crooked streets, past the sculpted plants, into the shops and the various hidden, peaceful spaces without vehicular fear. And we can do so at night. It is clean. The staff is friendly, and, as if by osmosis, the other customers are civil.

The technology usually works — the computers, the air-conditioning, the communication and transportation systems, and the light and sound technology of the rides and shows. There are day-care centers, kennels, and extensive provisions for the disabled.

Walt Disney World acts as an antidote to the normal, everyday experiences of many of its middle-class guests. They need only submit to Disney's total control of the operation and to the commodification of their own experience. It's very seductive. Huxley would have recognized it.

Thesis XI. The Critics Have Only Interpreted Walt Disney World, in Various Ways; the Point, However, Is to Make It into a Museum.

Notes

Chapter 1

1. A. A. Milne, *Winnie-The-Pooh* (New York: Dell, 1926), p. 38. The woozles that Winnie-the-Pooh and Piglet were tracking turned out to be themselves: They were walking in circles.

2. The Walt Disney World management calls all of its visitors "guests" and its customer service employees "hosts" and "hostesses." To preserve some accuracy I will often call the "guests" visitors or customers.

3. Johann Wyss, *Swiss Family Robinson* (New York: Dell, 1960).

4. This is Richard Schickel's title for one of the best books on Walt Disney. See Richard Schickel, *The Disney Version: The Life, Times, Art and Commerce of Walt Disney* (New York: Touchstone Books, 1985 [original 1969]). I will use the phrase often to describe the Disney view of the world.

5. The world of commodities is chaotic in the sense of chaos theory. One of the characteristics of chaos is the replication of pattern at different levels of scale. With its continuous colonization of life's niches and interstices, the market insinuates its social relations into the smallest possible spaces. See James Gleick, *Chaos: Making a New Science* (New York: Penguin Books, 1987).

6. Among its other tasks, anthropology is the discipline that creates exotic descriptions of non-Western peoples. These peoples are often presented as "natural" people, or at least as closer to nature than industrial/technological man. Whether film, report, or monograph, anthropological products must appeal to the market. Nature must be skillfully "invented" and packaged for sale. Exoticism sells.

7. Neil Postman, *Amusing Ourselves to Death: Public Discourse in the Age of Show Business* (New York: Viking Penguin, 1985).

8. Joel Achenbach, "Reality to Be Cancelled?" *Tropic Magazine, Miami Herald*, December 13, 1987. pp. 18-21.

9. This passage is quoted in Emily Martin, *The Woman in the Body: A Cultural Analysis of Reproduction* (Boston: Beacon Press, 1987), p. 23. It is found in Antonio Gramsci, "Notes on Italian History," in Quintin Hoare and Geoffrey Nowell Smith, eds., *Selections from the Prison Notebooks of Antonio Gramsci* (London: Lawrence and Wishart, 1971), pp. 103-104.

10. One example is the use of regional culture in television advertisements to sell commodities. We might also note the increasingly ironic depiction of masculinity in "light" beer commercials.

11. California's Disneyland has a very midwestern tone, reflecting an idealized ambience of Disney's midwestern youth. Florida's WDW brings southern California to the south. So far, Disney's parks are a region behind.

12. Many of the pavilions, incidentally, present stories about physical and geological evolution.

13. Langdon Winner, *The Whale and the Reactor: A Search for Limits in an Age of High Technology* (Chicago: University of Chicago Press, 1986), pp. 54-58.

14. Steve Birnbaum, *Steve Birnbaum Brings You the Best of Walt Disney World* (New York: Houghton Mifflin, 1985, 1988, 1989, 1990). Each of these was published the year before the date on its cover; for example, the 1986 guide was published in 1985. I will reference the Birnbaum volumes by publishing date.

Chapter 2

1. Dick Schaap, "Culture Shock: Williamsburg and Disney World, Back to Back," *New York Times*, September 28, 1975, section 10, p. 12.

2. For an early analysis of Tokyo Disneyland, see Mary Yoko Brannen, "'Bwana Mickey': Constructing Cultural Consumption at Tokyo Disneyland," n.d. Revised version of paper of the same title read at the session "Magic Kingdoms: The Reality of Illusion," American Anthropological Association Annual Meeting, Washington, D.C., November 15-19, 1989.

3. This phrase is taken from Leiss's book of the same name. He argues that the orientation toward justifiable domination of humans over nature has been a central and dangerous theme in Western history. See William Leiss, *The Domination of Nature* (Boston: Beacon Press, 1974).

4. Maria-Lydia Spinelli (personal communication) reminds me that this is what fascism boasted about: a clean body and a clean mind, technological progress, order, and cleanliness.

5. By symbolic capital, Bourdieu refers to publicly valued symbols of such things as honor, truth, justice, morality, and the like, which may be used by those who can legitimately claim them to generate real capital. See Pierre Bourdieu, *Outline of a Theory of Practice* (Cambridge: Cambridge University Press, 1977).

6. Weber used this phrase to describe historical situations in which two human practices, systems, or processes reinforced each other, not out of necessity or organic connection but because at the time they fit together in some way. His classic example was the sixteenth- and seventeenth-century fit between what he called "the Spirit of Capitalism" and "the Protestant Ethic," each of which, he claimed, reinforced the other.

7. See Raymond Williams, *Keywords: A Vocabulary of Culture and Society*, revised edition (London: Oxford University Press, 1976), for a short history of the different meanings of culture. For extended analyses, see his *Culture and Society: 1780-1950* (New York: Columbia University Press, 1983), and *The Sociology of Culture* (New York: Schocken, 1982).

8. These characteristics are taken from Roger Keesing, *Cultural Anthropology: A Contemporary Perspective*, 2nd edition (New York: Holt, Rinehart, Winston, 1981).

9. Much of the following section is drawn from Peter Berger and Thomas Luckmann, *The Social Construction of Reality: A Treatise in the Sociology of Knowledge* (New York: Doubleday, 1966).

10. As the work of Noam Chomsky and Edward Herman has shown us over and over again, *political* and *economic* boundaries *are* protected by a positive conspiracy. My analysis is meant to be consistent with theirs.

11. Leo Marx, *The Machine in the Garden: Technology and the Pastoral Ideal in America* (New York: Oxford University Press, 1964).

12. It is in part the unexceptionable naturalness of such creatures that Dorfman and Mattelart object to in their denunciation of the Disney message to Chile. See Ariel Dorfman and Armand Mattelart, *How to Read Donald Duck: Imperialist Ideology in the Disney Comic* (New York: International General, 1984).

Chapter 3

1. Guy Debord, *The Society of the Spectacle* (Detroit: Black and Red, 1983), p. 51.

2. Quoted in Godfrey Hodgson, *America in Our Time: From World War II to Nixon — What Happened and Why* (New York: Vintage, 1976), p. 13.

3. See Robert Nisbet, *History of the Idea of Progress* (New York: Basic Books, 1980), especially chapter 9.

4. This idea, which will be discussed more later, was first suggested to me in conversation by Howard Kaminsky.

5. For discussion of the U.S. system of manufacture, see H. J. Habakkuk, *American and British Technology in the Nineteenth Century* (Cambridge: Cambridge University Press, 1962). Also see Merritt Roe Smith, *Harpers Ferry Armory and the New Technology: The Challenge of Change* (Ithaca, N.Y.: Cornell University Press, 1977). For a capsule summary of early- to mid-nineteenth-century developments in the United States, see Richard D. Brown, *Modernization: The Transformation of American Life, 1600-1865* (New York: Hill and Wang, 1976).

6. Chapter XXV of *The Education of Henry Adams* (Boston: Houghton Mifflin, 1961 [1918]).

7. Cecelia Tichi, *Shifting Gears: Technology, Literature, Culture in Modernist America* (Chapel Hill: University of North Carolina Press, 1987).

8. For Ford and Barton, see "Culture Heroes: Ford, Barton, Ruth," in Warren I. Sussman, *Culture as History: The Transformation of American Society in the Twentieth Century* (New York: Pantheon, 1973).

9. C. B. McPherson, *The Political Theory of Possessive Individualism* (London: Oxford University Press, 1962).

10. See Stuart Ewen, *Captains of Consciousness* (New York: McGraw-Hill, 1976).

11. Karl Polanyi, *Great Transformation: The Political and Economic Origin of Our Time* (Boston: Beacon Press, 1957).

12. Marshall Sahlins, *Culture and Practical Reason* (Chicago: University of Chicago Press, 1977).

13. Max Weber, *The Protestant Ethic and the Spirit of Capitalism* (New York: Charles Scribner and Sons, 1958). See also Anthony Giddens, *Capitalism and Modern Social Theory: An Analysis of the Writings of Marx, Durkheim and Weber* (Cambridge: Cambridge University Press, 1973).

14. *The Autobiography of Benjamin Franklin* (New York: The Modern Library, 1981), p. 148. Thanks to Leo Marx for alerting me to this.

15. See Michael Kammen, *People of Paradox: An Inquiry Concerning the Origins of American Civilization* (London: Oxford University Press, 1980).

16. Adam Smith, *The Wealth of Nations* (New York: Penguin, 1970 [1776]).

17. Adam Smith, *The Theory of Moral Sentiments* (Indianapolis: Liberty Fund, 1977 [1789]).

18 This point is made by Robert Nisbet in his *History of the Idea of Progress* (New York: Basic Books, 1980), pp. 187ff.

19. See Jeremy Bentham, *Introduction to the Principles of Morals and Legislation* (New York: Hafner, 1948 [1789]).

20. Garry Wills, *Inventing America: Jefferson's Declaration of Independence* (New York: Random House, 1978).

21. For this and the following point, I am indebted to Michael D. Bayles and Kenneth Henley, eds., *Right Conduct: Theories and Applications* (New York: Random House, 1983).

22. John Stuart Mill, *Utilitarianism* (New York: Bobbs Merrill, 1957 [1861]).

23. Henry D. Thoreau, *Walden and Other Writings* (New York: Bantam, 1981).

24. Daniel Bell, *The Cultural Contradictions of Capitalism* (New York: Basic Books, 1976).

25. *Ibid.*, pp. xvi-xvii.

26. See Tichi, *Shifting Gears*, pp. 75-96.

27. See especially Richard Edwards, *Contested Terrain: The Transformation of the Workplace in the Twentieth Century* (New York: Basic Books, 1979).

28. Ford did not introduce consumer financing until 1928, nine years after General Motors had started its consumer financing subsidiary, the General Motors Acceptance Corporation. Thanks to Joyce Shaw Peterson for this information. See also her *American Automobile Workers, 1900-1933* (Albany: SUNY Press, 1987).

29. This label for pop culture design styles of the 1950s is the title phrase of Thomas Hine, *Populuxe* (New York: Knopf, 1986).

30. John Kenneth Galbraith, *The Affluent Society* (New York: Houghton Mifflin, 1976).

31. See David J. Riesman et al., *The Lonely Crowd: A Study of the Changing American Character* (New Haven: Yale University Press, 1973); Paul Goodman, *Growing Up Absurd* (New York: Random House, 1962); Herbert Marcuse, *One-Dimensional Man* (Boston: Beacon Press, 1966); and Michael Harrington, *The Other America* (New York: Penguin, 1971).

32. See Christopher Lasch, *The Culture of Narcissism: American Life in an Age of Diminishing Expectations* (New York: Norton, 1979); Richard Sennett, *The Fall of Public Man* (New York: Random House, 1977); Marvin Harris, *America Now* (New York: Simon and Schuster, 1981); and Bell, *The Cultural Contradictions of Capitalism.*

33. Jules Henry, *Culture Against Man* (New York: Vintage, 1963).

34. In a personal communication Maria-Lydia Spinelli suggests, "In the context of a crisis of efficacy and the breakdown of cooperative networks and extended family networks due to high mobility, consumption of certain luxuries becomes a need, not just a 'psychotic' need but a real one. Soma is a pacifier, commodities are not; they often make one's life easier and more livable. Granted, it snowballs, but I do not know how to live without a car and the concomitant expenses that go with it in southern California. I like commodities, not because they give me a false sense of security but because they make life more comfortable. Also they are vehicles of

expressiveness and send messages about identity (status included). Overlooking some of these messages is cutting oneself out of a major aspect of life."

35. See Tichi, *Shifting Gears*.

36. Aldous Huxley, *Brave New World Revisited* (New York: Harper and Row, 1965).

37. Neil Postman, *Amusing Ourselves to Death: Public Discourse in the Age of Show Business* (New York: Viking Penguin, 1985), p. 3.

38. *Ibid.*, p. 3.

39. *Ibid.*, p. 65.

40. *Ibid.*, p. 76.

41. *Ibid.*

42. *Ibid.*, p. 87.

43. *Ibid.*, p. 112.

44. *Ibid.*, p. 110. *The Christian Science Monitor*, a newspaper that has the audacity to print long, in-depth, analytical stories, has only a little over 200,000 paid subscribers.

45. Joshua Meyrowitz, *No Sense of Place: The Impact of Electronic Media on Social Behavior* (New York: Oxford University Press, 1985).

46. *Ibid.*, p. 38.

47. *Ibid.*, p. 41.

48. Erving Goffman, *The Presentation of Self in Everyday Life* (New York: Doubleday Anchor, 1959).

49. Meyrowitz, *No Sense of Place*, p. 99.

50. The dramatic enactments of social life are central to the thought of Kenneth Burke and Hugh D. Duncan. See Burke's *Language as Symbolic Action: Essays on Life, Literature and Methodology* (Berkeley: University of California Press, 1966), and *A Rhetoric of Motives* (Berkeley: University of California Press, 1969), and Duncan's *Communication and Social Order* (New York: Transactions Publications, 1985). Thanks to Charles Elkins for leading me to Burke and Duncan.

51. Meyrowitz, *No Sense of Place*, p. 79.

52. As Elaine Rapping argues in *The Looking Glass World of Nonfiction TV* (Boston: South End Press, 1987), these stories are told to us by newscasters who act as if they were our friends in a community they actually cared about.

53. Cited in Richard Reeves, *American Journey* (New York: Simon and Schuster, 1982), p. 240.

54. *Ibid.*, p. 240.

55. Meyrowitz, *No Sense of Place*, p. 87.

56. *Ibid.*, p. 85.

57. *Ibid.*, p. 87.

58. *Ibid.*, pp. 118ff.

59. Robert Bellah, Richard Madsen, William M. Sullivan, Ann Swidler, and Steven M. Tipton, *Habits of the Heart: Individualism and Commitment in American Life* (New York: Harper and Row, 1985).

60. *Ibid.*, pp. 152-155.

Chapter 4

1. Mike Wallace, "Mickey Mouse History: Portraying the Past at Disney World," *Radical History Review* 32 (1985), pp. 33-57. This quote is found on p. 34.

2. *Ibid.*, pp. 35-36.

3. This refers to the epigraph for Chapter 2.

4. Wallace, "Mickey Mouse History," p. 34.

5. As are Future World and World Showcase at EPCOT Center. The latter is obviously divided into lands, each of which represents itself in terms of a particular orientation to its own history. The former expands geography considerably, with its Spaceship Earth, its Land and Horizons, and its World (of Motion) and Universe (of Energy). Through these one Journeys (into Imagination) and sees Wonders (of Life). The Magic Kingdom represents time as space, whereas World Showcase often codes space in terms of time. One is reminded here of the central conceit in David Lowenthal's *The Past Is a Foreign Country* (Cambridge: Cambridge University Press, 1986).

6. For a discussion of some of the important issues contained in a postmodern geography, see Edward Soja, *Postmodern Geographies* (London: Verso, 1989).

7. Wallace, "Mickey Mouse History," p. 33.

8. See Hayden White, "The Historical Text as Literary Artifact," *Clio* 3:3 (1974), pp. 277-303, reprinted in Hazard Adams and Larry Searle, eds., *Critical Theory Since 1965* (Tallahassee: Florida State University Press, 1986), pp. 395-407. This quote is taken from p. 396.

9. *Ibid.*, p. 397.

10. *Ibid.* In discussing "the constructive imagination," White notes, "The late R. G. Collingwood insisted that the historian was above all a story teller."

11. *Ibid.*

12. Clifford Geertz, "Blurred Genres: The Refiguration of Social Thought," *The American Scholar* 29:2 (Spring 1980), pp. 165-182, reprinted in Geertz, *Local Knowledge: Further Essays in Interpretive Anthropology* (New York: Basic Books, 1983), pp. 19-35.

13. Wallace, "Mickey Mouse History," p. 35.

14. The present discussion of the Disney version of history, then, begins with Liberty Square, although one of Liberty Square's attractions — the Haunted Mansion — will be left to the section on fantasy. Let me pause once more to reiterate my debt to Steve Birnbaum's guides to WDW. Perhaps one has to be a bit obsessed by the place to understand how much information is crammed into these guides and how much work it must have taken to gather it. The guides are models of descriptive completeness.

15. *Walt Disney World* (The Walt Disney Company, 1986), p. 46. There are two editions of this commemorative book, one published in 1986 and a later one published with no date. I will refer to the former as *Walt Disney World* (1) and to the latter as *Walt Disney World* (2).

16. The Disney *Guide Book* puts the keelboats and the riverboat into Liberty Square, although both fit more appropriately into Frontierland. In a limited space, the staging areas have to fit somewhere.

17. Both the South and the farmers show up in the film at the Hall of Presidents, but they are represented as antagonists to the domination of northern urban capital and federal authority.

18. See Gary B. Nash, *The Urban Crucible: The Northern Seaports and the Origins of the American Revolution*, abridged edition (Cambridge, Mass.: Harvard University Press, 1986).

19. Marylin Springer, *Frommer's 1987-1988 Guide to Orlando, Disney World and EPCOT* (New York: Prentice-Hall, 1987).

20. The Americana shop at the American Adventure in World Showcase is called by the upscale name Heritage Manor.

21. See *Walt Disney World* (2), p. 47.

22. *Ibid.*, p. 48.

23. Steve Birnbaum, *Steve Birnbaum Brings You the Best of Walt Disney World* (New York: Houghton Mifflin, 1988), p. 89. The Birnbaum volumes will be listed by date of publication.

24. The others are King Stefan's Banquet Hall in Fantasyland and Tony's Town Square Restaurant on Main Street USA. Tony's is the place where Lady and the Tramp ate their famous spaghetti dinner.

25. The number is recorded in Birnbaum, *Steve Birnbaum*, 1988, p. 89.

26. Wallace, "Mickey Mouse History," p. 49. Let me reiterate a point made earlier in this chapter. The difference between "real" and "false" history is deeply problematic. History of any sort is an imaginative discourse built out of some subset of available information, shaped by one or more available literary tropes, and presented as a gambit motivated by conditions contemporaneous to its invention. Thus, there is thus no essentialist history to be "killed." Disney's histories are no more guilty of this capital crime than those of Gore Vidal, Carl Sandberg, or, for that matter, Henry Steele Commager and William Appleman Williams. What *is* important is to attend to the ideological metathemes that motivate a particular history. Disney's presentation of history as bricolage and commodified nostalgia stifles voices and suppresses conflict. This domestication of history, rather than the truth of any particular historical story, is something for us to notice. We notice Disney's ploys by paying attention to particular pieces of Distory.

27. For an excellent discussion of the political assumptions held by the document's creators and of the struggles through which it was made, see Gary Wills, *Inventing America: Jefferson's Declaration of Independence* (New York: Vintage Books, 1978).

28. Lincoln's words, here and elsewhere, are read by Royal Dano, who sounds a lot like Walter Brennan.

29. This theme is repeated throughout EPCOT Center, especially at the American Adventure and the Universe of Energy. As we shall see, it is grafted onto the larger, ubiquitous message about "meeting the challenges of the future."

30. Until the mid-1980s, the audience was known to snicker when Richard M. Nixon's name was called. By 1990 he had been rehabilitated, and his introduction passed without comment. See Joseph Lelyveld, "Disney's Hall of Presidents Not '76 Politics," *New York Times*, March 16, 1976, section 25, p. 1.

31. Audioanimatronic engineering has come a long way. By the time the Hall of Presidents was built, pneumatic and hydraulic systems had replaced cam-and-lever joints, giving the figures a good deal of flexibility. Vinyl plastic skin stretched over polyester resin and fiberglass skulls made the heads look uncannily human. In "The Walt Disney Robot Dramas," *The Yale Review* 66:2 (December 1976), pp. 223-236, James H. Bierman notes the following. (This quote is taken from p. 233.) "What really made the development of the figures possible was the invention of sound readers governing each valve which could respond to a computer-generated impulse that remotely controlled their movements. The thirty-two-channel magnetic tape which stores the show's information is capable of cataloguing over 64,000 pieces of information governing less than a quarter of a second of the show's action in ten

inches of tape. As a result the synchronization of sound, music, dialogue, lighting, and any other stage effects can be dependably perpetuated automatically. Human error is eliminated in audioanimatronic dramas."

32. In a series of exit interviews, Joseph Lelyveld reports in "Disney's Hall of Presidents" that "there was not a single person who declared it to be anything but inspiring." When he asked the same people about the then current (1976) presidential campaign, however, he found that "these emotional cross currents — a yearning to believe in Presidents along with a mistrust of those who seek the office — emerged in erratic counterpoint in most of the interviews."

33. *Walt Disney World* (1), p. 39.

34. Bald men who do not want to be part of the show might wish to ask for a seat in the smoking section in the balcony. A bald customer is always placed at the center table on the main floor, and his head is be used as a prop during the revue.

35. *Walt Disney World* (2), p. 38.

36. Birnbaum, *Steve Birnbaum*, 1989, p. 88.

37. The show host greets us with "Howdy, folks," to which we are to respond, "howdy." One attendant told the crowd in exasperation, "Folks, I don't write 'em. I just tell 'em — all day long." One wonders who wrote *those* lines.

38. Birnbaum, *Steve Birnbaum*, 1989, p. 88.

39. WDW's version of Splash Mountain will open between Pirates of the Caribbean and Big Thunder Mountain Railroad in 1992.

40. Incidentally, Cinderella's Castle is also 180 feet tall.

41. *Walt Disney World* (1), p. 41, specifies 630 tons of steel and 9,000 gallons of paint. I don't know why the discrepancy exists.

42. Birnbaum, *Steve Birnbaum*, 1990, p. 92.

43. Birnbaum, *Steve Birnbaum*, 1989, p. 90.

44. Actually, for this ride as well as for Space Mountain, Disney uses height as an index for age. Potential riders must be taller than the bottom of a sign telling them they must be taller than the bottom of the sign. I don't know how Disney handles "little people."

45. Along with the sternwheeler riverboat, WDW has two sidewheelers. As of 1983 the *Ports-O-Call* was still running on Bay Lake, powered by a walking beam steam engine. The *Southern Seas* had been converted to a diesel electric drive and renamed *Southern Belle*. See David Sarlin, "Disney World Sidewheelers," *Live Steam* (August 1983), p. 27.

46. Birnbaum, *Steve Birnbaum*, 1989, p. 89.

47. Throughout WDW there are signs that label trees, shrubs, and spice plants. It is a horticulturalist's delight. One of the two special programs designed for adults (the other is an art program that focusses on World Showcase) is a half-day horticultural program.

48. Passenger launches ply the waters between the Fort Wilderness dock, Discovery Island, the Contemporary Hotel, and the Magic Kingdom.

49. Birnbaum, *Steve Birnbaum*, 1989, p. 182.

50. *Walt Disney World* (2), p. 151.

51. *Ibid.*, p. 149.

52. The logo of which is Mickey's head with a "D" in the big circle-face and with two smaller circles for ears.

53. Birnbaum, *Steve Birnbaum*, 1989, p. 184.

54. *Ibid.*, pp. 184-185.

55. Every place and event at WDW must have a name; otherwise, apparently, it does not exist. It is a nominalist's (or a Parkinsonian's) heaven.

56. Wallace, "Mickey Mouse History," p. 52.

57. *Ibid.*, p. 38.

58. *Ibid.*.

59. *Ibid.*, p. 39.

60. James H. Bierman describes two earlier versions of this show in "The Walt Disney Robot Dramas." On p. 231, he writes, "The directors of W.E.D. Enterprises claim the . . . superiority of their actors to human ones. Not only do robots never forget a line or miss a cue, but the casting is always perfect. Performances are developed with a precision and control which the directors of living actors could never experience."

61. We note here that Father mediates between the family and the audience. He is the only one who speaks to us. Perhaps Father knows best.

62. For a counterargument about the liberating capabilities of domestic electronic labor-saving devices, see especially Susan Strasser, *Never Done: A History of American Housework* (New York: Pantheon, 1982).

63. At least it's in the Pacific Time Zone.

64. One wonders how these lines about choice now play to the self-designated "pro-lifers." Here is a nice conservative contradiction.

Chapter 5

1. Mike Wallace, "Mickey Mouse History: Portraying the Past at Disney World," *Radical History Review* 32 (1985), pp. 35-57. This quote is found on p. 49.

2. *Ibid.*, p. 43.

3. A Kodak spokesman cited by Wallace remarks, "You might entrance a teenager today, but tomorrow he's going to invest his money in Kodak stock." See *ibid.*, p. 43.

4. A General Electric spokesman noted, "The Disney organization is absolutely superb in interpreting our company dramatically, memorably, and favorably to the public. See *ibid.*, p. 43.

5. Steve Birnbaum, *Steve Birnbaum Brings You the Best of Walt Disney World* (New York: Houghton Mifflin, 1989), p. 120. The Birnbaum volumes will be referenced by year of publication.

6. Birnbaum, *Steve Birnbaum*, 1990, p. 119.

7. Birnbaum, *Steve Birnbaum*, 1989, p. 119.

8. Robert Nisbet has bemoaned the demise of the idea of progress. As show after show at WDW tells us, however, this idea has by no means died: It has merely retired to central Florida. See Robert Nisbet, *History of the Idea of Progress* (New York: Basic Books, 1979).

9. *Walt Disney World* (The Walt Disney Company, n.d.), p. 66; hereafter *Walt Disney World* (2).

10. Birnbaum, *Steve Birnbaum*, 1989, p. 120.

11. *Ibid.*

12. *Ibid.*

13. My colleague Barbara Watts, a historian of Renaissance art, tells me that whereas Leonardo was left-handed, Michelangelo was probably not.

14. Birnbaum, *Steve Birnbaum*, 1989, p. 121.

15. *Ibid.*, p. 127.

16. For a full list of the makes and models of the vintage automobiles shown along this ride, see Ward Kimball, "Disney's 'World of Motion,'" *Horseless Carriage Gazette* (September-October 1982), pp. 34-38.

17. Hector St. John de Crevecoeur, "Letter III," in *Letters from an American Farmer* (London: Dent, 1971 [1782]), pp. 39-55. Cited in Richard J. Ellis and Alun Munslow, "Narrative, Myth and the Turner Thesis," *Journal of American Culture* 9:2 (Summer 1986), pp. 9-16. This quote is from page 13.

18. Ellis and Munslow, *ibid.*, p. 15.

19. For a sampling of these understandings, see Leo Marx, *The Machine in the Garden: Technology and the Pastoral Ideal in America* (New York: Oxford University Press, 1964); and Sacvan Bercovitch, *American Jeremiad* (Madison: University of Wisconsin Press, 1979). For a counterimage to the empty wilderness of the early seventeenth-century United States, see William Cronon, *Changes in the Land: Indians, Colonists and the Ecology of New England* (New York: Hill and Wang, 1983).

20. See Gary Wills, *Inventing America: Jefferson's Declaration of Independence* (New York: Random House, 1979).

21. Seymour Martin Lipset, *The First New Nation: The United States in Historical and Comparative Perspective* (New York: Norton, 1979).

22. David M. Potter, *People of Plenty: Economic Abundance and the American Character* (Chicago: University of Chicago Press, 1954).

23. Frederick Jackson Turner, "The Significance of the Frontier in American History." Reprinted in *F. J. Turner, Frontier and Section*, edited by R. A. Billington (Englewood Cliffs, N.J.: Prentice-Hall, 1961). My page citations here are taken from Ellis and Munslow, "Narrative, Myth and the Turner Thesis." This quote is found on p. 10.

24. Ellis and Munslow, *ibid.*

25. *Ibid.*, p. 11.

26. *Ibid.*, p. 14.

27. *Ibid.*

28. David M. Johnson, "Disney World as Structure and Symbol: Re-Creation of the American Experience," *Journal of Popular Culture* 15(1) (1981), pp. 157-165. This quote is found on p. 157.

29. Birnbaum, *Steve Birnbaum*, 1989, p. 100.

30. *Walt Disney World* (2), p. 98.

31. Wallace, "Mickey Mouse History," p. 51.

32. *Ibid.*

33. Andrea Stulman Dennett, "A Postmodern Look at EPCOT's American Adventure," *Journal of American Culture*, pp. 47-53. This quote is found on p. 50.

34. As of early 1991, this display had been replaced by a show on quilting.

35. The eleven quotes follow. Corporate Guest Affairs has printed them for distribution (something I discovered after recording them myself).

America has been settled by people of all nations. All nations may claim her for their own. We are not a narrow tribe of men. . . . No, our blood is as the flood of the Amazon, made up of a thousand noble currents all pouring into one. . . . We are not a nation so much as a world.

- Herman Melville

You who have been born in America, I wish I could make you understand what it is like not to be an American — not to have been an American all our life — and then suddenly with the words of a man in flowing robes to be one. For that moment and forever after. One moment you belong with your fathers to a million dead yesterdays. The next you belong to America with a million unborn tomorrows.

- George Magar Mardikian

No matter what accomplishments you make, somebody helps you.

- Althea Gibson

Our way of living together in America is a strong but delicate fabric. It is made up of many threads. It has been woven over many centuries by the patience and sacrifice of countless liberty-loving men and women.

- Wendell Lewis Willkie

What after all has maintained the human race on this old globe despite all the calamities of nature and all the tragic failures of mankind, if not the faith in new possibilities and courage to advocate them.

- Jane Addams

Our greatest natural resource is the minds of our children.

- Walter Elias Disney

What kind of man would live where there is no daring? I don't believe in taking foolish chances, but nothing can be accomplished without taking any chance at all.

- Charles Augustus Lindberg

Throughout the centuries there were men who took first steps down new roads armed with nothing but their own vision.

- Ayn Rand

Bring me men to match my mountains. Bring me men to match my plains. Men with empires in their purpose. And new ideas in their brains.

- Sam Walter Foss

There are those, I know, who will reply that the liberation of humanity, the freedom of man and mind, is nothing but a dream. . . . They are right. It is the American dream.

- Archibald MacLeish

I think the true discovery of America is before us. I think the true fulfillment of our spirit, of our people, of our mighty and immortal land is yet to come.

- Thomas Wolfe

36. So Birnbaum, (*Steve Birnbaum*, 1989, p. 144) quotes a Disney designer.

37. *Ibid.*, pp. 144-145.

38. According to Dennett, "A Postmodern Look," p. 50, Franklin and Twain were to be joined by Will Rogers as the Spirit of the Twentieth Century, but survey research in several high schools suggested that nobody knew who Will Rogers was. Maybe they should have used Dick Clark.

39. It seems Twain has read the Melville quote in the rotunda.

40. For a full text of the speech see Dee Brown, *Bury My Heart at Wounded Knee: An Indian History of the American West* (New York: Holt, Rinehart and Winston, 1970), pp. 328-329.

41. Wallace, "Mickey Mouse History," p. 54.

42. *Ibid.*, p. 50.

43. This song is played at the entrance to EPCOT Center near Spaceship Earth. It is EPCOT's theme song.

44. See Steve Warren, "Disney: No Future for Gays — or Anyone," *Bay Area Reporter*, March 31, 1983.

45. The people and events shown are given in an EPCOT Resource Center printout (and in my own notes). The list replicated here is published in Dennett, "A Postmodern Look," p. 51. The full list is as follows: Iwo Jima flag raising, MacArthur signing peace treaty, end of war celebration in New York City, Ike and Mamie Eisenhower, Jackie Robinson (baseball player), Bob Hope in Korea, Marilyn Monroe in Korea, Eleanor Roosevelt and U.N. Building, polio poster child, Dr. Jonas Salk, Frank Sinatra, Louis Armstrong, Elvis Presley, Arthur Fiedler, Albert Einstein at blackboard, Norman Rockwell self-portrait, Walt Disney, John Wayne, Lucille Ball, Margaret Mead, Billie Jean King, John F. Kennedy delivering a speech, caisson on Pennsylvania Avenue, John Kennedy, Jr.'s, final salute, Martin Luther King, Coretta King in funeral procession, "Eagle" heading toward the moon, Astronaut with flag and lunar lander on moon's surface, Houston control room celebration, Walter Cronkite, U.S. helicopter taking off in Vietnam, Woodstock overview, Lee Trevino, Cassius Clay (1960 Olympics), and U.S. hockey victory (1980 Olympics).

46. See David Arnold, "No Room at EPCOT for Them or Their War," *Boston Globe*, March 19, 1983.

47. Wallace, "Mickey Mouse History," p. 52.

Chapter 6

1. This quote is cited in Edward L. Prizer, "The Disney Era in Florida," *Orlando-Land* (October 1981), p. 33.

2. Richard Schickel, *The Disney Version: The Life, Times, Art, and Commerce of Walt Disney* (New York: Simon and Schuster, 1968), p. 358.

3. *Sleeping Beauty* (1959), *101 Dalmatians* (1961), *The Sword in the Stone* (1963), and *The Jungle Book* (1967) were the last major animated features produced during the Walt Disney years. This period saw the rise of live action Disney, with such films as *The Shaggy Dog* (1959), *Kidnapped* (1960), *Pollyanna* (1960), *Swiss Family Robinson* (1960), *The Absent-Minded Professor* (1961), *The Parent Trap* (1961), and *Son of Flubber* (1963). 1964 brought the blockbuster *Mary Poppins*. Disneyland was a huge financial success.

4. Cited in Prizer, "The Disney Era," p. 33.

5. *Ibid.* Walker said the search became especially active after Disney got an airplane in 1963. One can imagine the search being intertwined with Disney's new toy.

6. John Rutherford, "What They Say About Walt Disney World," *Orlando-Land* (October 1981), p. S-27.

7. Cited in Prizer, "The Disney Era," p. 33.

8. John Rothchild, *Up for Grabs: A Trip Through Time and Space in the Sunshine State* (New York: Penguin, 1985).

9. This and much of what follows is reported in Leonard E. Zehnder, *Florida's Disney World: Promises and Problems (FDW)* (Tallahassee, Florida: The Peninsular Publishing Company, 1975). *FDW* includes an invaluable compilation of newspaper reports covering Disney's first ten years in Florida. Many of Zehnder's materials duplicate those available in the Orlando Public Library. When such is the case, I will also cite *FDW*. Some of this story is also told in Bob Thomas, *Walt Disney: An American Original* (New York: Pocket Books, 1976), pp. 358-362.

10. Prizer, "The Disney Era," p. 34.

11. *Ibid.*

12. See also "Disney Creates a Magic Kingdom in Orlando," *Florida Trend* (June 1983), p. 5C. As of 1983 there were still four scattered pieces of property — thirty acres in all — owned by heirs of the Mungar sales.

13. Rutherford, "What They Say About Walt Disney World," p. S-21.

14. Zehnder, *FDW*, p. 7.

15. Charles Wadsworth, "Hush Puppies," *Orlando Sentinel*, May 21, 1965. Cited in Zehnder, *FDW*, p. 10.

16. "Two More Large Tracts Sold: New Facility to Provide 5000 Jobs," *Orlando Sentinel*, May 20, 1965.

17. This confession is found in the editorial, "We Know We'll Get It But We Don't Know What," *Orlando Sentinel*, May 23, 1965. Cited in Zehnder, *FDW*, pp. 10-11.

18. "Mystery Buyer Tops $5 Million," *Orlando Evening Star*, May 28, 1965. Cited in Zehnder, *FDW*, pp. 13-14.

19. Disney himself used to check in as "Bill Davis." See Charlie Jean, "Central Florida's Greatest Mystery," *Sentinel Star*, September 28, 1981, p. 6A.

20. Zehnder, *FDW*, p. 28.

21. *Orlando Sentinel*, October 24, 1965. Cited in Zehnder, *FDW*, pp. 28-29.

22. "Walt Disney Productions Announces Plans for a Whole New 'Disney World Development' Near Orlando, Florida"; Cited in Zehnder, *FDW*, p. 85.

23. Everything but the sentences in parentheses is from Edward L. Prizer, "The Disney Decade," *Orlando Magazine* (October 1981), p. 36. Contents of the second set of parentheses are from Zehnder, *FDW*, p. 86. Part of this film is shown at the Walt Disney Story on Main Street USA.

24. Leonard Mosley, *Disney's World* (New York: Stein and Day, 1985).

25. Rouse had said in a 1963 commencement speech at the Harvard School of Design (cited in Thomas, *Walt Disney: An American Original*, p. 387), "I hold a view that may be somewhat shocking to an audience as sophisticated as this, and that is that the greatest piece of design in the United States today is Disneyland."

26. Michael Harrington, "To the Disney Station: Corporate Socialism in the Magic Kingdom," *Harper's* (January 1979).

27. *Ibid.*, p. 39.

28. Harrington calls them the sentiments of the Norman Thomas tradition. See *Ibid.*

29. *Ibid.* See Edward Bellamy, *Looking Backward: 2000-1887* (New York: Penguin, 1987 [1888]).

30. This description was tendered at a press conference at the end of 1966. Harrington cites it in "To the Disney Station," p. 38.

31. At this press conference he was asked, "How on earth . . . had he stumbled into this project, which sounded like one of those idealistic, socialistic communities of the early years of the American nineteenth century. Walt violently shook his head since the mention of the word socialism was anathema to him. 'No way, no way!' he said violently. 'It just happens that I'm an inquisitive guy, and where I see things I don't like, I start thinking, why do they have to be like this? How can I improve them? City governments, for example. We pay a lot of taxes and still have streets that aren't paved or are full of holes. And city street cleaners and garbage collectors who don't do their jobs. And property owners who let dirt accumulate and help create slums.'" This is cited in Mosley, *Disney's World*, p. 287.

32. *Ibid.*, p. 288.

33. A carefully crafted mystery remains about the disposition of Disney's body after his death. One version of what happened is that he was quickly cremated and his ashes buried in a small family ceremony at Forest Lawn Memorial Park in Glendale, California. The other version is that he was frozen and is "waiting" for the appropriate medical developments. This latter version seems to appeal to those who resisted Corporate Disney's reworking of Walt Disney's plans at EPCOT. Mosley reports one old Disney hand as saying, "If he had himself frozen and he does come back, there is going to be hell to pay at Disney. . . . He's going to be good and mad at what they have done to his City of Tomorrow. . . . When he comes back, a lot of heads at Disney are going to roll, that's for sure." (*Ibid.*, p. 299). John Rothchild considers this cryogenics business as typical Disney mythology, but I'm not so sure. See John Rothchild, "EPCOT: It's a Stale World After All," *Rolling Stone*, September 1, 1983, p. 34.

34. Mosley, *Disney's World*, p. 297.

35. *Ibid.*, p. 295.

36. Rutherford, "What They Say About Walt Disney World," p. S-24.

37. Zehnder, *FDW*, p. 47.

38. The following quote from Bob Thomas's biography of Walt Disney is cited in Becky O'Malley, "Mickey Say, Mickey Do," *New Times*, October 16, 1978, p. 42: "Walt and his president, Donn Tatum, were discussing plans for the Florida Property. Tatum reportedly observed that what Disney seemed to want was an experimental

absolute monarchy. Walt raised an eyebrow and asked puckishly, 'Can I have one?' 'No,' Tatum replied."

39. Rutherford, "What They Say About Walt Disney World," p. 37.

40. According to "Disney Unwraps Its Newest Extravaganza," *Business Week*, May 3, 1969, p. 34, no business can advertise itself as being so many miles from Walt Disney World.

41. Zehnder, *FDW*, p. 45.

42. Cited in *ibid.*, pp. 64-66.

43. News release no. 2, reproduced in *ibid.* , pp. 89-90.

44. Quoted in *ibid.*, pp. 87-88.

45. Quoted in *ibid.*, p. 89.

46. Some years later, supporters of the "bullet train" argued unsuccessfully for the Reedy Creek plan as a precedent for gaining control over the necessary railroad rights of way. See Victoria Churchville, "The Environmental Fears May Slow Bullet Train," *Orlando Sentinel*, November 21, 1982.

47. See Zehnder, *FDW*, pp. 97-99.

48. Quoted in *ibid.*, p. 104.

49. When he signed the bill that covered the enabling legislation, Governor Claude R. Kirk, Jr., made the following statement: "When some future generation studies the history of Florida, three events may well stand out above all others: the discovery of Florida by Ponce de Leon; the magic moment when Henry Flagler brought the railroad to Palm Beach and opened South Florida for development; and the equally magic moment when Walt and Roy Disney decided to make Florida their second home." Up for grabs, indeed! (See Prizer, "The Disney Decade," p. 36.)

50. See O'Malley, "Mickey Say, Mickey Do." Cited in Zehnder, *FDW*, p. 113.

51. Prizer, "The Disney Decade," pp. 42-43.

52. *Ibid.*, p. 43.

53. Because income from municipal bonds isn't taxable under federal law, Disney could pay investors a low return on their capital. Thanks to the Reedy Creek Improvement District ruling, a private company can raise money at municipal rates. See O'Malley, "Mickey Say, Mickey Do," p. 42.

54. "Disney Dollars," *Forbes*, May 1, 1971. Cited in Zehnder, *FDW*, p. 192.

55. "Riding the Coattails of Mickey Mouse," *Business Week*, September 11, 1971, pp. 72. Cited in Zehnder, *FDW*, p. 185.

56. "The Labor Peace of 'Disney World,'" *U.S. News and World Report*, January 4, 1971. Cited in Zehnder, *FDW*, p. 179.

57. WED, derived from W(alter) E(lias) D(isney), is the design, and engineering arm of the Walt Disney Company.

58. Prizer, "The Disney Era," pp. 43-44.

59. See "Disney World Wakes Sleepy Orlando," *Business Week*, November 14, 1970.

60. "A Brand New House for Mickey Mouse," *Business Week*, November 14, 1970. Cited in Zehnder, *FDW*, p. 169.

61. Jon Nordheimer, "New Disney World Is Rising," *New York Times*, December 29, 1970.

62. Zehnder, *FDW*, p. 175.

63. See Diane H. Rush, "Disney 'Imagineers' Come to Florida," *Business and Economic Dimensions Magazine* (January 1971). Also cited in Zehnder, *FDW*, p. 177.

64. Laura Kavesh, "Disney as a Neighbor," *Orlando Sentinel Star*, September 30, 1981, p. 12A.

65. Florida highways used to be studded with "Arrive Alive" signs.

66. Matt Walsh, "It's Not Easy Living with the Mouse," *Florida Trend* (December 1986), p. 74. Dick Nunis remembers that "we had some fun with that one."

67. Kavesh, "Disney as a Neighbor," p. 12A.

68. Walsh, "It's Not Easy," p. 74.

69. "Monitor," National Broadcasting Corporation, August 13, 1983.

70. Al Burt, "Al Burt's Florida (It's Only Make Believe)," *Miami Herald*, August 1, 1982.

71. O'Malley, "Mickey Say, Mickey Do," p. 48.

72. Burt, "Al Burt's Florida."

73. Dick Marlowe, "Disney World to Begin 'Casting' for Employees," *Orlando Sentinel*, March 30, 1971. Cited in Zehnder, *FDW*, p. 184.

74. "Disney World: Pixie Dust All Over Florida," *Orlando Sentinel*, October 18, 1971.

Chapter 7

1. This quote is cited in Karen Haymon Long, "Disney World: Peeking Through the Pixie Dust of a Booming Corporate Kingdom," *Gainesville (Fla.) Sun*, September 27, 1981.

2. Cited in Barry Stavro, "The Topsy-Turvy World of Theme Parks," *Florida Trend* (December 1981), p. 64. Rod Caborn was marketing manager for Busch Gardens in 1981. Stavro reports that Caborn said this admiringly.

3. For a good analysis of all of these events, see Godfrey Hodgson, *America in Our Time: From World War II to Nixon, What Happened, and Why* (New York: Vintage, 1976).

4. Edward L. Prizer, "The Disney Era in Florida," *Orlando-Land* (October 1981), p. S-4. Disney also underestimated the food problem at the opening of EPCOT Center. It took a while for movie people to realize that half of their revenue at WDW came from food and lodging.

5. Leonard E. Zehnder, *Florida's Disney World: Promises and Problems* (Tallahassee: The Peninsular Publishing Company, 1975), p. 242.

6. These figures are taken from the *1972 Walt Disney Productions Annual Report* (Walt Disney Productions, 1972). Cited in Zehnder, *ibid.*, p. 286. The rounded-off percentage figures are mine.

7. Marjorie Green, "Orlando: City Riding Boom," *Tampa Tribune*, January 2, 1972. Cited in *ibid.*, p. 243.

8. Prizer, "The Disney Era," p. S-5.

9. Denise Lang, "Salvation Army Seeking Transient Shelter Funds," *Orlando Sentinel*, April 1, 1972. Cited in Zehnder, *Florida's Disney World*, pp. 245-246.

10. Cited in Zehnder, *ibid.*, p. 272.

11. Prizer, "The Disney Era," p. S-6.

12. Green, "Orlando," Cited in Zehnder, *Florida's Disney World*, p. 244.

13. Zehnder, *ibid.*, p. 279.

14. Judy Wilson, "Orlando Continues Reign as Growingest U.S. Area," *Orlando Sentinel Star*, September 21, 1973. Cited in *ibid.*, pp. 304-305.

15. "Orlando Working Wonders," *Orlando Sentinel Star*, September 9, 1973. Cited in Zehnder, *ibid.*, pp. 303-304.

16. Zehnder, *ibid.*, p. 299.

17. Robert D. Shaw, Jr., "Nightmare in a Bedroom Town," *St. Petersburg Times*, January 7, 1973. Cited in *ibid.*, p. 291.

18. Cited in Joseph Budge, "Florida's Booming — and Beleaguered Heartland: The Mouse Gets the Blame," *National Geographic Magazine* (November 1973). Cited in Zehnder, *ibid.*, p. 313.

19. Dick Marlowe, "Disney Wonder...2 Years Old Today," *Orlando Sentinel Star*, October 1, 1973. Cited in Zehnder, *ibid.*, p. 308.

20. "Sales Tax Collections Up 22 Pct. in August," *Orlando Sentinel Star*, October 1973. Cited in Zehnder, *ibid.*, p. 302.

21. *Walt Disney Productions 1973 Annual Report* (Walt Disney Productions, 1973). Cited in Zehnder, *ibid.*, pp. 314-315.

22. Zehnder, *ibid.*, p. 315.

23. Clayton Reed, "Florida Banks' Index Loses 19% in a Single Month," *St. Petersburg Times*, December 8, 1973. Cited in Zehnder, *ibid.*, p. 321.

24. "Hotel Operators Plan Ad Drive: Officials Meet in Orlando," *Miami Herald*, January 10, 1974. Cited in Zehnder, *ibid.*, p. 323.

25. Prizer, "The Disney Era," p. S-10. Five hundred of these employees were called back in February.

26. Clayton Reed notes the following: "As the New York Stock Exchange price nosedived from $123.87 to $37.62 a share, its 28,602,000 outstanding shares of stock fell from about $3.5-billion in value to about $1-billion. The $2.5-billion sell-off is approximately equal to the total tax revenues of the State of Florida in a year." Clayton Reed, "With Tourist Parade Slowing Disney Diversifies Operations," *St. Petersburg Times*, January 13, 1974. Cited in Zehnder, *Florida's Disney World*, p. 327.

27. Prizer, "The Disney Era," p. S-10.

28. Reed, "Tourist Parade Slowing," and Prizer, *ibid.*, p.S-10. Cited in Zehnder, *Florida's Disney World*, p. 327.

29. Reed, "Florida Banks' Index." Cited in Zehnder, *ibid.*, p. 328.

30. Frank Eidge, "Florida Winter Tourist Season off 22%," *St. Petersburg Times*, May 8, 1974. Cited in Zehnder, *ibid.*, pp. 329-330.

31. "Attendance Drops at Walt Disney World and Disneyland," *Jacksonville Times-Union*, April 11, 1974. Cited in Zehnder, *ibid.*, p. 331.

32. Edward L. Prizer, "The Disney Decade," *Orlando Magazine* (October 1981), p. 56.

33. Prizer, "The Disney Era," p. S-12.

34. "Disney World Has to Close Gates as Tourists Crowd In," *Los Angeles Times*, March 26, 1975. Cited in Zehnder, *Florida's Disney World*, p. 335.

35. Prizer, "The Disney Era," p. S-12.

36. Prizer, "The Disney Decade," p. 57.

37. Prizer, "The Disney Era," p. S-15.

38. Prizer, "The Disney Decade," p. 58.

39. *Ibid.*

40. "1971-1981 Facts, Figures Tell Disney Story," *Jacksonville Times-Union*, October 15, 1981.

41. 1971 also saw the inaugural Walt Disney World Golf Championship. Jack Nicklaus won the first three tournaments. In 1974 this became the Walt Disney

World National Team Championship but reverted to an individual tournament a few years later. As such it was the last tournament of the professional golfing year, guaranteeing an interesting field as golfers fought for the year's money-winning title and for the last few exemptions for the coming year.

42. Now the Disney Inn.

43. "1971-1981 Facts, Figures Tell Disney Story."

44. See Mimi Whitefield, "Cotton-Candyless EPCOT Aims to Hook More Europeans," *Miami Herald*, September 20, 1982.

45. *Florida Trend* (September 1982), p. 51.

46. Frances Novak-Branch, *The Disney World Effect*, 1983. This study is self-published by the author.

47. Her figures cover 1970-1980. I will stay with them and skew the "Disney decade" by a year.

48. Novak-Branch, *The Disney World Effect*, p. 9.

49. *Ibid.*

50. *Ibid.*, p. 11.

51. *Ibid.*, p. 13.

52. *Ibid.*, p. 17.

53. *Ibid.*, p. 75.

54. Mitch Boretz, "Government Jobs Pay Big Role," *Orlando Sentinel*, May 30, 1982. Disney's payroll ranked fourth.

55. Novak-Branch, *The Disney World Effect*, p. 17.

56. *Ibid.*, p. 23.

57. *Ibid.*, p. 25.

58. *Ibid.*, p. 27.

59. *Ibid.*, p. 32.

60. *Ibid.*, p. 36.

61. Tourism is a pretty big gorilla. It's the nation's second-largest industry, behind only grocery stores. Tourism is one of the top three industries in thirty-five states. See Jeff Kunerth, "The Tourist Stops People Passed Up," *Orlando Sentinel*, October 1, 1982.

62. Novak-Branch, *The Disney World Effect*, p. 41. Orlando's airport was swamped by requests for rental cars.

63. *Ibid.*, p. 42.

64. *Ibid.*, pp. 45-46. The actual figures for Florida were 23,152,160 tourists in 1970 and 33,823,000 in 1980. Greater Orlando's numbers were 800,845 and 5,493,000 respectively. Incidentally, one can see in all the figures the change in attitude from the earnestness in 1970 with which all the numbers were counted to the last digit to the sophisticated blasé attitude of the 1980s, where everything is just rounded off to the nearest thousand.

65. *Ibid.*, pp. 48-49.

66. *Ibid.*, pp. 49-50.

67. *Ibid.*, p. 52.

68. *Ibid.*, p. 57.

69. "The investment multiplier is defined as the total change in income resulting from a change in investment." *Ibid.*, p. 66. Novak-Branch (p. 69) adjusts this index for the area's unusual population increase.

70. *Ibid.*, p. 70.

71. *Ibid.*

72. *Ibid.*

73. Overall attendance at WDW jumped 106 percent. See Vicky Vaughan, "Attendance Sends Disney to New Highs," *Orlando Sentinel*, April 20, 1983.

74. "Problems in Walt Disney's Magic Kingdom," *Business Week*, March 12, 1984.

75. "Walt Disney Grows Up," *The Economist*, July 23, 1983.

76. Thomas C. Hayse, "The Troubled World of Walt Disney Productions," *New York Times*, September 25, 1983.

77. *Ibid.* In addition, *Tron* showed strong sales in video cassettes and in a spinoff video game.

78. John Taylor, *Storming the Magic Kingdom: Wall Street, the Raiders, and the Battle for Disney* (New York: Alfred A. Knopf, 1987), p. 25. Much of the following discussion is taken from Taylor's excellent book.

79. *Ibid.*, p. 29.

80. "Problems in Walt Disney's Magic Kingdom."

81. *Ibid.*.

82. "Analysts: Rumors of Disney Takeover Greatly Exaggerated," *Orlando Sentinel*, February 13, 1984. Also see Sharman Stein, "Analysts: Takeover Fear Spurs Disney Credit Move," *Orlando Sentinel*, March 23, 1984., pp. A1, A8

83. The following chronology is taken from Sharman Stein, "Debts, Doubts Haunt Disney's Reality," *Orlando Sentinel*, June 17, 1984, p. A8.

84. Stuart Mieher, "Arvida Tries a New Balancing Act Under Disney," *Florida Trend* (November, 1984), pp. 73-78.

85. The Basses were no strangers to greenmail, having made substantial profits in buy-backs by Blue Bell in 1983 and Texaco in 1984. See Fred R. Bleakley, "Outrage over Disney Buyout," *New York Times*, June 13, 1984, pp. D1, D4.

86. Robert Knight, "Steinberg and His Ilk Twisted System when They Put the Screws on Disney," *Los Angeles Times*, June 20, 1984, p. A15. In late summer of 1989, Disney announced an agreement to purchase another U.S. icon, the Muppets (Henson Associates, Inc.), and similar, if nonanti-Semitic, grumblings were heard. After the sudden death of Jim Henson in the spring of 1990, the original deal was called off. By then, however, Disney had opened its Muppet show at the Disney-MGM Studios.

87. Bleakley, "Outrage over Disney Buyout."

88. By August 1989, when shares stood at 116 1/8, the Bass's original $400 million investment had grown to about $3 billion. See Joan Chrissos, "The Mouse Is Roaring," *Miami Herald*, August 6, 1989, p. 2F.

89. Although 7,200 acres were to be reserved for a wildlife preserve, that left almost 17,000 acres to play with. See Merwin Sigale, "Florida Is a Magic Kingdom for Disney Profits and Growth," *Miami News*, October 20, 1986.

90. John Taylor, "Bringing Disney's Last Dream to Life at Last," *Florida Trend* (December, 1985).

91. Reported in Michael Cieply, "Disney's Plan to Build Cities on Florida Tract Could Shape Its Future," *Wall Street Journal*, July 9, 1985. Also published in *The Miami News*, July 10, 1985, pp. 1A, 9A, as "Giant Disney Flexes Its Muscles: Florida Mega-Cities Next in Sight." By 1986 there was talk that Disney might build residential properties and then "de-annex" them — redraw its property lines to put them outside Disney property — thus avoiding improvement and service fees by putting

voters into another jurisdiction. See Geri Throne, "Orange County Fears Disney May Elude Impact Fees," *Orlando Sentinel*, October 5, 1986, p. B3.

92. See Vicky Vaughan, "Disney Magic Harsh Reality for Its Rivals," *Orlando Sentinel*, February 9, 1986, pp. A1, A22-A23.

93. Cieply, "Disney's Plan." See also Gail DeGeorge, "Disney on Expansion Binge: Some of Mickey's Neighbors Fear They May Not Survive," *Miami Herald*, August 3, 1986, pp. 1F, 3F, for responses to Disney's moves from around the state — especially from south Florida.

94. Within two months of its opening, the Disney-MGM Studios park was overcrowded. Michael Eisner announced that the park would double in size within three years. See Joan Chrissos, "New Theme Park Not Big Enough, Disney Discovers," *Miami Herald*, July 1989.

95. Pam Parks, "Exclusive Details on Disney's Pleasure Island," *Orlando Magazine* (September, 1986), pp. 26, 31-32.

96. Yumiko Ono, "Theme Parks Boom in Japan as Investors and Consumers Rush to Get on the Ride," *Wall Street Journal*, August 8, 1990, p. B1. By the next year attendance increased to 16 million. See James Sterngold, "Cinderella Hits Her Stride in Tokyo," *New York Times*, February 16, 1991, p. 6.

97. The first phase of this park, extending to 1997, was budgeted at $2.67-$2.83 billion. Said Robert Fitzpatrick, chairman of the Disney subsidiary that is designing and building the complex, "Europe isn't just another market for Disney, but a key part of its long-term strategy. . . . Euro Disneyland will be the most important thing for the company between 1990 and 2000." See Jacques Neher, "Mickey! Disney Cranks Up for French Park," *Miami Herald*, April 2, 1989, pp. 1F-2F..

By early 1991, it was reported that $4.4 billion would be spent by the time the park opened. See Stephen Greenhouse, "Playing Disney in the Parisian Fields," *New York Times*, February 17, 1991, Section 3, pp. 1, 6.

98. *Ibid.*, p. 6.

99. "French Accept Mickey, His Pals," *Miami Herald*, March 22, 1987, p. 28A.

100. For further information on the structure of investment at Euro Disneyland, see *The Walt Disney Company 1990 Annual Report* (The Walt Disney Company, 1990), p. 29.

101. These figures, expressed in millions, are found in "Disney's Magic on Film Is Money in the Bank," *Miami Herald*, July 26, 1989, pp. 5B-6B.

102. *Ibid.* Under the leadership of Jeffrey Katzenberg, Disney revenues from film and television quintupled from $320 million in 1984 to $1.6 billion in 1989. See Frank Rose, "Taking Care of Business," *Premiere* (November 1990), pp. 102-112.

103. Andrea Gabor and Steve L. Hawkins, "Of Mice and Money in the Magic Kingdom," *U.S. News and World Report*, December 22, 1986.

104. Corie Brown, "Disney Is Doing It Right: Why the Studio Has Dominated Ticket Sales Recently," *Boston Sunday Globe*, August 5, 1990, pp. B33, B36.

105. Vicky Vaughan, "Disney's Shares Rise on Market," *Orlando Sentinel*, December 4, 1986.

106. Dick Marlowe, "The New Disney Magic: Maximizing Profits," *Central Florida Business*, June 23-29, 1986, p. 3.

107. Here is a simplified financial picture for 1984-1990.

	Revenues	Net Income
1984	$1.4 billion	$97.8 million
1985	$1.7 billion	$173.5 million
1986	$2.2 billion	$247.3 million
1987	$2.9 billion	$444.7 million
1988	$3.4 billion	$522.0 million
1989	$4.6 billion	$703.3 million
1990	$5.8 billion	$824.0 million

Adapted from Chrissos, "The Mouse Is Roaring," p. 1F. From 1986 on, figures (rounded off) are taken from *The Walt Disney Company 1990 Annual Report* (The Walt Disney Company, 1990). The compound annual growth rate of revenues for 1986-1990 is 28 percent. Note also that the average annual profit increase for the years 1984-1989 was 48 percent. See "Reality Intrudes into the Magic Kingdom," *The Economist*, April 21, 1990, pp. 71-72.

108. David Altaner, "Walt Disney Co. to Sell Arvida," *Fort Lauderdale News*, January 30, 1987. In 1987, its job done, Arvida was sold to JMB Realty Corporation for $400 million, nearly double what Disney had originally paid. In a sidebar to this sale, The Walt Disney Company filed suit to prevent twenty Arvida executives from exercising around $20 million in stock options, claiming that Arvida was being sold before those options could be legally exercised. See "Walt Disney Co. Sues Arvida Executives," *Miami News*, April 16, 1987.

109. Peter Adams and Vicki Vaughan, "A New Set of Wings for Disney," *Orlando Sentinel*, January 31, 1987, pp. A1, A16.

110. By March 1, 1989, the Orlando metropolitan area, with 69,513 hotel rooms, had overtaken New York and Los Angeles. The local industry's 84 percent occupancy rate was significantly higher than the 65 percent break-even point. See "No Rooms at the Inn? Orlando Area Has Plenty," *Miami Herald*, June 5, 1989.

111. For this quote and the figures above, see Vicki Vaughan, "No Longer Dwarfed by Disney, Orlando's Booming on Its Own," *Orlando Sentinel*, September 28, 1986.

112. Edward L. Prizer, quoted in Charlie Patton, "Disney World Transformed 'Sleepy Orlando,'" *Jacksonville Times-Union*, September 28, 1986, pp. A1, A11-A12.

113. In 1986 Orlando had its status as a "big league city" ratified by the National Basketball Association when it accepted the Orlando Magic as a franchise, to begin play in 1989-1990.

114. John Wark, "Disney's Self-Isolation Stymies Area Governments," *Orlando Sentinel*, July 8, 1985, pp. A1, A6.

115. Matt Walsh, "It's Not Easy Living with the Mouse," *Florida Trend* (December 1986), pp. 70-75.

116. Cited in Gail DeGeorge, "A Sweet Deal for Disney Is Souring Its Neighbors," *Business Week*, August 8, 1988, p. 48. See also Andrew Holleran, "The Mouse and the Virgin," *Wigwag* (August, 1990), p. 25.

117. See Martin Merzer, "Disney's Mouse Roars in Orlando: Expansion at Disney World Puts Squeeze on Competitors," *Miami Herald*, April 27, 1989, pp. 1A, 19A.

118. See Dan Tracy, "Maglev Loses Out on Epcot Stop," *Orlando Sentinel*, September 29, 1989, pp. 1A, 10A.

119. "Disney Works Its Magic Again," *Florida Trend* (September 1989), p. 25. See Charles Fishman, "Talk About a Tax Base: Try Disney World," *Southpoint* (January

1990), p. 14; and Holleran, "The Mouse and the Virgin," p. 29, for reports on Disney's recent tax relations with Osceola County, whose property appraiser removed the agricultural classification from around ten thousand acres of land in 1989, thus revaluing the land from $28 million to $85 million and causing its taxes to rise from $395,000 to $1.4 million.

120. Matt Walsh, "It's Not Easy Living with the Mouse," p. 75.

121. See Vicki Vaughan, "Raising the Rent Tax Stake," *Orlando Sentinel*, February 2, 1985; "Senseless Fight on Resort Tax," *Orlando Sentinel*, October 14, 1985; Vicki Vaughan, "Tourism Panel Votes for Surtax," *Orlando Sentinel*, January 31, 1986.

122. "Magic Kingdom of Aloof," *Orlando Sentinel*, July 10, 1985.

123. Walsh, "It's Not Easy Living with the Mouse," pp. 72-73.

124. "Magic Kingdom of Aloof."

125. Holleran, "The Mouse and the Virgin," p. 25.

126. *Ibid.*, p. 26.

127. Many local newspapers carry the stories of these visits and are supplied with photos and information by WDW public relations people. Stanley Elkins has written a delightful, biting novel about bringing a slew of dying children to the Magic Kingdom. See Stanley Elkins, *The Magic Kingdom* (New York: Dutton, 1985).

128. Phil Williams, "Disney Dominance: A Tale of Mice and Millions," *Florida Today*, July 27, 1986, pp. 1E-3E. At the turn of the decade into the 1990s, Disney opened seven new resort hotel areas: the Grand Floridian, Caribbean Beach, Swan, Dolphin, Beach Club, Yacht Club, and Port Orleans resorts.

129. *Ibid.*

130. Cited in Merzer, "Disney's Mouse Roars in Orlando," p. 19A. Merzer also cites the following comment. "We are Orlando," says Tom Elrod, Disney World's senior vice president for marketing. "We're the sole reason people visit here." *Ibid.*

131. *Ibid.*

132. *Ibid.*

133. This quote is found in Richard Hollis and Brian Sibley, *The Disney Studio Story* (New York: Crown, 1988), p. 7.

Chapter 8

1. According to Heidi Yorkshire, over 15 million Mickey Mouse hats, with their big ears, have been sold over the years. Today some half a million are sold annually at the Disney parks and other toy stores. See Suzy Gershman, "Big Ears: Down the Decades with the Mickey Mouse Hat," *Travel & Leisure* 20:3 (March 1990), pp. 105-106.

2. See "Reality Intrudes into the Magic Kingdom," *The Economist*, April 21, 1990, pp. 71-72; and Larry Lipson, "Mickey and Disney Gang Go Down the Fast-Food Lane," *Miami Herald*, August 18, 1990, pp. 1E, 3E.

3. See *The Disney Management Style* (Walt Disney Productions, 1977), p. 18.

4. Note the rhetorical use of family imagery, an imagery that is itself "naturalized" through its "branching" tree metaphor.

5. I am also switching the places of WDW and Disneyland as shown in the chart. This makes my presentation more fully reflect present realities.

6. *The World-Wide Disney Team* (Walt Disney Productions, 1982).

7. In 1953 Walt Disney formed a private company — Retlaw, which is Walter spelled backward — to control merchandising rights to his own name in the inter-

ests of his immediate family. Andrew Holleran traces some of the Company's internal difficulties to an ongoing feud between Walt's people and Roy Disney's people, which was triggered by this event. See Andrew Holleran, "The Mouse and the Virgin," *Wigwag* (August 1990), p. 23.

8. *The Walt Disney Company 1990 Annual Report* (The Walt Disney Company, 1990).

9. At the fin de siècle of the twentieth century Disney doesn't have to wait seven years for children to be Disneyfied. As parents of young children know, Disney marketing has been so successful that children seem to be born not only with Chomsky's language acquisition device in their heads but with a preternatural knowledge of Mickey Mouse. Here perhaps lurks an interesting issue for Lamarkians (or sociobiologists).

10. Although the latter especially get a significant boost by being incorporated into the show at the Studio Tour as examples of various cinematic techniques.

11. *Disney Management Style*, p. 19.

12. The prerelease marketing of *Dick Tracy* (1990) is a good example of this approach.

13. *Disney Management Style*, p. 18.

14. This quote is taken from Richard Holliss and Brian Sibley, *The Disney Studio Story* (New York: Crown, 1988), p. 134. They add (*ibid.*): "Re-issued six times up until 1983, it has earned in the region of $47 million at the American box office. The 50th anniversary re-issue in 1987 generated an additional $40 million in under eight weeks."

15. Pierre Bourdieu, *Outline of a Theory of Practice* (Cambridge: Cambridge University Press, 1977).

16. Name recognition is also crucial. As a simple measure of Disney's success, think of the unique ubiquity of reference to Disney and Disney symbols in world culture. Anytime anyone refers to something as being like or not like Disneyland or Disney World or as "Mickey Mouse," he or she is taking Disney as a shared and taken-for-granted central reference point. I once started to count written and spoken instances, but I gave up. There were too many to keep track of. Talk about a hegemonic position!

17. In August 1989, the *Miami Herald* published the following excerpt of an interview. "Another interesting point is the pricing decisions that went into the firm's MGM Studio Tour. Disney originally planned to charge $15 a person. However, surveys showed that people weren't very interested in going to the studio at that price. After spending so much money to fly to Florida, stay in a hotel and feed the kids, the $15 price seemed too low; those surveyed felt that at $15, the studio couldn't possibly be as good as the Magic Kingdom, which cost $29. When the company surveyed people with a $22 price, they were more interested; however, people didn't get really interested until the price was $29. Thus, you pay $29 for the tour." I have lost the full reference for this quote.

18. In 1989 Disney threatened suit against the American Academy of Motion Pictures because of its unauthorized use of the Snow White character in an Academy Awards show skit.

19. See *Disney Management Style*, p. 24.

20. For a look behind those smiles, see John Van Maanen's unpublished manuscripts, "Whistle While You Work: On Seeing Disneyland as the Workers Do," and "Whistle While You Work: Task Organization and Peer Culture at Disneyland."

I would be surprised if Van Maanen's descriptions were much different at the Florida park.

21. Actually, Eisner and Wells stepped up Disney ad machinery. The need to make EPCOT a household word had led to substantial advertising in the fall of 1982.

22. N. W. Pope, 1980 president of the Bank Marketing Association, claimed that first-time visitors to WDW described their experiences in detail to at least ten groups of friends or relatives. This is reported in John Schnurlein, "Mickey Mouse Can Be a Marketing Guide, Too," *San Jose Mercury News*, June 15, 1980.

23. "EPCOT Center Marketed Without Ad Budget," *Marketing News*, October 11, 1985, p. 18.

24. The following is reported in Thomas R. Elrod, "With Benefits to All: Disney's Target Marketing," *Broadcasting*, November 21, 1977, p. 14.

25. Thus Sears or whoever could run its own promotions.

26. Cited in Edward D. Sheffe, "EPCOT: Making the City of Tomorrow Known Today," *Madison Avenue*, p. 98.

27. *Ibid.*, p. 99.

28. For example, all three major networks covered the opening of EPCOT Center as news. WDW also received a lot of air time when it hosted part of the Constitution bicentennial celebrations.

29. Press response to the offers of free trips to the fifteenth anniversary gala were interesting in this light. Because the mainstream print press (having abdicated its responsibility to do anything civically useful during the Teflon Age) had invented the pseudo-issue of press ethics, countless presspeople felt called on to resuscitate their high horses and thereupon publicly refuse their junkets. "We will," they said, backpattingly, "pay our own way like the independent critics we are."

30. Lore Croghan, "At Disney World, Some of the Fun Is in the Ad-House," *Adweek*, August 18, 1986, p. 8.

31. All of which are also placed front and center in Disney's annual celebrations of New Year's Eve and the Fourth of July.

32. Alice Hinkle, "Disney World Ads Promote Family 'Guilt Trips,'" *Lexington (Mass.) Minute Man*, March 7, 1986.

33. "Disney Trippers," *The Nation*, October 10, 1988, pp. 296-297.

34. "Ibid." Gretchen Elizabeth Carlson, Miss America 1989, was also rewarded with an evening with Willard Scott, as co-host of a televised 1989 4th of July Show.

35. "Ibid."

36. Suzy Hagstrom, "From $5,000 Sword to Toys, Disney Retail Sales Grow," *Orlando Sentinel Star*, April 4, 1982.

37. *Ibid.*

38. Selwyn Crawford, "Shop for a Piece of Faraway Lands," *Orlando Sentinel*, October 1, 1984, p. 13.

39. This was said to Crawford by Monroe Greenstein, a senior analyst with Bear, Stearns & Co. Reported in Crawford, *ibid.*

40. See the *Walt Disney Company 1990 Annual Report* (The Walt Disney Company, 1990). Disney reports its consumer products revenues separately from its theme park and resorts revenues. It is unclear how much merchandising is included in the latter reporting category; $573.8 is a minimum figure.

41. See Suzy Gershman, "The Good, the Bad and the Tacky," *Travel & Leisure* 20:7 (July 1989), pp. 25-30.

42. Cited in Lynn Trexler, "Disney's Unlikely Retail Success," *Apparel South* (May/June 1982).

43. Suzy Gershman, "Mickey's Merchandise: The Best Deals In and Around Walt Disney World," *Travel and Leisure* 19:7 (July, 1988), p. 146.

44. Trexler, "Disney's Unlikely Retail Success."

45. Gershman, "Mickey's Merchandise", p. 146. Gershman (*ibid.*)nevertheless goes on to tell us about all the bargains available at WDW, claiming, "At Disney, you actually get what you pay for."

46. Ibid.

47. One of the pioneers of LPM was Herman "Kay" Kamen, who brought this concept to Walt Disney in 1932 and built the company into a huge character licensor. See James Roman, "Billion Dollar Baby: The Lucrative World of Licensed Product Merchandising," *USA Today*, September 1981. Also see Holliss and Sibley, *The Disney Studio Story*, pp. 20-21.

48. See Patricia Bellew, "EPCOT: It's Not Mickey Mouse," *Miami Herald*, September 28, 1981. For a good extended discussion of character licensing in general, see Tom Engelhardt, "The Shortcake Strategy," in Todd Gitlin, ed., *Watching Television* (New York: Pantheon, 1986), pp. 68-110.

49. Mitch Boretz, "Disney Finds Large Market for Its Toys," *Orlando Sentinel*, July 24, 1982.

50. Because of quality control and loss of income, Disney must find some way to combat counterfeiters. In the spring of 1989, thousands of "Disney" items were confiscated from traders in Thailand and burned. See "Counterfeiters Fire up Disney: Fakes Cost Company Millions in Royalties," *Miami Herald*, June 24, 1989.

51. In 1981, James Roman, "Billion Dollar Baby," reported that this royalty was 6 percent, but its agreement with Tokyo Disneyland puts the figure at 5 percent.

52. See Boretz, "Disney Finds Large Market."

53. *Merchandise* (Walt Disney Productions, n. d.), p. 2.

54. For a useful typology of the souvenir, see Beverly Gordon, "The Souvenir: Messenger of the Extraordinary," *Journal of Popular Culture* 20:3 (Winter 1986), pp. 135-146.

55. *Merchandise*, p. 4.

56. W. DeWayne Booker, a merchandise manager for Walt Disney World Shopping Village in 1982, told this to Suzy Hagstrom. See Hagstrom, "From $5,000 Sword to Toys."

57. *Merchandise*, p. 11.

58. At the Magic Kingdom, people may store their own purchases in the lockers under the train station.

59. See Hugh Dalziel Duncan, *Culture and Democracy* (New York: Bedminster Press, 1965), pp. 123-131.

60. "Making Money in 'Never-Never' Land," *Florida Trend* (December 1981).

61. "Candy's Magical Merchandising at Disney's Magic Kingdom," *Candy Wholesaler* (June 1980).

62. Among the exceptions to this practice are the imported candies sold in World Showcase and the candy made by those companies that have leased the privilege of using Disney figures on their labels — which is available especially at the resort hotels.

63. Candy is also the attraction at Sweet Success on Hollywood Boulevard at the Studio Tour.

64. Hot coffee, iced tea, and citrus products are also sold.

65. Dave Henry, "Coca-Cola and Walt Disney World: The Adventures Keep Coming," *REFRESHER USA* (June 1981), p. 27.

66. *Ibid.*, p. 28.

67. See Lynn Wyner White, "Ray Budd," *Flowers &* (April 1983), for the following.

68. *Ibid.*

69. See Lynn Phillips, "2 Brothers Ride Disney Coattails to Success," *Orlando Sentinel*, June 6, 1983.

Chapter 9

1. "Making Money in 'Never-Never' Land," *Florida Trend* (December, 1981).

2. Second to Cinderella's Castle, that is.

3. "Disney World Railroads: Functional First, Fun Secondarily," *Railway Age*, June 10, 1974. See also Steve Birnbaum, *Steve Birnbaum Brings You the Best of Walt Disney World* (New York: Houghton Mifflin, 1988), p. 82.

4. Broggie is a Disney engineer who, like Walt, was an antique train buff.

5. Walt had a one-eighth-scale train in his own backyard. Named after his wife, it was the first Lilly Belle. This is the second.

6. Richard V. Francaviglia, "Main Street USA: A Comparison/Contrast of Streetscapes in Disneyland and Walt Disney World," *Journal of Popular Culture* 15(1) (1981), pp. 141-156. This quote is found on pp. 155-156.

7. *Ibid.*, p. 154.

8. Francaviglia notes (*ibid.*, p. 141) that Disney's idealized main street designs and images have influenced town planning and the restoration of main streets across the United States. We have traveled a strange full circle of simulation because many of our folk ideas about what idyllic small towns looked like came from the movie industry in the first place. Then Disney built a movie-version small town, which is now being copied by small towns as they revivify their downtown districts. What they have correctly picked up from Disney is the fantasy façading of stores and shops because main street is also a mall, a place to enact Hugh Dalziel Duncan's "drama of shopping." See Hugh Dalziel Duncan, *Culture and Democracy* (New York: Bedminster, 1965), pp. 123-131.

9. Richard V. Francaviglia, "Main Street USA: The Creation of a Popular Image," *Landscape* (Spring-Summer, 1977), p. 21.

10. Francaviglia, "A Comparison/Contrast," p. 143, suggests that Town Square gives Main Street the feel of an eastern Pennsylvania town. It has a "mature, manicured Victorian quality."

11. *Ibid.*, p. 152.

12. All are two-story buildings with three-story façades. Main Street is wider here than at Disneyland, and the buildings are more imposing — taller and fuller in scale.

13. There are few clocks inside the Disney park — one each at the Railroad Station, at City Hall, on Main Street, at Cinderella's Castle, and at the Hall of Presidents. Our experience is supposed to be timeless.

14. In "To the Disney Station," *Harpers* (January 1979), pp. 35-44, 86, Michael Harrington called Main Street fraudulently neat. He noted that there are no politics in City Hall, only information downstairs and a public relations department upstairs. Although this may be an inappropriate representation of City Hall activities during the McKinley era, it is certainly ethnographically prescient as a description of U.S. politics in the last quarter of the twentieth century. All we would

have to do is relabel the first-floor offerings as "disinformation" and expand the public relations space. City Hall may not be a simulacrum after all.

15. The Magic Kingdom opened in 1971.

16. The Hospitality House is also the place to go for reservations to the Diamond Horseshoe Revue on the border of Liberty Square and Frontierland.

17. Birnbaum, *Steve Birnbaum,,* p. 181.

18. According to Birnbaum (., p. 80), there is one maintenance crew whose sole job is to change the little lights around the roofs.

19. See Marylyn Springer, *Frommer's 1987-1988 Guide to Orlando, Disney World and Epcot* (New York: Prentice Hall, 1987), pp. 135-136.

20. Birnbaum, *Steve Birnbaum,* p. 81.

21. *Ibid.,* p. 35.

22. Because Disney doesn't page people, the parks need some other mechanism by which to get information around the parks. All Disney employees are trained to check regularly for any information that might circulate through computerized logbooks.

23. A crew keeps the woodwork painted, working from Town Square to the Plaza and then starting over again. As Birnbaum, (*Steve Birnbaum,* p. 80) reports, "The greenish, horse-shaped cast-iron hitching posts are repainted twenty times a year on the average — and totally scraped down each time."

24. *Ibid.* This may be a low estimate for the holiday season, when people spend a good bit of time hanging out by the giant Christmas tree that is put up each year.

25. This commemorates the original secret land-buying scheme.

26. *Walt Disney World* (Walt Disney Productions, 1986), p. 17.

27. There are two recent additions on the lagoon at the intersection of World Showplace and Future World. Disney Traders and Port of Entry sell souvenirs and gifts, many of them items from countries not pavilioned at World Showcase.

28. Golden Age Souvenirs is on Lakeside Circle. Endor Vendors, the Indiana Jones Adventure Outpost, and the Indiana Jones Wagon are on the Backlot Annex. The Disney Studio Store and the Loony Bin (with its Roger Rabbit stuff) are on the Backstage Studio Tour, and the Animation Gallery is on the Animation Tour. With its artwork from Disney animated features, the Animation Gallery sells some of the most expensive items at WDW.

29. See Thomas Hine, *Populuxe; The Look and Life of America in the '50s and '60s, from Tailfins and TV Dinners to Barbie Dolls and Fallout Shelters* (New York: Alfred A. Knopf, 1986).

30. In its ads, Disney calls its architecture here "California crazy." For a discussion of this, see Jim Heimann and Rip Georges (with an introduction by David Gebhard), *California Crazy: Roadside Vernacular Architecture* (San Francisco: Chronicle Books, 1980).

31. Remember that this Hollywood sign is sitting in central Florida. It is a mileage chart that is not a real mileage chart but is a sign of a mileage chart that would be real if it were there rather than here.

32. For a fuller description of Oscar's, see Jay Clarke, "Disney Movie Mania — Travel Editor's Rating: The Park's a Winner," *Miami Herald,* May 29, 1989, p. 8J.

33. This phrase is taken from Richard Schickel, *Intimate Strangers: The Culture of Celebrity* (New York: Fromm International Publishing Corporation, 1986).

Chapter 10

1. *Ibid.*, p. 11.

2. See Louis Mumford, "The First Megamachine," in Donald Miller, ed., *The Louis Mumford Reader* (New York: Pantheon, 1986), pp. 315-323. The following quote is found on p. 320.

3. See Mumford, "Technics and Human Development," in *ibid.*, pp. 304-314.

4. Much of this information is found in Peter Blake, "Walt Disney World," *Architecture Forum* 136 (June 1972), pp. 24-41.

5. *Ibid.*, p. 38.

6. Walker, "EPCOT '82," p. 8. See also "Delicate Hydraulics Keep Mickey Mouse's Feet Dry," *Engineering News-Record*, January 27, 1972, p. 25.

7. Walker, "EPCOT '82," p. 8.

8. *Ibid.*

9. See Conrad Kottak, "Anthropological Analysis of Mass Enculturation," in Conrad Kottak, *Researching American Culture* (Ann Arbor: University of Michigan Press, 1982), especially pp. 55-65.

10. The following is taken from "From Swamp Land to Dream Land," *Engineering News-Record*, November 25, 1982, pp. 35-38. See also "EPCOT," *Civil Engineering* (June, 1983).

11. See "From Swamp Land to Dream Land," p. 37.

12. See Dan Wascoe, Jr., "Moving People from Fantasy to Reality," *Mass Transit* (August, 1983), p. 11.

13. As of 1991 watercraft link the Disney-MGM Studios and the EPCOT hotel complex (Swan, Dolphin, Beach Club, and Yacht Club).

14. The bus is an alternate route for those who don't want to ride the monorail or ferry from the TTC to the Magic Kingdom.

15. At both the TTC and EPCOT Center, bus stops are off to stage left, away from major pedestrian paths and partially camouflaged by arboreal landscaping. This is also where tour buses park. Disney drivers are "cast members"; their public lounging between circuits is kept to a minimum. Tour bus drivers, however, are not part of the show. Thus, in typical multifunctional Disney fashion, they have been provided with a drivers' lounge to give them a place to go and to keep them out of sight.

16. Noel Perrin, "The High Cost of Magic," *Audubon* 86 (May 1984), p. 28-30.

17. Wascoe, "Moving People from Fantasy to Reality," p. 38.

18. *Ibid.*, p. 39.

19. Walker, "EPCOT '82," p. 26.

20. Wascoe, "Moving People from Fantasy to Reality," p. 40.

21. See "Disney's Technology Is Universal," *World Construction* (June 1983).

22. Wascoe, "Moving People from Fantasy to Reality," p. 40.

23. Cited in *ibid.*

24. See "World of Make-Believe Is Also Technological Innovator," *National Engineer* (May 1983).

25. *Ibid.* Also see the following: Katherine W. Hickerson, "Walt Disney's EPCOT Center Is Showplace for Public Works Technology," *Professional Engineer* (Winter 1982); Tom Scherberger, "High Costs End Garbage Experiment," *Orlando Sentinel*, February 27, 1983; John Wark, "Disney Research Seeks Savings, Image Boost,"

Orlando Sentinel-Star, March 3, 1981 ,pp. 1E-2E; Peter Blake, "Walt Disney World," *Architectural Forum* (June 1972), pp. 32-34.

26. See Walker, "EPCOT '82," p. 8; "World of Make-Believe Is Also Technological Innovator"; Hickerson, "Walt Disney's EPCOT Center"; H. W. Haeseker and Steven C. Helle, "Walt Disney World," *Public Works* (December 1980), pp. 34-35; *Boyle Engineering Corporation Newsletter*, (June 1980); Katherine Long, "State Fears Disney Discharge May Be Ruining Lakes," *Orlando Sentinel*, April 23, 1986.

27. See Haeseker and Helle, "Walt Disney World," p. 35, as well as Hickerson, "Walt Disney's EPCOT Center." p. 39.

28. Hickerson, "Walt Disney's EPCOT Center," p. 39.

29. Sources for the following are John J. Foster, "Electrical Users and Utility Combine for Walt Disney World Energy Management," *Electrical Energy Management* (November 1980), pp. 10-12; Robert Doering and Robert Redgate, "Development of Energy Management System at Walt Disney World via Centralized Computer Control," *Computers and Industrial Engineering*, 1981; "Energy Is Prime Feature at Showcase of the Future," *Insulation Outlook* (July 1982); Hickerson, "Walt Disney's EPCOT Center"; "World of Make-Believe Is Also a Technological Innovator"; Mark Weintz, "Disney World Shows Visitors Glimpse of Alternate Energy," *Solar Times* (January 1981); Perrin, "The High Cost of Magic," p. 30.

30. Perrin, *ibid.*

31. *Ibid.*

32. *Ibid.*

Chapter 11

1. This Peter Blake quote is taken from Derek Walker, "Architecture and Theming," *Animated Architecture* (December 1982), p. 28.

2. D. L., "Disney World Is Just a Bit Much with All That Odorless Perfection," *Dayton Journal-Herald*, July 5, 1980.

3. Charles Moore, quoted in William Chaitkin, "The Metaphysical Themepark," *Animated Architecture* (December 1982), p. 14.

4. Robert Craft did *not* care for WDW. In Jeff Simon, "Pleasure- Are We Having More Fun and Enjoying It Less?", *Buffalo Evening News*, April 30, 1982, p. 3, he is quoted as follows: "Any demonstration of mass mindlessness is depressing. What makes this all the sadder is that children are so greatly in need of good models, wise teachers, examples of beautiful and inspiring works of art. There is no more pernicious and powerful force against all these than Walt Disney's Walt Disney World."

5. Robert Venturi, cited by Paul Goldberger in "Mickey Mouse Teaches the Architects," *New York Times*, October 22, 1972, Section 6, p. 40.

6. Thomas More's original *Utopia* meant "no place."

7. See Don Mather, "Rediscovering Civility," *Lake Worth Herald*, September 20, 1984.

8. For reports on services for the disabled, see *The Disabled Guest's Guidebook*, available at WDW; Patrick M. Vaughan, "Disney World on Wheels," *Accent on Living* (Bloomington, Illinois) (Summer 1985); and *Steve Birnbaum Brings You the Best of Walt Disney World* (New York: Houghton Mifflin, 1985, 1988, 1989, 1990).

9. It is so normal to see the disabled that one can understand how unremarkable it might be to see the kinds of terminally ill children brought to WDW in Stanley Elkins's novel, *The Magic Kingdom* (New York: Dutton, 1985). In fact, one of Disney's

public relations gambits is to welcome some children whose "last wish" is to see Mickey Mouse.

10. As outlined by Louis Mumford, "The Ideal Form of the Modern City," in Donald L. Miller, ed., *The Mumford Reader* (New York: Pantheon, 1986), pp. 162-175.

11. Louis Mumford, *The City in History: Its Origins, Its Transformations, and Its Prospects* (New York: Harcourt, Brace and World, 1968).

12. Louis Mumford, "The Ideal Form of the Modern City," p. 171.

13. Michael Harrington, "To the Disney Station: Corporate Socialism in the Magic Kingdom," *Harper's* (January 1979), pp. 35-44, 86.

14. See "EPCOT Center: It's a Very Carefully Planned Place," *Philadelphia Enquirer*, October 21, 1982.

15. *Ibid.*

16. See Richard V. Francaviglia, "Main Street USA: The Creation of a Popular Image," *Landscape* (Spring-Summer 1977); also Francaviglia, "Main Street USA: A Comparison/Contrast of Streetscapes in Disneyland and Walt Disney World," *Journal of Popular Culture* 15:1 (1981), pp. 141-156.

17. Francaviglia's term.

18. What I say here about lines applies to EPCOT Center as well.

19. See, for example, Robert Alan Arthur, "Grandpa Cullum's Flawless Two-Day Plan for Disney World," *Esquire* (July 1975), pp. 40, 51.

20. According to John Van Maanen, employees at Disneyland call the areas in which customers wait "bull pens"; park officials call them "reception areas." See John Van Maanen, "Whistle While You Work: On Seeing Disneyland as the Workers Do" (unpublished manuscript).

21. Jim Fitzgerald, "Disney Plays Tricks with Mickey Mouse Lines," *Bellevue (Michigan) Gazette*, May 2, 1984.

22. The use of air-conditioning also creates some rather odd problems. For example, to maintain its spooky, dreary atmosphere, various parts of the Haunted Mansion tableaux are covered with dust. The problem is that the air-conditioning fans blow the dust away. As Birnbaum reports (Birnbaum, *Steve Birnbaum*, 1985, p. 82), dust is purchased in five-pound bags from a West Coast company so it can be spread around at night "by a device that looks as if it were meant to spread grass seed." He recounts a local story that "enough has been used since the park's 1971 opening to bury the mansion." One presumes that for legal reasons, the dust is sterilized. Now, there's a commodity niche — commercial sterilized dust.

23. Bob Sehlinger and John Finley, *The Unofficial Guide to Walt Disney World* (New York: Menasha Ridge Press, 1985).

24. Actually, they do stop every so often to load handicapped guests. Many people who complain about the starting and stopping of rides assume, usually incorrectly, that mechanical malfunctions are at fault.

25. Van Maanen notes that sometimes contests develop between shifts of workers at a particular ride to see how fast people can be moved through the attraction. Some loaders try to beat their "personal best" at turnstile records. See Van Maanen, "Whistle While You Work," pp. 49-50.

26. *The Unofficial Guide*, p. 68.

27. *Ibid.*, p. 71.

28. CommuniCore is a somewhat Orwellian contraction of Community Core.

29. For a time after October 1987, this central area was filled with the accoutrements of the EPCOT Daredevil Circus Spectacular. This very un-Disneylike attrac-

tion did not last long. By the end of 1989, daredeviltry was pretty much confined to the Indiana Jones Epic Stunt Spectacular at the Studio Tour.

30. See Howard P. Segal, *Technological Utopianism in American Culture* (Chicago: University of Chicago Press, 1985); also Segal, "The Technological Utopians," in Joseph Corn, ed., *Imagining Tomorrow: History, Technology and the American Future* (Cambridge, Mass.: MIT Press, 1986), pp. 119-136.

31. Both Michael Harrington and Mike Wallace note that Walt Disney's father was acquainted with Bellamy's book. They argue that Walt Disney may have been imbued with some utopian notions as a child. Corporate Disney's version of utopia is, in any case, quite different from Walt's. See Harrington, "To the Disney Station," p. 39, and Mike Wallace, "Mickey Mouse History: Portraying the Past at Disney World," *Radical History* 32 (1985), pp. 33-57.

32. Segal, *Technological Utopianism*, p. 21.

33. *Ibid.*, p. 23.

34. *Ibid.*, p. 24.

35. Quoted in *ibid.*, p. 26.

36. Quoted in *ibid.*

37. Quoted in *ibid.*

38. See Arlie Russell Hochschild, *The Managed Heart: Commercialization of Human Feeling* (Berkeley: University of California Press, 1983).

39. Segal, *Technological Utopianism*, p. 27.

40. For information on air-conditioning systems, see P. A. Kelsey, "Walt Disney World Prototype Solar-Powered Office Building Will Provide 80% A/C Needs," *Air Conditioning, Heat, and Refrigeration News* 143 (January 23, 1978); and "Energy Efficient Villas Built for Disney World Vacationers," *Air Conditioning, Heat, and Refrigeration News* 143 (March 20, 1978).

41. Segal, *Technological Utopianism*, p. 30.

42. Harold Albert Loeb, *Life in a Technocracy: What It Might Be Like* (New York: Viking, 1933), p. 75. Cited in *ibid.*

43. Segal, *Technological Utopianism*, p. 11.

44. *Ibid.*, p. 5.

45. See John Wark and Laura Kevesh, "Innkeepers Forced to Be Policemen," *Orlando Sentinel-Star*, September 8, 1981, pp. 1A, 4A.

46. Cited in Laura Kavesh and John Wark, "Thieves' Paradise: Pickings Are Easy in Central Florida," *Orlando Sentinel-Star*, September 6, 1981, pp. 1A, 4A.

47. *Ibid.*

48. Janet Grant, "Disney Helps What Is Lost Get Found," *Orlando Sentinel-Star*, May 18, 1986.

49. Gail M. Martin, "Safety and Health in the Magic Kingdom," *Job Safety and Health* (July 1977), pp. 7-14.

50. One rare such incident concerned the death of a young visitor from amoebic meningoencephalitis. Orange County officials claimed the child internalized the causative amoeba at River Country. Saying they had planned the action before the child's death, Disney officials cut back the daily attendance quota at River Country in order to lower the amount of water bacteria the amoeba eats. See Keay Davidson, "Amoeba Strikes Again," *Orlando Sentinel-Star*, August 1980.

51. These figures are found in Anastasia Toufexis, "No Mickey Mousing Around," *Time* (March 11, 1985), p. 54.

52. Although one young bandsman did receive a potential $42 million settlement in 1983 when a platform collapsed during a band rehearsal, breaking his neck and spinal cord. See "Collegian, 21, Paralyzed at EPCOT Settles for $42 Million," *Miami Herald*, May 11, 1983.

53. James Koslowski, "Walt's World in Litigation Land," *Parks and Recreations* 20:1 (January 1985), pp. 28-33, 100.

54. According to estimates by lawyers on both sides, Disney wins around 85 percent of jury trials. See Stephen Adler, "Snow White for the Defense: Why Disney Doesn't Lose," *American Lawyer* (March 1983).

Chapter 12

1. Dean MacCannell, *The Tourist: A New Theory of the Leisure Class* (New York: Schocken Books, 1976), p. 13.

2. See Alexander Moore, "Walt Disney World: Bounded Ritual Space and the Playful Pilgrimage Center," *Anthropological Quarterly* 53 (1980), pp. 207-218.

3. *Ibid.*, p. 208.

4. Arnold Van Gennep, *Rites of Passage* (Chicago: University of Chicago Press, 1961).

5. Moore, "Walt Disney World," p. 209.

6. Conrad Kottak, "Analysis of Mass Enculturation," in Conrad Kottak, ed., *Researching American Culture* (Ann Arbor: University of Michigan Press, 1982), pp. 40-74. See especially pp. 55-65.

7. Victor Turner, *The Ritual Process: Structure and Anti-Structure* (Chicago: Aldine, 1969). Also see "Pilgrimages as Social Processes," in Victor Turner, *Dramas, Fields, and Metaphors: Symbolic Action in Human Society* (Ithaca: Cornell University Press, 1974), pp. 166-230.

8. Moore, "Walt Disney World," p. 210.

9. *Ibid.*, p. 215.

10. Gregory Bateson, "A Theory of Play and Fantasy," in Gregory Bateson, *Steps to an Ecology of Mind* (New York: Ballantine, 1972), pp. 177-193. This phrase is found on p. 183.

11. For a full discussion of reasons for travel, see Eric J. Leed, *The Mind of the Traveler: From Gilgamesh to Global Tourism* (New York: Basic Books, 1991).

12. MacCannell, *The Tourist*, p. 10.

13. *Ibid.*, p. 21.

14. *Ibid.*, p. 153.

15. *Ibid.*, p. 13.

16. *Ibid.*

17. This is the only example of human hucksterism this transparent in all of WDW. Corporate hucksterism, of course, is ubiquitous.

18. Colonel Hathi was the leader of the elephant "dawn patrol" in Disney's 1967 movie *The Jungle Book*.

19. Steve Birnbaum, *Steve Birnbaum Brings You the Best of Walt Disney World* (New York: Houghton Mifflin, 1985), p. 77. The Birnbaum volumes will be referred to by year of publication.

20. *Walt Disney World* (The Walt Disney Company, 1986), p. 34.

21. This movie is a Disneyfication of Johann Wyss's *The Swiss Family Robinson* (New York: Airmont Books, 1963 [1812-1813]), itself a gloss on Defoe's classic work. Treehouse: movie set: Wyss: Defoe — simulations of simulations.

22. The items available to Wyss's Robinsons, both on their shipwrecked boat and on the island, form a similarly unlikely cornucopia.

23. We must remember Friday, however, as well as Crusoe's own salvaging of manufactured items from the ship.

24. Note that except for anthropologists and those who served there during World War II (or in the Peace Corps), interest in Polynesia has occluded the fact that Micronesia and Melanesia are also in the Pacific.

25. It's probably also ageist.

26. The Caribbean motif continues in the color-coded Caribbean Beach Resort. The aqua-and-pink gingerbread hotel modules are named for Caribbean Islands — Barbados, Aruba, Jamaica, Martinique, Trinidad. Old Port Royale mimics the Farmer's Market at EPCOT's The Land pavilion with its food court. The pool has a Banana Cabana bar and a simulated fort built out over part of it with smoking canons. The posted speed limit here is twenty-seven miles per hour, whimsically telling us to slow down and relax.

27. These include the Coral Isle Café, the Papeete Bay Veranda, the South Seas Dining Room, the Tambu Lounge, Captain Hook's Hideaway, Robinson Crusoe, Esq., Trader Jack's Grog Hut, the Polynesian Princess, and News from Civilization.

28. Birnbaum, *Steve Birnbaum*, 1985, p. 175.

29. For some of the following, see Birnbaum, *Steve Birnbaum*, 1990, pp. 180-182.

30. As does River Country, Typhoon Lagoon requires a separate admission.

31. This storm seems to have passed through the Caribbean. Why they call it Typhoon rather than Hurricane Lagoon is a geographical mystery.

32. We might remember that Pleasure Island was also the place where the boys turned into donkeys in *Pinocchio*.

33. The yakoose is a cross between a yak and a moose.

34. Note also there is *real* staff here — *real* waitpersons and bartenders. When they go home, there is a *real* cleanup crew.

35. Note that the word "showcase" itself suggests commerce — the placing of wares under glass.

36. *Walt Disney World*, p. 94.

37. More than once in Europe I have heard people say, "This is just like the one at Disney World."

38. Much of the following information on World Showcase is found in the various guidebooks, Disney commemorative books, and information pamphlets about WDW. The most important for my purposes are Birnbaum (1985, 1988, 1989, 1990); Bob Sehlinger and John Finley, *The Unofficial Guide to Walt Disney World* (New York: Menasha Ridge Press [distributed by Simon and Schuster], 1985); Richard R. Beard, *Walt Disney's EPCOT Center* (New York: Henry N. Abrams, 1982); *Walt Disney World*; Joel A. Glass, *Fodor's Fun in Disney World and the Orlando Area* (New York: Fodor's Travel Publications, 1988); Marylin Springer, *Frommer's 1987-1988 Guide to Orlando, Disney World and EPCOT* (New York: Prentice-Hall, 1987); and the *Epcot Center Guidebook* and the *Epcot Center Entertainment Program* (published weekly).

39. The previous exhibit was "The Splendors of the Golden Age — Three Centuries of Spanish Colonial Art," which contained artifacts and clothes from the colonial period of Mexico's history.

40. See Richard Defendorf, "Mariachi," *Orlando Sentinel*, May 25, 1986, pp. 17-18.

41. As the 1991 Persian Gulf war underscored, Americans tend to learn their geography through television maps of war zones. If the United States does not go to war, its citizens remain geographically ignorant.

42. *Stavekirker* (Oslo: Normanns Kunstforlag, n.d.).

43. There is a discrepancy between the Disney sign (c. 1250) and the date (c. 1200) given in the Norsk Folkemuseum brochure (Oslo: Chr. Olsen-Mittet, n.d.). The Disney sign also says that there were over one thousand of these churches. Perhaps Disney is overcoming official Norwegian modesty.

44. This replaces the former exhibit, "One Thousand Years of Discovery," a display of pre-Christian artifacts, including a Kuli stone with incised runes.

45. For a description of the Akershus, see Stephen Tschudi Madsen, *Akershus Slott* (Oslo: Haslum Grafisk, 1985).

46. The best collection of these studs is actually in Sweden, in Stockholm's Old Town (Gamla Stan).

47. Li Bai was apparently a somewhat unsavory character in real life. See *China* (Alexandria, Va.: Time-Life Books Library of Nations, 1986).

48. In recent years, "Treasures of the Forbidden City," an exhibit of imperial domestic artifacts, and "Artistry in Time," a collection of intricate mechanical clocks, have visited this museum.

49. In January 1991, Der Bücherwurm presented Jutta Levasseur, master egg painter, while porcelain artist Werner Rauschert, representing W. Goebel Porzellanfabrik, performed at Glas und Porzellan. See *EPCOT Center Entertainment Program*, January 20-26, 1991.

50. See Beard, *EPCOT Center*, p. 182.

51. Birnbaum, *Steve Birnbaum*, 1985, p. 126; Beard, *EPCOT Center*, p. 186.

52. Yet with all of this, the Campanile is on a different side of the piazza than it is in Venice's Piazza San Marco.

53. Beard, *EPCOT Center*, p. 189.

54. *Ibid.*, p. 191.

55. See Patrick Connolly, "Artist Enjoys Seeing Smiles as He Performs Candy Sculpture," *Nashville Tennessean*, October 9, 1986.

56. Bastilla is a devastatingly rich Moroccan dessert.

57. The French term reminds us of Morocco's colonial history.

58. According to Birnbaum, this is "a motion picture designer's technique . . . which involves exaggerating the relative smallness of distant parts of a structure to make the totality appear taller than it really is." See Birnbaum, *Steve Birnbaum*, 1986, p. 177.

59. All three restaurants plus the boulangerie around the corner are operated by these three chefs, but Les Chefs de France is their centerpiece.

60. See Roland Barthes, "The Eiffel Tower," in Roland Barthes, *The Eiffel Tower and Other Mythologies*, translated by Richard Howard (New York: Hill and Wang, 1979).

61. There are some city crests here and there inside the shops, but one must already know what they represent to know what they represent.

62. Birnbaum, *Steve Birnbaum*, 1986, p. 119.

63. Cited in Jim White, "Disney Shop Fosters Hoser Image Abroad," *Toronto Star*, May 11, 1983.

64. "By comparison," White writes (*ibid.*), "External Affairs spent $3.5 million in six months at the recent Knoxville, Tennessee, World's Fair. Powles (director of world exhibitions for external affairs in 1983) says that by partaking in different regional fairs, Canada gains access to different regional audiences."

65. *Ibid.*

66. Ken Smith, "Disney World's EPCOT Center Gives U.S. View of Canada," *London (Ontario) Free Press*, March 10, 1983.

67. Hazel Howe, "Canada Featured in Newest Disney World Center," *The Expositor*, October 16, 1982.

68. Jim White, "Toronto Is Pork Chop City, Right?" *Toronto Star*, May 11, 1983.

69. The use of city and provincial names to label entrées seems to have been discontinued as of spring 1991.

70. This section draws from Smith, "Disney World's EPCOT Center," which continues, "Also included in the setting are Rose of Sharon, purple leaf plum, a weeping willow, flowering dogwood, swamp and black birch — 400 big trees and shrubs in all. To this has been added azaleas, 250 roses, hundreds of perennials, and 20 varieties of annuals numbering approximately 8,000 for each of the five seasons they have every year."

71. See Beard, *EPCOT Center*, p. 164.

72. *Ibid.*, pp. 164-165.

Chapter 13

1. Joel Achenbach, "Reality to Be Cancelled?" *Tropic Magazine, Miami Herald*, December 13, 1987, pp. 18-21. This quote is on p. 20.

2. Frederic Jameson, "Postmodernism, or the Cultural Logic of Late Capitalism," *New Left Review* 146 (1984), pp. 53-92.

3. Achenbach, "Reality to Be Cancelled?", p. 18.

4. *Ibid.*, p. 20. Two further comments in passing. As Achenbach points out (and as Charles Elkins independently reminded me), airline travelers — who normally pay no attention to live flight attendants when they give their preflight safety explanations — sit riveted to the screen when the same spiel is shown on video. Further, not only have we become comfortable with artifice and falsehood, but they have become explicit marketing tools. Eh, Joe Isuzu?

5. Birds are also presented as an attraction on Discovery Island.

6. Umberto Eco, *Travels in Hyperreality* (New York: Harcourt Brace Jovanovich, 1986), p. 9.

7. Note the series of levels here. Such dolls — Broccoli, Eggplant, and Tomato — are images of audioanimatronic figures, themselves modeled both on vegetables and on a 1950s caricature of Latin musical groups.

8. This term is borrowed from Elaine Rapping. See her *The Looking-Glass World of Non-Fiction TV* (Boston: South End Press, 1987).

9. But then Williamsburg doesn't have any robots, and the film stars Jack Lord and not Michael Jackson.

10. The best book about Disney movies is Richard Holliss and Brian Sibley, *The Disney Studio Story* (New York: Crown, 1988). This book contains a complete Disney filmography.

11. For an extended analysis of the technology of animation as well as a report on the "glory days" of Disney productions (especially the 1930s and 1940s), see Frank Thomas and Ollie Johnston, *Disney Animation: The Illusion of Life* (New York:

Abbeville Press, 1981). Although generally hagiographic, this large and useful book contains some information about Walt Disney as a difficult boss and about the progressive cost-effective corner cutting practiced as the expenses of animation rose over time.

12. As Schickel defines it, Disneyfication is "that shameful process by which everything the studio later touched, no matter how unique the vision of the original from which the studio worked, was reduced to the limited terms Disney and his people could understand." See Richard Schickel *The Disney Version: The Life, Times, Art and Commerce of Walt Disney* (New York: Simon and Schuster, 1968), p. 225.

13. Peter L. Berger and Thomas Luckmann, *The Social Construction of Reality: A Treatise in the Sociology of Knowledge* (New York: Doubleday Anchor, 1966). See particularly pp. 104-116.

14. Will Wright, *Sixguns and Society: A Structural Study of the Western* (Berkeley: University of California Press, 1975), p. 186.

15. John M. Ellis and Maria Tatar have traced the path by which the European stories that became collected as *Grimm's Fairy Tales* were domesticated in succeeding reissues of the original collection. Among other things, such domestication drastically altered the presentation of female characters and the style of punishment for misdeeds. See John M. Ellis, *One Fairy Story Too Many: The Brothers Grimm and Their Tales* (Chicago: University of Chicago Press, 1983); and Maria Tatar, *The Hard Facts of the Grimm's Fairy Tales* (Princeton: Princeton University Press, 1987).

16. See especially Bruno Bettelheim, *The Uses of Enchantment: The Meaning and Importance of Fairy Tales* (New York; Random House, 1977).

17. Regarding "properties," Schickel writes of Walt Disney himself, "the egotism that insists on making another man's work your own through wanton tampering and by advertising claim is not an attractive form of egotism." See Schickel, *The Disney Version*, p. 296.

18. The only time Disney dispensed with a story line altogether in a feature-length film was in the animation of *Fantasia*. This attempt to blend the kind of characters the studio was used to animating — Mickey Mouse as the sorcerer's apprentice, various kinds of fairies, racist versions of dancing Chinese mushrooms, and the like — with clichéd middlebrow examples of classical music was, perhaps because there was no familiar story line (and because the music was usually pretty loud), the scariest of all Disney movies to many children. Reissues of *Fantasia* have been moderately successful in part because of its appeal audiences of young adults filled with mind-altering substances.

19. Cited in Schickel, *The Disney Version*, p. 18.

20. *Ibid.*, p. 220.

21. *Ibid.*, p. 43.

22. *Ibid.*, pp. 51-52.

23. *Ibid.*, p. 129.

24. *Ibid.*, p. 192.

25. *Ibid.*, p. 101.

26. *Ibid.*, p. 156.

27. *Ibid.*, p. 51.

28. *Ibid.*, p. 101.

29. Stephen Jay Gould, "Mickey Mouse Meets Konrad Lorenz," *Natural History* 88:5 (May 1979), pp. 30-36. See also Elizabeth A. Lawrence, "In the Mick of Time: Reflections on Disney's Ageless Mouse," *Journal of Popular Culture* 19:2 (Fall 1986),

pp. 65-72; and Robert W. Brockway, "The Masks of Mickey Mouse: Symbol of a Generation," *Journal of Popular Culture* 22:4 (Spring 1989), pp. 25-34.

30. Actually, there are few fathers, either. Disney's world is one in which children go it alone without parents. Such a world may be derived from one aspect of psychological wish fulfillment, but it includes loneliness and danger as well.

31. Kay Stone, "Things Walt Disney Never Told Us," *Journal of American Folklore* 88 (1975), pp. 42-50.

32. *Ibid.*, pp. 44-45.

33. This is Schickel's phrase. See Schickel, *The Disney Version*, p. 275.

34. Another brand of animation is evident at WDW. Derived more directly from the style of the cartoons made for the War Department during World War II, these films are particularly evident at Future World. Didactic in intent, these cartoons — *The Water Engine* at World of Motion and *Atlas* at The Living Sea — are excellent examples of the Disney mission to make education, in the interest of multinational corporations, fun. *Atlas* and the opening movie at Universe of Energy which points to *Fantasia* in style are, in fact, progressively educational in their presentation of physicochemical evolution.

35. At the Disney-MGM Studios there is an attraction devoted entirely to sound and sound effects. The Monster Sound Show, with audience participation, tells us how Foley artists — sound effects specialists — do some of their work. In the accompanying "Soundsations," we sit with headsets on as the character we play hears a glass of soda poured, is accosted by a mad director, and gets a haircut. The sound of the blow-dryer as it passes from one side of our head, across our neck, and on to the other side is so effectively done that we "almost" feel the hot air as it passes.

36. Canned regional or folk accents are heard at attractions such as Country Bear Jamboree, where folk caricatures define the show.

37. Standard American English is, of course, an accent. It's merely the one that has gained hegemony in the United States.

38. The use of the label "cast members" for Disney workers highlights the cinematic structure of WDW while obscuring the fact that the people so called, like cast members in general, are also employees.

39. One of the arguments made by management in response to attempts by low-paid employees in character outfits to join the performers' union for actors and musicians is that because these employees do not have speaking parts, they are not actors and should not be compensated accordingly. Here's a nice catch-22.

40. Thomas and Johnston, *Disney Animation*.

41. In *The Disney Studio Story*, Holliss and Sibley list all of Disney's Academy Award nominees and winners. Among them are fifteen nominations for best musical scoring (two winners) and thirteen nominations for best song (three winners). This does not include the nominations and winner from *The Little Mermaid*.

42. There has, however, been some opposition to the presentation of ghosts and the like based on religious principles.

43. Mike Wallace, "Mickey Mouse History: Portraying the Past at Disney World," *Radical History Review* 32 (1985), pp. 33-57.

44. I find the the Carousel of Progress song easily the most obnoxious one at WDW. Yet when asked by Father to sing along during the later parts of the show, a number of visitors *do* try to join in. Some even seem to look embarrassed because they don't yet know the words. It's not clear who is going to know that they don't know the words because they have been invited to sing along by a robot.

45. Not without reason has EPCOT Center been called the Experimental Prototype Commercial of Tomorrow.

46. The "preshow" reminds us, had we forgotten, that Journey into Imagination is sponsored by Kodak.

47. Jackson has a special suite at one of the Walt Disney World Hotel Plaza hotels where he keeps his Disney memorabilia.

Chapter 14

1. Steve Birnbaum, *Steve Birnbaum Brings You the Best of Walt Disney World* (New York: Houghton Mifflin, 1988), p. 93. The Birnbaum volumes (1985, 1988, 1989, 1990) will be referred to by year of publication. Beginning with the 1989 edition, the volumes have been published in New York by Avon Books and Hearst Professional Magazines, Inc.

2. *Walt Disney World* (The Walt Disney Company, 1986), p. 30, introduces Fantasyland thus: "The inspiration for Fantasyland, of course, was provided by Disney's classic animated films, namely *Snow White and the Seven Dwarfs*, 1937 (Snow White's Scary Adventures); *Pinocchio*, 1940 (Pinocchio's Village Haus Snack Bar); *Dumbo*, 1941 (Dumbo, the Flying Elephant); *The Adventures of Ichabod and Mr. Toad*, 1949 (Mr. Toad's Wild Ride); *Cinderella*, 1950 (Cinderella's Castle and Cinderella's Golden Carousel); *Alice in Wonderland*, 1951 (Mad Tea Party and the Mad Hatter Hat Shop); *Peter Pan*, 1953 (Peter Pan's Flight and the Tinkerbell Toy Shop); *Sleeping Beauty*, 1959 (King Stefan's Banquet Hall restaurant); *The Sword in the Stone*, 1963 (Merlin's Magic Shop); and *The Aristocats*, 1970 (The AristoCats gift shop)."

3. See Birnbaum, *Steve Birnbaum*, 1985, p. 75.

4. Incidentally, the total cost for fireworks at the various Disney shows is in excess of $30,000 per night. See Charles Leerhsen, "How Disney Does It," *Newsweek*, April 3, 1989, pp. 48-54.

5. Maria-Lydia Spinelli (personal communication) notes the change from Disneyland to WDW: "The castle at Disneyland is Sleeping Beauty's Castle. The juxtaposition is just a process of internal change within the park, from royalty . . . to upward mobility would-be royalty. Cinderella is the fairy tale counterpart of Horatio Alger."

6. Behind the host and hostess podium is a computerized graphic display with bulbs that light up when a table is ready. Someone upstairs in the restaurant pushes a parallel display button when a table is reset.

7. *Walt Disney World*, p. 27.

8. Passing overhead from Fantasyland to Tomorrowland, the Skyway offers one of the few public looks at how some of the magic is put together. Especially over Fantasyland we can see the relationship among building structure, functional use, and street-level façade. Every so often, one even catches a glimpse of maintenance personnel on the roof.

9. Incidentally, the *Magic Kingdom Guide Book*, which is given to every visitor, cleverly camouflages structural design. Stylized maps of each "land" are numbered and brightly colored in red (attractions), blue (restaurants and snacks), and green (shops). Buildings and landscaping outside the focal area are depicted in something like peach. Especially at the Adventureland-Frontierland and Liberty Square-Fantasyland borders, our attention is drawn away from the sharing of structures. Both the Fantasyland and Liberty Square maps, for instance, show a large blank space

(where the theater for the Hall of Presidents and Fantasyland Theater are situated) just beyond colored land boundaries. The Liberty Square map goes one step further by depicting half of this space in white, with the identifying Liberty Square legend printed across it.

10. Birnbaum, *Steve Birnbaum*, 1985, p. 83.

11. *Ibid.*, p. 84.

12. As employees at Disneyland have told Maria-Lydia Spinelli (personal communication), "It wears off in a week." There is a good bit of evidence, however, that for the right person, pixie dust can last forever. A lot of Disney people remain delighted with their park jobs. Although I've never worked there, I certainly remain pixie dusted.

13. Edward W. Said, *Orientalism* (New York: Random House, 1979).

14. The theme song here, sung in other languages during the ride, returns to English. One reading of the sameness of physiognomy, the eventual sameness of costume colors, and the return to English is that the world would be a better place if children all looked like American Anglos. One wonders what the message would be if all the children in the "white" room were dressed in rust and had brown skins. Another reading is that the designers of this attraction have unconsciously presented an argument for miscegenation. I like that interpretation.

15. Maria-Lydia Spinelli (personal communication) suggests that many people who like this ride are sensitive to these realities. They are often deeply touched by the hope that love and harmony may do away with war, violence and hunger.

16. Birnbaum, *Steve Birnbaum*, 1985, p. 85.

17. Interestingly, my copies of the *Magic Kingdom Guide Book* list this ride only as Snow White's Adventure. One can clearly see the space where the word "Scary" has been whited out of the typesetting.

18. It is also a pungent comment on citizens' interest in national electoral politics.

19. Birnbaum, *Steve Birnbaum*, 1985, p. 83.

20. *Ibid.*

21. Distribution of attractions, shops, and restaurants at the Magic Kingdom is shown as follows.

Magic Kingdom Venues

	A	S	R	Total	%[a]
Adventureland	4(20%)[b]	11(55%)	5(20%)	20	16%
Frontierland[c]	6(33%)	6(33%)	6(33%)	18	15%
Liberty Square	4(27%)	6(40%)	5(33%)	15	12%
Fantasyland	11(39%)	9(32%)	8(29%)	28	23%
Tomorrowland	10(56%)	4(22%)	4(22%)	18	15%
Main Street USA[d]	4(16%)	14(56%)	7(28%)	25	20%
Total[e]	39(31%)	50(40%)	35(29%)	124	100%

A = Attractions, S = Shops, R = Restaurants

[a]These figures represent the percentage of all Magic Kingdom venues contained in each of the lands. This column actually sums to 101 percent due to rounding.

[b]These percentages represent the proportion of types of venue in each land. The first three percentages in each row sum to 100 percent.

[c]These figures do not include Splash Mountain.

[d]Main Street also has six service establishments: Sun Bank, Magic Kingdom Baby Center, First Aid Center, Stroller Shop, City Hall Information Center, and Hospitality House.

[e]These figures represent the total number of attractions, shops, and restaurants in the Magic Kingdom. The percentages represent the proportions of all Magic Kingdom venues filled by each of these kinds of venues. They sum to 100 percent.

22. This illusion is similar to, but more successful than, the one at Future World's The Living Seas.

23. *Steamboat Willie* opened on November 18, 1928.

24. Clarence Nash was the original voice of Donald Duck. Carl Barks invented much of Duckburg and its citizens.

25. For many years, Hyperion was the address of the Walt Disney Studios in California.

26. A mother speaks to a small child: "This is where Mickey and Minnie go nite-nite." I'm not sure this is quite what Walt Disney would have had in mind.

27. Goofy's lavender-and-purple place parodies the peeling plaster with bricks showing behind it motif we have seen at the Italy Showcase and elsewhere. The exposed bricks are a clearly non real shade of pink.

28. Richard R. Beard, *Walt Disney's EPCOT Center: Creating the New World of Tomorrow* (New York: Harry M. Abrams, 1982), p. 83.

29. *Ibid.*, p. 86.

30. William J. Sertl, "Hollywood Drive: Disney-MGM Studios in Orlando," *Travel & Leisure* 19:12 (December 1989), pp. 140-146, 192-196. This quote is found on p. 196.

31. Dean MacCannell has argued that work displays are one of the markers of modern tourism. See his *Tourist: A New Theory of the Leisure Class* (New York: Schocken, 1976).

32. The Disney-MGM Studios is a bit smaller than the Magic Kingdom and EPCOT Center. It can accommodate 25,000 people on a daily basis, whereas the others can hold 60,000 and 45,000, respectively. See Joan Chrissos, "New Theme Park Not Big Enough, Disney Discovers," *Miami Herald*, July 1989.

33. See Mark Crispin Miller, *Boxed In: The Culture of TV* (Evanston, Ill.: Northwestern University Press, 1988).

34. The extras include at least one black Nazi.

35. See John P. Peecher, editor, *Making of Return of the Jedi* (New York: Ballantine, 1983).

36. For further examples of this style, see Rip Georges and Jim Heimann, *California Crazy: Roadside Vernacular Architecture* (San Francisco: Chronicle Books, 1980).

37. See Thomas Hine, *Populuxe* (New York: Knopf, 1986).

38. There is a functioning radio studio on the left end of this building.

39. Jimmy Foley was one of the first great sound effects people in Hollywood. Sound effects people are often called Foley artists.

40. This technology is also part of the show at the Wonders of Life in Future World.

41. The shows include "The Nightly News," "I Love Lucy," "The Ed Sullivan Show," "General Hospital," "Bonanza," "Gilligan's Island," "The Golden Girls," "Cheers," "The Three Stooges," and interviews with Howard Cosell (after a young guest "hits" a home run at Shea Stadium), Johnny Carson, and David Letterman.

42. Explanations of the technology itself are developed on the Backstage Studio Tour.

43. The plaza is landscaped to look like an upside-down Mickey Mouse from the air. Echo Lake forms his right ear. His left ear, the outline of which passes through the Hollywood Brown Derby, is planted in the same shape and at the same angle as Echo Lake. Landscaping in front of the Chinese Theater forms Mickey's smiling mouth, and plantings in the plaza make up his eyes and nose.

44. *The Disney-MGM Studios: A Pictorial Souvenir* (The Walt Disney Company, n.d.).

45. *Ibid.*

46. Vehicles go through two at a time. One gets kidnapped in each scene.

47. Again I refer the reader to Frank Thomas and Ollie Johnston, *Disney Animation: The Illusion of Life* (New York: Abbeville Press, 1981), for a rich description of the process of animation.

48. This list is taken from *Disney-MGM Studios Guide Book* (The Walt Disney Company, 1989).

49. *Disney-MGM Studios: A Pictorial Souvenir.* This may be a comment about the person next to us as well.

50. Birnbaum (1989, p. 161) notes that with over two-and-a-quarter million garments, WDW has the biggest working wardrobe in the world.

51. Sometimes the shuttle passes down the street, sometimes not. Recently the street has been closed off to shuttle traffic. The vehicle that delivers the Teenage Mutant Ninja Turtles to Washington Square for their periodic appearances is currently (1991) the only moving vehicle on New York Street.

52. Once the shuttle tour is over, visitors can return to the set on foot to notice the detail.

53. It is also an ironic comment on the terror with which many children endured *Night on Bald Mountain* in particular and *Fantasia* in general. See Elinor J. Brecher, "*Fantasia* at 50: Of Course It's Scary. Disney Has *Always* Been Scary," *Miami Herald*, October 7, 1990, pp. I1, I6.

54. Seven, actually, but I have mentioned the Caribbean Beach Resort elsewhere, and the Port Orleans Resort has just opened.

55. Gary Delshon, "Architecture for the Masses: Disney Makes Statement in Grand Manner," *Sacramento Bee*, September 30, 1990, pp. H1, H16.

56. Beth Dunlop, "Dolphin, Swan Take Classic Shapes," *Miami Herald*, May 27, 1990, p. 2I. See also Beth Dunlop, "Disney Reshaping Architecture World," *Miami Herald*, May 27, 1990, pp. I1, I2.

57. See Dunlop, "Disney Reshaping Architecture World," *ibid.*, p. I1 and Suzy Kalter Gershman, "Disney's Grand Hotels," *Travel & Leisure* 20:2 (February 1990}, p. 66.

Chapter 15

1. Guy Debord, *The Society of the Spectacle* (Detroit: Black and Red, 1983), p. 4.

2. Joel Achenbach, "Reality to Be Cancelled?" *Tropic Magazine, Miami Herald*, December 13, 1987, pp. 18-21. This article was expanded in "Creeping Surrealism: Does Anybody Really Know What's Real Anymore?" *Utne Reader* (November-December 1988). See also Achenbach, "Fake Up, America!" *Mother Jones* (September 1988), pp. 13-15.

3. Achenbach, "Reality to Be Cancelled?"

4. Disney has built a studio tour theme park at WDW — not a studio theme park but a studio *tour* theme park. The actual studio part is there merely to make the entertainment areas credible. The back lots are simulated. What have been constructed are not back lot façades but fake back lot façades. Michael Harrington has described WDW as a Potemkin Village. What we really have here is a fake Potemkin Village.

5. Here's Achenbach again in "Reality to Be Cancelled?": "This is a country in which, when a 13-year-old California girl turned in her parents for drug use and soon found herself in an orphanage because her parents were in jail, the president's wife congratulated the girl and said, 'She must have loved her parents a great deal.' This Orwellian scene was made even more poignant when Hollywood film companies immediately began scrapping over movie rights."

6. Disney's artifice is one of the central draws at WDW. Robert Campbell cites the entertainment power of the "machinery of illusion" in "Fabulous Fakery," *Boston Globe*, February 27, 1990, pp. 57, 59.

7. Umberto Eco, *Travels in Hyperreality* (New York: Harcourt, Brace, Jovanovich, 1986), p. 8.

8. For an excellent discussion of Jameson and Baudrillard, see Steven Connor, *Postmodern Culture: An Introduction to Theories of the Contemporary* (Oxford: Basil Blackwell, 1989), especially pp. 27-64. See also Douglas Kellner, editor, *Modernism/Jameson/Critique* (Washington, D.C.: Maisonneuve Press, 1989). Does Bo, one wonders, know 'drillard?

9. Frederic Jameson, "Postmodernism, or the Cultural Logic of Late Capitalism," *New Left Review* 146 (July-August 1984), pp. 53-92.

10. *Ibid.*, p. 66.

11.. Here Jameson refers to Guy Debord, whose *Society of the Spectacle* is a major signpost on Jameson's journey. Debord begins his short book with a quote from Feuerbach ("Preface" to the second edition of *The Essence of Christianity*), suggesting that the triumph of images is not new: "But certainly for the present age, which prefers the sign to the thing signified, the copy to the original, fancy to reality, the appearance to the essence . . . *illusion* only is *sacred*, truth *profane*." What *is* new is the degree to which images have become the connotative tactical materials of commodification. See Debord, *Society of the Spectacle*, p. 1.

12. Jean Baudrillard, *Simulations* (New York: Semiotext(e), Inc., 1983), p. 6.

13. *Ibid.*, p. 8.

14. *Ibid.*, p. 1.

15. *Ibid.*, p. 95.

16. *Ibid.*, p. 101.

17. *Ibid.*, p. 148.

18. *Ibid.*, p. 26. Baudrillard has also discussed Disneyland in his misguided Californianization of America, *America*, translated by Chris Turner (New York: Verso Books, 1988). Another strong statement about the hyperreal autonomy of the model is found in *In the Shadow of the Silent Majorities* (New York: Semiotext(e), 1983), pp. 83-84: "Deterrence of all real potentiality, deterrence by meticulous reduplication, by macroscopic hyperfidelity, by accelerated recycling, by saturation and obscenity, by abolition of the distance between the real and its representation, by implosion of the differentiated poles between which flowed the energy of the real: This hyperreality puts an end to the system of the real, it puts an end to the real as referential by exalting it as a model."

19. Some brief comments on the deconstructionist notion of "undecidableness" are in order. The deconstructionist stance reminds me of the teenager who, by proving that no one else can understand the complete meaning of any word in his or her utterance, shows that communication is impossible. The demonstration, of course, relies on the possibility of clear communication of the problem. It struck me, when I used to do things like this, as slightly masturbatory.

What underlies this stance is a thwarted desire for the holiness of essentialism. Because the world in general and language in particular do not yield essentialist truths, the deconstructionist — in a huff — opts for an essentialist version of antistructure in which all is random, nothing is decidable. There are liberating moments in this but better, I think, Bateson's "difference that makes a difference" than Derrida's "différance."

Much poststructuralism is written in a discourse of dominance. In "The Patron Saint of Neo-Pop," New York Review of Books, June 1, 1989, p. 29, Robert Hughes calls it "French jargon as an impenetrable prophylactic against understanding."

Deconstruction is precisely the philosophical position one might expect under the hegemony of the commodity form — a paradigm instance of postmodern culture under late capitalism. It is easy to see how in a manner most dialectic, deconstruction has resuscitated pragmatism as a viable philosophical stance.

20. Karl Marx, *Capital: A Critique of Political Economy* (New York: Modern Library, 1906), p. 41.

21. Paul Smith writes, "Capital's claims for the legitimation of contemporary social and economic structures are made largely at the level of the *consumer*, who is never the consumer of just a commodity but equally of the commodity's text and

ideology." See Paul Smith, "Visiting the Banana Republic," in Andrew Ross, editor, *Universal Abandon? The Politics of Postmodernism* (Minneapolis: University of Minnesota Press, 1988), pp. 128-148 [p. 139].

22. This is the title phrase of Adrian Forty, *Objects of Desire: Design and Society from Wedgewood to IBM* (New York: Pantheon, 1986).

23. See, for example, Neil Postman, *Amusing Ourselves to Death: Public Discourse in the Age of Show Business* (New York: Penguin, 1986), pp. 58-60.

24. C. B. McPherson, *The Political Theory of Possessive Individualism* (London: Oxford University Press, 1962).

25. Gary Wills, *Nixon Agonistes* (New York: New American Library, 1971).

26. See Stuart Ewen, *Captains of Consciousness: Advertising and the Social Roots of the Consumer Culture* (New York: McGraw-Hill, 1976), and Stuart and Elizabeth Ewen, *Channels of Desire: Mass Images and the Shaping of American Consciousness* (New York: McGraw-Hill, 1982). See also Stuart Ewen, *All Consuming Images: The Politics of Style in Contemporary Culture* (New York: Basic Books, 1988), and Michael Schudson, *Advertising, the Uneasy Persuasion: Its Dubious Impact on American Society* (New York: Basic Books, 1984).

27. As Judith Williamson has suggested in *Consuming Passions: The Dynamics of Popular Culture* (London: Marion Boyars, 1986), the act of shopping itself has taken on moral heft: "Shopping is a socially endorsed event, a form of social cement. It makes you feel normal. Most people find it cheers them up — even window shopping. The extent to which shoplifting is done where there is no natural need (most items stolen are incredibly trivial) reveals the extent to which peoples' wants and needs are *translated* into the form of consumption" (p. 23).

28. W. F. Haug, *Critique of Commodity Aesthetics: Appearance, Sexuality and Advertising in Capitalist Society* (St. Paul: University of Minnesota Press, 1986). My colleague Howard Kaminsky brought Haug to my attention.

29. In his introduction to Jean Baudrillard, *Selected Writings* (Palo Alto, Cal.: Stanford University Press, 1988), Mark Poster describes this result: "But the commodity embodies a communicational structure that is a departure from the traditional understanding of the sign. In a commodity the relation of word, image or meaning and referent is broken and restructured so that its force is directed, not to the referent of use value or utility, but to desire" (p. 1).

30. See also Jack Solomon's popular treatment of semiotics, *The Signs of Our Times* (Los Angeles: Jeremy P. Tarcher, Inc., 1988).

31. Are commercials embedded in television shows, or is it the other way around?

32. Neil Postman, *Amusing Ourselves to Death: Public Discourse in the Age of Show Business* (New York: Viking Penguin, 1985). See also Elayne Rapping, *The Looking Glass World of Nonfiction TV* (Boston: South End Press, 1987).

33. See Irving Rein, Philip Kottler, and Martin Stoller, *High Visibility: How Executives, Politicians, Entertainers, Athletes, and Other Professionals Create, Market, and Achieve Successful Images* (New York: Dodd, Mead, 1987).

34. George Felton, "Students of 'the Pitch,'" *Newsweek*, September 29, 1988, p. 22.

35. Jules Henry, *Culture Against Man* (New York: Vintage, 1965).

36. Jameson, "Postmodernism, or the Cultural Logic of Late Capitalism," p. 61.

37. I found Evans's ideas in his unpublished manuscript, "Deflective Attention," n.d.

38. In Edward Henderson, "Homo Symbolicus, A Definition of Man," *Man and World* 4:2 (May 1971).

39. Evans, "Deflective Attention," p. 9.

40. *Ibid.*, p. 12.

41. *Ibid.*

42. *Ibid.*, p. 13.

43. *Ibid.*, p. 14.

44. The use of a mantra performs this function in meditation. Ostensibly meaningless, its repetition is meant to override connections between signifiers and signifieds as they pass through consciousness. Husserl claimed that all consciousness is consciousness "of" something; but meditative consciousness is "empty" consciousness, awareness without meaning. Meditation is a good example of absorbed attention.

45. Evans, "Deflective Attention," p. 15.

46. *Ibid.*, p. 19.

47. *Ibid.*, p. 17.

48. *Ibid.*, p. 14.

49. *Ibid.*, pp. 20-21.

50. *Ibid.*, p. 17. Jameson argues that this is a schizophrenic experience: "Schizophrenic experience is an experience of isolated, disconnected, discontinuous material signifiers which fail to link up into a coherent sequence. The schizophrenic thus does not know personal identity in our sense, since our feeling of identity depends on our sense of the persistence of the 'I' and the 'me' over time." See Jameson, "Postmodernism and Consumer Society," in Hal Foster, editor, *The Anti-Aesthetic: Essays on Postmodern Culture* (Port Townsend, Wash.: Bay Press, 1983), pp. 111-125 [p. 119]. Indeed, Jameson's cultural schizophrenia — a metaphor rather than a clinical concept — and commodity Zen may be one and the same.

51. Raymond Williams, *Keywords: A Vocabulary of Culture and Society,* revised edition (New York: Oxford University Press, 1983).

52. This passage from Herder is cited in R. Williams, *ibid.*, p. 89.

53. Jim Collins, *Uncommon Cultures: Popular Culture and Post-Modernism* (New York: Routledge, 1989). This quote is found on p. xiii.

54. In *The Culture of Criticism and the Criticism of Culture* (New York: Oxford University Press, 1987), Giles Gunn reminds us that even this elite version of "culture" was a field of contention: "The Romantics used the term *culture* as a weapon in the cause of social and political change; the Victorians turned it into an emblem of social and political reaction" (p. 9).

55. See Andreas Huyssen, *After the Great Divide: Modernism, Mass Culture and Postmodernism* (Bloomington: University of Indiana Press, 1986).

56. *Ibid.*, p. 17.

57. *Ibid.*, pp. 53-54.

58. Cecelia Tichi, *Shifting Gears: Technology, Literature, Culture in Modernist America* (Chapel Hill: University of North Carolina Press, 1987).

59. Huyssen, *After the Great Divide*, p. 21.

60. See Sandy Carter, "Popular Music and the Left," *Zeta Magazine* 2:7-8 (July/August 1988), pp. 107-110.

61. Wilfred Fluck, "Popular Culture as a Mode of Socialization: A Theory About the Social Functions of Popular Cultural Forms," *Journal of Popular Culture* 21:3 (Winter 1987), p. 31.

62. *Ibid.*, p. 33.

63. These comments are borrowed from Michael R. Real, "The Disney Universe: Morality Play," in Michael R. Real, *Mass-Mediated Culture* (Englewood, N.J.: Prentice-Hall, 1987), p. 47.

64. Huyssen, *After the Great Divide*, p. 152.

65. Haug, *Critique of Commodity Aesthetics*, p. 6.

66. For an extended discussion of the way peoples' actual needs and social locations lead them to different interpretations of popular cultural texts, see John Fiske, *Television Culture* (New York: Methuen, 1987).

67. See Collins, *Uncommon Cultures*, pp. 1-17, for a good discussion of the decentered fragmentation of culture.

68. Anders Stephanson, "Regarding Postmodernism — A Conversation with Frederic Jameson," in Ross, *Universal Abandon? The Politics of Postmodernism*, p. 26.

69. Real, "The Disney Universe."

70. *Ibid.*, p. 48.

71. *Ibid.*, p. 47.

72. *Ibid.*, p. 76.

73. This notion of a "postmodernism of reaction" is Hal Foster's idea. In "Postmodernism: A Preface," in his *The Anti-Aesthetic*, pp. ix-xvi, Foster writes, "In cultural politics today, a basic opposition exists between a postmodernism which seeks to deconstruct modernism and resist the status quo and a postmodernism which repudiates the former to celebrate the latter: a postmodernism of resistance and a postmodernism of reaction" (p. xi-xii).

Chapter 16

1. Ellen Goodman, "At Large," *Summit* (1981); reprinted in *Literary Cavalcade Scholastic Magazine* (January 1982).

2. According to Ray Bradbury, Walt Disney had wondered why a permanent exposition couldn't be built. Why build something and tear it down after the fair's short life? Why not keep the shells and just change the displays from time to time?

3. See William Leiss, *The Domination of Nature* (Boston: Beacon, 1974).

4. Steve Birnbaum, *Steve Birnbaum Brings You the Best of Walt Disney World* (New York: Avon Books and Hearst Professional Magazines, Inc., 1989), p. 128.

5. *Ibid.*, p. 129.

6. Richard R. Beard, *Walt Disney's EPCOT Center: Creating the New World of Tomorrow* (New York: Harry M. Abrams, 1982), p. 71.

7. Richard Holliss and Brian Sibley, *The Disney Studio Story* (New York: Crown, 1988), p. 230.

8. Beard, *Walt Disney's EPCOT Center*, p. 71.

9. J. Tevers McFadyen, "The Future: A Walt Disney Production," *Next* (July 1980).

10. T. M. Shine reports the following: "In the sled in front of me in General Electric's 'Horizons,' I saw something else: A middle-age woman was taking in the leisurely life of the future when she turned to her husband and said, 'I hope I don't live to see this.' She has already lived to see it, thanks to Disney, but what she doesn't want to do is experience it." See T. M. Shine, "EPCOT: The Not So Wonderful World of Disney," Miami *New Times*, November 2-8, 1988, pp. 9-13. This quote is on p. 13.

11. Beard, *Walt Disney's EPCOT Center*, p. 73.

12. "Listen to the Land" (Kraft, Inc., 1987), p. 33.

13. Soup and Salad, the Bakery, the Barbecue Store, the Cheese Shoppe, Picnic Fare (a "handwich" stand), an ice cream stand, the Potato Store, and the Beverage House.

14. Salad makings and some of the fish offerings are reputed to come from The Land's own greenhouses and aquacells.

15. Near the Land Grille Room is a window display of packages of Kraft products and those Kraft sells under other labels. Included are Knudsen's ice cream, Breyer's ice cream, Früsen Gladye, Breakstone's cottage cheese, Landes bagels, Carroll Shelby's Texas Chili Preparation, Sealtest, and Tombstone pizza. They don't tell us that Kraft is currently owned by R. J. Reynolds, whose theme song might well be "Listen to the Lung."

16. Beard, *Walt Disney's EPCOT Center*, p. 118.

17. Paul Gerber was the project's writer-producer-director. See Mary Agnes Welsh, "The Land," *Kraft Ink Magazine* (August 1982). According to Welsh, the film is projected at thirty frames per second rather than the usual twenty-four, thus giving a richer, brighter picture with less flickering. There are thirteen sound tracks, played on thirteen speakers for pinpoint sound.

18. In *The Future World of Agriculture* (Walt Disney Productions, 1984, hereafter *FWA*), Wendy Murphy writes, "The purpose of this motion picture is to give the millions of visitors to The Land some sense of personal involvement in the world of farming and food production" (p. 29).

19. "In Holland the wind has been made to serve man," reads a picture caption in Beard's *Walt Disney's EPCOT Center* (p. 117), summing up the Disney-Kraft tone.

20. Cited in Murphy, *FWA*, p. 30.

21. *Ibid.*

22. This image brings to mind the crying Indian warrior of a few years back in a televised ad about the threatened environment.

23. Paul Gerber is quoted in Welsh, "The Land": "Our goal was to make a beautiful, majestic and positive film about humans and the environment. But we also wanted to make visitors aware of their responsibility to protect the land, water and air . . . we want to debunk the myth that only in recent times have people sought to modify the environment. . . . As the film's narrator points out, 'nothing has changed, except the approach.'"

24. Murphy, *FWA*, p. 30

25. Some people remain unstirred. One overhead comment: "That was a good movie, but it made me sleepy." Perhaps even Future World is capable of too much soporific pedagogy.

26. John Neary, "Brave New Garden: The Outlandish World of Merle Jensen," *Horticulture* (August 1983), pp. 21-25.

27. This is the same crew that put together the Biosphere II self-contained living project in Arizona. See Georgia Tasker, "Biosphere II: Real Live Ark for the Future," *Miami Herald*, January 28, 1990, pp. 1G, 3G.

28. Jensen is quoted in Mary Jane McSwain, "EPCOT Previews Garden's Future in Land Pavilion," *Daytona Beach Morning Journal*, March 1, 1983.

29. As always with live spiels, our understanding depends on the combination of mouth-to-microphone distance, equipment squealing, and the amount of "airline conditional" speech written into the script. The latter is speech with consistently misplaced emphasis, the kind one sometimes hears on airplanes as attendants tell us about the equipment. It always sounds as if the speaker has a tangential relationship at best with the words and couldn't care less about what they mean.

30. Beard, *Walt Disney's EPCOT Center*, pp. 107-108.

31. Murphy, *FWA*, p. 23.

32. I use the word "profitable" advisedly here. Speaking of his Arizona lab, Merle Jensen has said (quoted in Neary, "Brave New Garden," p. 25), "If it doesn't mean dollars down the line, if it isn't something that somebody can put into effect, then it's not going to come about." For all of Disney's words about sharing, we know that somewhere down the line some corporation is going to control and market as much of this technology and as many of these seeds and materials as possible.

33. For a general argument in praise of artificial plants, see Roger Vick, "Artificial Nature: The Synthetic Landscape of the Future," *The Futurist* (July-August 1989), pp. 29-32.

34. Birnbaum, *Steve Birnbaum*, 1989, p. 124.

35. Murphy, *FWA*, p. 23.

36. "Listen to the Land," p. 2. This is a souvenir pamphlet.

37. The pineapples here are artificially stimulated to flower by ethylene, a naturally occurring plant hormone. See *ibid.*, p. 4.

38. Alfred Borcover, "Disney View of Future Farm and Food," *Chicago Tribune*, November 4, 1982. See also "Robot Farm Workers, No-Soil Fields Seen in Ag's Future," *Salem (Oregon) Capital Press*, August 5, 1983.

39. Paddlefish are a source of caviar. The tilapia and catfish end up on plates upstairs.

40. "Listen to the Land," p. 6.

41. *Ibid.*, pp. 10-12. See also Murphy, *FWA*, p. 24.

42. At the opening of EPCOT, Robitaille had a staff of thirty-two scientists — entomologists, plant pathologists, agricultural engineers, aquaculturalists, and agronomists. Later his staff would include graduate students and recipients of agricultural grants. See Borcover, "Disney View of Future Farm and Food."

43. Bill Kilby, "Serious Business Abounds at EPCOT," *Jacksonville (Illinois) Journal-Courier*, March 21, 1986.

44. Tissue cultures are the regeneration of whole plants from tiny pieces of a parental plant. This is practiced here on asexually propagated clones — pineapples, bananas, sweet potatoes, and strawberries. See "Listen to the Land," p. 22.

45. All persons who enter the greenhouses must step into a bleach solution to avoid bringing in soil-borne plant diseases. *Ibid.*, p. 25.

46. Lady bugs for aphids, parasitic wasps (*Encarsia formosa*) for leafminers. *Ibid.*, p. 25.

47. Heat pasteurization of the sand at 180 degrees Farenheit for 1-3 hours.

48. Cited in Kilby, "Serious Business Abounds at EPCOT."

49. As with the advice offered by regulars to tourists, this is a chance for regimented "guests" to claim, "I am somebody!"

50. Peg Boyles, "Two Paths to the Future," *New Hampshire Times Weekly*, May 2, 1983. Boyles anticipates Albert Borgmann's argument (see the following chapter) about the importance of protecting "focal things" and "focal practices" under the onslaught of the rule of technology.

51. Brian Tokar, "Engineering the Future of Life," *Zeta Magazine* (July-August) 2:7-8, 1989, pp. 110-116.

52. Hope Shand, "Test Tube Agriculture; Biotech: Threat or Promise?" *Dollars & Sense* (June 1990), p. 18.

53. "Nor is EPCOT a community where anybody lives or is ever likely to. The real inhabitants of EPCOT are the hundreds of audioanimatronic robots — humanoid, animoid, vegetoid — whose mechanical gestures lag exactly one-half spastic beat behind their speech, screech, and bellow, as if all of nature were delivering a Richard Nixon oration." Arnold Wasserman, "Un and Loathing at EPCOT," *Industrial Design Magazine* (March-April 1983), pp. 34-39. This quote is on p. 34.

54. See Murphy, *FWA*, p. 28.

55. Robert Holland, "Disney's Living Seas Opens in EPCOT Center," *Underwater USA*, March 1, 1986, pp. 38-39. This quote is on p. 38.

56. "Disney himself would probably have called it 'the world's sixth largest ocean,'" suggests John Culhane in "Visit to an Underwater Fantasia," *Reader's Digest* (July 1986), pp. 137-141. This quote is on p. 137.

57. Holland, "Disney's Living Seas," p. 39.

58. Future World pavilions have advisory boards that help create the presentations. According to the *Miami Herald*, the board for The Living Seas was particularly prestigious. The *Herald* quotes Michael Eisner as calling this pavilion "a nice change of pace, a new beginning." See "In Living Seas, Everything's Real but the Reef," *Miami Herald*, January 26, 1986.

59. This sounds much like the Mark Twain, Alexander Graham Bell, Andrew Carnegie, and Susan B. Anthony robots at the American Adventure's 1876 Philadelphia Exposition.

60. See Philip Gatsoulis, Mark E. Fordham, and Paul E. Cooley, "Disney Engineers Voyage to the Deep," *Civil Engineering* (March 1986), pp. 50-53. As usual, Disney has elicited statistical superlatives from the reviewers of The Living Seas. This is a central idiom through which people try to grasp Disney engineering. As is also often the case, people disagree slightly on all the figures. Reference to statistics, not to exact particulars, is important. If I cite a reference for every figure here, this section will never end; so the figures here are ballpark figures.

61. According to Gatsoulis *et al.*, *ibid.*, pp. 50-51, "This will be the first time that marine mammals including sea lions, seals and dolphins will be kept with fish in the same synthetic seawater." Birnbaum (*Steve Birnbaum*, 1989, p. 123) lists sea bass, parrotfish, puffers, barracuda, butterfly fish, angelfish, sharks, croakers, hog snappers, dolphins, sea lions, and diamond rays. The tank also contains one-person submarines, minirobotic submersibles, and scuba divers (including Mickey Mouse). By the summer of 1990 there were manatees as well.

62. See Culhane, "Visit to an Underwater Fantasia," pp. 137-141. According to Murphy, "The little ones were introduced first, so that they could find places to hide out." Cited in *ibid.*, p. 140.

63. "In Living Seas, Everything's Real but the Reef."

64. Birnbaum, *Steve Birnbaum*, 1989, p. 123, gives the recipe as "dry dog food, chicken's laying pellets, a complete aminoacid solution, and a vitamin B complex solution, all held together by dental plaster."

65. Holland, "Disney's Living Seas," p. 39.

66. Gatsoulis *et al.*, "Disney Engineers Voyage to the Bottom of the Sea," p. 53.

67. *Ibid.*, p. 51. These include an 85,000 square-foot, 4.2-million-gallon earthen reservoir adjacent to the water treatment facility, designed to hold most of the water from the main aquarium should it need to be drained; a 38-foot-high aeration tower; and three 300,000-gallon reinforced concrete storage reservoirs for holding and making up additional seawater. See *ibid.*, p. 53.

68. *Walt Disney World* (The Walt Disney Company, 1986), p. 94.

69. Here, as with "The Bird and the Robot" at GM's World of Motion, we get a propagandistic robotic "sell."

70. People laugh regularly at this show. No one complains about the evolution stories. Either the creationists are elsewhere, or they are splitting their beliefs from the cartoonic moment.

71. Quoted in Culhane, "Visit to an Underwater Fantasia," p. 140

72. Holland, "Disney's Living Seas," p. 38.

73. Glossed over, of course, is the need for military power to back it up. It is as if exclusive economic zones somehow "get posted" — on a bulletin board? — and that's that.

74. See Holland, "Disney's Living Seas," p. 39, for a description of what it's like to dive the reef with Mickey.

75. Derek Walker, "EPCOT '82," *Architectural Digest* (October 1982), pp. 1-28. This quote is found on p. 8.

76. Leo Marx, *The Machine in the Garden: Technology and the Pastoral Idea in America* (New York: Oxford University Press, 1964).

77. In the Magic Kingdom, the flowers are changed four or five times a year in order to keep them fresh and seasonable. See Howard Bloomfield, "Mickey Mouse Grows Trees, Too," *American Forests* (July 1976), pp. 16-19, 55.

78. Eilers Maynard, "Plants Are Part of the Show at Disney's EPCOT Center," *Jacksonville Journal*, March 8, 1986.

79. See George Tasker, "EPCOT: 12,000 Trees in $8-Million Landscape," *Miami Herald*, May 22, 1983; also Pam Parks, "Disney Report," *Orlando Magazine* (January 1982), and "A 225-year-old Yucca from Texas Graces Mexico," *Orlando Magazine* (May 1983).

80. See Parks, "Disney Report," p. 47.

81. *Gardens of the Walt Disney World Resort* (The Walt Disney Company, 1988).

82. As of 1982, there were only fifty-one accredited zoos throughout the United States. "Discover Birds, Peace at This Attraction," *Fort Pierce (Florida) News-Tribune*, January 31, 1982.

83. Discovery Island, together with the conservancy area elsewhere on the property, bears the closest connection to the studio's history of wild animal films.

84. Birnbaum, *Steve Birnbaum*, 1989, p. 186.

85. It also passes rest facilities. The men's room is labeled "his tern," the women's room "her tern." A major paper is waiting out there about Disney restroom labeling.

86. *Discovery Island: A Very Special Zoological Park* (The Walt Disney Company, 1986).

87. See the Discovery Island park brochure; also "Discovery Island: Where Feathers, Fur, Claws, and Paws Are in Good Hands," *Cocoa (Florida) Today*, July 25, 1983.

88. The story is most completely told in Peter B. Gallagher, "Mickey, Minnie, Donald, . . . Buzz?" *Tropic Magazine, Miami Herald*, January 21, 1990, pp. 9-13.

89. See Garth Bray, "Disney Zoo Kills Birds," *Multinational Monitor* (November 1989), p. 32.

90. The company was also ordered to pay the same sum to the Florida Audubon Society's Center for Birds of Prey and agreed to contribute $75,000 to the state's fish and game programs that promote conservation. See *ibid.*

Chapter 17

1. J. Tevere MacFadyen, "The Future: A Walt Disney Production," *Next* (July 1980).

2. Jennifer Allen, "Brave New EPCOT," *New York*, December 20, 1982, pp. 40-43. This quote is on p. 41.

3. Quoted in *ibid.*, p. 43.

4. Langdon Winner, *The Whale and the Reactor: A Search for Limits in an Age of High Technology* (Chicago: University of Chicago Press, 1986), p. 47.

5. *Ibid.*, p. 10.

6. *Ibid.*, p. 6.

7. Thanks to some technologies, it can no longer be said that the air humans breathe or the water in which fish swim is unremarkable and to be taken for granted. Such metaphors about the media of life no longer make sense.

8. In Winner, *The Whale and the Reactor*, p. 93, Winner notes that for most of the twentieth century, the prospect of unhindered personal consumption and the use of goods seemed to make most people happy. In fact, that is what "freedom" came to mean in the eyes of many.

9. *Ibid.*, p. 9.

10. *Ibid.*, p. 11.

11. *Ibid.*, p. 13.

12. *Ibid.*, p. 22.

13. *Ibid.*, p. 27.

14. *Ibid.*, p. 19.

15. *Ibid.*, p. 31. Winner asks his readers to think about what civil liberties and other "freedoms" they give up in order to live with (and benefit from) particular technologies. We might ask what "freedoms" visitors give up in order to be at WDW.

16. *Ibid.*, pp. 47-48. Number 5 reminds us of Disney's relations, as the Reedy Creek Improvement District, with the state of Florida and Orange and Osceola counties.

17. *Ibid.*, p. 103. Many of the items on this list are showcased at the Communi-Cores, on which we focus in the next chapter.

18. Albert Borgmann, *Technology and the Character of Contemporary Life: A Philosophical Inquiry* (Chicago: University of Chicago Press, 1984).

19. *Ibid.*, p. 34.

20. *Ibid.*, p. 36.

21. *Ibid.*, p. 39.

22. Borgmann employs a philosophical rather than an economic notion of the commodity. That is, a commodity is something useful to human life rather than just something that has a market price. Borgmann's meaning echoes Marx's opening definition at the beginning of *Capital*, volume 1.

23. Borgmann, *Technology and the Character of Contemporary Life*, p. 41.

24. Borgmann parses the device into the machine — the means that produce the effect — and the commodity — the end or effect. Like Max Weber, he argues that machines often produce unintended effects, especially in eliminating the social practices in which commodities often were previously enjoyed. For example, the social practice of cooking together is eliminated by prefabricated frozen meals.

25. Borgmann, *Technology and the Character of Contemporary Life*, p. 56.

26. *Ibid.*, p. 61.

27. *Ibid.*, p. 94.

28. *Ibid.*, p. 135.

29. This hegemony is unremarkable even to the "extension of the technological paradigm to the global scale where the earth itself is seen and treated as a device, namely, as a spaceship." *Ibid.*, p. 144. Disney followed this usage in its Spaceship Earth.

30. *Ibid.*, pp. 103, 63.

31. Borgmann notes (*ibid.*, p. 140) that "technology now mimics the great breakthroughs of the past, assuring us that it is an imposition to have to open a garage door, walk behind a lawn mower, or wait twenty minutes for a frozen dinner to be ready."

It always takes me a few days after I return home from WDW to get used to opening my own doors again. As I often get bruised once or twice before I readjust, I have the opportunity to get mad at a world that makes me do things for myself.

32. See John H. Douglas and the editors of Grolier, *The Future World of Energy* [hereafter *FWE*] (New York: Grolier, 1984), p. 17.

33. Michael Harrington, "To the Disney Station: Corporate Socialism in the Magic Kingdom," *Harper's* (January 1979), p. 43.

34. Marilyn Williams, "This Energy Story Should Dazzle," *(Exxon) Profile* (1982), p. 5. The article goes on to report that in order to ensure a "broad-based message," Disney personnel periodiocally met with an "independent" board of directors: "The five advisors reflected the energy views of such wide-ranging interests as aerospace, electric power, transportation, natural gas and construction." We can rest easy now that we know what "broad-based" and "wide-ranging" mean.

35. Solar, wind, and the like (my additions).

36. Harrington, "To the Disney Station," pp. 43-44.

37. The building was built in collaboration with United States Steel, which had a manufacturing site on the property. The rooms were constructed at the onsite plant, as they were for the Polynesian, and then lifted into place by huge cranes. The building techniques were certainly modern.

38. The original was sponsored by Eastern Airlines, which withdrew its support in 1988 as a Frank Lorenzo cost-cutting move. Disney and Delta overhauled the attraction, which reopened in 1990.

39. Steve Birnbaum, *Steve Birnbaum Brings You the Best of Walt Disney World* (New York: Avon Books and Hearst Professional Magazines, 1989), p. 100.

40. *Ibid.*

41. *Ibid.*

42. And back again, although riders have to get off and go through the line again. The line is always longer at Fantasyland.

43. The attendant at the turning point has the most isolated job inside the Magic Kingdom and is always ready for conversation.

44. Birnbaum, *Steve Birnbaum*, p. 99.

45. WED stands for W(alter) E(lias) D(isney). WED is the engineering and design arm of the Walt Disney Company.

46. Beneath which is the Space Bar, a soft drink and Handwich (a specially registered Disney sandwich) spot, sponsored by Wise Foods.

47. This ride is sponsored by Thomson Consumer Electronics, an RCA brand.

48. Advertised on the PeopleMover as Florida's third-highest mountain.

49. These tracks are back-to-back but are not identical. A full visit requires rides on both tracks.

50. Birnbaum, *Steve Birnbaum*, p. 98.

51. *Ibid.* Birnbaum also notes (*ibid.*), "Legend has it that the meteors visible to guests in the queue are actually projections of chocolate chip cookies."

52. Richard R. Beard, *Walt Disney's EPCOT Center: Creating the New World of Tomorrow* (New York: Harry N. Abrams, 1982), p. 56.

53. These cells provide about 15 percent of the energy needed to run the attraction. See *Walt Disney World* (Walt Disney Company, 1986), p. 71.

54. The entrance is here, between the building and the triangle.

55. Birnbaum, *Steve Birnbaum*, p. 131.

56. *FWE*, p. 18.

57. In case we miss the dynamism, here's Beard's breathless description of the show. See Beard, *Walt Disney's EPCOT Center*, p. 59. "All the various forms of energy, in their basic states, are depicted in a spellbinding series of images. We see representations of nuclear energy, contained within the atoms of all matter, and of the chemical energy that binds atoms into molecules and crystals. Galaxies metamorphose into spirals, swirls, and crystals, and then into organic objects such as butterflies and roses, portraying chemical energy. Clouds meet in a zap of lightning to produce electrical energy. And next, mechanical, heat, and light energy are introduced, all through a succession of fleeting, sometimes disorienting, but ever compelling images. The screen's rippling panels intensify the phenomena pictured on it: Water appears wetter, fire hotter."

58. As if a captive awaiting rescue. The "rescue," of course, is death for the trees.

59. Although to use a friend as a tool raises familiar ethical issues.

60. The Walt Disney Educational Media Company has published a free comic book, "Mickey and Goofy Explore the Universe of Energy," to accompany the Universe of Energy. In it Goofy responds to Radok's film with a democratic list, but Mickey sets him straight about the overriding importance of oil. "Goofy: Wow! There's oil, natural gas, coal, hydro-electric, nuclear and solar power!" "Mickey: Today, oil is the most important energy source for transportation! It supplies our energy needs for cars, planes, trucks and trains!" "Goofy: Gee, this subject is getting pretty deep!" "Mickey: Deep is right! We have to drill deep into the ground to get our oil! Oil is one of the oldest and most valuable resources on earth!"

61. As Beard puts it (*Walt Disney's EPCOT Center*, p. 60), "a sobering thought, but one tempered by the promise of man's innate ingenuity."

62. According to Birnbaum (*Steve Birnbaum*, p. 131), the vehicles are 29 feet long, 18 feet wide, and — when fully loaded — weigh on the order of 30,000 pounds. Each vehicle is driven by a single six-horsepower electric motor. The eight battery storage energy pack is recharged when the cars are stationary (Douglas, *FWE*, p. 22). The back row of each vehicle contains a broad space and boarding rails for mobility-impaired guests. Depending on who you listen to, car capacity ranges from 96 to 98 persons, so six full vehicles can transport 576 to 588 passengers per 38-minute show. Two shows are run simultaneously, as two moving theaters move through the different parts of the pavilion.

63. Beard, *Walt Disney's EPCOT Center*, p. 60.

64. This 4 1/2-minute film required a return to the classical inking and drawing techniques the studio had abandoned years ago as too costly. Ub Iwerks's multiplane camera was unretired after twenty-five years in order to create an effective sense of depth on the huge screen. See *ibid.*

65. Again, note that this is evolution, not creationism.

66. The description in the commemorative *Walt Disney World* (p. 70) reminds us how hard it is to stop mocking Disney language: "The formation of fossil fuels is re-enacted in a drama featuring life-sized dinosaurs which eventually become coal and oil."

67. Beard, *Walt Disney's EPCOT Center*, pp. 62-63.

68. *Walt Disney World* calls it a dimetrodon. Douglas's *FWE* calls it an edaphosaurus.

69. All of these dinosaurs are the largest animated creatures ever fabricated. They hold center stage against a 515-foot scenic background that took 6,000 man-hours to paint. See Douglas, *FWE*, p. 20.

70. This lava is actually a harmless gelatinous material that contains, among other things, a type of commercial styling gel (Birnbaum, *Steve Birnbaum*, p. 131). Orange dye and black-light pigment have been added to the mix to give it a fiery glow (Beard, *Walt Disney's EPCOT Center*, p. 67).

71. A critical note about the ride and these dinosaurs is sounded by Alfred Heller in "A Funny Thing Happened on the Way to Tomorrow: Stalled in EPCOT's World of Motion," *World's Fair* (Winter 1983). As he describes Exxon's ideological message, "The only decent thing these ancient, fire-breathing lizards ever did was to turn into fuel for the use of our own exquisite civilization, as atonement for their previous behavior. Somehow, the whole performance frees you from any guilt you might have felt about your wasteful habit of taking the old gas guzzler down to the corner for a six pack."

72. Here again is some euphoric Disney hyperbole from *Walt Disney World*, p. 71. The emphases are mine. "Next on a screen stretching 200 degrees around us, we are *immersed* in an *exciting* live-action film dealing with today's *energy challenges* and the technologies that may *power our tomorrows*. We discover the *staggering* tasks involved in the search and recovery of fossil fuels, the *enormous* effort it took to build the Alaskan pipeline, and the almost *overwhelming* task of delivering the world's oil via supertanker."

73. Beard, *Walt Disney's EPCOT Center*, p. 64.

74. In the Disney comic book about the Universe of Energy, Mickey and Goofy spend 75 percent of their sixteen pages discussing the "information" in this film.

75. Remember that Disney has its own nuclear power license. The best treatment of Disney's nuclear arrangements, including a 1967-1980 chronology, is in a September 1981 article in *New Florida*, the title and author of which I have lost (although the last part of the title is "of Walt Disney's Nuclear Dream"). In this article, Harvey Jones, the company's top utilities executive in 1981, is quoted thus: "If you take a nuclear submarine and put it underwater, you can run Disney World. Maybe not run it efficiently, but you could do it. You could just build cement around the submarine to protect the environment, if you're talking about feasibility" (p. 36).

On June 28, 1979, the state of Florida cited Disney for "noncompliance with material leak test requirements" (p. 38). Apparently, Disney people were told "they weren't doing things right." "Regardless, state inspectors found no radioactive leaks at Walt Disney World, where the nuclear storage site and the waste disposal are located about a mile from the amusement area parking lot" (p. 38).

76. In the comic book, Mickey mentions this uncertainty as part of his lecture to Goofy about becoming "energy wise." The arguments Mickey makes are aimed directly at Goofy's economic self-interest. Goofy apparently is interested in no one

else and nothing else — except stupid puns. "Mickey: First, we can all try to conserve energy. . . . Also, we need to explore for new supplies of crude oil and natural gas!" "Goofy: You mean, ol' Bessie's [Goofy's car] gonna last me a long time?" "Mickey: Sure, Goofy! Oil can supply your car's energy needs for many years to come!" "Goofy: Great! And we can always buy oil from foreign countries, too!" "Mickey: Sometimes we can't depend on other countries! Since 1973, our foreign oil supply has been cut off TWICE!" "Goofy: Oh, yeah — I remember how ol' Bessie had to wait in loooonnnggg lines for gasoline." "Mickey: And because gasoline was scarce, it became very expensive, too!" "Goofy: Gawrsh, Mick. . . . That 'scarce' me a lot!" "Mickey: Yes, Goofy — but it will help if we can find new sources of oil in our own country!"

77. This, of course, is a prespill film. Exxon is trying to convince the audience that transporting crude oil over eight hundred miles of fragile tundra and then shipping it out through extremely damageable bays and channels on barely attended tankers is normal. Oil spills may then be seen as abnormal and accidental.

78. We might note the use of the word "provide." Disney and its allied corporations interject this concept into much of their discourse. They will be the nurturing providers, the parents, the caretakers. The things they want their audience to do, now and in the future, will be the result of opportunities provided for that audience. Although such provisions may be parental, they will also be economical. If they are not so, they should not be provided — for provision ought rightfully to take second place to economics in the corporate heart.

79. When corporations need us, "it's up to the individual . . . we need you to help shape tomorrow's world." When they don't need the individual (he or she might have black lung), the individual disappears. In any case, as John Rothchild points out, what is really happening is that we are strapped into cars, often going backward. See John Rothchild, "EPCOT: It's a Stale World After All," *Rolling Stone*, September 1, 1983, pp. 33-36. This quote is on p. 36.

80. These predictions were made at the beginning of the 1980s — a kind of post-Three Mile Island nuclear industry whistling in the dark.

81. I can't resist. I'm sorry. "For the Universe of Energy finale, images and colors move and change, creating a total energy experience and summarizing our energy possibilities. This show reemphasizes the theme that, by working together and exploring new energy frontiers, we can build a bridge to a more secure energy future" (*Walt Disney World*, p. 71).

82. Biomass includes such materials as wood, corn, sugarcane, and water plants and organic wastes such as sawdust and municipal trash.

83. Douglas, *FWE*, p. 23. Birnbaum (*Steve Birnbaum*, p. 133) suggests that "although the overall subject matter is serious, the exhibits are so diverting that it's entirely possible to spend an hour or more in the area without being aware of the passage of time." I have, however, seldom seen anybody linger to do any reading or see the films all the way through. People *do* do the hands-on stuff and the games.

84. We can also play interactive touch-screen computer games. In one we attempt to drive a football quarterback, with dispatch and fuel efficiency, through an urban street grid to the stadium.

85. Electrical specifications for EPCOT Center as a whole can be found in Arthur Freund, "EPCOT Center — A Monumental Project," *EC&M* (September 1982), pp. 53-60. See also John J. Foster, "Electrical Users and Utility Combine: For Walt Disney World Energy Management," *Electrical Energy Management* (November 1980), pp.

10-12; and Mark Weintz, "Disney World Shows Visitors Glimpse of Alternative Energy," *Solar Times* (January 1981).

As mentioned in Chapter 10, Noel Perrin ("The High Cost of Magic," Audubon [May 1984], pp. 28-29) is very forceful about the downside of Disney's various energy systems.

86. Howard Curry, a nuclear plant worker from Fredrick, Maryland, was disgusted with the exhibit. In Peter Larson, "Adults Aren't Mindless Visitors — Try More Facts, Less Glitter," *Orlando Sentinel*, October 24, 1982, Curry says, "The main concern people have is if nuclear power is safe . . . this exhibit doesn't address anything about that." In post-Chernobyl times, the critique still stands.

87. There are a lot of critiques about the finite resources-foreign source problem. For a representative example, see Michael Rounds, "Disney Town Too Optimistic," *Rocky Mountain News*, January 10, 1984. Obviously, increasing domestic oil production means a lot of offshore drilling. In an interview with *Multinational Monitor* in March 1990 ("Greenpeace: An Antidote to Corporate Environmentalism," pp. 26-29), Peter Bahouth, executive director of Greenpeace USA, describes the situation Exxon would have us forget in its swarm of dinosaurs: "To us, the issue is not double hulled tankers and making it safer for oil companies to transport oil. The real issue is that they are pushing the use of oil to the extent that they are; that they are fighting to maintain oil subsidies; that they are working against a level playing field in terms of the prices of nonrenewable energy resources; that they are actively campaigning against things like conservation and public transportation. The bigger issue is our energy use; the corporations don't necessarily help to solve it." This quote is on p. 27.

88. Dave Barry, "Is Nothing Sacred? A Cynic Visits EPCOT, Flees the Challenge of the Future," *Miami Herald*, September 4, 1983, pp. 6-9, 18.

89. Valery Moolman and the editors of Grolier, *The Future World of Transportation* [hereafter *FWT*] (New York: Grolier, 1984). This quote is from p. 19.

90. This film is about the use of eminent domain by Detroit to tear down a neighborhood — "Poletown" — to allow GM to build a Cadillac plant.

91. See Stephen M. Fjellman, "Taming the Robot: The Bird and the Robot at Walt Disney World," *Science as Culture*, in press, for a more complete analysis of this show. It is interesting that the GM exhibit at the now-defunct Flint auto museum was also about industrial robots, presented as "friends" to people GM had just thrown out of work. The company has no shame.

92. As Joseph Bohn points out in "GM Takes Center Stage with EPCOT Pavilion," *Automotive News*, May 24, 1982, "Consumers are led to believe their needs, desires and ability to pay will ultimately determine the outcome."

93. Moolman, *FWT*, p. 23.

94. *Ibid.*, p. 24.

95. The World of Motion hands out information sheets with specifications for both of these vehicles. See "The Lean Machine" and "General Motors' Aero 2000" for complete specifications. The yearly "GM Visitor's Handbook" is nothing more than an advertisement with a map of the Transcenter.

96. According to the 1989 "GM Visitor's Handbook."

97. Moolman, *FWT*, p. 74.

98. As with The Land, the incline leads to a built-up entrance.

99. Birnbaum, *Steve Birnbaum*, p. 129.

100. Made up, Birnbaum tells us (*ibid.,* p. 130), of bits and pieces of old Goofy cartoons

101. According to Birnbaum (*ibid.*), "These are the same type of flight simulators employed by military and commercial airline pilot training."

102. The seat belts are monitored by a visual display at the left front of the theater. Green lights go on as the belts are connected. Gaps in the display signal problems or recalcitrance for all to see. This gives the attendant something to do. The ride does not start until all the lights are on.

103. This ride is a Disney gloss on the movies *Fantastic Voyage* and *Inner Space.*

104. All, that is, but the underappreciated, whiny hypothalamus — "ignored as usual." The hypothalamus is an industrial robot that looks like binoculars on a stick. None of these characters-actors are women.

Bobby's rational right brain is Charles Grodin, doing his accountant role to the hilt. His emotional left brain is Jon Lovitz. Hans and Franz pump Bobby's heart. In perfect casting, Sam Kinison is the screaming adrenal gland, stressing out at will, and George Wendt, in lobster bib, is Bobby's stomach — alternately pleading for food (at lunch an entire hamburger arrives) and ducking butterflies when love hits.

105. Larson, "Adults Aren't Mindless Visitors — Try More Facts, Less Glitter."

106. Winner, *The Whale and the Reactor,* p. 27.

107. Rothchild, "It's a Stale World After All," p. 36.

108. Beverly Beckham, "Pursuing Donald Duck, Tinkerbell and Wonder," *Quincy (Mass.) Patriot-Ledger,* June 1, 1983.

Chapter 18

1. Cited in Robert L. Sample, "The Exciting World of EPCOT Center: Tomorrow's Technologies Displayed at New Disney Attraction," *Administrative Manager* (November 1982), pp. 49-52. This quote is found on p. 52.

2. *Walt Disney World* (The Walt Disney Company, 1986), p. 68.

3. The metaphors and allusions used to tell the various computer, robot, and other machine stories at Future World draw on images — the sorcerer's apprentice, Groucho Marx (the Bird at *The Bird and the Robot* in GM's World of Motion) — that adults rather than children would know.

4. By now it will be clear that the future will be marked by all sorts of clever place names in which words will be abbreviated, run together, and internally capitalized. Names will be functional and sleek. Many of us, no doubt, will live in the UniStates watched over by SkyCams.

5. Although the television monitors boast what are called touch-sensitive screens, the viewer never actually touches the screen, which is protected by an impact-resistant, weather-tight transparent plastic shield. Infrared light-emitting diodes form a pattern about one-quarter of an inch in front of the screen. When a person's finger touches the plastic protective shield, some of the tiny beams in this matrix of light are interrupted, allowing the computer to identify the exact coordinates of the spot touched. A microprocessor computes the location at which the beam was interrupted and sends these data to a computer. The computer uses this information to determine which video and audio sequences to display. See Jack Hollahan, "AV Exhibit: Communication on Demand," *Audio-Visual Communication* (February 1983).

6. See Marjorie Costello, "Going Interactive: Disney Gets in Touch with Videodiscs at EPCOT," *Vidoegraphy* (January 1983), pp. 27-32.

7. Hollahan, "AV Exhibit: Communication on Demand."

8. Steve Birnbaum, *Steve Birnbaum Brings You the Best of Walt Disney World* (New York: Avon Books and Hearst Professional Magazines, 1989), p. 132.

9. See Robert Doering and Robert Redgate, "Development of Energy Management System at Walt Disney World via Centralized Computer Control," *Computer and Industrial Engineering* 5 (1982), pp. 86-87; also Edith Myers, "Mickey's Astuter Computer," *Datamation* (1981), p. 98.

10. Richard R. Beard, *Walt Disney's EPCOT Center: Creating the New World of Tomorrow* (New York: Harry N. Abrams, 1982), p. 125.

11. *Ibid.*, p. 126.

12. *Ibid.*

13. *Ibid.*

14. *Ibid.*

15. It would be interesting to know how many visitors from outside the United States take the poll. One might expect their answers to be a bit more expansive than those of the average American (although the choices given don't have much range), but many may exclude themselves due to language.

16. See Sample, "The Exciting World of EPCOT Center: Tomorrow's Technologies Displayed at New Disney Attraction," p. 50.

17. It has done so since World War II and its cartoons for the U.S. military.

18. Paul D. Lehrman, "Future Shock: The Alarmingly Superb Technology of EPCOT," *Boston Phoenix*, March 22, 1983.

19. See Stephen M. Fjellman, "Taming the Robot," *Science as Culture*, in press.

20. Paul D. Lehrman, "Future Shock: The alarmingly superb technology of EPCOT."

21. Computers are also used for hotel reservations, distributed inventory, film distribution, travel arrangements, item tracking, payrolls, employment timekeeping, food ordering and distribution, and point of sale activity.

22. Jeff Smith, "Entertainment Control System: EPCOT's Central Nervous System," *Theater Crafts* (November-December 1982), pp. 14-15, 45-50. See also Myers, "Mickey's Astuter Computer," p. 98; Douglas B. Seba, "Mickey Mouse Computers," *Online* (July 1983), pp. 85-87; Tom Mannes, "Disney's EPCOT Is Computer Festival," *Electronics*, November 3, 1982, pp. 86-87; Lehrman, "Future Shock: The Alarmingly Superb Technology of EPCOT."

23. ECS also controls the light and sound for live shows through cue files entered into each day's show schedule data base.

24. See John Haupt, "Parade Route Lighting: Now You See It — Now You Don't," *Theater Crafts* (November-December 1982), pp. 16, 50-52. Haupt describes the vertical lifts and pneumatic arms in use to position lighting from its hiding places. He also notes the use of "negative light" — dark spaces that follow an event, creating an "envelope" of lighting and music to emphasize its highlights. The system allows lighting to be used as a parade architectural design element.

25. See Robb Resler, "Disney's Experimental Prototype Community of Tomorrow," *Theater Crafts* (November-December 1982), pp. 13, 42-43; and Robb Resler, "Sound and Audio at EPCOT: Relaying Signals from ECS," (*Theater Crafts*) (November-December 1982), pp. 18, 54-56.

26. Lehrman, "Future Shock: The Alarmingly Superb Technology of EPCOT."

27. Smith, "Entertainment Control System," p. 47.

28. Pete's Dragon alone has over 25,000 bulbs. See George Korda, "A Latesummer Night's Dream," *Cocoa (Florida) Today*), August 22, 1980, p. 8.

29. For a full list of restaurants and locations, see Birnbaum, *Steve Birnbaum*, pp. 200-202. The mere fact that people could think up so many cute themed names is impressive.

30. See Roca Grindin, "The Mystique of Training at Disney World," *Restaurant Business*, February 10, 1984, p. 242.

31. Robert W. Tolf, "A Taste-Test Surprise Near Tomorrowland," *Florida Trend* (July 1983).

32. If reservations weren't taken until 10:00, the morning was also shot.

33. Here are the World Showcase restaurants (t = table-service).

Mexico
San Angel Inn Restaurant (t)
La Cantina de San Angel

Japan
Teppanyaki Room (t)
Tempura Kiku (t)
Matsu No Ma Lounge (t)
Yakitori House

Norway
Restaurant Akershus (t)
Kringla Bakeri og Kafé

Morocco
Restaurant Marrakesh(t)

China
Nine Dragons Restaurant
Lotus Blossom Café

France
Les Chefs de France (t)
Bistro de Paris (t)
Au Petit Café (t)
Boulangerie Patisserie

Germany
Biergarten(t)
Sommerfest

United Kingdom
Rose and Crown Dining Room (t)
Rose and Crown Pub

Italy
L'Originale Alfredo di Roma
    Restaurant (t)

Canada
Le Cellier

United States
Liberty Inn

34. The success of the Mitsukoshi establishments has been a spur to other Japanese companies planning moves to central Florida. See Sue Hong, "Japanese Love It Here, Even Greasy Hamburgers," *Orlando Magazine* (May 1983), pp. 67-69.

35. Ruth Gray, "More Magic from the Kingdom: EPCOT Food Will Feature an International Flavor," *St. Petersburg Times*, September 30, 1982.

36. Keith Keogh, executive chef of Future World's Coral Reef Restaurant, has twice been named Florida's seafood chef of the year. See "It's a Small World After All: International Dining Is a Highlight of Visit to EPCOT," *Baltimore Sun*, May 18, 1986. Many of the hotel restaurants have been highly praised, as has the Empress Room at Pleasure Island.

37. See, for example, Melissa Wall, "EPCOT Center's Restaurant Marrakesh Offers Flavor of Moroccan Cuisine," *Newport News (Virginia) Times-Herald*, June 19, 1985.

38. Here are two representative statements from foreign workers in the showcases. They are found in Jim Sullivan, "Around the World in a Day: At EPCOT, if It's 1 p.m., It Must Be France," *Boston Globe*, August 3, 1986, pp. 15, 38. "We asked her [Scottish saleswoman Lorraine McCrorie] whether EPCOT's United Kingdom felt like home to her. 'It's very, very well made. . . . It's an American conception of what they expect countries to be like . . . and it's what Disney gives them. It's very detailed.'" "'This is just a small section of Germany, of Bavaria,' said Monica Schoilch, 20, a hostess from Heidelburg. 'I just talked to a couple of Germans today, and they said, 'If all these tourists come here and think that's Germany, what a bad thing.' It's artificial. It isn't created to educate people. It was created to entertain. But I get the impression that most people think they're being educated.'. . . 'It's a part of Germany,' explained her friend and co-worker Joachim Luke, 'like Indian tents are a part of America.'" These quotes are on p. 38.

39. Rob Morse, "It's Disney, But Is It French?" *Florida Magazine*, November 28, 1982.

40. Vicki Vaughan, "Building on EPCOT Success: Restaurateurs Moving from Pavilions to Seek Profits Outside the World," *Orlando Sentinel*, October 27, 1986, pp. 1, 12.

41. See William D. Cissna, "World Showcase: The Beers at EPCOT," *All About Beer* (August 1985).

42. See "Disney 'Food and Fun' Package," *Institutions-Volume Feeding*, October 15, 1972, pp. 81-88.

43. Cited in Sheila Friedeck, "Food Plays Role in Disney Fun, Fantasy," *Beaumont (Texas) Enterprise*, March 5, 1986. Friedeck continues, "The grocery list includes imported cheeses from New York for the Italy Showcase; wafer-thin crepes flown in from Paris for the Morocco Showcase; cactus strips for the Mexico Showcase; and seafood flown in the same day it comes off the boat for several Disney restaurants."

44. For information on purchasing patterns, see Amy Clark, "Disney Magic Keeps Cooking for 14 Million," *Cocoa (Florida) Today*, August 17, 1980.

45. William J. Primavera, "The Techniques and Technology of Walt Disney World," *Restaurant Hospitality* (February 1982), pp. 31-34. This quote is found on p. 32.

46. For a good general description of the center, see Peter Berlinski and Joan Marie Lang, "EPCOT's Upscale World of Foodservice," *Restaurant Business*, June 1, 1983, pp. 104-118.

47. Friedeck, "Food Plays Role in Disney Fun"; see also Linda Cicero, "Magical Mealtimes: Food Preparation at Walt Disney World is Awe-Inspiring," *Austin American Statesman*, August 7, 1986, pp. E1-back page.

48. In "Food Plays Role in Disney Fun," Friedeck reports, "Alcohol is monitored with stickers. For example, a bottle of Scotch is signed out for the Rose and Crown, the English pub, then tagged with that bar's sticker. When empty the stickered bottle is exchanged for a stickered new one."

49. Janis D. Smith, "Touring Mickey's Kitchen," *St. Petersburg Times*, February 23, 1984.

50. These labor-saving devices help keep food costs quite low for the value. See interview entitled "Jim Armstrong, Walt Disney World," *Restaurant Business*, September 1, 1985.

51. Friedeck, "Food Plays Role in Disney Fun."

52. The bulk of the following is taken from Paul King, "The Marketing Challenge — 'Backstage' at Walt Disney World," *Food Management*, July 1, 1986, pp. 74-78, 142-148.

53. The following guidelines were published in "Muttonchops Need Not Apply," *Harper's Magazine* (June 1990), p. 40. "Each individual's appearance should add to the show and not detract from it. For this reason, anything that would be considered offensive, distracting, or not in the best interest of our Disney show will not be permitted." People are hired as "cast members"; thus, they can be told that it is reasonable for the Company to dictate the dos and don'ts of their costume and appearance. See Shirley Corbett, "It Takes Reality to Put 'Magic' into Magic Kingdom," *Portland (Maine) Sunday Telegram*, August 10, 1980. The continuing joke is that with his moustache, Walt Disney would never have been hired at his parks.

54. For some of these, see Norwood Pope, "At Walt Disney, Mickey Mouse Markets Inside, Too," *American Banker*, July 29, 1981.

Chapter 19

1. Jennifer Allen, "Brave New EPCOT," *New York*, December 20, 1982, p. 43.

2. Quoted in Edward L. Prizer, "The Disney Decade," *Orlando Magazine* (October 1981), p. 36.

3. See Ariel Dorfman and Armand Mattelart, *How to Read Donald Duck: Imperialist Ideology in the Disney Comic* (New York: International General, 1975).

4. Mike Wallace, "Mickey Mouse History: Portraying the Past at Disney World," *Radical History Review* 32 (1985), pp. 33-57.

5. Bateson uses this phrase to characterize an "elementary unit of information." See "Form, Substance, and Difference," in Gregory Bateson, *Steps to an Ecology of Mind* (New York: Ballantine, 1972), pp. 448-465. This quote is found on p. 453.

6. Hal Foster, "Postmodernism: A Preface," in Hal Foster, editor, *The Anti-Aesthetic: Essays on Postmodern Culture* (Port Townsend, Wash.: Bay Press, 1983), p. xii.

7. Joel Achenbach, "Reality to Be Cancelled?" *Tropic Magazine, Miami Herald*, December 13, 1987, p. 18

8. Neil Postman, *Amusing Ourselves to Death: Public Discourse in the Age of Show Business* (New York: Penguin, 1985).

9. Frederic Jameson, "Postmodernism, or the Cultural Logic of Late Capitalism," *New Left Review* 146 (July-August 1984), pp. 53-92.

10. *Ibid.*, p. 66.

11. Jean Baudrillard, *Simulations* (New York: Semiotext(e), Inc., 1983), p. 8.

12. Antonio Gramsci, "Notes on Italian History," in Quintin Hoare and Geoffrey Nowell Smith, editors, *Selections from the Prison Notebooks of Antonio Gramsci* (London: Lawrence and Wisehart, 1971), pp. 103-104. I found this passage in Emily Martin, *The Woman in the Body: A Cultural Analysis of Reproduction* (Boston: Beacon Press, 1987), p. 23.

13. Mandel's most thorough discussion of contemporary political economy is found in Ernest Mandel, *Late Capitalism* (London: Verso, 1978 [1972]).

14. See James Gleick, *Chaos: Making a New Science* (New York: Penguin, 1987).

15. Alexander Moore, "Walt Disney World: Bounded Ritual Space and the Playful Pilgrimage Center," *Anthropological Quarterly* 53 (1980), pp. 207-218.

About the Book and Author

Walt Disney World is a pilgrimage site filled with utopian elements, craft, and whimsy. It's a pedestrian's world, where the streets are clean, the employees are friendly, and the trains run on time. All of its elements are themed, presented in a consistent architectural, decorative, horticultural, musical, even olfactory tone, with rides, shows, restaurants, scenery, and costumed characters coordinated to tell a consistent set of stories. It is beguiling and exasperating, a place of ambivalence and ambiguity. In *Vinyl Leaves* Professor Fjellman analyzes each ride and theater show of Walt Disney World and discusses the history, political economy, technical infrastructure, and urban planning of the park as well as its relationship with Metropolitan Orlando and the state of Florida.

Vinyl Leaves argues that Disney, in pursuit of its own economic interests, acts as the muse for the allied transnational corporations that sponsor it as well as for the world of late capitalism, where the commodity form has colonized much of human life. With brilliant technological legerdemain, Disney puts visitors into cinematically structured stories in which pieces of American and world culture become ideological tokens in arguments in favor of commodification and techno-corporate control. Culture is construed as spirit, colonialism and entrepreneurial violence as exotic zaniness, and the Other as child.

Exhaustion and cognitive overload lead visitors into the bliss of Commodity Zen — the characteristic state of postmodern life. While we were watching for Orwell, Huxley rode into town, bringing *soma*, cable television, and charge cards — and wearing mouse ears. This book is the story of our commodity fairyland.

Stephen M. Fjellman is professor of anthropology at Florida International University in North Miami. He received his Ph.D. from Stanford University and has taught at Harvard University and Florida International University.

Index

3.3
2
44
192